D1218730

DOCUMENTARY HISTORY OF THE FIRST FEDERAL CONGRESS OF THE UNITED STATES OF AMERICA

4 March 1789–3 March 1791

SPONSORED BY
THE NATIONAL HISTORICAL PUBLICATIONS AND RECORDS COMMISSION
AND
THE GEORGE WASHINGTON UNIVERSITY

This book has been brought to publication with the generous assistance of the National Historical Publications and Records Commission.

NHPRC

DOCUMENTING DEMOCRACY

National Historical Publications and Records Commission

This volume has been supported by a grant from the National Endowment for the Humanities, an independent federal agency.

NATIONAL
ENDOWMENT
FOR THE
HUMANITIES

VOLUME XX

CORRESPONDENCE

SECOND SESSION: JULY–OCTOBER 1790

CHARLENE BANGS BICKFORD

KENNETH R. BOWLING

HELEN E. VEIT

WILLIAM CHARLES DIGIACOMANTONIO

Editors

The Johns Hopkins University Press, Baltimore

This book has been brought to publication with the generous assistance of the Boone Endowment of the Johns Hopkins University Press.

Printed in the United States of America on acid-free paper
2 4 6 8 9 7 5 3 1

The Johns Hopkins University Press
2715 North Charles Street
Baltimore, Maryland 21218-4363
www.press.jhu.edu

ISBN-13: 978-0-8018-9447-3 (hardcover: alk. paper)
ISBN-10: 0-8018-9447-6 (hardcover: alk. paper)

Library of Congress Control Number: 2009933941

A catalog record for this book is available from the British Library.

To
Justice David Souter and former Senator Charles McC. Mathias
for their vitally important interest in and support for
the NHPRC, documentary editions and the First Federal Congress Project

CONTENTS

ILLUSTRATIONS

Correspondence: Second Session

July 1790

Thursday, 1 July 1790

Cool (Johnson)

George Clymer to Henry Clymer

***

The Senate this morning gave a third reading to the residence bill. ~~and of a short~~ [?] ten years at Philada. and from thence to eternity on the Potowmack—To morrow it comes into our house—what will be its fate there on the various readings you will excuse me from telling, for I have very little foresight of what is to happen especially in this land of un[*c*]ertainty—Excuse me to your Mama [*Elizabeth Meredith Clymer*] in not writing her—but if this letter contains any thing of news which she has not heard before before, tell it to her.

ALS, Clymer Papers, PHi. Undated; addressed to Market Street, Philadelphia; written at 10 P.M.; franked. The omitted text provides instructions for a business transaction.

Richard Henry Lee to Thomas Lee Shippen

I promised my friend Mr. [*Burwell*] Stark, who by the time this reaches you will be in Phila., to inform him thro you how the Bill went in the Senate respecting the future Seats of the general government—I have now the pleasure to inform both you and him that the bill for adjourning Congress to Philadelphia after this Session, there to remain for ten years, and then to go to the Potomac; was this day passed in Senate by a majority of two votes—Tis well known that one Gentleman in the minority [*Wingate*] would have voted with the majority had it been necessary—but there being enough & he the last Voter, jokingly he voted in the negative.

It rests now with the H. of Representatives, where we are assured by many members, that a Majority will pass it into a Law—Thus, well has ended this very troublesome business—Truth is great & will prevail—For surely it is true that the convenience of a real majority of this Union is consulted by being in your [*ci*]ty rather than in this—farewell.

[*P. S.*] Let me know if you get this letter & when.

ALS, Shippen Family Papers, DLC. Place to which addressed not indicated.

William Maclay to Benjamin Rush

This day at a few minutes before 3 O'Clock, A Bill for removing the federal Offices to Philada. before the first Monday in December. and remaing. there for Ten Years, and fixing the Residence of Congress, after that period, on the Potowmack, passed the last reading in the Senate, and was ordered down for the concurrence of the Representatives. the Division on the last Question was 14 to 12. We expect it will be enacted into a Law, without further Opposition. For God knows We have had enough of it, in our House. so painful a perseverance I never experienced before in any Business. But We are at last crowned with Success, at least as much as was Attainable, in our Circumstances. In Much Haste.

ALS, Rush Papers, DLC. Addressed to Third Street, Philadelphia; postmarked; franked.

Theodore Sedgwick to Pamela Sedgwick

The Letter I wrote you last evening I expected to have sent by Mr. Foot of Lenox. He went away without my knowledge, I cannot omit just adding at present, that never I am sure was I so anxious to get home as at present. This day in the senate a bill has passed to fix permanently the seat of government at potomack, the residence being previously at Philadela. where it is to remain 10 years from the first Monday in december next. I have all this evening been aiding in preparing a motion for the assumption which is to be made tomorrow in the senate. If it should succeed there It will soon be in the house where I presume it must pass, and the moment it does nothing else shall detain me a *moment* from repairing to the arms of the best of women and the dearest object of the affection of your Theodore.

ALS, Sedgwick Papers, MHi. Place to which addressed not indicated.

Samuel W. Stockton to Elias Boudinot

***

What shall *we say* about the dilatory proceedings of Congress, for we think more than we *dare* say—Every body from the highest to the lowest among us are calling loud agt. the *amazing* & shocking delay in the by far, most important business of the nation—The widows & orphans are to starve to death & the innocent creditor must suffer & be ruined because some people cant have their own way—it is too much and great dissatisfaction is taking place & very much encreasing every day—You are among those who bear a uniform consistent part, & who receive the applause of the just—If Congress rise before the provision is made to support the *public credit*, I fear that every thing will be lost that is valuable in the government—& I shall not expect any thing, but loud complaints & tumults—Pray let us hear from you on the expectations you have on this subject—I am in fear of losing the Mail as it has arrived some time.

ALS, Stimson Boudinot Collection, NjP. Written from Trenton, New Jersey; sent "Per Post." The omitted text relates to private business transactions.

Michael Jenifer Stone to [*Walter Stone*]

I received your Letter inclosing the Paper—In which there is a *Compliment paid* to Mr. Gale and myself for voting the *Interest of Maryland divested of Locality*. The Peice has been reprinted here 8 Days ago.[1] Not on account of its value (for nothing can possibly be more Stupid) but for residence purposes.

*** I have written Several times to you and twice to Frederick But recieved no answer nor any account [*of*] them.[2]

***

This day at 3. oClock the Bill for fixing the Seat of ~~Congress P~~ Government [*Residence Act S-12*] passed the Senate 14 to 12.

The provisions of the Bill are—That at the beginning of the next Session of Congress and for 10 years thereafter the Congress and all the officers of Govt. who by their Duty are obliged to attend at the Seat of Govermt.—and all the Offices be and remain at—the City of Philadelphia. And at the Expiration of the 10 years And for ever thereafter the Seat of Government shall be—on the Banks of the river Potowmack! The place to be Elected by the *President* of the United States! ~~The Buildings~~ [*lined out*] As the Bill originated in the Senate they could not appropriate Money to make the Buildings. This Bill in Statu quo,[3] will most undoubted pass in the House of Representatives if all the members are alive 'till Saturday night—Joy! Joy to Myself! Joy to My Country! Joy to the United States! Joy to the Lovers of Mankind! that this touchey subject is like to be finished—That this torment to all our proceedings is likely to rest forever—Perhaps I may be too sanguine in my Hopes that the Bill will pass—and the benificial effects that may arise from it—I own that my Heart is full of this Subject and that in my Opinion nothing better could have been obtained for the United States or for Maryland—And that (except the temporary residence being divided between Phila. & Baltimore) it is as much as Maryland ought to wish—Indeed tho' in a year's time Baltimore might have been fitted for the residence of Congress—yet as the weight of representation would have been against us it is pretty Evident we should either not have gone at the appointed time or having been fixed there we should suddenly have been dragg'd away—never to return. But in the Course of 10 years—with the Impulse which the Country attachd to the Potowmack will receive by the *Idea* that the permanent Seat of Congress is on her Banks may gather the weight of representation into our Scale. If the Govt. is *never* fixed on the Potomack the *Law* will be worth Millions to that Country—It will convert it into a field which Speculation will enrich and adorn. What is 10 years! in the Existence of a Govt.?—I believe the Center of Population will be Westward of Potowmack in 50 years—and when the Govt. is *fixed* it will probably remain Stationary long after the place is not considered proper—It's remaining so long in N. York till the present is a full proof of this. By the law in its present form we gratify a political Principle of great importance—We shall probably throw Pensylva. into the Southern Scale.

I have thrown these hints together without Study or method.

***

ALS, William Briscoe Stone Papers, NcD. Place to which addressed not indicated. The conclusion of this letter was written on 2 July and is excerpted under that date. The recipient's identity is based on the letter's similarity to the tone of other letters Stone addressed to Walter Stone, and on the exclusion of the probability of its being John Haskins Stone, who is mentioned in the letter. The omitted text relates to family business transactions, including the settlement of the estate of their brother Thomas, and an outline of the Residence Act.

---

[1] The piece is printed as Memnon to Messrs. Goddard and Angell from Baltimore's *Maryland Journal* under 9 June, volume 19; no New York printing has been found.

[2] Clothes and travel goods that Stone had requested.

[3] In its present state.

George Thatcher to Thomas Robison

Your favour of the 14th. June is before; and would have been noticed before this time, but I have waited to see what would be substituted in room of the proposed excise—and now send you inclosed the Copy of a report of a special committee,[1] proposing an additional impost—whether these additional duties will take place or not, I cannot yet determine.

There is, at present, no prospect of an excise being laid, this Session, unless the State debts should be assumed—in which case I rather think an excise will pass—Mr. [*Ebenezer*] Mays has been well recommended by Messrs. [*John*] Fox & [*Daniel*] Davis Representatives, for the Town of Portland.

I also send you a Bill reported to the House, a day or two since, for the encouragement of the Trade and Navigation of the United States—and which I am of opinion will pass into a Law before Congress adjourns—It is a pretty general opinion that some regulations should be made, by Congress, whereby the merchants & traders of the United States are put on as good footing as those of other nations.

FC, Thatcher Family Papers, MHi.

[1] House committee report on ways and means, presented by Fitzsimons on 29 June; see *DHFFC* 6:2040–42.

George Washington, Diary

Having put into the hands of the Vice President of the U. States the communications of Mr. Gouvr. Morris, who had been empowered to make informal enquiries how well disposed the British Ministry might be to enter into Commercial regulations with the United States,[1] and to fulfil the Articles of Peace respecting our Western Posts, and the Slaves which had been carried from this Country,[2] he expressed his approbation that this step had been taken; and added that the disinclination of the British Cabinet to comply with the two latter, & to evade the former, as evidently appears from the Corrispondence of Mr. Morris with the Duke of Leeds (the British Minister for Foreign Affairs) was of a piece with their conduct towds. him whilst Minister at that Court; & just what he expected; & that to have it ascertained was necessary—He thought as a rupture betwn. England & Spain was almost inevitable, that it would be our policy & interest to take part with the latter as he was very apprehensive that New Orleans was an object with the former; their possessing which would be very injurious to us; but he observed, at the same time, that the situation of our affairs would not Justify the measure unless the People themselves (of the United States) should take the lead in the business.

***

The following Gentn. & Ladies dined here to day—viz.—The Secretary of State, Secretary of the Treasury and Secretary at War & their Ladies—Mr. Dalton & Mr. King & their Ladies Mr. Butler & his two daughters—Mr. Hawkins, Mr. Stanton & Mr. Foster & Mr. Izard. The Chief Justice & his Lady, Genl. Schuyler & Mr[*s?*]. Izard were also invited but were otherwise engaged.

Washington Diary, ViHi.

[1] For more on G. Morris's commercial negotiations with Great Britain, see *DHFFC* 2:451–73.

[2] In addition to requiring the British army to leave U.S. soil, Article 7 of the Treaty of Paris (1783) required them to do so without carrying away enslaved Blacks. The treaty made no stipulations about returning former slaves who had run away and emigrated during the war.

Caulkers Wanted

Six d*****s [*dollars*] a day will be given for good caulkers to repair and caulk the new ship C— [*Congress*], R. M[*orris*]. commander. The seams of her bottom having never been properly squared, and the plank of green stuff, it is proposed to give her a thorough repair before she is properly fitted for the great and important voyage to *Philadelphia*. The Captain flatters himself he will be able to conduct her, in safety, to her desired port, having *ingratiated* himself in favor of the *crew*. The owners assure the public, that whatever they may think proper to ship in said vessel shall be punctually delivered to the person authorised to receive the same, agreeably to the *bill of mortality*, on which depends the *absolute fate* of the *united company*.

J. P. and R. H. L.

NYJ, 2 July; reprinted at Boston and Hartford, Middletown, and New London, Connecticut. J. P. and R. H. L. are John Page and Richard Henry Lee.

Letter from Hartford, Connecticut

Consistency in all actions is what ought particularly at this time, to characterize the Americans. A man of but tolerably plain understanding always pays his just debts and gets a good roof over his head before he allows himself to think of possessing the extravagancies and superfluities of life. It appears to me that a mode of thinking and acting is adopted among our public men in this country which (to use an old phrase) is not calculated for our meridian. I am afraid vanity and folly are conspicuous in too many of our public proceedings. There are a certain class of gentlemen whom nothing but *titles* will serve, the mere mimicry of the slavery of Europe, and such as no free American can endure to think of with patience; others, before proper provision is made for the payment of a single creditor, or before they are proprietors of a single foot of land, are pestering the public with their plans for a new seat of government. While foreign benefactors are despising us for our ingratitude in neglecting to make provision for the repayment of money generously loaned, and while the widow and the orphan, the bankrupt soldier and the defrauded officer are looking from the depths of distress for relief, our federal legislature are attempting to plunge still deeper in debt, by purchasing a sufficiency of territory, and erecting suitable buildings for their permanent residence. *Federal Hall* and *New-York* (it appears) are theaters on which they cannot display themselves with sufficient lustre. It can be proved that the discussion of this subject alone has cost the United States at least eight or ten thousand dollars.

NYDA, 9 July; reprinted at Philadelphia; Baltimore; Edenton, North Carolina; and Charleston, South Carolina.

Other Documents

William Bradford to Elias Boudinot. ALS, Wallace Papers, PHi. Written from Philadelphia; addressed to Elizabethtown, New Jersey.

Wishes the question of residence were settled "any how," so that Congress could address more important matters; has heard that the Senate voted for a temporary removal to Philadelphia, but questions whether the decision will be rescinded or postponed; family news; at first opportunity, will send a copy of (Alexander James) Dallas's book (*Reports of Cases Ruled and Adjudged in the Courts of Pennsylvania, Before and Since the Revolution* [Philadelphia, 1790]); asks Boudinot to provide a list of congressmen who have subscribed to it and to promote its sale; Susan (Boudinot Bradford) suffers her old back aches.

Benjamin Goodhue to Stephen Goodhue. ALS, Goodhue Family Papers, MSaE. Addressed to Salem, Massachusetts; franked; postmarked.

Concerning the use of order of $200 he has advanced to Boston bank, he has written to Fanny (Frances Goodhue) "to take out of it so much as she wants for her own use"; "we have nothing new, every thing is yet uncertain."

Stephen Goodhue to Benjamin Goodhue. FC:lbk, Goodhue Family Papers, MSaE. Written from Salem, Massachusetts.

Reports there is nothing new on state politics, except what is in the newspapers.

Benjamin Goodhue to Samuel Hodgdon. No copy known; acknowledged in Hodgdon to Goodhue, 3 July.

Thomas Jefferson to William Short. ALS, Jefferson-Short Letters, ViW. For the full text, see *PTJ* 16:589–90.

Believes with certainty that the Residence Act will pass the Senate that day, although it depends on only one vote; is also very sure of its receiving a majority in the House.

Joseph Manigault to Gabriel Manigault. ALS, Manigault Family Papers, ScU. Addressed to Charleston, South Carolina.

Izard, Smith (S.C.), and their wives, who "are all well," waited on him immediately upon his arrival at City Tavern; "Smith says there are still hopes of the State Debts being assumed."

Samuel Meredith to Margaret Meredith. ALS, badly damaged, Read Papers, PPL at PHi. Place to which addressed not indicated; written at 10 P.M.

Received her letter through Clymer; usually writes very early in the morning, because that is when the post leaves; has little doubt that the Residence Act will pass; no one doubts of Washington's signing it, "as he has a predelection for Potomack & no dislike to Philad."; dined that day at (John) Harrison's (Tavern, 18 Gold Street), where "some hote & Hasty words passed" between "two of the Great opposing Parties," Morris and Schuyler; supposed Schuyler remembered "with pain" having broken faith in the previous session's bargain (with the Pennsylvanians), which would have given New York at least the temporary residence for three years; (her brother) Cadwallader "is well and enjoying the Victory I left him about a half hour agone"; instructs her to send some of his shirts by way of Fitzsimons.

William Peck to Henry Knox. ALS, Knox Papers, Gilder Lehrman Collection, NHi.

Asks "that you will send for Colo. Wadsworth to call on you this Morning" before Congress convenes; "This request I make by his particular desire; as he wishes to have an interview with you" before the President sends the Senate his nominations for federal officers in Rhode Island.

George Thatcher to Thomas B. Wait. No copy known; acknowledged in Wait to Thatcher, 10 July.

Jeremiah Wadsworth to Catherine Wadsworth. ALS, Wadsworth Papers, CtHi. Place to which addressed not indicated.

Rejoices at Daniel's continuing recovery; had a head ache the night before and is very sleepy; had some wine shipped home until his return, "which would be on a Visit next Week if I did not hope that in a fortnight I could come for good & all"; longs to be home but must wait a few days, "tho' the strawberrys run away"; asks to forward an enclosure to Decius.

William Widgery to George Thatcher. ALS, Thatcher Papers, MeHi. Written from Boston; postmarked. Widgery probably refers to Pain Elwell, Jr. (1767–1840), of Waldoboro, Maine.

Requests by the first post Thatcher's opinion on assumption; the (Massachusetts) legislature will not discontinue or suspend the excise until Congress assumes the state debts; has shown Thatcher's (unlocated) letter to (David) Mitchell, who "thought the person you mentioned to me ought not to have the Berth you mention in the Excise"; recommends instead Pain Elwell.

John Sevier, Journal. Claiborne Collection, Ms-Ar.

Loaned Parker twenty silver dollars.

[Georgetown, Maryland] *Times and Potowmack Packet*, 28 July, from non-extant [New Bern] *North Carolina Gazette*, 1 July.

The grand lodge last Friday (25 June) appointed "the Most Worshipful Grand Master" Samuel Johnston a delegate to a continental convention to be held for establishing a Supreme Grand Lodge for the United States.

Letter from New York. *FG*, 2 July.

"Yesterday the senate finished the second reading of the bill for determining the future permanent and temporary residence of Congress—the former is to be on the east bank of the Patowmack after the expiration of ten years, during which time the latter is to be in the city of Philadelphia. The bill will be brought in engrossed today, and there is no doubt of its passing."

Letter from a Member of Congress to Fairfax County. [Alexandria] *Virginia Gazette*, 8 July. The editors believe R. B. Lee authored the letter.

"This day a bill passed the Senate for establishing the permanent seat of the government within 60 miles of tidewater, on the Maryland shore, on the banks of the Patowmack, at the expiration of ten years. The temporary residence, in the mean time, to be the city of Philadelphia. The place for the permanent seat will be chosen under the direction of the President. This bill will certainly pass our House—after which the public business will be harmoniously arranged."

Letter from New York. [Portland, Maine] *Cumberland Gazette*, 12 July.

"It is proposed in Congress to adjourn on the 15th of this month; but I believe the business of the present session will not then be completed."

FRIDAY, 2 JULY 1790

Cool (Johnson)

William Davies to Governor Beverley Randolph

*** The bill for settling the accounts with the individual States [*HR*-77] has passed the house of Representatives, giving the Commissioners of the General board nearly the same powers as before, except that the quota of each State is settled in the bill and two more Commissioners are to be added to the present. It was originally proposed to transfer to the Auditor & Comptroller a considerable portion of the business, but those gentlemen represented the impossibility of attending to it; & the clause was struck out—The settlements made with individuals since Sepr. 1788 by the different States are not to be admitted against the Union. The Representatives applied to me for information on the subject, and finding the amount did not exceed £3000 or £4000 at the utmost, they determined to favor the motion, supposing that Virginia would ultimately be a gainer by it, some of the States having made many settlements of a later date, particularly New York, who as soon as there was a prospect of the assumption of the State debts, opened an office for receiving claims ~~that were~~ for services or supplies during the war.

ALS, Executive Papers, Vi. Place to which addressed not indicated.

James Monroe to James Madison

Your favour of the 17th. of June I have recd. & am sorry to find the most important measures of congress still remaining unsettled & in a very fluctuating state. The assumption will be dislik'd here from what I can learn, under any shape it can assume—under the discussion it has recd. the publick mind appears to be made up on the subject, & will not readily yeild to any accommodation respecting it. you however can best judge of these things & I only mention the above fact as one of those circumstances to be taken into the calculation in any final determination on the subject.

A bill has pass'd the govt. I find for settling the accts. of the U.S. with Individual States [*HR*-77]; by wh. two Com[*missione*]rs. are to be added to those already in office. one will probably be taken from this State, at least

I presume that will be the case. Mr. [*John*] Dawson has I doubt not from the friendship subsisting between you communicated his desire of that appointment. As I know him to be a young man of parts, merit & attention to business, I heartily wish him to succeed. He stands well in the publick estimation in his present office, & I think his appointment wod. be satisfactory to the publick.

[*P. S.*] If you see our friends in B. W.[1] inform them their sister & niece are only in tolerable health.

ALS, Madison Papers, DLC. Written from Richmond, Virginia; franked; postmarked.

[1] Number 90 Broadway was the residence of Elizabeth Monroe's father, the widowed merchant John Kortright (1728–94), and her unmarried siblings, Hester, Mary, Sarah, and John.

Robert Morris to Mary Morris

I Congratulate you my Dearest Friend upon Our Success, for at length the Senate has passed a Bill fixing the Temporary Seat of Congress at Philadelphia for Ten Years, after which it is to be permanently fixed on the Banks of the Potomack (provided the buildings &c. are ready). The next Session of Congress is to Commence on the first day of December next in Philada.

This bill had the third reading & passed in the Senate yesterday 14 to 12, This Morning it will be sent to the House of Representatives where it must have three readings and will undergo a fiery Trial, but our People are Confident that they have a Majority which will carry it through and there is no reason to fear the Presidents Consent, so that we have a much better prospect of perfecting this Momentary Affair to our Satisfaction now than we have had at any time this Session, but I cannot help remembering what happened the last Year, We were nearer to our Object then than we are now, and yet we lost it. at the Moment when we were most sure.

The Majority in the House of Representatives is so small, that many Contingencies may happen to dash the "Cup from the Lip"[1] therefore it is best not to be too Sanguine. The Yorkers are Cunning and intrigueing They Spare no pains to Coax & Cajole those with whom they think there is the least Chance of Success, They lay all the blame of this Measure on me, and abuse me most unmercifully both in the Public Prints*[2] private Conversations and even in the Streets, and Yesterday I was nearly engaged in a Serious quarrell with one of them[3]—However I dont mind all they can do & if I carry the point I will like a good Christian forgive them all.

Mr. Franklin delivered last Night your letter of the 29th. He tells me he was of your party at Grays Gardens[4] and that you were all well &c. I will not now reply particularly to the Contents of your letter—because (but dont say a word to any soul of it) I have a mind to do it in person tomorrow Evening if possible. I am now writing at 5 oClock in the Morning and cannot tell untill after the business of the day Wether I can go or not, but I will if I can, farewell till you see or hear again from your affectionate.

ALS, Morris Papers, CSmH. Addressed to Philadelphia.

[1] A reference to the anonymous proverb, "There's many a slip 'twixt the cup and the lip."

[2] The asterisk may have related to an enclosure.

[3] Schuyler; see Samuel to Margaret Meredith, 1 July, above.

[4] Philadelphia's first public pleasure garden was designed by Samuel Vaughn in the early 1780s around the site of an old tavern that stood on the eastern terminus of Gray's ferry (or "the lower ferry") over the Schuylkill River, the busiest overland access to Philadelphia from points south.

John Samuel Sherburne to John Langdon

I sincerely thank you for the trouble you gave yourself to make those Enquiries of the Secy. [*Hamilton*] by his answers I find I have been misinformed with regard to the tenor of his letter to the presidt. [*governor of New Hampshire*] on that subject, had his sentiments been earlier known. I imagine our Court [*legislature*] might have been induced to make [*lined out*] partial compensation—One Year's payment from 4th. march 1789 has been made by the Gen. Govt. can you tell if any & what measures will be taken for a second years payment this session—From the business before you, we begin to apprehend you will spend another summer at N. York—Will the funding bill in any form pass this session, & will the Assumption take place, are objects of great speculation here. Our Court appointed me one of a committee to instruct our Represents. against assuming, but I found means to prevent their agreeing on any report, whereby the design failed—The party in our Court that is most jealous of the federal Govt. is composed chiefly of the very persons who were most zealous for its adoption, they prevented the Cession of both light house & castle.[1] however I have no doubt they will both be ceded at our next meeting.

***

ALS, Langdon Papers, NhPoA. Written from Portsmouth, New Hampshire. The omitted text relates to private legal affairs.

[1] The island of New Castle, New Hampshire, guarding the approach to Portsmouth about one mile from the mouth of the Piscataqua River, was first fortified in 1632. Military stores were first housed there in 1692, when it was named Fort William and Mary after the reigning

British monarchs. The first (wooden) lighthouse north of Boston was built on the grounds of the fort in 1771. Unused during the Revolutionary War, it was relit in 1784. Both the fort and lighthouse were ceded to the federal government in 1791.

Michael Jenifer Stone to [*Walter Stone*]

***

I have been ill with Reumatic pains and Sensations nephretic. Of the former I have got relieved but not in the least of the Latter. when two Bills—to wit that respecting the Seat of Govt. and that to provide the ways and means for payment of the Debt are through I mean to travel Eastward and taking the Landward routé Home Shall probably touch at the Berkely Springs in [*West*] Virginia.

ALS, William Briscoe Stone Papers, NcD. Place to which addressed not indicated. This is the conclusion of a letter begun on 1 July, printed above.

Jonathan Trumbull to Ebenezer Huntington

We have been in a most distracted situation since you left us, nothing but cabal & Intrigue respecting the place of Residence—& the matter not yet over—a Bill is passed in the Senate—makig. the Potomac the permanent seat of Congress—after 10 Years residence in Phila. to which we are to go the next Sessions. all this is Bargained between *Penna.* & the *Virginia* Interests—& the Matter *fixed* as they suppose beyond the power of the *Northern Faction*—this remains to be tried in the House of Rep. on Tuesday next—the Cabalistic Question has so compleatly occupied all Minds that every other great Object has been arrested to wait its event—or indeed, as you know—on the result of this, hangs the Decision of all other great transactions—a melancholly consideration this indeed—but thus are human Events some times circumstanced—This Situation will prevent Wadsworth's & my attendance at Hartford on the 7th. as we had intended—you'll please make our excuse to the Socity.[1]

ALS, Miscellaneous Papers, NN. Addressed to Norwich, Connecticut.

[1]The Connecticut Society of the Cincinnati convened its annual session at Hartford on 7 July. After a belated July Fourth observance, it elected Wadsworth as president, Trumbull secretary, and this letter's recipient assistant secretary. Wadsworth and Huntington were also appointed two of the delegates to the general meeting of the national society in May 1791 ([Hartford] *Connecticut Courant*, 12 July).

Henry Wynkoop to Reading Beatty

You are altogether mistaken respecting the Adjournment to Philadelphia, the Bill passed the Senate yesterday, will come down to us this day, probably as we have a decided Majority be Assented to tomorrow, by this the permanent Residence is fixed on the Potowmac & the temporary for ten Years in Philadelphia, to which place all the public Offices are to be removed by the first monday in December next; thus we have a Prospect at length to put an end to this disagreable Busyness, & upon Terms, tho' not altogether so advantageous to Pensylvania as might have been wished, yet the the best possible to be procured, and such as must be considered a great Acquisition to the State, for the Financial Arangements once established there, it is improbable that their Removal to an inland Situation will be convenient to Government, The Credit of this Measure is due to our Senators, Mr. Morris who is ridiculed, insulted & abused here, is entitiled to the Gratitude & Esteem of every Man who regards the Interest of Pensylvania.

The funding Bill is yet with the Senate, the aditional Ways & Means you will see in the papers, which were adopted in Committee of the whole yesterday & probably will pass the House this day tho' not without Opposition, cheiffly arising from the non-assumption of the State Debts. could You command the money You would do well to furnish Yourself with Indents sufficient to redeem Your Continental Certifficates, by doing that you add the whole of Your Interest to the principal Stock, by this even at 2 pr. Ct. Your Annuity will be equal & perhaps more & that in actual Specie, than You received at 6 pr. Ct., on account of the encrease of Your principal; I have directed [*Herman Joseph*] Lombaert to get mine in Philadelphia, here they were a few days ago at about 7/. to the pound.

The Indian Corn You must have, tho' I relied on that to supply myself with some necessary Cash.

ALS, Wynkoop Papers, PDoBHi. Place to which addressed not indicated. Written in the morning.

Newspaper Advertisement

To be Sold or Exchanged

For a PLACE in the COUNTRY,

That elegant BUILDING known by the Name of

FŒDERAL HALL!

It has lately undergone a thorough Repair, its Situation is GRAND, being in a fine airy Spot of the City, and its confines bordering close to a Place of public Worship. It is as eligible a Stand for a Speculator or Broker as any in the United States, and as such it has been occupied for some time past. Likewise,

The *Thirteenth Part* of an almost
NEW CONSTITUTION,

Which will be SOLD, under said cost, the Partnership of the present Company being *dissolved*, the Business in future will be carried on under the Firm of R***** M***** [*Morris*] and Company.

NYMP, 2 July.

OTHER DOCUMENTS

George Clymer to Henry Clymer. ALS, Clymer Papers, PHi. Addressed to Philadelphia; written at 3 P.M.; carried by Morris.

The House received the Residence Act today; "the struggle will be hard and the issue not very certain."

William Coombs, David Coats, and Moses Brown to Benjamin Goodhue. ALS, Letters to Goodhue, NNS. Written from Newburyport, Massachusetts. For this letter and background on the petition it relates to, see *DHFFC* 8:418–20.

Elaborates upon grievances contained in their (unlocated) petition on the Impost [HR-2], Tonnage [HR-5], and Coasting [HR-16] acts.

Thomas Fitzsimons to Benjamin Rush. Excerpt of two page ALS, Philadelphia Autograph Company, *Unique Collection of Autograph Items of and Associated with the Bench and Bar* (ca. 1950):item 55. Franked; postmarked. The ellipses are in the source.

"My time at present will only permit me to tell you that the bill for fixing the temporary residence of Congress for 10 years at Phila. and after that time on Potomack passed the Senate yesterday. . . . it must be considered as almost miraculous considering what we have had to contend with to get away from this place is of itself a miracle. . . ."

Benjamin Goodhue to Stephen Goodhue. Undated fragment of AL, Goodhue Family Papers, MSaE. Place to which addressed not indicated. Dated from internal evidence.

"a bill has just pass'd the Senate for establishing the residence of Congress 10 years in Philada., afterwards on the Patowmac and will probably pass our House—the Patowmack scheme is so absurd that very few expect Congress will ever go there—but continue in Philada.—this may give a new turn to bussiness—none of Delagation vote for the Patowmac but abhor it."

Benjamin Huntington to William Ellery. No copy known; docketed on Ellery to Huntington, 21 June.

Pamela Sedgwick to Theodore Sedgwick. ALS, Sedgwick Papers, MHi. Written from Stockbridge, Massachusetts.

Sends letter by (James?) Orton and hopes it meets Theodore en route home; she had depended on his coming with the (New York and Vermont) Commissioners, but now she thinks he will not come until Congress rises; would have been happy to visit him in New York, especially while Mrs. [*Susan Kemper*] Jackson is there, but thinks it is now too late; asks for Agrippa (Hull) to get her a mirror, and to enquire at Kinderhook (New York) for dress stays for Eliza (Mason Sedgwick); they can postpone purchasing parlor furniture for the present.

NYJ, 2 July.

A committee has been appointed by the Massachusetts legislature to consider instructing its U.S. Senators "to use their utmost influence and endeavors to obtain *a reduction of the compensations, salaries and pensions, in general*, which have been granted by" Congress.

Letter from New York. *PP*, 6 July; reprinted at Fredericksburg, Virginia.

"The Residence Bill has been read in the House of Representatives, and Tuesday next is appointed for taking it up.

This day the report of the committee of ways and means was agreed on in a committee of the whole, and a committee appointed to bring in a bill agreeable to the report."

SATURDAY, 3 JULY 1790

Cool (Johnson)

Nathaniel Appleton to Caleb Strong

I have to acknowlege your civilities to me when in New York, & your kind offer to promote my desires, as I have been so long in public employ, of being reappointed Commissr. of Loans in this State—If the Funding bill should not be completed when this reaches you, I would beg leave to remind you of some conversation that passed between us, respecting the compensations to the Commissioners; when I consider the magnitude of the business that must take place in this State, when the domestic Debt shall be re Loand, &

especialy if the State Debts should be assumed; I am confident it cannot be conducted with proper dispatch, & with satisfaction to the public Creditors, with less than three or four Clerks, at the expence of 1000, or 1200 Dollrs. therefore the sum ~~stat~~ of 1500 Dolls. stated in the Bill, as it went up to the Senate, would leave no compensation to the Commissr. especialy if he has Office rent & fuel to provide, I then suggested the propriety of Congress fixing suitable Salaries to the Commissrs. according to the~~ir Ideas of the~~ probable magnitude of the business & the importance of the trust, that will fall to them respectively, & then leaving it to the discretion of the Secretary of the Treasury to allow such Clerks to each of the Commissrs. as he shall judge reasonable, for the proper dispatch of the business—or let Congress after fixing the Salaries, allow a small commission on the sum reloaned as a compensation for the hiring of Clerks, perhaps one twentieth ⅌ Cent on one or two thousand might answer—when it is considered that every Certificate, of which I suppose there are not much less than 200,000 now extant, must be critically examined by the Officers, & compared with the Registers & Checks before they can be passed, that counterfeits maybe detected, some of which are so accurately executed as to evade the notice of the most cautious purchaser, & when it is also considerd, that every Certificate brought in must be registerd in all its particulars as Vouchers for the amount of the new Certificate issued—I say when any one adverts to these circumstances he can form some Idea of the magnitude & importance of the trust to be reposed in the Commissrs., I therefore can't suppose any Gentleman will be disposed to turn them off with mere Clerks wages—no Treasurer in either of the 13 States can, in my opinion, have half the business to transact, which will fall to the Share of the Commissrs. of the large States, while they are reloaning the Debt & you may well remember that the Treasurer of this State [*Alexander Hodgdon*] has 6 or 8 Clerks in his employ.

FC:dft, Appleton Papers, MHi. Written from Boston. Appleton indicated that the letter was "not sent."

Benjamin Goodhue to Michael Hodge

I have not wrote for some time past because I could not communicate anything, and the same reason would forbid my doing it now. If I was not apprehensive you might think me inattentive—Residence funding and Assumption have been and still are so disagreably entangled, that at present there is not sufficient light afforded as to form a a tolerable conjecture of the fate of either—when a subject is not taken up on its own merits distinct from extraneous considerations all is involved in uncertainty—I yet hope a due sense of National obligation may induce us to perform what is justly expected from us—the Residence bill for Philada. and Patowmac has pass'd the Senate and is now before us and tho' our State have and will oppose the bill including so objectionable a place as the Patowmac, yet the Yorkers are so sore at the idea of loosing Congress that they threaten not to vote for the Assumption, tho' we are not as yet accessary—we are perplex'd on every side beyond what any one can conceive, who is not a member.

ALS, Ebenezer Stone Papers, MSaE. Place to which addressed not indicated.

Samuel Hodgdon to Benjamin Goodhue

*** Since the Post came I am honored with your Letter of the 1st instant, was glad to find Berry[1] was forwarded—but more so to hear that Congress were likely to get over a question that has sunk them exceedingly in the minds of all *good Men*—the consequences you apprehend may be experianced, unless the appropriation is severed from the [*Residence*] Bill[2]—which I hope will be the case—A Century to come will not I trust find Congress to the southward of *Susquehanna*—the centre of *population*, not *territory*, should in my opinion determine, the place suitable for their residence at *all* times.

*** shall thank you for a Line as often as you have leisure.

ALS, Letters to Goodhue, NNS. Written from Philadelphia; dated 3 June, but internal references as well as Goodhue's endorsement identify it as 3 July.

[1] John Berry, of the New York City stationer's firm of Berry and Rogers, was reimbursed in April 1790 for providing stationery to the House (*DHFFC* 8:825). Hodgdon's reference may be to helping to secure additional supplies contracts.

[2] The bill appropriated money for "the necessary expence" of the removal from Philadelphia to the Potomac in 1800.

Benjamin Huntington to Governor Samuel Huntington

Congress are in an awkward Situation Between Assumption—Ways and Means—Increasing Duties—Excise—Permanent Seat without money to Build it—Temporary Residence and Funding System all these Matters very uncertain, I Believe the Assumption cannot be take Place this Session I shall give the earliest Information when any of these Matters become Certain.

ALS, privately owned in 1995. Addressed to Connecticut; franked; endorsed "private" by the recipient; answered 7 July.

Richard Bland Lee to Theodorick Lee

I have received your letter from Dumfries [*Virginia*] of the 25th. Ult. ***

The Bill in faver of the Potowmack has passed the Senate after a very dubious struggle. It will be considered by the house of Representatives on Tuesday next. It will be encountered by some difficulties but none I hope insurmountable. I thank you for your attention to my election. I wish I could hear the fate of the wheat. I apprehend the worst.

ALS, McGregor Library Collection, ViU. Addressed to "Sully," Loudoun County, Virginia, "By way of Alexandria"; franked; postmarked.

Nathaniel Rogers to John Langdon

I have the pleasure of acknowledging the receipt of your friendly & polite favor of the 15th. ultimo—To be consi[*dered*] in the number of your friends is an honor I shall always be ambitious to deserve.

*** we are begining to electioneer for delegates to Congress. the meetings are to be on the last Monday of August before which hope the pleasure of seeing you.

I cant help remarking that there seems to be no end to congressional disputes a Question determined to day taken up tomorrow & so on but from present appearances (of every other that of permanent or temporary residence seemes of the least necessity for unless they are better agreed they will sit where they are till doms day [*doomsday*]—from the way of doing business it is impossible for *me* to know from the news paper accounts whereabouts they are too [*?*] true now & then we are told that this & that act, for compensation to A. & B. had passed & this & that Officers Salary was raised & that new Officers are to be appointed & since I think of it & it would be *very* convenient If my friend should bring me in for a share in the next distribution of the loaves & fishes[1] I should not be affronted—President [*Governor Josiah*] Bartlet was dangerously Ill on thursday since which I have not heard If he should die what a glorious figure we should cut with our Senior Senator at the head Coll. E[*benezer*]. Smith[2]—I should have done myself the honor of answering your letter sooner but tho't then it was probable Congress might adjourn before it would reach you but perceiveing there is no end to their last word send this not doubting it will find you at N. York.
[*P. S.*] Judge Livermore will undoubtedly be reelected.

ALS, Langdon Papers, NhPoA. Written from Newmarket, New Hampshire. The omitted text reports on the good health of Langdon's family and reveals the political motives behind the upcoming impeachment trial of Woodbury Langdon.

[1] Mark 6:41–44.

[2] Under New Hampshire's constitution that took effect in 1784, the president of the state Senate would serve as acting governor until the vacancy was filled by a special election.

Baron de Steuben

Those who have any doubts on their minds; (says a correspondent) as to the justice of the pension granted by Congress to the Baron DE STEUBEN, are referred to the Speech of Mr. GERRY, inserted in THE CENTINEL of May 8th, last[1]—where are faithfully shewn the sacrifices, services and merits of that *able* disciplinarian, and veteran friend to America—and where too, they will see, that the faith of the United States was pledged by Congress to him, that he should receive adequate compensation for the sacrifices he had made in Europe—and the amount of those sacrifices regulated the sum he is to receive. The Baron is now in the vale of his years—and it would have reflected disgrace on our country,

Like *Belisarius*,[2] had the world been told,
We left him naked, wretched, poor, and old,
To seek a refuge in the silent grave,
Or beg his bread in realms he fought to save.

[Boston] *Columbian Centinel*, 3 July; reprinted at Exeter, New Hampshire, and New York City (*NYMP*, 10 July).

[1] The then *Massachusetts Centinel* printed a portion of Gerry's speech of 19 April from *NYDA*, 21 April (*DHFFC* 13:1081–83).

[2] A Roman general (d. 565) who lost favor with the Emperor Justinian and according to legend was blinded and reduced to begging on the streets.

OTHER DOCUMENTS

William Few to Joseph Clay. Summary of ALS, *Libbie Catalog*, 17–18 November 1904, item 1124.

Relating to business in Congress and the establishment of the seat of government on the Potomac River.

Theodore Sedgwick to Pamela Sedgwick. No copies known; two letters mentioned in Theodore to Pamela Sedgwick, 4 July.

Philemon Waters to George Washington. ALS, Miscellaneous Letters, Miscellaneous Correspondence, State Department Records, Record Group 59, DNA. Place from which written not indicated; delivered by Burke. For the full text, see *PGW* 6:7–8.

Expects federal government will purchase a large territory of Creek land and seeks a grant there as redress for an unsatisfied bounty claim against Virginia's royal government in the Ohio Valley, for service in the French and Indian War; mentions Sumter and Burke as references.

SUNDAY, 4 JULY 1790

Cool (Johnson)

Abigail Adams to Mary Cranch

A Memorable day in our calender a Church[1] beloning to the dutch congregation is this day to be opened and an oration deliverd, this Church was the scene of misiry & horrour. the prison where our poor Countrymen were confined, crowded & starved during the war & which the British afterwards destroyed. it has lately been rebuilt and this day is the first time that they have met in it. they have done us the favour of setting apart a pew for us. the Clergyman is dr. [*William*] Lynn one of the Chapling to congress and I think a better preacher than most that I have heard to day; an oration is to be deliverd by dr. [*John Henry*] Livingstone the other Minister belonging to this Church, but as to an orater, the oratory of a Clergyman here consists in foaming loud speaking working themselves up in such an enthusiam as to cry. but which has no other effect upon me than to raise my pitty. o when when shall I hear the Candour & liberal good Sense of a [*Richard*] Price again, animated with true piety without enthusiasm, Devotion without grimace and religion upon a Rational System.

My Worthy Friend Mrs. [*Abigail*] ~~Rog~~ Rogers is returning to Boston, She has engaged to convey this to you with a Magizine which has for a Frontispeice a View of this House,[2] but the great Beauty could not be taken upon so small a scale Which is the Noble Hudson. as far distant from the House as the bottom of the Boston Mall is from the Governours [*John Hancock*] House if you see Mrs. Rogers, as it is probable you will at commencment,[3] she will tell you how delightfull this spot is, and how I regret the thoughts of quitting It, I shall miss her more than half N. York besides. We are very well, but impatient to hear from you and Family. I wish Congress would so far compleat their buisness as not to have an other Session till the Spring.

I really think I would then come home and pass the Winter with you; Mr. Adams wants some excercise ever since the 4th of janry. he has not mist one hour from attendance at Congress. he goes from Home at ten and seldom gets back till four, and 5 hours constant Sitting in a day for six months together. (for He cannot leave his Chair) is pretty tight service. reading long Bill, hearing Debates, and not always those the most consonant to his mind and opinions putting questions, stating them, constant attention to them that in putting questions they may not be misled, is no easy task whatever Grumblers may think, but Grumblers there always was & always will be.

ALS, Abigail Adams Papers, MWA. Addressed to Braintree, Massachusetts; carried by Abigail Rogers.

---

[1] The Middle Dutch Church was built in 1731 for the city's second Dutch Reformed Church congregation on Nassau between Liberty and Cedar streets. Used as a hospital and a riding school during the British Army's occupation of the city (1776–83), only the exterior walls stood when repairs were begun in 1788 (*New York*, pp. 130–31).

[2] The *New York Magazine* volume 1, no. 6 (June 1790) featured the only known rendering of "Richmond Hill" during the Adams's occupancy, drawn and engraved by Cornelius Tiebout; see *DHFFC* 9:244.

[3] Harvard College's summer commencement was an important social event in the Boston area.

John Dawson to James Madison

I am favourd with your letter of the 24th. ulto., & request that you'll accept my thanks for it, & for your attention to the business with Twining. I fear that my chance for payment from that quarter is a very bad one—shoud the bill give him any Money I must repeat my request to you to secure some for me as realy it is an object of some consequence, & a debt which ought to be paid.

I am sorry to hear that the eastern members have not relinquishd the asumption business—I do not know any event which woud cause~~d~~ such general discontent in this state—fixing the seat of the goverment on the Potomac is surely a desireable thing; but even this woud not compensate for the evils which woud result from the adoption of the other measure; especially as there woud be very little chance of a compliance at the end of twelve or fifteen years.

In one of the papers which you were kind enough to forward to me I observe that a bill has passd the H. of R.—for settling the accounts of the U.S. with the individual states—by this 2 additional Commissioners are to be appointed—the gentlemen at present in office are I think, from N.H. P. & S.C.—& as it is a business in which all the states will feel particularly interested, I presume some person will be appointed from this state—if you have thought of no person more proper than myself I will thank you to mention my name to the President as I am realy tired of the inactive station I am at present in.

ALS, Madison Papers, DLC. Place from which written not indicated. For background on Nathaniel Twining's petition and the act to compensate him, see *DHFFC* 8:241–46.

Elbridge Gerry to John Wendell

By the post last evening I received your favour of the 24th of June, with sundry inclosures which shall be sent agreable to their directions I was always of opinion that some of the salaries were too high & gave my negative to them, & to the judiciary establishment also, which I considered as an oppressive act: but it was necessary to organize the government, before a revenue could be provided for the support of public credit. the uneasiness of the people arises more from a disappointment of the immediate benefits they were promised from the operation of the new constitution, than from other causes. I always predicted discontents from this cause, for when the proper line of policy was to prepare the people at the time they were ratifying the constitution, for a patient submission to the administration thereof untill the good effects could be attained, they were elated with promises that as soon as the government could be put in motion commerce manufactures & agriculture would flourish the value of lands would be enhanced, the public debts would be funded, money would be plenty &c. &c. &c. & their inevitable disappointment produces uneasiness. I know very well that the measures of congress have been impeeded & vitiated in some instances by local & private veiws & prejudices, & in a greater degree than at this period I expected: but had they been unexceptionable, discontents would have been the result of the impolicy alluded to. there is more-over every reason in my mind to expect they will increase & therefore I wish to be releived from the cares of my present situation, as I see no prospect of giving public satisfaction: & without this I wish never to be in any public office whatever. I agree with you in the indispensible necessity of enabling citizens who are able & willing to pay their debts, & there can be no doubt of projects sufficient to make medium plenty very soon: the difficulty in my mind is, that the projects will be too numerous or too far extended as soon as the foundation is laid by a collection of the revenue. I have tho't of an expedient which if ~~it~~ on further examination it should meet my own approbation may hereafter be suggested in order for improvement but I confess to you, that in the present crude state of our system for establishing public credit, too much precaution cannot in my mind be taken ~~to~~ with respect to a paper medium.

The death of Colo. [*Thomas, Jr.*] Gerry was very unexpected & gave me a great shock, which has been since followed by the loss of my very particular friend Colo. Bland of Virginia. the distresses arising from such events & the pressure of public concerns have lately impaired my health, altho I consider it as an indispensible duty implicitly to acquiesce in the dispensations of divine providence.

Mrs. [*Ann*] Gerry is happily in bed this morning with a lively girl [*Eleanor*].

[*P. S.*] I have deliverd your message to my brother in law Mr. [*John*] Thompson who returns his compliments.

ALS, Autograph Collection, PHi. Addressed to Portsmouth, New Hampshire; franked; postmarked.

James Madison to James Monroe

You will find by one of the Gazettes herewith sent, that the bill fixing the permanent seat of Government on the Potowmac, and the temporary at Philadelphia, has got through the Senate. It passed by a single voice only, Izzard and Few having both voted against it. Its passage through the House of Representatives is probable, but attended with great difficulties. If the Potowmac succeeds, even on these terms, it will have resulted from a fortuitous coincidence of circumstances which might never happen again.

The provision for the public debt has been suspended for some time in the Senate by the question relating to the seat of Government. It is now resumed in that House, and it is to be hoped will soon be brought to an issue. The assumption sleeps, but I am persuaded will be awakened on the first dawn of a favorable opportunity. It seems, indeed, as if the friends of the measure were determined to risk everything rather than suffer that finally to fail.

We hear nothing further of the controversy between England and Spain.

PJM 13:261–62, from Madison, *Letters* 1:521–22.

John Page to St. George Tucker

I thank you for your frequent Hints respecting my Election—I have done all that I can reconcile to my own Principles If my Constituents can suffer themselves to be imposed upon by a Man who takes Advantage of my Absence & News-paper Misrepresentations—if they think an untried Person whom they scarcely know is to be prefered to one who has been tried *"as it were by Fire,"* be it so—they Use *"the Prerogative of free men,"* & I shall enjoy the Luxury of Retirement, made sweet, by the sweetest Partner [*Margaret Page*] of domestic Happiness—Adieu my dear Tucker.

[*P. S.*] I have not forgotten your Hints respecting your Brother [*Thomas Tudor Tucker*]; if possible I shall carry him to Rosewell—neither have I forgotten your favorite Trunk. I think I shall shew it to you. when we meet—I say nothing of politicks because Friendship has nothing to do with it—& because I am sick of it, & you will have enough of it in the Papers & from every idle Person with whom you can meet.

ALS, Tucker-Coleman Papers, ViW. Addressed to Williamsburg, Virginia; franked; postmarked 6 July.

Philip Schuyler to Stephen Van Rensselaer

Your favor of the 27th ult. I had the pleasure to recieve on the first instant. I am much obliged by the communication, and hope my dear Little child [*granddaughter Catherine Schuyler van Rensselaer*] is before this compleatly recovered.

A Bill has passed the Senate by a Majority of two fixing the permanent seat of Congress from the year 1800 at potomac and at such place there as commissioners to be appointed by the president shall locate, and that next sessions shall be held at Philadelphia, and every other until the year 1800. It will probably pass the house of representatives with a majority of two or three. this measure has been carryed by a compact in which the parties have sacrificed what many of them deemed national objects of prime magnitude and on that Account [*lined out*] is very reprehensible, as well as because It has evinced a want of that decency which was due to a City whose citizens had made very capital Exertions for the accomodation of Congress. and who had paid every attention [*to*] Its members.

My expectations on the funding system have been so repeatedly disappointed that I can no longer rely on assertions and must wait the event. a final decission either way will probably be had towards the end of the ensuing week.

ALS, Smith Collection, NjMoHP. Place to which addressed not indicated.

Theodore Sedgwick to Pamela Sedgwick

I yesterday wrote you two very short letters by Mr. Verplank.[1] The last I wrote at Mr. Benson's request and both in such violent hurry that I consider myself obliged to ask your excuse. For some time the citizens here have been in violent agitation on account of the proposed removal of congress from this place to Philadelphia. The event has become probable from a coalition between the Pensylvanians and the southern members. There is a caricature right hand is Mr. Jefferson instead of a walking staff: in his fob Col. Hamilton & at the chain Madison hanging as a bauble, The senators who should seem confused by the motion of the building are looking out of the windows and perceiving the cause they exclaim, "where are you going to carry us Robert?" He answers by a label "where ever I please": — In the back ground are represented the members of the house of Representatives with myself in front. These words are put into my mouth. "Stop Robert you rascal and take my assumption with you." To which he answers, "I'll be d—nd if I do": — Indeed the rage here against Mr. Morris, who has done every thing in his power to sacrifice the

Theodore Sedgwick to Pamela Sedgwick, 4 July, ALS, p. 2. This letter contains the only known description of a lost cartoon that linked assumption and the seat of government question, before the terms of the "Compromise of 1790" were widely known. In addition to Jefferson, Hamilton, and Madison, Sedgwick identified himself in the cartoon, leading a House delegation that demands that Morris carry assumption along with him to Philadelphia. (Courtesy of the Massachusetts Historical Society.)

"What think ye of C_o_n_ss now. View of C_o_n_ss on the road to Philadelphia." Cartoons were an uncommon form of political commentary during the American Revolution. The editors know of no event that generated more of them than Congress's decision to move from New York to Philadelphia in 1790. Evidence of four, or perhaps five, cartoons exists. The most famous, expertly accomplished and multicolored, circulated outside of New York; see *DHFFC* 9:311. The most significant one attributed George Washington's signature on the Residence Act to "self-gratification"; it will appear as an illustration in *DHFFC* 21. On 8 July the editor of the *New York Morning Post* described "Y. Z. Sculp"'s etching, shown here, as the most villainous ever issued in the United States because of its implication that one of the fourteen Senators of the majority had been bribed by Robert Morris, who was shown carrying a bag of money and pulling the twelve minority Senators along the "Road to Philadelphia" by strings through their noses. From left to right, the dialogue for the "Majority" Senators on the "Ladder of Preferment" [A] reads "my Name is Robert Coffer R.M.," "Stick to it Bobby," "we are going at the rate of 6 Dollars pr. day," "Money & preferment," and "This is what Influences me." The dialogue of the "Manority" is more complex: "It is bad to have a gouty Constitution"; "I am affraid bobbys dance will not mend it"; "I hope the Philadelphians will not serve us as they once did," a general reference to events when Congress previously resided there from 1774 to 1783 (or perhaps a specific reference to the Continental Army mutiny there in June 1783); "so do I for I am tired of traviling," a reference to the fact that Congress had met in five places between 1783 and 1790; "What will they move to prolong our next session"; "the divil & Bobby will help them to something"; "This looks like disinteresesested proceedings"; "O yes & well becomeing the servants of the people"; "This move has deprived us of our fish & lobsters"; and "Ay and Oysters too." (New York: Anonymous, 1790, Collection of The New-York Historical Society.)

print designed and it is said executing,[2] which is to represent Mr. Morris with the federal building on his shoulders, in one of his pockets Mr. Jay and in the other General Knox. In his right hand is Mr. Jefferson instead of a walking staff, in his fob col. Hamilton & at the chain Madison hanging as a bauble; The senators it should seem roused by the motion of the building are looking out of the windows and perceiving the cause they exclaim, "where are you going to carry us Robert?" He answers by a label "where ever I please." In the back ground are represented the members of the house of Representatives with myself in front. These words are put into my mouth. "Stop Robert you rascal and take my assumption with you." To which he answers, "I'll be d—nd if I do." Indeed the rage here against Mr. Morris, who has done every thing in his power to sacrafice the interest of the public and the reputation of the government to his own emolument is such that it perhaps might not be safe for him to be here tomorrow, when the anniversary of independence will be celebrated. He has prudently pretended business and is gone to Philadela.

In the senate they have committed the proposition for assumption, for which there is a majority of 2 or 3 members. it will probably be there determined by tuesday or wednesday, when it will come down to the house, By that time I hope we shall have done with the paltry business of residence. I dont know what untoward circumstance may intervene but I most ardently hope we shall compleat it by the end of this week. I pray you dearest & best beloved of my soul not to be very anxious or impatient the little time I have to be absent—it cannot be many days.

ALS, Sedgwick Papers, MHi. Place to which addressed not indicated.

[1] Gulian Verplanck, the sole commissioner for New York state to have attended the meeting with Vermont commissioners scheduled for 6 July in Stockbridge, Massachusetts ([Stockbridge, Massachusetts] *Western Star*, 13 July; Pamela to Theodore Sedgwick, 8 July, below).

[2] No copies are extant; it may not have been executed.

William Smith (S.C.) to Edward Rutledge

After com[*plimenti*]ng you, my worthy friend, on this ~~auspicious~~ illustrious day re[*nown*]ed so by the exertions of yourself & other Patriots, I ack[*nowle*]dge the obligations I am under to you for several Letters co[*ntai*]ning an interesting detail of your proceedings at Columa. Some I read with satisfaction; others with indignation at the almost incredible treachery of some of our low country people—had the Seat of Govt. not been fixed at Columbia I shod. have been entirely satisfied with the Constitn.—as it is, I am more & more pleased with it; the Census has thrown a new light on this

Subject & your reflections on the weight of population must make every low-country citizen extremely thankful for your exertions. Tho I am sincerely chagrined at the Success of the back country in their favorite object, yet the circumstance of that triumph on their part creating unanimity in passing the Constitution will ~~prompt~~ compel me soon to acquiesce in the determination; but I must have time for it, for I can't yet get over it. Besides the folly & absurdity of the measure, it will I fear shed a malignant influence on all the proceedings of the Legislature.

Many severe strictures have been passed on ~~the~~ our [*new state*] Constitution by the Constitution-mongers here, who argue from theory alone, & who would make Constitutions to be read & not to be acted upon. Madison told me he thought we made no figure at Constitn.-making; I was obliged to enter into a history of So. Car. politics, & then he thought better of it—the T[*wo*] Treasuries,[1] without one Treasure, is a cause of merriment a[*t o*]ur expence—the rotation of officers—the Exclusion from continental & state offices at the same time, the *fifteen* members for Charleston, the large representation for a small State, as they think ours, the want of power in the Executive, the details, &ca. are objects of censure; the consequence is that I have a great deal of trouble, for whenever I hear any of these comments, I enter into the state of parties, the local considerations which were necessarily attended to & the whole detail of the business.

I wrote you a few lines a day or [*torn*] by an opportunity, which I had just heard of at the time of [*torn*]. I mentioned the safe arrival of your amiable Son [*Henry Rutledge*], whom I [*torn*] great pleasure. Your young friend [*son*] Hal will always [*carry?*] with him strong personal recommendations; his manners & understand[*ing*] will procure him friends & admirers in every part of the continent. [*I*] feel the strongest prepossessions in his favor; I should feel them on [*your*] account alone were there no other inducement: with the assistance of your Letters he will not fail to meet a hearty welcome wherever you are known; & where you are not personally known, you are by reputation.

I herewith send you the Bill for settling the accounts between the U.S. & the Several States [*HR*-77] as it passed the Represents.—the Senate have struck out the Clause appointing two additional Commissrs. & I am afraid will curtail the time for bringing in Claims—our house were not disposed to grant so long a time, as most of the States have already sent in their Claims—I am very intimate with the leading eastern men, some of them have a regard I beleive for me & they voted for a long time, because I requested it: I hope they will not give up to the Senate.

I see by the Constitution the Election for Delegates [*Representatives*] will come on in October—some of my Correspondents have asked me whether I will Serve again—I wished not to have made up my mind till Sepr. if possible to delay giving an ansr. till then, but my constituents have a right to know my determination which I make with considerable apprehensions of making a wrong one, tho I have very seriously thought on the subject. The very flattering testimony of approbation I have been honored with from you & other friends is extremely encour[*agi*]ng, & your opinion that I shod. not meet with opposition [*removed the*] terrors of another contest: altho I came off victorious on the former occasion, yet I dislike the anxiety these struggles necessarily excite: As my friends think I am worthy of the station, & that my attention to business & ~~my~~ zeal for my country's welfare supply the ~~deficiency~~ place of splendid talents I am ready to offer my services, such as they are, to my countrymen; promises I hope are not necessary & that my past conduct will be an earnest of my future labors. I make some pecuniary sacrifices, but I shall be indemnified in the reflection that they are for a country I love & that every benefit which it shall receive will be [*torn*].

***

ALS, Smith Papers, ScHi. The ALS is torn; the missing letters and words are taken from the *SCHM* printing. Addressed to Charleston, South Carolina; franked. The omitted text discusses family and business affairs. The conclusion of this letter was written on 5 July and is printed under that date, below. For the full text, see *SCHM* 69(1968):120–22.

[1] Under Article X of the state constitution, one treasurer was to reside at the new capital of Columbia, while another remained at Charleston.

George Thatcher to David Sewall

The inclosed [*Residence*] Bill passed the Senate, and came to the House on Fryday—And Tuesday is assigned to take it up. This bill is the result of a very singular combination of circumstances—and however proper the Bill may be—& however advantageous it will prove to the U. States for the permanent Seat of Government to be fixed so far south as the Patomock, nothing but an extraordinary convention of circumstances could, at this time, have produced it—Every passion good and bad has had its influence—every degree of art—simulation and dissimulation has been practiced during the discussion and passage of the Bill thro the Senate—It has a thousand times brought to my mind a passage of the bible—I think, in Psalms—and if I mistake not nearly in these words—"surely the wrath of man shall praise the—and the remainder ~~of of his wrath~~ thereof thou wilt restrain"[1]—I dont know that I have receited the words exactly—but sufficiently so to refer you to the place where they may be seen.

When I see public men giving their votes for, & advocating measures, which their reason & cooler understanding, at the very time, condemn—

and, which measures finally turn out to the good of the Community, or of the human race in general, I look upon them as a literal fulfillment of the declaration contained in the foregoing words—And I dont know of an instance where it was more compleatly so than the present—For I beleive it will be acknowledged, by some of the actors themselves, that the very worst of passions, have been chiefly instrumental in effecting this Bill—What will be done with it in the House I cannot yet say—but am rather of opinion it will be agreed to—a majority of the House are, some from one motive, & some from another, in sentiment—if not in league, with the party who carried it in the Senate.

This subject of Residence has cost much time, & been the cause of vast delay of public Business—for which the members of Congress have been justy censored—and yet, in the present state of things, passions & prejudices, I must acknowledge that I dont see how it could have been otherwise—It seems like "the offences that must happen, & yet woe to the men by whom they come."[2]

The papers inform us of Mr. Daltons fall[3]—and we Representatives look upon it as laying the ax at the root of the tree, the declaration whereof is, "be ye also ready"[4]—and blessed is the man who shall be found prepared.

Yours of the 28th. June came to hand last evening—I am almost surprised at the increase of legal Business in the County of York [*Maine*]—and am inclined to think a prediction made four or five years ago by Crazy Jonathan [*Thatcher*], is begining to come to pass—viz. that the increase of Justiciary power will have quite a different effect on the Community from what was generally expected.

The Secretary of War, to whom was refered the petition of Joseph Hardison, has reported favourably—& a committee is appointed to bring in a Bill, allowing pay to the captive, from the time of capture to the end of the war.[5]

FC, Thatcher Family Papers, MHi.

---

[1] Psalms 76:10.
[2] Matthew 18:17.
[3] Thatcher refers to Dalton's loss of his Senate seat.
[4] Matthew 24:44.
[5] For background on Joseph Hardison's petition for back pay and related documents mentioned here, see *DHFFC* 7:402, 417–18, 420.

George Thatcher to Sarah Thatcher

Having wrote you two or three pretty long Letters the last week—I shall, at this time, barely acknowledge the receipt of yours of the 24th. & 26th.

June—And tell you that I hope to leave this place by the Twentieth of this month.

I cannot account for your not receiving a Letter from me on the day you wrote your last—for I am pretty confident that I wrote you the sunday before—I do not recollect of having omitted writing a sunday for some months.

I have frequently noticed the kindness of our friends to you; and shall always be happy in returning the like with good interest—The dear Children or their mamma cannot be more desirous of my return than I am anxious to get home.

ALS, Thatcher Family Papers, MHi. Place to which addressed not indicated.

Oliver Wolcott, Jr. to Oliver Wolcott, Sr.

***

With respect to public business in the country I can form no definite calculation—Congress are still disputing whether they shall fund the debt—the assumption of the State Debts this session is an improbable event—*direct Taxes*, are the political abhorrence of the day—and I believe that a majority cannot be induced to vote for any thing resembling an *Excise*—thus it seems all the Revenues are expected to be derived from duties on Importations.

I have no doubt that the government will either come to nothing, or that ~~a~~ different ideas will be adopted, that the immense debt of this country is to be be charged upon the commercial capital and that all other property is to be excused from any direct contribution; I regard as a visionary illusion of the mind—When the change of sentiments which I have mentioned shall happen there will be respectable appointments in the Revenue Department in the Country. ***

I wish it was in my power to give you a pleasing account of the state of our public affairs—nothing is yet done, nor can I determine from the votes in Congress what any one wishes or expects to do.

The question respecting the State Debts is not given up, continual negociations are making with regard to it—the question of residence is also continually entangling every measure which is proposed and a a party which can be gained in favor of one proposition, is frequently lost by the resentment which another party can excite by bringing up some other question.

There are in Congress all the varieties of opinions that can be imagined, some believe that the public debt has qualities which are most sacred—these insi[*s*]t that nothing shall be done which does not imply the greatest veneration for the public Creditors—others imagine that their Claims are principally founded in accident or fraud—and wish to disavow the obligations of the late Government—In the mean between these extremes, the truth probably lies, and if any thing is compleated, the result will be a proposal for a new Loan of the public Debt, at about four ℔ Cent Interest.

With respect to residence, I think we shall finally settle in Philadelphia, where the consequences stated in your Letter will be perceived.

Some indications of a spirit, too imperious, have appeared. Indeed, all the disputes of this session, may in my opinion be traced to the rival claims for preeminence, between Massa. & Virginia, New York & Pensylvania—These States have very important interests at stake, which cannot easily be reconciled, and the consciousness which they have ~~have~~ of their weight in the government, prevents them from exercising all the moderation, which our present circumstances require.

***

ALS, Wolcott Papers, CtHi. Place to which addressed not indicated.

From New York

The TEMPORARY RESIDENCE is fixed, in the Senate, for 10 years, at *Philadelphia.* The PERMANENT RESIDENCE on the *Potowmack*; at Carrolsburg[1] some think. The question on the permanent business was carried for the Potowmack, yeas 16, nays 9. The question in favour of *New-York*, as the *temporary residence* was at first carried by a majority of *one.* On *Tuesday* the Bill was called up, and debated nearly three days, when the question being put to strike out *New-York*, and insert *Philadelphia*—it finally passed in the affirmative, yeas 14, nays 12.

The Assumption will soon be determined—now the residence is like to be finished. For this vexatious subject, has engrossed a great part of the attention both in, and out of Congress.

[Boston] *Columbian Centinel*, 10 July; reprinted at Portland, Maine; Exeter and Keene, New Hampshire; and Newburyport, Massachusetts.

---

[1] In 1770, Daniel Carroll of Duddington platted the town of Carrollsburg in Prince Georges County, Maryland. It was near the confluence of the Potomac River and its Eastern Branch, or the Anacostia River, several blocks south of the present U.S. Capitol.

Other Documents

Martha Dangerfield Bland to George Washington. ALS, Washington Papers, DLC. Written from "Cawson," Prince George County, Virginia. For the full text, see *PGW* 6:9–13n.

Inquires about some of Bland's unsettled public accounts as a Continental Army officer in 1777 and a member of Congress in 1781; she (as sole executrix of her husband's estate) is "left *alone* to Conduct all his private affairs with his whole fortune perfectly independent and large enough for every rational wish."

Thomas Fitzsimons to Benjamin Rush. Summary and excerpt of three page ALS from *Collector* 59(1946):item 1402. Franked; postmarked. The ellipses are in the source.

"Mentions opposition in 'our Congregation' and advice which Rush has given him. 'The [*Residence*] bill sent down from the senate will be taken up by us on tuesday till which time we postponed it that after once taking it up we might not suffer anything else to interrupt it. Our Enemys are using every stratagem that art or malice can advise. . . . While some of our friends are so weak that we tremble for their stability—The Abuse of us by the people of this place is outrageous, and I learn that we are not much better used at home.' . . ."

Governor Samuel Huntington to Benjamin Huntington. ALS, Huntington Autograph Book, NRom. Written from Norwich, Connecticut.

Considers the final settlement of the states' accounts with the United States to be "of great Importance, & absolutely Essential for National Confidence & prosperity"; encloses letter for forwarding to London; "your Lady [*Anne Huntington*], appears to me gradually declining notwithstanding some unexpected favourable Symtoms at the first approach of warm weather this Spring"; news of health and deaths of other friends and family.

Thomas Jefferson to Francis Eppes. ALS, Jefferson Papers, DLC. Place to which addressed not indicated. For the full text, see *PTJ* 16:598.

Residence and the assumption "have so chafed the members that they can scarcely go on with one another"; assumption will never be settled in the present form, but neither can it be wholly rejected without "preventing the funding the public debt altogether which would be tantamount to a dissolution of the government"; assumes the Residence Act will pass the House.

Thomas Jefferson to Nicholas Lewis. FC, Jefferson Papers, DLC. For the full text, see *PTJ* 16:599–600.

Believes the Residence Bill will pass the House on 6 July by a considerable majority.

Thomas Jefferson to Edward Rutledge. FC, Jefferson Papers, DLC. For the full text, see *PTJ* 16:600–601.

Describes Congress's attempts to counteract Great Britain's trade restrictions; it is thought that pending proposals for reciprocal restrictions will not be agreed to; "the fear is that it would irritate Great Britain were we to feel any irritation ourselves"; the debates show that "there are good men and bold men, & sensible men, who publicly avow these sentiments"; the Residence Act will probably pass the House.

William Samuel Johnson to Samuel William Johnson. ALS, Johnson Papers, CtHi. Addressed to Stratford, Connecticut; franked; postmarked.

Cautions Samuel Johnson against too much fatigue; "be at all times attentive to the preservation of your health," especially when adapting to new climates; enumerates construction, clothing, food, and other items sent home; "We are all, thank God, in very good Health."

James Madison to Fontaine Maury. No copy known; acknowledged in Maury to Madison, 20 July.

Jeremiah Wadsworth to Harriet Wadsworth. ALS, Wadsworth Papers, CtHi. Place to which addressed not indicated. Signed "your affectionate friend & parent."

Receipt of her letter the night before made him as happy as he could be at that distance from home; "public duty commands my stay here," but for no more than a fortnight, he hopes, when he will return home; "Uncle Trumbull" and (his brother) John are both there and well.

Mercy Warren to Elbridge Gerry. Listing of ALS, *Libbie Catalog* 17 March 1891, item 6397.

Monday, 5 July 1790

Hot (Johnson)

Pierce Butler to James Iredell

If my little interest has been instrumental in placing you [*as an associate justice of the Supreme Court*] where you will do honor to the recommendation, and render so essential service to the country, my feelings are more highly gratified than I will venture to express. In paying a tribute to sincere friendship, I have at the same time not only discharged my public duty, but served the United States.

May you live long, my dear Sir, to enjoy the honorable station, where the unanimous voice of such of your fellow-citizens as had a right to a voice on the occasion has placed you, is my ardent wish.

I am very glad that my country, South Carolina, and countrymen meet with your approbation. I thank you for the copy of our [*state*] constitution. I hope it will answer the purpose for which the Convention were called. I have seen systems that I like as well. It is not for me though to say any thing against it. I can live under it as well as others. Congress are still sitting: if I did not hope to have the pleasure of seeing you soon here I would tell you what we have been doing. The House of Representatives are now debating the questions of Permanent and Temporary Residence. . . . Mr. Johnston was really dangerously indisposed with (the influenza): in this situation, contrary to my pressing recommendation, he suffered himself to be brought in a chair to the House to vote on the question of Temporary Residence. He is now recovered, &c.

Iredell 2:291–92. The ellipsis is in the source.

DeWitt Clinton to Charles Clinton

. . . The chief subject of conversation is the intended removal of Congress from this place. A bill has passed the Senate providing for the permanent residence on the banks of the Patowmac and a temporary residence of ten years in Philadelphia. This bill is now discussing in the house of Representatives—its enemies have used every act to shackle its progress and divide its friends but as yet their endeavours have been fruitless—an amendment was proposed to divide the temporary residence between N. York & Philadelphia and fix the permanent at Baltimore but it was negatived by 37 against 23. The probability is that the bill will be executed & that Congress will in a few days adjourn to meet at Philadelphia in December. The Citizens are extremely irritated and must now feel that the promised authors of the Millenium are like other men—governed by local interests. . . .

Excerpt of two page ALS, *Charles Hamilton Catalog* 6(1965):item 47; mistranscribed as 7 July. Addressed to Ulster County, New York. The ellipses are in the source. The correct date, a more specific address of Little Britain, Ulster (now part of Orange) County, New York, and the phrase "from this place" in the first sentence are from *Parke-Bernet Catalog* 1436(1953):item 96.

John Brown Cutting to John Adams

There are so many rumours concerning the present state of the dispute between Spain and Britain and so many individuals interested to misrepresent it that it is with much diffidence that I venture to offer you any opinion on that subject.

The british parliament the members of which are now chiefly elected will not be assembled before the middle of august. Till then very little that can be depended on relative to the spanish rupture will be known—unless some unforseen event shou'd precipitate hostilities.

Mr. Fitzherbert the british ambassador is now at Madrid[1]—negociating. I believe it may be relied on that he is instructed to demand 1. Satisfaction for the seisure of the british Ships in Nootka Sound—and for the destruction of the factory establish'd on the coast. 2. An acknowledgment of a right in great Britain to navigate the South Seas and carry on fisheries and commerce throughout those seas and coasts. 3dly. Payment of a million sterling the computed cost of the present armaments here. The second of these points is that which Spain is most loth to give up—and from which the minister of this country is determin'd not to recede.

Both nations however are willing to negotiate—Britain because she is not ready to begin maritime hostilities with vigour till her west india merchantmen come in with seamen to mann the fleet—which at present is very thinly mannd: Spain because tho' ready herself—her new ally Portugal is not—and because she is desirous to ascertain what reliance may be had on her old ally France for aid in the war.

Meanwhile both parties to this dispute must be desirous of the friendship of the United States. I hope our country without embroiling herself will obtain considerable points of both. The court of Lisbon have already appointed M. Friere their late resident at this court[2]—to be minister resident with Congress. And I understand from good authority that the navigation of the Missisippi is already tacitly ceded to the United States—by orders issued to the Vice Roy of Mexico. Be this so or not the present period seems a most auspicious one to gain whatever points the United States are most desirous of ~~the~~ gaining either of Spain or Britain.

Shou'd the latter be disposed to treat—I hope the moment will not be neglected to agree upon some criterion whereby the american seamen may be properly discriminated from the british and consequently protected from the insults of their press gangs and the management that is now practiced to get them on board their ships of war For two months past I have diligently discharged the duty which I think incumbent upon a republican citizen—

in contributing to rescue our seamen from an abhorred servitude in the british fleet Altho' I have succeeded in most instances—in some I have wholly failed. Whatever of industry or ability I possess has been on this occasion exerted and for the present this exerition is likely to continue because it is likely to be needed.

But as I have repeatedly written both to yourself and to Mr. Jefferson on this subject—I shall not trouble You with a fresh repetition of what I consider it my duty at the time zealously to represent.

I send you a parcel of newspapers—The Editor is violently ministerial; but is reputed to possess better sources of foreign intelligence than most of his co-temporaries.

ALS, Adams Family Manuscript Trust, MHi. Written from London.

[1] Alleyne Fitzherbert (1753–1839), Baron St. Helens—for whom his friend the explorer George Vancouver named Mount St. Helens (in present-day Washington state) in 1792—served as Britain's minister plenipotentiary to Russia from 1783 to 1788, prior to his reassignment to Spain, 1790–94.

[2] Cypriano Ribeiro Freire (1749–1814) served as Portugal's chargé d'affaires in London until 1790, when he was reassigned to the United States. He did not arrive at Philadelphia until 1794, and resided there until 1799.

Alexander Hamilton to John Adams

I have the honor to inform the Vice President of the United States and to request him to ~~inform~~ cause an intimation to be given to the Honoble. The Members of the Senate that at one oClock to day, an oration will be delivered at St. Pauls Church in commemoration of the declaration of Independence by a Member of the Society of of the Cincinnati and that seats are provided for his and their acc[*ommod*]ation.[1] Peculiar circumstances prevented [*an*] earlier communication. The Requis[*ite*] number of tickets ~~accompany this~~ have [*been*] sent to the Secretary of the Senate.

ALS, Hull Collection, DSI.

[1] Following an escorted procession of Cincinnati members from City Tavern to St. Paul's Chapel, the oration was delivered by Henry Brockholst Livingston beginning about 1 P.M. Maclay records that he and other Senators took their seats next to the Washingtons, in pews so crowded that Maclay could not hear the oration well, although "some said it was fine" (*DHFFC* 9:312–13; for Washington's own detailed summary of it, see *DGW* 6:85–86). "Both Houses of the Congress of the United States with many strangers of distinction were present" (*NYJ*, 6 July).

Abraham Holmes to Charles Jarvis

***

It is considered by the Citizens of this Town that the droping a Gentleman [*Dalton*] who fill'd a dignified station is *ominous* of Good, especially when they read the observation ~~in th~~ of the Correspondent in the Chronicle,[1] as they view him being in *terrorem*[2] to the rest, and that this event tels them in Language not easily misunderstood *"be ye also ready."*[3] and I feel not a little proud that Massachusetts has given the first proof of political Mortallity.

***

ALS, Samuel Adams Originals, NN. Written from Rochester, Massachusetts; place to which addressed not indicated.

[1] [Boston] *Independent Chronicle*, 24 June, volume 19.
[2] As a warning.
[3] Matthew 24:44.

Henry Sewall to George Thatcher

Yours of the 15 of April was duly and gratefully received.

We are sorry that the subject of providing for the public debt has met such difficulty in Congress, and that the magnitude and importance of the question has not sooner suggested to the discernment of that Body some mode of conciliation and decision.

The attention of Congress has been so far engrossed by other objects, and the time so far elapsed, that our expectations of seeing any thing done this session for the support of the subordinate officers in the *judicial department*, are almost expiring. With the present fees, as measured by those in the supreme court of the state and the small accession of business with which we are as yet favoured, we cannot long support our stations, and our patriotism will not much longer supply the place of emolument. Not the least provision is made for paying any kind of fees in criminal cases, either to officers or jury. We have already had one capital trial, which took up a very considerable part of the last term; and we have no way to come at any compensation. This is an object of consequence to us, and we would presume to hope that you will neglect no opportunity of exerting yourself in our behalf. Genl. [*Henry*] Dearborn says, If you do not support us, we shall not be disposed to support you at the approaching election. Let that be as it may—the officers must be supported, or the judicial business will drag heavily, the reputation of the department be impaired, and the due course of justice impeded.

Would a petition from this quarter assist you in obtaining a *post* [*road*]

from Portland [*Maine*] to Hallowell—or can you effect it without? We think we are entitled to this attention from the general Government, and cannot see any reason why it should not be granted.
[*P. S.*] N. B. I take the liberty to trouble you with a line to Mr. [*John*] Fenno.

ALS, Chamberlain Collection, MB. Written from Hallowell, Maine; franked; postmarked Portland, 15 July.

William Smith (S.C.) to Edward Rutledge

This morning, being the day on which our Independance is celebrated, the Address of our Convention was presented by the whole Delegation[1]—it was read by Butler—the answer will please you—there was a part of it which I beleive did not much please the Reader; the President says he takes a pride in being a *Native* of America.[2]

We have just returned from an Oration delivered by Brockholst Livingston.[3]

ALS, Smith Papers, ScHi. Addressed to Charleston, South Carolina. This concludes a letter begun on 4 July, above.

---

[1] The congratulatory address to Washington, voted by the South Carolina constitutional convention on 31 May and forwarded to the state's congressional delegation by the convention's president, Charles Pinckney, on 14 June, was presented at the President's house between 11 A.M. and 1 P.M. The occasion corresponded with the Washingtons' open house held in official observance of Independence Day, which fell on a Sunday in 1790. The guests included members of Congress and other public officials, foreign dignitaries, and members of the Society of the Cincinnati. The Senate adjourned early on a motion to attend upon the President as a body (*DHFFC* 9:312). Butler's letter of 6 July, below, indicates that the convention's address was presented before the assembled guests while they were being treated to "Wine punch & Cakes." For the text of the address and Washington's reply, see *PGW* 6:16–19n.

[2] Smith hints at Butler's sensitivity on this point, as a native of Ireland.

[3] See Alexander Hamilton to John Adams of this date, n. 1, above.

A Correspondent

A Correspondent observes, that the elaborate Speech of Mr. Ames [*on assumption*], which has been so grossly puffed in our several papers,[1] appears a redundancy of words, rather than a display of nervous reasoning—Whole columns are filled with a jingle of high-flown *phrases*, without scarcely a determinate idea. Provided we are to estimate speeches by the spaces they occupy in the papers, Mr. Ames must be considered the American Demosthenes; but should force, decision and plain sense, be the criterion, it is presumed he would fall vastly short of obtaining the palm of eloquence. Eight columns, with so few ideas, are seldom impos'd in the public as a specimen of elocution becoming a Legislative Body, as the time is too precious to be taken up with rhapsody and declamation.

Boston Gazette, 5 July; reprinted at Hartford and Norwich, Connecticut; New York City (*NYMP*, 10 July; *NYP*, 10 July; *NYJ*, 13 July); Philadelphia; Baltimore; and Fredericksburg and Richmond, Virginia.

---

[1] Ames's speech of 25 May, originally printed in *NYDA* on 29 May (*DHFFC* 13:1432–46), was reprinted at Boston in the *Columbian Centinel*, 30 June, 3 July, and *Independent Chronicle*, 1 July.

An Electioneering Anecdote

WHEN Dr. [*Charles*] Jarvis had declined, being considered as a Candidate, and had even publickly erased his name from the list of Senators, Mr. [*Nathaniel*] Gorham appeared the most likely to succeed in his election—But this last gentleman had been concerned in the Jenisse [*Genessee*] purchase, and was viewed as a kind of delinquent by the [*Massachusetts*] house of representatives. As there was nothing against him but this, and a thousand apologies might be made for his apparent neglect of payment, it was very possible that this circumstance might be overlooked and forgotten in the process of electioneering—to prevent this, a paper was sent down from the Senate by the President [*Samuel Phillips, Jr.*] and was read by the Speaker of the House [*David Cobb*], almost at the very hour when the election was to take place—this paper produced the discussion that was to be naturally expected from its appearance—some vindicating this gentleman's conduct and others condemning. The result was, that the votes were transferr'd to Mr. [*George*] Cabot, who obtained his election by a majority of one. It would be wrong to pronounce this a stroke of political intrigue, as the known impartiality of the characters immediately concerned must prevent such suspicions. It is very certain however, that Mr. Cabot would never have succeeded in his election but for this circumstance.

[Portland, Maine] *Cumberland Gazette*, 5 July. Printed in italics. Cabot was elected in place of Dalton.

OTHER DOCUMENTS

[*George Champlin*] to Joseph Stanton. FC, Champlin Papers, RHi. Place from which written not indicated. The author was identified from his handwriting and references corresponding to the contents of Stanton's letter to Champlin, 29 June, volume 19.

The residence question "has taken up so much of their time. and retarded business of much more Importance to the Union" with an issue "Intirely local"; now that it is resolved, hopes Congress will quickly settle more important business; believes that "great interest has been made ~~to~~ In the North [*the Providence interest*]" against the appointment of "our friend here [*Henry Marchant*]"; "your friendship in their favour will be kindly rec'd."; Stanton's family is well; looks forward to continuing the correspondence.

George Clymer to Henry Clymer. ALS, Clymer Papers, PHi. Addressed to Market Street, Philadelphia; written in the morning; franked; postmarked. Dated "Monday Morning," and internal evidence indicates it was written shortly after George's letter to Henry dated 2 July.

Returned last night from a two day excursion.

James Madison to Benjamin Rush. ALS, Rush Papers, DLC. Addressed to Philadelphia. For the full text, see *PJM* 13:263.

Introduces the bearer, Count Paolo Andreani.

Henry Marchant to John Adams. ALS, Adams Family Manuscript Trust, MHi. Written from Newport, Rhode Island; franked; postmarked. Unlike Providence, nearby Newport endured a hostile occupation by three thousand British troops in 1778–79.

Office seeking: Walter Channing for commissioner of loans; preference should be given to an office seeker from Newport, Rhode Island, over one from Providence because of the former's greater suffering during the Revolutionary War.

Thomas Posey to James Madison. ALS, Madison Papers, DLC. Written from Fredericksburg, Virginia. For the full text, see *PJM* 13:263–64.

Inquires whether, and how, arrears of subsistence (rations) due him can be collected by a power of attorney; needs to collect his arrears of $153 as soon as possible, but has heard there is no money for the purpose at the seat of government; no news to report; Congress's proceedings "generally furnish us with the most interesting intelligence"; reports on crops.

William Samuel Johnson, Diary. Johnson Papers, CtHi.

"Independ[*enc*]e. Celebratd. Oration &c."

George Washington, Diary. ViHi.

The members of the Senate and House of Representatives came to the President's house "with the compliments of the day."

[Connecticut] *Litchfield Monitor*, 5 July; reprinted at Hartford, Connecticut. The poem "Progress of Dullness" was written by the "Connecticut Wit" John Trumbull, not the congressman Jonathan Trumbull; see A Republican #4, 7 June, volume 19.

"*In addition to the Catalogue of Books reported by the Committee of Congress, a correspondent recommends* 'The Progress of Dulness,' *written several years since by an hon. Member.*"

[Charleston, South Carolina] *City Gazette*, 19 July.

"A gentleman, who is a member of congress, mentions in a letter to his friend in this city, dated July 5th, that it was expected congress would adjourn in about six weeks."

Tuesday, 6 July 1790

Hot (Johnson)

Pierce Butler to Weeden Butler

The Mail for England is to be closed on tomorrow it must Convey a letter from me to Chelsea, though at present my mind is not free, My Dear Mrs. [*Mary Middleton*] Butler's continued indisposition and some little difficulties in Our Legislative proceedings rather unfit me for writing at this time; the Eye of friendship will make allowances.

***

Our Parliamentary proceedings You shall have when printed. they will be more Voluminous than the last I sent, and more Elucidatory of Our Situation, Connection and little Jaring of Interests The House of Representatives, or lower House, are now Occupied with a Bill I brought into Senate, and which has pass'd Our House, for Establishing the Permanent Residence of Our Government—It was long Debated in Senate—I suppose it will undergo a like process in the lower House—Here local Attachments step in. The Bill got through Senate with some difficulty and fix'd Our Permanent Residence at the end of ten Years from this time where I wish'd, on the Eastern Bank of the River Patowmack the Temporary Residence, from the present session, to be in Philadelphia—Our Funding system still unfinish'd—*post tennebra lux*[1]—I wish Our session was well ended and Our Members at their peaceful Homes—It is certain that the business is the most trying and arduous that can in all probability present itself for some time.

***

You will be so good to apologise for me to my Son [*Thomas*] for not answering His letter by the Packett—I realy have not leisure—I will write to Him by the first Merchant Vessel that Sails after the Packet for England—I agree intirely with You that Young Folks shou'd first hear and think before they Speak from themselves; but the habit of repeating aloud to a Considerable Audience from Select Authors has a good Effect, it prepares them for a more easy delivery of their own productions when they are Capable of Composing, Classing and Arranging—the Boys here repeat from Demosthenese, Cicero, Shakspear, and other Authors, as their Preceptors direct or make Choice—I have heard two of them, one Nine Years old, the other Seven, deliver the discourse between Brutus and Cassius[2] with astonishing propriety and Correctness—habit assuredly has a great effect—to this hour when I have to speak on any important question I feel the greatest diffidence and no small Embarrassment—Last Monday it fell to my lot as first Senator from Carolina to deliver an address from that State to the President of the United States—The Audience were brilliant and Numerous; Many of them Nice Judges—I felt aukward before I began, not having had time given me; but from adopting the plan I recommd. to my Boy of Repeating Slowly and distinctly I got through with some Eclat.

My Dear Wife directed me to thank You in Her Name for Your kind letter—She is not able to write for herself—I left Her and my daughter Frances at the Seaside to try what Change of Air will do—She is quite a Shadow.

I will not trouble You, my Dear Sir, with a repetition of my great anxieties and ardent desires to have my Boy qualified in a *more than ordinary Manner* for a public Character—He is with You; I feel full Confidence from this circumstance, that He will gratify my fond wishes.

ALS, Butler Papers, Uk. Addressed to Cheyne Walk, Chelsea "near London"; postmarked 8 July; answered 30 August. The omitted text discusses mutual acquaintances and European news, including P. Butler's sympathy for the revolution in the Austrian Netherlands (Belgium).

---

[1] Light after darkness.
[2] From Shakespeare's *Julius Caesar.*

William Crocker to George Thatcher

Altho' I have nothing of consequence to communicate—yet shall trouble you with this scrawl—I arrived here on saturday last. your bundle was placed agreeable to your orders. have not heard from your family, not having seen a person from their place of abode. Please give my compliments to Mr. King & Lady [*Mary Alsop King*], nor do I forget thier good Father [*John Alsop*], whom I ought first to have mentioned—Please inform Mr. King that his friends & Relations at Scarborough [*Maine*] were well yesterday. I had not timely notice of our Vessell's sailing—otherwise I shou'd have again call'd upon you & others. If anything offers worthy your notice and attention in the Eastern part of this state (where I expect soon to be) shall endeavour your information of the same.

Before I left ~~my~~ the place of my abode, I was possessed of opinion, that the World of America had their Complaints reduced, Censory done with; & that universal satisfaction respecting our Rulers of the states in Union, prevaded the United states of America—But in this place I am disappointed of that pleasing & agreeable satisfaction. The conduct of Congress have not here, ~~have~~ had a fair & unprejudiced tryal, by the Judgment of some of those characters, by no means the least respectable. Wrong representations, induce many well meaning persons to think, & Speak very different of that body of which you are a member, than truth would Justify. you would be surprised to hear the Questions that I have been asked—but I forbear—there is an evil in the political world—I hope it will not long exist—the seeds of discord have been sown, & softened by a few evil minded persons, who have not forgot their old employ, I do not say by any one of the Inhabitants of Portland—~~I do not~~ nay do I mean to excuse my Countrymen—I know their Intentions are good, but they are deceived. you will pardon me my good Sir, when I inform you that I lament the opposition in Congress—this I conclude in some degree origionates ~~from of~~ from the Local situation of our Representatives, & a misconceived Idea of *Interest* which should admit of no seperation; ~~but~~ the good of the states in Union I wish might be the View, (& excusing the common prejudices Of human Nature) I doubt not but will be fully attended to by that Honorable body.

Enough upon this subject.

I despise detraction as much as any man in the World, if what follows should in some degree partake of a species of that Iniquity; self Justification only can plead an excuse, & by which I claim a title to forgiveness. any representation or account of my Character or eligibility for publick office Receive as truth coming from anyone Individual upon this Globe except one whose Name was mentioned when I had the happiness of Seeing you last; I conclude you will not be at a [*loss?*] for his name. You will my good Sir pardon me for the freedom I take I write to a person in whom I can confide.

ALS, Chamberlain Collection, MB. Written from Portland, Maine; franked.

Richard Henry Lee to Thomas Lee Shippen

Your letter of the 4th. I received this day, and whatever may be the opinion of others with respect to me, I am happy to find that yours, which I much value, states me as I realy am—Not suffering private regards to supplant public duty—I think that whilst I live I shall never forsake this principle.

It was not difficult to foreseee that all the arts of division practised in the Senate would be repeated in the H. of R. and so, this day, the first that they entered upon the consideration of our bill, has been wasted in debate upon a proposed amendment to substitute Baltimore for Potomac—no que[*s*]tion yet taken upon that—Tomorrow will probably be passed in determining whether N.Y. shall be preferred to Phila. &c. &c. &c.—Our friends seem determined hereafter to prevent the Adversary's stratagem for delay & division, by letting them talk, and the former be contended with voting—Thus perhaps, this troublesome business may be ended on thursday when it is expected that the bill will be carried ~~without~~ [*lined out*] by a Majority of one or two at least—Should this Bill succeed it will be a very strong proof of the prevelance of truth over its contrary—for every act that can be devised has been practised to overcome truth and public convenience—Stratagem in every shape—threats of Mob—Severance of the Union—And even beauty has condescended to aid a misjudged policy in this business—for this day the House has been crouded with ladies, as much as to say, as you Vote, so will we smile—A severe trial for susceptible minds—And a very unfair (if I may say that Ladies can do anything unfair) whilst the Abundant beauty of Philadelphia had not an equal opportunity of shewing its wishes—May heaven protect you & us all.

ALS, Shippen Family Papers, DLC. Place to which addressed not indicated.

Benjamin Lincoln to Theodore Sedgwick

I have had the pleasure of receiving your favour of the 28 ulto.

Mr. Dalton had not made himself ~~uppo~~ unpopular Mr. [*Nathaniel*] Gorham had his *fast* friends, Dr. [*Charles*] Jarvis had his also Mr. [*George*] Cabot shared the others and was elected, When the waters were Troubled there was no person to put Dalton into the pool[1]—poor man, could not help himself.

I thank you most cordially for your frequent letters—The moment I have any thing worth your attention I will communicate it.

ALS, Sedgwick Papers, MHi. Written from Boston.

[1] Ancient Jerusalem's pool of Bethesda was said to cure the ailments of the person who was the first to step in after its waters were troubled by an angel (John 5:4).

James Madison, Notes

Distances travelled by the members of the House of Reps. to N. York as charged and allowed in the Congs. first assembled there.

From	New Hampshire	Travel 927 Miles		
	Massts.	2061		
	Connecticut	640		
	Rhode Island	200		
	N. York	570		
			3471	
From	N. Jersey	Travel 291		
	Pennsylva.	1289		
	Delaware	173		
	Maryland	1448		
	Virginia	4578		
	N. Carolina	3121		
	S. Carolina	4512		
	Georgia	3120		
			18,532	
				22,003

Ms., Madison Papers, DLC. The editors believe that Madison compiled these figures for a speech he made on this date; see *DHFFC* 13:1648.

Newspaper Article

The 4th clause of the *Residence bill*, as from the Senate, to be read a third time in the House of Representatives *this day*, is an oblique hint to the house *to grant sums of money for erecting buildings*—the 5th provides for *ten years* residence at Philadelphia—the 6th for the *expences* of *removal* to that city, and from thence to the Potowmack. As it is probable the bill will be *amended*, and PARADVENTURE *rejected*, we have omitted insertion of it until its *fate* be known.

NYJ, 6 July.

Residence

A correspondent observes—such has been the tame complaisance of the P[*hiladelphia*]. faction, that they have endeavored to remove all objections and to accommodate all humors and weaknesses. A member of the j—t c—m—e [*joint committee*] declared—*upon honor*—That Philadelphia was *immensely, prodigiously, monstrously* hot—Mr. F—ns [*Fitzsimons*] immediately declared, that he meant to move, if the session was a warm one, that each member should be furnished with a fan, and that his friend the S—r [*Senator Morris*], should provide for this expence, under the head of *contingencies*—My friend, patron and master says, he has imported an assortment from India, and will furnish both houses with *fans*, by *contract*, at his own price. It is thought that any plan which will cool the *heated children* after the violent game of *move all* and *push pin*, will be popular.

It is whispered, says a correspondent, that Mr. F. (in the bill to provide for the *temporary* residence of Congress in Philadelphia, which will prove a *permanent* one) means to insert a clause for the free transportation, per post, of *salmon*, from the *assumptive* or *consumptive* state of Connecticut, and *sheepshead* and *blackfish* from the fly market,[1] to mitigate the New York Representation. The old men, who have young wives, mean to contract with the minister of the lower house for the free transportation of *oysters*. Such a negotiation has taken place with the P. faction. We do not doubt, but the old gentlemen will succeed, if the ladies unite their influence in this novel and extraordinary negotiation.

NYJ, 6 July; reprinted at Poughkeepsie, New York.

[1] The oldest of New York City's many open air markets, located at the foot of Maiden Lane.

Letter from Montreal

Some very recent movements at Quebec indicate the extreme suspicion and jealousy of our government in respect to the fortified posts within your boundaries, still occupied by British troops.[1] Those posts are continually strengthening, a convincing proof that Lord Dorchester expects your attention will be turned this way as soon as your government is consolidated, and you find you have the means to reinstate yourselves in the possession of what, it is possible, you may lay a just claim to. At the same time permit me to say, these posts are by no means the object of a war. The value of the fur trade is inconsiderable, in comparison of what it is commonly represented to be, and Canada itself is so poor a province in its present state, that considering its expence to the crown, one would think not even national pride would deem it an object worth any great consideration.

NYDA, 28 July.

[1] See George Beckwith, Notes of Conversations with Different Persons, n. 7, April 1790 Undated, volume 19.

Other Documents

William Samuel Johnson to Samuel William Johnson. ALS, Johnson Papers, CtHi. Addressed to Stratford, Connecticut; franked; postmarked.

"We are, thank God in perfect Health"; acknowledges the excellent smoked beef.

Samuel Johnston to James Iredell. ALS, Iredell Papers, NcD. Addressed to Edenton, North Carolina; franked; postmarked.

Acknowledges several recent letters; (sister) Hannah Johnston Iredell recovering from smallpox and influenza; (wife) Frances Cathcart Johnston "is not well she has lost her Apetite, dont sleep well and of course has very indifferent Spirits"; Johnston recovers slowly; "I was down at the Sea on Saturday & Sunday last which has been of some Service to me, yet it is with difficulty that I can write"; for political news, refers to William Dawson and the newspapers he carries; reports the Senate's passage of the Residence Act.

John Meyer to Tench Coxe. ALS, Coxe Papers, PHi. Addressed to Philadelphia; postmarked.

Principal speakers in that day's House debate on the Residence Act were R. B. Lee, Burke, Laurance, and Gerry; "It is thought (with what degree of probability I cannot say)" that that day's motion by Sherman to substitute Baltimore for Potomac "is likely to defeat the Bill."

George Thatcher to William Taylor. No copy known; acknowledged in Taylor to Thatcher, 1 December.

WEDNESDAY, 7 JULY 1790

Cool (Johnson)

Daniel Hiester to James Hutchinson

By this Post I suppose You expect to hear the desission on the Question of Residence but it was not decid[*ed*] yesterday. Mr. Sherman moved to strike out Potowmac and insert Baltimore for the permanent residence. this took up the whole day without taking a question on it. It may be a business of some days, for our opponents mean to accomplish their purpose by the number & variety of amendments they have to propose, almost any one will be fatal to the bill—We have very little to come and go upon we expit that Gen. Jackson has left us—if so the whole depends on Mr. Gillman with him we shall be 32 ag[*ains*]t. 31—tomorrow I [*lined out*] ~~tell~~ will tell You the Proceedings of this day.

ALS, Miscellaneous Manuscripts, PPAmP. Dateline torn off; addressed to Philadelphia; franked; postmarked 7 July.

John Langdon to Joseph Whipple

Your favir of the 28th. ult. I've Recd. I am not much pleased with the proceedings of N[*ew*]. H[*ampshire*]. their not Cede[*in*]g. the light House, is to me very Astonishing; as it appears to me, not a Single reason, can be given against the Measure—It is impossable for me to say when Congress will Adjourn it may be in a fortnight. or it may be two months; the fundg. System, the assumption, and Residence, are Questions that *Continue* (Violently) to Agitate Congress. I think it cannot be long er'e a Determination Must take place—My horses have Stood at Livery, for two months, expectg. to set out for home, from week to week; my Patience is totally exhausted; and I am half distracted to get home—but as some of our members are foolish enough to think me of some Importance here—I cannot get away, but I am Determined it shall not be very long before I set my face to the North.

P. S. pray let me know what money you have in your office, and whether an order for 500 or 1000 Dollars can be paid if I should send or bring one ~~order~~.

ALS, Sturgis Family Papers, MH. Place to which addressed not indicated.

Richard Henry Lee to Thomas Lee Shippen

Last evening I informed you how the business of Residence went on—this day has been passed [*lined out*] in practising the same Monœuvres that we were entertained with in Senate—Baltimore has been rejected with many other questions proposed for the purpose of dividing the friends of the bill, but they have all proved unsuccessful—The house adjourned to day upon a motion for dividing the time of temporary residence between this City & Phila. The same was tried with the Senate & rejected, the same fate is like to attend it in the H. of R. Your friend Count [*Paolo*] Andriani is gone to see you—I have frequently called on him at his lodgings, but have not had the happiness to find him at home—I still continue weak since my Influenza attack which renders writing unpleasant to me, and only tolerable when I write to friends whom I value as much I do you, and they are very few.

ALS, Shippen Family Papers, DLC. Place to which addressed not indicated.

William Maclay to John Nicholson

The Residence bill has stood the attacks of it's Artful and powerful Enemies for Two Days in the House of Representatives. It remains as yet intire. Every attempt to amend. in other Words to destroy it, has hitherto failed. Tomorrow we hope the final Question will be put upon it, and indeed untill the final Question is carried We cannot consider the Matter as Safe. for we are like those who war not only with open Violence but with every secret [*Friend?*].

We have a new bill for the Settlement of the Accounts between the individual States and the United States [*HR-77*], before the Senate. I really doubt much whether anything but delusion and delay is meant by it. at least by One part of Congress. The Warm Assumption Men, declare against the Utility of a Settlement altogether. And indeed a general Assumption will, in my Opinion deprive Us of the Means of equalizing the Accounts. Our imposts Taxes &ca. must all be equal. how then is the delinquent State to be called on? if a portion of her State debt, should be left on her, equal to the balance which she may owe the Union. all follows easy and familiar. But Hamilton and his Adherents. Are for fictitious Credits. to do Justice to the advancing States. And thus they would raise a Mass of National Debt, That Madness herself would be freightened to look at. I hope in my next to give You Joy, on the Residence being fixed.

ALS, Nicholson Papers, PHarH. Addressed to the "Controller Genl of the state of Pennsylvania"; franked; postmarked 8 July; received 9 July; answered 21 July.

Samuel Nasson to George Thatcher

I had the pleasure of a Line from you Dated feel Happy to know that you are Soon to return home, I am accidentaly at Boston Set out tomorow for home. you are wanted at this time, October is near at hand Sorry I am to Give you pain but pure frindship pleads an Excuse I fear much for you have none of your freinds been so sincear as to inform you that Strange and more Strange but five at least are put up would you know who I Say Nathl. Wells a mr. [*Josiah*] Thatcher of Goraham [*Maine*] [*Peleg*] Wadsworth [*William*] Wedgery Dorband Lithehowe [*William Lithgow?*]—I am a tell tale Say Some but must I Betray a Freind, you Never got me a Office, therefore I Cannot be the means of throughin you out of office you look back and think of all the persons that you have been Instrumental of gitting into place or trust Remember a Certan [*John*] Lee that has been Chosen to Office I now tell you that you had better been asleep I fear much but yet hope all you say you Cannot find out the fault mr. Dalton has been Guilty of. Remember the High Competition [*compensation*] made to all that hold offices—I yet hope the best Hurry home Call upon your Freinds think allso of me when you return.

I hast to Your Freinds.

ALS, Chamberlain Collection, MB. Written from Boston; franked; postmarked 8 July.

Roger Sherman to Rebecca Prescott Sherman

I think it is not very likely that Congress will rise quite So Soon as the 15th of this month there are Some matters unfinished that must be compleated this session—but I hope they will not have occasion to Sit many days later it will make our journey to the eastward pretty late, but we may go & return in September, Which will be a good Season for travelling, Mr. Hartwell[1] writes that Joseph Billings & Deacon Elihu Crane two of my acquaintance have died Since I was there—Governor [*William*] Livingston of New Jersey is dangerously ill—I enjoy good health, want much to be at home—I should have come home last friday If any vessel had been ready to Sail, as no business was done on Saturday or Monday. The anniversy of Independence was celebrated on Monday. I dont expect to come home until Congress closes the session, Enclosed are some verses for Pattsy & Sally[2] & No. 1. for You.

ALS, Sherman Collection, CtY. Place to which addressed not indicated.

---

[1] Probably some relation of Sherman's first wife, Elizabeth Hartwell (ca. 1725–1760) of Stoughton, Massachusetts.

[2] Sherman's youngest children, Martha and Sarah.

William Short to Thomas Jefferson

***

Some days ago a person who has resided many years at Algiers, called on me in company with M. Volney[1] whom you know, to speak of a means of procuring peace with that Regency [*Algiers*] on advantageous terms. It was for Congress to equip some frigates themselves, or to authorize a company to do it, & to cruise in the Mediterranean, particularly on the coast of Egypt against the Turkish merchant vessels. He said it was unquestionable that the [*Turkish*] Porte could force Algiers to conclude a treaty with any power whatever—that finding their commerce harassed, the Turks would gladly exchange their interposition at Algiers for its security—& that thus the United States who would be sure of failing so long as they should address the Algerines by embassies or entreaties, would be as sure of succeeding whenever they should speak to the fears & interest of the Turks—this is the leading idea of his plan, which he seems to have considered under all its circumstances. He went into several details respecting it, which he is to communicate to me in writing.[2] He has reasons for not chusing to be named; but wishes his ideas to be communicated to Congress. His calculation is that three frigates manned by two hundred men each would suffice—He does not propose their cruising off Algiers because a greater number would then be necessary—because a much longer time would be requisite for making an impression on the Algerines by this means, & consequently the success much less certain—He proposes cruising against the Turkish merchantmen because the prizes would much more than indemnify for the expences of equipment, & because it is much the most expeditious & certain mode of effecting the business at Algiers. His favorite idea is that the affair should be mercantile—viz. that all the expences should be furnished by individuals on the condition of their having all the profits, & he desires to be interested in the enterprize by placing a part of his fortune in it. He wishes that Congress should give the letters of marque[3] for reasons that are obvious. ***

I communicated to Mr. Necker the Resolve which you inclosed me in a former letter.[4] He received with pleasure that proof of the attention of Congress to their foreign engagements. He is very anxious to know their decision relative to the loan lately made at Amsterdam.[5] I still think as formerly that a person properly authorized by Congress might make that loan the basis of others so as to effect on advantageous & sure terms such as they will judge proper probably to have made for the discharge of their debts due this country, & which it is so essential to attend to without delay, from a variety of considerations.

***

You will no doubt have learned that several American sailors were impressed in London,[6] & that they were rescued by the zealous exertions & activity of Mr. [*John Brown*] Cutting. Since then one other has been impressed whom Mr. Cutting has been unable to get released. He is on board of the fleet & will probably be forced to serve so long as they have any occasion for him. You will certainly have received from Mr. Cutting the particulars of this affair which seems to deserve the earliest attention of Congress, & points out the necessity of some arrangement being made for preventing such cases in future.

*** The person of whom I spoke in the beginning of this letter, told me that he thought the remaining captives [*at Algiers*] might be redeemed at the same price for the common sailors & about 12,000.lt [*livres tournois*] for each of the Captains. He added that the Spanish Consul was at present in the greatest favor with the Regency, & would be the most proper person for being charged with such a commission. The same person told me that he had understood the present Emperor of Morocco had begun his reign by shewing dispositions to observe the treaties made by his predecessor. He thought it probable that ours[7] would be continued. In general however I have understood that we should be obliged to renew it. This is the opinion also of [*William*] Carmichael, from whom you will certainly first learn the result. ***

FC, letterpress copy, Short Papers, DLC. Written from Paris. For the full text, see *PTJ* 17:14–20. The omitted text reports the status of the American captives at Algiers, objections to the plan proposed for making peace with the Barbary states of North Africa, United States trade with France, French politics, and progress on the resolution of the Nootka Sound Crisis. For background on the Algerine captives, see *DHFFC* 2:425–49, 8:1–4.

---

[1] Constantin-François, comte de Volney (1757–1820), was a member of the French National Assembly who, in the late 1780s, authored two books on Turkish and Middle Eastern affairs.

[2] Volney's anonymous companion supplied Short with the more elaborate proposal (in French) on 12 July. Jefferson apparently received it, together with Short's summarized version of it included in his dispatch of 7 July, shortly before he and Madison met with Washington at Mount Vernon on 11–12 November. Its controversial contents prompted Jefferson not to retain a copy in State Department records, although translated transcriptions were made for Adams as well as Washington, perhaps with the intention of Adams's circulating its contents among members of the Senate prior to Jefferson's two reports of 28 December on Mediterranean trade and on the Algerine captives (*PTJ* 18:406–8; *PGW* 6:587–88). Adams's copy (Adams Family Manuscript Trust, MHi) is printed in *PTJ* 18:416–22.

[3] A government's legal commissions for private ships to make reprisals on ships of another state; a form of legalized piracy.

[4] In a dispatch dated 6 April, Jefferson requested Short to communicate to France's minister of finance, Jacques Necker, an enclosed copy of the COWH resolution to make adequate provision for the foreign debt, agreed to unanimously on 29 March (*PTJ* 16:316).

[5] In the fall of 1789, Dutch bankers negotiated a loan to the United States to meet its various short-term foreign obligations through June 1790. At about the same time, Jefferson

and Dutch authorities were considering opening a larger loan to America to pay off its entire French debt, as an alternative to the proposal by a combination of Dutch and American speculators to purchase the French debt outright, which Necker suggested to the French National Assembly in November 1789 (*PTJ* 15:471–75; *PAH* 6:210–18; *DHFFC* 4:129).

[6] Part of Britain's "heavy press" in preparation for war with Spain over the Nootka Sound affair. A Boston merchant later told Short that more than three hundred American sailors had been pressed into service that summer, exceeding the abilities of their shipowners to liberate them (Short to Jefferson, 5 September, *PTJ* 17:489).

[7] The Confederation Congress ratified a treaty with the Emperor of Morocco on 18 July 1787 (*JCC* 32:355–64). In order to renew the treaty with the emperor, Congress passed the Moroccan Treaty Act on 3 March 1791.

Other Documents

Governor William Blount to Benjamin Hawkins. No copy known; mentioned in Blount to Steele, 10 July.

Governor William Blount to Hugh Williamson. No copy known; mentioned in Blount to Steele, 10 July.

William Davies to Beverley Randolph. ALS, Executive Papers, Vi. Addressed to Richmond, Virginia; answered 20 July.

> "The bill for the settlement of accounts [*HR-77*] is before the Senate, and the Eastern members will endeavor to Strike out the addition provided in the bill, of two more Commissioners, from an apprehension if it so passes, that one of the additional members of the General board will be taken from Virginia. What may be the result cannot yet be foreseen, tho' Col. [*R. H.*] Lee thinks the opposition to this part of the bill will not be successful."

John Dawson to James Madison. ALS, Madison Papers, DLC. Written from Richmond, Virginia. For the full text, see *PJM* 13:266. On 16 July, Congress inserted a one cent per pound protective tariff on imported lead, which had been exempted from duty under the first session's Impost Act.

> Introduces the bearer, Stephen Austin, who seeks "assistance from the general government in some [*form*] or other" for a lead shot manufactory in Virginia.

Volckert Douw to Philip Schuyler. ALS, Schuyler Papers, NN. Written from "Green Bush," near Albany, New York.

> Reminds Schuyler of their conversation when Douw was in New York about compensation for their trouble and expense hosting Indians when they were at treaty negotiations; has kept no detailed accounts, but estimates the charge at £100.

James Freeman to George Thatcher. ALS, Chamberlain Collection, MB. Written from Boston; franked; postmarked 8 July.

Has forwarded (Dudley) Hubbard's books; is ready to deliver Dr. Enos Hitchcock's book (*Memoirs of the Bloomsgrove Family*) when Thatcher arrives in Boston; recommends Dr. Joseph Priestly's "History of the Church" (*History of the Corruptions of Christianity*?), which he may be able to loan to Thatcher.

Samuel Meredith to Margaret Meredith. ALS, Read Papers, PPL at PHi. Addressed to "Green Hill," near Philadelphia.

"the whole day yesterday was taken up in debates in which the Ingratitude of Congress was pointed out, & every mode taken to set the Gallery in a ferment but I believe nothing of this kind or any thing else will do, unless some persons who are depended upon should fall sick"; "I shall immediately after finishing this, go with Mr. Morris to breakfast with the President."

John Meyer to Tench Coxe. ALS, Coxe Papers, PHi. Addressed to Philadelphia; postmarked.

Reports proceedings on the Residence Act; "there is a fair prospect, that the whole will pass without any amendment. at least our members seem to despair."

Governor Beverley Randolph to the Virginia Delegation. FC, Executive Letterbook, Vi. Written from Richmond, Virginia. For the full text, see *PJM* 13:267.

Encloses certificate "respecting the situation of the Lead Mines in this State"; a lead manufactory established in Richmond (by Stephen Austin) promises national benefits, with the federal government's encouragement; the proprietors would be content with a small duty on manufactured lead.

Theodore Sedgwick to Pamela Sedgwick. No copy known; acknowledged in Pamela to Theodore Sedgwick, 16 July; may actually be a reference to his letter of 4 July.

William Short to Thomas Jefferson. ALS, Jefferson Papers, DLC. Written from Paris; marked "*Private*," as distinguished from his official letter of this date, printed above. For the full text, see *PTJ* 17:10–14. This entry concerns Jefferson's conflict over the diplomatic custom of exchanging gifts upon an ambassador's departure from his host country. Jean François de Tolozan, the

Introducteur des Ambassadores at the French court, had declined to accept the customary honorarium due him from Jefferson, as long as the outgoing U.S. ambassador declined Louis XVI's costly present, as dictated by the Constitution's Article 1, section 9, paragraph 8. For background on Jefferson's dilemma, see *PTJ* 16:xxxi–xxxii, 356–63, 584.

Tolozan recently told Short that Jefferson could constitutionally accept the gift if he had Congress's permission, which Tolozan knew could be easily obtained; Short replied that he supposed Jefferson did not want to be the first to solicit such permission.

Sir John Temple to the Duke of Leeds. ALS, Foreign Office 4/8 pp. 259–60, PRO. Place to which addressed not indicated.

The residence question seems as far as ever from being settled; the struggle between New York and Philadelphia is carried on with "more anxiety & heat" than any other issue yet debated in Congress; the prevailing idea in New York is that war between Great Britain and Spain would improve Anglo-American relations.

Thursday, 8 July 1790

Cool (Johnson)

Abigail Adams to John Quincy Adams

*** my advise to my children is to look well to their own affairs. ~~and if they are calld into publick Life consider well if they can afford to aid their country to the sacrifice of their own~~ I hope they will never be calld to act in such perilous times as has falln to the share of their Father, if they should I would ~~hope~~ have them keep in mind a maxim which tho it has not met with the reward which it ought to, has ever been a source of satisfaction to himself. it is never to suffer private interst to Bias his judgment but to sacrifice ease convenience and interst for the general welfare of the country to this principal you must attribute his declared opinion for a Removal from hence to Philadelphia. for tho he Stands upon Record as voting against both N. York & Philadelphia, It was oweing to his dislike to the [*Residence*] Bill which confined them to Philadelphia for ten years & an agreement to make potowmack the permanant Residence. as he conceived that ten years hence it might not be ~~the Residence~~ most proper place, It will be a greivious thing to me to be obliged to leave this delicious spot.[1] your Sister & the children your Brother[2] & other connection, yet for the sake of peace harmony and justice I am submissive I have just been reading the speach of mr. [*Richard*] Bland

Lee, and I am much pleased with the candour and good sense it contains I am still in hopes that the Assumption will be obtaind but I do not think that Congress will rise till August. ***

ALS, Adams Family Manuscript Trust, MHi. Place to which addressed not indicated. The editors have dated this letter based on the fact that Lee's "very handsome and pathetic speech" of 6 July was published the morning of 8 July (*DHFFC* 13:1636–42, 1660–61); however, the letter may have been written any time before 11 July, when Abigail wrote John Quincy another, obviously later letter (Adams Family Manuscript Trust, MHi).

[1] "Richmond Hill."
[2] Abigail Adams Smith, her sons William Steuben (1787–1850) and John Adams Smith (1788–1854), and her brother Charles.

Paolo Andreani to Francisco de Miranda

*** Hamilton is very oppressed by everyone, and among his greatest enemies are Jefferson and Madison with whom I find myself lodged at Mrs. [*Vandine*] Elsworth's. The first of these two works against Hamilton in the government, and the second uses his eloquence openly in Congress to the same end, and unfortunately they are both held in high esteem by the public, and are very dominant. But Jefferson it appears to me that he brought from Europe everything bad that he saw there, and very little of what exists there of good: thus he is proud of his position as Secretary of foreign affairs, as much as Kaunitz in Vienna,[1] and with regard to hospitality it seems he does not remember that he is Virginian. Madison stripped of his political harassments is a man of merit. He is a good orator and has a great number of philosophical views in all areas: he is perhaps the most educated man that I have met here; and I think he aspires to become the minister in Paris replacing his friend and idol Jefferson. I would like to paint you a picture of Washington, if I could claim to have known him. The first time that I visited him, I had that veneration for him that I will have my whole life; and that day he interested me more than since. On that occasion he was alone in his room and not surrounded by anyone, except by his glory and his name; and the other times I found him in the middle of the pomp of a Court, which, though miserable, dare I say ridiculous, is nonetheless a Court. In this respect, my dear Miranda, things have changed since your visit, and changed rapidly, and what is worse not for the better. Washington opposed it for as long as he could; but he had to give way to public feeling, and have levees in form; and be eternally surrounded by four good aides de camp, and I do not know how many Secretaries. The levee is once per week at 3 o'clock in the afternoon, for the convenience of the members of Congress; and there the President of the United States sees the world like the King at St. James [*Palace, London*] *** What is more extraordinary, he and the whole court is in complete costume with sword, while the visitors are in formal dress; but with hairstyles and shoes like the dandies in London or Paris, to say the least. *** Vice President Adams is the most pompous man I know and the most selfish that exists.[2] What are they doing in France? he said to me the other day; I believe that they are madmen and that they did not understand my work. Well I'll go there myself and explain it to them.[3] What do you say, you my dear friend, of this beginning? God prevent his becoming President! the country would change faces in little time. {It was some days ago that I dined at Mr. Adams's with Mr. Washington.}[4] That day I was surprised to see the President of the United States arrive at a private lunch with such formality. He was alone with his wife in a six horse coach with glass panes, preceded by two postillions on horseback and followed by two Aides de Camp also on horseback, and two in a reserve coach. What do you say my Friend of this procession which is unknown to you? The Congress has almost completed the current session without deciding anything important; and the members have neglected the finance affairs for debates on the location to choose as an interim residence for Congress—After much imbroglio it seems that today Philadelphia has won; but as one must debate the question again in Congress, one is not quite certain of the outcome of this affair.

***

Cesare Marino and Karim M. Tiro, eds., *Along the Hudson and Mohawk: The 1790 Journey of Count Paolo Andreani* (Philadelphia, 2006), pp. 99–104. The source of this copy (in French) is *Archivo del General Miranda*, Vincente Davila, ed. (14 vols., Caracas, Venezuela, 1929–33), 6:57–62. Francisco de Miranda (1750–1816), a native of Venezuela, served as a captain in the Spanish Army during the Revolutionary War, after which he became a celebrity while traveling throughout the United States and Europe to generate support for the liberation of Spain's colonies in South America. He settled in London in the summer of 1789 (John Ezell, *The New Democracy in America: Travels of Francisco de Miranda in the United States, 1783–84* [Norman, Okla., 1963], pp. xviii–xxi).

---

[1] Wenzel Anton, Prince von Kaunitz-Reitburg (1711–94), chancellor and diplomat of Austria at key points during that country's wars of expansion in the mid eighteenth century, was notorious for his eccentric conceit.

[2] Adams formed an equally unflattering impression of Andreani during their acquaintance in the summer of 1790. In a conversation with Tobias Lear in Philadelphia on 4 April 1791, Adams recalled that "not having formed a very good opinion of him, he had paid him but little Attention" (Lear to Washington, 5 April 1791, *PGW* 8:67–68).

[3] Adams referred to his *Discourses on Davila*; he had made an almost identical comment to Otto (Otto to Montmorin, 13 June, printed in volume 19).

[4] The bracketed sentence is the editors' translation from the French transcription in *PGW* 6:600n. The luncheon was probably that hosted by Adams at "Richmond Hill" on 30 June, for which Andreani sent a reply card accepting an invitation on 22 June (Hull Collection, DSI).

Andrew Craigie to Daniel Parker

***

I wrote you on the 3d. of June since which had nothing very material has been determined in by Congress respecting the funding System—The lower House has passed the funding Bill but the Bill of ways & means has not been agreed on as yet—The Fact is the whole Business has been delayed by the Question respecting residence which will now be settled there being a Bill before Congress ~~which~~ for the Purpose. There is no doubt but the Bill will pass & the Consequence will be that the funding & Assumption will immediately be agreed to by Congress. ~~It is now understood that an Bargain has been ma~~ By the *best information* that can be procured on the Subject it is evident that an accommodation has been made (call it a bargain if you please) by which the Residence temporary & permanent—the funding & assumption are secured. This is not publicly known altho' by some people suspect—I have good reasons to beleive that the New England Delegates ~~are~~ are not ~~concerned in~~ parties to the Agreement. By the Augt. packet I make no doubt but I shall send you [*lined out*] good Accts. respecting the funding & assumption. *** Never ~~did~~ a Business assumed so many shapes & hold out such different prospects as the Assumption has done—one Day it [*seem?*]ed impossible that it should fail—the next ~~day it has been almost~~ it was given up in the ~~by~~ public Opinion for lost—but I have now very little doubts of its success.

***

FC:dft, Craigie Papers, MWA. Sent by packet. The omitted text concerns certificate speculation.

Benjamin Goodhue to Stephen Goodhue

I recd. yours of 1st. instant, I would not have any more insurance on the Fanny—I hope you will purchase boards or somthing else, if you suppose they will answer–I don't beleive the story of the French ports being shut, its too, idle to gain credit[1]—I suppose Mr. [*Samuel, Jr.*] Phillips may be attending your Court [*legislature*], therefore have wrote him—We have nothing new—the residence bill is before us and I think will pass as it came from Senate—when this [*lined out*] contentious bussines is settled which I hope will be tomorrow or next day it is expected bussines may go on briskly and and an end soon be put to the session. I still think we shall adjourn the last of this or the begining of next month, the members are generaly very uneasy and want to be at home.

[*P. S.*] We have hopes of the Assumption tho' are not very sanguine.

ALS, Goodhue Family Papers, MSaE. Addressed to Salem, Massachusetts; franked; postmarked.

[1] On 29 June the *Salem Gazette* reported that France had closed its West Indian ports to American commerce.

John Meyer to Tench Coxe

The [*Residence*] Bill has past in the committee without any amendment, and will have the first reading in the house to morrow.

Mr. Burke's motion was, that congress should continue two years longer in New York, then adjourn to Philadelphia, and remain there 'till the time fixed by the Bill for going to the Potomack, which is in the year Eighteen hundred; Though this proposition was allowed to be very reasonable, still it was rejected, under pretence, that the senate would in all probability not agree to any amendment.

Hence we may judge of the firmness of the majority, which forebodes the fate of the Bill in a favorable manner. The minority mean to try now the constitutionality of the business, with what Success remains yet a problem.

ALS, Coxe Papers, PHi. Addressed to Coxe at Philadelphia as "assistant Secretary of the Treasury"; franked by Hamilton; postmarked.

Pamela Sedgwick to Theodore Sedgwick

From Your Letter my dearest Life of the 23d of June you Gave me Great Reason to expect you at home by the 6th of this month.

Mrs. Penfield Sent me word by your desire as She said that I might certainly rely on seeing you Last week—on Saterday Evening my Eys ware paind at Looking Evry noise was attended to until Thuesday Eveing is Pappa Come is Pappa come was [*lined out*] Ecchod Twenty Times evry one of those days from evry Part of the House—Think then my love what must have been my dissopointment—Thuesday Eveing a Man calld at the office who said he Belongd to Lenox [*Massachusetts*] had been to N. York and see you last week on Thursday That you propoesd writeing by him and he calld as he sopoesd at a wrong house for a letter and found none but that you told him you should not be home short of a fortnight.

So fond was I of beleiveing that you would Certainly come—that I suffered my self to think their might be some mistake in this account—but Last Eveing Mr. [*Gulian*] Verplank arived and put the Matter of your comeing beyond a doubt—he handed me your Letter of the 3d Instant and Told me you would not leve N. York until Congress should rise that theay had yet much Business on hand and are now deeply Engaged on the quesstion of Residence.

I am Greived I am mortified my dearest Mr. Sedgwick that Those who have the reputation for wisdom should not act wisely—It must be matter of surprise I think To almost evry Person in the united states that congress should make The matter of their Temporary Residence a Subject of so much consequence at this time—The Lovers of Good Goverment have with a pleasing Partiallety Lookt up to Those Fathers of The People and Calld them Gods ~~and~~ have Anticipated evry thing Great and Noble from Their conduct—but Alass theay are but Men and Subject to all those Passions that Debase and Render Humane Nature contemptable—do I write Treasone.

I hear you Say Yes and that I am medling ~~with~~ with a subject I am Totally Ignorant of—Be It so Then To my Lord & Master ~~to~~ I submit—all my opinions on Politicks—to be corrected amended and If he should pleas wholly expunged—but you will suffer me to be a Little Angree with Congress for so long detaining my Husband From my Arms. The Vermont Commissioners[1] are all Arived here I think but their is only Mr. Ver Plank as Yet come on the part of N. York—Wheather theay will or can go on to do Business—I know not—I have sent To Mr. Verplank to dine with me Tomorah and you may be assured my Dearest That I shall take pleasure in paying him evry attention in my Power for your Sake.

Your Letter by Chapman[2] I have not yet receivd.—pray have you receivd my letter written by the Post the week before Last—in It I mentioned with regard to [*Ebenezer*] Kingsleys Affairs—This goes by Mr. [*Silas*] Peepoon—It is not improvable to me but he may have It in his Power to give you some Information with regard to Kingsley that may be of advantage to you you will ask this Information only in confidence.

It is not impossible my dear that he may now have It in his Power to secure you.

This Moment Chapman is arived and brought me your Letters. I am paind inexpressably Paind my dearest that my Letter should have given you disagreeable Fealings—be assured my Love that It was not my Intention To give you Trouble—but I sopoesd my duty obliged me to give you Information that It might Possibly save you futer Trouble. Too long my dearest Love have I experienced your unmerited Tenderness for me and assiddious attention to the interest of our dear Little Charge to entertain a thought that you would by ~~what you Thought~~ any means that ~~y~~ To you appeard Hazardous Involve your family in Misfortune—If you have been Imposed on by a Villin be assured I do not beleive It to be to so Large an amount as to ruin your Estate Tho It may be a very Inconvenient circumstance to you yet If It pleas God to spare your Life and Health I make no doubt you my dear will be able to get Throu with It shold the worst Happen while you live ~~my~~ and enjoy Health I shall not fear the want of daily subsistance and my share of the comforts of Life.

Its but Little that we want here below nor want that Little Long—happy indeed shall I be If I can reallise my Perfect state of dependance on that Power which has daily Loaded me with his Benifits.

The World is the Lords and the fullness Thereof[3]—by no Wisedome or Prudence can we my Love Secure to our Children even futer worldly Blessings Therefore let us Cheerfully Leave them in the hands of Their Gratious Creator of whose Goodness we have had Large experience.

AL, Sedgwick Papers, MHi. Written from Stockbridge, Massachusetts.

[1] Vermont's commissioners—Nathaniel Chipman and Israel Smith—had passed through Bennington, on 4 July, en route to Stockbridge ([Bennington] *Vermont Gazette*, 5 July).

[2] Pamela possibly repeats Theodore's error in referring to Joseph Chaplin as "Chapman" in his letter of 17 June.

[3] Psalms 24:1.

Peter Silvester to Peter Van Schaack

***

They have been debating in our house Upon the bill which originated in the Senate for fixing the Temporary & permanent seats of Govt. every question in the Committee of the whole was lost on the side of the middle & Eastern States just before the Adjournment yesterday a motion was made to Stay a little longer at New York say about two years before a removal to philadelphia which will be taken up & decided upon to day but the Southern Gent are tenacious for the bill as it stands & will not suffer a tittle of an alteration suspecting the bill will be lost if it is returned to the Senate with any alteration—the debates have been warm & many of the Citizens are much agitated—they think it unkind after all their exertions for accommodating Congress for them abruptly to remove & that to a Temporary seat.

ALS, Van Schaack Papers, NNC. Place to which addressed not indicated. The omitted text concerns a private financial transaction.

George Thatcher to Samuel Goodwin

The *Bill accompanying this was a few days ago, reported to the House of Representatives, not so much with an expectation of passing it into a Law,

*A Bill for effectually providing for the national defence, by establishing a uniform Militia throughout the U. States [*HR*-81].

this Session, as to disseminate its principles among the people for their examination; that Congress, at their next session may avail themselves of their sentiments upon so important a subject.

Tho I was one of the Committee who reported the Bill, I do not look upon it a very perfect System—but every time I run it over, I think I can point out imperfections—The whole subject lies much more within your comprehension than mine; and I shall thank you for any notes and observations you may be pleased to favour me with.

FC, Thatcher Family Papers, MHi.

Paine Wingate to Samuel Hodgdon

I have receivd your favour of 6th instant and deliverd the enclosed letter to Mr. [*George*] Joy. I have not time now to write you but a line. This day the house of Representatives in a committee of the whole agreed to the Bill of Residence without any alteration, as sent from the Senate. To morrow it is expected that it will pass by a bare majority. In that case Congress will probably meet at Philadelphia next Decr. I intend to write to Mr. [*Timothy*] Pickering before I leave New York, which I hope will be in two or three weeks at furthest. The Postmaster-general [*Samuel Osgood*] says if Congress shall leave N. York he shall resign. Would not that be a place agreeable to Mr. Pickering if he had the offer? If so, I wish his friends would think of it.

ALS, Pickering Papers, MHi. Addressed to Philadelphia; franked; postmarked 9 July; received 10 July.

A New Yorker to Mr. Morton

FELLOW CITIZENS!

THROUGH the channel of this paper, I beg leave to inform you, that, in my opinion, they could not take a more effectual method to disgust Congress and prejudice them against this City, than suffering a pack of fellows to circulate the most villainous print that ever appeared in America.[1] It is intended to destroy the characters of several gentlemen of unblemished reputation, by insinuating, that they have taken bribes for their votes. How do you think those Gentlemen must feel when they hear those *Reputation Butchers*, hawking their Pictures about the streets? I hope somebody will immediately put a stop to their trade, and mark the Man, with infamy, who executed them, or employed others to do it. I think he may be found within one hundred miles of the Crane wharf. Strange as it may appear, the Wretch pretends to be very religious.

NYMP, 8 July, edited by William Morton.

[1] A "View of C—O—N—SS on the road to Philadelphia" was one of at least five political cartoons hawked on the streets of New York in July. Of the three that survive, one is an illustration in this volume; two others are described in Theodore Sedgwick to Pamela Sedgwick, 4 July, above, and DeWitt Clinton to Charles Clinton, 20 July, below.

Interesting Intelligence

Received by JOHN DONALDSON, *Esq. who arrived in the Fourth-street stage, this afternoon at three o'clock.*

Yesterday at 3 o'clock, P.M. in the House of Representatives of the United States, the residence bill, as sent down from the Senate, was reported to the House by a committee of the whole. (For this bill see the Federal Gazette of the 6th inst.)

By this bill the permanent residence is to be on the Patowmack, and the temporary residence (for ten years) in Philadelphia.

This morning the house was to determine the question without debate. There is no doubt of its passing, there having been a majority of *seven* in favour of it in committee of the whole.

FG, 9 July.

OTHER DOCUMENTS

Pierce Butler to Thomas Butler. ALS, Butler Papers, Uk. Addressed to the Rev. Mr. Butler's, Cheyne Walk, Chelsea near London; postmarked; answered 30 August.

Thomas's applications to his studies "must be greater than that of Boys in general, or You can not accomplish what is my object for You"; left Thomas's mother (Mary Middleton Butler) and Frances at the seaside last Sunday; his mother is "rather mended"; Sally (Sarah), Harriot, and Eliza (Anne Elizabeth) are "with me in town"; "We have a coll [*cool*] pleasant House open to the Harbour"; wishes he could transport Thomas to New York for a week; would not want to keep him from his studies any longer than that, "for my whole Soul is bent on seeing You a distinguished ornament to Your Country," and hopes "that I may have a honest pride in saying *He is my Son.*"

Andrew Craigie to Samuel Rogers. FC:dft, Craigie Papers, MWA.

"It must have given you uneasiness to observe the Delay & embarrassments which have procrastinated the public Business of Congress—& you will be surprised ~~to find~~ in being told that it has altogether been owing to the Question respecting residence which has connected itself with almost every Subject that has come before Congress—That Question being settled I expect every Thing will go on harmoniously—~~I beg you will~~ I send you [*John*] Fenno's papers [*GUS*] in continuation which will give you the News. There is no doubt but Congress will fix permanent residence on the potomack & the temporary in Philadelphia."

Thomas Jefferson to William Short. ALS, Jefferson-Short Correspondence, Swem Library, ViW. For the full text, see *PTJ* 16:590n.

There remains no doubt that the Residence Act will pass the House the next day or the day after.

Richard Henry Lee to Thomas Lee Shippen. ALS, Shippen Family Papers, DLC. Place to which addressed not indicated.

"The debates have ended this day with rejecting every proposition of amendment to our bill, which augurs well for its final passage—Tomorrow, or the next day, will probably put a period to this business and secure our next Session with you."

Benjamin Rush to William Maclay. No copy known; acknowledged in Maclay to Rush, 10 July.

George Washington, Diary. ViHi.

Dined with Senators Wingate, Strong, Maclay, R. H. Lee, and Johnston, and Representatives Gilman, Ames, Sturges, Schureman, Fitzsimons, Wynkoop, Vining, Smith (Md.), Madison, Sevier, and Sumter.

Memorandum Book. Item 187, p. 76, PCC, DNA.

The Connecticut Senators delivered to the state department a deed for a lighthouse.

FRIDAY, 9 JULY 1790

Cool (Johnson)

Abraham Hunt to James Madison

Although I have not the honor of being personally Known to you, I flatter myself that you will pardon the Liberty I have taken in Soliceting your countenance to a Petition on my behalf, which is lodged with Mr. Ames of Massachusetts to forward to Congress.

***

To so an able an Advocate for the Oppressed to the delight of Suffering poverty, & the soldiers Friend. I cheerfully commend my Cause, persuaded of a truth, that whether the prayer of the petition is granted or not, that I shall be one amid the thousands of freeborn Soldiers but too hardly dealt with, who rise up & call Maddison Blessed.

ALS, Madison Papers, DLC. Written from Boston. For the full text and background on the petition, which sought commutation of military pay, see *DHFFC* 7:154.

John Steele to John Gray Blount

By Mr. [*John*] Osborn I cannot omit to drop you a line, relative to congressional business. The assumption project seems dead, at least for the present session, and no prospect of its resurrection unless the residence bill now before us shoud be rejected. The Pennsylvanians hold the ballance, they are at present well with the southern interest, they are satisfied with having the temporary residence in Philada. ten years, at the expiration of that time to move to the permanent seat of Govt. on Potowmac; but shou'd this measure fail, we not only loose the coalition with the Pennsylvanians, the seat of Govt. etca. but force them into a junction with the Eastern Gentlemen, who woud be willing to fix the seat of Govt. on Delaware or even renounce their religion, (if they have any) on condition of having the state debts assumed. This bill on which so much depends, has passed the senate finally, and by several votes taken in this house, we have reason to believe that it will pass ~~this~~ by 33 votes agt. 28.

What is the reason you have not written to me? What is the reason my friend W[*illiam*]. Blount has not? I have recd. two letters from him, but these were on business only. on my arrival at this place, I made out a catalogue of correspondents. you were both included, but I suppose your old Gladiator[1] here is so attentive in giving you the news, that my letters wou'd be redundant. I rejoice that your brother is appointed [*governor of the Southern*

Territory], not that I suppose the Office a great acquisition, or that it will add any dignity to his character, more than he is otherwise entitled to, but that it will put him out of the reach of, and raise him above his enemies. There are various opinions here respecting the boundary between the Cherokees, and No. C[*arolin*]a. The Secty. at War has some strange ones indeed. It wou'd be tedious to detail them now, will therefore postpone it untill I have the pleasure of seeing you at Fayetteville [*North Carolina*] next Novemr. However I conceive it a great point gained to our land holders, that the business will fall into the hands of a man, of all others the most proper.

ALS, John Gray Blount Papers, Nc-Ar. Addressed to Washington, North Carolina. The letter is dated 10 July, but it was clearly written before the final House vote on the Residence Bill on 9 July.

[1] Probably a reference to Williamson, but perhaps to Abishai C. Thomas.

Henry Van Schaack to Theodore Sedgwick

One of the most polite friendly and best worded billet that ever was penned by woman (I recevd. yesterday from my Dr. friend Mrs. [*Pamela*] Sedgwick) brought me here to dine with her—Mr. [*Gulian*] Verplanck Mr. Ticknor [*Isaac Tichenor*] & Mr. & Mrs. Jacob her guests, we were chearful and happy but shod. have been more so if you had been with us and headed your Table—This is a pleasure we shall expect to enjoy a month or two hence when you return. Your Session is Spinning out to an enormous length by the injudicious maneuvering of some of the southern people about the removal of Congress—what can possess those people to obtrude this paltry business when so many essential matters remain undone? If you do not break up soon you will be called the long Parliament and I sometimes fear you will dwindle away ~~into the Rum~~ and be called the Rump.[1]

I recieved a long letter from you a few days ago but as I have it not with me I cannot reply to it particularly—Let it suffice that I thank you for it as I do for all the letters you have wrote me.

All the Vermont Commissioners are here but one—Mr. Verplanck the only one from New York—Was I from Vermont I should feel sour enough about this kind of treatment. How those Gentlemen are agitated I know not. as an indifferent person and a sincere wellwisher to an accommodation between the contending parties I cannot refrain blaming the York Commissioners exceedingly—Not a line from them—The least the albanians[2] cod. have done wod. have been to have wrote an Excuse for not coming. The Vermonters and Mr. VPlanck take their departure to morrow and probably will never meet here again for which I am extremely sorry I assure you.

Your family is well and so is mine—come to us as quick as you can for I never longed to see you so much as I now do. I wish you wod. bring Benson with you that he may breath some pure air ~~here~~ among *us* Yankees tell him ~~that~~ I am extremely disappointed that I did not meet him here—I had Schemed it so that ~~he~~ [*lined out*] you and he and some of the agreeable ones in the Commission were to have Spent next Sunday with me—Good Night I go off early to morrow for home.

ALS, Sedgwick Papers, MHi. Written from Stockbridge, Massachusetts.

[1] The English Parliament that sat from 1640 to 1648 was known as the Long Parliament; the one that sat from 1648 to 1653 as the Rump Parliament.
[2] In this case, a synonym for New Yorkers.

Henry Wynkoop to Reading Beatty

Was in hopes before now to have inform'd You of the final Determination of the question of Residence, but that is not yet in my power, the Bill passed by the Senate was taken up on tuesday in Committee ~~of~~ of the whole & Debated until yesterday when it was reported without any Amendment, the lowest Majority I think was six Votes, this Day it will be taken up in the House, when as usual, we shall have Yeas & Nays in abundance, tho the Majority is decided & there is not the most distant Prospect of defeating the Bill, yet the Opponents are determined to dispute it's Progress in every part, if it be got thro to day I shall slip home tomorrow, that I may have an Opertunity of viewing the Feilds of Grain before Harvest, but this at present is doubtful. Your Conjecture respecting Indents is right, on redeeming the Continental Certifficates the State must be furnished with Indents to the Amount of the Interest paid by her, otherwise she must retain that Sum out of the Certifficates themselves; Wish You & Cressey [*Christina Wynkoop Beatty*] could dine with me at Vreden's Berg on Sunday & yet thro' uncertainty, dare not ask You.

ALS, Wynkoop Papers, PDoBHi. Written in the morning. Place to which addressed not indicated.

Newspaper Correspondence

A CORRESPONDENT observes, that the absolute decorum of the citizens of New-York, on the late debates on a subject so interesting to them, redounds to their immortal honor. He further observes, that he is at a loss to determine the cause of Mr. V—g's [*Vining*] panic-struck alarm on Tuesday last[1]—unless it be a *self-conviction* of having supported a measure unjust in its operation.

How will the *Virginia* gentlemen be finally disappointed! says a constant attendant on the debates. Let us calculate—In less than *ten years* the eastern influence will be augmented by *four* or *five* members—Rhode-Island *one*, Vermont *two* (perhaps three) and this state *one* more on the new census. And can the southern gentlemen flatter themselves, that any one member, north of MARYLAND, will *then* give a vote to go south of *Philadelphia!*

The indefatigable labours, forcible remarks, and judicious propositions of Mr. *Gerry*, and Mr. *Burke*, on the *residence bill*, have not escaped the citizens of New-York, unnoticed.[2] The excellent speeches of Mr. Gerry, before and after that of the *little* gentleman from D— [*Delaware*] (with that also, if it can be obtained) shall be inserted soon.[3]

The complexion of the house of Representatives, says a correspondent, on the question of amendment to the *residence bill*, augurs, that the citizens of New-York *may pay off the* HALL BILL, without further *castle buildings* of *deriving advantages* from the *erection* of FEDERAL EDIFICES. What was told you, with Ciceronian eloquence, and federal enthusiasm, *ye* CONVENTIONEERS, and which converted many of your *nays* to *yeas*![4] ______________ ! Well—it is too late to repent when the Devil is come.

NYJ, 9 July.

[1] For summaries of Vining's speech of 6 July, see *DHFFC* 13:1659–60, 1667–68.

[2] For Gerry's speeches of 6 and 8 July, see *DHFFC* 13:1648–53, 1658–59, 1666–67, and 1688–89. For Burke's speeches of 6, 7, and 8 July, see *DHFFC* 13:1656, 1662–65, 1668, 1673, 1680, and 1687.

[3] Gerry provided *NYJ* with a "copy" of this 7 July speech; see *DHFFC* 13:1677–79. Other versions appear at 13:1669, 1674–75.

[4] Congress had been sitting at New York City for three and a half years when the New York state convention considered ratification of the Constitution in 1788. Fear of losing Congress to another state caused several Antifederalists from the southern part of the state to switch their vote, enough to insure ratification (*Creation of DC*, pp. 87–88).

Letter from New York

The residence bill is now nearly completed, and Philadelphia will have the honor next winter of entertaining our Congress. Your delegates and your city have been roughly handled in the course of the debates. The abuse of Mr. Morris has been both indecent and unmerited, for every part of his conduct in this business has been fair and candid. I hope your citizens will not raise their rents, &c. otherwise you will suffer in the opinion of your best friends.

FG, 12 July; reprinted at New York City (*NYDA*, 15 July; *NYDG*, 17 July); Wilmington, Delaware; and Winchester, Virginia.

Letter from Elizabethtown, New Jersey

Being here on my way home, I embrace this moment, while supper is getting, to inform you that the Residence Bill passed at half after three o'clock this afternoon, without amendment; majority four votes. The ground was disputed by inches throughout, and the contest severe. This matter is now at an end, and that in a way advantageous to Pennsylvania in general, and Philadelphia in particular.

PP, 13 July; reprinted at Charleston, South Carolina. Written in the evening.

Letter from Stockbridge, Massachusetts

The Commissioners from the State of Vermont have been here, agreeable to appointment—but the gentlemen from Albany not attending—and there being only one Commissioner from the State of New-York, they were under the necessity of adjourning without doing any thing further than agreeing to meet on the 27th Sept. next, either at New-York or Bennington, which place, to be agreed upon.

GUS, 17 July.

Other Documents

James Madison, Sr. to James Madison. No copy known; acknowledged in James to James, Sr., 31 July.

Letter from New York. *PP*, 13 July; reprinted at Charleston, South Carolina. Written at 4 P.M.

Congratulations on the Residence Bill, which "passed this moment by a majority of three—32 to 29; with the Speaker [*F. A. Muhlenberg*] it would have been four"; the bill will go to the President this afternoon.

From New York. [Boston] *Columbian Centinel*, 14 July; reprinted at Portland, Maine; Exeter, New Hampshire; and Northampton and Springfield, Massachusetts. Misdated 8 July.

"The FUNDING BILL will be completed and pass in a few days; and there is a strong talk of an Assumption of the State Debts—I guess, at 3 per cent. Congress will assuredly rise by the last of this month."

SATURDAY, 10 JULY 1790

Cool (Johnson)

Nathaniel Barrell to George Thatcher

I dont at all like that weakness you complain of at the Stomach—it dos not indicate longevity, and as you are fond of life I wish you could long enjoy it— ***

You see the time is fixt to elect new members for Congress—I hope you will be again chosen, but I fear there is a combination forming against you—I am told 'tis determined by the General Court [*legislature*] (as a mark of their resentment for the extravagant compensations the Stuben pension, the Idle dissipation of the Revenue, &c. too many charges to enumerate here bro't against Congress) to make a total change of men—I tell them 'twill be unjust to punish indiscriminately good & bad, that you, Mr. Gerry, & Ames, so farr as I could judge from what were publishd of the debates, had uniformly opposd those destructive measures & had always been on the right side—every artifice is bro't to oust you amongst which 'tis said you coupled Bibles & Wool Cards together, and proposd a heavy impost on them equal to a prohibition, thus lightly esteeming what they would have others think they conceive to be of the highest importance, the sacred book which contains the words of eternal life, while if it could be properly investigated twould appear they themselves have no further use for it than to promote their worldly interest, and at this present, use it as a proper engine to calumniate you, & destroy your popularity—I just hint these matters that you may be upon your guard and counteract their designs—my feeble abilities can be of but little service to you. but so far as they ~~may go upon~~ can be extended you may promise yourself both my interest and vote.

ALS, Chamberlain Collection, MB. Written from York, Maine; postmarked Portsmouth, New Hampshire, 14 July.

Governor William Blount to John Steele

Be pleased to accept my sincere Thanks for your Kind Congratulations on being delivered from my State Enemies and for the very active and friendly part you took in bringing about an Event so much to be wished by me, but independent of these Considerations the Appointment[1] *itself* is truly important to me more so in my Opinion than any other in the Gift of the President could have been, the Salary is handsome and my Western Lands had become so great an Object to me that it had become absolutely necessary that I should go to the western Country to secure them and perhaps my Presence might have enhanced there Value—I am sure my present Appointment will. I am so sensible of your Attention to me in procuring this Appointment that my Feelings of Gratitude surpass what I have Language to express of which I hope I shall have it in my power to give you more substantial Proofs by my actions. I my dear Sir had never censured you even in the Moment of Disappointment nor at any other for any part you had acted or had not acted at Fayette-Ville,[2] your Conduct there was in my Opinion perfectly proper, I assured myself of your good Wishes and Services as far as you could go without damning yourself and further I do not wish or expect my Friends to go and perhaps had you have gone even that length that I might not have been saved. I am much better pleased with Things as they are than I should been if I had succeeded for beside the appointment the Importance of which I have before mentioned, my private Affairs *really* required my Attention, they have had it and I have closed several pieces of old and weighty Business to me to effect which I have attended on the last Circuit the Superior Courts of Hillsborough, Edenton, New Bern and Wilmington tho very little of my Business was in the Courts but with the People at them. May it not be said that Jo[*seph*]. McDowell and his Friends have rendered me essential Service? I shall not thank them but leave them to the Happyness of their own Reflections on the Occasion. Beside Business and Absence from Home the Fever and ague with which you saw me labouring at Fayette with very little Intermission has attended me untill my Return from Wilmington Court, to these reasons allow for a little native Indolence and yourself and my other northern Friends may readily account why they have been so long without hearing from me—On the 6th Instant I receved my Commission and on the 7th wrote to the Secretary of State signafying my Acceptance and to Williamson & Hawkins on the Subject of my unprepared Situation to set out immediately for my Government of the Ten[*nesse*]e. I should stay before I did &c. &c. the Contents of which I make no doubt will be communicated to you and my other Friends—I hope it will not injure the Feelings of yourself nor others that I have given this Business into the Hands of these two old Politicians—I at present intend to pass through Salisbury [*North Carolina*] and ~~in~~ if I should meet you there and have a confidential *elbow*-Conversation for an hour it would be one of the happiest of my Life—I at present hope for it. There are many Things I want to know that cannot be had any way else. I am informed Alexander McGillivray passed through Hillsborough [*North Carolina*] a few days since with fifteen other Chiefs of the Creek Nation my Informant who by the by is not a very good one says he spoke freely of the contemptableness of the State of Georgia and in exalted Terms of the federal Government, expressed a great desire to form a lasting Treaty with the latter which he de[*c*]lared to be the Object of his Visit to Congress but said as a

Condition that the Lands the Georgians had ~~restored~~ taken from him must be restored and my Informant understood he meant those Lands near the Town of Savannah that descended to him from his Father which that State had declared confiscated.

I am very happy in finding this Man is gone on to Congress for I had feared much Trouble with [*lined out*] him but I think he is now "fallen, fallen, fallen"[3] from that great Character which has heretofore been given him—You and myself I beleive agreed in rejoicing at his Treatment of the Commissioners of Congress last Fall[4] but surely it was a great proof that he was a weak or an uninformed Man as to what he ought to have known. Nothing is more certain than that a Majority of those Commissioners (being northern Men) if not the whole went forward to treat with him with great Prejudices against the State of Georgia and on the other Hand with very favourable Impressions of him—Then was the Time he ought to have treated and not to have conducted himself in such a Manner as to compel those Commissioners in defence of *themseves* to report favourable of the State of Georgia and unfavourably of him and now to complete his Downfall he comes to Congress to show himself and supplicate of them what they had offered him on his own Soil—He is I suppose like most other great Men if so the more he is seen the less he is admired—But be all this as it may I hope and doubt not but his coming will be turned to the best possible Account, and if a Treaty could at Congress be formed with him in which good natural Boundaries could be fixed I should find myself much relieved in my duty as Superintendant of Indian Affairs—I should suppose fifteen Chiefs and himself quite enough to treat with. I am told a Colonel [*Marinus*] Willett is with them—a Man I never heard of before.

ALS, Steele Papers, NcU. Written from Greenville, North Carolina; sent by "Post"; answered 29 July.

[1] Blount was appointed governor of the Southern Territory on 8 June.

[2] Probably a reference to Blount's defeat in the election of North Carolina's federal Senators by the state legislature then meeting at Fayetteville, in which Joseph McDowall—another unsuccessful candidate—may have had a role.

[3] From Revelation 14:8.

[4] The commission composed of David Humphreys of Connecticut, Benjamin Lincoln of Massachusetts, and Cyrus Griffin of Virginia that met with a Creek delegation at Rock Landing, Georgia, from 20 to 27 September 1789.

John Brown to Harry Innes

*** the mode of transporting letters to Kentucke being such as to induce me to believe that a great part of mine have been lost or miscarried ***

My dear friend I can give you but very little satisfactory information relative to the proceedings of Congress which for some time past have been the result of accident & chance rather than of the ~~the~~ cool deliberations of a considerate Legislature The questions relative to the Assumption of the State Debts & to the Residence of Congress have taken up the greater part of the present long Session & have distroyed that disinterestedness & Unanimity which marked the proceedings of the last year Happily the question respecting residence so irritable in its nature & involving not only the general interests of the community but also the rival interests of particular States & places was yesterday determined—An Act has passed in consequence of a combination between Pennsylvania & the Southern States establishing the temporary residence in Philada. for ten years & the permanent residence upon the Potowmack—I send you herewith a Copy of the Act—The fate of Assumption is still uncertain—in the House of Representatives there has hitherto been a majority of three or four against it but I begin to fear that we shall be forced into this measure under some modification or other as it appears impracticable to get along without it—In the House of Representatives the further consideration of this subject was long since postponed & a Bill passed funding the Foreign & domestic Debt of U. States but the Senate have hung up that Bill & brought forward the Question of Assumption The friends of this measure in both houses have declared their determination to oppose every attempt for the support of public Credit unless coupled with this their favorite object which has been advocated with all the zeal which State & Individual Interest could inspire & which has called up all the Jarring Interests of the States & given birth to Combinations Parties Intrigues Jealousies &c. to such a degree as to give serious alarm to the friends of the Government I send you a Copy of the Resolutions upon this subject now under consideration of the Senate—I now despair of having it in my power to reach Kentucke before the Election as an Adjournment is not expected to take place untill some time in August & in the present critical State of our affairs I do not feel my self at liberty to desert my trust in order to secure my further appointment I therefore must rest this matter with my friends 'tho at the same time well aware that my presence might be necessary to remove impressions which misrepresentations of my Views & Conduct circulated by those who oppose my election may have made—If my letters had found a safe passage to Kentuckey your friendly advice would have been unnecessary I have written many—& to my friends in different parts of the District—My friend at Pittsburg who forwards my letters informs that many of them had certainly been lost having sent them by Mr. [*John*] May & in other Boats which had fallen into the hands of the Indians—a large packet forwarded by a Gentn. on his way for that Country was a few days ago returned he having declined the Journey after proceeding as far as Easton [*Pennsylvania?*].

Authentic information has not yet been recd. that War has been actually declared between England & Spain, but vast preparations are making by both & from the present temper of those Nations as well as a variety of other circumstances there is every reason to believe that that event either has or will shortly taken place—information has been recd. (Via Hallifax [*Nova Scotia*]) that a fleet of seven Sail of Frigates & Sloops of War with a Regiment on board had actually sailed from Jamaica in order to reduce the Floridas & New Orleans—let this account be true or false 'tis certain that to get possession of the Mississipi is the great object the British at present have in view—What consequences ~~might~~ may not the U. State have to apprehend should that Key to the Western World fall into her hands? Would not the whole of that extensive & important Country infallably become tributary to the avarice & subservient to the Views of that ambitious Nation? I need not enlarge upon this interesting Subject or trouble you with my Ideas as to the manner in which it would affect the Interests of your Country—The great & almost certain loss of Inhabitants in case of attempts to colonize within the non Spanish Territory—the monoply of Trade—discouragement to manufactures—introduction of Factors—increase of Slaves by incouragement to cultivation of Tobacco—undue influence over the Councils of & probable seperation of the western Country from the Atlantic States are consequences so obvious as only require to be mentioned to be seen—We wait with great solicitude for further intelligence upon this head—we are not prepared for war & 'tis difficult to say how we shall be able to preserve a Nutrality.

You ask me what is meant by proceeding in Chancery agreeable to the Civil Law—Nothing more than agreeable to the mode of proceeding in Chancery in England—in contra distinction to proceedings at common Law.

As I send this thro the Wilderness[1] the mode of Conveyance prevents the pleasure of enclosing you News papers &c. Nothing in them but abuse of Congress for change of Residence & tardy proceedings.

ALS, Innes Papers, DLC. Place to which addressed not indicated. The omitted text concerns private financial transactions that Brown undertook for Innes and Brown's effort to establish a cotton factory in Kentucky, aborted owing to the arrest of the manager.

[1] The road through Cumberland Gap that connected the Great Valley of Virginia to Kentucky.

Samuel Dexter to Elbridge Gerry

Your just way of estimating men and things will induce you to consider this letter both as the effusion of private friendship and a regard to the public good.

By these same sentiments I was influenced when I contributed on a former occasion, though but in a small degree, yet to the utmost of my power, to the election of a gentleman, whom ~~tho'~~ I viewed as extremely ill treated for his endeavours to serve his country, yet disposed and well qualified to render it further service.[1]

With pleasure I have heard, from time to time, many who made objections at the time of voting for representative for this district, acknowledging to me their misapprehensions, expressing their entire satisfaction in the choice finally made, and approving, in the strongest terms, the conduct of their delegate in congress. These men, among whom were divers of the clergy, and other sensible persons, I trust have not altered their sentiments. But great pains are taking, and will be taken, to persuade such as were the most ready to vote for you at first, to give their suffrages at the approaching election for N. G. [*Nathaniel Gorham*] Esq. of Charlestown [*Massachusetts*]; and I believe I may add, under his influence. I enter not into particulars, but in general I say, as a public man I have never been greatly pleased with him. I assert not that his finances are low; but on the supposition that they are, I observe, that a man in different circumstances is (ceteris paribus)[2] more suitable to hold a place in the national legislature. That he is *a man of infinite cunning* but few in this county seem to be sensible. His own townsmen are so more than others.

The articles of charge recently brought against you are

1. That you, probably, intend to be an inhabitant of New York.

2. That altho' you did not vote for the compensation to the Senators and Representatives, yet you had said to some of your friends it was because *they were not high enough.*

3. That you ~~had~~ have more zealously promoted the pension of Baron [*Frederick William*] Steuben than any other member.

4. That you have been active in forwarding the plan of a congressional library. and

5. That you are in favour of placing the officers of the late Navy on the same footing with the officers of the army.

To the first article your friends answer, that they suppose you intend to return to your seat at Cambridge, when public business does not render it more convenient for you to be absent. To the second, that the charge is doubtless *false.* To the third, that you knew the services of Baron Steuben better, probably, than any other member in the house, certainly much better than either of the other Massachusetts members. ~~To~~ The fourth some of them justify as a proper measure, and none of them censure. The last they are unable to form a proper opinion concerning.

Your prudence, wisdom, assiduity, firmness, unwearied constancy and zeal in regard to the public debts, particularly ~~as~~ to the assumption of the debts of the individual States, meet the entire approbation of all. On these I principally rest the hope of your reelection. Those your friends mention on all occasions, among other good things which they think proper to say. The clergy, in general, are for you; but some of them exercise a sort of prudence to which I am a stranger. It will give me great satisfaction should we succeed. If you do not think me incapable of adulation you do not sufficiently know me. Perhaps none of your friends have asked you whether you should like to be rechosen. 'Tis sufficient for us that we wish for it ourselves. No person that will be a candidate can carry it against you, unless N. G. Esq. should succeed. If he should, it will give me much chagrin. You need not doubt my disapbrobation of him, any more than of my attachment to yourself.

My compliments to Mr. Ames, who I heartily wish may be reelected. But there will be a [*lined out*] party warmly opposed to him in Boston. It is hoped, however, to use an hibernian phrase, that his enemies will find themselves *in a great minority*.

P. S. If you think proper to consider any part of the foregoing letter as confidential, I have no objection to it. I do not want *needlessly* to make enemies; but I stand ~~in~~ not in need of the friendship of any man so much as to restrain me from speaking & writing with the utmost freedom on political matters.

ALS, Gerry Papers, DLC. Written from Weston, Massachusetts.

[1] During Weston's town meeting to vote for federal Representative on 18 December 1788, Dexter publicly vouched that Gerry only wanted to amend the Constitution, not repudiate it (*DHFFE* 1:641).

[2] All other things being equal.

Benjamin Goodhue to Michael Hodge

I herewith inclose you a revision of the collection law [*HR-82*] which has been reported to the House, and is to be taken up tomorrow, and I expect will pass through our House pretty soon and with probably few alterations, I expect we shall in a day or two report the Coasting Act [*HR-89*] revised—you'l see the compensation to Officers in some cases are increased beyond their rate of fees, and I should have made additions to you and others in my neighbourhood, who I am conscious realy stand in need of it, but in as much as grants are generaly odious, among those who do not distinguish between those that are properly made and others, (& many improper ones have been made) I thought it expedient with the advice of Mr. Hamilton not to add any from my County but to delay it for a while—the Secry. means to collect from the several Officers the amount of Fees that it may be a subject of revision in future, and you may rest assured that he is sufficiently disposed to do all in his power (whh. is not small,) amply to provide for them—I expect we shall adjourn in 3 or 4 weeks and I hope through many fears that We shall after having suffer'd more I am sure then any of our Constituents can conceive of ~~at~~ finish the great bussines, which to our dishonour has been so long neglected.

ALS, Ebenezer Stone Papers, MSaE. Addressed to Newburyport, Massachusetts.

Thomas Hartley to Jasper Yeates

I received your Favor of the 4th. inst. and am glad to understand that your Family as well as my Family are well and I should be glad to meet Mrs. [*Catherine Holtzinger*] Hartley at Lancaster [*Pennsylvania*], but I fear she will not like to be absent from Home so long. On to Morrow a Week or next Day Week I am in Hopes I shall be able to get away—(tho' I think Congress will not adjourn so soon—) and shall proceed to Lancaster ~~as soon~~ as early as possible.

Your account of Mrs. [*Ester Bowers Sayre?*] Atlee is very distressing, but I hope she has got better.

The Bill for fixing the Temporary Residence of Congress at Philadelphia for ten Years and permanent Residence at Potomac passed our House without any Alteration or Amendment—32. to 29—My Immagination has been engaged to inquire if any Trick can be played agst. us but at present I cannot discover any—The History of this Business I shall give you more particularly—when I see you but you may be assured it will be curious The Senate have suspended the Funding Bill till our Ways and Means Bill has been offered them—Monday or Tuesday will discover whether we shall fund or not—The Question of Residence being now out of the way—~~Things~~ Affairs may go on better—Indeed Things look rather better than when I wrote you last, but I do not mean in this Observation to include the Sower Faces of the New Yorkers—and you may well suppose that our Delegation are not very agreeable here.

We affect great Moderation when in public but in a Corner we do take a Laugh.

We are just now disputing upon the Post Office Bill [*HR-74*]—I have made my Speech & take this Oppertunity to write to you.

ALS, Emmet Collection, NN. Place to which addressed not indicated.

William Maclay to Benjamin Rush

I trust, at last, my dear friend, I may give You Joy, in the almost certain prospect, of seeing Congress soon in Philadelphia. May they gain as much

Credit by their Conduct in that City, as I fear they have lost, under the influence of this. Indeed I consider it as high time to find a Scape Goat on whom to lay our political Transgressions. Many things that are considered as such, have really been the offspring of this place, and here may they remain.

I have received & thank You for your Friendly letter of the 8th instant. I know I have given offense to the Class of Men You Mention. Be it so. I have in the Affair You allude to, I trust I shall in every other, Act as if I were immortal. let them take my place, and give it to whom they please, my peace of mind they shall not take. The Business of the Residence has been attended with many difficulties, and engaged our Utmost address. I will not however give You any detail of our Arrangements in Writing. It will be proper food for some future Evening.

ALS, Rush Papers, DLC. Addressed to Third Street, Philadelphia; franked; postmarked 11 July.

Peter Muhlenberg to Benjamin Rush

Though I have no doubt you are allready informd, that the Bill establishing the permanent, and temporary, residence of Congress has past both Houses; I enclose a statement of the Votes taken on the occasion and venture to congratulate you on obtaining; not alltogether what we wishd, but what we could possibly get. I do not know if the measure will prove satisfactory but I am well convincd, it was the only one from which we had a prospect of success—The Motions to introduce Germantown [*Pennsylvania*]—Susquehanna &c. &c. were only intended to ensnare, & divide us, & had we in one instance divided, the Bill must have been lost.

General Matthews and myself, first introducd the plan to our Friends, and tho it did not promise much at first, yet, when acceded to by some of The Southern Members of The Senate, and the Virginia Representatives, we were enabled to carry it through, notwithstanding the strong opposition, and without giving just cause for the charge of *Bargaining.*

ALS, Gratz Collection, PHi. Addressed to Philadelphia.

Thomas Pleasants, Jr. to James Madison

***

My recommendation of Mr. Thomas Thompson, and his solicitation for an appointment of Consul, was in expectation that an emolument would be annexed. but as that is not the case; and having no hopes of advantage from a Residence in the Canaries, he begs leave to wave that appointment.

at Madeira Lisbon, Opporto, Cadiz, Barcelona, Bilboa, or any other place in Europe that afforded a Certain, and Regular Market, for the produce of the American States, and especially of this State, he might from his acquaintance here, have expected, to have done something in the line of business. but with Teneriffe, or any other of the Canaries, there is so little intercourse, that without an emolument it would never answer his purpose. indeed without an emolument, I am inclined to think, the appointment in no Case, would be worth the acceptance of an American, not already settled, or who had not views to a settlement in business, at the place to which, he may be appointed. 'Tho Mr. Thompson for the above reason, would decline an appointment to the Canaries, yet he is loth to loose sight of the matter altogether, and therefore wishes to be Continued upon the List, in hopes that if any thing should turn up hereafter, more to his advantage, that he may not be forgot: and to that end, has wished me to mention the matter to Mr. Jefferson, which I have declined; but I believe he hath engaged Mr. Thomas [*Mann*] Randolph jr. to do it, who may refer to what I have written you, in that Case, and it should be mentioned by Mr. Jefferson, you may Communicate to him my Sentiments respecting Mr. Thompson.

I am not acquainted with the Subject of Finance—or sufficiently informed of the situation and extent of the state debts, to be able to form a just opinion in regard to their assumption. but as the Requisitions of Congress from time to time upon the several States, have not been equally Complied with, it seems unjust that the States that have paid, should be taxed in the same proportion, with the states that have not paid.

It also seems to be impolitick, perhaps unsafe, to increase the national debt, so as not to be able to pay the Interest, without having Recourse to direct taxation.

The Northern, and Eastern States have already made Considerable progress in Manufactures—which will increase, and advance much faster than in the Southern States. and as their Manufactures increase, their Imports will Lessen—and as their Imports Lessen their Taxes will decrease—and thus the great Burthen of the debt will fall upon the Southern States.

The People of the North, are more attached and awake to their Interest, than those of the South—and having it more in their power too, are upon the Watch, and seize every opportunity of Speculating upon their Southern Brethren. and if the State Debts are assumed, it will be found that they are Chiefly possessed by the people of the North—for these among other Reasons that have been given, I am inclined to the opinion, that it would be better, at least for the Southern States, that each State, should provide for, and Work out their own particular debt in the best Manner they Can.

Tho' the situation of America loudly Called for some alteration in their General Government—and the Change that has taken place is perhaps as free from objections, as any System that Could have been framed yet I have always apprehended great difficulty in uniting a people, whose Interests, are so diametrically opposite, under one General Government. and without more Condescèntion, Liberality, and Disinterestedness in the Representatives—less attachment to local, and particular Interests, and greater attention to the General Good, in short unless they are in fact the Representatives of the U. states, and not the partisans of particular States, all that the Enemies of the Government have foretold will probably Come to pass—Tho' not much in the Way of Information, I sometimes mix with the people—and think I discern apprehensions, among the more thinking part, that the affairs of the Government does not go on well—and a prevailing Wish that Mr. H—y [*Patrick Henry*] was in Congress. the subject of Slavery hath excited great uneasiness here, and will probably Cause still greater to the southward. 'tho there is no doubt, but Slavery is a Moral, and political, Evil, and that Whoever brings forward in the Respective States, some General, rational, and Liberal plan, for the Gradual Emancipation of Slaves, will deserve Well of his Country—yet I think it was very improper, at this time, to introduce it in Congress, as well, because they had not power to do any essential good, as that it interfered with other, perhaps more important business, and that its discussion Could not fail to produce great Intemperance of debate, which ~~would~~ tends to Weaken the Government.

It does not strike me that the Regulations, hitherto made by Congress, will operate upon the Trade With Britain, so as to induce their Government to Make a Commercial Treaty with the States. for what advantage Can they expect to derive from a Treaty that they are not already possessed of? Their Ships are permitted to bring to America the products and Manufactures of all Countries, while American Vessels are restrained from Carrying to Britain any thing but the growth and produce of the States.

Their Ships without restraint or Controul, navigate between their Islands and America and import, and export whatever they please—while American Vessels are restrained from all intercourse with their Islands.

When the Connection between two Countries are Reciprocal, the Conditions on which the Trade between those Countries is carried on should be Reciprocal also. The Connection between this Country, and the British W. India Islands is Reciprocal (indeed they are in a great measure dependent upon us, and it is at least problematical, if we should not be better without anything from them) therefore we should equally participate in Carrying on the trade, or have nothing to do with them.

But it will be said, by such a Measure we should be the greater sufferers, for in that ~~place~~ Case, where should we find a Market for our Lumber and provisions?

If the Trade to the South of Europe Was safe for American Vessels, it would increase their Number. and as Ship-building increased it would occasion a demand for all our White Oak, and the best part of the pine timber—and the south of Europe is the great Market to which we must look ~~up to~~, for the sale of our provisions.

But admitting Europe should not afford an exit for our surplus provisions; so great is the dependence of the W. India Islands upon this Continent and they derive their supplies so much cheaper and better from hence, than from Europe, that there is but little doubt but their ports would soon be thrown open to American Vessels—or, if it should not produce that effect, that our provisions would still find the way to them thro' the Dutch, and Danish Islands where they would be Carried in American Vessels.

But should neither of these be the Consequence, I do not see that we should suffer by the loss of a trade; the ballance of which, is so greatly against us, and for articles of Luxury too, of which one is of the most pernicious Kind. as to Lumber it would be better that the trees remained in the forest, than that they should be got up into this article, to be transported in *British ships*, as it may be proved that the Value, in most instances, but especially in White oak Staves, and timber, is not equal to the labour of getting, and the expence of Carrying it to Market, so that the Timber is wholly lost.

It is indeed of no small Importance to the British Trade for they not only obtain this article so Necessary to their Islands 100 ℔ Ct. Cheaper than they Could derive it elsewhere, but it also affords employment for their Ships, at a time when they would otherwise be Idle, and exposed to Worms, and Hurricanes. in short it appears to me that the supply of this, to them necessary article, would alone Compel them to open their ports to American Vessels.

But another, and perhaps Still greater objection, would be the effect that it would have in Reducing the Revenue. surely the saving of half a Million in the annual Consumption of Rum only, would enable the people in some other way to pay a greater tax than the amot. of the Impost on this article. but admitting this was not the Case, I do not think it of Sufficient weight, to prevent an experiment, that bid so far to produce such good effects.

It is at least doubtful whether it is good policy to prevent foreign Merchants from holding an Interest in American Ships. at least if not openly permitted, I think it should be Connived at. for if the Timber is not Wrought up here—it will be Conveyed to Europe in European Ships to be Wrought up there. and thus our Ship-builders will Remain Idle, while additional employment is given to their Ships & builders. If a foreign Merchant found it his Int. to Connect himself with a Mercht. here in building a Ship, why restrain him from doing it? It would in effect be the same as selling the Ship to him When built. besides in the Infant State of the Trade of this Country, the Merchants here want Capital, and are therefore naturally led into such foreign Connexions as will help them forward in business—and it may be in their power to hold part of a Vessel, when they Could not own the Whole.

I have in a former Letter observed how Important to the Commerce of the U. states it is, that their Vessels should be able to Navigate in safety the Mediterranean—and to that end a treaty with the piratical States of Barbary, should be obtained—it is of more Consequence than all the W. India Trade—as in that event, the exportation of Grain, and flour, Might in a few years be transfered to American Vessels only.

I observe that the British Merchants, have begun to prosecute the Recovery of their old debts, before the people are in a situation to pay, and if the business goes on with Rigour, it will be apt to produce disagreeable Consequences. I have thought, that it would be best for both parties, that the payments were placed upon such Installments, as afforded to the debtor hopes of emancipation, without such a Change and sacrifice of property as must follow a Rigorous Collection—and that would at the same time ultimately secure the Creditor: but I am at a loss to know how this is to be brought about. The Government of the States, Cannot interfere without the consent of the Creditors—and they, I should suppose would not, after the delays that have already happened, be prevailed upon, but thro' the Medium of their own Government, to come into the Measure—who probably would not Concern with it, unless it became, a National affair, and to this the states would probably object.

But if nothing of this kind should take place, I am persuaded that it will be a Measure Not only Necessary to the Debtors; but sound policy in the States, to pass an act, permitting foreigners to hold Land for a given time. for the debts Cannot be paid but by a great Change of Real property. there is not money among the people to purchase the property at its intrinsick Value, and if the Creditors could hold the lands, they would probably in many instances, enter into a Reasonable accomodation with their Debtors, by taking lands in payment. this while it afforded Relief to the debtor, would be a transfer of property to the benefit of the State: as the Creditor would settle himself, or some of his family upon the Lands, or Negociate a sale in Europe to some person who would Come out and settle upon them; which in either Case, would be an acquisition of people, and in many instances, property too, to the States.

I have insensibly run into these Cursory observations, which have swelled my letter far beyond the bounds that I intended—and tho' they may Contain nothing worthy your attention—still I am persuaded that they will be well Recieved.

ALS, Madison Papers, DLC. Written from Raleigh Parish (Amelia County), Virginia. The omitted text concerns a letter from an "Honest Clergyman" that Madison asked Pleasants to forward. For the full text, see *PJM* 13:269–74.

Governor Beverley Randolph to Thomas Jefferson

*** Mr. Stephen Austin one of the Proprietors of the lead mines in this State[1] proposes to make application to the Congress of the United States for some encouragement in order to enable them to furnish this Country with manufactured Lead in all its various Forms. He also wishes to contract with the general government to supply such Quantity of Lead as may be wanted for their Magazines & cæt: In order to give every aid to his application I take the Liberty to introduce Mr. Austin to you & to request the Favour of you to assist him by your advice & Recommendation to those who may have Power to forward his views.

I believe you are well acquainted with the Fertility of these Mines. From the Information which I have received I conceive they are capable of producing such a Quantity of Lead as will intitle them to the Countenance of Government. The inclosed certificate speaks fully of their present Situation & future Prospects.

[*Enclosure*]

Arthur Campbell, R[*obert*]. Sayers, and William Migomry [*Montgomery*] to the Governor and Council of Virginia, 23 June

We, professing ourselves friends to the promotion of American Manufactures, especially those of Necessary Articles, and being requested by Mr. Stephen Austin to view the present State of the Works now carrying on at the Lead Mines, Do certify, that there are between fifty and sixty men employed as Miners, Artificers, and Labourers; that there are seven Pits sunk, of about seventy feet in depth, which are so productive, that from six to eight tons of Ore, may be raised in a day; that the appearances give Confidence to conclude, that the bodies of Ore, that may be found in the Hill is inexhaustible; that at present a very simple but improved manner of beating and Washing the Ore are adopted; that there are in forwardness materials for erecting a New furnace, which may be ready for use in less than two Months, but that built by the late Colonel [*John*] Chiswell is now so repaired, that above one ton and an half of Lead may be Smelted every day while it Stands.

From these beginnings, and from the Activity and professed Views of the Owners, we are sanguine enough to believe, that with a small encouragement from the General Government, so as to compensate in a degree for so distant a Land Carriage, that Lead will be produced and Manufactored, in the course of the ensuing year, Sufficient for the Consumption of the United States.

It has been mentioned to us that a duty of one Cent per Pound on all foreign Lead imported will operate as an ample encouragement to bring about a completion of their Views. We are not so well acqua[*inted*] with the Commercial Interests of the United States as to urge the adoption of such a Proposition; but wish to remind our Rulers, that the time has been, tha[*t*] much depended on the preservation and success of this same Manufacture: That similar Occasions may hap[*pen*] in the Course of future Events, that will show the goo[*d*] policy of being independent of all the World for so necessary an Article.

ALS, Jefferson Papers, DLC; Ms., Miscellaneous Letters, Miscellaneous Correspondence, State Department Records, Record Group 59, DNA. Written from Richmond, Virginia; enclosure written from the "Lead Mines." The editors are printing this letter because we believe it is the same, or nearly the same, as that which Randolph sent to Virginia's Senators; see Lee and Walker to Randolph, 25 July, below.

[1] Virginia's famous lead mines were located along the New River, near its confluence with Cripple Creek, in present-day Wythe County. In his *Notes on the State of Virginia* (1781), which misidentified the New River as part of the Great Kanhaway (Kanawha) River, Jefferson reported that the mines yielded up to sixty tons annually, transportable to Richmond over a 130 mile land carriage. So crucial were the mines to Virginia's war effort that they were operated by the state government until 1782. Moses Austin, who had opened a lead shot manufactory in Richmond with his brother Stephen in 1789, settled at the mines later that year, established the mining town of Austinville, and was granted a claim to the surrounding 1400 acres by the state in May 1791 (Jefferson, *Notes on the State of Virginia*, "Query VI"; *PTJ* 17:23–24; *PGW* 6:42–44).

Theodore Sedgwick to Pamela Sedgwick

I dont know in what terms to write to the best beloved of my heart. For four or five weeks past we have been in such a state that I thought it impossible that the business should detain me here above four or five days. So it seems at present, but let me pray you dearest and best beloved, not to permit yourself to be too impatient for 14. days from the date of this, by which time if ever the important question [*assumption*] is settled it must be determined.

Mr. [*Martin*] Hoofman imediately on his return called at my lodgings. I was out walking with Col. Hamilton and conversing on the great subject. On my return I went there. You would to be sure have thought me a very child, had you heard the innumerable questions I put to him. when he told me that you and the children were all well—that Roberts leg was almost recovered—that he was pleased with my little ones, that he thought my wife a very excellent woman. when he spoke handsomely of his reception and approved our situation and improvements. I could with good will have taken the honest Deacon in my arms and kissed him.

Mary Hoffman, who saw Eliza [*Sedgwick*] at the pool [*Lebanon Springs, New York*], speaks very handsomely of her. I am induced to believe she is a Girl of taste.

By [*James?*] orton who will leave New York on wednesday or thursday I shall again write you, which I verily hope and beleive will be my last.

ALS, Sedgwick Papers, MHi. Place to which written not indicated.

Frederick Wolcott to Henry Van Schaack

The last evening I reached Home on my return from New York. The Smiles of my Friends, and the receipt of your [*lined out*] polite and friendly favour of the fourth Inst., made me very happy; and for a few Hours almost induced me to forget my *capital* Infirmities. The morning I left N. York I wrote You a letter which You have probably received. I informed You that the funding system would not be compleated this Session. There are in Congress all the varieties of opinions that can be imagined. Some believe that the publick Debt has properties which are most sacred—these insist that nothing shall be done which does not imply the greatest veneration for the publick Creditors—others imagine that their claims are founded principally in accident or fraud—and wish to disavow the obligations of the late Government. In the mean between these extremes, the truth probably lies—and if any thing is compleated, the result will be a proposal for a new Loan of the publick Debt, at about four ℔ Cent interest.

I perceive that the Disputes of this Session have added but little to the popularity of Congress—I believe however that the Representatives of each particular State are very popular at Home. The Virginians respect their Representatives for opposing the assumption; the People of Massachusets are pleased that theirs appear in favour of the measure. Whilst there remains such a difference of sentiment in the different States, we may never expect that Congress will proceed very harmoniously in establishing general principles.

In popular Governments the Representatives of a People will seldom vindicate measures which are generally odious to their Constituents. I think it is pretty evident that the science of Politicks, among the geat Body of the People in the Southern States, has not made the progress it has in New-England. This must lay the Representatives of that part of the Union under very great embarrassments. However We may lament the desultory proceedings of Congress, I think We should acknowledge that they are of very great *negative benefit* to Us. They prevent the establishment of *tender Laws*, the making of paper money, & an infinite variety of Frauds which some of Us are inclined to practise. The People of Massachusets & Connecticut are the most dissatisfied with our publick measures. The obvious reason is, that previous to the establishment of the present system, our Politicks were in so happy a train that they required no checks from a general Government, and we can experience no benifit from the Union unless by some positive acts of legislation—But it is of infinite consequence to the deluded People of *Rhode-Island* that they have a Master who will prevent their destroying themselves.

It must be a great exertion of generosity in you to pardon me for this shocking Scrawl. ***

ALS, Van Schaack Papers, Newberry Library, Chicago, Illinois. Written from Litchfield, Connecticut.

[*David Daggett,*] A Republican to Messrs. Printers (No. 7)

THE Baron [*Frederick William*] Steuben has finally obtained from Congress, a stipend of 2500 dollars per annum. Who pays this sum? The people either directly or indirectly. Of the inhabitants who shall contribute to this, not one third are individually possessed of as much property as this pensioner receives annually—not one man in three possesses an estate worth 2500 dollars. This, however, I agree, does not prove that the grant ought not to have been made, tho there *are* arguments of weight against it.

For what has this compensation been allowed? This is a question which we have a right to ask and to which we may demand a catagorical answer. It will be replied to this inquiry the Baron rendered essential services to the United States during the war—agreed. But are not the demands of justice equal? Is not every man who has furnished the public with property, entitled to his stipulated reward? And can Congress, without a blush, shut their ears against one class of creditors and extend relief to another? If the public are unable to perform *all* their contracts, they should give no preference. An individual, in bankrupt circumstances, who conducts differently towards creditors equally meritorious, shews a disengenuity of heart, which is justly reprobrated. And are communities bound by no principles of morality, which should actuate a private person in his intercourse with his neighbour?

But, it may be said, the debts of the union will *all* finally be paid—we are not under a national bankruptcy—admit that idea—will it hence follow, that one obligation shall be paid on demand, and another, equally binding, be postponed half a century? This would be as glaring and unjust a preference as the one alluded to above.

But the Baron Steuben rendered us most signal services—so have *many* others. But he sacrificed the most flattering prospects to yield us his assistance—so have *hundreds* of others. But he has beggared himself in the American cause—so have *thousands* of others. But Congress made him the most positive and unequivocal promises of an adequate reward—so they have to every individual to whom they were indebted. But humanity and compassion would induce Congress to relieve him from his necessities. And is he *alone* the object of their humanity? Where is the whole class of public creditors who lent their property or afforded their services to the United States? Where are the hundreds and thousands whose whole fortunes have been swept from them by the conflagration of a single hour, or have been swallowed up in the whirlpool of depreciating currencies? Where is the generous soldier "who" (in the striking language of a late elegant sermon) "has nobly braved fatigues and dangers and death for our sakes, who has faithfully adhered to our cause, while thousands and ten thousands of his brethren perished around him, by the horrors of sickness and the sword and the far greater horrors of British prison-ships, and British jails?" Where are the numerous widows and orphans, whose fondest hopes and only prospects have been cruelly disappointed in a single moment, by the death of a husband, or a parent, and who are, at once, expressive monuments of the desolation of a war, and the ingratitude of our country? Where is the numerous band of invalids, whose dislocated joints, meagre countenances, and debilitated constitutions, address us in the most feeling language, and present claims which a heart less hard than adamant, could not reject?

Are none of these worth the attention of Congress? Shall no provision be made for such as I have described, while an individual, entitled to no more compassion than they, is allowed a decent fortune, every year, during life? This may be just in men who act above the reach of controul, but we must be excused from according with such sentiments. This is not "rendering to all their dues—tribute to whom tribute is due—custom to whom custom;"[1] nor is it in imitation of the conduct of the Ruler of the Universe, who "regarded, with an equal eye, the poor and the rich, and is no respector of persons;"[2] nor is it "filling the hungry with good things, and sending the rich empty away."[3]

One thought further, and I will quit the consideration of this pension. Will the man whose family is beggared by the loan of his money to the public, or will the soldier, who is now compelled to labour twenty four hours to earn half a dollar, consent to pay their proportion of compensations so manifestly partial and unjust? If they will, they richly deserve, and doubtless will receive the ignominy attendant upon such meaness of spirit.

[New Haven] *Connecticut Journal*, 14 July; reprinted at Boston and Springfield, Massachusetts; Lancaster (in German) and Philadelphia, Pennsylvania. For information on this series and its authorship, see the location note to A Republican to Messrs. Printers (No. 1), 15 May, volume 19.

[1] Romans 13:7.
[2] Probably a paraphrase of James 2.
[3] Luke 1:53.

Letter from New York

The residence bill passed yesterday afternoon, and will be prepared to receive the signature of the President on Monday. The New-Yorkers are very angry at our delegates, but they should blame nobody but their own senators, who last year, by breaking an engagement with our people, deprived their city of four years temporary residence, and of all the advantages, which the back parts of their state would have derived from the perpetual residence of Congress on the Delaware.

FG, 14 July; reprinted at Baltimore.

Letter from an Influential North Carolinian

The Representatives from the Eastern States and the Senate as a body, have discovered such an appetite for *political power*, and so little knowledge of the temper, dissentions, and prejudices of the people of America, that I declare I have the most serious apprehensions of their overturning a government, it has cost us so much trouble and pains to establish. You have no idea, my friend, how much our best federalists are alarmed at the present parties and proceedings of Congress. A direct tax, or an excise at present would undoubtedly unhinge the government, it is far from being permanently fixed, and the people of the United States are in the habit of being gratified with revolution and novelty. I am very happy to find that the post-office bill [*HR*-74] is nearly on the footing I wished it. The post-line will still serve a large part of the commercial gentlemen by being direct thro' the towns at the heads of the river navigation, where the business of the state is principally done; but there is one object extremely important that will be obtained; the body of the people will have an opportunity of being informed of the proceedings of Congress which are now become very important to them; a circumstance which will prevent those jealousies at least, which proceed from ignorance and distrust.

NYDA, 30 July; reprinted at New York City (*NYP*, 31 July); New Brunswick, New Jersey; Philadelphia; Baltimore; Fredericksburg, Virginia; and Edenton, North Carolina.

Other Documents

James Abeel to Silvanus Bourn. ALS, Bourn Papers, MH. Place to which addressed not indicated.

Last week, Thomas Lloyd, the congressional shorthand reporter, "was sent to prison, but remained only two days"; wishes "some of the Members of Congress" be sent there "as some of them deserve it."

Charles Carroll to Richard Caton. No copy known; mentioned in Carroll to Mary Caton, 11 July.

Andrew Craigie to Daniel Parker. FC:dft, Craigie Papers, MWA.

The decision on the residence question "will restore Harmony to Congress & as it was the result of accommodation there is no doubt but the public Business will now go on with dispatch & the funding System with the assumption be immediately compleated"; mentions a (private?) bill being negotiated in Amsterdam, which "I suspect Fitzsimons has the direction of."

Benjamin Goodhue to William Coombs, David Coats, and Moses Brown. No copy known; acknowledged in Coombs, et al., to Goodhue, 19 July.

Thomas B. Wait to George Thatcher. ALS, Chamberlain Collection, MB. Written from Portland, Maine; postmarked Portsmouth, New Hampshire, 12 July; received 15 July.

Thanks for loan of money; asks if his predictions of a long Congress are correct and when Congress will adjourn.

Hugh Williamson to John Gray Blount. ALS, John Gray Blount Papers, Nc-Ar. Addressed to Washington, North Carolina. For the full text, see *Blount* 2:78–79.

Has sold the 1786 North Carolina certificates that Blount sent; proposes further speculation in them; has not heard from William Blount since his appointment as governor of the Southern Territory.

George Washington, Diary. ViHi. For the full text, see *DGW* 6:93. For Beckwith's communications, see *DGW* 6:87–88. The "important matter of it" was the impending war between Spain and Great Britain.

Visited the site of Fort Washington with the Adamses and others; asked the Vice President to turn his "attention to the Communications of Majr. [*George*] Beckwith, as I might in the course of a few days," call for an opinion about "the important matter of it."

Memorandum Book. Item 187, p. 77, PCC, DNA.

As attorney for David Ramsay, Burke delivered copies of Ramsay's *History of the Revolution in South Carolina* (1785) and *History of the American Revolution* (1789) to Jefferson and applied for copyrights. (Page 79 of the same source indicates that Burke obtained a receipt from Jefferson on 16 July.)

Sunday, 11 July 1790

Fisher Ames to Thomas Dwight

I think I have not recd. a line from you since the 24 June—At this time of joy & sorrow in the family of your respectable neighbour, where you sometimes go, changes are taking place which will be interesting to their happiness. Maria [*Worthington*] is almost married, & perhaps on her way to N. Brunswick, Pray let me hear from you in regard to that family, & our other friends.

Tomorrow a Comee. will report in Senate in favour of the Assumption—and on Tuesday I suppose it will be taken up. But we begin to relax in our sanguine hopes of success. It is plainly in our power—The Game is in our ~~hopes~~ hands—Last week the removal bill passed in favour of Philadelphia & Potowmac. That incumbrance out of our way, it is not to be doubted that we could carry our long contested point—But in Senate some gentlemen advocate a simple four per Cent provision for the debt, making no compensation as the Secretary has reported for the two per Cent[1]—This has been agreed to as an Amendment to the funding bill, wch. is still in that house—Several Senators friendly to the funding and assuming say—That such a measure (four per Cent, and no equivalent for the two per Ct.) is agt. justice—agt. national policy—agt. eastern policy, for it is forgiving, or rather throwing, away one third of the property now collected in the Middle & Eastern states—disgraceful to the public—weakens the attachment of individuals &c. That if we can pay 4 per Ct. now, we can pay two more in ten years—Even if we shd. fail, the evil wd. be foreseen & guarded agt. & then we shd. have gained strength & could bear it better—4 per cent, tho dishonest, affords no relief—it is an unnecessary anticipation of an uncertain contingency &c. &c. I confess I incline to this opinion—The other is ~~this,~~ that as we may fail ten years hence, it is better not to promise This difference of opinion is becoming serious Those who insist on the Secretary's proposals say, that unless assurances are given that these offers shall be made to the Creditors, they will vote agt. the funding assumption & every thing connected with what they call so improper a plan—Neither party seems to advance towds. accommodation, & it now seems inevitable that the assumption will on Tuesday be rejected in Senate—Thus my friend, we hope & fear—we then become sanguine & then absolutely despair—I begin to fear that we are but 15 years old in politics, wch. is the age of our nation since 1775, & that it will be at least 6 years before we become fit for any thing but Colonies—we want principles—morals, fixed habits—& more firmness agt. unreasonable clamours. I shall give you the Vapours–I finish.

ALS, Ames Papers, MDedHi. Place to which addressed not indicated.

[1] For the amendment to the Funding Bill, see *DHFFC* 5:914–15n.

Fisher Ames to John Lowell

You may remember when I had the pleasure of your company from Salem to Beverly [*Massachusetts*] that I expressed this opinion That the second session of Congress would not be a popular one—I had seen so much of the conduct of members that I was convinced that their ideas & expectations in regard to Govt. were different from those which prevail in New England. But what remains of the attachment to the new Govt. I begin to apprehend will be lost in a short time.

Last Friday, the Bill for removing Congress to Philaa. passed—This contest has spoiled all other business—That being no longer in our way, it is not to be doubted that the friends of the funding & assumption have it in their power to do both. But an amendment was made some time ago in Senate to the funding bill to strike out the offers to the creditors & to give a simple four per Ct. Several Senators friendly to our wishes as to the state debts make this point, i.e. an equivalent for the two per Cent as proposed by the Secy., a sine qua non of the Assumption—Mr. Elsworth, in particular, will not renounce his four per Cent—and of course it is to be expected, that the Assumption will be lost, & by a friend—we have reached the summit of the Mountain—like Sysiphus—on Tuesday, I expect the stone will be at the foot again, and it will be next to impossible to roll it back again[1]—Many talk of an adjourmt. The funding is not to [*be*] made safe without the assumption—shd. we adjourn, after so many months of hope & fear & anger on the part of the public, I am apprehensive that we shall bring our Govt. into danger—I have no doubt that we ought to fund, tho we shd. not assume. But to cut off one third of the debt, which it is said the middle & eastern people have engrossed, to tarnish our honour, is so much agt. justice, agt. national, agt. eastern policy that I think we ought not to agree to it upon any pretence of political or artificial expediency. we want principles, morals, habits in Govt.—we are, I am afraid, colonies still—I am mortified to find this Govt. so much addicted to the policy of R[*hode*]. Island.[2]

Many affect to wonder that we talk of the force of contract—They say, let us promise no more than we can perform—our new promises must not be broken. True—but let us perform what we can—The plan of 4 per Ct. gives no relief—The Secy. proposes no more till ten years have elapsed—Then we shall be able to pay it—or if not able, the creditors may then be asked to compound—now we anticipate, we aggravate an evil wch. otherwise we might avoid—we not only seem but we try to do justice by the Sec.'s plan, & we may expect to effect more than if we did not try—The sense of justice will produce a sense of attachment. The Govt. by sticking to a principle will be safer than by wandering after a delusive policy.

I forget that to your mind these remarks are superfluous.

ALS, Diedrich Memorial Collection, MiU-C. Place to which addressed not indicated.

[1] In ancient folk legend, Sisyphus was condemned to the eternal punishment of rolling a rock up a hill, only to have it roll back just before reaching the summit.

[2] A reference to Rhode Island's pro-debtor fiscal policies.

Charles Carroll to Mary Caton

I yesterday acknowledged in my letter to Mr. [*Richard*] Caton the receipt of your letters of the 24th past & 5th instant.

Capt. White is expected to return to this city in a short time, by him I Shall Send the feathers, bouquet, & muslin dress; I shall get Mrs. [*Van*] Courtland, at whose house I board, to procure these articles; She has Seen better days, & is connected with the best families in this place and is a good judge of dress: I however will see the things myself before they are bought.

When I have an oppertunity I will enquire of the President the character of Driskill your overseer.

***

I have some expectations that Congress will be able to go thro' the necessary business of the Session by the middle of next month, as the questions of temporary & permanent residences are now settled; and in my Judgt. well settled; if the general good of the whole Union is regarded: Maryd. no doubt would have been more benefited, (& I am sure I should) by having the permanent residence fixed at Baltimore Town; but this measure was not obtainable, nor was that town held out with any serious ~~expectation~~ intention of removing the seat of Govt. to it; Its advocates (half a dozn. excepted) proposed Balt. in opposition to Potwomack, to keep Congress here 3 or 4 years longer, at wh. time ~~there~~ it would be impossible to effectuate the removal—All the eastern State, N.Y. Jerseys, & the eastern part of Pense.

would ~~have~~ then oppose~~ed~~e the execution of the law; the southern States (I mean Virga. N.C. & S.C. & Georgia) are not [*lined out*] much attached to Baltimore, ~~or to~~ nor would they insist on ~~its~~ the laws being executed at the hazard of the union—Maryland will be greatly benefited by having the permanent seat of the Govt. within its limits; the seat of Govt. of the U.S. will give consequence & opulence to our State, which will put it on a par with either of its neighbours, and being more compact & much more united it will enjoy advantages superior perhaps to those of any other State in the union. I am persuaded in five years after the removal of Congress to Powomack, the Susquehanna will be opened, which will add greatly to the growth & pro[*s*]perity of Balt. Town & the State of Maryd. Thus I have reasoned, & tho' I do not expect to live to see the accomplishment of these predictions, I am confident if the Seat of Govt. of the U.S. is fixed on the Potwomack in Maryd., they will be verified; keep this letter by you, and when these great events shall happen, shew it to your children; they, and the descendants of my fellow citizens will perhaps then applaud that foresight, which contributed to procure such solid advantages to Maryd. at the expence of contemporary popularity.

ALS, Carroll-McTavish Papers, MdHi. Addressed to the care of "Richard Lawson & Co.," Baltimore; franked. The omitted text concerns family matters and household management.

Christopher Gore to Rufus King

To morrow morning my nephew will go to Andover for your ward[1]—and will return on tuesday—if he chooses to remain till commencement I shall take the liberty of detaining him.

The success of Philadelphia is truly mortifying to all who wish to see base means unsuccessful—I truly regret that those whose characters we thought correct shoud bend to such measures as are dishonorable for the purpose of gaining any object—Mr. Ames observes to me that he can very justly say that his hands are free from the guilt of bartering one thing for another.

The appearances are against our National prosperity—and all real friends to our country have grown weary with disappointment—but nothing seems to have happen'd more contrary to their expecta[*tions*] than the base 4 per Cent, as proposed by the Senate—That a proposal so undisguised, & unjust shoud come from that branch of the legislature was not within our expectation—the odds to Massachusetts in point of real property between this and the Secretary's report will be so great, that I think our members ought to hazard every thing rather than accede to such schemes—Indeed, my friend, the untoward projects of influential men in Congress, which are daily rising to view, leave small prospects of our country's attaining to that dignity & honor, which we fondly hoped at the adoption of this Constitution—farewell.

ALS, King Papers, NHi. Written from Boston; franked; postmarked.

[1] John Gore (1769–1817) retrieved Cyrus King from Phillips Academy in Andover, Massachusetts, from which King's younger half brother graduated in 1790. The academy was founded by Samuel Phillips, Jr., in 1778 and incorporated in 1780.

Thomas Jefferson to James Monroe

*** Congress will now probably proceed in better humour to funding the public debt. this measure will secure to us the credit we now hold at Amsterdam, where our European paper is above par, which is the case of no other nation. our business is to have great credit and to use it little. whatever enables us to go to war, secures our peace. at present it is essential to let both Spain & England see that we are in a condition for war, for a number of collateral circumstances now render it probable that they will be in that condition. our object is to feed, and theirs to fight. if we are not forced by England, we shall have a gainful time of it. a vessel from Gibraltar of the 10th. of June tells us O'Hara[1] was busily fortifying & providing there, & that the English Consuls in the Spanish ports on the Mediterranean had recieved orders to dispatch all their vessels from those ports immediately. the Captain saw 15. Spanish ships of war going to Cadiz. it is said that [*Benedict*] Arnold is at Detroit reviewing the militia there. other symptoms indicate a general design on all Louisiana and the two Floridas.[2] what a tremendous position would success in these objects place us in! embraced from the St. Croix [*Maine*] to the St. Mary's [*Georgia*] on one side by their possessions, on the other by their fleet. we need not hesitate to say that they would soon find means to unite to them all the territory covered by the ramifications of the Missisipi. ***

ALS, Monroe Papers, NN. For the full text, see *PTJ* 17:25.

[1] Major General Charles O'Hara (ca. 1740–1802) was posted to the British garrison of Gibraltar, controlling access to the Mediterranean, after a distinguished tour of duty under Lord Cornwallis in the Revolutionary War.

[2] East and West Florida and Louisiana were the three Spanish colonies contiguous with the United States. The latter, ceded by France under the Treaty of Paris (1763), lay between the Mississippi River and New Spain to the west. The Floridas, separated by the Apalachicola River, were ceded by Great Britain in 1783 and stretched from the Mississippi east to the Atlantic and from the Gulf of Mexico north to a disputed latitude between thirty-one degrees and thirty-two degrees twenty-eight minutes.

George Thatcher to Thomas B. Wait

I have just finished reading the second volume of Emilius; and about thirty pages in the third—It is four years since I read these books before—much too long a time! This Treatise on education, together with the dissertation on the inequality of mankind, ought to be attentively read once in two years.[1] Readers, in general, are too apt to hurry from one book to another, before they have fully reduced the ideas and sentiments of the first to their own—To do this is to read understandingly, and to good purpose—But to read an ingenious book, & then lay it aside, is like a cursory, external view of a very complex machine. Some books cannot be read too much. Among such I place Hartley, & Helvetius on man—Emilius—Eloisa,[2] and some of [*Joseph*] Priestleys works.

Three years ago I come to a Resolution to read Hartley once a year—And within two years I have extended this determination to Helvetius.

It is not unusual to hear people say one may read too much—and if they were to read less they might gain more information—This is not true, if they read as they ought to—that is fully comprehend, and reduce to their own sentiments, all they read—As well may it be said a man may travel to much to make travling usefull—whereas the man who knows how to improve from Travel cannot see too much so long as there remains any city or country he has not examined—Some countries are less productive of objects for usefull reflection than others; but there are none altogether barren—so it is with books; and tho it is prudent, from the shortness of Life, to select the best, yet those of inferior merit may sometimes be run over—for in the progress of knowledge and improvements the retrograde steps of ignorance and ~~barbarism~~ stupidity must be noted.

I fancy there are very few Gentlemen who will subscribe to my catalogue of Books—but having read them all more than once; and, on this subject, thinking myself a competent Judge, (thro vanity if you please), I shall persevere in my opinion and resolution. Having passed the common point of union, in sentiment with the bulk of people, ~~in general~~ we are constantly diverging from each other—and the angle of diversity is already so extended, that it is hardly to be expected I shall meet with many of them again in this world—In the next we may—For all things tend to light, knowledge and universal Happiness—what an animating—what a glorious prospect is this! while education and Government, which are only different names for the same thing, or different parts of the same instrument, will effectually bring about this desirable period.

In plain Language, I say, I want to see you—I ought first to have said I wish to hear from you—because I may expect this before the other—and it is, I verily beleive, two full months since I had that pleasure, If I except Mrs. [*Sarah Savage*] Thatchers writing me, about ten or twelve days since, that you had that day or the day before dined with her.

FC, Thatcher Family Papers, MHi.

---

[1] Jean-Jacques Rousseau's *Émilius and Sophia* followed by eight years the publication of his groundbreaking *Discourse on the Origin and Foundations of Inequality among Men* (1754).

[2] *Observations on Man* (1749) by the English philosopher David Hartley (1705–57); *A Treatise on Man: His Intellectual Faculties and His Education* (1777) by the French philosophe Claude Adrien Helvetius (1715–71); Rousseau's *Eloisa* (1761).

From New York

Congress met yesterday, and took into consideration the amendments of the *Senate* to the *Post-Office Bill* [*HR*-74], and disagreed to the first. The House contends that the members are more competent to pointing out the different Post-Roads through the United States, than the *Post-Master General.*

It is in contemplation to make an attempt to keep *Congress* here two years longer, notwithstanding the Bill that was passed. The majority is small for going—but *three.*

Notwithstanding the people here are much agitated at the idea of Congress removing, they preserve their dignity and federalism untarnished—a circumstance which will do them honour; and heighten their importance in the Union.

[Boston] *Columbian Centinel*, 17 July; partially reprinted at Salem, Massachusetts; and Newport, Rhode Island.

Other Documents

François Baudin to Thomas Jefferson. ALS, Washington Papers, DLC. Written from St. Martin, Isle of Rhé, France.

Office seeking: consul at Isle of Rhé; Morris has informed him, on the basis of a conversation with Jefferson in March, that he will likely be appointed.

Oliver Ellsworth to Abigail Ellsworth. Typescript, Ellsworth Papers, CtHi.

"It has finally been found necessary to agree that Congress shall next meet in Philadelphia," it being more central and the southern members no longer willing "to come so far north as New York"; expects to take their daughter Nabby (Abigail) with him to Philadelphia.

Thomas Fitzsimons to Benjamin Rush. Four page ALS, *Carnegie Bookshop Catalog* 155(1950):item 124 and *Charles Hamilton Catalog* 65(1973):item 116. The ellipses are in the source.

"Extremely fine political letter describing the maneuvers of the various factions in the choice of the national capital"; "the bill '. . . Establishing the Permanent & Temporary seat of the Government of the U.S.'"; Fitzsimons "refers to 'Intrigue & Cabal' against him"; ". . . we suffered them to say what they pleased with my [*very?*] little opposition—the final Vote was 32 to 29. . . . We (Pennsylvania Delegation) never should have consented to the Establishment of the permanent seat out of Pennsylv'a." "but that we were determined there was no other mode by which we would get it from hence. . . ."

Benjamin Goodhue to Joseph Hiller. No copy known; acknowledged in Hiller to Goodhue, 22 July.

Benjamin Huntington to John Trumbull. ANS, Trumbull Collection, CtY. This note appears on the reverse of a printed receipt dated 17 April, acknowledging payment of three guineas for one half of a subscription for prints of Trumbull's paintings of the deaths of Gen. Joseph Warren at Bunker Hill and of Gen. Richard Montgomery at Quebec. An identical receipt was made out the same day to Madison (Broadside Collection, DLC).

Requests that Trumbull provide a receipt for payment in full, which Huntington chooses to settle at the present.

Thomas Jefferson to Thomas Mann Randolph, Jr. ALS, Jefferson Papers, DLC.

"the bill for the removal of the federal government to Philadelphia for 10. years & then to George town has at length past both houses, so that our removal is now certain: and I think it tolerably certain that the President will leave this place on a visit to Mount Vernon about the last of August or first of September. that will fix my visit to Monticello to the same time. I am in hopes yourself & the girls may take your arrangements to pass three or four weeks there with me, suppose from the middle of Sep. to the middle of Octob."

William Samuel Johnson to Samuel William Johnson. ALS, Johnson Papers, CtHi. Addressed to Stratford, Connecticut.

Financial business; "We are all well."

George Thatcher to Sarah Thatcher. ALS, Thatcher Family Papers, MHi. Place to which addressed not indicated.

Household management; "I continue to hope we shall adjourn some time the next week—our business is nearly finished—eight or ten days will determine whether the state debts can be assumed, this session, or not—& after that I shall set off with myself."

William Samuel Johnson, Diary. Johnson Papers, CtHi.

"St. Pauls. Taken with the Gout."

Letter from a "gentleman of fortune and distinction in Virginia." [Edenton] *State Gazette of North Carolina*, 13 August, under a 23 July New York dateline; reprinted at Baltimore. The editors believe the writer may have been Henry Lee, who expressed similar sentiments to Madison earlier in the year.

"I converse with nobody that would not prefer a dissolution of the Union, to an assumption of the state debts, or indeed, to any other measure so glaringly and shamefully prompted by injustice and local prejudices."

Monday, 12 July 1790

Welcome Arnold to Theodore Foster and Joseph Stanton

Undoubtedly you have been apprised of an Act of the Legislature of this State having some time since passed for incorporating Sundry of the Citizens of this State by the name of the "River Machine Company"[1] for the purpose of rendering the River leading to Providence more navigable.

The General Assembly convinced of the importance & utility of the objects of the Association were pleased to grant a duty on tonnage of Vessels of specified burthens for the carrying into effect the purposes of the company The proceedings of the Legislature referrd to we have the honor herewith to enclose.[2] By the accession of this State to the Union the company are deprived of the benifit of the tonnage duty granted by our Legislature.

The exclusive right of levying such duties being vested by the constitution in the Legislature of the United States; as the completion of the objects of the aforementioned association are absolutely necessary to the safe navigation of this River and as those objects cannot be effected without a continuance of the Tonnage levied by the Legislature of this State the Proprietors of the machine have instructed me to write you on the subject and to solicit your assistance in the procurement of an Act of Congress for the

Imposing of similar duties of Tonnage to those which were granted them by our Genl. Assembly.

I have to acquaint you that the Machine is compleated and now actually employed in deepening the Channel; but unless the company shall receive some aid from the Public, the objects of their association will become entirely frustrated, having no doubt of your being fully convinced that the object of our present application is highly Interesting to the trade & Navigation of the United States as well as to that of this State in particular I rest assured of your immediate & most effectual efforts to obtain an Act of Congress for a continuance of the Tonnage formerly granted by the Legislature of this State & to be in like manner appropriated to compleat the purposes of the General Assembly in passing the aforesd. Act for incorporating the company. The cost of the Machine far exceeded the expectations of the company, the expence of the materials and erecting the Machine Amounts to twelve Hundred dollars and the money collected in virtue of the Act of Assembly previous to our accession is only sixty dollars, the daily expence of working the Machine ~~the~~ is four dollars exclusive of wear & tear.

It is needless to suggest that in the Act which Congress may pass on the subject it will be proper that the collection of the duty should be vested in the Collector of this District.

[*Enclosure*]

An Act for continuing to certain Persons by the Name of the River Machine Company in the Town of Providence certain chartered Rights and Privileges granted to them by the Legislature of the State of Rhode Island & Providence Plantations before the Accession of that State to the Present National Constitution.

Whereas the Legislature of the State of Rhode Island and Providence Plantations before the Accession of the said State to the National Government granted a Charter of Incorporation to Sundry persons by the Name of the River Machine Company in the Town of Providence who have by Subscription raised a Fund and have been at a very considerable Expense in building a Machine called a Mudd Engine for the Purpose of deepening and clearing the Channel of Providence River and making the same more navigable which if duly carried into Execution agreeably to the purpose of the said Association and the Intention of the Legislature in granting the said Charter will be greatly beneficial to the Trade and Navigation of the United States as well as to that of the State of Rhode Island and Providence Plantations in particular.

And Whereas the said Persons agreed to raise and have raised among themselves by Subscription the Sum of One Thousand Spanish Milled Dollars divided into Forty Shares which hath been applied in the Purchase of Materials for and the Building a Machine called a Mud Engine for the

Purpose of Clearing the said River and rendering the Same more navigable as aforesaid and by the said Charter of Incorporation in order to reimburse the aforesaid Company the Money which should be raised and applied by them for the aforesaid Purpose & Duty of Two Cents per Ton was granted on all Vessels of the Burthen of Sixty Ton and upwards those laden with Wood & Lumber excepted arriving in the Port of Providence within the Term of Twenty Years next after the Time of passing the said Act providing however that if the Produce of the said Duty should exceed the Disbursements of the said Company the Surplus should be appropriated to other Improvements of the Navigation of said River under the Direction of the said Company and by Reason of the Accession of the said State to the National Government the said Duty ~~deprived of the Benfit of the said Duty~~ [*lined out*] ~~some is continued with the consent of the National Legislature~~ cannot be collected without the consent of Congress and as it is reasonable and will be beneficial to the Public that the said chartered Rights and Privileges herein after mentioned should be continued to the said Persons incorporated as aforesaid.

BE IT THEREFORE Enacted by the Senate and House of Representatives of the United States of America in Congress assembled That Moses Brown Welcome Arnold Joseph Nightingale John. J. Clarke Cyprian Sterry Thomas Lloyd Halsey Isaac Brown Daniel Tillinghast Obadiah Brown Nicholas Brown George Benson John Mumford Joseph Martin Samuel Butler Amos Atwell Zephariah Brown Reuben Potter Benjamin Tallman John Jenckes David Anthony Joseph Russell William Russell Philip Allen Zachariah Allen Jonathan Arnold John Brown John Francis and Edward Thurber and their Associates be and they hereby are made and constituted a Body corporate and Politic in Fact and Name by the Name of the River Machine Company in the Town of Providence, for the Purpose of ~~making~~ deepening and clearing the Channel of Providence River and making the same more navigable.

AND BE it further Enacted that the Persons aforesaid their Associates and Successors be empowered as a Body Politic and incorporate to have and to hold the same Sum or any greater Sum, provided the same shall be raised by Subscription among themselves and shall be thought necessary to affect the laudable Purpose of their Association as a Fund appropriated for procuring a Machine or Machines as aforesaid keeping the same in Repair and working the same in deepening clearing and making Providence River more navigable and that the same be vested in the said Company their Associates and Successors.

LS and Ms., Foster Papers, RHi. Written from Providence, Rhode Island; signed by Arnold as president of and "in Behalf of the Providence River Machine Company." On 11 August Congress passed the Navigation Act [HR-93], which consented to Rhode Island's levying this special tonnage duty until 10 January 1791, at which time Congress agreed to the Navigation Act [HR-103] extending its consent for another year.

In the same collection in the hand of the mover, Sedgwick, is his motion of 30 July: "That a committee be appointed to report a bill declaring the consent of congress, that the laws of the legislature of Rhode Island & imposing duties on the tonage of ships & vessells, entering at providence in the said state, to be appropriated for the purpose of rendering more navigable providence river shall be valid."

---

[1] The Company for Dredging the Providence River was chartered in January 1790 with an initial capital of forty subscribed shares of $1000 each (Joseph S. Davis, *Essays in the Earlier History of American Corporations* [1917; reprint, 2 vols., New York, 1965], 2:284–85).

[2] The state's act allocating tonnage duties for the Company's purposes was also passed in January 1790.

Benjamin Huntington to Governor Samuel Huntington

I have Inclosed a Printed [*Residence*] Bill which was originated in the Senate and in a most Extraordinary Manner was Concurred in the House without Amendment it was obtained by a bare majority in the Senate and by a Party agreement passd the House by a Vote 32, against 29 The friends of the Bill in the House Declared they would not consent to the least amendment even of a Comma because it would make it necessary that the amendment Should be considered in the Senate who were not in humour to Pass it a Second Time The Debate began on Amendments in the House on Tuesday as you will see by the Dayly Advertizer and Continued in a Most farcical train untill it Closed on Friday The Bill is badly Draughted and unconstitutional in some of its Parts but the Majority had agreed not to alter it and it is Passd and will Doubtless Receive Sanction from the President as the Permanent Seat is on the Potomack—I hope we shall be able after this to go upon Business of Some use to the Union and that before the Connogocheque Seat is Built the Eyes of Congress will be so far opened as to Repeal the Act.[1]

***

ALS, American Manuscripts, CSmH. Marked "Private." A postscript dated 13 July concerns private business.

---

[1] The Residence Act [S-12] set the mouth of Conococheague Creek at Williamsport, Maryland, as the western limit for the permanent seat of government.

Thomas Jefferson to George Washington

Th. Jefferson had a conference yesterday with mr. Madison on the subject recommended by the President. he has the honor of inclosing him some considerations thereon, in all of which he believes mr. Madison concurred. he has sketched the heads only, as the President's mind will readily furnish the developement of each. he will wait on the president at one aclock on some other business, and then and at all other times be ready to enter more into the details of any part of the subject the president may chuse.

[*Enclosure*]

[*Hea*]ds of consideration on the conduct we are to observe in the war between Spain & Gr. Britain and particularly should the latter attempt the conquest of Louisiana & the Floridas.

[*T*]he dangers to us, should Great Britain possess herself of those countries.

she will possess a territory equal to half ours, beyond the Missisipi

she will seduce that half of ours which is on this side the Missisipi

by her language, laws, religion, manners, government, commerce, capital.

by the possession of N. Orleans, which draws to it the dependence of all the waters of Missisipi

by the markets she can offer them in the gulph of Mexico & elsewhere.

she will take from the remaining part of our States the markets they now have for their produce by furnishing those markets cheaper with the same articles. tobacco. rice. indigo. bread. lumber. ~~furs~~ naval stores. furs.

she will have then possessions double the size of ours, as good in soil & climate.

she will encircle us compleatly, by these possessions on our land-board, & her fleets on our sea-board.

instead of two neighbors balancing each other, we shall have one, with more than the strength of both.

Would the prevention of this be worth a war?

consider our abilities to take part in a war.

our operations would be by land only.

how many men should we need to employ? their cost?

our resources of taxation & credit equal to this.

weight the evil of this new accumulation of debt

against the loss of markets, & eternal expence & danger from so overgrown a neighbor.

But this is on supposition that France as well as Spain shall be engaged in the war. for with Spain alone, the war would be unsuccessful, & our situation rendered worse.

No need to take a part in the war as yet. we may chuse our own time.

Delay gives us many chances to avoid it altogether.

In such a choice of objects, Gr. Britain may not single out, Louisiana & Floridas.

she may fail in her attempt on them.
France and Spain may recover them.
if all these chances fail, we should have to re-take them.
the difference between retaking, & preventing, overbalanced by the benefits of delay.
Delay enables us to be better prepared:
to obtain from the allies a price for our assistance.
[*s*]uppose these our ultimate views, what is to be done at this time?
1. as to Spain?
if she be as sensible as we are that she cannot save Louisiana & the Floridas,
Might she not prefer their Independance to their Subjection to Grt. Britain?
does not the proposition of the Ct. d'Estaing[1] furnish us an opening to communicate our ideas on this subject to the court of France, and thro them to that of Madrid? and our readiness to join them in guaranteeing the independence of those countries?
this might save us from a war, if Gr. Britain respects our weight in a war.
and if she does not, the object would place the war on popular ground with us.
2. as to England? say to [*George*] Beckwith
'that as to a Treaty of commerce, we would prefer amicable, to adversary arrangements, tho the latter would be infallible, and in our own power:
that our ideas are that such a treaty should be founded in perfect reciprocity; & wd. therefore be it's own price:
that as to an Alliance, we can say nothing till it's object be shewn, & that it is not to be inconsistent with existing engagements:
that in the event of a war between Gr. Brit. & Spain we are disposed to be strictly neutrel:
that however, we should view with extreme uneasiness any attempts of either power to seize the possessions of the other on our frontier, as we consider our own safety ~~as~~ interested in a due balance between our neighbors.' (it might be advantageous to express this latter sentiment, because if there be any difference of opinion in their councils, whether to bend their force against North or South America, or the islands, (and certainly there is room for difference) and if these opinions be nearly balanced, that balance might be determined by the prospect of having an enemy the more or less, according to the object they should select.)

AN and Ms., Miscellaneous Letters, Miscellaneous Correspondence, State Department Records, Record Group 59, DNA. The docket on the enclosure, in the hand of Washington, states, "On the Subject of the War betw[*ee*]n Great Britain & Spain Opinion."

[1] On 20 March, Charles-Hector, comte d'Estaing, wrote Washington to suggest an elaborate "triple alliance" by which France, Spain, and the United States would share sovereignty over Louisiana and Isle de France (the Mauritius Islands in the Indian Ocean), as a common front against the British and Dutch in North America and the East Indies (*PGW* 5:256–63). d'Estaing (1729–94), the former commander of French naval forces in America (1778–80), was at the time a commander in the National Guard under Lafayette, who endorsed the plan. William Short wrote to John Jay on 4 April, enclosing d'Estaing's letter and cautioning that his proposal did not enjoy the Spanish ministry's support. The letter was received in New York on 17 June, but the Administration held off on a formal response until 10 August, when Jefferson wrote Short to express "our thankfulness . . . tho' it might be out of our system to implicate ourselves in trans-Atlantic guarantees" (*PTJ* 16:301, 17:123).

Joseph Jones to James Madison

*** We are taught to believe Congress will hold their next Session in Philadelphia and that we shall at least be amused with the hope of the permanent seat on the Potomack—If these things are so the Pensylvanians must have seen through the policy of N. York and the eastern states and have deserted them and joined us rather than be duped by their machinations—however it be I confess I had lost all hopes of a decision to come southwardly at this Session and indeed had taken it for granted we were fixed for a length of time at N.Y. The famous [*Alexander*] McGilveray with some leaders of the Creek nation have gone on to N. York to treat with the President and from their apparent disposition it is probable a treaty promising future quiet may be accomplished. ***

ALS, Madison Papers, DLC. Written from Fredericksburg, Virginia. The omitted text discusses crops; invites Madison to visit Fredericksburg upon adjournment, which *GUS* indicates will be soon; and mentions Jones's own plan to visit Monroe in early August. For the full text, see *PJM* 13:276–77.

Samuel Meredith to Henry Hill

Some of our best Friends in Senate & House of Representatives are affraid that the Parsimony of the Philadelphians, will hinder them from doing any thing clever with respect to the accomodation of Congress which I should be extreemly mortified to find was the case, to avoid which those Gentlemen who have heretofore taken a principal lead in those matters ought to forward every thing that would lead to the accomodation of them; The New Yorkers have acted in a very spirited manner & laid out in the Federal Hall near

£26,000—they are now building a House of 80 feet by 70 for the use of the President, levelling the ground of the Fort [*George*] &c. which will cost at least £10,000 more, the first was done by a Tax on the Citizens & they raised £15, or £16,000—the first year, the residue the Assembly agreed should be raised by Lottery, now with us to do every thing that ought to be done perhaps it would not cost more than £15,000 which we as a Town are much better able to bear than they are half the sum—when you consider that the residence is to be 10 Years certain, & that the Value of every kind of property will encrease in a very great degree what would so triffling a sum as the one mentioned amount to when laid upon the Citizens of Philad. if even paid for in one year, which I should suppose not necessary as the Bank no doubt would lend them the sum payable in two or more years considering the [*lined out*] advantages they will reap from the lodgment of the Publick Money, as well as that of Individuals who will necessarily be drawn to the Seat of Goverment, where all Strangers, Speculators &c. will take up their residence, who will spend an amazing Sum of money, which by estimate of the Secy. of State (if I am informed right) will amt. to 200,000 Guineas ℔ Year—to reap fresh advantages as these will it not be worthwhile to incur a small expence, which will in future add to the beauty as well as the Convenience of the City These reflections are drawn forth by the Gentlemen I alluded to in the first part of my Letter as well as from my own doubts of the spirit of our people unless aided by the Conduct of some leading Characters, I already anticipate the rapid rise of Philadelphia, which I have not the least doubt will more than double itself in the 10 Years—as you do not like dealing in the funds, I would advise you take the property offered by your Sisters in England, what lay in the City you would beyond a doubt make great advantage of, and that very suddenly, excuse me [*torn*] of the moment.

AL, signature cut off, John Jay Smith Collection, PPL at PHi. Addressed to Philadelphia.

Louis Guillaume Otto to Comte de Montmorin

The hypothesis upheld by one of the noblest geniuses of this century that virtue is the principle of a republic[1] would do much honor to humanity if it could pass without alteration through the crucible of experience. For eleven years I have examined carefully one of the freest people on earth and I have found here so little virtue in the political sense of this word that I am very far from subscribing to the opinion of this philosopher who knew republics only through books or through isolated and too rapid observations. The intrigues, the cabals, the underhanded and insidious dealings of a factious and turbulent spirit are even much more frequent in this republic than in the most absolute monarchy where they are concentrated in the palace without infecting the mass of the nation. Here the intrigues begin in the smallest parochial assemblies whence they pass to those of the district, from there to the state legislatures and from the latter to Congress where they act through accelerated movement with more energy. But as it is impossible to deceive an entire nation about its true interests, it generally happens that the private egoism concentrated in that of the nation leads to an honorable end by means which are hardly so and by men who desire the good only because it is personally useful to them.

For six months now, My Lord, Congress has been occupied with a bill to fund the public debt. All money operations are in suspense; the speculators are in action; the creditors of the state are in distress. One asks onself in vain why Congress does not agree on this important matter. Some want to fund at six per cent, others at four, others desire that Congress charge itself with the debt contracted during the war by the individual states, others do not want the debt funded. Today they agree on a principle; tomorrow they reject it. It is approved again by a large majority but it does not pass the Upper House. The latter proposes another plan which is also rejected. The individual members vote obstinately sometimes for and sometimes against the same question. It is surprising to see that almost at the same time a measure can appear good and bad, just and unjust. Underhanded negotiations are suspected. One strives to penetrate this mystery and finally finds that all this irresolution was due to the intrigues and secret agreements of the delegates of two states, namely Pennsylvania and Massachusetts.

Pennsylvania, being in the center of the states and almost that according to population, has for a long time seen with chagrin that the government established its temporary residence in New York. It has been supported by several Southern states which complained of being too far from Congress. Having served as residence during the war, the city of Philadelphia above all aspired again to the honor of being considered the capital of the country. For three years its attempts have been frequent but unavailing, Congress having always alleged as a pretext the uselessness of changing residence before having chosen a permanent capital. The true motive for its refusal was the jealousy which the wealth and prosperity of the city of Philadelphia inspired in the other cities of the continent. Boston being one of its most active rivals, the delegates of Massachusetts have always used all their influence to thwart the Pennsylvanians. To surmount this difficulty, the latter began from the opening of the present session of Congress negotiations with the Senators and Representatives of Massachusetts affording a way for them to vote for a question of extreme interest to Massachusetts provided they obtained for their part the transfer of the residence to Philadelphia. The Massachusetts delegates seemed to favor this proposition which had as a basis that the Pennsylvanians would make the motion in Congress to charge the United States with the debts of the particular states, a motion which passes here under the name of *assumption of the debts*. This assumption was well received by a committee of the House, all the partisans of the Philadelphians having voted for it; but at the moment when the House was actually to enact it, the Pennsylvanians stopped the debates by all sorts of evasions in order to have the time to introduce the question on the residence. They feared rightly that the people of Massachusetts, not very scrupulous in political matters, would break their word after having obtained what they desired. Their apprehensions were much better founded since they were themselves of bad faith and they had used the question of the *assumption* only as a snare to get those of Massachusetts to vote for a change of residence. The latter distrusted the Pennsylvanians equally and when it was a question of the residence they showed themselves unfavorable to Philadelphia without, however, opposing it openly. Thus it is that for six weeks Congress was divided between the two questions which had no outward relation between them and of which the public has been able to guess the secret relations only through the indiscretion of some delegates. Mr. Robert Morris, formerly Superintendent of Finances, Senator of Pennsylvania, is at the head of party which is fighting for the residence. Seeing that the people of Massachusetts were too astute for him, he changed tactics all at once and impressed on the Virginians that in order to weaken the too great preponderance of the Northern delegates, this moment should be seized to fix by a law the permanent residence of Congress on the Potomac. "I answer to you," he added, "for my colleagues provided that you determine by the same law that while waiting till the city of Congress can be built, this assembly adjourn to Philadelphia and that it leave this city only in the year 1800." The Virginians, much more credulous than the Northerners and eager besides to get out of New York at any cost, fell into the trap. The bill accordingly was proposed in the Senate and passed there by a majority of two. In the House of Representatives it met with much opposition. The debates there being public and the crowd very large, each member wished to show his zeal for or against New York and to give an exhibition of his eloquence. The discussion lasted an entire week and never had Congress and the New York public been more excited. Finally Philadelphia triumphed by a majority of three. There remained a last resort for the champions of New York. It was to persuade the President of the United States not to sign the bill. Every day there appeared addresses to this supreme magistrate entreating him not to consent to a measure which was represented as unconstitutional, impolitic and unjust to the people of New York. For five days the President left the public in suspense. Finally he signed and the bill became a law. By virtue of this act all the offices of Congress will be transferred to Philadelphia at the beginning of next December and the government of the United States will be established there until the year 1800, when a suitable site will have been chosen and prepared for the reception of Congress on the Potomac. Everyone here judges this change of residence according to his passions. As an impartial spectator, I think with the New Yorkers that despite the law about the ten years the Philadelphians will find the means to hold Congress in their city for twenty or thirty years. I agree also that there was no pressing motive to discuss at this moment a question as thorny as that of the residence. On the other hand I think with Mr. Jefferson that with regard to the public spirit New York ought rather to be considered as a suburb of London than an American city; and as for the coming change of place, Philadelphia is infinitely better suited for the residence of the American Government. As to the President, there is no doubt that as a Virginian and an inhabitant of the banks of the Potomac he is very much inclined towards the execution of the law which has just been passed; but even supposing that he were still in office in 1800, it would be very difficult to make Congress leave the richest and most populated city of the continent to repair to a village.

O'Dwyer, pp. 438–41. Otto's letters included in *DHFFC* were usually written over the course of days, and even weeks, following the day they were begun.

[1] A dominant theme of Montesquieu's *Spirit of the Laws* (1748).

Govenor Beverley Randolph to James Madison

I have received your Favour of the 23d. of last month. I hope the addition of two commissioners for settling the accounts between the U.S. & individual States will ~~I hope~~ remove the Danger in which Virginia stood from the prejudice of two of those already in commission.[1] The remedy for this evil will be more compleat should the new appointments be fill'd with Southern men.

I am sorry to find that we are still haunted by the Assumption Business. Should it be adopted in any Form I fear it will give great Disquiet in this State. Besides the Injustice of the measure it is considered here as intended in Effect to produce a perfectly consolidated Government. You know that any Thing having such a tendency will occasion grave Ferment among us. The most influential Character in our Legislature [*Patrick Henry*] considers it as unconstitutional & will I beleive oppose it upon that ground. Even admiting that this ground is not tenable Such Jealousies are excited against it that I beleive not a single advocate will be found to support a system so unjust in it's Principle & so baneful in it's effects.

The late vote of the Senate on the subject of the temporary & permanent

Seat of the general government was very unexpected. I always supposed that the Potowmack would meet with greater opposition in that House than in the House of Representatives.

ALS, Madison Papers, DLC. Written from Richmond, Virginia.

[1] Randolph refers to Commissioners John Kean and John Taylor Gilman. See Report of the Commissioners for Settling Accounts between the United States and Individual States, 8 May, volume 19.

Samuel W. Stockton to Elias Boudinot

*** This day I heard that Govr. [*William*] Livingston is better but Scarcely expected to get over it—Judge [*David*] Brearly proposes in a day or two to set out for the warm Springs in Virginia—but whether he will ever return again, is to me a matter of great doubt. In my last I mentioned to you my ideas respecting that office [*federal district judge for New Jersey*] shd. it become vacant. you had best think of it in time if agreeable to you—The act has at length passed for the temporary & permanent residence—In my present opinion, the *temporary* reside. will be more *permanent* than the *permanent Residence*, which seems paradoxical; but I beleive they will, with proper management change Yet, and before long, the permanent residence from Potowmack to *Del*[*aware*] & I dare say *by this time* the New Eng[*land*] People & N. Yorkers would be happy to join the Pensylvs. & Jerseymen~~t~~ in that measure.

The public Creditors are almost raving—The widows & orphans of that class must in a little time starve to Death—The President I trust, will preserve his integrity & consistency by never puting his hand & giving his consent to a bill pretending to provide for public credit, unless it shd. have the principles of common Justice in it.

ALS, Stimson Boudinot Collection, NjP. Written from Trenton, New Jersey; carried by John Stevens, Jr. The omitted text concerns private business.

Jonathan Trumbull to William Williams

It is some time since I have written to you—mostly because I had nothing of much consequence to inform you, unless it were to give you an account of our troubles our Contentions & our follies—I can now only give you the result of all then—with a conjecture of what may be its consequence.

The great Question of Residence which has so long agitated us—& thrown a Block in the Way of all other great Business—is at last finished—a Bill has passed both Houses for removing from this City to Philadelphia—

while Congress are to remain for *ten years*—after which they are to retire to the Banks of the Potomac for a permanency—I inclose you the Bill that you may see the whole of its provisions—& also a News paper—that you may be informed of the variety of Votes on the Occasion—& the particular states in favor of the Bill—the same near division also obtained in the senate—It was a *nice* division—& was finally effected by a close *alliance* between the state of Pennsylvania (the Ballancing state) & the Old Dominion—involving certain stipulations for particular purposes, between the high contracting parties—tho' it is my belief that the latter will in the event, be miserably duped, by Congress never moving further West or south than the state of Pennsylvania.

This Block being out of the way—we shall now proceed to the great objects of the present session—funding—Assumption—Ways & Means &c. but whether we shall be able to effect them this session is a doubt with many there being a violent opposition from some quarters & the tempers of the Members being much sowered by the late transactions—for myself however—I rather think we shall do something—the whole Busines has been in great forwardnes for long time—& if it fails will be owing to the particular stipulations of the aforementioned contracting parties—The Assumption will undoubtedly take place, either this or the next session—public Credit is rather rising notwithstandg. our situation—paper is 9/. to 9/4—a proof of public Confidence in the eventual issue.

A Bill for settling the great Acct. of the Nation [*HR*-77] is almost completed—also the Post Office Bill [*HR*-74]—& sundry others of smaller Importance which have got along in the Intervals of our Intemperance—The New England States with N. York & Jersey—are exceedingly agitated with the Residence Bill—& the Delays of the important Business—but neither their uneasiness nor their Clamors could prevent its progress.

FC, letterbook copy, Trumbull Papers, DLC.

Other Documents

William Davies to Governor Beverley Randolph. ALS, Executive Papers, Vi. Place to which addressed not indicated. The letter encloses a chart listing the various balances due upon each state's settlement of its accounts with the United States.

House members from some middle and southern states do not seem satisfied with the Senate's amendment striking the addition of two members to the board of commissioners for settling accounts, under the Settlement of Accounts Act [HR-77]; notes that the Residence Act will add to his office's expenses by mandating its removal to Philadelphia in December 1790, with the other public offices attached to the seat of government.

Elbridge Gerry to Samuel R. Gerry. ALS, Gerry Papers, MHi. Addressed to Marblehead, Massachusetts; franked; postmarked New York, 13 July; answered 25 July.

Thoughts on the death of their sister (Elizabeth Greenleaf); such frequent & heavy strokes by the loss of our nearest friends *** have put my philosophy to a severe test & have impaired my health"; his wife (Ann Thompson Gerry) and the new baby (Eleanor) "are remarkably well."

Seth Harding to James Madison. ALS, Madison Papers, DLC. For the full text, see *PJM* 13:274–76. For background on Harding's invalid pension petition, see *DHFFC* 7:401, 420–21. The dating of this letter is based on the date Harding's petition was presented to the House.

Solicits Madison's support for enclosed (unlocated) "rough peace [*piece*] of writing"; "Sir I consider you as one of the grate rulers of this young kingdom and to whome the unfortunate and distressd, can onely look to for redress"; refers Madison to Sherman for further documentation.

John Murray to Benjamin Goodhue. ALS, Letters to Goodhue, NNS. Written from Philadelphia.

Thanks "My very kind indulgent Friend" for the attention paid him and his wife (Judith Sargent Murray); is glad Congress "are like to go on in the way of peace in future"; "it is necessary that" "something may yet be done for the good of the publick"; "it will be well if the *confidence* of the People can be obtained and preserved" and if "Congress can preserve a *reputation*"; wishes Congress had remained at New York "till they had found an everlasting Habitation"; will return to Boston despite solicitations by his Philadelphia friends "to fix my *permanent residence* in this Metropolis" and despite his belief that "it would be more advantage to me as an individual to fix my residence in this City than it will be to the Congress as a Body."

John Page to St. George Tucker. ALS, Tucker-Coleman Papers, ViW. See 8 August, below.

Theodore Sedgwick to Thomas Dwight. No copy known; acknowledged in Dwight to Sedgwick, 19 July.

John Swanwick to John Langdon. ALS, Langdon Papers, NhPoA. Written from Philadelphia.

Has credited Langdon's dividends from his Bank of North America stocks to Langdon's account with Willing, Morris, and Swanwick; the Bank—"this valuable Institution"—continues to be successful and "from the prospect we have of soon possessing the government of the Union in this City cannot fail to derive the greatest additional benefits"; congratulates Langdon "on these agreable Circumstances."

Oliver Whipple to George Thatcher. ALS, Chamberlain Collection, MB. Written from Portsmouth, New Hampshire; addressed to Thatcher "on public service"; postmarked. In the letters referred to, Whipple sought a federal office.

Sent letters to Thatcher and King under the care of Tobias Lear when he returned to New York in the spring (about 20 May); has not received answers to either letter; supposes "the more weighty Matters of *Funding*, Assumption &c. &c. have prevented your giving me one Line on the Subject"; "I must intreat you will condescend once, to hear your Friend & that you will mention the Subject of my Letter" to King "if he did not receive" it; asks Thatcher to deliver an enclosed letter to Chief Justice Jay.

Daniel Hiester, Account Book. PRHi.

Attended "Monday Club" (or Mess Day) with the Pennsylvania delegation at Fraunces Tavern.

William Samuel Johnson, Diary. Johnson Papers, CtHi.

"Went to Senate & continued to go till 15th. Then confined for some Days & went only on pressing Occasions which increased my Disorder & I attended only 10 or 15. times till Augt. 12th. When Congress adjourn'd."

The 1790 Veto Controversy

Raising the issue of constitutionality was a tactic used by the minority on several occasions during the FFC as a last ditch attempt to defeat a bill before it passed Congress. Most famously, Madison contended that the Bank Bill was unconstitutional during its final reading in the third session. In the first session he had argued that the Seat of Government Bill was unconstitutional because the President would be signing a bill that related to the adjournment of Congress in violation of the Constitution's Article I, section 7.

In an essay dated 12 July and published in *NYDA* the next day, Smith (S.C.), writing as Junius Americanus, used Madison's argument about the Seat of Government Bill to attack the constitutionality of the Residence Bill. This was the first public declaration that a bill on the President's desk was unconstitutional: "every citizen who has taken an oath to support the Constitution *violates that oath* if he silently suffers any law to pass which appears to him, in the smallest degree, repugnant to it," Smith stressed most pointedly and publicly to Washington.

Washington strongly supported the Residence Bill because it fulfilled his dream of locating the permanent seat of federal government on his beloved Potomac River; nevertheless, Smith's challenge—previously raised in the House—caused Washington concern and he immediately turned to Secretary of State Jefferson for an opinion on the bill's constitutionality. When Jefferson had not responded by 15 July, Washington sent him a note asking if he had formed an opinion yet; Jefferson responded that he had and later in the day sent Washington his formal opinion declaring the bill constitutional. In the process Jefferson sought Madison's comments on his opinion, which Madison supplied.

The newspaper debate did not end with Junius Americanus. On 15 July a piece signed "One of the Gallery" attacked Madison, Page, and D. Carroll for having changed their position since they had argued in the first session debate that the Seat of Government Bill was unconstitutional on the same grounds that Smith (S.C.) raised about the Residence Bill.

The issue seemed to have gone away following the President's signing the bill on 17 July, but it only slept. A newspaper article on 9 August, perhaps written by Madison, argued that "those who objected to the constitutionality of the former bill, and concurred in that of the latter, voted consistently with the constitution, and with themselves." A piece signed "Truth," perhaps Smith (S.C.), found this argument "paltry" in a response that brought to conclusion the first veto controversy in American constitutional history.

[*William Smith (S.C.),*] Junius Americanus to the President of the United States, 12 July

With esteem for your person, and the sincerest reverence for your high public and private character, I humbly request your candid perusal of the following observations: They have been occasioned by a serious attention to the Bill which has recently passed the two Houses of Congress, and now waits your sanction: they spring from an affection for the constitution, and an anxious solicitude to guard it from invasion.

In the fifth section of the bill, is this clause, "*at which place the session of Congress, next ensuing the present shall be held*:" A doubt has arisen, whether that clause be conformable to the constitution; in which it is declared, by the 3d clause of the 7th sec. art. 1st. that "every order, resolution or vote, to which the concurrence of the Senate and House of Representatives may be necessary, (*except on a question of adjournment*,) shall be presented to the President." From this *exception* it is obvious, that it was intended by the Constitution, to reserve *to the two Houses* the right of adjourning to such time and place as they should deem proper: To relinquish that right is to betray their own privileges, and is a departure from that line of legislation which the constitution hath wisely chalked out.

An attentive inspection of that instrument, which we have all engaged to support, evinces that there are various modes by which the several component parts of the government are to manifest their will. In matters which relate to *each house* in its *separate capacity* a *single vote of each house* is alone sufficient to have the force of law; thus by the 5th section, "Each house shall be the judge of the elections, returns and qualifications of its own members, and may punish a member for disorderly behaviour, and even expel him."

In cases wherein the two branches of the legislature are concerned, a *joint vote* is prescribed; thus by the 4th clause of the 5th section, "it is inhibited to either house to adjourn, during the session of Congress, for more than three days, *without the consent of the other*, or to any other *place* than that in which the two houses shall be sitting:" Where the two houses disagree as to the *time* of adjournment, it is provided by the 3d sec. of the 2d art. That "the President may adjourn them to such a *time* and he shall think proper;" where they differ as to the *place*, Congress must re-assemble at the *place* where they were last sitting: In this case the President has no agency, nor is it intended by the constitution that he should.

Such are the provisions established in matters which concern *each house separately* and the *two houses collectively*: in none of them is the President called upon to act, except in the *single* instance above mentioned, where he performs the part of an umpire, and where his interposition is necessary, because the *time* of meeting *must* be fixed; the *place* is unnecessary, because if none be appointed, they will of course return to the former place.

But in matters of a general nature which concern the public at large, the wisdom of the Constitution requires something more than the act of the two houses; the President must *approve* them; it is therefore declared that every *order, resolution or vote*, to which the concurrence of the Senate and House of Representatives may be necessary (*except on a question of adjournment*) shall be presented to the President.

Here are then *three* modes of passing orders, resolutions or Votes: the *first* by *each house*; the *second* by the *two houses*; the third by the *two houses and the President*. The question now occurs, Is it consistent with the constitution to depart from the modes above prescribed?

If it be in one instance, it must be so in all. If it be constitutional to require the assent of the President in cases where the two houses, without such assent, are competent to decide, it must likewise be constitutional to require the assent of the Senate in cases where the House of Representatives are alone capable of determining: it would therefore be a constitutional act for the two houses to decide, by a *concurrent resolution*, on the *privileges of each house.* Some of the members of the House of Representatives hold their seats under a resolution of *that house alone*; did the idea ever suggest itself that there would be no impropriety in sending such resolution to the Senate for their concurrence? Would not such an idea have been severely reprobated? Why? Because each house is the judge of the qualifications of its own members; because, to have required the concurrence of the Senate, would have been a violation of the rights of the House of Representatives; and is less respect due to the rights of the two Houses?

If it be an infraction of the constitution to require the concurrence of the two houses where one house can decide, is it less an infraction to demand the approbation of the President, where the two houses can decide? Suppose the President should refuse his assent; the bill would then be lost, unless it be passed by a *two thirds* of both houses, but a *majority* of the two houses have a *constitutional right* to adjourn to such place as they shall think proper; either then the two houses will have relinquished a power they possess by the constitution, and a majority will be insufficient to adjourn where they please, or, a *bare majority* of the two houses will give effect to a measure which has been formally *disapproved* by the President: whereas the constitution expressly declares in the 2d and 3d clause, 7th sect 1st art. that it shall be repassed by *two thirds* by the Senate and House of Representatives, before it can take effect.

In what absurdity will Congress be involved when the period of adjournment arrives? If the question respecting the place of adjournment be already determined by the bill, then the two houses have relinquished a right which all legislative bodies possess, of reserving to themselves to the very last day of adjournment, the power of declaring at what place they will re-assemble. When this point is settled by a concurrent vote of the two houses, they may at any time prior to the adjournment, rescind the resolution. At the last session Congress resolved to adjourn on the 22d of September; the vote was not sent to the President, such an absurdity was never thought of: when the 22d arrived, they saw the difficulty of adjourning on that day, and the vote was rescinded; had it been approved by the President, they must have had his approbation to the prolongation of the session, which he might have withheld; if there would have been an absurdity in requiring his assent to *the time*, there would have been a greater absurdity in requiring it to *the place*, for he has the power of interfering when the two houses disagree as to the *time*, none as to the *place*.

If the question be still unsettled, notwithstanding the clause in the bill, and this was admitted by its advocates, then this inconsistency occurs, that a clause is agreed to, knowing it to be inoperative, and that its inefficacy results from its unconstitutionality. To make this more striking, place the argument in the shape of a syllogism; the constitution is violated when any law or part of a law is past, which is repugnant to it, but the friends of the bill admitted that the clause *was nugatory*, because it was repugnant to it, therefore in passing it they violated the constitution.

It is no answer to the argument to alledge that the clause will do no harm. If it be intended that it should be carried into effect, it controuls the will of the majority of the two houses, against the express words of the constitution; if it be nugatory, and the same thing must hereafter be determined, by a concurrent vote of the two houses, such inconsistency will expose Congress to public censure and derision. It will be asked why do Congress determine by a concurrent vote of the two houses that which they have already decided by law? If the public are told that the law was nugatory, and that Congress were apprized of it when they passed it, they will lose all respect for their proceedings; it will be said, if an act has already passed on the subject, a resolution can neither inforce or repeal it: If an act was void, it was because it deviated from the constitution, and it should not have been passed.

If laws are made which are unconstitutional, because they may do no harm, Congress will soon proceed to those which may and will do harm. The example is a dangerous one, and will be quoted on future occasions. Every law does not undergo the revision of the judiciary; this will certainly not; the President of the United States can alone arrest its progress. Having his sanction, the public will consider every part of the bill as valid, because they know he would not approve any bill that contained a syllable that was unconstitutional; the clause will then be deemed binding, because every part of the bill must have its operation, for words in a law which command a particular act to be done, cannot be viewed as mere surplusage: If the law remains unrepealed or invalidated by the judiciary, the thing commanded to be done must be carried out into effect; a bare resolution of the two houses, without the approbation of the executive, cannot repeal a law, which has his approbation, because it requires the same power to repeal a law as to pass it: The two houses will then be precluded from exercising their constitutional privilege.

A gentleman[1] who supported an objection to the bill of last session, on the ground that a law fixing the *temporary seat of government was unconstitutional*, attempted the other day to prove that it is not unconstitutional to fix by law, even *the session of Congress*. If there was any force in his arguments against fixing by law, the *temporary seat of government*, the arguments against fixing, by law, the *session of Congress*, must be conclusive: But he is reconciled to the measure this session, because his objection was overruled in the last by a majority. When a member of his knowledge of, and attachment to the Constitution, suffers himself to be so influenced by a *precedent* which he must himself acknowledge to be a *bad one*, it is time to apprehend danger from precedents, and to put a stop to them. *No precedent can justify a wrong measure*; but the bill of last session did not pass into a law. Where then is the precedent? He has agreed to make one this session. It is remarkable too that the objection last year was totally inapplicable, for it related to fixing the seat of government, which must be done by law, whether it be the permanent or temporary seat.

The constitution provides that a district of territory shall, by the cession of a state and the acceptance of Congress, become the *seat of government*; that acceptance must be declared by law; for both houses must concur in the measure and every vote in which they both concur, must be sent to the President, except on a question of adjournment, but the two houses may afterwards adjourn *from that place to any other.* This is undeniable from the various clauses already quoted. Congress may also declare, by law, prior to their establishing the permanent seat of government, where the temporary seat shall be, that the public officers, foreign ministers, and the judges of the supreme court, may know where to assemble; but it does not follow that the two houses are to sit at that place.

This distinction between the seat of government and the seat of Congress, has been however denied by that gentleman. He contended, that Congress being a part of the government, the seat of government must be *wherever they hold their session.* It would then follow, either that during the recess of Congress there would be no seat of government, or should they, by concurrent vote, adjourn to any other place than that fixed by law as the seat of government, there would be two seats of government.

The executive and judicial, and the officers of state, are component parts of the government; the judicial is as much a part of the government as the legislative, and yet it is declared by law, that the supreme court shall hold their sessions at the seat of government; the executive is also as much a part of the government as the legislative, and yet the President may reside where he pleases.

This, however, is clear, that the gentleman was *persuaded last session* that it was *an unconstitutional act to fix, by law, the place where Congress should hold their next session*; his words were these, "from the constitution it appeared, that the concurrence of the two houses was sufficient to enable them to adjourn from one place to another; nay the legal consent of the President was in some degree *proscribed* in the 7th Sec of Art. I. where it is declared that every order, &c. to which the concurrence of the senate and the house of representatives may be necessary (except on a question of adjournment) shall be presented to the President, &c. *any attempt therefore to adjourn by law*, is a violation of that part of the constitution which gives the power *exclusively* to the two branches of the legislature. By another clause in the constitution it is declared, that neither house, during the session of Congress, shall, without the consent of the other, adjourn for more than three days, and to any other place than that in which the two houses shall be sitting; from hence he inferred, that the two houses by a concurrence, could adjourn for more than three days, nor to any other place which they thought proper; by the other clause he had mentioned, the *executive power is restrained from any interference with the legislative on this subject*; hence he concluded it would be dangerous to attempt to give to the President a power *the constitution expressly denied him.* He did not suppose that the attempt to vest the executive with a power over the adjournments of the legislature would absolutely convey the power, but he conceived it wrong to make the experiment. He submitted it to those gentlemen who were attached to the success of the bill, how far an *unconstitutional* declaration may impede its passage through the other branch of the legislature."

On the same occasion, another member of the H. of Representatives addressed the House in these words, "the Susquehannah being agreeable to the wishes of a great part of my constituents, I felt myself under an obligation to vote for it, *and nothing would restrain me from giving my consent to the bill, but that clause which requires the concurrence of the President*, respecting the seat of government until Congress meet at their permanent seat. To this clause I have *strong constitutional objections.* I have endeavoured to remove this conviction from my mind, in order to give my assent to the bill, but as I am under the sacred obligation of an oath to support the constitution, as I cannot efface the conviction from my mind that *it is contrary to the constitution*, and as we could not succeed in striking out the clause, I feel myself under the disagreeable necessity of giving my dissent to the bill."[2]

If the clause was unconstitutional last session, is it less so this? If it was an infraction of the constitution to fix by law the temporary seat of government, is it not a more palpable one to fix by law the place where Congress shall hold their next session: can the vote of last session render the measure constitutional? Admitting that some members had then violated the constitution, was not a greater obligation imposed on others to resist any further invasion? For what will become of the government if such encroachments are allowed to succeed, and its friends do not step forward and oppose them?

This is the moment when public measures should be narrowly watched; in the cool hour of calm discussion, when the subject is little interesting to the passions, there is no danger; on the slightest suggestion of unconstitutionality, a clause would be struck out; but when the mind pursues a favorite object with a passionate enthusiasm, men are too apt, in their eager embrace of it, to overlook the means by which it is attained. These are the melancholy occasions when the barriers of the government are broken down, and the boundaries of the Constitution defaced! There is a danger in another respect; from the apparent unimportance of the clause objected to. In the eye of the law the offence is equally great; in the eye of reason and prudence it is greater, because the public are more inattentive to the incroachment, and because the *success of one step infallibly leads to another.* It is a wedge which having entered the gap, makes way for further progression. The Constitution is the rock of our political salvation; it is the palladium of our rights; it is the safeguard of the rights of the States as well as individuals; it is our only bond of union; the smallest deviation from it is a mortal blow to those rights, and ought to be opposed by every citizen who wishes the preservation of the Union; nay, every citizen who has taken an oath to support the Constitution, *violates that oath* if he silently suffers any law to pass which appears to him, in the smallest degree, repugnant to it.

That the clause in question is repugnant to it is admitted, but it is justified on the principle that *it will be inoperative*; this is however a mistaken idea, for it will have an operation, unless formally annulled by the judiciary, and it is impossible the construction of it can ever go before the federal courts; it can't be alledged that it will be nugatory, and that a subsequent resolution of the two houses may adjourn to some other place, for then there would exist this solecism in politics, of a *smaller power rescinding the act of a larger*; there would also exist this *absurdity of one place being fixed by law* and *another by a simple resolution of the two houses*; if both the law and the resolution should name the same place, then there would exist *another absurdity* of a *resolution without* the President's approbation *enforcing a law* which *had received his sanction.* It cannot be justified on the ground that the two houses may, if they think proper, *waive* their *right* of determining for themselves, and request the concurrence of the President, because such a relinquishment of their privileges is not only a *departure from the plain words of the Constitution* which they have *sworn to support*, but is a transfer of rights which they enjoy as *members of the legislature*, not *as individuals, as trustees for the public*, not as their *own property*; they therefore betray the trust reposed in them, when they wantonly, and with their eyes open, *curtail or alienate those privileges.*

The circumstance of the clause being only a small part of the law, does not alter the case; the law ought not to pass, if there be any part of it inconsistent with the constitution; if the President signs it, he approves the whole; if he objects to any part, he must return it with his objections, and the two houses may expunge the exceptionable part, and then the president can give it his sanction. The bill may still pass with the *sound* part; if the *unsound* part should not be cut out, it will *contaminate* the whole, and be perpetually a *good* cause of repeal. There will always remain on the minds of *scrupulous* men, *conscientious doubts* respecting the efficacy of a law, which *contains within it an unconstitutional clause*, which may considerably *tend to defeat its operation.* Even the sanguine promoters of it, will look at it with different eyes from what they do now, when their ardent zeal shall have cooled; they reprobated it once themselves, as highly unconstitutional. What will not some men do to attain a favorite object? The reflection is mortifying and degrading!

Can there be a doubt, that, if the law consisted of only this one clause, that there would have been a general clamor at the absurdity of sending it to the President—even had the two houses been so ignorant of the constitution as to pass such a law would not the President have returned it with this answer, that *by the constitution he had nothing to do with it*. What would have been the consequence of such a measure? Either the two houses would discover what they ought to have known before, that they could do without his assent, or they must have repassed by *two thirds*, what by the constitution a *majority is competent to*: and does it make any difference, in point of constitutionality, whether the *objectionable clause* is a *whole law* or only *part of a law*? No man of common understanding will assert it.

Will not the public lose respect for the acts of Congress, when they see them blindly pursuing favorite measures, to the total disregard of the constitution? What appearance will it have to *pass laws* which are *admitted not to be binding*? What folly to require the assent of the President, when it would be as *effectual without it*?

Some of these arguments were stated. It was acknowledged that the clause was *nugatory, because it was unconstitutional*, but it was *retained*—why? Because the bill was *unalterable: sic volo, sic jubeo*;[3] these things ought not to be.

NYDA, 13 July; reprinted at New York City (*NYDG*, 14 July; *NYP*, 15 July); Philadelphia; Baltimore; and Charleston, South Carolina. Two one word corrections noted in *NYDA*, 14 July, have been made to the text. In 1965, *PTJ* editor Julian Boyd made a convincing case for Smith's authorship of this piece (*PTJ* 17:191–92). In addition, *NYDG*'s coverage of the House debate of 9 July informed its readers that the Speaker ruled as not in order an attempt by Smith to enter a "proposition" regarding the constitutionality of the Residence Bill on the Journals (*DHFFC* 13:1690), and the piece was republished in Smith's congressional district in a newspaper ([Charleston] *Columbian Herald*, 10 August) different from the one (*City Gazette*) that routinely reprinted pieces from *NYDA*.

---

[1] At this point in the text an asterisk leads the reader to a note referencing Madison's speech in *CR*, 21 September 1789. See *DHFFC* 11:1492–94 for this speech.

[2] For D. Carroll's speech of 22 September 1789, see *DHFFC* 11:1498–99.

[3] So I wish, so I command.

Newspaper Article, 13 July

We are informed, that a committee of both houses waited on the President of the United States, yesterday, with the residence bill, the return of which is uncertain.

Reports have circulated, that the unconstitutionality of the bill will prevent the President's signing it: others say, that if it is passed into a law, some members of the late majority will move for a suspension: but it is difficult to say what will be the result.

NYDG, 13 July; reprinted at Charleston, South Carolina.

George Washington to Thomas Jefferson, 15 July

Have you formed an opinion on the subject I submitted to you on Tuesday? Have you heard whether the Bill was disputed in both or either House of Congress on the ground of the Constitution, or whether this objection (in its full force) was held in petto[1] for the last move, in the present Stage of the business? If it was debated, as above, whether the arguments adduced by the Author of the Address to the P— were made use of, and how treated? & what would be the consequence supposing such a case, as he states, should arise?

ALS, Jefferson Papers, DLC. Signed, "Yours sincerely and Affectionately."

[1] In his heart.

Thomas Jefferson to George Washington, 15 July

I have formed an opinion, quite satisfactory to myself, that the adjournment of Congress may be by law, as well as by resolution, without touching the constitution. I am now copying fair what I had written yesterday on the subject & will have the honor of laying it before you by ten oclock. the address to the President contains a very full digest of all the arguments urged against the bill on the point of unconstitutionality on the floor of Congress. it was fully combated on that ground, in the committee of the whole, & on the third reading. the majority (a Southern one) overruled the objection, as a majority (a Northern one) had overruled the same objection the last session on the Susquehanna residence bill. so that two majorities, in two different sessions, & from different ends of the union have overruled the objection, and may be fairly supposed to have declared the sense of the whole union. I shall not lose a moment in laying before you my thoughts on the subject.

FC, Miscellaneous Letters, Miscellaneous Correspondence, State Department Records, Record Group 59, DNA.

Thomas Jefferson to George Washington, 15 July

Th. Jefferson begs pardon of the President for being later in sending the inclosed than he had given him reason to expect. the sole cause has been that the act of copying took him longer than he had calculated. he will have the honor of waiting on the President to answer any thing which he may have omitted materially in these papers.

[*Enclosure*]

Opinion on the Constitutionality of the Residence Bill

A Bill having passed the two houses of Congress, & being now before the President, declaring that the seat of the federal government shall be transferred to the Patowmac in the year 1790 [*1800*], that the session of Congress next ensuing the present shall be held at Philadelphia, to which place the offices shall be transferred before the 1st. of December next, a writer in a public paper of July 13. has urged on the consideration of the President that the constitution has given to the two houses of Congress the exclusive right to adjourn themselves, that the will of the President mixed with theirs in a decision of this kind would be an inoperative ingredient, repugnant to the constitution, and that he ought not to permit them to part, in a single instance, with their constitutional rights: consequently that he ought to negative the bill.

That is now to be considered.

Every man, and every body of men on earth, possesses the right of self-government: they recieve it with their being from the hand of nature. Individuals exercise it by their single will: collections of men, by that of their majority; for the law of the *majority* is the natural law of every society of men. when a certain description of men are to transact together a particular business, the times & places of their meeting & separating depend on their own will; they make a part of the natural right of self-government. this, like all other natural rights, may be abridged or modified in it's exercise, by their own consent, or by the law of those who depute them, if they meet in the right of others: but so far as it is not abridged or modified, they retain it as a natural right, and may exercise it in what form they please, either exclusively by themselves, or in association with others, or by others altogether, as they shall agree.

Each house of Congress possesses this natural right of governing itself, & consequently of fixing it's own times and places of meeting, so far as it has not been abridged by the law of those who employ them, that is to say, by the Constitution. this act manifestly considers them as possessing this right of course, and therefore has no where given it to them. in the several different passages where it touches this right, it treats it as an existing thing, not as one called into existence by them. to evince this, every passage of the constitution shall be quoted, where the right of adjournment is touched; & it will be seen that no one of them pretends to give that right; that on the contrary every one is evidently introduced either to enlarge the right where it would be too narrow, to restrain it where, in it's natural & full exercise it might be too large & lead to inconvenience, to defend it from the latitude of it's own phrases, where these were not meant to comprehend it, or to provide for it's exercise by others where they cannot exercise it themselves.

"A majority of each house shall constitute a quorum to do business; but a *smaller number* may adjourn from day to day, & may be authorised to compel the attendance of absent members." Art. 1. sect. 5. a majority of every collection of men being naturally necessary to constitute it's will, and it being frequently to happen that a majority is not assembled, it was necessary to enlarge the natural right, by giving to "a *smaller number* than a majority" a right to compel the attendance of the absent members, & in the mean time to adjourn from day to day. This clause then does not pretend to give to a majority a right which it knew that majority would have of themselves, but to a number *less than a majority* a right which it knew that lesser number would not have of themselves.

"Neither house, during the session of Congress, shall, without the consent of the other, adjourn for more than three days, nor to any other place than that in which the two houses shall be sitting." ibid. each house exercising separately, it's natural right to meet when and where it should think best, it might happen that the two houses would separate either in time or place, which would be inconvenient. It was necessary therefore to keep them together by restraining their natural right of deciding on separate times & places, & by requiring a concurrence of will.

But as it might happen that obstinacy, or a difference of object might prevent this concurrence, it goes on to take from them, in that instance, the right of adjournment altogether, and to transfer it to another, by declaring Art. 2. sect. 3. that "in case of disagreement between the two houses with respect to the time of adjournment the President may adjourn them to such time as he shall think proper."

These clauses then do not import a gift, to the two houses, of a general right of adjournment, which it was known they would have without that gift, but to restrain or abrogate the right it was known they would have, in an instance where, exercised in it's full extent, it might lead to inconvenience, and to give that right to another who would not naturally have had it. it also gives to the President a right, which he otherwise would not have had, "to convene both houses, or either of them, on extraordinary occasions." thus substituting the will of another, where they are not in a situation to exercise their own.

"Every order, resolution, or vote, to which the concurrence of the Senate & house of representatives may be necessary (except on a question of adjournment) shall be presented to the President for his approbation &c." Art. 1. sect. 7. the latitude of the general words here used would have subjected the natural right of adjournment of the two houses to the will of the President, which was not intended. they therefore expressly "except questions of adjournment" out of their operation. they do not here give a right of adjournment, which it was known would exist without their gift; but they defend the existing right against the latitude of their own phrases, in a case where there was no good reason to abridge it. the exception admits they will have the right of adjournment, without pointing out the source from which they will derive it.

These are all the passages of the constitution (one only excepted which shall be presently cited) where the right of adjournment is touched: and it is evident that none of these are introduced to give that right; but every one supposes it to be existing, and provides some specific modification for cases where either a defect in the natural right, or a too full use of it would occasion inconvenience.

The right of adjournment then is not given by the constitution; and consequently it may be modified by law, without interfering with that instrument. It is a natural right, &, like all other natural rights, may be abridged or regulated in it's exercise by law; & the concurrence of the third branch in any law regulating it's exercise is so efficient an ingredient in that law that the right cannot be otherwise exercised, but after a repeal by a new law. The express terms of the constitution itself shew that this right may be modified *by law*, when, in Art. 1. sect. 4. (the only remaining passage on the subject not yet quoted) it sais "the Congress shall assemble at least once in every year, & such meeting shall be on the 1st. Monday in december, unless they shall, *by law*, appoint a different day." then another day may be appointed *by law*; & the President's assent is an efficient ingredient in that law. nay further, they cannot adjourn over the 1st. Monday of December but by *a law*. this is another constitutional abridgment of their natural right of adjournment: and completing our review of all the clauses in the constitution which touch that right, authorises us to say no part of that instrument gives it; and that the houses hold it, not from the constitution, but from nature.

A consequence of this is, that the houses may by a joint resolution remove themselves from place to place; because it is a part of their right of self-government: but that as the right of self-government does not comprehend the government of others, the two houses cannot, by a joint resolution of their majorities only, remove the executive, & judiciary from place to place. these branches possessing also the rights of self-government from nature, cannot be controuled in the exercise of them, but by a law, passed in the forms of the constitution. the clause of the bill in question therefore was necessary to be put into the form of a law, & to be submitted to the President, so far as it proposes to effect the removal of the Executive and Judiciary to Philadelphia. So far as respects the removal of the present houses of legislation thither, it was not necessary to be submitted to the president: but such a submission is not repugnant to the constitution. on the contrary, if he concurs, it will so far fix the next session of Congress at Philadelphia, that it cannot be changed but by a regular law.[1]

The sense of Congress itself is always respectable authority. it has been given very remarkeably on the present subject. the address to the President in the paper of the 13th. is a complete digest of all the arguments urged on the floor of the Representatives against the constitutionality of the bill now before the President; & they were over-ruled by a majority of that house, comprehending the delegations of all the states South of the Hudson, except South Carolina. At the last session of Congress, when the bill for remaining a certain term at New York, & then removing to Susquehanna or Germantown was objected to on the same ground, the objection was overruled by a majority, comprehending the delegations of the Northern half of the union with that of South Carolina. so that the sense of every state in the union has been expressed, by it's delegation, against this objection, South Carolina excepted, and excepting also Rhode island, which has never yet had a delegation in place to vote on the question. In both these instances the Senate concurred with the majority of the Representatives. The sense of the two houses is stronger authority in this case, as it is given against their own supposed privilege.

It would be as tedious, as it is unnecessary, to take up & discuss one by one, the objections proposed in the paper of July 13. Every one of them is founded on the supposition that the two houses hold their right of adjournment from the constitution. This error being corrected, the objections founded on it fall of themselves.

It would also be a work of mere supererogation to shew that, granting what this writer takes for granted (that the President's assent would be an inoperative ingredient, because excluded by the constitution, as he says) yet the particular views of the writer would be frustrated. for on every hypothesis of what the President may do, Congress must go to Philadelphia. 1. if he assents to the bill, that assent makes good law of the part relative to the Patowmac, and the part for holding the next session at Philadelphia is good, either as an ordinance, or a vote of the two houses, containing a compleat declaration of their will, in a case where it is competent to the object, so that they must go to Philadelphia in that case. 2. if he dissents from the bill, it annuls the part relative to the Patowmac; but as to the clause for adjourning to Philadelphia, his dissent being as inefficient as his assent, it remains a good ordinance, or vote, of the two houses for going thither, & consequently they must go in this case also. 3. if the President witholds his will out of the bill altogether, by a ten days silence, then the part relative to the Patowmac becomes a good law without his will, & that relative to Philadelphia is good also, either as a law, or an ordinance, or a vote of the two houses, & consequently in this case also they go to Philadelphia.

AN and Ms., hand of Jefferson, Miscellaneous Letters, Miscellaneous Correspondence, State Department Records, Record Group 59, DNA. The heavily edited draft opinion is in the Jefferson Papers, DLC.

[1] Madison's Comments, immediately below, apparently referred to this paragraph.

James Madison, Comments on Jefferson's Opinion, 14–15 July

This reasoning is inforced by the clause (Art. 2. Sect. 1. ~~cl. 3~~) which says the list of votes of the electors shall be transmitted to the Seat of Govt. directed to the President of the Senate, who in presence of the Senate & H. of Reps. shall open the certificates &c. The seat of *Congs.* then must be at the Seat of Govt.~~—otherwise the list of votes wd. be directed to a~~ It is admitted that the Seat of Govt. can not be where the *Ex. part* of the Govt. does not sit. The 3 branches then must sit together & each ~~being~~ having a will independent of the other, all must concur in saying where the common seat shall be, that is, ~~it~~ [*lined out*] a law ought to pass for the purpose.

Ms., in pencil, hand of Madison, Jefferson Papers, DLC. The dating of this document is based on the fact that it was composed on the reverse of a note Madison received from Hawkins on 14 July, printed above, and prior to sometime on 15 July when Jefferson delivered his opinion on the matter to the President, above. Jefferson attached Madison's opinion to a draft of his own.

One of the Gallery, 15 July

A Correspondent observes that the charge generally brought against lawyers of changing sides when it suits their purpose ought not to be confined to that class of men, but may with great propriety be extended to *certain public characters*, who, if they are not influenced by a fee, yet act under an impulse equally strong. What shall we say to those men who, *a few months ago* declared most-solemnly that it was an *unconstitutional act to fix by law the session of Congress*, and now *give their votes for a clause which fixes by law the next session of Congress?* Those who have read the speeches of Mr. M—n, Mr. P—e, and Mr. C—l, as recorded in the 2d. volume of the Congressional Register, pages 425, 427, and 432, must now see with great astonishment mingled with grief the names of those gentlemen on the Journal giving sanction to a law which they think unconstitutional.[1] Mr. P—e in his speech published a few days ago says that the law to be inconsistent with the constitution should direct the adjournment to take place *without the consent of the Senate*, because the constitution is; that "neither house shall adjourn *without the consent of the other*,"[2] ingenious quibble! Compare it with his speech of last session, Congressional Register, 2d. vol. page 427, where he asked, "where was the necessity of adhering to a clause, which its warmest advocates must allow had *no binding force*, as it related to its main object, namely, the *continuance of the two houses to sit in this city*." He says in the latter part of his speech "that it might indeed be said upon a question concerning *common adjournments* the two houses would do well to retain the right of adjourning *without the consent of the President*; but this is *an extraordinary case*." (a very extraordinary case, truly, Mr. P! and so there must be an extraordinary deviation from the constitution to suit this case!) There are two sorts of adjournment, a *common* one and an *uncommon* one: the common one, when Congress are to fix by law that the temporary seat of government shall be at New-York is *not binding* and unconstitutional: the *uncommon* one when they are to adjourn to meet at Philadelphia, must be fixed by law and have the consent of the President; *without this check*, says the conscientious patriot, after getting to Philadelphia on an adjournment, they may be brought back to New-York; pray, Mr. P. will this check prevent Congress adjourning back to New-York, if they are so disposed; if I remember right, the law only says the *next session* shall be at Philadelphia, and where is the check if the clause has *no binding force*, as was said by Mr. P. last session: It would be a prudent thing for some persons to think before they speak. *Litera scripta manet!*[3]

What is become of another person's *oath* which stuck in his throat last session, and prevented his voting for the Susquehannah? Has he swallowed it since that time? Or is it so long since he took it that he has forgot it? Or have the waters of the *Patowmac* the virtue of the *Lethe*, that those who drink of them lose their memory?[4]

NYDA, 15 July.

---

[1] For Madison's and Page's speeches of 21 September 1789, see *DHFFC* 11:1492–97. For D. Carroll's speech of 22 September, from *NYDA*, later printed in *CR*, see *DHFFC* 11:1498–99.

[2] For Page's remarks on 8 July 1790, see *DHFFC* 13:1685.

[3] The written letter remains.

[4] The reference is to D. Carroll's speech of 22 September 1789; see *DHFFC* 11:1498–99. The Lethe was a river in Hades, whose waters induced the dead to forget their life among the living.

[*James Madison?*] Newspaper Article, 9 August

The public attention having been drawn to the meaning of the constitution, as applied to two bills, one before the last, the other before the present session of Congress, the following candid view of this subject is submitted by one who has carefully attended to the whole discussion.

By the [*first*] article of the constitution the power of adjourning to *another* place is vested in the two houses, whose joint vote for the purpose is not to be submitted to the President.

The bill at the last session for continuing the *seat of government* at New-York, for a term not exceeding four years, was a violation of the said article.

Because the seat of government included the seat of Congress, as being an essential part of the government; and as is proved by the clause requiring the votes of the electors to be sent to the *seat of government* to be opened *in the presence of the two houses.*

Because the bill of consequence imposed a restraint on the right of the two houses alone during the said term, to adjourn from New-York.

The clause in the late act fixing the temporary and permanent seat of government, which declares 'that the ensuing session of Congress shall be held at Philadelphia,' is not a violation of the said article of the constitution.

Because the article refers to an *adjournment.*

Because an adjournment refers to the *same Congress.*

Because a new election of representatives makes a new Congress, notwithstanding the sameness of the senate as a new house of commons makes a new Parliament, notwithstanding the sameness of the house of lords.

Because, therefore, as the ensuing session might have been that of a new Congress, by the intervening election of a new house of representatives, the approbation of the President would in that event have been operative, and even necessary.

Because even on a contrary event the clause attempts no restraint on a future Congress, but binds only the two existing houses, and that equally, whether the President approves or disapproves their joint vote of adjournment involved in the clause.

From this view of the subject it is evident, 1st. that those who objected to the constitutionality of the former bill, and concurred in that of the latter, voted consistently with the constitution, and with themselves.

2d. That those who concurred in the former and objected to the latter, voted inconsistently both with the constitution and with themselves.

3d. That the President in signing the latter added one more to the reiterated proofs given of a judgment not to be bewildered by false reasoning, and of a *patriotic* firmness not to be affected by *local* discontents.

NYDA, 11 August; reprinted at Philadelphia. Julian Boyd (*PTJ* 17:202–3) makes a compelling argument for Madison's authorship.

[*William Smith (S.C.)?,*] Truth, 11 August

A PALTRY attempt in yesterday's paper to impose on the public requires some notice—the writer asserts that the bill of last session for *continuing the seat of government* at New-York was *unconstitutional* and the bill of this session for *adjourning to Philadelphia, constitutional*: the citizens of this country are too enlightened to be deceived by the flimsey reasoning which is employed to support these points. Let us examine them. Fixing the seat of government, says the author, at New-York for four years was a violation of the article of the constitution which vests the power of adjourning in the two houses alone, because the seat of government included the seat of Congress, and because the bill imposed a restraint on the right of the two houses alone during the said term to adjourn from New-York. Hence he infers that it was unconstitutional to fix by law the seat of government because Congress is part of the government—how then does he pretend to justify the bill of this session which fixes the government for ten years at Philadelphia? Will not Congress constitute a part of the government and be included therein as much at Philadelphia as at New-York, or does the difference between four years residence in the one bill and ten years in the other make one bill violate the constitution and the other conform to it? Where then is the proof of unerring judgment in approving a bill which, according to this sagacious writer, restrains Congress from adjourning for the space of ten years from Philadelphia.

It is then evident, that this author is mistaken in his first position, viz., that the seat of government cannot be fixed by law for a term of years; or that if he be right in his first position, he must be wrong in his second, viz. That the bill of this session is constitutional, because the said bill contains a clause similar to the one in the bill of last session, which he declares unconstitutional.

A slight attention to the subject, will also refute his second position; he says that the clause in question does not violate the constitution, because the article refers to an *adjournment*, and because an adjournment refers to the *same Congress*. The writers reasoning in this part, is so involved in confusion, that it is difficult to trace it. His distinction between the *same* and *another* Congress, is perfectly absurd as applicable to this question and unfounded from the very words of the Constitution; nay, he refutes himself, for in the very outset of his remarks, he says, 'by the article of the Constitution the power of adjourning to another place is vested *in the two houses*, whose joint vote for the purpose is *not* to be submitted to the President.' Where does he find any distinction between an adjournment of the same Congress and meeting of the new one? there is none in the Constitution. But here his own argument turns strongly against himself for the clause in the bill declares that the *next session of Congress* shall be held at Philadelphia, and not the *session of the next Congress*; the law therefore binds the *same* Congress, who had a right to adjourn themselves by concurrent resolution.

Would the assent of the President be *necessary* to a concurrent resolution of one Congress directing where another should assemble? No; because the Constitution vests in the *two houses alone* the power of adjournment *in every case.* If the old Congress should assign a place for the meeting of the new one, they would of course assemble at the place where the offices of state were held, and where the former Congress had held their session; if a place should be assigned, the new Congress would assemble there, but they would have the power by concurrent resolution to adjourn to any other place; the assent of the President therefore to the act would be nugatory, for it would not be binding on the new Congress, who would by virtue of the Constitution possess the power of adjournment, in any case then the assent of the President to a vote of adjournment is unconstitutional.

The author refutes himself in more than one place; he acknowledges that the clause *attempts no restraint on a future Congress*; then the assent of the President is *not valid*, quoad[1] a new Congress; but says he, it *binds only the two existing houses* and that *equally* (wonderful conclusion from his premises!) *whether the President approves or disapproves their joint vote of adjournment* involved in the clause. So that tho' he in one paragraph insinuates that the *approbation of the President would have been very necessary*, as applicable to a *new Congress*, yet in a subsequent one he contends that the clause *attempts no restraint on a future Congress*; and tho' he insists on the constitutionality of the clause, yet he admits that the signature of the President adds no validity to the vote of adjournment, but that it would be *equally binding without it*; and why? Because as he has above declared the *two houses alone possess the power of adjournment.*

There is reason then to apprehend that false reasoning has been too successfully employed in bewildering a judgment that has heretofore given reiterated proofs of its soundness, and in subduing a *patriotic* firmness which should have resisted every impression arising from *local motives*, which, upon this and another late occasion (the unnecessary detention of a very necessary bill)[2] appear to have had far more influence than was proper.

NYDA, 12 August. Julian Boyd argues that Smith authored this piece; see *PTJ* 17:205.

---

[1] As to; with respect to.

[2] Washington held the Settlement of Accounts Bill [HR-77] until the tenth day before signing it.

TUESDAY, 13 JULY 1790

St. John de Crèvecoeur to William Short

*** I Saw & conversed with him [*Jefferson*] the day before I left new York & he [*illegible*] declared He had not the Least Idea of the Person Intended to replace him at Paris; the Bill Empowering the President To appoint Ministers & consuls [*Foreign Intercourse Act HR-52*] was past the Lower house but had not been Taken up by the Senate; I make no doubt Mr. Jefferson as a friend & peculiar confident of the President must have a Great Influence in the appointt. of his Successor, if a Successor is as yet Sent; I have often mentioned your name without being able to form any Jugemt. of his Intentions; I did more I asured him that Mr. Maddisson was the Person pitched upon by the Public "I have not heard the Least Syllable about it"—was his answer; I hope & pray you May be continued & have an oppetunity of Seeing the conclusion of this Grand & Interesting Scene[1] which Transacting under your Immediate Inspection; ***

ALS, Short Papers, DLC. Written from L'Orient, France; addressed to Paris; postmarked. Dated "July 90"; the editors accept the date written on the manuscript, at a later time, perhaps by an archivist. The omitted text reports on events in the United States.

[1] The French Revolution.

Thomas Dwight to Theodore Sedgwick

In one of your late letters, you enquire the reason that Mr. Dalton is not only not reelected but that he had no votes, I have endeavored to inform myself, and find no other reason assigned than that he voted for the compensations as they are now stated—no exceptions it is said, were made to his political character or conduct. but upon this subject, and it is indeed a constant source of complaint in our government—a perpetual check to the *dear blessing* of popularity.

Our election of Fed Reps. takes place as you will have learn'd, in October next the pot even now begins simmering, it will soon boil—the same, or similar dirty, base tricks will be play'd over in the approaching, as, in the last election and with what success God only knows—I am weary of attempting to make calculations on popular conduct—it is almost invariably directed by wantonness and caprice—or is changed by the most trifling and unexpected causes—gratitude is one of the scarcest virtues—and a great and good politician who has snatchd his Countrymen from devouring flames need not be surprised, if in return they should throw *him* in. I will give you from time to time the progress of our Demons so far as I can trace ~~them~~ it.

I have to beg a favor of you Sir, which I am sorry to trouble you with, but will endeavor to repay—In December last a ~~vessel~~ schooner named the Friendship commanded by Capt. Joseph Whitfield sailed from this [*Connecticut*] river with beef belonging to myself and some of my neighbors—she was first to make the town of Alexandria in Virginia as we have heared nothing of her since she sailed, we are suspicious that she is either lost or runaway with, by the Captain—if you have any friend from that quarter who could write a line to Alexandria and have enquiry made whether such a vessel has ever been entered there and if so for what port she cleared and when—it will greatly oblige me—to save trouble I enclose on a separate paper the name of the Captain and vessel and ask such questions as I wish to have answered.

Mr. [*Jonathan*] Bliss and Miss Mary Worthington were married on sunday evening last they wish you to accept their sincere thanks for your kind congratulations Mr. Bliss says it would give him very great pleasure to see you and Mr. Strong, but that pleasure he fears must at present be deferred—He tells me to assure you both, of his sincere wishes for your happiness.

ALS, Sedgwick Papers, MHi. Written from Springfield, Massachusetts.

Benjamin Goodhue to Stephen Goodhue

I have nothing new to write you, the Senate have this day been employ'd on the inclosed resolutions[1] but what will be the fate of them is wholy uncertain, now residence is out of the way they I mean the yorkers and some others who are fond of 6 ℔ Ct. on the funded debt have conjured up another difficulty, and say unless they can have 6 pr. Ct. which the Senate have struck out of the funding bill and inserted 4 ℔ Ct. instead of it, restor'd they will be against the Assumption, so that this ill fated measure has to combat every opposition from every quarter—I long to be at home and unless we can do somthing soon I suspect they will be so weary of contending as to adjourn the whole of it over.

ALS, Goodhue Family Papers, MSaE. Addressed to Salem, Massachusetts; franked; postmarked.

[1] For the Senate committee report of 12 July on assumption of the state debts, see *DHFFC* 5:923–26; it was ordered printed that day.

Christopher Gore to Rufus King

The embarrassed situation of Congress and our public affairs is truly distressing to all those who love & respect the American name—We feel & fret at the delay of great business for such paltry objects as where the business of our country shall be done—and to me it is truly mortifying that Pensylvania shoud be gratified when her representatives have behaved so disgracefully.

I sincerely hope our friend Ames has conducted to the satisfaction of all honourable men I feel no doubt of the purity of his intentions ***

ALS, King Papers, NHi. Written from Boston; franked; postmarked New Haven, Connecticut, 16 July; the omitted text discusses Cyrus King's departure by stage for New York City late the following week.

Theodore Sedgwick to Pamela Sedgwick

Last evening I recd. your very kind letter sent by Mr. [*Silas*] Pepoon. He went on directly to Philadelphia & left the letter behind him. Eliza's Stays were not sent as I have hoped every three days since they were made to be able to be myself the Bearer. I thank you my dearest sweet Love for this Letter, it is a display of those amiable qualities which originally engaged my affections to you, and which every moment since, as they have been more fully displayed have encreased the ardor of my attachment. Indeed my love it is naturally to be supposed that the conduct of congress, on the subject of the residence must have depreciated the character of the members in the public estimation. I have however nothing on this account with which I can charge myself or be charged by the public. I was against the introduction of it, never intended its progress, and indeed believed and do still believe that any determination is preferable to the state the government was in. Indeed I am not greatly dissatisfyed with the result.

I am beyond measure chagrined that such delays take place in the progress of the great business now before us. But it has been unavoidable. Today the question was put in the senate on the assumption and carried 14. against 12. yet as there will be another reading there it is not certain it will succeed. A difference exists in opinion in that as well as our house with regard to the terms on which the debt shall be funded. A few on each side have declared that they will consent to nothing unless they are gratifyed in their particular wishes. Both are in my opinion greatly to blame. all however are friends of the assumption, and each of these small parties can prevent a majority. Both seem determined, and none of them possessing any principle of accomodation. On one side are Ellsworth, Carroll and Read, on the other Morris, Schuyler and King. If neither recede we may after all dispair of the event, and this day or tomorrow will determine.

I have written Theodore [*Sedgwick, Jr.*], he will probably shew you the letter. I have purchased you a dozen very pretty de[*s*]sert spoons & have sent them to get your name & a handsome cypher ingraved. I hope in a few days to present them to you. Should [*James?*] Orton tarry till morning I will write you again. In the mean time may the choicest of heavens blessings attend the dearest & best of women & wives.

P. S. The letter to Theodore I have not written, but will a few words while Orton waits—I intended to have written Mr. [*Henry*] Van Schaak, and all the children but cannot now.

ALS, Sedgwick Papers, MHi. Place to which addressed not indicated.

Paine Wingate to Jeremy Belknap

I should not have written to you this day, was it not for the sake of enclosing a letter I have just received for you—I am ashamed to repeat so often that we have yet done nothing decisive respecting the funding system—This day the Senate have spent on the question of assumption, but came to no determination. I think this point must be finally determined, at least for this session, in a day or two, but in what manner is very doubtful. It would be tedious for you as well as for me to enter into a particular account of this matter. We have got one embarrassment to business out of the way, that is respecting residence. As soon as the assumption is decided we shall then do something effectually or agree to do nothing more this session. At any rate I hope & believe we shall adjourn pretty soon when I hope to have the pleasure of seeing you & perhaps may give you a more satisfactory account of matters.

ALS, Belknap Papers, MHi. Addressed to Boston; franked; postmarked.

A Plebeian to Mr. McLean

WHEN a respectable number of citizens of a large community feel themselves aggrieved, it is a difficult task to persuade them that the measures, of which they complain, are necessary for the public good.

The citizens of New-York have always shewn a disposition to make the residence of Congress as convenient and agreeable in this city, as could be expected: in some instances they have even exerted themselves beyond all conceptions. To a man, whose honest and reasonable feelings are not subservient to the higher notions of policy, it would therefore almost appear, as if those citizens had sufficient reasons to consider the very abrupt manner in which Congress has resolved to leave them, as a hardship.

As to the public welfare being concerned in a speedy removal from New-York, it is true Mr. M*****n [*Madison*] has only given us an explanation by a calculation of mileage; but the necessity of it he has shewn in so clear a manner as ought to be satisfactory to New-York, and to all the states that voted against the bill—for, says he, "we shall lose the bill; and I would therefore beg gentlemen to remember, that as they regard the passing of the act, and the obtaining a southern and more central position, *so they ought to oppose any and every amendment that should be offered.*"[1]

And at another time he argues thus (addressing himself as it were to particular members) "We have it now in our power (says he) to procure a southern position. The opportunity may not again speedily present itself. We know the various and jealous interests that exist on this subject. We should hazard nothing. If Patowmac is struck out, are you sure of getting Baltimore? May not other places be proposed? Make any amendment, sir, and the bill will go back to the Senate. Are we sure that it will come back into our possession again? By amending, we give up a certainty for an uncertainty. In my opinion, we should act wisely if we accepted the bill as it now stands, and *I beg leave to press it on gentlemen not to consent to any alteration, least it be wholly defeated, and the prospect of obtaining a southern position vanish forever.*"[2]

Now I would ask, whether the citizens of New-York ought not to yield to such forcible arguments, be silent, and sacrifice self-interest to the exigencies of absolute necessity and the public welfare? Who is there so base as to say we have been at considerable expences, which were incurred on a reasonable expectation that Congress would remain a few years with us? or does the state of New-York form so diminutive a part of the union that Congress should treat us with contempt?

But Mr. M*****n tells us that the bill will be lost; and Mr. M*****n is a wise man, who has studied all the ancient and modern authors upon government, and has read Machiavel in the original language.

There is another consideration, which ought to have its due weight with the good people who think themselves injured by the sudden removal of government: the city of Philadelphia is properly situated, and in many respects well calculated for the residence of Congress, and though it be a little on one side of the geographical center, there are good reasons to believe that the proceedings of Congress will in that city go on with the same progress as heretofore in New- York, that the national debt will be funded within a few years, the state debts assumed, and that hereafter there will be no more dispute about the center.

NYDG, 13 July, edited by Archibald McLean.

---

[1] Madison's remarks about mileage took place on 6 July (*DHFFC* 13:1648). The quoted remarks are from Madison's speech of 7 July (*DHFFC* 13:1673).

[2] The quoted remarks are from Madison's speech of 6 July (*DHFFC* 13:1648).

Timon to Mr. McLean

DURING the debate on the residence bill in the House of Representatives, it was remarked by some of the friends of the Virginia and Pennsylvania compact in the gallery, that the principal opposers were opposed to the New Constitution; thus attempting to conjure up the ghost of antifederalism, in order to run down the characters of two or three of the most valuable members in the house.

The citizens of New-York are generous, and they would ill support their liberal fame did they not express their gratitude to Messrs. Gerry, Burke, Smith [*S.C.*], Sherman, Wadsworth, Laurance, and several other worthy friends of the residence minority, whose exertions in opposing a measure which is not only fraught with dangerous consequences to the city of New-York, but to the harmony of the union in general, merit universal applause. They have shewn themselves enemies to rotation, instability, disunion and intrigue.

No good, no wise, no true politician can demonstrate that a ten years residence in Philadelphia will be the means of establishing a permanent constitution; neither will it be approximating to the centre of the territory of the union, although it may be a few miles nearer the Patowmac. But centrality is become the fashionable doctrine in these days, and the ambitious impolitic few say, that we shall never have a good government until our chief magistrate be made hereditary, and we are all reduced to the humiliating alternative of worshipping, perhaps, an idiot in the cradle! from such centrality, *libera Nos Domina!*[1] Such movings round a centre of territory, or round an arbitrary monarch's baboon in his cradle, deserve no better fate than the moth that whirls round the flame and centres there.

The worst enemies of the present experimental constitution, could not have devised a surer mode of attack to effect its destruction, than by rendering the proceedings of the first Congress ridiculous in the eyes of the world: for so certain as the people imbibe a contemptible opinion of their representatives, so surely will the constitution become obnoxious, and instead of affording the government every possible support, they will despise and disobey the laws.

It is therefore a just inference to say, that the advocates for rotation (before any salutary laws are established for the support of public credit and the safety and welfare of the union) *are not the friends of this country.*

The subtle logician may endeavour to deny my conclusion, and the avaricious statesman may hire his scribbling hacks to struggle against reason and sound policy: but truth will ever stand against the fire of anti-constitutional assailants, the storms of intrigue, and the blasts of aristocracy.

NYDG, 13 July, edited by Archibald McLean. The ancient, semi-legendary Timon of Athens was best known through Shakespeare's play of that name, portraying reckless generosity's decline to misanthropy, and, no doubt, reflecting New Yorkers' complaints of the nation's ingratitude for removing the seat of government.

[1] Lord, free us!

Civis to Mr. Greenleaf

ATTENDING, on Friday last, in the House of Representatives, on the important debate of the residence bill, I was struck with amazement at the rude behavior of certain gentlemen, who are near the person of the P—t of the U— S—, I mean their sneering conduct on that day to the virtuous minority. Query, are the free citizens of New-York, after their many exertions, to be insulted?

NYJ, 13 July, edited by Thomas Greenleaf. The "gentlemen" in question could have been all or some of the President's aides; at this time, they included Tobias Lear, David Humphreys, William Jackson, Thomas Nelson, and Robert Lewis.

OTHER DOCUMENTS

Benjamin Goodhue to David Sewall. No copy known; acknowledged in Sewall to Goodhue, 30 July.

James Madison to George Nicholas. No copy known; acknowledged in Nicholas to Madison, 31 December.

Hugh Williamson to John Gray Blount. ALS, John Gray Blount Papers, Nc-Ar. Place to which addressed not indicated. For the full text, see *Blount* 2:79–80.

Proposals, in addition to those in his letter of 10 July, for speculation in 1786 North Carolina state certificates; when people buy them knowing their legal status, "it is a fair Subject of Speculation and if they mistake the Proportion between the true Soldiers and the men of Straw it is not the fault of the Seller of the Certificate but of themselves who guess wrong"; asks if any subscribers have been obtained for their map.

WEDNESDAY, 14 JULY 1790

Samuel Meredith to Margaret Meredith

*** the President has not yet put his Name to the [*Residence*] Bill & there has been a peice addressed to him on the unconstitutionality of it,[1] which

I believe will have very little weight with him, however I confess on many accots. I should wish it done, in the first place it would tend to make up the Minds of the people here to a removal, it would likewise enable our people to begin their opperations for the accomodation of Congress, which I am very much affraid ~~our people~~ they will do in a nigardly way, I wish I may be disappointed, for if they do, the Contrast between the New Yorkers & us will be remarkable, for they certainly have gone to an enormous expence, the half of what they have & are laying out would answer the purpose very well & as we are twice as large & rich it would fall but a fourth part as heavy on the Community. I have wrote Mr. [*Henry*] Hill on the Subject thinking he as well as the Philadelphians want a little spurring ***

ALS, Read Family Papers, PPL at PHi. Addressed to "Greenhill," near Philadelphia.

[1] See [*William Smith (S.C.),*] Junius Americanus to the President of the United States, 1790 Veto Controversy, 12 July, above.

William Smith (S.C.) to [*Edward Rutledge*]

The Seat of Governmt. Bill [*Residence Act S-12*] has passed the two houses; it fixes the temporary Seat at Philada. for 10 years, to commence from next Decr. & thereafter proposes to fix the permanent Seat on the Potowmac, where it will, in my opinion never go: the whole of this has been a manœuvre to throw Congress into Philada.—the Bait of the Potowmac has taken in Some of the Southern Members, who will sorely repent it ere long. Butler consented to the Bill merely on that account. That question being disposed of, the Senate have taken up the Assumption, in the funding Bill it was resolved by the Senate to fund the Continental debt at 4 per Cent: this offended mightily some of the Members who are said to be deeply interested, viz., Morris, Schyler & King who swore they would not consent to the Assumption, unless the continl. debts were funded at 6 per cent; Butler joined them in this, (altho it is not long since he was opposed to funding at all) & declared he wod. vote agst. the Assumption, if the 6 per cent was struck out: on the other hand, Elsworth, Strong & some others would not agree to the Assumption if more than 4 pr. Ct. was given to the continl. creditors; Mr. Izard was neutral & promised to agree to that which wod. ensure the assumption; in this gloomy state were things yesterday; Hamilton has taken a great deal of pains to bring them to rights; from the tenacious temper of the contending parties, it was seriously apprehended this morning early that both assumption & funding Bill would be thrown out altogether; I called on Mr. Izard as I went to the House—he was full of despondency—when we got near the federal Hall, we met Hamilton with a Smile on his countenance; he told us that a parley had taken place & that it was proposed that the *principal* of the public debt shod. be funded at 6 per cent, & the *interest* at 4—& the *State debts* at 4.—that the Assumption shod. be taken up & agreed to, then the funding Bill—& then both committed to a committee of compromise—this arrangemt. Seems to have Succeeded for they have actually agreed to the Assumption by a majority of 2—the numbers being 14 to 12—what the final result will be is yet uncertain, but there appears some prospect of Success—I am sorry however to find that several persons here are buying up our Securities very fast, & that Contracts are made for the delivy. of them to a considerable amount—you shod. put people on their guard against the Speculators & prevent their Selling.

You [*South Carolina*] passed a Law last Session ceding our Lighthouse to the U.S. but you clogged the Cession with a condition that the U.S. should pay certain expences which amounted to about £190 Sterling; the cession has therefore not been accepted, & you were in a fair way of having the expence of maintaining the Lighthouse thrown upon you after the 15th. next month, which would soon have exceeded £190. I have therefore prevailed on the house to consent to a Bill [*Lighthouses Act HR-84*] prolonging to next July the time within which you may make the Cession & I hope the next Legislature will make an unconditional ~~cession~~ one.

ALS, Pinckney Family Papers, DLC. Place to which addressed not indicated. The identification of the recipient is based on the docket in his hand. The letter was continued on 17 July, below.

Hugh Williamson to John Gray Blount

Since I wrote you on Yesterday the Senate have by a Majority of two agreed to assume the Debts of the several States at least 21 Millions of Dlrs. of the same, and this to be apportioned according to favouritism among them. I fear that a Majority will eventually be found in our House for adopting because I verily fear that some of the Members have an Interest in deep Speculations. Before the Measure passes we shall put their Honesty to a severe Tryal. If People to the Southward have as much Virtue as they ought to have in Order to remain free they will disappoint the Hopes of those who expect to get 20/ in the Pound for what cost them in Carolina about 2/6. Don't omit the 86ers.[1] And if others are purchasable on good Terms why not buy at a rising Market!

ALS, John Gray Blount Papers, Nc-Ar. Addressed to Washington, North Carolina; carried by Dr. Osborne.

[1] See Williamson to Governor Alexander Martin, 6 March, volume 18, for information on these North Carolina certificates.

Newspaper Article

The New-York papers teem with invectives against Congress, on account of the vote to meet the next Session, at Philadelphia—and caricature prints, are called in to aid the abuse of language. In one of them is represented, the Hon. Mr. M[*orris*]. of the Senate as bribing the majority for their votes, and leading the minority by the nose. The following is a specimen of the *milder* species of abuse.

From the New York Daily Gazette.

SALE AT AUCTION.

THIS DAY, at two o'clock, P.M. without reserve, for the benefit of the original owners, (the present holders having neglected to make good their arguments and thereby forfeited their title)

The ship New Constitution.

Well built, and gilded on the head and stern, warranted sound in her timbers, except a *couple of plank* which sprung yesterday, supposed to be on account of the attraction of the South Pole, and during the time that the crew were hoisting anchor to sail for Philadelphia.

N. B. Ten years credit will be given to any Virgianite, Pennsylvanianite, or Boobysite,[1] from Maryland or North-Carolina; and those who may be desirous of treating at private sale are requested to call the *Nocturnal Divan Room*,[2] in Disunion-Street.

[Boston] *Columbian Centinel*, 14 July; reprinted at Keene and Portsmouth, New Hampshire. The quoted article is from *NYDG*, 1 July.

[1] A reference to Morris.
[2] A reference to the privy council of Turkey, popularly considered a secret body.

[*Philip Freneau,*] Nabby, the New York House-Maid, to Nanny, her friend in Philadelphia

WELL, Nanny, I am sorry to say, since you writ us
The Congress at last has determin'd to quit us;
You now may begin with your brushes and brooms
To be scowering your knockers and scrubbing your rooms;
As for us, my dear Nanny, we're much in a pet,
And hundreds of houses will be to be let;
Our streets, that were just in a way to look clever,

Will now be neglected and nasty as ever;
Again we must fret at the Dutchify'd gutters
And pebble-stone pavements, that wear out our trotters.
My master looks dull, and his spirits are sinking,
From morning till night he is smoking and thinking,
Laments the expence of destroying the fort,[1]
And says, your great people are all of a sort—
He hopes and he prays they may die in a stall
If they leave us in debt—for FEDERAL HALL—
And STRAP[2] has declar'd, he has such regards,
He will go, if they go, *for the sake of their beards.*
Miss *Letty* poor lady, is so in the pouts,
She values no longer our dances and routs,
And sits in a corner, dejected and pale
As dull as a cat, and as lean as a rail!
Poor thing, I am certain she's in a decay,
And all—because Congress resolve not to stay!
This Congress unsettled is, sure, a sad thing,
Seven years, my dear Nanny, they've been on the wing;[3]
My master would rather saw timber, or dig,
Then see them removing to Connegocheague,
Where the houses and kitchens are yet to be fram'd,
The trees to be fell'd, and the streets to be nam'd;
Of the two, we had rather your town should receive 'em—
So here, my dear Nanny, in haste I must leave 'em,
I'm a dunce at inditing—and as I'm a sinner,
The beef is half raw—and the bell rings for dinner!

NYDA, 15 July. This poem is a sequel to one that appeared on 29 June, volume 19.

---

[1] Fort George was taken down in order to build a mansion for presidents of the United States.

[2] A barber.

[3] Congress moved from Philadelphia to Princeton, New Jersey, in June 1783; from December 1783 through August 1784 it met at Annapolis, Maryland; in November and December 1784 it sat at Trenton, New Jersey; and since January 1785 it had met at New York City.

OTHER DOCUMENTS

Charles Bessonet to Thomas Fitzsimons and Robert Morris. ALS, Coxe Papers, PHi. Written from Bristol, Pennsylvania.

Asks them to propose to Congress that it purchase his drawbridge over Neshaminy Creek (in southern Bucks County, Pennsylvania), for £2400 and make it part of the federal post road; hopes Congress "will rightly consider the publick Spirit with which I have acted."

Theodore Foster to Governor Arthur Fenner. No copy known; acknowledged in Fenner to Foster, 17 July.

Elbridge Gerry to Henry Marchant. No copy known; acknowledged in Marchant to Gerry, 26 July.

Benjamin Hawkins to James Madison. Ms., hand of Hawkins, Jefferson Papers, DLC. The identification of the recipient is based on the fact that Madison used the reverse of the note to compose for Jefferson his opinion on the constitutionality of the Residence Bill, printed under the 1790 Veto Crisis, 12 July, above.

Tally of the 14–11 vote this day in the Senate to assume $21,000,000 of state debt; Gunn abstained.

Azor Orne to Benjamin Goodhue. ALS, Letters to Goodhue, NNS. Written from Marblehead, Massachusetts.

Office seeking: asks Goodhue to use his influence in behalf of his son Joshua as Marblehead collector, to succeed the recently deceased Richard Harris.

Benjamin Stelle to George Washington. ALS, Washington Papers, DLC.

Office seeking: loan commissioner for Rhode Island; expects "Some of my Friends in the Senate" will interest themselves on his behalf.

Hugh Williamson to John Gray Blount. ALS, John Gray Blount Papers, Nc-Ar. Addressed to Washington, North Carolina; presumably carried by Osborne. For the full text, see *Blount* 2:82.

Urges Blount to send him as many of the certificates of 1786 as possible; "I verily wish that every Shilling of that Emission was sold in this Town, because I suspect that the Buyers here are generally acting for British or other Foreign Speculators"; wishes to buy £2000 of any certificates other than that emission which are not counterfeits.

NYJ, 16 July.

The Senate agreed to the resolutions for assumption.

GUS, 17 July.

The Senate agreed to the resolution assuming the state debts by a majority of two.

Letter from New York. [Boston] *Columbian Centinel*, 21 July; reprinted at Portland, Maine, and Exeter and Portsmouth, New Hampshire.

"*Congress* are now proceeding with much dispatch, in finishing a number of Bills which have been under consideration. The delay of these Bills has given them an opportunity of making several very important amendments, which the want of information at first precluded."

THURSDAY, 15 JULY 1790

George Rogers Clark to John Brown

I received your favor on the new construction for boats. The little machine remains as it did when I wrote to you on the subject, without my being able to make any improvments or find a defect. The papers you were so kind as to enclose, gave much satisfaction to the neighbors. I hope you will continue those favors.

As to the Narrative;[1] I have been at a great deal of trouble in attempting to recover several copies, that I was in hopes were in the hands of Captains Harrisson and Brashears,[2] at the Natchez, and others, but found myself disappointed, and have set about the business without those helps. I have tasked myself to spend two days in the week, and have got through about one hundred pages. I wish, before I close this business, to receive every querie of importance on the subject that yourself and Mr. Madison could imagine. The more I enter into this business, the better I am pleased at the undertaking, and frequently, I suppose, experience the same feeling that actuated me at the time of those transactions. I believe, that through myself, every thing past, relative to this country may be known. If this should fortunately meet with a quick passage, I may probably get an answer from you in two months. Judging from the progress I make, to be nearly closing this business by that period.

Please present my respects to Mr. Madison.

[Kentucky] *Frankfort Commonwealth*, 25 July 1838, Draper Collection, WHi. Written from Jefferson County, Kentucky.

---

[1] In a letter to Clark dated 5 July 1789, Brown had expressed both his and Madison's interest in Clark's composing a narrative of his Revolutionary War campaigns (*DHFFC* 16:946n). In response to a letter in which Jefferson hoped that Clark would persevere despite his alcoholism, Harry Innes wrote on 30 May 1791 that Clark was then engaged in the work and would complete it that summer (*PTJ* 20:481). The result was undoubtedly Clark's undated *Memoirs* (Milo M. Quaife, ed., *Conquest of the Illinois* [Chicago, 1920]), a manuscript copy of which also exists in the Draper Collection, WHi.

[2] Richard Harrison served as a lieutenant of artillery in the militia of his native Virginia before becoming a captain in Clark's Illinois Regiment. By 1785 he seems to have been

militia captain in the Natchez District, in the employ of the Spanish. Richard Breshear was another captain in Clark's regiment from 1778 to 1781. In 1787 he led thirty Americans from the Ohio Valley in an unsuccessful effort to plant a trading colony on Chickasaw Bluffs (present-day Vicksburg, Mississippi) (Lawrence Kinnaird, ed., "Spain in the Mississippi Valley, 1765–1794," *AHA* 1945, 2:142, 236).

Roger Sherman to Simeon Baldwin

I received yours of the 12th instant. Since the Bill respecting the Seat Government passed. business goes on harmoniously in the House, that matter I believe is quieted for Seven years at least—The time for adjournment is postponed to the 27th of this month—The Senate have before them the funding Bill, and the assumption of the State debts—There is a Bill before House for increasing the impost [*Ways and Means*]. as soon as those Bills are finished Congress may rise, there are Some matters of less importance which may be passed or postponed to next session—It was *morally* impossible for Congress to proceed faster than they have done—The pieces Signed Republican have been thought by Some, ill Natured & injudicious.[1]

I did not expect that Oliver would enter College next Fall.[2] I had rather he should be a year or two older before he enters. I wish to have [*torn*] well fitted. I have got Jeremiah OCain's Petition referred to the Secretary at War. & delivered him the two depositions that Mr. Thatcher left with me.
[*P. S.*] Report is not made on Pitman Collens's Petition.[3]

ALS, Sherman Collection, CtY. Addressed to New Haven, Conn.; franked; postmarked.

[1] The pieces, authored by David Daggett, are printed individually, beginning with 15 May, volume 19.

[2] Sherman's son Oliver (1777–1820) graduated from Yale in 1795.

[3] For the Ocain and Collins petitions, see *DHFFC* 7:84–85; both concerned impressed ships.

William Smith (Md.) to Otho H. Williams

Although uncertain, where, *or if ever*, this may reach you, I sit down to communicate, what you may be anxious to learn.

In the first place then, you are to know, that, the permanent seat of the government, for the U.S. of america, is fixed by Law, on the Banks of Potowmac, *at the mouth of Canogocheauge* after halting ten years, on its passage from hence, at the City of Phila. from whence, some think it will be extreamly dificult, if not impossible to remove it after so long possession.

When I say, at the mouth of Canogocheauge, I dont mean absolutely so, for the President has the power of Locating the Spot, any where from that place to the Easteren branch [*Anacostia River*], or Carrollsburg, but you will no doubt agree in opinion, with those who think it impossible, he should give a preference to any other place, when that is in his Option. The deciding on this important question, has occupied the whole time of Congress for near three weeks past, & has precluded almost all other business of consequence. The Senate has this day passed a Bill, *14 to 12*, for assuming the State debts. what may be its fate in our house is rather uncertain. That house has also changed the face of our funding Bill, by striking out all the Alternatives, & giving 4 ℔ Cent interest *only*.

The only news from abroad is the appearance of a war betwixt Great Britain & Spain, & great preperations making on both Sides; indeed it is Said with some degree of certainty that hostilities are already commenced, although it is believed the quarrell will yet be made up.

I had the pleasure of hearing by your letter, dated at Genl. [*Daniel*] Morgans, that you were all well & in good spirits. A letter from Jenny [*Janet Smith*] Hall, yesterday, informed me all friends at Eutaw & balto. were well, but that my Mill dam was carried away by fresh, & that Capt. C. Ridgely died Suddenly of an appoplectic fit, which is a Striking proof of the folly of over anxious cares in amassing the trash of this earth.[1]

Inclosed you have a coppy of the Residence bill as passed—I Say passed, although it has not yet recd. the Presidents assent, however little doubt remains on that head.

ALS, Williams Papers, MdHi. Addressed to Sweet Springs, Virginia.

[1] Charles Ridgely (1733–28 June 1790) was a sea captain, planter, and proprietor of several ironworks in Maryland. He played an active role in the revolutionary movement as a provincial legislator, followed by a career in the Maryland House of Delegates from 1777 to 1789. He was an antifederalist during ratification. Smith alludes to the personal fortune that the childless Ridgely symbolized in his Baltimore County estate, "Hampton," the largest house in America when it was completed, the year of Ridgely's death.

Joseph Tucker to George Thatcher

You will much oblige me to deliver the Inclosed letter to Major [*Michael*] Connolly, or give it to Mr. Van Renssalaer, who sees him every day—I want him to Complete some business for me, so as to forward it by you on your return, I hope you will Endeavour to have my other bussiness Accomplished this Session, if in your power, I am Sorrow to put you to so much trouble, and do not know if ever I can have it my power to make you any returns for your kindness—if major Connolly should pay you any money for me please to purchase a New York lottery Ticket—I have nothing new to Send you from this quarter—the fishing bussiness has been very Successfull here this

Season—the people (some of them at least) are Clamorous against Congress; they Say they were Sent to Ease them of there greviences and are now themselves become there greatest—but those people that rail so, you know are the the fickle sort who would make a King, to day and Crucify him tomorrow, they want a Congress, that can pay of[*f*] the public debt without money—and Support themselves on the honours of there appointments.

ALS, Chamberlain Collection, MB. Written from York, Maine; postmarked Portsmouth, New Hampshire.

X. X. to the Free Electors of Worcester District

THE time is now affixed for electing a Representative for the District of Worcester, in the next Congress—The attention of the people will again be called for that purpose, and the great question to be determined is, who they will elect to that important and very consequential office. Our present Representative was elected by a respectable majority of the voters in the district—and whether he has done well or ill will be determined by the people's electing him again, or by their choosing some other person. I was his supporter before—I ever esteemed him as a man of good natural capacity, and from his being long in the Legislature of Massachusetts I supposed he possessed a competent share of political information to answer the purpose. Although I am a plain unlettered man, I take great pleasure, and much pains whenever I have leisure, in reading the debates in Congress, and so far as I have been able to attend them, I am convinced, that the people, the free electors of every district in Massachusetts, ought at this period to divest themselves of every little prejudice, and elect a man who can do justice to his constituents, and will attend to the general good of the whole Union. I do not mean to suggest by this, that I would not have them choose our present worthy representative. If the people incline, I shall be satisfied, although I am much in favour of rotation in republican governments, it being a lesson for every man who holds an elective office to learn his dependence on the people. That we ought to send our best men, is a fact incontrovertible. A person representing a great district in the great Court of our Empire, ought to possess liberal political information, and to native strength of mind, a thorough knowledge of the foundation, rise and progress of modern and ancient governments, and the causes of their declension—a perfect knowledge of the natural and relative situation of our particular country—the ability and strength of it, with its various resources. From such a knowledge benefit is to be expected; the great secret of all government being to prevent the dissolution of it; as every government, like the human body, carries within it that morbid matter which sooner or later must inevitably destroy it.

There is no man will disagree in the truth of the foregoing observations. Many people in the district have said that Mr. Grout will not be reelected—if that is the prevailing sentiment, which I must doubt, it will be necessary to turn the attention of the electors to such a person as will best answer the great and important purposes of federal legislation. If the electors intend not to choose their present representative, I hope at least, they will think of a man better qualified—for it is folly in the extreme to turn out of office or place a man against whom the people have no reasonable objection. I am aware that many people have said Mr. Grout is not a man of a liberal education—we all know it—and does that argue that he is not fit to go to Congress? By no means. There are many, very many, great people, who have been well educated without passing through a college—nor is it essentially necessary. But if the people are determined not to vote for Mr. Grout, let them fix on some man of firmness—who is able to assert, maintain and support the rights of the northern or eastern States—who will attentively consider their interests—a man of religion and morality, property and fidelity. It is absolutely necessary that the northern or eastern states should send their best men to Congress. We know the interests of the southern states are different from ours—our habits and our views, our customs and education, are different—great men only can reconcile us. Let the electors beware how they vote on that important day. There are wolves amongst us in sheeps clothing, who pretend they can save millions to the people if they could be at helm—who pretend, when they are amongst ignorant people, that all political knowledge, including the great business of financing, pertains to them alone—when, in fact, they are as ignorant as they are impudent, and wish for nothing but to vault into the political saddle; and having once got seated you hear no more of them—No, my friends, if you will turn out Mr. Grout, fix upon a man of property and ability—and take this solemn truth with you, that let the pretensions of people be what they may—there are but few, very few, persons in our district who are fit to represent us.

[Worcester] *Massachusetts Spy*, 15 July.

From New York

Yesterday the Hon. Senate accepted the report, and passed the Resolutions for ASSUMING the part of the State Debts mentioned therein, by, I hear, a majority of TWO.

This day the Committee of the whole went through the *Ways and Means* bill and reported the same to the House, without amendment. Mr. MADISON, in the House moved a limiting clause, which occasioned a debate until the time of adjournment.

The *House* has resolved to adjourn the 27th inst. *Fund* they certainly will, if not *Assume.*

[Boston] *Columbian Centinel*, 21 July; reprinted at Portland, Maine, and Exeter and Portsmouth, New Hampshire.

Letter from New York

The bill for a permanent residence at Potowmack, after ten years' residence at Philadelphia, is completed.

Yesterday the Senate agreed, 14 to 12, to assume twenty one million dollars of the State debts—four million only from Massachusetts. This day they have committed the proposition, and the funding bill, which originated in the house, to a special committee, to be incorporated together. The Senate having stricken from the Bill all the alternatives, and reduced the whole to a single proposition of four per cent, it is doubtful whether the assumption will finally pass or not in that house, as three of the fourteen members have, in positive terms, declared that unless the alternatives are restored, or the four raised to six per cent, they will vote against the whole bill.

This day the house agreed to adjourn on the 27th instant—uncertain.

[Worcester] *Massachusetts Spy*, 23 [22] July; reprinted at Portsmouth, New Hampshire; Boston; and Elizabethtown, New Jersey.

Other Documents

William Davies to Governor Beverley Randolph. ALS, Executive Papers, Vi. Addressed to Richmond, Virginia.

The conference committee on the Settlement of Accounts Act [HR-77] has not met yet.

Thomas Fitzsimons to Miers Fisher. ALS, Fisher Papers, PHi. Place to which addressed not indicated. Most of this letter refers to the Accommodations for Congress at Philadelphia and is printed in that section with Correspondence: Third Session.

Acknowledges Fisher's letter of 12 July; it will be shown only to Clymer; "My Countryman Burke is oftener heared than attended to & never less than when he expresses himself by Illiberal reflections."

Thomas Fitzsimons to Benjamin Rush. Summary of three and one half page ALS, *Parke-Bernet Catalog* 484(1943):item 138.

"On public debt and other national affairs."

George Osborne, Jr. to John Langdon. ALS, Langdon Papers, NhPoA. Written from Portsmouth, New Hampshire; answered.

Asks Langdon to purchase and mail to him, free of postage, a set of the laws of the United States agreed to at the last and present sessions; will pay Langdon on his return home; this will not only oblige Osborne "but do the state essential service" because it "has employed me to print them"; Osborne has forwarded some account to the secretary of war and "requested him to pay the amount to you"; wishes Langdon "all that happiness & felicity, which a life devoted to its country is calculated to produce—and a happy return to the arms of your Family and Friends."

Abishai Thomas to John Gray Blount. ALS, John Gray Blount Papers, Nc-Ar. Addressed to Washington, North Carolina; carried by Dr. (John C.) Osborn. For the full text, see *Blount* 2:82–83.

Assumption will be "loudly opposed no doubt" in the House "but without effect, some of your lukewarm Antis will shift sides" and a debt of $21,000,000, "which Congress have no business to interfere with in my estimation," will be assumed; it is thought Congress will adjourn early next month, to reconvene in December.

Letter from New York. *PP*, 17 July; reprinted at Baltimore. Written at 3 P.M..

"I have the pleasure of informing you of the President's signing the Residence Bill."

Friday, 16 July 1790

William Maclay to Benjamin Rush

Our indefatigable labours are at last crowned with compleat Success the Signature of the President, to the Residence bill was this day, announced to Congress, by one of his private Secretaries [*Tobias Lear*]. The Prospect of the funding System at present in the ~~Sate~~ Senate is. The Principal of the Domestic Debt, funded on the Principles of the Secretary's 3d alternative. the interest which comprizes one third of the Whole. to be funded at three ⅌ Cent. an assumption of State Debts to the amount of 21,000,000. this last I sincerely hope will meet damnation in the House of Representatives. settle & pay is all right, but to promise to pay before we know What. I consider as political Madness. I am with sincere wishes to be soon in Philada.

ALS, Rush Papers, DLC. Addressed to Third Street, Philadelphia; carried by Mr. Brown.

Pamela Sedgwick to Theodore Sedgwick

Oweing to a Slight Cold that I have Taken I am so misseriably feeble that I have hardly Strength to write a line—knowing however that only a line from Stockbridge throu Your Generous Partiallety may affoard You some little amusement amidst the Fatigues of Business—I Cannot omit saying that since you have my dearest Love Entered The Public stage that I wish you the Meekness of a Moses the Wisdom of a SolloMan, and I think the Patience of a Job—may be of use to you—These Party disputes and Public Intrigues I Always hated but my Love since you have Embarkd on this Turbelent ocean I can only wish your bark may be drifted safe to the Haven of Tranquility—since I have been writeing your Favour of the 7 Instant was handed me. from It I learn you are still in Trouble—and know not when this Vexsatious business will be Throu—Heaven grant It may be soon—but Mrs. Shandy[1] Like I am you must think all Submission.

The Caricature Picture[2] is Truly Laughable but greived I am that the General Goverment should at this Early Period be made a Subject of Buffoonery—I really Tremble for the week State of our Goverment—and Think Such Ill Judged Ridecule may be Big with fatal Consequences.

The Season Grows so warm that I fear the Air of N. York will prove unfavourable To Health This is an additional reason with me to wissh the seccion may soon very soon be Ended. after the longe Scene of Bissiness and Turbulence You have gone throu—I flatter my self that the Tranquil Seens of Domestick sameness may not prove Irksome To my beloved Friend for a few months—The fond Prattle of your Little ones will be Entertaining to you—and the no small Injoyment of One who dearly Loves You will be pleasing to your Generous Heart.

Master Theodore has not forgotton his Pappa But is so Taken up with working in the Hay that He cannot Spare a moments Time—Harry & Robert have little Thoughts About Pappa Robert can walk Tollerably well and is very desirous to show evry one how well he can walk and how smart he can run—Your Nephu Theodore is still here Waiting for the Moveing of the Waters[3]—he has receivd no Awnser to the Letter he wrote to you as yet—and He is So low Spirited that I have not had the Heart to Tell him what you said in your Letter to me of the 30th Instant—I wait Still hopeing That Some thing favourable may Turn up for him—Adieu my Dearest best Love may Heaven soon return you to your Long expecting Truly affectionate Pamela Sedgwick.

[*P. S.*] If this Letter should reach you before you Leve N. York [*lined out*] I hope It may not Eliza prays her pappa to get a pattern of Lite Colourd Calico [*torn*] self a Gown—wishes it may be a Small figure—and [*torn*] by her Pappa will you be so good as to bring me ~~a few~~ 6 or 7 Y~~ards~~ds. of dark Colourd Calico.

ALS, Sedgwick Papers, MHi. Written from Stockbridge, Massachusetts.

[1] The submissive wife and mother of Tristram Shandy in Lawrence Sterne's novel.
[2] See Theodore to Pamela Sedgwick, 4 July, above.
[3] That is, he was waiting for Sedgwick's help in securing a federal appointment; from the biblical allusion to angels healing the sick at the pool of Bethesda (John 5:4).

Joseph Stanton, Jr. to James Sheldon

The Temporary & permanent Residence of Congress is fixed at last, the Latter to Commence at the Patomack 10 years hence, The former at philadelphia Untill that time Arives, It has engrossed the Attention of Congress a whole week, Before it past Both Houses, Great warmth in the debates, Between Two rival Cities, New york & [*and P*]hiladelphia, It made me think of Some of Our Assembly proceedings, I wish'd not to leave N. york so Abruptly, Gratitude Seems to make it Necessary to have given another Sessions to N. york for their Exertions to Accomidate Congress, and their Respectfull treatment to the members, But the question is merely Local, The Grand point is for Congress to attend to the Intrest of the Union Let them Set where they may, the funding Bill & the assumption of the State debts is now on the Anvil, They are questions of Great magnitude, I Sincerely wish you had a Voice in the Determination of them, Sir a Line from you (by way of advice) Will have Every Attention paid.
P. S.
I have Sent you two New york papers for your Amusement & Information; I expect [*torn*] will Adjurn By the first of August. ***
excuse the Scrawl I have not time to Coppy It.

ALS, Dreer Collection, PHi. Addressed to Richmond, Rhode Island; franked. This is probably the two page ALS, dated 1790 and summarized in *The Collector*, May 1912, as "describing the vote for the transfer of the government from New York to Philadelphia."

John Vining to Walter Stewart

I have but a moment to avail myself of the Intelligence from senate, and to communicate to you the Principles of their Report of this Morning, which will furnish you with a probable ground of conjecture as to the Event of the Business, at least in that branch of the Legislature—It is said that a compromise of 4 instead of 3 per Cent will possibly take place—but of this

I will inform you more particularly when the Stage which carries the mail will allow me more Time.

The residence bill was handed to the Senate in propria Forma about 1/2 past Eleven this Morning, and the *report* is that you have gained the Hut from Meredith, but as he doubts, we must wait the decision of a more favorable Moment then the present to make the Enquiry—when you shall be informed of your success.

ALS, Stewart Bound Volume, NHi. Addressed to Philadelphia; answered 22 July.

Newspaper Article

Whether the President of the United States has signed *the bill*—was *the question* in all companies yesterday, and on which many minds appeared to be much agitated. A certain female personage was heard to say, that she expected soon to leave the city—says one. Aye, says another—then the matter is all over—the bill is signed without any doubt! You blockhead, says a third, do you really suppose the President will sign it—he never will—for an adjournment can be constitutionally effected without the agency of the President, and his feelings spared on so delicate a subject.

Bets are still open, at various rates, though *some* say it was signed on Monday last.

NYJ, 16 July.

Letter from Norfolk, Virginia

Having lately been on a jaunt to Cape-Henry, I could not but admire at the ill-directed parsimony, or rather down right negligence of the people of this state, or neighbourhood, in not having taken some method of preventing the foundation of their formerly intended light-house from being entirely covered up by the sands, that are continually drifted about and constantly accumulated by the winds on this Cape. At present there is not a trace of that work remaining, and possibly the expence of digging to it through the sand now heaped several feet above it, would be more than the value thereof when found; so that the federal government will have to begin all of anew, and at a place, too, where the article of stone is so extremely remote and scarce. It would perhaps be proper to hint, that the European new improvements in light-houses ought to be adopted on the American coasts. Lenses and reflectors render the light much larger and more brilliant,[1] and will therefore be seen at a much greater distance than the lights now in use, always appearing the same in a storm or calm, and not flashing and disappearing, like fire stirred or affected by the wind, as is the case with those that direct our mariners at present.

NYDA, 2 August.

[1] In 1784 Swiss chemist Aimé Argand patented an oil lamp in which a single wick emitted as much light as seven candles and which gave a more steady light as well. He later improved the strength of this light with parabolic reflectors.

Other Documents

George Clymer to Henry Clymer. ALS, Miscellaneous Manuscripts, DLC. Written at 10 P.M.

Legal business; the Residence Bill is at last completed by the President's signature; the Senate is again on the subject of assumption, which he supposes will come before the House in a few days; "it is this which prevents me from taking a trip home to morrow which I had some thoughts of."

Thomas Fitzsimons to Miers Fisher. ALS, Fisher Papers, PHi. Addressed to Philadelphia; franked. The remainder of the letter concerns accommodations for Congress at Philadelphia and is printed in that section with Correspondence: Third Session.

"Our [*Merchants*] Seamans bill has passed & we have sent to the Senate a New Collection bill [*HR-82*]—Which I trust will Remedy most of the inconveniencys Experienced from the Old."

Henry Wynkoop to Reading Beatty. ALS, Wynkoop Papers, PDoBHi. Addressed to "Falsington," Bucks County, Pennsylvania.

Adjournment was postponed the day before until 27 July; the funding of the debt and the "consequent revenue Systems are yet far from being completed, Report was yesterday that the President had signed the residence Bill, but no official Information was given."

GUS, 17 July; reprinted at New York City (*NYDG*, 19 July).

"We hear that a committee of the Senate reported on the funding business yesterday—which report was accepted, and is in substance as follows, viz. Principal of the Domestic Debt of the United States, 2/3ds at 6 pr. cent. the other 1/3d. at 6 pr. cent. in 10 years, agreeable to the fourth alternative in the Secretary's Report. Indents at a present interest of 3 pr. cent. State Debts 1/3d. at 3 pr. cent. the other 2/3ds. on the same terms as the principal of the debt of the United States."

Saturday, 17 July 1790

John Brown Cutting to John Adams

I embrace the opportunity afforded me, by a vessel that sails to day for Philadelphia to send you some newspapers and to tell You that the condition of the american seamen here claims the immediate attention of the Government of the United States.

In the absence of any person invested with consular or ministerial authority from Congress—I cou'd not endure to see my fellow citizens first subjected to the outrage's of british press gangs—and then drag'd on board british ships of war to be scourged at the mere will and base discretion of every mean or malignant petty officer of the navy into the performance of ~~duties~~ services which our native seamen dread and detest—In this crisis I came forward and did and have done and am continually doing all that a zealous persevering individual cou'd or can do in his private capacity.

It is now necessary to state that every seaman of the United States is impress'd for and retain'd in the services of his britannic majesty as a british subject—unless the Captain who ship'd him in America will positively swear that he was actually born in the United States and is a subject of them. No Commander of a british bottom in the American Trade can take such an oath: consequently every american seaman who happen'd to arrive here since the 4th of last May in a british bottom is now on board a british ship of war. Several applications have been made to me by seamen in this predicament—and some of these accompanied with strong evidence that the applicants were really natives of the United States. In the next place there are several natives of G. Britain and Ireland who command american bottoms—but are unable—possibly unwilling to identify their american seamen by such an oath. And lastly when an american commander of an american bottom has sworn point blank that such and such seamen are natives & subjects of America—And in consequence thereof I have press'd the Lords of the Admiralty for their discharge and for a written exemption against another in press and have obtain'd both—both have been violated—by a new press-gang. On Wednesday evening last for instance such discharges and protections were totally disregarded: almost every american seaman in the thames—as well as mates of vessels and apprentices—were swept off in the night—some of these have been hardly treated by inferior officers of the british navy.

It must be owned there are intrinsic difficulties in some cases to furnish even reasonable proof that a particular seaman is a subject of the United States but in some of the cases to which I allude the most clear and absolute proof had been given and in the manner prescribed by the Lords of the Admiralty themselves.

Perhaps no immediate remedy that wou'd be effectual can be invented by Congress. A palliative wou'd be—the appointment of a consul here who might substitute prudence and management sustain'd by a suitable authority from the american government—[*lined out*] in lieu of *clear rules of proceeding and loftier powers* than coud be now exercised here with utility to our country.

Clad with that mild and modest capacity I am vain enough to believe that even I shoud be enabled just now, to render the United States essential service—which the experience and local knowledge of the past six weeks have afforded me peculiar facilities for performing in future But at any rate, I feel it my indispensable duty to continue exerting every nerve in endeavour to procure the release of as many of these impressed american seamen as possible Before the late rigourous impress I had paved the way for liberating many of them—who have returned home rejoicing Nor do I now despond of procuring the discharge of some—to the birth and citizenship of whom their commanders are this day again to swear. Patience, vigilance prudence and unwearied perseverence—are our only weapons.

I consider a war between Britain & Spain is inevitable—between Prussia and Austria as in the highest degree probable *Manifestos* are expected to be published this evening.

I write this in the greatest haste.

ALS, Adams Family Manuscript Trust, MHi. Written from London.

Governor Arthur Fenner to Theodore Foster

I had [*lined out*] made a rough draft of a short letter to you before I ~~had~~ red. yours of the 14th the post left providence before I finished it you will see by that my sentiments respecting the Motion you mention. I have enclosed that letter for want of time to Copy it. Your letter of the 14th contains matters of Consequence too great to answer immediately You are sensible of the Situation of this State or the People, the assumption will alarm them very much and how far it will do for you to proceed in that matter I am at present at a Loss. Your standing requires great caution it is my opinion at present that you had better wave every matter that can be waved and not very essentially affect the Interest of the State. it appears to me however that it will be to the Interest of the State if the Assumption is finally carried for the State to take a share in the matter as most certainly we shall pay our proportion of the other State demands out of the Monies arising from our Revenue chest but as long as you can pospone the matter do it by all means I shall take oppertunities to consult our Friends in the Country and communicate to you their sentiments as soon as possible This is post morning and I cannot write you but a short sketch of my mind I recd. your letter on sunday evening and have been so much engaged in my Farming Bussiness that I could not attend to write you fully but will attend to the subject of your letter and give you an Answer fully as soon as I have consulted Friends.

I want you to write a few lines to some of our country friends—among the rest to Benj. Sands of Newshoreham it will please him he intends to be a Deputy the next choise.

I seem at present strong in the Faith that you will be re elected but as I mentioned in my other letter here enclosed it is a Lottery—perhaps you will be here timely if you come home before the setting of the Assembly it may help some I suppose the choise can be had or made at september Sessions and perhaps it may be the best to make it then—This letter you must also excuse it is Wrote as fast as I can talk almost and have not time to copy it.

[*Enclosure*]

I recd. your two letters with the Newspapers and am much Obliged by the information through the Channel of your Letters and papers. I am very sorry that you was so unfortunate in the *Lottery*[1] however I shall exert my little influence to get you re-elected it said that J. Hazard has a mind to try again ~~but~~ it will be in vain in my opinion, your Chance I think to be good, The Representative is not fully settled—yet [*Thomas*] Holden, [*Job*] Comstock & [*Peleg*] Arnold are talked of by the Majority. I am informed that J[*abez*]. Bowen intends to try his Luck The Newport Gentlemen say they have no Person in View to serve in that Capacity: if that is really so there will be no difficulty in getting in one of the Majority. And in my Opinion, J. Comstock stands the foremost or in other words the most likely to succeed.[2]

The Congress ~~are~~ is looked upon generally as the Minority looked upon our general Assembly you will see by some of the Boston & Connecticut Papers that they are uneasy. the removeal from New York is considered here as a Partial, & ungrateful Act such as Body like Congress ought Not to know You mentioned in your letter that you intended to lay a plan before the Senate respecting the Public Debt in which you expected considerable support.

Permit me to Caution you respecting the matter the motions made ~~is~~ are generally known ~~from~~ by whom made, let your plan be such as will have a tendency to lessen the Value of the Public Securities and it will answer, but even if it will have that effect in the end, and at the first View it appears to Establish them, it will render you unpopular You must be very Cautious how you proceed if you could be the means of giving the securities an Irish Hoist[3] it ~~may~~ will help you in your reelection—I never see the Minority so much Cast down as they now appear to be, They are very complasant & Free, wish to lay all party a side &c. &c.—you know them—be you not deceived by them if they should correspond with you by Letter—The Appointment of our worthy Friend [*Ebenezer*] Thompson has given some of the Merchts. (I mean those who used to run goods) a Violent Shock they are disappointed, if [*William*] Peck had been appointed in my Oppinion the Revenue would not have been worth to Congress so much as it is now by thousands of Dollars the appointment is a perfect Check upon ~~the~~ their designs and has put them out more than any thing that has taken place. I am so much unwell that I cannot attend ~~much~~ half my time to my Bussiness. I am in hopes of getting beter so that I can secure your Election my efforts shall not be wanting but it is a Lottery almost you know but I have heretofore been rather fortunate than otherways in those Lotteries. Please to give my ~~kind~~ love to your worthy Colleague [*Stanton*] and informed him, I recd. his Letter and shall answer it as soon as I have any thing that I can communicate I have nothing now but ~~the~~ what I have communicated to you which you can communicate to him or that of it which you please he wished to know how we were going on in the Representative way.

Your Family, Mine and all our Friends are well. You must excuse ~~this~~ this broken letter as I have not time to enter into a proper Chain of the Bussiness I wish to communicate have therefore only given hints I shall in my next perhaps attend to the Substance.

P. S. This was my Rough draught but the Post is waiting therefore cannot Copy it excuse imperfections.

ALSs, both written as drafts, the enclosure first, Foster Papers, RHi. Written from Providence, Rhode Island; delivered from the post office by A. Foster on the evening of 24 July.

---

[1] Foster drew a two year Senate term when he and Stanton were classed.

[2] The election of Rhode Island's first Representative, Benjamin Bourn, took place on 31 August.

[3] A kick.

Benjamin Goodhue to Insurance Offices

A new tonage Act [*HR-78*] has passed in which provision is made, that Vessels with Registers going from district to district in the same state or an adjoining State are exempted from tonnage, restitution is also order'd to be made of foreign tonage where its been paid by our Vessels—likewise a new Collection law [*HR-82*] has pass'd the House and will probably the Senate, in which many inconveniences are remedied—a new Coasting Act [*HR-89*] will probably pass before We adjourn—a new impost [*Ways and Means*] Act is before the house augmenting the duties agreably to what you see publish'd in the papers, but I hardly think it will ever go through both Houses, if it should fail as I expect, its uncertain what means may be adopted to supply.

The Senate have the week past had under consideration the funding and assumption, a majority of whom were of opinion that 4 ⅌ Ct. was as great an interest as the circumstances of the Country would warrant an engagement to pay, others strenuously insisted on a greater interest, and this difference of opinion for some time had the appearance of frustrating the whole bussines in that Body, a large Committee was chosen to see if an accommodation could not be made, after much difficulty they agreed to report as follows, and which will probably obtain in Senate on Monday—the principal of the debt of the U. States say, 27,000,000, to have 2/3ds funded at 6 ⅌ Ct. and in 10 years to have 26 dollrs. funded at a like interest agreably to the 3d proposition in the Secry's. report, the Indents or interest due say, 13,000,000 to be funded at a simple 3 ⅌ Ct.—debts to be assumed 2/3ds. to be funded the same as the principal of the contin'l. debt, the other 1/3 on a simple 3 ⅌ Ct.—the Assumption is to be annexed and form a part of the funding bill, the amount of the debts to be assumed 21,000,000[1] of which Massachts. 4,000,000—{the above is the effect of compromise in the Senate, and} I hope will meet the acceptance of our House, tho' I expect much opposition—the Senate as {I'm inform'd are much fixed and will not materialy receede from those propositions}—I anxiously hope that an imprudent pertinacity of opinion on those great objects may not be the means of postponing this bussines to the next session. for we have spent time enough to have it brought to an issue—Congress are weary of the session and its not probable they can be Kept together more then 2 or 3 weeks longer.

ALS, Goodhue Papers, NNS. Addressed to Salem, Massachusetts; franked; postmarked 18 July.

[1] To this point, the letter was printed almost verbatim in the [Massachusetts] *Salem Gazette*, 27 July, and reprinted at Dover, New Hampshire, and Hartford, Connecticut. After this point, only the words in wavy brackets appeared in the newspaper version.

Benjamin Lincoln to Theodore Sedgwick

I have been honoured with your favour covering ~~your~~ the report for a new collection law {*HR-82*} The thirty third Section[1] I do not comprehend. It is said that there shall be allowed for *draught* & *tare* for the first hundred weight or one hundred and twelve pounds one pound This cannot mean the tare of the cash if it doth not it will not agree with the Proviso. By Sec. 24[2] The oaths to the Master Consignee &c. are to be administred by the Collector in presence of the Naval officer this will clog the business I do not know what security is to be derived from the measure The evidence of a mans being sworn ~~always~~ allways attends the proceeding for the oath is written and subscribed by the person taking it. As to the business of ascertaining the amount of the duties upon articles the quantity of which are not ascertained In that case we take a general bond for a sum sufficient to cover the duties the condition of which is that they will in twenty day pay or give security for the whole amount of the duties arising on the Cargo imported in the vessell described There seems to be some Militation between the close of Sec. 28[3] and the proviso in Sec. 31[4]—Sec. 40[5] provides that for all teas imported from China the duties shall be secured by giving bonds for ~~tuelve~~ twelve months or depositing the teas if the teas are deposited the duties cannot be collected untill the experation of Eighteen months this will operate wrong as it will in this case be for the interest of the importer to deposit his teas which is by no means as safe as bonds for in case of accident to the teas the whole duty may be lost Teas are an article liable to damage I think the idea should be reversed bonds taken for Eighteen months or if the importer be urged & insisted upon a deposit that it might be sold at the expiration of one year In the last clause of the 25 Sec.[6] it is enacted that all good &c. so unladed or delivered shall be liable to forfeiture unless the goods are landed & they are not liable by this clause to secure. I think in some cases it ought to be other wise when for instance the master of a vessel is owner of the loading and part of it has been landed ~~accord~~ contrary to Law by which the vessel shall be liable should not the remainder of the Cargo being the property of the Captain be liable also.

I thank you for your frequent communications pray continue them You cannot be more sorry than I am at the impatience of our country they will however come right I trust Our members are not unpopular No members from this State to Congress ever I presume stood better with the wise & good.

ALS, Sedgwick Papers, MHi. Written from Boston; franked; postmarked 18 July. Lincoln's discussion of provisions of a Collection Bill [HR-82] under consideration in the House of Representatives makes it clear that Sedgwick had sent him a copy of the bill. Given the length of the bill and the date of this letter, the editors believe that the copy sent to Lincoln had to be a printing of the bill as introduced on 8 July. The Senate later added a section (23) to the bill, thus changing all the section numbers after that point.

[1] Section 34 of the final act.
[2] Section 25 of the final act.
[3] Section 29 of the final act.
[4] Section 32 of the final act.
[5] Section 41 of the final act.
[6] Section 26 of the final act.

Henry Marchant to Elbridge Gerry

Yesterday I recd. my Commission [*as Rhode Island district judge*] and the Time is very short, before the Court is to be held—I find by the Act of Congress [*Judiciary Act*] the Judge is to provide a Seal for the court, and I wish to avail myself of Mr. Gerry's Taste and Judgment as to the Device and the Artist to be imployed—I would not have it large—I should think an Inch over sufficient, cut in Silver or Steel as may be thought best. I should like the Arms of this State being an Anchor, somewhere introduced—Perhaps as a Crest—with the Word Hope over it. A pair of Scales in a blue Field suspended by a Hand in even Ballance, or such other Device as you shall think proper. Round the Edge I would have the Words *Rhode Island District* I find no Provision made for procuring the Seal, nor for Fees of the Grand Jury for Their Attendance, Our State Grand Jurys are paid by an order from the Clerk of the Court on the Genl. Treasury, I should think it might be by an Order drawn on the Collector. Nor is any Provision made for a Tender, Messenger or Waiter upon the Court; one at least during the sitting of the Court must be had—I would be obliged if Mr. Gerry would make Enquiry of Judge [*James*] Duane how He has done, or what is to be expected—How Charges arising in a Criminal Prosecution, and there are many which no Table of Fees ever provided for, are to be paid—especially when the Prosecution fails, or the Prisoners are unable to pay—Also how the Goalers Fees and the Sustenance he affords to Prisoners are to be paid—Our Treasury was always open to such Charges where the State was a party—The Seal is wanted immediately, and I will see you paid on the first Notice, or Receipt of it. Well my Friend pardon this Trouble—accept of my Thanks, for every Instance of His Friendship.

ALS, Gerry Papers, MHi. Written from Newport, Rhode Island. Franked; postmarked.

Benjamin Rush to James Madison

Count [*Paolo*] Andreani is just such a man as you have described him to be in your letter.[1] Is it not disgraceful to our Country to suffer its natural productions to be explored & described only by foreigners? Are we safe in committing so important a part of our history to men who are imperfectly acquainted with our language, and who from receiving their first impressions of us thro' the medium of British publications, cherish prejudices against us unfriendly to successful inquiries After truth [*lined out*] upon all Subjects?

The Residence bill gives general Satisfaction in Philadelphia. your Goverment here will be less sophisticated than in New York. There is an *Aer loci*, which governs like the *lex loci* in all countries.[2] The atmosphere of Philada. is *diphlogisticated* from all *foreign* mixtures. From the influence of the Quakers & Germans on our manners, There is perhaps more republicanism in our city, than in any other city in the United States.

I hear that the Senate have voted to pay 3 ℔ cent on the domestic debt, & the remaining 3 in 7 or 10 years. This is the least mischievous mode of adopting an unjust debt. It will prevent the Certificates from suddenly drawing off all the Cash of our Country from Agriculture—Commerce & manufactures. It will moreover prevent our country from being depopulated by our cities. It will prevent innumerable bankruptcies, & imigrations—and lastly it will prevent a thousand Suits which would be immediately commenced against honest debtors to employ the money when Obtained from them in purchasing Certificates. In short—it will give an *equitable level* to every Species of property in our Country, and thereby render the Goverment the equal guardian of the interests of all its citizens.

ALS, Madison Papers, DLC. Written from Philadelphia; postmarked 19 July.

---

[1] Madison's letter of 5 July, calendared above, described Count Paolo Andreani at the outset of his North American tour as being motivated by a "philosophical curiosity," which had already earned him a reputation among scientific circles of the European Enlightenment (*PJM* 13:263). After a six week crossing from England and a brief stopover in Halifax, Nova Scotia, Andreani's North American sojourn began with his arrival in New York City on 6 June. Apart from a side trip to New Haven, Connecticut, in mid-July, Andreani remained in New York until 14 August, when he sailed up the Hudson and penetrated the Mohawk River Valley into the heart of Iroquois country. His Italian language journal of the month long trip recorded significant ethnographic observations on Native Americans and the Shakers of northern New York State, which he circulated (in manuscript form) among interested acquaintances in Europe. Andreani spent the winter of 1790–91 in Philadelphia before embarking again for Canada via the Hudson, where he traveled counterclockwise along the Great Lakes shorelines as far as Minnesota before returning via Detroit and Lake Erie back to Canada in the fall of 1791. Andreani was elected to the American Philosophical Society while in Philadelphia again briefly before embarking for England in June 1792. For extensive background on Andreani's travels in 1790–92, and the translated and edited text of his research trip in New York in 1790, see Cesare Marino and Karim M. Tiro, eds., *Along the Hudson and Mohawk: The 1790 Journey of Count Paolo Andreani* (Philadelphia, 2006).

[2] The "atmosphere of a place" is as decisive as the "law of place" in influencing political culture.

William Smith (S.C.) to [*Edward Rutledge*]

Your broth[*er*][1] [*torn*] yesterday & is well.

In the Senate, the Assumption being carried, the funding Bill was taken up & both referred to a Committee of compromise, viz., Butler, King Morris, Elsworth, Strong Read, R. H. Lee—the three first for 6 per cent—the three next for 4—all six for the Assumption; the last against the Assumption: they brought in a report yesterday morning; the result of mutual concessions; it is as follows; viz., That the principal of the continental debt be funded on the ~~third~~ terms contained in the third alternative of the Secys. Rept. (viz. $^2/_3$ds now funded at 6 per cent & the remainder at the end of 7 years) and that the arrears of interest including Indents on the said domestic debt be funded at 3 per Cent;

Principal, say	27,000,000	at 6 pr. Ct.
Interest & Indents	13,000,000	at 3 pr. Ct.
	40,000,000	

That the amount of the debts of the respective states which may be assumed by the U.S. be funded as follows, two thirds on the terms contained in the third alternative (as above) & the other third at an interest of 3 per cent—

on the third alternative	14,000,000
at 3 per cent	7,000,000
	21,000,000

This report was agreed to yesterday; Morris, however, is against it. Should he persist in his opposition, the Senate will be equally divided & the V. Presdt. will give the casting vote for it: the votes now stand thus:

Ayes—	Noes
Langdon	Wingate
Elsworth	Morris
Strong	Maclay
Johnson	Basset
Dalton	Henry
Schyler	Lee
King	Walker
Patterson	Johnston
Elmer	Foster
Read	Stanton
Carrol	Hawkins
Butler	Gunn
Izard—13.	Few—13.

There are hopes however of Morris & perhaps Few, but slender ones. We expect to carry it in our house but by a bare majority. both houses are full—not a single member absent.
We are 63–62 on the floor,[2] & we rec[*eived*] 32 without Sumpter, which is a majy. of ~~one~~ two.

We hear that a Pilot-boat is dispatched by the Speculators to buy up on these prospects in Charleston [*South Carolina*]—exert yourself to prevent it, & insert something in the prints to warn people from selling at 3/ or 4/ when they may get soon perhaps 10/. We have agreed to adjourn the 27th. but I imagine the business will not be accomplished by that time. The Excise Bill [*Duties on Distilled Spirits Bill HR-62*] being rejected, we have added one third to the Impost much against my consent the [*Ways and Means*] Bill has passed our house.

ALS, Pinckney Family Papers, DLC. Place to which addressed not indicated. This is the conclusion of a letter begun on 14 July, above.

[1] John Rutledge, Jr.
[2] When the House sat as a COWH the member off the floor was its chair; otherwise, the member off the floor was the Speaker.

William Smith (S.C.) to George Washington

Mr. Smith (S.C.) begs leave to recommend to the notice of the President of the United States the following gentlemen who have applied for the following offices; viz.,
For the office of Commissioner in the State of S. Cara. under the funding Bill;
Mr. Peter Bonnetheau.
Mr. Daniel Stevens.
For the office of Inspector of the Revenue, should the Excise Bill pass;
Mr. Edward Trescot.
Col. John Mitchell.
Mr. Daniel Stevens.
Mr. Peter Bonnetheau.
For the Command of one of the Revenue Cutters;
Capt. William Hall.
Capt. Jacob Milligan.

AN, Washington Papers, DLC.

Ebenezer Thompson to Theodore Foster

My last was by the post which hope is safe to hand. Since which I have had the pleasure of perusing your last letter to the Governor [*Arthur Fenner*]—I cannot see the propriety of the Senates apportionment of the several sums to be assumed of the State Debts—Massachusetts they say shall be 4,000,000 Dollars in the same proportion Rhode Island should be 500,000 New York is 1,600,000 dollars and by the best account they do not at present owe half the sum and I understand Maryland is in the same predicament, most of the other States except Rhode Island is apportioned nearly agreeable to former requisitions of the Old congress—I have not had any opportunity to talk in particular of this matter with the Governor: but I think in case the State Debts are assum'd in whole or in part by the General Government, which I hope will not be done, it will be most prudent to Insist that this State shall be put nearly on the same footing, with regard to the money that may be loaned from its inhabitants holding State Evidences as Massachusetts and the other States—(New Hampshire an exception) which will make our State full 500,000 Dollars—but in any instance it will be very impolitic for our Senators to Vote for the assumption: on the contrary to oppose it in all its Stages. from what principles the Committe of Senate apportioned to our State only 200,000 Dollars I cannot Devine nor do I see what led them to the particular sums as express'd in the report, it could not be from Estimate of the Debt due from each State to individuals if so Conneticutt and some other States would have been much larger sums—Since writing the above I have had some conversation with the governor and his Sentiments on the foregoing appeared to be nearly Similar with my own.

ALS, Foster Papers, RHi. Place from which written not indicated.

Thomas B. Wait to George Thatcher

The time is now drawing near when I am to have the happiness of seeing, feeling, and conversing with you. and I am looking anxiously for the period—for I have much, very much to say to you; and on a subject~~s~~ too that pretty nearly concerns you.

I have my doubts whether you will be reelected. Opposition arises from quarters ~~from~~ whence it was the least expected. *Ambition* and *Friendship* are very unneighbourly passions—they will not live lovingly together in the same habitation—where the former prevails there is no room possitively no room for the latter. You may, perhaps, long have *believed* this doctrine—Now you are about to *experience* the truth of it. But no more of this matter. "*It makes me angry while I sing.*"[1]

There are two littel pieces of business which I would thank you to attend to—*One* is to enquire the price of an iron screw and nut suitable for a Book Binder. I have lately seen them advertised in N. york. The *other* is, to ~~acquire~~ procure a specimen and the prices of the Types manufactured in Newyork; and also, to [*lined out*] deliver the inclosed to Mr. [*Adam Gerard*] Mappa, and receive his answer in writing on the same piece of paper.

Do my friend attend to these requests; and write an answer by the first post.

ALS, Chamberlain Collection, MB. Written from Portland, Maine; postmarked Portsmouth, New Hampshire, 19 July.

[1] From "A Cradle Hymn" (1715) by the British clergyman and famous hymn writer Isaac Watts (1674–1748).

A Marylander to Mr. Hayes

I FIND that our town has lost the permanent residence of Congress, in the lower House, by a majority of *three*, and what is peculiarly provoking, we have lost it in the lower House by *four* of our own members, out of *six*. Can they ever expect, when in Baltimore, to be invited to any gentleman's house, or that they will not be hissed and execrated, whenever they walk the streets? Some injuries *may* be forgiven, but not those, which are *irreparable*. Baltimore-town might have been benefited, and our own members prevented it. Had it been done by members from other states, it might have been borne with some patience. I do not consider the question on partial grounds, but on a broad bottom. The eastern members originally thought of fixing the permanent residence of Congress on the Delaware, and the southern ones on the Patowmack; therefore, on principles of accommodation, some intermediate place ought to have been agreed to, which was either this town, if a mart was preferred, or on the banks of the Susquehannah, if an inland situation was more eligible. Mr. *Gale* was very instrumental in defeating the fixing the permanent residence on the Susquehannah last fall, which surprised people, as in this state Senate he had ever been deemed a warm friend to Baltimore town, and it is not very pleasing to find an enemy, where one expects a friend. He was originally the favorite member of our whole delegation, while Mr. *Seney*, whom we hardly knew, has turned out our warm friend. Messrs. [*D.*] *Carroll, Contee*, and *Stone* were never expected to be our friends, but Mr. *Henry* was, and we are unhappily deceived in him, and the Patowmack interest very agreeably, considering how strenuously they opposed *his* appointment as a Senator.

The other Senator from Maryland [*C. Carroll*] is a man of talents, integrity and character; but as he is known never to lose sight of his own emolument, it was always expected, he would be in favor of Patowmack, on account of a large manor he holds on the Monocacy, which communicates with that river, and of course will eventually enhance the value of his lands there; whereas his personal property near this place, is *tolerably* well secured, as far as mortgages, bonds and security can do it. It is adding insult to injury to say, that in opposing Baltimore, *he* made a sacrifice of *his own interest*. When Maryland was convulsed on the subject of paper money, several years ago, and this gentleman was attacked in the papers, and represented as dangerous from his opulence, he answered it, and among other things asserted, that only *five* of our state Senators were indebted to him.[1] It is to be hoped, that his colleague and our member from the lower district of the Eastern-Shore [*Gale*], were not *among them*, or if so, that they were not thereby in the least influenced to vote against us. This insinuation has been thrown out in many private companies, and ought to be refuted, if untrue.

Many people say, if (what was termed) the antifederal ticket had been carried, Baltimore might have stood a better chance;[2] but except in putting Mr. [*William Vans*] *Murray* in the place of Mr. *Gale*, we should not have been benefited. Mr. *Seney* was in both tickets; Mr. [*John F.*] *Mercer*, as a Virginian, and holding property in that state, would have voted for the Patowmack as well as Mr. *Contee*, and so would Mr. [*George*]*Dent* and Mr.[*Abraham*] *Faw*. Mr. [*Samuel*] *Sterett* would act as Mr. *Smith* has done. Had Col. [*Uriah*] *Forrest* been our Senator, he would have advocated the Patowmack, and Mr. *Henry* and Mr. *Gale* entertain similar sentiments on that head. Had not party rage run so high in our Assembly, and the antifederalists insisted on single districts, our present exceptionable mode of representation would not have taken place. The federalists proposed four members from the Western-Shore at large, and two from the Eastern-Shore, in which case Mr. *Sterett* would have been chosen, and Messrs. *Contee* and *Stone* not even thought of. Our present representation in Assembly was negotiated last fall by gentlemen, who foresaw the necessity of uniting the town and county in support of a ticket favorable to our interest, for Congress before next October, and prepare us for turning out such of our members, as might prove inimical. The Patowmack interest will probably endeavour, if possible, to revive the distinctions of federal and anti, in order to divide us, while they will be unanimous. As the government is now established, and explanatory amendments to the constitution are ratified, all causes of political difference are done away, and we shall be stupid indeed, if caught in such a cobweb snare. Any Assemblyman, which may benefit from this town, will agree upon a successor to Mr. *Carroll*, as a Senator, who declines serving any longer.

If Baltimore-town and its vicinity, act with proper spirit, the same exertions will be made to turn out the four members, who have proved themselves decided enemies, as in the election of October, 1788. Any man, who votes for either of them, must be considered as the inveterate enemy to the prosperity of Baltimore-town. Members of Congress ought to consider themselves as representing the state at large, not any particular spot in it. The Pennsylvania delegates acted in that manner, and have performed their duty; they agreed (as one of their members told me) to be unanimous in supporting the establishment of the permanent or temporary residence of Congress in *any part* of the state, which should be advocated by members from other states, they moved together last fall for the Susquehannah, as the permanent residence, and lately for Philadelphia, as the temporary one, and if our Senators and members had but considered themselves as representing Maryland at large, instead of representing only such people as reside on or near the banks of the Patowmack, we should have had the permanent residence *here*. When members act contrary to the sense and interest of a *majority* of their constituents, is it not a species of high treason? Ought not such men not only to be left out as members of Congress, but even by law expressly and individually disqualified from ever holding even the office of constable among us? They are certainly to be considered more as enemies to Maryland, than nonjurors[3] were during the war, because the nonjurors never had it in their power to injure the state, and their treble taxes did more good than personal service.

[Baltimore] *Maryland Gazette*, 20 July, edited by John Hayes. Written from Baltimore.

[1] Samuel Chase attacked Carroll in an anonymous letter printed in the [Baltimore] *Maryland Journal* on 2 March 1787. Carroll replied in the issue of 16 March; in it he stated that "four" state senators were indebted to him. In addition to Henry and Gale, D. Carroll was also a member of the Maryland Senate at the time.

[2] The reference is to Maryland's first congressional election in early January 1789.

[3] Someone who refused to take an oath of allegiance to a government.

Other Documents

Francis Cabot to Benjamin Goodhue. ALS, Letters to Goodhue, NNS. Written from Salem, Massachusetts.

Office seeking: Joshua Orne as collector for Marblehead, Massachusetts, to replace Richard Harris, whose death "as it respects the revenue, I confess I rejoice at"; Cabot's brother George has written Hamilton on Orne's behalf and will write Goodhue if time allows.

Richard Curson to Sarah Livingston Jay. ALS, Ridley Papers, MHi. Written from Baltimore on Saturday night; place to which addressed not indicated. The recipient's identity is based on internal evidence and the endorsement's handwriting.

Reports that Congress will go to Philadelphia for the next session; "If you dont like it, blame your friend Mr. Morris."

Benjamin Goodhue to Samuel Phillips, Jr. No copy known; acknowledged in Phillips to Goodhue, 29 July.

Stephen Goodhue to Benjamin Goodhue. FC:lbk, Goodhue Family Papers, MSaE. Written from Salem, Massachusetts.

Expects Congress will have adjourned before the letter reaches him; Fanny (Frances Goodhue) and the children all well; reports on crops; refers to newspapers for political news; "we do not Expect the State debts will be assumed but hope they will be assumed to quiet the mind of the People."

Joseph Howell, Jr. to Josiah Harmar. ALS, Harmar Papers, MiU-C. Place to which addressed not indicated.

Those favoring the removal of Congress from New York "have been Caricatured particularly Mr. Morris ~~to~~ on whom the Citizens of this place lay all the blame"; those opposed to removal expected "that the President would not sign the Law, however their hopes are now *done over*"; Creek peace treaty delegation under Alexander McGillivray expected to arrive in New York that night.

Henry Marchant to John Adams. ALS, Adams Family Manuscript Trust, MHi. Written from Newport, Rhode Island.

Asks whether a letter to the President acknowledging his appointment (as federal district judge) is expected, in addition to Marchant's letter to Jefferson acknowledging receipt of the commission; asks whether his letter to the President in care of Adams, and other letters from friends supporting his appointment, were ever delivered; thanks for the "essential and successful Weight" of Adams's influence in Marchant's favor; hopes he and any of his family will make Marchant's house their home while traveling through Newport en route to Boston.

[Boston] *Columbian Centinel*, 17 July.

"Letters received by the last mail from New-York, say, that the Committee of Senate, to whom the FUNDING BILL was committed, would report in favour of an Assumption of the State Debts; and that there was a probability of its being accepted in the Senate."

NYWM, 17 July; reprinted at Charleston, South Carolina.

"A number of members" who voted for the Residence Act intend to support a motion to suspend the move to Philadelphia so that Congress can remain at New York until 1792.

SUNDAY, 18 JULY 1790

Fisher Ames to Thomas Dwight

I sympathise with the afflicted family as sincerely as you imagine[1]—The social principle has more force in the country than in town—it's strength is not dissipated among a croud—It is stronger still among those of the same famly—~~than~~ Long habit, uncommon merit and a strong mutual sense of it have bound that charming sisterhood together—while I lament the pain the separation costs them. I cannot forbear considering their long union under the same roof as a wrong done our sex—This Hesperian fruit shd. not be inaccessible, You are going to gather it, and to make my mouth water—o shame, you cry, what an expression! Then blot it out.

A Commee. was lately appointed in Senate to reconcile if possible, the different opinions which prevail on the point of the funding bill—Some propose one scheme & others another—This Comee. have reported—to fund the principal of the U.S. debt, and 2/3ds of the principal & interest of the state debts on the 3d. proposal of the Secy. The Indents & interest of the U.S. debt & the other 3d of the state debts at 3 per Cent—This last is not warranted by the terms of the public engagements, nor will it give satisfaction—However, the Report was adopted in Senate, in toto—and is incorporated into the funding bill—& to be decided tomorrow. I think on some terms we shall fund & assume—and in 3 or 4 weeks at the latest see our wives & sweethearts.

Is Mr. [*Samuel*] Lyman coming out again in force? I hope Mr. Sedgwick will be chosen—his ground cannot, I think, be made good, by any of his rivals.[2]

The removal of Congress to Philaa. is a grievous thing to the N. Yorkers. They have cause to complain of the intrigues of the Pensylvanians.

I had heard many weeks ago that I was courting here. I am obliged to my Roxbury [*Massachusetts*] friends for disposing of me—I have long found it hard to get rid of myself.

ALS: first and second pages in Ames Papers, MDedHi; third page and address sheet in Ames Papers, Stanford University, California. Place to which addressed not indicated.

---

[1] The reference is to the Worthington family of Springfield, Massachusetts. They are "afflicted" because of sister Mary's move to Nova Scotia following her marriage to Jonathan Bliss on 11 July.

[2] The ALS prior to this point is at MDedHi; the text from this point is provided from the manuscript at Stanford.

Charles Carroll and John Henry to Governor John Eager Howard

Almost all the States have appointed persons of ability and proper talents to Superintend the settlement of their respective accounts with the United States, and to support the validity & justice of the charges contained in those accounts.

We Submit to your Excellency and the Council the propriety of a Similar appointment on behalf of our State, which may be the more necessary, should the State debts be assumed by the United States, of which event there is now a prospect, and even a probability.

ALS, hand of Carroll, Signers of the Declaration, WHi. Addressed to Annapolis, Maryland; franked; postmarked. Maryland's previous agent for settling accounts was John White, who was appointed postmaster at Baltimore in November 1789 and died on 20 May 1790.

Pierpont Edwards to Jeremiah Wadsworth

When I last saw you at Hartford, you gave me some information respecting Mr. Shermans Conduct, relative to the bill, determining the Compensations to the representatives and senators [*Salaries-Legislative Act HR-19*]—Perhaps I have not a perfectly accurate recollection of what you said, Justice is due to all men; and no man ought, by pretence of having had no hand in an unpopular measure, which however met with his entire approbation, to screen himself from the odium that happens to be the result of it—This is Jesuitism which illy befits an honest fair man. The freemen ought to know the ground on which Mr. Sherman should stand, so far as the matter of Compensations is to have any weight in their minds—I have therefore, with my usual frankness, when the Wages of Congress have happened, in my presence, to be the subject, tak[*en*] pains to put Mr. Shermans Conduct, in a proper point of Light—According to my recollection you said, that after the bill had passed the House of representatives, and was under the Consideration of the senate, Mr. Sherman [*a*]ppli[*e*]d to Judge Ellsworth, and told him, that whatever the senate did on the subject, by no means to consent to lower the wages below six Dollars—Is this as you informed? pray write me in the course of this week—I have not made use of your Name, but have asserted it as a fact, and have challenged Mr. Sherman to deny—you are too honest to deal with such an old Jesuit—He will descend to practices [*to maint*]ain his popularity which you abhor.

I have in the Course of my life, given you a great deal of trouble about my own personal concerns; I have not yet done troubling you in this way.

My object, you are sensible, is the Judiciary department of the United States; I am [*therefore?*] anxious as to every thing which may affect the favorite object of my pursuit. My success will, in a great measure, depend upon the opinion, which the Judges of the supreme Judicial Court, (who happen to have been acquainted with me) form of me as a man of abilities in my profession—I was concerned in so much of the bussiness before the last Circuit Court, that Jay must have had a tolerable opportunity to decide upon me as a speaker, as a Lawyer and as a man. I have heard of much which he has said of me; perhaps more than he ever uttered; Cou'd I know his real [*two lines torn and illegible*] prospects, which woud have a very powerful Influence upon my future Conduct. If he thinks but indifferently of me, I may, with great propriety, abandon all my hopes from the Judiciary—[*two lines torn and illegible*] I have all [*illegible*]; and you in the [*illegible*] will take measures to be informed, or not, as you think proper. I am cited to appear before Judge [*Richard*] Law, to shew reason against the remission of some penalties, incurred by on[*e*] Savage, [*by?*] an infraction of the Collection Law [*HR-11*]—Am I to do the service for the United States without reward? No provision is as yet made, to defray this expence.

ALS, Governor Joseph Trumbull Papers, Connecticut State Library, Hartford. Written from New Haven, Connecticut.

Thomas Fitzsimons to Benjamin Rush

Our fellow Citizens, would hear on saturday that the Residence bill was Signd by the President, and of course be Relieved, from their Anxiety on that Score—I believe they need not apprehend the Success of any Measure that may be attempted to prevent the Removal tho we are yet threatned with such an attempt. If I am to believe reports our people have allready evidenced their desposition to take advantage of the Removal. the Rent of some houses applyd for ~~in~~ have in the first instance been Nearly doubled—had this been Known before the business was settled—there can be no doubt it would have been made a proper Use of—however after they get there high Rents will Occasion the building of more houses, and bring Rents like other things to their proper Level. I shall not fail as often as Occasions present to make it Known, how powerfull the Agency of Mr. Morris was in Accomplishing this Removal—tho I expect before Long to see before ~~the~~ long the City Members Accused of Improper Conduct for Effecting it—pains has and will be taken to persuade that we Might have Obtained the permanent seat in the State—and there is no doubt we could have Obtained a Law for it—but we believed ~~that~~ Such a Law would Not have been executed & had what we Supposed sufficient grounds for that opinion. Whether a Removal at the end of ten Years may or may not take place Can only be presumed. we took that possibility into our Calculation. Mr. Jefferson has made an Estimate of the expenditure at this time at the seat of Congress, and makes it two hundred thousand pounds. Sterg.—I am glad to find you are turning Your attention towards Your Next representation and have not a doubt You will make it better than the present. it is the duty of every good Citizen to promote the Election of the Men most likely to serve the public interest, and on Such Occasions private Attachments ought to have no weight—the present Representatives have not in any instances disgraced the State or sacrificed its interest. they ~~have~~ or some of them at least have been advocates for these Measures which has given so Much offence and will not be surprized or offended at the Consequences you predict. our funding System is yet to be decided on as the Senate are about making Considerable Alterations in the one Agreed to in our house and it remains yet to be determ[*ined?*] whether any or What provision will be ma[*de*] [*seal*] that subject—I think we shall adjourn the end of this Month.

ALS, provided by ARA Foundation, Philadelphia, 1977. Addressed to Philadelphia; franked; postmarked 19 July.

Benjamin Goodhue to Stephen Goodhue

I think our bussines will soon come to a close and I have very little doubt. but we shall adjourn in 3 weeks done or not done. for it signifys nothing to be forever contending, the members are wearied out and will not stay— the Senate have come to some kind of compromise in the funding bussines, in which they were much divided as to the rate of interest, which will be about equal to 4 ℔ Ct. and I am informed they are determind if this does not take effect, they will postpone the whole, some are violently contending for more interest—it is proposed to assume about 4,000,000 Dollrs. from Massachts.—I think it will be opposed in our House by some who are for an higher interest, but hope it may succed— ***

ALS, Goodhue Family Papers, MSaE. Addressed to Salem, Massachusetts; franked; postmarked. The omitted text concerns a personal financial transaction.

Thomas Hartley to Jasper Yeates

I this Day expected to set off for York Town but alas my Friend I am totally prohibited and cannot even be at the York Court—The most important National Business is still unfinished—Funding has been under the Consideration of the Senate—and it seems they have tacked the State Debts to the Bill (we sent up) by way of Amendment—What we shall do I know not—The Senate have changed the whole System—There is however an Idea of paying six per Cent Interest to the Creditors of the union Debt and three per Cent upon Indents and State Debts—Calculations go so near as a single vote—The New Yorkers also intend to bring forward a Bill for dividing the Time of temporary Residence with Philadelphia—Mr. Gerry gave Notice Yesterday—Should they fail in that—they will attempt to embarrass us at the Adjournment.

I am also upon a Conference on the Post Office Bill [*HR-74*]—The Senate want to strike out all the Cross Roads and leave the whole Roads and Revenue in the Hands of the President and Post Master General—which would be unconstitutional and highly dangerous—Many other Bills of Importance are under Consideration & my Friends absolutely interdict me from going now—and say that I cannot answer for my Conduct were I to depart now—Forgive me my Sins—a handsome Situation I am in—(& my Devotion is increased by a Methodist Preacher who is within a few Perches of me speaking loudly) A few Days will close the Session—I trust to Providence and my Friends—I know my Brethren at the Bar will be generous—and as to my Friends I really throw myself upon their Mercy—I shall join you as early as possible.

ALS, Yeates Papers, PHi. Addressed to York, Pennsylvania; franked.

James Monroe to Thomas Jefferson

My last from Richmond in ansr. to yours of the 20th. of June has no doubt been recd. The more I have reflected on the subject, the better satisfied I am of the impolicy of assuming the state debts. The diminishing the necessity for State ~~legislation~~ taxation will undoubtedly leave the national govt. more at liberty to exercise its powers & [*lined out*] encrease the subjects [*lined out*] on wh. it will act, for that purpose, and if that were absolutely a necessary power of the govt., & no objections [*lined out*] applied to the transfer itself of the publick creditors from one govt. to the other, without their consent, (for such a modification as leaves them not even a plausible alternative, amounts to the same thing, & such I understand the report to be) or to the probable inefficiency of the national govt. comparatively with those of the States in raising the necessary funds, I shod. perhaps have no objections to it at present. Even in our time we may hope to see the whole debt extinguish'd or nearly so, & we must be the favor'd people, if no occasion shod. hereafter arise, that wod. make it necessary for the gen. govt. to tax highly, & raise considerable revenues. Such exigency can never apply hereafter to those of the States, so that merely for the sake of preserving an equality [*lined out*] at present, I shod. think it useless to balance the debt, between them. But as I believe this (upon speculation only) a defect in the government, & presume thro that medium, the preponderance of one over the other, will be settled [*lined out*]. I wod. avoid throwing any thing occasionally into that scale from wh. I apprehended most danger. On the other hand as the govt. now rests on its own means, for the discharge of its engagements, I wod. always use its powers for the purpose, nor wod. I endanger the publick credit rather than exercise a power, wh. was of questionable propriety, or in some instances thought so. Thus things wod. have their regular course, proper experiments wod. be made, & we shod. ultimately be landed where we shod. be. The weight of all the State creditors thrown into the national scale at present, might also perhaps produce some disorder in the system, as it wod. occasion a fortuitous but severe pressure from that quarter, [*lined out*] affecting them from the heart to the extremities, before either their legislators by moderate experiments, had acquir'd sufficient knowledge for the purpose, or the people given sufficient proof of what they could, and what they would bear. Will not this from necessity as well as policy, compell them to glean whatever they can from trade, pressing that resource upon trial likewise, beyond what perhaps for the sake of revenue, it can bear, & introducing a system of œconomy in other respects very oppressive on some parts of the U. States: For in the present State of arts & industry in America, the moment that medium is pass'd, that forms the basis of a wise commercl. policy for the whole, diffusing its beneficial effects to every part, will it degenerate into a tyrannous sacrifice of the interests, of the [*lined out*] minority to that of the majority; and that precise medium wh. will be most productive in point of revenue & beneficial in other respects, can only be discover'd by gradual operation & gentle experiments, which the assumption, for the reasons above will entirely prevent.

As to the residence I will only hazard one Idea. we find that for its removal to Phila. the representatives of that State rely on those of this, & the other southern States or some of them. They do not expect that the Eastern States will vote to remove it further from them—place it in Phila. & how doth this principle apply? will our & their members harmonize so well afterwards, will they unite in forwarding it to Georgetown? or will it not rather immediately bring about an harmony of sentiment & cooperation elsewhere? & shall we not be left dependent on a resolution of Congress which holds its tenure upon the pleasure of 2. States, who (whatever their true interests may be) have always shewn they consider'd it as consisting in keeping the seat of govt. as near home as they could. As soon as they get fix'd in Phila. (& the shorter the term allotted for their residence there the more active will this principle be) the representatives of that State will look with a jealous eye toward their brethern of the South. any attempts to forward the erection of buildings at Georgetown will at first be recd. coolly & afterwards with disgust. common interest in this as in other respects will unite them, and we shall soon find a well form'd plan, regularly pursued, that shall be best calculated to promote them. we have often found that an union on some great question, which was consider'd as primary or ruling in the view of parties, gave a tone to their proceedings on many others; how much more reasonable then is it to expect it, when there are so many predisposing causes to promote it? I shod. therefore wish to see the funds appropriated & comrs. appointed to carry on the work, plac'd as completely without the reach of Congress as possible afterwards, before we acceded to any thing upon this subject only much less wod. I give a consideration for any thing less.

I hinted in my last I wod. mention to you a subject of importance to myself in cypher, but as you expected to return to France when you left it tis possible you ~~left it in France~~ omitted to bring it with you. as tis a matter wh. does not press immediately, and wh. perhaps you may conjecture, & tis possible we may meet before I come to any decision on it unless I have a private opportunity, I shall decline mentioning it untill one of those events takes place. we are well & hope you are completely restor'd.

ALS, Jefferson Papers, DLC. Written from Albemarle County, Virginia; received 26 July.

James Sullivan to Elbridge Gerry

After more than one months absence I returned yesterday to this Town and had the pleasure of your favours of the 17 & 26th June.

I am very sorry to find the people at large so universally dissatisfied with the proceedings of Congress. perhaps there never was a more unpopular assembly in any part of the world. it may wound your feelings to have this so plainly mentioned, but it would be cruel in a friend not to do it. the idea of a compromise of measures, and giving ~~up~~ up a principle to obtain an End, strikes our People very disagreeably. the assumption of the State debts is dictated by Justice and Supported by sound Policy. but to obtain this by agreeing to vote for the residence of Congress at any place, is going into that mode of politicks which has long disgraced [*lined out*] other Countrys and is a very unwelcome measure to our Sober people. that Congress ~~Shall~~ Should think of a permanent place of residence, or of quakers or negros, before they had Settled their System of finance, and Settled it upon principle, is a galling thing to the men who love the honor of the nation and delight in those Sentiments which lead to purity of politicks and the Luve of freedom.

ALS, privately owned by Ned Downing, 1998. Written from Boston; franked; postmarked; addressed to Langdon by mistake.

George Thatcher to Samuel Nasson

Yours of the 7th. inst. dated at Boston, reached me three days ago.

Your friendship to me I cannot call in question—indeed it has so often been manifested that any one acquainted with your conduct must be blind not to see it; and I must be more than ungratefull not to acknowledge—If I have not made due returns thereof it certainly is owing to the want of opportunity, and not of disposition.

Some of my friends, as well as yourself, have informed me, that there will be a number of Candidates at the ensuing election of federal Representative—and that my election is doubtfull—To which I shall observe that all political power resides in the people—they can raise up and put down whom they please; and it is my sincere wish they may always enjoy this right secure and unimpared—And that when ever a man, they have put into office, behaves, in any manner, unbecoming the trust deposited in his hands, that they will exert their right and turn him out—And when ever the people shall choose to elect a Gentleman in my room, I shall say blessed is this power of the people—long may they enjoy it—And may the man they have chosen, in my stead, be able to render them more service than I have—but certain I am his desire and integrity to do this can never exceed mine.

You tell me "it had been better for me to have been asleep, than have been the means of geting mr. [*John*] Lee appointed Collector"—true—if I had consulted my own popularity, I should not have recommended him to the President—For at that time I plainly foresaw the loss of some friends, and the acquisition of some political enemies—But I discharged an important Duty I owed to the Public—and having done this I wait, with pleasure, all the consequences. And permit me to say—that Mr. Lee, as an officer, does honor to the place he holds.

I lament, with you, many things that have been done by Congress; and could wish they were otherwise—But we must not expect every thing to take place just as we, in Massachusetts, would have it: We must remember the other States have their wants, their ideas of right, & public Good, as well as ourselves—And what appears wrong to us may appear right and proper in their estimation.

The high compensations and Salaries given by Congress, and their slow progress in business are the principle causes of complaint among the people—The former of these I have frequently wrote you my sentiments upon. and to the latter I will just observe—That when the Constitution was first adopted it seemed to be a general opinion that the first Congress must be in session their whole time—Scarcely a man but who said it would require two full years for Congress to organize the Government, make all Laws necessary for the regular course of Business in the Union—and to fund, & provide ways & means for discharging the Debts of the United States. Notwithstanding these were the sentiments of most people eighteen months ago, & tho Congress have been in session scarcely twelve months of the two years, yet we hear the complaints from every quarter, more especially from Massachusetts, of the slow progress Congress make in business. Of the Laws for the foregoing purposes how many are there not compleated, or nearly compleated? I assure you but very few—And here I must observe that a great variety of seemingly small matters, resulting from the war & unsetled state of accounts & the finances of the Union under the Confederation, are daily forced upon Congress, to the exclusion of such things as persons who are far off and unacquainted with their particular circumstances may look upon of greater importance and require the first attention of the general Legislature.

I most readily agree that the Business of Legislation is not so rapid in Congress as in the Legislatures of some of the States, if we consider the time only, and not the difficulties attending the discussion of Subjects—But it does not follow from that criterion, that Congress is guilty of wilfull negligence—or that the members protract the Session for the sake of their Compensation—You who have been in our General Court are a competent Judge of those charges of delay—You must frequently have been a Witness of the variety of Interests—the opposition of sentiments—the contradiction of propositions among the members till a Session has been drawn out nerely three months. Now, my friend, consider this subject properly and I beleive you will acknowledge, that all these causes of delay must be much stronger & more numerous in Congress where the interests of thirteen Sovereign and independent States, are debated and decided upon, than in the Legislature of an individual State. If Jealousies, and fearfull apprehensions of of one anothers views take place among the Representatives of a State in their Legislature how much more are these things to be expected in the Congress of the United States. There is some diversity of Interest in the different parts of the same State—and even in the same County, & I beleive I may extend the idea to a Town—For I find the Justices in Sessions, & the Select men, when they are about apportioning a Tax on the Inhabitants of the County or respective Towns, talk much about the difference of Interests, arising from the quality of land—the situation of Trade—to keep a Tavern or some other local circumstance—If we take these circumstances into consideration and form a Judgment of the difficulties and causes of delay attending the Business of Congress it appears to me, every candid, impartial man will say that the members of Congress deserve applause for their dispatch, rather than censure for a delay of Business.

It is very true that many people are uneasy—public measures do not go right according to their ideas of what would be for the ~~public~~ general Good—they look about for the cause of this irregularity—but it is out of their sight, and thus, in the dark, they are apt to fix upon the first objects that are presented to their view, however remotely they may be connected with the supposed evil—And nothing is more natural then for the people to look towards those in administration ~~f~~ as the real causes of public errors—This eagle-eyed Jealousy I hope never to see, in the least, blinded—It is the very life of Liberty—and therefore I had rather cherish, than discourage it. I would have the people at all times examine the conduct and principles of those they entrust with power—and always to remember that they are the only true source of it.

Watch your Legislators with an impartial and candid Jealousy—Attend to your Schools—Instruct your Children in the general principles of Literature—Be industerous and honest—And, Americans, you have nothing to fear.

Altho this Letter is already too long I cannot close it without adding—that a Committee from the Senate has reported to that house, that Twenty one millions of the State debts ought to be assumed (four millions of which is of the Massachusetts debt), and funded two thirds thereof at six per cent & one third at three.

A week or ten days will decide this question, and the present Session.

FC, Thatcher Family Papers, MHi.

George Thatcher to Sarah Thatcher

Since my last yours of the 3d. 5th & 10th have come to hand—the last gave me the melancholly account of your disappointment on account of my not seting out for home at the time first proposed—I am, my dear, as much hurt at my delay as you can be—a thousand reasons that never existed before, in my absence from home, conspire to increase my anxiety to return—I would have set out before now, but there is some Business before Congress which cannot be left—and my Colleagues insist on my tarrying till that is finished—I feel the most ardent struggle between my affection to you, & a real duty to the public—should I leave Congress, just at this time, & the assumption of the state debts be lost by reason of my absence I could never answer it to the people of Massachusetts—You must forgive my delay, but be assured it shall not be a moment longer than real necessity demands—Keep up your spirits—be cheerfull—Invite our friends to visit you as often as they can—Our friend Mercy is good company—pray tell her from me—that she must tarry with you as much as her business will permit.

We have fixed on tuesday the 27th inst. for an adjournment—And it is the opinion of every member that we shall get away all next week—And the moment I am released I will fly to my dear Sally.

If you should not get the money from Boston, borrow of Mr. [*Jeremiah*] Hill or any of our friends—they will lend you.

ALS, Thatcher Family Papers, MHi. Place to which addressed not indicated.

George Thatcher to Oliver Whipple

Yours of the 12th inst. came to hand last evening, and very justly reminds me of an omission I am ~~very~~ rarely guilty of to my particular friends—among whom I certainly place you as one.

Yours by Mr. [*Tobias*] Lear was received immediately on his arrival to this City; and would have been answered before this time, but I waited, to know the probable event of an excise Bill, then before the House, and unexpectedly arrested in its progress, & thereby the whole subject put out of my mind.

I shall feel myself happy if it should be in my power to serve you in the object of your wishes[1]—And tho I may have some influence in the appointments, within the District I represent I cannot flatter myself that it will have energy enough in another State to effect an appointment contrary to the recommendation of its immediate Representatives. If I can discover the Sentiments of any of your Senators or Representatives to be in your favour, I shall readily support them—otherwise my voice in your favour might not serve you—but even in this case it shall not be wanting.

Your Letter to the Chief Justice of the United States is forwarded to him. I will particularly mention the Subject of your Letter to Mr. King.

FC, Thatcher Family Papers, MHi.

[1] Whipple wished to be appointed federal excise collector at Portsmouth, New Hampshire.

From New York

The *Funding Bill* has passed the Hon. Senate—By this Bill the *Principal* of the *Domestick Debt* of the United States is funded, *two-thirds* at 6 per cent. immediately, the other *third* at 6 per cent. to commence in the year 1800, agreeably to the fourth alternative in the report of the Secretary of the Treasury. *Indents* at a present interest of 3 per cent. *State Debts, one third* at *three per cent*—the other *two thirds* on the same terms as the *principal* of the debt of the United States.

The FUNDING BILL passed the *Senate* yesterday only. It is expected this will bring the Funding Business to an issue, as it is the result of a compromise between the *four* per centers, *six* per centers *Assumptionists* and *Anti-assumptionists.*

With respect to *Residence*, or seat of Government, many flattered themselves with a hope that the bill would not receive THE PRESIDENT's approbation. It is however signed. The citizens of this place are wounded by the measure of removal—they, however, behave to a charm. The ebulitions in our papers are not pleasing to many here. The great body of citizens, we do not conceive, are benefited by an uncertain residence—as supplies do not keep pace with demands for necessaries of life; but the hope of a longer residence has occasioned improvements in this place, which would not otherwise have happened, perhaps in half a century. These will remain solid advantages.

We have no expectation, that the time of removal to *Philadelphia*, will be procrastinated; though some suppose another effort will be made, by way of a Bill for suspending the Act two years.

PEACE

[Boston] *Columbian Centinel*, 24 July; reprinted at Portland, Maine, and Concord and Portsmouth, New Hampshire.

OTHER DOCUMENTS

John Adams to Eliphalet Fitch. FC:lbk, Adams Family Manuscript Trust, MHi. Addressed to Jamaica.

Has forwarded to the President Fitch's packet of pamphlets regarding the slave trade.

Benjamin Contee to Levi Hollingsworth. ALS, Hollingsworth Papers, PHi. Addressed to Philadelphia; postmarked. Enclosures not found.

"I recd. yr. favr. yesterday covering the inclosed—& made the remarks you see on the sealed side & dispatched it by the messenger of the House of Representatives [*Cornelius Maxwell*]—it was returned to my lodgings late in the Eveng. from which I conclude that Mr. Manuel had left Town; especially as he told me in the early part of the week (when I happened to see him) he intended to do, as on Wednesday—I therefore conclude it proper to inclose you back the letter.

The presdt. of the U.S. approved the Residence Bill on Friday morng."

Robert Morris to Walter Stone. ALS, Stone Papers, DLC. Addressed to Port Tobacco, Maryland; postmarked 19 July.

Has forwarded Stone's letters to Mr. Christie in London; office seeking: has given Stone's letter respecting the consulate at London to the secretary of state and "told him I would answer for your integrity & Honor," but has not heard anything back; "You give good Advice respecting public service and I will *try* as I often have before done, to carry my own resolutions on that Subject into Execution."

James Sullivan to John Langdon. ALS, Langdon Papers, NhPoA. Written from Boston; franked; postmarked; addressed to Gerry by mistake.

Found Langdon's wife (Elizabeth) and daughter (Eliza) well on 16 July; discusses Woodbury Langdon's impeachment and thinks "you had better write your friends upon the subject"; "the people are generally dissatisfied with and disappointed with the Measures of Congress"; "Mrs. Langdon says she will take your directions respecting meeting you at our house."

Daniel Hiester, Account Book. PRHi.

Dined with the Pennsylvania delegation at Charles Brenan's Tavern on Greenwich Road.

Monday, 19 July 1790

William Coombs, David Coats, and Moses Brown to Benjamin Goodhue

We have received your favor, of the 10th current, and feel ourselves obliged to you for the intelligence it contains, and sincerely hope the important objects, of the Assumption of the State Debts, providing a fund for Payment of the public Debts &ca. will be effected, before the rising of Congress, to general satisfaction.

We thank you, for the Information you give us respecting the Tonnage Act [*HR-78*], providing for the Restitution of foreign Tonnage &ca., but could have wished a like provision had been made, for the Restitution, of American Tonnage also, in all cases, where it has been paid twice, when according to the Spirit and meaning of the Act of Congress, it ought to have been demanded only once, as explained and shewn in the Petition,[1] we had the honor to transmit you. And if it is not too late, we are desired by the Merchants of the Town, to request you to endeavour, after the insertion of such provision in the Act, if you shall think there is any prospect of Success. The Collector here continues to demand and receive it, after he forbore to receive the foreign Tonnage, tho' we cannot learn that it has been demanded and paid in any District, except this, in Massachusetts.

We have had opportunity to peruse the new proposed Bill for Collection of the Revenue Duties [*HR-82*], and beg leave to suggest to you, our Ideas respecting some few matters in it.

We conceive it not reasonable that the Surveyors fee, for measuring our Vessels should be paid by the Owner, but out of the Revenue, as it is a necessary Act for Collecting the Tonnage.

The fees for gauging Casks is we think much to high, half that sum would be ample satisfaction, and is so esteemed as we conceive, by those who are capable of doing it. The fee of two Cents per hundred for weighing Fish, to entitle the Exporter to a Drawback is very high; one weigher in this Port, has made seven or eight Dollars a Day, and may make twice that Sum—The Wages allowed the Mariners, at forty eight shillings a Month, on board the Cutters we think is too high, and that it ought not to exceed the ordinary Wages of Mariners, in the Merchants Service, which are from six to Seven Dollars a Month.

Our motive in mentioning these matters, (unless the first may be an exception) you will readily see is not interested, it is to prevent more of the Revenue's being appropriated to the Support of the Officers, than is necessary, and to cause the same to be applied to the great purposes for which it is raised.

When this is the case, the Duties will ever we believe, be paid with chearfulness, and satisfaction given to those who pay them.

It may look interested for us to object to the Article of the Cutters, but as we know of no attempts to evade the payment of the Duties, by Smuggling, in this District, and believe the same to be true in many others, we venture to suggest to you whether the Number of them is not greater than is at present necessary.

We Communicate to you the Sentiments of the Merchants in this Place, in what we have written, and do it at their request—and still requesting the honor of your Correspondence, and the Communication of such matters as you shall think important or interesting.

ALS, Letters to Goodhue, NNS. Written from Newburyport, Massachusetts.

[1] For background on this petition from the Merchants and Traders of Newburyport, Massachusetts, see *DHFFC* 8:418–20.

Thomas Dwight to Theodore Sedgwick

I am greatly obliged by your favor of the 12th inst.—the more I see and hear of the divisions in Congress on questions of almost every kind the more am I convinced of the very great injury which will ultimately arise from drawing a line between Northern & Southern interests—and the more do I fear a separation by means of such prejudices—the business of assumption, is I know a favorite one with N. England-men, who may be perhaps full as sanguine in their wishes, and expectations on the subject, as they ought to be; yet never can they persevere too long, in their endeavours, to obtain that, which is clearly their right. The men who have connected this business with that of residence ~~and~~ who ~~will~~ counteract their own political sentiments for the sake of carrying a point, which can only affect a small local interest are (I think with you,) as despicable as their conduct is injurious to the nation—if such jobbing, such shameful jockeying is to be the common mode of carrying private points in our public councils—if to prove that black is not white & have it admitted, it is become necessary to make a bargain and give a very valuable consideration—I think we may safely predict a speedy end to our existence as a nation—the present constitution does not furnish power enough to keep us long together on such terms.

That you have suffered more than, almost any pecuniary consideration could atone for I do not doubt—publick life has generally its pleasures as well as pains—but in the late sessions of Congress I think our N. England representation cannot have been envied for the ease and pleasure which they have enjoyed—your anxiety and impatience must have been intolerable and I do not see any present prospect of relief to you.

Our General Court Caucusses have undoubtedly arranged the business of the next elections what these arrangements are, we can as yet only conjecture—no considerable movements are made—the Boston papers, particularly the Court paper [*Boston Gazette*] that vehicle of sedition, are beginning with invectives agt. the present members—popular opinion is such an ignis fatuus[1] that no man can with any degree of probability conjecture whither it will lead us, by the next October there will I think be efforts to displace some of the present, members, but this is no more than wild guessing.

***

[*Ebenezer*] Kingsley is now at Becket, and does not pretend to shut his doors agt. any body—Colo. [*Jonathan*] Smith who has been to see him says he is a poor humble shoe licking devil, willing to be kicked, if it will gratify his creditors—my brother [*Josiah Dwight*] and many other of your friends will not be made to believe as yet, that you Sir, are not a sufferer by his failure—they now s[*ay?*] you have given him a letter to somebody [*a*]t Hudson [*New York*] which will render you responsible for a considerable sum—I hope and pray it may not be true.

Be so kind as to make my ~~respectful~~ compliments to all the Gentlemen of your family whom I had the pleasure to see when at N. York.

ALS, Sedgwick Papers, MHi. Written from Springfield, Massachusetts. The omitted text relates to news of friends.

[1] Fool's fire, i.e., deceptive.

John Steele to Governor Alexander Martin

I beleve I mentioned to you in a former Letter that the House of Representatives had passed a bill [*Post Office HR-74*] to change the post road of the United States and instead of following the old rout, it proceeds from Petersburg to Halifax Tarboro', Fayetteville, Campden, Augusta To this modification the Senate have disagreed a Committee of Conference on the difference between the two Houses is appointed, and the result is uncertain.

The accounts from Edinburg [*Scotland*] and those from Havre de grace [*France*] of the same date respecting the Spanish War are diametricaly opposite—The one Announces hostillities the other pacification, through the ~~pa~~ intervention of the national Assembly. Neither being relied on, we are placed in a state of the greatest suspence.

My conjectures of the event of the Assumption project have heretofore been flattering; but the Scene seems at present wofully changed, *This cup*[1] tho' a bitter draught for No. Carolina must be swallowed. It has not yet indeed passed our House, but the Senate has passed it by 14 votes to 12 and coupled it with the funding bill 15 to 11. not withstanding we have rejected the same proposition five times this decision of the other branch will I fear have a very improper influence. The Senate secluded from the public Eye secret in their negotiations, and superior in direction and prerogative will always in great questions mannage the other House by intrigue—Perhaps my fears on this occasion may be groundless. God grant that they may! but were I to hazard an opinion it would be that the Assumtion would take place Having been uniformly in favor of this Constitution I feel alarmed at every proposition which can possibly affect a peaceful administration of it and I must confess this augurs very unfavorably indeed.

It is thought we shall adjourn about the 1st. of August to meet at Philadelphia next Decemr. you will have seen e'er this reaches you the public prints containing an act to establish the temporary Seat of Govt. of the United States [*Residence Act S-12*]—a great point gained by the southern delegates and was it possible to reject the Assumption once more I would return to my fellow citizens perfectly satisfied.

Copy, Governors' Papers, Nc-Ar.

[1] A reference to Jesus' prayer in the Garden of Gethsemane (Matthew 26:39).

Z to the Honourable the Senate of the United States

With the most humble intentions, I take the liberty of addressing your honorable house in this public manner. Possessing few literary advantages, nothing could induce me to this, but the influence of some supposed violation or wrong. As I conceive a further introduction would be a loss of that time which you know how to apply to more valuable purposes, I shall cease excuses, humbly desiring nothing, either contained in this address, or which may result from the manner of expression, should give the smallest offence, as the writer of this has the greatest veneration for the wisdom and prudence of your honorable house.

But to the subject of this address: I have heard, to my utter grief and astonishment, that a committee of the Senate has reported (which report is said to be accepted) the following funding system:

Principal of the domestic debt, two thirds at a present interest of 6 per cent.—the other one third at 6 per cent. in ten years—indents, at a present interest of 3 per cent.

As to the rest of the proposition, relative to the funding and assumption of the state debts, I shall omit, as not interested in the motive of this address.

What the reasons are, which could be urged for so enormous a disproportion between the interest and the principal of domestic debt, I cannot tell: I shall only attempt some statement of arguments, which stand most opposed to that which is, in my opinion, so impolitic an arrangement. Those arguments I shall consider as they regard *justice* and *national policy.*

With respect to the first, I cannot perceive the justice of funding the indents at little more than one half the rate of the principal, for which no other reason can be alleged than that the interest ought to have been paid a great many years ago. This does not look like justice: I think it would have a greater appearance of justice, to pay off the whole amount of old interest before we contract for a new; this to be done either by the natural funds of the country as quickly as they are received, or by making new loans; or if inability prevents these measures, surely it is but just we should make all possible provision which the resources of the country will still admit. On this ground, I conceive the whole of the interest ought immediately to be funded at 6 per cent. subject to be paid off by annual installments. This, I conceive, should certainly be done, even If necessity required that the principal of the debt should be funded at only 4 per cent.

The only argument I have heard alledged in favour of the proposition, was the cry of—Will you then pay interest upon the interest? Let us not be deceived by words.

Those very men themselves, who make this outcry, perceive the necessity of the measure and agree to it; but at the same time are for steering what they call a middle course. I fear the course they steer is neither just nor honorable. Let us suppose the indents for interest immediately funded at 6 per cent.; then let me ask, where is the advantage received by the holder? Why, truly, this is the advantage: he ought to have been paid the same amount in money from three to ten years since. Is this so! During this period the principal was still receiving some emolument by the sale of interest: Is not this a sufficient advantage, whilst he that purchased the indents 5 years ago (at which time they commanded double the price of the principal) has never received any advantage by them since, but the simple hope that Congress would one day surely make provision for them before the principal?

That this address may not seem a bold intrusion on your patience and the public, we shall find these sentiments not originating with an uninformed individual, but upon record; upon those records, the spirit of which you are bound by an oath to fulfil. In the requisitions on the several states by the former Congress, it is there expressed, that every state which did not by a limited period pay in a certain proportion of specie, should for every dollar of indents, so unpaid, be liable to pay one dollar and one-fourth in specie.

I really wonder how men of the first information, after reading the various resolves of the late Congress upon this subject; could come forward with any proposition for paying less than either the whole of the principal, or at least the whole of the interest.

If this thing takes place, surely we shall have more reason to applaud the policy of the late Congress than of the present. The former Congress, without resources and without money, raised those very indents to 16s, in the pound. The present Congress, possessed of both, have not raised them to one half of that sum; and, least they should do too much, are disposed to retract from what, by the report of their Secretary and the concurrence of the lower House, has been expected by every part of the United States many months ago. Surely, this is but sporting with the opinions of men!

NYDG, 19 July. The piece continued in *NYDG* on 20 and 21 July, and concluded on 23 July, below.

[*David Daggett,*] A Republican to Messrs. Printers (No. 8)

THE *great*, the *all-important* question is, at length, brought to an issue *for the present.*

Congress have finally determined that Philadelphia shall be the temporary, and Conogocheque, an Indian settlement on the Potowmac, the permanent place of residence. We rejoice at these glorious tidings! Happy times! Blessed æra! Philadelphia "who sits mistress of the world," is to embosom the grand council of America, till the year 1800, and then, a wigwam, at Conogocheque, is to be their "city of refuge," "their abiding place."[1]

We can but congratulate ourselves, that we live in an age, when patriotism is so conspicuous in our supreme legislature, and when the public good alone is the object of their exertions. Had that honorable body been composed of such *stupid* politicians as the Congresses of 1774 and 1775 were, perhaps they would have been contented to have tarried at New York, for the present—at least till the *trifling* question about funding the national debt had been determined; perhaps they would have considered themselves under obligations to remain in a city which had expended 40 or 50,000 pounds for their accommodation, and thus defeated the darling project of removing to Philadelphia. But, *happily* for the interest of the union, there are certain *great* and *illustrious* characters in that body, who have never lost sight of this *momentous* question—nor has it been attended to with coldness or indifference—the debate has been conducted with a *noble* ardor, as well as the most *forcible* and *pungent* argumentation. It is true, the discussion of this question has been attended with some *trifling* expence of time and money. It was agitated eleven days during the last and eight, during the present session, and the yeas & nays have been taken upon it fifty times; but there has been *no animosity or irritation* created—nor the least symptom of *partiality* or *prejudice*—15 or perhaps 20 000 dollars may have been expended, and it will cost Congress 30 or 40,000 dollars more to remove to Philadelphia. But who regards this? Are not our finances flourishing? Is not our public faith unimpeached? And are not all our creditors perfectly satisfied? Let Congress then sport with forty or fifty thousand dollars—who is *niggardly* enough to make any objection, especially when it is expended in such an *interesting* question as that, whether Congress sit at New York or Philadelphia? Why, my fellow citizens, 'tis indeed a matter of the first *magnitude*—a question as important to the union, as *whether there were any rain-bows before the flood, or whither Alexander the copper-smith over compensated the apostle Paul for the injury which he did him.*[2]

Again, there are many invincible arguments in favour of Philadelphia. In the first place, the very name of PHILADELPHIA, signifies originally, BROTHERLY LOVE, and that virtue may possibly be very necessary to some *future* Congress, tho the present members appear to possess it in an eminent degree. 2ndly, the city is much more elegant than New York—and who does not more regard the beauty and splendor of the place *where* Congress sit, than the manner in which they conduct business? 3dly, the theatre is constantly open in Philadelphia; and as Congress are frequently *fatigued* with the *multiplicity* and *arduousness* of their business, and as they appear by their attempt to purchase a library, to be anxious to complete their education, is it not important that they should be near theatrical exhibitions, where mind can, at once be relieved, and also furnished with useful *political* information? 4thly, the honorable R. M—s [*Morris*] lives at Philadelphia, and can any person, *in his senses*, suppose, that the seat of government ought not to be fixed where he dwells? 5thly, Philadelphia is nearer the ancient dominion, Virginia, than New York, and the very next stride is to place Congress upon that *American Nile*, the Potowmac, at a place called Canogocheque, a spot apparently as much designated by nature for the residence of a Congress as Kamschatka [*Russia*], or Otahieta [*Tahiti*].

Thus "the nations that sit in darkness will see great light." "the wilderness shall bud and blossom like a rose,"[3] and Canogocheque exchange her wigwams for palaces, and her tawny inhabitants for the brilliant circle of a polished court.

Viewing the subject in this light we are compelled to say, to the last vote of Congress, AMEN.

[New Haven] *Connecticut Journal*, 21 July; reprinted at Bennington, Vermont; Newport, Rhode Island; Hartford, Litchfield, and Middletown, Connecticut; New York City (*NYJ*, 27 July); Philadelphia; and Baltimore. For information on this series and its authorship, see the location note to A Republican to Messrs. Printers (No. 1), 15 May, volume 19.

---

[1] These concepts come from Joshua 20.
[2] II Timothy 4:14.
[3] Isaiah 9:2, 35:1.

OTHER DOCUMENTS

Elbridge Gerry to Samuel Dexter. No copy known; acknowledged in Dexter to Gerry, 31 July.

Pennsylvania Delegation (except Maclay) to Philadelphia Mayor Samuel Miles. Printed with the documents related to Accommodations for Congress at Philadelphia in Correspondence: Third Session.

Pennsylvania Delegation to Governor Thomas Mifflin. No copy known; mentioned as received in Pennsylvania Supreme Executive Council Minutes, Record Group 27, PHarH; see also *DHFFC* 9:326–27.

Thomas Thompson to John Langdon. ALS, Langdon Papers, NhPoA. Written from Portsmouth, New Hampshire.

Acknowledges Langdon's "very polite" reply to Thompson's "very Impertinate but very sencer Scrall" concerning a commercial venture; Langdon is expected at Portsmouth within two weeks; wishes him a pleasant journey and "a Happy sight of all your connections."

CONGRESSIONAL BIOGRAPHIES

One of the most interesting, controversial, and mysterious public opinion series written by or about members of the FFC appeared in the New York press as the second session drew to a close. Readers of *NYMP* and *NYDG* on Monday, 19 July, were either entertained or provoked by the first two anonymous pieces entitled "Congressional Biography." Before the series ended a week later, a total of ten such biographies would appear in three different newspapers, along with a poem aimed primarily at Vice President Adams. Nine of the ten pieces all but broadcast their subjects' names. The only thing that is known for certain about the person parodied in the tenth (*NYMP*, 23 July) is that he was a Virginian; indeed, it was clearly the author's intent to keep his subject's identity vague.

The pieces were written by at least two authors, about whom nothing is known except that, from the style and specific choice of reference (regarding Representative Vining in particular), one of them apparently wrote elsewhere under the pseudonym Theatricus (20 July, below). No discernible system underlies the creation, order, or publication of the biographies. For that matter they are not really biographies at all, but highly editorialized portraits. The series lacks a common theme, the closest being comment on the members' support for or opposition to the successful effort to move the temporary seat of the federal government from New York City to Philadelphia.

The series climaxed on Saturday, 24 July, when it was attacked by A Constant Reader, later identified by one of the biographers as Representative Vining. The same day the authors of the series wrote a letter to the editor of *NYMP*, the newspaper that had printed more than half the biographies, promising more pieces, denying a libelous intent, and offering to defend the editor against both lawsuit and arrest. The letter's claim that a member of Congress had not only complained about the piece on the unidentifiable Virginian but also had threatened to send an officer of the House, likely the sergeant at arms, to haul the printer to Federal Hall implies that an important moment in the history of congressional immunity and the freedom of the press was at hand. Unfortunately, no other documentary evidence of the event exists.

On Monday, 26 July, one of the biographers responded to Vining's attack of Saturday, but the series was already dead, probably brought to its sudden demise by the newspaper editors' reluctance to get embroiled in a possible libel suit or confrontation with Congress.

Exhibition Corner;
or,
Congressional Biography

****** ****** [*Pierce Butler*], ESQUIRE

DESCENDED from a line of HEROES, whose virtues he disdained, has affected the glory of his ancestors, by boasting himself the Representative of their genuine greatness—In public life, he affects to be the haughty bully of the Senate, in private, the little tyrant of the vassalage, who are either necessiated to suffer under his Cruelty, or the pimping knaves whom he has introduced into the service of this *devoted* Country.

Advanced by a series of unprecedented occurrences from a majority[1] in the enemy's line, he has risen from the *ranks*, to one of the *highest stations* in this Republic, without having once distinguished himself in the day of trial. Without being nurtured in the doctrines of a Republican system, his ambition led him to the public execration of a Monarchial government he consented to ingratiate himself with the joint leaders of the Aristocratic faction, disguising the narrow selfishness of his designs under the semblance of a disdainful contempt for the principles and conduct of his *Colleague** in office [*Izard*], and sheltering the errors of timidity, ignorance, and misinformation, under the appearance of arrogance and asperity; after having deluded the unsuspecting *Residence Minority*[2] by signalizing himself under the mask of friendship: After having treated the most circumspect, with insolence and derision, he retreated over to the *Majority*, leaving the world to declare the odium of so ignoble a proceeding: Thus stigmatized by infidelity to the Citizens of New York, Treachery to his private friends, and cruelty to those whose unfortunate situations deprived them of the means of calling him to an account. I say, that thus covered over, with the blackest robes of ingratitude, treachery, dissimulation and unmanly unprovoked revenge. His character will ever be detested, either on the banks of the Patowmac, or amongst the discerning inhabitants of Pennsylvania.

M. N. P.

*An Honest gentleman.

NYMP, 19 July; reprinted at Boston and Worcester, Massachusetts.

---

[1] That is, a commission as major in the British Army, which Butler held from 1766 until he sold it in 1773.

[2] The coalition that advocated extending the temporary seat of government's stay at New York.

Congressional Biography

Mr. A * * S [*Ames*]

LET the dictates of truth, biassed only by sincerity, pay equal respect to his eloquence and moderation. His candour was much suspected in the commencement of the present session: but his exemplary conclusions are honorable and valid. Conscious of the dignity with which he has discharged his trust, he should not value the murmurs of designing enemies, nor the tumults of declared traitors to the happiness of America, who have weakly attacked his character in the eastern newspapers: those envenomed shafts will be buried in oblivion, when records, more permanent than marbled praise, will acknowledge his merit. His faithful perseverance in the cause of his constituents, as well as in that of the general welfare, will bear testimony of his abilities and honor.

D. G.

NYDG, 19 July; reprinted at Boston and Worcester, Massachusetts.

Exhibition Corner;
or,
Congressional Biography

****** ******, Esq.

Messrs. A. B. C. G. H. M. P. S. V. W.

OR mute, or parrot, knave, or popping jay,
Each worthy member fobs six crowns per day.
Unhappy States! how are we duped, to send
So many Delegates with scarce one friend?
Was it for this ye suffer'd, fought, and bled,
To see, at last, a silly peacock tread
Down your freedom, ridicule your cause,
And e'en subvert your government and laws?
Shall patriots bow, to things dress'd up in silk,
To mere whipp'd sylabubs of asses milk?
Shall peruk'd[1] pedantry impose his drug,
"Discourses on Davilla?"
— Out the bug.
Send his "*Defence*,"[2] that train so wise and civil,
Both drug and Doctor[3] headlong to *** ***** [*the devil*].

Cetera Desunt[4]

NYMP, 20 July. The editors believe this piece was probably aimed at Congress in general rather than specific individuals.

---

[1] Wigged.

[2] *Discourses on Davila* and *Defense of the Constitutions* were two recent publications on government by Adams.

[3] Adams held an honorary LLD, granted by Harvard in 1787.

[4] The rest are omitted.

Sketches of Congressional Biography

J— J— [*James Jackson*], Esq.

J—n, if thou hast an enemy on earth, he must be of infernal extraction.

Thou hast thought with deliberation, and acted with independence. Thou hast been the enemy of intrigue and petty meanness; the patron of fair representation, and the steady supporter of that truth which ingrafts national honor on national prosperity.

When I hold up a character, like this, to public view, I must tell my fellow citizens, that

THIS IS A MAN,

eminent without artifice, just without pride, sanguine without prejudice, elegant without deceit, faithful without ostentation, and uniformly brave in the contempt he shews for the sycophants of the cabinet. To sum up all, I may justly assert, that J—n will ever be enrobed with the love of his fellow citizens.

D. G.

NYJ, 20 July; reprinted at Philadelphia.

Congressional Biography

R. K. *** [*Rufus King*] Esq.

IN an age when, rectitude is treated with derision, and virtue reprobated with indignity, it is difficult for an honest politician to steer his course clear of the rocks and shoals that are ever cast in his way, by the hackneyed antiquated knaves of government.

Mr. K. however, exhibits an example of firmness, prudence and respectability, seldom to be met with in young senators. Possessed of talents which, when called forth in the service of his country, shone with a lustre that obscured the mean abilities of many whose influence, not their merit, had placed them in exalted stations, he has exerted his abilities with dignity and effect. His judgement is mature, his conceptions strong, his reasons seldom to be controverted.

In discharging the duties of every office hitherto delegated to him, he has come off with *eclat*; and we have no cause to suspect that he will depart from the paths of true patriotism.

We shall only add our wishes, that he may never suffer his character to be branded with the curses which his countrymen have in store for the betrayers of their liberties. May his conduct remain exemplary as a representative, and virtuous as a man—blessed in domestic felicity, and admired by the true friends of America.

D. G.

NYDG, 20 July.

Exhibition Corner or Congressional Biography

(continued)

Messrs. B***ke and G***y [*Burke and Gerry*]

Possessed of judgment and penetration to circumvent the designs of those, who, dreading the superiority of their talents, sought to gratify an inveterate resentment, by openly stigmatizing those worthy friends with unpopular Epithets, and marking them out as the opposers of good government,[1] Messrs. B**ke and G***y have endeared themselves to their Country and to their friends, by exhibiting superior abilities, as Statesmen and Politicians.

By scrutinizing the conduct of a dangerous Aristocratic faction, with manly warmth, they have been threatened with Ministerial Vengeance, by even the Underlings of all the Understrappers in office. But, firm to their trust, those Patriots steer forward, hand in hand, stemming the torrent of Corruption, and GUARDING THE LIBERTIES OF MANKIND.

NYMP, 21 July.

[1] Both men were Antifederalists.

Congressional Biography (continued)

A****** B****** [*Abraham Baldwin*], Esq.

EXALTED, at a period when his abilities shone with their most distinguished lustre, to the dignity of a delegate to the grand [*federal*] convention in 1787, he discharged that important trust to the entire satisfaction of his constituents.

Being so honored with a seat in the great assembly of the United States, he is revered by men whose interests he protected, and admired by the most zealous advocates of a party whose prejudices were diametrically opposite to the principles of his conduct. His oratory is eloquent, with a precision of arguments peculiar to himself. Possessed of talents which nature had bestowed without reserve, he has improved them by an unvaried application. Cautious in the assertions he maintains, and rapid in the animated progress of his language, he astonishes his adversaries with the sublimity of his reasoning, while, by the judicious texture of his arguments, he renders the authority of his decision unanswerable even by the giant S***.[1]

With regard to the late dispute of temporary residence we must suppose he voted agreeable to the wishes of his constituents; and we therefore scorn to detract from his general character, even supposing his vote, in this instance, may have administered to cut the gordian knot.

D. G.

NYDG, 21 July.

[1] Scott's height provided an easy mark for anonymous identifications in the press; he appears again as "the great giant S***t" in "the Valedictory," *NYMP*, 21 August. Scott had reached some of his greatest oratorical heights in speeches opposing Baldwin's own highly publicized attacks against the Quaker antislavery petitions the previous spring.

Sketches
or
Congressional Biography

(continued)

"O! all ye host of Heaven! O Earth!
What else?
And shall I couple Hell? O fie! hold,
hold, my heart;
And you, my sinews, grow not instant old,
But bear me stifly up!"

SHAKESPEAR[1]

****** ******, Esquire

LIKE a tall gibbet, erected on the road side, to deter the unthinking passenger from following an evil course of life—THIS CHARACTER is hung up to warn the yet malefacting Libertine, who may have slept (through a motive of curiosity) from the chambers of debauchery to those of Contemplation—O ye Americans! What is it that bewitches you to send Delegates without principle! O thou eldest sister of the Union, why do you not make some enquiry into the *Morals* of your Representatives? Know you not that there are other qualifications besides riches and influence necessary in a Legislator?

Yet out of *Ten Members* should you at any time *choose One* who would commit a crime, at the perpetration of which even a Satyr would blush, then would I be warranted in saying, that your judgements would be eternally d—n—d, and your State disgraced beyond the power of Oblivion to obliterate.

D. G.

NYMP, 23 July; reprinted at Georgetown, Maryland.

[1] Shakespeare's *Hamlet*, Act I, scene 5.

Sketches of Congressional Biography

(Continued)

J— M—, [*James Madison*], Esq.

HAD there not appeared in the New-York Journal, some very illiberal effusions of folly and resentment against this gentleman,[1] we should not yet have touched upon his political character, having previously intended to watch his congressional proceedings until the end of the session, and then to have attempted a sketch of the part he had acted on the great stage of national exhibition.

Reserving, therefore, part of our design, we shall not, at present, enter into many particulars. The abuse from a *Citizen*, we disclaim and despise, because it is unfounded and unjust. Mr. M—n's conduct, in the struggle for discrimination we think most honorable; and, with regard to his manœuvres to carry the residence bill, we mean not to take any other notice of them hereafter, than as they are connected with subjects of much higher importance, which, we fear, were suffered to lie over neglected too long, in order to give precedence to this discordant, temporary, temporising hobby-horse.

Mr. M—n has always deserved and commanded the respect of his countrymen, not only on account of his own natural, and acquired abilities, but, because he stands high in the estimation of our hitherto favorite guardian and deliverer [*Washington*].

In defiance of his influence upon the *Philadelphian Residence*, we admire and love him; and did he not too often evince a strong aristocratic principle lurking *somewhere*, he would stand the best chance of any man in America to be the most patriotic character we could boast of.

D. G. & P. N.

NYJ, 23 July.

[1] A Citizen to the Citizens of New York, *NYJ*, 20 July, below.

[*John Vining,*] A Constant Reader to Mr. Morton

The Biographer Biographized

Friday, 23d July 1790

THIS Renowned Champion, whom the polite and accomplished Citizens of New-York have advanced to the dignity of Biographical "Bully" exhibits specimens of redoubtability terrible only to Dwarfs and Pigmies. This "*Toad Eater*"[1] of ______ hops among the Croud in EXHIBITION CORNER and squirts his venom indiscriminately on all around him, without regard to decency, place, or pension. The "*Bull Dog*"[2] of Faction, without Touch or Scent, he neither pursues his game nor seizes his prey. The "*Pimp*" of Discord, he weilds his weapon of Envy and Malevolence too feebly to wound, and too awkward to intimidate—A "*Puppy*"[3] among whelps, he knows not how to bark, nor when to bite–Like Œolus's harp,[4] his music has no melody, and like Sicyphus's stone, his burthen rolls back upon the Ass that moves it. Stupid by nature, and ignorant from necessity, his panegyric is nonsense, and his satire, dulness. Without talents to write, or wisdom to discriminate, his words have no meaning, his language conveys no sense.

He snarls at his friends, and grins at his foes,
and leaves marks of his folly wherever he goes.

NYMP, 24 July, edited by William Morton. The author of To J. V., 26 July, below, identifies Vining as A Constant Reader.

[1] A sycophant or parasite.

[2] A relentless, tenacious person.

[3] A term of contempt between men.

[4] Eolus or Aeolus was ruler of the winds, according to Homer's legend. The harp named after him operated like a zither, by wind blowing over it, and could produce only a single tone depending on wind speed.

To the Editor of the Morning Post

WE have received your letter, informing that a Member of Congress had this day sent several commanding messages, to desire your attendance at Fœderal Hall, respecting a Publication in your paper, and threatening you by one of the Messengers of the House of the United States, &c. as you have desired our instructions how to act.

WE now assure you, that there was not any LIBEL in the Publication alluded to, that the Constitution of the United States does not empower any Member of Congress to send threatening messages by any Attendant on the House, or any other Officer, to the Citizens of New-York, or any other City; that you are not under any obligation to give up the name of the Author in this instance; that if you are sued, or arrested, we will support and indemnify you; and finally, that we disregard the threats of any man, or set of men in the Universe, being resolved to make what use we judge proper of the LIBERTY OF THE PRESS.

The characters we have drawn, and mean occasionally to depict, are not exaggerated, but should any person *prove* the contrary, and leave their names in a proper manner, at your Office, should we then deem the said persons such as are worthy of our notice, we will most probably visit them after the close of the present session. Yours, &c.

D. G. & P. N.

N. B. The one which you intimate to have received, mentioning the name of a very worthy member from Virginia, (Colonel G—n [*Griffin*]) as being connected with the character alluded to in yesterday's publication, is a boyish attempt at confounding a saint with a public criminal. We esteem and respect Colonel G—n; it is only *the galled horse should wince.*

NYMP, 24 July.

To J*** V*****, Esquire

The Letter V. stands so close upon the tail of the Alphabet, that it would probably have been a week or ten days hence, before D. G. had come round to you, if at all. It is some doubt however with me, whether he would not have entirely omitted your name, and instead of ranking you among his Congressional Substances, passed you by as a shadow. Vanity, to exhibit a specimen of your Erudition, has induced you to volunteer in defence of the V—g—a [*Virginia*] Grey hound, whose lungs being long since exhausted, has been reduced to melancholy alternative of calling the assistance of a yelping ***** [*bitch*].

In order to be explicit, I say you are the Writer of the worse than School Boy collecting of cant phrases which appeared in the *Morning Post* of Saturday last.[1] Mr. ****** [*Vining*] being a little deficient in Ovid,[2] your knowledge of Æsop's Fables,[3] (for 'pon my soul I believe you can boast little more) enabled you to jumble together a few borrowed sentences from the *numerous* authors which you never read. What a *blessed pair* of Scholars ye are! Do good People but read the last *Morning Post*, and be struck dumb with astonishment: It is the Performance of a Member of Congress, not naturally born but sprung like VENUS from the *froth* of the river D—l—w—re.[4] A young River God, who languishes for the Nymphs of the Potowmack, and therefore voted for a *Ten Years* Residence on the Banks of the Delaware. A second Solomon,[5] who came post haste to harangue against the ASSUMPTION, and then voted for it. But it would be a vain attempt in us to enumerate his many

Consistencies. We shall therefore dispatch him by appropriating an Employment to fill his vacant hours.

Having already hung his *worthy* friend up on the gibbet of public detestation,[6] we shall couple Mr. V***** with Robert the Coffer [*Morris*], and start them naked together from New York in the Dog Days, to the Tune of *Connygojigg.*[7]

Hark away my good Dogs!
Hark away !
DIANA[8] TRIPES,
And all the Potowmack Harriers *in full Cry*
R. H. L[*ee*]. *Whipper-in to the Pack*

NYMP, 26 July.

[1] A Constant Reader, *NYMP*, 24 July, above.

[2] One of the most widely published ancient Roman poets (43 B.C.–A.D. 17).

[3] The ancient Greek world's foremost moralist through the use of fables (fl. early sixth century B.C.).

[4] Worshipped as the goddess of love and fertility in much of the ancient Mediterranean world, said to have been born from sea foam.

[5] King of ancient Israel (d. ca. 930 B.C.), most famous for his wisdom.

[6] Apparently the unidentified subject of the congressional biography dated 23 July, above.

[7] A dance or jig making a pun on the name of Conococheague Creek, the western most point on the Potomac River at which the seat of government could be located under the Residence Act.

[8] The ancient goddess of hunting.

TUESDAY, 20 JULY 1790

De Witt Clinton to Charles Clinton

I reced. by the bearer some newspapers which contain all the news in circulation. The removal is now determined—The Law declares that the next sessions shall be held at Philadelphia—The Constitution [*declares*] that the two Houses may or shall pass a vote of adjournment—without the assent of the President—It was then insisted that this clause in the Law which required the additional sanction of the President was unconstitutional—A piece was addressed to the President to prove the unconstitutionality of the Law[1]—sanguine expectations were formed by the ardent that the President would object to the bill—but their hopes were frustrated—The straw that now supports their sinking spirits, is a new law to qualify the former & fix the residence here for two Years. The people are much exasperated—Their federalism—their ships [*the Hamilton*] & processions federal halls and Palaces—are unrewarded—The ingratitude of Congress stares them in the face—The rents of Houses will fall—Boarding Houses will be empty—Mechanics will lose some of their business—and the indolent will have no federal hall at which to saunter away their morning hours. [*lined out*] but the poor will have cheaper markets cheaper houses, & clothes—The excessive luxury of the town will diminish—Splendid levees will no longer disgust the republicans nor the eternal rattling of coaches disturb the studious. The prints contain some angry pieces [*lined out*] & several caricatures have been circulated ridiculing the principal advocates for the removal—The best that I have heard of is one that represents Robert Morris the great engineer of the departure carrying federal hall on his back—Jay in one Pocket Hamilton in the other and the Members of Congress peeping their Heads out of the windows & asking where are we agoing to which Morris replies "Where I please." another represents some of the Congress as mere toys of Morris—Mr. Maddison for instance hanging at his watch fob There is one in which Morris is carrying a ladder of promotion on his back to Philadelphia filled with the majority & dragging the minority after him one of the former holds a purse of gold in his hand and says "This is what influences me" intimating that some of the members were bribed—some *Heroes* have talked of shutting up the Hall & refusing it to Congress in future but these are I presume mere explosions of wind—The Holy Name of the P—t is not much respected in the mouths of the profane.

The true History of the removal is this—Last sessions there was a solemn agreement made between the Members of Congress from New York & Pensylvania that the temporary residence should be four years in this City & the permanent on the banks of the Deleware [*at Germantown, Pennsylvania*]—a bill was brought in to that effect and on the verge of passing—Mr. Maddison went to some Merchants of this City, informed them that this might be a disadvantage to the City for if nothing was done in the business, Congress might stay a longer time here—that if they could Influence our Senators to vote for an amendment he would propose it would defeat the bill—The Merchants waited upon King & Schuyler. The latter closed with their wishes without hesitation, the former reluctantly—The bill was defeated because our Senators violated their faith—Virginia & Maryland that wished the permanent residence on the Potowmack formed this sessions a league with Pensylvania that was much exasperated at the conduct of our Senators & the event has turned out most unfavorably to this city. Our Commissioners ware [*were*] to meet those of Vermont a few days ago at stockbridge in Massachusetts—The Vermonters attended but none of ours except Mr. [*Gulian*] Verplank—consequently the meeting was adjourned without doing any thing The palace for the Governor is an immense building perhaps there will not be a larger house in America—It will take several thousand to furnish it—It goes on slowly—The Old fort [*Fort George*] is levelled—Docks are building out in that part of the city—Broadway is repaving—The departure of Congress will throw a damp on these spirited improvements. After our state representatives are apportioned according to the census, the Majority will probably be for Albany as the seat of government—federal Hall will then be a theatre of common-council legislation or a ball room—the palace will make a good bedlam[2] or ~~ple~~ house for the Mayor and this devoted City will never be the residence of sovereign powers—Consuls will be Ambassadors—Aldermen Legislators—Mayor & Recorders supreme Court Judges—Sheriffs ~~District~~ state Marshalls Constables, Sheriffs—The Governors of Bridewell[3] Roman Censors—~~the~~ In short, the little will be great—ambition will be gratified.

ALS, Extra illustrated *Old New York*, NHi. Addressed to Little Britain, New York.

[1] [*William Smith,*] Junius Americanus to the President of the United States, printed under 1790 Veto Crisis, 12 July, above.

[2] The colloquial name for Bethlehem Hospital, the London asylum for the insane, founded by the Catholic Church in 1377, confiscated by Henry VIII, and given to the City of London in 1547.

[3] A reference to the former royal palace that served as a London prison after the reign of Edward VI.

John Steele to Joseph Winston

This session is now near a close, without the prospect of obtaining any further amendments to the Constitution. Mr. Bloodworth and my self have made two attempts, but they were rejected by large majorities.[1] I must confess that tho' I have been uniformly in favor of the system, I am nevertheless anxious to have some material part of it modified on such a manner as wou'd unite all parties, give general satisfaction, and destroy those invidious party distinctions that have heretofore subsisted.

A vessel arrived here yesterday from Havre de Grace [*France*], and another from Glasgow [*Scotland*], which bring accounts of the same date which are diametrically opposite, respecting the Spannish-War. The one anounces hostilities, the other a pacification, neither being relied on entirely we are best in a state of extreem suspence with regard to the event. It is a dispute highly interesting to the United states, and I am very much affraid, that we shall be forced into the contest. The advantages which we may derive from a state of neutrality are so great that nothing can induce me to give my consent to any measures which might tend to lead us into the struggle.

We have passed a bill in the House of Reprs. to establish a post road from Petersburg to Halifax, Tarboro' Fayetteville, Campden, and Augusta[2]—This wou'd be throwing political information into the heart of the three southern States, and it wou'd enable me to be more usefull to my constituents in particular, because from Fayetteville my letters wou'd certainly find conveyances; whereas at present I am not sure that one letter in ten ever reaches the person it is intended for: But the Senate has disagreed to this bill, and a committe of conference is appointed to settle the difference between the two houses—what the result will be is uncertain. Notwithstanding we have rejected the assumption of the state debts five times in the Houses of Reprs.—The senate has lately passed it by 14 votes to 12—this decision I am affraid will have an improper influence on some wavering members.

The senate secluded from the public Eye, secreet in all their deliberations, few in numbers, and superior in prerogatives, and duration will always on great questions mannage the other house by intriegue.

We have fixed with uncommon difficulty the permanent seat of Govt. on the Potowmac and untill the buildings are compleated congress will hold their sessions in Philadelphia—This is a great point gained by the Southern delegates, and were it possible to reject the assumption-project once more and disappoint these reptile speculators who are preying upon Government, I woud return to my fellow citizens perfectly satisfied.

ALS, Steele Papers, NcU. Addressed to Stokes County, North Carolina.

---

[1] On 30 March Williamson presented to the House the eight Amendments to the Constitution proposed by the 1789 North Carolina convention that ratified the Constitution (and all but one of the twelve Amendments agreed to by Congress in September 1789). They were read and tabled; for the proposals and Bloodworth's and Steele's efforts on their behalf, see *DHFFC* 12:872, 13:1360, 1373, 1481.

[2] The Post Office Bill [HR-74] would have provided for a post road that ran from Petersburg, Virginia, through Halifax, Tarboro, and Fayetteville, North Carolina, and Camden, South Carolina, to Augusta, Georgia.

George Thatcher to David Sewall

Your conjectures of the motives that governed the Pennsylvanians in advocating the Patomack Bill are certainly just—and I have no doubt but future events will sanction them as predictions much better founded than many of Mohammeds supposed prophesies.

The importance, and consequences of a fixed seat of Government for the United States was first brought before Congress in the year 1788—I was then in Congress—and from that time to this have frequently revolved the subject in my mind—and have finally come to an opinion, that if the thirteen States, and such other as may be erected within the Limits setled by Treaty of eighty three, are to ~~be~~ continue~~d under~~ united under one Government and one nation, according to the principles of the present Constitution—the Seat of Government ought to be upon the Potomac, or some where between that River & the Susquehanna—I dont know that any place within these bounds is now the centre of population—but for two or three hundred years to come I beleive it will be there more than three fifths of the time. Natural population has always been the most rapid in the northern and eastern States—whether this will always be the case I am not fully convinced; but if it is owing to accidental causes acting, in the southern States, to retard the natural course of the increase of the human species, & which may hereafter be removed[1]—the numbers will then increase more rapidly in the southern and western, than in the northern & eastern States—because nine tenths of emigrants, which are continually poring into ~~America~~ the Unted [*United States*], will resort to Pensylvania and south thereof. These considerations, however point out to me the impropriety of fixing, at this time, a permanent seat of Government—but selfish motives, and what may be called temporary causes, have forced Congress into the measure—It is natural to ask, will Congress now take it upon them to say where it will be most convenient for the Legislature of the United States to reside fifty years hence—or one, two, or three centuries to come? It is impossible for the greatest human sagacity to do this. too many events, altogether contingent to the Understanding of man, are necessary to be taken into the calculation, in order to settle this point—All this will be granted—that as a majority are for fixing on the seat of Government, it appears to me it must be done under a supposition of one of two alternatives taking place—viz.—that the present thirteen States, and such others as may hereafter be created within the Limits setled [*by*] the Treaty of eighty three, are to continue under one general Goverment for ever—or that, at some definite period of time, the Territory within the foregoing Limits, is to be divided into separate & distinct Governments—each having a Legislature & seat of Government in and over itself.

If the seat of Government be established on the first of these alternatives, we must anticipate three or four hundred years, at least—or the utmost period of time, the ordinary events whereof can be discovered to have any possible connection with the present state of things—And tho the great chain of future events is so concealed from our inspection, that the most certain principles we can lay down to regulate our present conduct by, so far as it is to effect those distant senes, can only be compared to the glimmering rays of a Glow-worm in the blackest night; yet to me it seems more wise and prudent to act upon this, than the other alternative.

Who can enumerate the inconveniencies & miseries that would probably arise from debating, bublicly [*publicly*], the seat of Government on a supposition of a division of the American Empire?

These, and like reflections have reconciled me to the Patomack Bill—tho

I am not clear but the Susquehanna might have been more convenient—But the evils of the Law are not, and cannot be yet felt—after the seed is put into the Ground a considerable time will elaps before the sprout appears. Some Laws are to the body-politic what poison is to the natural man—their effects are not felt till they are become irremidible. What will be the state of the American mind, american prejudices & passions, eight or ten years hence, I will not take upon me to say—at this moment, however, they revolt against the Law for going to the Patomac; and nothing but the evils, it is supposed to conceal in its Trojan womb,[2] being so distant as not to be felt, prevents its being the occasion of immediate confusion—Some of these evils were pointed out by members, in the minority, when the Bill was before the House—and apparently laughed at by the majority—I say apparently—because I am persuaded many apprehended them, but hoped for the best—relying on a ten years contemplation of the Law to reconcile its opposers to its ~~opperation~~ fitness—and the minds, prejudices & passions of the people to acquiess in its operation—others laughed—because they had no doubt but the Law will be repealed before the time it is to take effect as to the permanent residence—and before that time Congress would be seated in Philadelphia—where they presumed it would remain.

Laws that are good, and which would operate beneficialy to the people they are to govern, were it not for some unreasonable prejudice the people have conceived against their operation, must be ranked among the acts of imprudent Legislators unless such prejudices are removed—Upon this principle, and in conformity to some unreasonable prejudices the Athenians had contracted, repugnant to a higher degree of happiness than what they then enjoyed, *Solon* declared his Constitution was a less perfect one than he would have offered them had they been free of these prejudices, which rendered them incapable of submiting to a better Government—He had but a choice of evils—an imperfect Government with a continuation of peace & the degree of happiness the Athenians then enjoyed—or a more perfect System with the probable risque of confusion and misery—and Ages have done justice to his wisdom and prudence in adopting the former.

When there exists an unreasonable prejudice in the minds of a people against a Law, the most effectual method of introducing it, and preserving peace & harmony, is to publish it some time before it is to take effect—This affords time to examine the Law and its natural consequences—and if a spirit of Liberality and candor, with free enquiry, prevails generally among the people, they will perceive that all their apprehended evils must flow from their unreasonable prejudices and not from the Law itself—By contemplating the Law, with its natural consequences, the public mind will be brought willingly to embrace it—Upon the same principles a Law, originating in party spirit, and which has not the general good for its object, (could the time of its operation be put off to some distant period, & time given for the special causes that gave rise to it, to subside) might be prevented from ever taking effect at all.

In proof of this I should even dare to refer you to Laws now existing in Massachusetts—which, had the time of their operation been fixed to the present moment, would have been repealed the last Session of the General Court, if not before—There are moments of political phrensy when the people cannot determine a good Law from a bad one—there are also moments of madness when the leaders of the people will force down Laws of the latter character, from Revenge, or some other abominable passion—But I entertain too high an opinion of the general good sense and enlarged views of Americans to apprehend these periods will ever be of long duration—The circumstances of America are vastly more favourable to a rational Legislation than any other Country under Heaven.

The Patomack-Law is a subject of much speculation—Will it be repealed before eighteen hundred? Then the president of the United States must be a Citizen of Pensylvania, or some eastern State—If it is not repealed, will Congress, at the time appointed, remove the Government and all its appurtenant-Offices to the Patomack? If Pennsylvania & the eastern States please they will continue in Philadelphia—And the moment Congress gets seated in that City it *will* be their pleasure to remain there—What then will the southern States say—they will plead the present Law—and the minority, with those in the majority who advocated the Law only for the sake of removing to Philadelphia, will laugh at the Southern States for being duped by the Pennsylvanians.

But if the Law is founded on rational grounds, and the public good actually requires the seat of Government at, or near the Patomack, the arguments & declamations against it are all founded on prejudice, which ten years reflection will wipe away; & at the time appointed the seat of empire will be removed thither, and all parties chierfully acquiess—But suppose this should not be the case—the Law is not repealed—and the seven eastern States are not in a humour to comply with it, will not the Southern States take dudgen, and declare, as the eastern part of the Union have openly violated one Law, they have a right to disregard all the others & the constitution itself, & set up a Republic themselves? This opens the door of speculation too wide to be shut by any thing but random conjectures—conjectures more wild than Chines[*e*] fables—or heathen mythology.

When I took my pen & began this Letter my designe was, in a few lines, to acknowledge the receipt of yours of the 12th. inst. But instead of that have wrote a dissertation—And having cursorily run it over I have strong doubts whether it is lawfull *in bono conscientiæ*,[3] for me to send it; as it will impliedly lay you under an obligation to read it—But as it is probable you will turn to the end to see who signed it, you may possibly see this Line—wherein *I Give you full Liberty to put the whole into the fire before you read another word.*

P. S. By the face of the inclosed order you will perceive it was made out and registred on the 12th. inst. which is the same date with your Letter requesting an order upon Collector [*Richard*] Trevett And your Letter did not reach me till the evening of the 17th. The order being made out in my name was owing to a mistake of the Treasurer [*Samuel Meredith*], which he did not discover till it was ~~to late to~~ registred & too late to be rectified—To remidy which I have indorsed it for value received.

FC, Thatcher Family Papers, MHi.

---

[1] Probably a reference to black slavery and its eventual abolition.

[2] A reference to the wooden horse with Greek soldiers in its belly that the Trojans hauled into Troy.

[3] In good conscience.

Oliver Wolcott, Jr. to Frederick Wolcott

***

The comptroller [*Nicholas Eveleigh*] is unable to attend constantly to the business of his office, which renders my attention somewhat more necessary.

It is not strange that the people of the country should feel disappointment at the delays of Congress. You may, however, be assured that a great majority are honestly attempting to serve the public. They disagree, it is true, as to the manner in which this is to be effected, and this is to be imputed, in a great measure, to the real difficulties which attend the subjects of their deliberation.

The business of the residence is settled. We are to remove before the 1st of December to Philadelphia, and if we live so long, in ten years, to the Indian place with the long name on the Potowmac [*Conococheague Creek*].

The great question is now respecting the interest. Our friend, Mr. Ellsworth, in the Senate, has been of opinion that it was not expedient to attempt to fund the public debt at a higher rate of interest than four percent. That this sum, punctually paid, would answer the expectations of the creditors, the requirements of justice, and would better secure the public honor than a promise of a higher provision, which would, under the circumstances of this country, be attended with greater risque of failure.

He has also been dissatisfied with the Secretary's proposal of leaving one-third of the debt unfunded for ten years, as this measure would tend to encourage speculations, and would leave, after ten years, a great burden upon the country, with little advantage to the creditors, who would probably alienate their demands to foreigners, who would purchase that part of the debt at a low rate.

These opinions have been supported by him with all that boldness and reason which give him a predominant influence in the Senate. He has, however, been warmly opposed, and a compromise, it is said, has been made to fund the principal of the domestic debt in the following manner:

For every $100 principal, 66 2/3 to be funded presently at 6 per cent., and 26 88/100 after ten years at the same rate. The indents and all arrearages of interest, which amount to about one-third of the debt, to be funded at three per cent. This, it is said, will give about 4s. 3 per cent. interest for the entire debt.

A resolution has passed the Senate for funding the state debts at the same rate as the continental debt; but all these things may, and probably will assume a different modification before the session is completed.

The House have passed an additional impost act, by which the duties are increased about 33 1/3 per cent. This has not yet passed the Senate.

These are the principal matters of which I am able to inform you at this time, as the post will leave the town directly. ***

Wolcott 1:49.

[*Andrew Brown,*] Newspaper Article

Whatever has a tendency to destroy internal harmony amongst the people of the United States ought to be deprecated by every American citizen as hostile to the union of the States, and consequently destructive of liberty. Civil discord is fraught with such alarming evils, that no man, unless he be callous to every patriotic, to every humane feeling, can behold even the appearance of it without horror. Our escape from anarchy is too recent to be yet forgotten. Rescued from the dangers of disunion with which we were lately threatened, be it our chief study to guard against them in time to come.

We have already proved to the world, that Montesquieu and other writers on government were mistaken, when they asserted the impossibility of holding a vast and extensive territory united under a free republican government. We have formed the most extensive republic that ever has been known in the world; but let it be remembered, that we have formed it upon the great basis of a true and equal representation of the people, in the remote as well as in the central parts of the empire. This health-diffusing principle, like the circulation in the animal body, administers vigour to the most distant extremities of the body politic.

But another rock, on which republics have been often wrecked, is civil strife, arising from the apparent clashing of local interests, or from some such unworthy motive. It is necessary to guard against this bane of republicanism, by convincing the citizens of America of the great political truth, that the interest of the whole will best promote that of every part, and that the prosperity of individual states is inseparably connected with that of the union.

It is presumed that if due attention were paid to this consideration, the different parts of the union would not be so easily set at variance with each other. The question of temporary residence lately agitated in Congress would not make the citizens of New-York and Philadelphia consider their interests as opposite, or their dispositions as inimical to each other. They would view the decision of Congress in no other than a general light. respect only being had to the common convenience of the union. It would be absurd, and highly derogatory from the dignity of Congress, to suppose them capable of being influenced by a partiality for either city, or by any other motive than that of general convenience. Their decision is certainly viewed in no other light by the most respectable and best informed citizens either in Philadelphia or New-York. And whatever mistake or misrepresentation may advance to the contrary the Editor of this paper, having spent the greater part of last week in New-York, is happy in being able to assure his readers, from his own observation, that the people of that city have shown no disposition, on this occasion, either to abuse the citizens of Philadelphia or to insult Congress, as has been mistakenly imagined by some. That indecent reflections have appeared in some of their newspapers is true; but what candid man will believe that such publications convey the sentiments or meet the approbation of the citizens at large? They certainly do not. On the contrary, the Editor has been assured from good authority that precautions were actually taken by the police and the most respectable inhabitants, to suppress any disorderly proceedings which a misguided multitude might engage in; but the event showed that their apprehensions were groundless. The decision of Congress, though not pleasing, was nevertheless received with the utmost decency and decorum. The Editor was in the gallery of the House of Representatives on Friday last, when the approbation and signature of the residence bill by the President were announced; and though the crowd was great, no indecency of behaviour was shewn.

These facts the Editor thinks it [*h*]is duty to communicate, in justice to the citizens of New-York, and from a desire of preserving peace and harmony between New-York and Philadelphia, by contradicting such injurious reports as have for some time past, been in circulation. May the citizens of this Metropolis, like those of New-York, be distinguished by a polite attention to Congress. The great exertions made for their accommodation do honor to the liberality and patriotism of that city.

FG, 20 July; reprinted at Boston and Baltimore.

Z to the Honourable the Senate of the United States

On the proposition for lowering the rate of interest on indents, when funded, below the rate of interest on the principal.

Gentlemen,

YESTERDAY I attempted to shew the injustice of the proposed arrangement: I shall now attempt to prove its impolicy, by [*ef*]fective reasoning.

1st. That the interest is almost totally retained in the hands of our own citizens; but that a great proportion of the principal debt is transferred to foreigners. The truth of this may, in a great measure, be judged by the treasury books: but there is still more retained by citizens in trust for foreigners, and a considerable sum in original certificates sent both to London and Amsterdam, neither of which can appear by those books.

2d. That it must effect the credit of the newly funded debt, principal as well as interest, the holders of which will reasonably conclude, that if deficiencies of interest are neither to be paid off nor even funded on equal terms, they have then no security in case deficiencies in the funds should in future arise. In short the whole arrangement must be granted as highly dangerous to the holders of principal as well as interest, in all future occasions or contingencies, by an accidental derangement of the finances of the union, by a civil commotion, by a foreign war, some expedient similar to those very indents might, for a time, become necessary. The promoters of this new arrangement ought to consider, that they blast all hopes of the utility of such an expedient in future.

3d. That a violation in the rate or payment of interest, is more immediately ruinous to the credit of the nation, where that violation is not the effect of necessity, which it confessedly is not in the present case. The richest nation in the world, under a repetition of these circumstances, could not possibly enjoy credit any longer. The British credit has been supported by no other means, but a regular payment of interest and arrears of interest, whenever it accrued: by adhering steadily to this, they enjoy a more extensive credit than the rest of the habitable world; yet every wise man, to whom they stand indebted, knows perfectly that they neither are nor ever will be able to discharge the principal, the amount of which is more than the whole island of Great Britain would command, if sold acre by acre, with the king, lords and commons to boot.

4th. The impolicy of this measure may be seen by comparison. There are sums of interest due to foreign powers: these, we presume, must be paid in specie. It is hoped the forms of government give us no just right to do so greatly worse for our own citizens. It is admitted that, in case of the revenue being deficient, good policy prescribes that the loss should fall upon our own citizens, rather than upon foreigners: but in this loss each part should bear a just proportion. If good policy prescribes that we should pay the whole interest we owe to foreign powers in specie, I think the same policy will direct that we should do as much towards the payment of our domestic interest so long due, as far as our situation and circumstances will admit. All that our citizens expect is, that the interest should be funded on terms at least equal to the principal: I think there is nothing unfair in this.

But the proposition of paying 6 per cent. for principal, and only 3 per cent. for interest, is the reverse of all this. It is an imaginary and impolitic distinction raised like a phantom in the minds of some men, who, without knowing any certain reason, think merely, in general, that it is hard to pay interest for interest. I say, if it was unjust to pay interest for interest, it would hold equally the same at 3 per cent. as well as six; but I am confident it is not unjust at all. The interest ought to have been paid in money, if not, certainly it is just to pay for the delay. It was always conceived, that whenever the United States were possessed of resources, they would make provision for the actual payment of these in money, before they would make provision for the payment of any new interest that might accrue. The forms of private contracts are no ground of calculation in this case: a private man, possessed of an estate, who neglected payment of interest, would soon have his estate sold for the arrears. The common law, in this case, provides a sufficient remedy: if the plaintiff neglects his suit, he has himself alone to blame; but, in the case under consideration, there were no courts of justice or common law to which to have recourse: therefore, the same power alone which, through the necessity of the times, inflicted the wound, ought now to provide the remedy.

NYDG, 20 July. The piece began in *NYDG*, 19 July, and continued in the issues of 21 and 23 July.

A Citizen to the Citizens of New York

RESIDENCE

THE liberal and federal conduct of this city deserved from government polite and delicate treatment. Polite conduct they would have experienced, if the g—t [*government*] was administered by men, who had the sentiments, the education, the manners, and habits of *g—l—n* [*gentlemen*]. If America has any of this *breed* left, they are to be found in the *capitals*. These citizens have yielded their pride, their wealth, their luxuries, their commerce, for the speculative advantages of a *chimerical union.* The proud and high minded inhabitants of this city must be extremely mortified to be governed by a majority of rustic boors, who are sudden and forced vegetables in the hot bed of federalism. *Jockeys* versed in all the stratagems of *quarter races—Attornies* hackneyed in all the tricks of *county courts* and *elections—Planters*, whose social collisions are with their hogs, negroes, and horses.

This generous and ill-treated city has expended £25,000 to accommodate the g—t of the n—n [*government of the nation*]. A faction, formed upon chimerical, profligate, immoral, and impolitic principles (with a leader [*Morris*], who disgraces the councils of a republic, who enjoys his personal liberty, through the lenity, and timidity) of his creditors, turn their backs, and shake off the *dust of their feet*, towards this hospitable and generous city.

The conduct of *discriminator* [*Madison*], who was always represented as a *monk* in his solitary and virtuous habits, has disappointed the world. Open doors has let light on the obscurity of his character, *the screen is thrown down*, and the *sentimental Joseph* stands revealed and exposed.[1] If the imagination could, with any critical propriety, weave the events of ten years in the plot of the comic drama, the *denouement* would be to his confusion & disgrace. He would stand like the detected *surface*, entangled in his own web, the contempt and the jest of the whole *dramatis personæ*, and would exhibit to the audience an admonitory lesson against *little intrigue* and political *hypocricy.*

We can have no reliance on the liberal manners, or politeness of a *cloistered pedant*, when we consider his society and *connections*—Politeness is an accidental and artificial virtue, acquired by certain social situations, which pedantry or ambition cannot command; a man might as well look for his *debts* in the antient dominion [*Virginia*] as *politeness.* It is a plant which will not flourish in the neighbourhood of tobacco, which is as fatal to its tender nature, as the barberry-bush is to wheat. *Gratitude* is a virtue, which may shew itself as illustriously in a *cottager* as in a *courtier*—in a *pedant* as in a scholar—it does not depend on a *forced* education or refinement of manners. The violation of the laws of hospitality, is one of the few crimes, which the untutored savages punish and abhor. The violation of gratitude is considered, by civilized society, as a more flagrant offence than the violation of chastity, on the altars of the church. It is always marked with peculiar odium and infamy, and the charity of the world never excuses an offence, which the scripture denominates worse than *witchcraft.* We cannot excuse the heart of the *closet politician*, when he errs from the paths of gratitude, we cannot admire the sagacity of his understanding, when he becomes the dupe of an *insidious contract*, and the tool of a dishonorable faction.

This state has surrendered to the union a very unequal share of revenue, yet they are treated with the supercilious contempt of the majority. This state was nearly out of debt, and was the envy of the union. If the state debts are assumed, we shall be forced into burdensome and dishonorable connections with insolvent states, and we shall loose our natural superiority and independence. It is time, my friends, to reflect, whether the advantages of the union, now the residence is removed, can qualify a *certain sacrifice*. The citizens are injured, and a compensation is due from the liberality and justice of government.

NYJ, 20 July; reprinted at Philadelphia.

[1] In Genesis 45:1–4, a tearful Joseph revealed himself to his brothers.

Theatricus to Mr. Greenleaf

I SEND you a short account of the *farce*, called the *Junto Triumphant*, lately performed at the *New Theatre*, by *Discord's F—d—l* [*federal*] *Company of Comedians*. The principal characters were—

THE JUNTO

Machieval [*Morris*]—A deep designing fellow, and leader of the junto.
Fritz. [*Fitzsimons*]—A creature, & dependent of Machievals.
Virginius [*Madison*]—Principal speaker of the junto.
Thersites—By a gentleman from M—l—d.[1]
Georgius Bulldog [*Jackson*]—A noisy chap, who pretends to act disinterestedly.
And *Froth* [*Vining*]—Pimp for the party.

DISSENTERS

Patriot [*Ames*]—A great politician and speaker.
Councellor John [*Laurance*].
And *Sir Brullihan O' Blunder* [*Burke*].
Mr. *Self-Interest*—Prompter.

The first act begins with Machieval's escape from bailiffs, who pursues him across the stage with protested bills. The characters were in general well supported, and the performers had their parts to admiration, except *Froth*, who was much confused at some mistakes he made; but we suppose he did not expect to see a full house, or he would have been more cautious, as he endeavours much to please the audience, particularly of the female class.

NYJ, 20 July, edited by Thomas Greenleaf; reprinted at Poughkeepsie, New York. The style and specific choice of references identify the probable author as one of the contributors to the Congressional Biographies, 19 July, above. (See especially the references to Vining in the *NYMP* pieces of 20 and 23 July.)

[1] Most likely D. Carroll, but perhaps Stone or even Contee or Gale. Thersites was a stoop shouldered, bowlegged, and pointy headed Greek soldier in Homer's *Iliad*.

OTHER DOCUMENTS

William Constable to Alexander Ellice. FC:lbk, Constable-Pierrepont Collection, NN.

The debt will be funded at four percent, with alternatives.

Fontaine Maury to James Madison. ALS, Madison Papers, DLC. Written from Fredericksburg, Virginia. For the full text, see *PJM* 13:280–82.

Encloses his account with Madison for the period 5 July 1788 and 13 July 1790; "There seems to be great exertions in some of the districts for the next Congress"; in Madison's, "I hear of no opposition—Mr. [*Francis*] Corbin is very active in Middlesex and the counties which compose that [*Page's*] district."

Governeur Morris to William Short. ALS, Short Papers, DLC. Written from London; FC, letterbook copy, Morris Papers, DLC, indicates it was addressed to Paris.

Letter from New York dated 4 June informed him that the Foreign Intercourse Bill [HR-52] was lost but that another would be brought forward immediately; another letter from the same correspondent, dated 16 June, makes no mention of a new bill.

GUS, 21 July.

"On the third reading of the Funding Bill in the Senate, a motion to strike out the assumption of the state debts was negatived by a majority of two."

WEDNESDAY, 21 JULY 1790

Thomas Fitzsimons to Benjamin Rush

***

I have not the Smallest inclination to be in any degree Accessory to the Robbery of the Army and as little to Sacrifice the honor and interest of this Country—I Lament that a Series of Unjust and Ill advised Measures should have Rendered absolute Justice to the first Impracticable at same time I have satisfyd myself that funding the public debt at 3 ℔ Ct. would not only be unjust but Impolitic, and being of that Opinion I Can Neither Advocate nor assent to such a Measure—I Know that in public Life it is too often Necessary to Sacrifice ~~Opinion~~ to public Opinion but there & as farr as honor would Warrant I have Sacrificed Mine but there are Occasions when every Man in public life ought to Act upon his own—I shall lament extreamly if my doing so should have the Consequences You apprehend—but so far as they respect myself I have been long determined to Abide them—I Never expect my friends to serve me at the expence of their Judgement or the Sacrifice of their Opinions. they must Allow me to Conduct myself upon the same principles—It is yet very uncertain whether any or What provision sho[*uld*] be made for the public debt ~~but~~ my end[*eav*]ors will be used to Obtain a Reasonable one before we Adjourn—it gives me no small Concern that I should differ so Widely in Opinion on this business, with a friend on Whose Judgement I have great Reliance—I hope it will Occasion No interruption in our other pursuits or our Regard for Each Other.

ALS, Gratz Collection, PHi. Addressed to Philadelphia; franked; postmarked. The omitted text relates to the Pennsylvania gubernatorial election and assures Rush that the upcoming meeting of the state constitutional convention "will test the business and we shall be with You at that time."

Edmund Pendleton to James Madison

*** I am happy to find that Potowmac stands on so good grounds as the Permanent seat of Congress; I could not help wishing that the Temporary Residence had remain'd at New-York, as a recompence for their expence in y[*ou*]r Accommodation; to save the expence & trouble of a double removal of the Public Offices, and from a conviction, that Philidelphia is in bad order for yr. reception, & must incur a considerable expence to be in order: besides I doubt, from from former experience, whether those Citizens may not more intermeddle with the Fœdral proceedings, than they have at [*New*] York. However you Gentn. on the Spot could much better judge of all these, & other circumstances, than we at a distance.

I hope some Accommodating Spirit has allayed the fury of debate on the great Subject of Assumption, to prevent your Session terminating in a temper which must injure Government in Character & Interest—At the same time caution seems necessary, that we do not by yielding too much, fortify & Cherish an Opinion, some Gentn. appear to have entertained, that they are to dictate to the union, against the sense of a majority on a full discussion. I wished to have earlier mentioned to you the subject of the British debts, & submitted to you whether it would not be expedient & indeed necessary for Congress to pass a law on that Occasion, as I know there will otherwise be considerable difficulties in the minds of the State Judges at least, in deciding suits which may come before them on the present footing. Tho' too late for this Session, I mention them for your Reflection in the Recess.

The Treaty [*of Paris, 1783*] is "there shall be no legal impediment to the bona fide recovery of debts on either side"—Is this a law of Repeal in itself, &

what is the extent of it? does it repeal all acts of limitation, & such as regulate the modes of proving debts? Or is it rather a covenant by the contracting parties to remove legal impediments by their respective laws, & meant to be confined to such as the War had introduced?

Was not the latter the sense of the Congress who made the treaty, when they called on the States to repeal the several laws containing such Impediments? The New Constitution "all Treaties *made*, or which shall be made, under the authority of the United States, shall be the *Supreme law* of the land."

What law is here meant? is it like those of the Medes & Persians, unalterable?[1] or may not the contracting powers annul it by consent? Or a breach on one side discharge the other from an Obligation to perform it's part? And how are these circumstances to be communicated to each ~~Gov~~ Station but by their respective Governmts.? It seems placed on the ground of the Other laws of Nations, to which all Municipal laws must yield, & is directly opposed to the State Constitutions & laws. But must not the National Government regulate all National Affairs? does not the Coupling *Treaties* with the Constitution & *laws* of the United States, indicate that the latter are to introduce & give force to the former in the Society? the former question here Occurs, whether this Treaty be a law in itself repealing all others, or an Executory Covenant to pass laws for the purpose? Do Congress mean the debts shall be paid, if Britain refuses to perform the Treaty on her part, giving up the Western posts &c.? And do not all these circumstances combine to prove the propriety of a law of Congress to settle the Subject? Perhaps you'l consider these as mere sceptical whims; if so pray throw them by & take no further notice of them, tho' I fear unless they are removed, & I am obliged to decide on the question, they will have a serious affect on the Judgment of Dear Sir Yr. very Affe. friend.

ALS, The Gilder Lehrman Collection, on Deposit at the New York Historical Society, New York. [GLC 99.144] Written from Virginia. The omitted text apologizes for Pendleton's "arrears" in letters and describes a state court of appeals case.

[1] Daniel 6:8.

George Thatcher to Nathaniel Barrell

My last contained some general observations on the dissatisfaction among the people at the delays, as well as the doings of Congress—and the probability of a change of Representatives the ensuing election.

This shall give you some facts and sentiments relative to myself, and in answer to your favour of the 10th. inst. which came to hand last evening—

and I assure you, that sometimes, and upon some subjects, I delight as much in talking about myself as fond mothers do about their darling children—There is one difference, however—they most always dwell on such qualities and actions as are esteemed, by their company, to be virtuous, and amiable; and for the most part recommends children to the approbation of those they converse with—whereas I shall bring to view those things that, in the present state of opinions and sentiments, have a quite contrary tendency—But truth and duty to my fellow creatures command me to speak—and silence would be criminal.

The most ardent wish I have is, that all people may be instructed in those things that make for their real happiness—An enlightned, intelligent people only can be happy—while ignorance and misery are inseperable companions. When I compare the past state of things with the present I am delighted—but when I extend the comparason to future periods—the prospect is ravishing—my soul is in extacy; and I forgive, as well as forget the little Bickerings, calumnies and troubles of the present moment, & live upon the general joy & harmony which all will then enjoy—What is it to me, whether I am in Congress, or out? Others may conduct affairs as well as myself—and the increasing felicity of mankind can be equally enjoyed on the Banks of the Saco [*River*], or the Hudson—To return to your Letter.

The Journals of the House of Representatives will witness that I have uniformly opposed those grants and measures of Congress, which have caused so much uneasiness among the people of Massachusetts—I have done my duty—On this account I am above slander—I have vanity to think, that in some respects, I have served particular parts of the district of Maine better than any man in it would have done, had he been in my room—on this account I shall always triumph over those who were my competitors at the last election: And I feel myself equal to any man in the district of Maine to render it such service, in Congress, as it may require—and sure I am that no man exceeds me in wishing its happiness and prosperity—Hence, on this account, I shall never be mortified at seeing another succeed me in the future elections.

Indeed I shall think it rather strange if the general uneasiness at the proceedings of Congress, joined to the Cry of impiety and irreligion, against me in particular, should not oust me at the coming election. It is natural for pole-cats to kill chickens—and for wolves to devoure Lambs: So it is for *religious* people to persecute those who differ from them in sentiment. Ignorance and superstition have, in all Countries, and at all times been at war with reason. Religion has long served as a shield for vilany to attack honesty under; and it is not unusual for the greatest scoundrals to cry out, God and the Church, in order to run down those who stand in their way.

But these things, my friend, must be endured with patience and resignation—time and information, in the true principles of what is usefull to man and Society, will work a cure.

Tho I am the victim of this monster, I feel happy in thinking, he will soon be drove from the American shores—his power is weakned every day; and the most it can effect is to prevent a mans election, or cause him to be stared at for a while—The reason and good sense of the pople will not long be duped by hypocrasy, superstition and folly—I feast on the idea that people are daily growing wiser, better and more happy. This is a luxurious *compensation* for any thing I may suffer by the pious Calumny of the ignorant.

What astonishing advances have been made towards rationality in thinking & acting within one century past—Had I lived in that time I certainly should have been banished—perhaps, worse might have befallen me. At that unhappy period, to be a Quaker, a Baptist a Witch or a Socinian[1] was almost equally dangerous—The same spirit of *holy error* led people to persecute each of these denominations; and now induces many to cry out *Impiety* & *irreligion* against those whom they wish to hunt down—with this difference however; and which strongly marks the superior felicity of the present times—that then this spirit was so potent as to govern the Laws; but now 'tis feble, and governed by them. Happy happy times—soon—very soon, will it be in subjection not only to the Laws, but to reason itself—And it shall be my constant endeavour to accelerate and hasten so desirable a state of Society.

You tell me "that every artifice is made use of to oust me at the ensuing election amongst which 'tis said that a I coupled *Bibles* and *wool-cards* together, and proposed a heavy impost on them, equal to a prohibition"[2]—This is truly laughable—yet it tends to shew the spirit, I will not say of *the people*, but, of *some people*.

If it be impious to write *Bibles* and *wool-cards* on the same bit of paper, what shall we say of those who keep the *Bible* and *wool-cards* in the same house and, perhaps, some times in the same room? I will honestly confess I have always had a *Bible*, a *Testament* and *wool-cards* in my house & I never once heard them call each other hard names—nor did I ever know them to quarrell. I can well recollect particular times when I have set by the side of Mrs. [*Sarah Savage*] Thatcher reading the *Bible*, while she was diligently making use of these said *wool-cards*; and I never perceived but she worked with them as well as tho the *Bible* had been at an hundred miles distance—and I declare further, that I beleive, I read the Bible as understandingly, and as savingly, as if the said *wool-cards* had been in the Garret or in some merchants shop at Boston—Hence I conclude there is nothing hurtfull to individuals, or Society in coupling the *Bible* and *wool-cards* together; or their being in the same House, the same room; or even nearer together—And consequently I shall give it as my opinion, in which I dont know that many will join me, that there is nothing impious, irreligious or criminal in this action of coupling the *Bible* and *wool-cards* together.

"But tis said I proposed a high impost on them equal to a prohibition"—Query—did this Impost extend to *Bibles*—or the *wool-cards*, or to both? I have before shewn there is no *criminality* in coupling *Bibles* and *wool-cards* together: And I beleive it will be a much more difficult task, than my religious constituents imagine, to shew why *wool-cards* should be imposted in this manner, and not *Bibles*—since the American printers can as easily supply America with *Bibles*, as the Card-makers can with *wool-cards*. I very well recollect there was great opposition to the impost on *wool-cards*, but none to the impost on *Bibles*—for *Bibles* are imposted—Perhaps the Impost was designed to reach both *Bibles* and *wool-cards*, in equal degree—Be it so—and in the name of good policy why should it not? Are not American Bibles as good as British or Irish? Does not America furnish good paper, good Tipes, & good printers in abundance? Are there not already published, or publishing, in different parts of the United States Bibles of almost every size—viz. folio, quarto and octavo? Have not the printers come forward and requested Congress to afford them some encouragement as well as other mechanics and manufacturers in the Union? And what reason can be assigned why they should not be duly encouraged—I say according to the magnitude of their undertaking? If Bibles are of the first utility—it is of importance that we should not depend on a foreign nation for our supply—every one must recollect how much we suffered during a long war thro the scarcity of Bibles[3]—while we had *wool-cards* eno' because the latter were manufactured in america, & not the former—now I would have them both equally encouraged, & then we shall be always able to supply ourselves.

I have said "we have *good printers*" in America—perhaps, some of my religious constituents will object, that they are not *religious printers*—I confess I dont know how this may be; but I repeat it, they are *good printers*—I speak of my own knowledge—they print equal to any, and ~~superior~~ much better than many of the British and Irish *Bible printers*—And with proper encouragement would supply the United States with good Bibles as cheep as we now get them from England—should I be asked if they would be *religious Bibles*? I shall decline giving an answer till they let me know what they mean by religion—and a *religious Bible*—and hence I conclude again that it would not have been injurious to the United States to have imposted *Bibles* and *wool-cards* with a pretty high duty—and if you please equal to a prohibition—And I shall dare to give it as my opinion, let religious people say whatever their Religion may suggest, that there is *nothing impious, irreligious*, or *criminal in coupling Bibles* and *wool-cards* together, *and proposing a high duty on either or both.*

I have thus allowed the facts as charged against me, in order to shew, that if the facts were true, they do not amount to a crime of a civil, or religious nature.

But to be honest—I never did propose an impost on *Bibles* and *wool-cards* in my life—It was, as nearly as I can recollect, on Bibles, Testaments, spelling-books and other school-books printed in America—this I moved—which was seconded—Then a very authordox, religious man, who set by me, and approved my motion, (the same who seconded it) desired me to add playing cards to the list—which I accordingly did. Then it ran thus—*on all Bibles, Testaments, speeling Books & all other school-books printed in the United States, also on all playing Cards*—But I never mentioned any sum, either high or low, at which I would have them imposted—I ment to leave that to the merchants & those better acquainted with the subject.

I have now stated to you the facts just as they took place; and will only add, that if some people knew I had coupled *Bibles* with *playing-cards* they would be more outrageous, and ball [*bawl?*] out irreligion, with more zeal, than when they heard I had coupled the *Bible* with *wool-cards*—And if any one mentions this matter to you as an objection to my religious, moral or political Character—do you be honest and tell him plainly I never coupled the *Bible* and *wool-cards* together; but it was the *Bible* and *playing-cards*—Tell him he has been missinformed; and if this is a more impious copulation than the other—nevertheless, it being the truth, I would have him know it.

Your friendship for me is so great I am fearfull it will lead you to state some things that are not true, the better to recommend me to the people—This I must caution you against. Friendship is sometimes as bland as Love; and to make others esteem our friends as we do ourselves, we are exceedingly apt to attribute to them those qualities and virtues which are the best calculated to produce this effect: But as much as I respect the opinion of people and court their applause I cannot wish for their approbation at the expence of truth. I should be unhappy if I thought people put their trust and confidence in me, upon a presumption that I possessed certain virtues or dispositions which I was conscious did not belong to me.

As yet people think religion an essential qualification of a Legislator, or any person in public trust—And more have objected to my being their Representative, because I am, they say, a man of no Religion, than on any other account whatever—Remove this—and I am of opinion very few would withhold their votes—But in trying to obviate this I cannot agree for you to hold out an idea that I beleive any or scarce any of the Tenets that enter into the Creed which people, in general, look upon as necessary to make a religious man; I had rather be as I am, and deemed irreligious than thought such an one—Such as I am seen and known to be, by him who trys the reins and searches the hearts of all men,[4] I am willing to appear to my fellow-creatures; and in no other Character—I had rather never be again noticed by the voice of my Country, than receive their unanimous vote on the ground of my holding to many of the things which I know they look upon essential to a religious Character—Among which I will mention a few.

The doctrine of original sin—or depravity—Imputation of sin, or Righteousness, with the doctrine of Atonement—The Trinity or a plurality of persons in the Deity—The divinity and preexistance of Jesus—the Divinity & personality of the Holy Ghost as taught by athenatius[5]—that a man can be saved without virtue; or damned who is virtuous—or that there is any other way of recommending ourselves to the approbation of the Deity, than by the practice of moral virtue—If 'tis said, on this Ground, I am no Christian—I reply, tis indifferent to me what I am called—I beleive Life and immortality are brought to light by the Gospel—That Jesus is the son of man; and, as the Apostle declares, a man highly favoured of God—that he wrought the miricles attributed to him in the four Gospels—that at the last day the Resurrection will take place as set forth in those Books; and man will be happy or miserable *precisely* according to his works in the Body—I dont beleive much about the Devil, or Hell fire—and am pretty strongly inclined to think the whole system of creation tends to perfection & happiness—and that finally, when God will be all in all, all beings will be happy—that the pain and misery the wicked undergo are by way of discipline.

Now if a beleif of the foregoing positions, and perhaps some others of a similar kind, which, in my hurry, I have omitted, are sufficient to denominate me a Christian—then I am certainly one—otherwise I am not—But as I said once before, it is indifferent to me what I am called—provided Justice is done me—And I am more fearfull that people will, after all, attribute to me too much, than too little faith.

I will once more return to your Letter, and after an observation or two take my leave—And as this may be the last Congressional Letter you will receive from me, you will the more willingly excuse its undue length—You must recollect, I told you, at the begining, I was going to write about myself—and compared myself to a fond parant listning to his own discourse about his darling children.

I have noticed that the people of Massachusetts express more uneasiness at the proceedings of Congress, so far as they relate to the grants of money, than those of any other state. And tho it is well known to their Representatives have, with greater unanimity, than is to be found among the Representatives of other States, opposed those Grants; Yet Massachusetts is the only State where the people seem so determined upon a general change of their Senators and Representatives—I do not recollect a single measure or act of Congress that is reprobated by the people of Massachusetts, but what their Senators, or Representatives, or both, have uniformly opposed. All this must be known to the people if they read the News papers—What then can enrage them to such a degree as to aim at a general change?

Why our District should wish to oust me is easily accounted for—first others wish to come in my room—& secondly my religion & that of the people are very different things—Now these two circumstances are eno' to oust me, let my political character be ever so unexceptionable—But the second objection is made to none but myself—why then should they be turned out. They have uniformly advocated the very measures the people wish to have taken place—but they were in the minority—which is no crime.

Whether the next representation, from Massachusetts, will be more wise, more powerfull, more economical, or more successfull than the present is impossible now to say—but sure I am they will not have the difficulties and perplexities to encounter that have fallen to our Lot. Ours is the task to conduct the Ship thro shoals, rocks & quick sands—in dark and tempestuous weather—theirs to command her in a serene sky, fair wind and placed sea—How immense the difference! Will these wide extremes of circumstances be duly weighed in estimating the services of the present & future members of Congress? I doubt it—The people are more apt to dwell upon the good effects of a Law than the great difficulties that might have attended it—But some philosophic Historian will hereafter lay open to public view the arduous task of organizing the Government, and adapting one Code of Laws to thirteen Sovereign & Independent States—Farewell.

My things, books & papers are all put up, and on the morrow will be shiped for Boston, & thence to Biddeford [*Maine*], where I hope to follow them the next week—I shall there continue my Speculations in the midst of domestic enjoyments, regardless of politics, and politicians, excepting as they become subjects of disenterested discussion.

FC, Thatcher Family Papers, MHi.

[1] The Quakers and Baptists had been persecuted for challenging the validity or practice of traditional Church hierarchies and sacraments; the Socinians for challenging the divinity of Jesus and consequently the Trinity.

[2] The only known reference to Thatcher's stand on taxing Bibles during the debate on the Impost Act is in Lloyd's Notes for 17 April 1789. Although difficult to interpret, the Notes suggest Thatcher was against exempting Bibles from the 7½ percent rate proposed on other books together with all paper products (*DHFFC* 10:177). Ultimately all printed books were dutied at the five percent rate for non-enumerated items.

[3] To remedy a shortage, in September 1777 the Continental Congress adopted a committee's recommendations to import twenty thousand Bibles from Europe. Just one month prior to this letter, the Senate received and tabled a petition to endorse an official version of the Bible; see *DHFFC* 8:306–7.

[4] A paraphrase of Psalm 26:2 and Jeremiah 11:20.

[5] Athanasius of Alexandria (ca. 293–373) was an Egyptian bishop and theologian of the early Christian church credited with helping to enshrine the then-debated doctrines about the divinity of Jesus and the nature of the Trinity.

Z to the Honourable the Senate of the United States

On the proposition for lowering the rate of interest on indents, when funded, below the rate of interest on the principal.

5th. HOW impolitic a step would this be, with regard to the state debts, one-third of the principal of which is proposed to be funded at 3 per cent. Suppose the same proportion to hold good, the interest would be funded at 1½ per cent. I imagine this would ill suit the state of New-York, whose certificates for interest at present command 7s. 6d. in the pound, and have often sold for much more. There are other states besides New-York in a like situation.

6th. It is impolitic to violate all the laws of the former Congress on this head, who strove to provide for those very indents on better terms than all the power of the present Congress would be able to carry into effect: they provided for them something better than a funding system, if the laws of the confederacy had been sufficient to enforce its performance.[1] But these resolutions of Congress being executed in a partial manner by most of the states, failed of the desired effect: still indents have been known to pass current for cash, in the state of Virginia, at 16s. in the pound (which was five times as much as the principal then sold for) therewith to purchase houses, estates and merchandize, to the amount of near one million of dollars, being carried into that state from all parts of the continent, where they are still retained to a large amount. The states of New-York and Pennsylvania are those which suffered most, next to Virginia. Certainly, Congress are bound, by all the ties of honor and of justice, to make the most ample compensation their present ability will admit, to men who thus (when public credit was at the lowest ebb) relied solely on the honor of Congress, and I believe nothing else.

I shall lay down one short statement, which I believe contains a fair convincing proof of the real state of the case. It is acknowledged on all hands, that if we were possessed of sufficient funds, it would be nothing more than justice to discharge the amount: it is also acknowledged, that if we could even make a new loan in Europe for the purpose, it would be nothing more than what is perfectly just. Then pray let me ask those speculative reasoners, whether it be not more just, more politic and wise, to pay the amount of this interest to our own citizens?

As a copy of the bill, pending in your house, is now published for general observance, we can the more readily combat those principles on which the obnoxious parts of this bill is grounded. In the first and second sections of this bill, we find the reason of the proposition in yesterday's address, approved by your honourable house, with respect to the foreign loan, viz. that it is nothing more than just to contract and pay interest for a new loan to discharge old arrears of interest. For effecting this and other purposes, the President of the United States is, in this bill, authorised to cause to be borrowed a sum not exceeding 12 millions of dollars, to be applied to the discharge of said arrears of interest and other purposes therein mentioned. Here we see a loan of 12 millions authorised, for the express, and in a great measure the sole purpose of discharging arrears of interest. It is true this regards the foreign loan, and we immediately acknowledge the distinction imposed by necessity between this and the domestic debt; but it is conceived that, if necessity obliges us to make this distinction, we must lift our eyes to you to hold an even balance, and to make an equal, uniform and just proportion in the domestic debt and its several parts. Let us then try the proposition of the bill by these principles.

The *interest* of the *foreign debt* is to be discharged in specie; the new arrangement of the *principal* of the *foreign debt* will probably fix it at an interest of 4 or 5 per cent. It is then proposed to fund the *principal* of the *domestic debt*, 2/3ds. at an immediate interest of 6 per cent. and nearly the other third at 6 per cent in 10 years; at the same time it is proposed to fund the *interest* at only 3 per cent. Whether this bears a just and uniform proportion the world may judge.

That we should fund the principal of our domestic debt at a higher interest than what we shall in general pay to foreigners; that we should pay off the foreign arrears of interest in money, yet neither pay our domestic interest, nor ever fund it on an equal basis with the principal: these things must be allowed greatly unaccountable. Is it a regard for foreign powers that changes our policy so much, with respect to foreign and domestic interest? If this is the case, would not the same policy affect the principal? I have heard some other causes mentioned which I do not think right to offer.

NYDG, 21 July. The piece began in *NYDG* on 19 July, was continued on 20 and 23 July, and is printed under those dates.

[1] Indents were federal promissory certificates that Congress issued in lieu of the interest on the federal debt that it could not afford to pay. They came into effect after 27 April 1784, when Congress adopted the report of the grand committee on the arrears of interest.

[*Jeremiah Wadsworth*] to [*Pierpont Edwards*]

*** As to the business of compensations you understood me perfectly—Mr. Ellsworth was as explicit as you understood me, and I presume will not forget it. The history of that business was as follows: A committee was appointed to bring in a bill for establishing compensations for the senate, and House of representatives [*Salaries-Legislative Act HR-19*], one of which I was. At our first meeting we voted, by a majority, eight dollars for the Senate, and five for the Representatives. We were in a very unpleasant situation, as this vote was obtained by those, who were for six dollars, joined with others, who were for eight dollars for the Senate, *in order to force us, who were for five dollars, to give it up.* We then agreed to meet again. After consulting *our several delegations*, we did so, and a compromise took place, to report six dollars for Senate and Representatives. This compromise was made *by us who were for five dollars*, with those who were for more; and after *consulting our delegation*, Mr. Sturges was *the only member*, who objected to six; *he always voted five*, till some members called for the yeas and nays—after a large majority, in a committee of the whole, had repeatedly voted for the six dollars. I then explained the doings of the committee, and declared, I considered the calling of the yeas and nays as a measure intended to intimidate; hinted at popularity as a probable cause for their being called. And, as every member knew there would be a great majority for the bill, it would be easy to say *no*, and yet the bill would pass; but I should not take such a part, as I considered it disgraceful. *Sturges* then said, *yes*; and afterwards declared *his reasons* to be the same *as mine.*

No representative from Connecticut, but Sturges, ever hinted at a less sum than six dollars to me. True it is, Mr. Sherman was not then in the House, having just before obtained leave of absence for a week. But on the 10th day of September, (see Journals of the House of Representatives, page 134, 135, 136) *when there was a chance to defeat the bill, if Mr. Sherman had been desirous of doing so*, he would have voted that it was *not in order to reconsider*—had that vote *obtained*, the bill *was lost. This is a true history of the business.*

***

[Hartford] *Connecticut Courant*, 11 October 1790, printed within a letter to Sherman. This letter is a reply to Edwards's letter of 18 July, above.

Other Documents

Edmund Pendleton to John Page. Listing of ALS in *Leavitt Catalog*, 20 May 1868, item 226. The catalog is in error. Pendleton did not correspond with Page during the FFC; the editors believe this listing should have been for the letter of this date that Pendleton wrote to Madison, above.

John S. Sherburne to John Langdon. ALS, Langdon Papers, NhPoA. Written from Portsmouth, New Hampshire.

Has long expected a line from Langdon, whose friends have long been expecting him home; apologizes for not writing more often; wonders when Congress will rise; "we expect you will not steal upon us in the manner you did last year, but give us such seasonable notice of your approaches, that we may have an opportunity of indulging our wishes on the occasion"; requests details or a copy of the Invalid Pensioners Act [HR-80];

no news to report; "the streams of intelligence must flow from you who reside at the fountain."

GUS, 21 July.

The question on passing the Funding Bill is expected today in the Senate.

Washington's Portrait in Federal Hall

From 6 April 1789, when New York's Mayor James Duane formally notified Congress that the City's Common Council had granted it exclusive and unqualified use of City Hall (by then already known as Federal Hall), any alternative use of the building became subject to congressional approval. In the first session, such approval had been granted to the New York Society Library for a third floor corner chamber, and to the municipal government for two first floor rooms to be used by Federal Hall's city appointed caretakers. Both instances are recorded either among the debates or the official papers of Congress.[1] The only known request in the second session was made on 21 July, when Mayor Richard Varick made a request to Adams for space for the celebrated artist John Trumbull to execute a portrait of President Washington that had been commissioned by the City Corporation. No letter from Varick to Speaker Muhlenberg on the matter is known to be extant; it is possible the Speaker did nothing on the grounds that the Senate had "jurisdiction" over the second floor. Although Varick hoped that the Speaker and the Vice President could make the decision without bothering to consult the House or Senate, Adams's reply of 22 July indicates that he, at least, did so.

NYDA, 21 July, and A Burgher in *NYJ*, 30 July, explicitly acknowledged the connection between Congress's recent decision to leave New York and the City Council's decision to honor the man who might have vetoed that decision. To A Burgher's charge that the city's "*canvas* compliment" was fiscally imprudent, Vox Res Publica (the voice of the people), in *NYJ*, 20 August, added outrage over honoring a President before his death, especially when he may have usurped a constitutional role over congressional adjournments. Such opinions reveal the earliest cracks in Washington's venerated public image under the guise of criticizing his painted image.

As a matter of public policy, New Yorkers may have felt justified in questioning the timing, expense, and anti-republicanism of honoring a living President in public art. But displaying the portrait, even before its completion, was an apparent public relations success. There was well established precedent for using public buildings as art galleries, and even art studios. For example, in 1785 the artist Robert Edge Pine was working on and exhibiting several paintings in the Pennsylvania State House (now Independence Hall) in Philadelphia. These included a portrait of Washington as a general, and a history painting of his resignation as commander in chief in 1783—interestingly, both themes that Trumbull would take up himself.[2] Since 1784 Congress had also boasted its own small art collection: companion life size portraits of its generous allies, France's Louis XVI and Queen Marie Antoinette. But those majestic portraits were painted by French artists, commissioned by the French monarchy, and imported as gifts from France.[3]

Federal Hall, already New York City's principal tourist destination and the acknowledged masterpiece of an American architect, now offered visitors further evidence of the country's artistic autonomy. This legacy of the American Revolution was christened the "Rising Glory" movement by the poet Philip Freneau, who coincidentally penned one of the few contemporary accounts of the popular impact of Trumbull's painting.[4] Freneau's poem, "Picture of New York, August 1790" (printed under 17 September, below), satirized New Yorkers' craze for lotteries by lamenting that it distracted them from coming to "View TRUMBULL's forms sublimely blaze, / And *feel* the paint—with wondering gaze."

Washington's portrait for New York City, begun no earlier than 22 July, was not painted from life. His diary does not indicate any sittings for Trumbull after 19 July, when the artist was apparently nearing completion on a smaller portrait which he had undertaken to paint as a gift for Martha Washington. It was this smaller portrait that Trumbull would use as the model for the slightly larger than life size work commissioned by the city.[5]

According to Trumbull's autobiography, published half a century later, the original portrait was realistic enough to make a delegation of astonished Creek Indians mistake the image for the man himself when a prankish Washington displayed it to their "untutored minds" during a visit to the presidential mansion in July 1790.[6] Other commentary bears witness to a similar impression created by the city's copy. The internationally known scientist Dr. John Jeffries, no stranger to European courts and their art, saw Trumbull's unfinished work on 1 August and declared it "very fine" (although the original "small Picture," he thought, remained "at present the best likeness"). Jeffries saw the painting in "the Conference Room," where the French royal couple's portraits hung. This was the large room that Mayor Varick specifically requested. Judith Sargent Murray visited Trumbull's work space just prior to witnessing the signing of the Treaty of New York in the House chamber below, and noted that it was as crowded as if the President himself were there.[7]

By 8 August the copy was sufficiently completed for Smith (S.C.) to pronounce it "magnificent," and to begin lobbying Charleston's citizens to match New York's zeal by commissioning of Trumbull a similar tribute to Washington—which they did in May 1791. Presumably the portrait for

New York City was completed by 2 September 1790, when the Common Council ordered the city treasurer to pay Trumbull £186. The portrait was hung at the head of the west staircase after its completion, to be joined by Trumbull's life size portrait of Governor George Clinton in 1791. Both paintings are still in the possession of the City of New York.[8]

[1] *DHFFC* 8:653, 688, 690.

[2] Robert G. Stewart, *Robert Edge Pine: A British Portrait Painter in America, 1784–1788* (Washington, D.C., 1979), p. 28.

[3] "Furnishing Plan for the Second Floor of Congress Hall," Independence National Historical Park, October 1963, Part C, Section 1, pp. 18–27.

[4] Freneau borrowed the phrase from the ancient Roman philosopher Seneca for his 1771 Princeton commencement address (Mary S. Austin, *Philip Freneau: The Poet of the Revolution* [New York, 1941], pp. 78–79). For background on the Rising Glory movement, see Kenneth Silverman, *A Cultural History of the American Revolution* (New York, 1987), pp. 228–35.

[5] Helen A. Cooper, *John Trumbull: The Hand and Spirit of a Painter* (New Haven, Conn., 1982), pp. 118–19.

[6] John Trumbull, *Autobiography* (New Haven, Conn., 1841), pp. 164–65.

[7] Jeffries Diary, 1 August, below; Judith Sargent Murray to Winthrop and Judith Sargent, 14 August, in *Murray*, p. 255.

[8] Smith to Edward Rutledge, 8 August, below; Cooper, *Trumbull*, pp. 104, 120; *Iconography* 5:1274.

Mayor Richard Varick to John Adams, 21 July

The Corporation of this City have applied to the President of the United States to permit Colo. John Trumbull take his Portrait to be placed in the City Hall, to which the President has consented & Mr. Trumbull has suggested to me that as the Portrait will be large the Room in the Hall in which those of the King and Queen of France are placed will be most eligible to perform the Painting in & that he will take Care that no Possible Injury or Inconvenience shall be occasioned by this Indulgence to him.

The whole of the Hall being devoted to the use of Congress I take the Liberty of thus addressing You Sir as well as the Speaker of the House of Representatives on the Subject of soliciting your Permission, under a Persuasion that your respective Assent will be sufficient without troubling the Senate or House of Representatives.

I pray Your Answer on this Subject.

ALS, Adams Family Manuscript Trust, MHi

Newspaper Article, 21 July

Yesterday the Mayor waited on the President of the United States, and presented the request of the Corporation that he would honor them with permitting Mr. Trumbull, to take his portrait to be placed in the City-Hall, as a mark of the respect the Citizens of New-York entertain of his virtues.

The President was pleased to express the favourable impressions occasioned by this application, and cheerfully granted the request.

We understand that this circumstance has been for some time contemplated, but the measure was not brought forward in the Corporation, until the question of the residence of Congress was finally settled, lest any charge might have been imputed against the disinterestedness of the citizens on this occasion.

The Picture will be placed, we are informed in that part of the Representatives Chamber, behind the Speaker—and will be so elevated, as to be out of danger from being handled and sufficiently conspicuous from every part of the Room.

NYDA, 21 July.

John Adams to Richard Varick, 22 July

I received Yesterday the Letter you did me the honour to write me, Soliciting Permission for Mr. Trumbul, to paint the Portrait of the President in that room of the City Hall, in which the Portraits of the King and Queen of France are placed.

This morning I took the Liberty to read your Letter, Sir, in Senate, and have the order of the members to inform you, that they consent with Pleasure to Mr. Trumbuls request. I am happy, sir in the Oppertunity, of obliging Mr. Trumbul as well as yourself.

ALS, privately owned in 1970.

The Chatechism of Prudence, 30 July

Is it prudent in a city, which is reduced to pay its debts by *lottery*, to incur the superfluous expences of *disinterested* flattery? Is this *canvass* compliment to be discharged by a *Picture Lottery*, and entrusted to *responsible* and *respectible* commissioners? If the expences of this *disinterested* compliment are to be discharged by assessments, will the citizens, deluded by federal tricks, and oppresed by federal burdens, chearfully submit to a *Picture Tax!*

A BURGHER—*whose eyes are open*

NYJ, 30 July.

Munificence, 20 August

IF the ______ mean to patronize American genius, and they are infected with the liberal enthusiasm of *Amateurs*, they have an ample field. The American genius might exercise the powers of the brush, in a picture which should represent the fathers of this city assembled in *common council*, when the important question—*picture* or *no picture*—agitated the expressive countenances of aged wisdom. This picture would be a proper ornament, for that monument of federal folly and prodigality, which is soon to assume the humble title of *City-Hall*. This picture would call forth the variety of his genius, and on this canvass the grave and comick powers of his pencil may be illustrated. It is an inauspicious moment, for the wise fathers of a republican city, to pay a prodigal compliment to the ______ when the c—sti—ti—al propriety of his conduct is ambiguous, and devides the opinion of the wise.

The injudicious flattery of the people have often intoxicated their rulers, and sanctioned their usurpations. When a free people flatter without judgment, it indicates a servility of spirit, and slavery is at no great distance. A republican people should be frugal of flattery to any living character; and should reserve their plaudits until the curtain drops on the actor. They can then view the whole conduct of the actor; and if meritorious, let the air resound with your applauses!

Then let *busts* adorn the niches of your municipal palaces, let the marble, seemingly alive, and the equestrian statue, adorn your squares. Flattery to the living rulers is always dangerous, and seldom sincere. American republicans, watch with jealousy the living rulers, and perfume the ashes of the worthy dead. This posthumus praise is wise in point of prudence, and safe in point of policy.

VOX RES PUBLICA

NYJ, 20 August.

THURSDAY, 22 JULY 1790

Joseph Hiller to Benjamin Goodhue

Your favour of the 11th. instant came safe to hand. Many of the alterations in the new bill [*Collection Act HR-82*], you kindly favored me with, appear adequate to the design: tho' perhaps in the opperation defficiences may present that will require amendment. I may not presume to judge from other evidence after the scrutinies it must have passed thro. I beg leave, however, to ask whether the 8th. Section embraces the present Case of Marblehead, there being no other than a Collectorship in that District.

Is any thing further intended by the 33 Section[1] than articles which pay a specific duty on every 112 lb. such as at present do Cables, Cordage, Twine & unwrought Steel. Are the customs established ~~in the~~ amongst Merchants respecting the Tare and Draught allowed on hogsheads of Sugar &c. which pay a duty per pound, to govern weighers.

Should not a provision similar to the last in the 4th. Sectn. be made in the 9th. for Masters, by absence, ignorant of the law. Is the further credit allowed to be given in the 58th. Section,[2] to be given by simply refraining to put the bond in suit as directed by the 43d. Section?[3] perhaps the answer to these questions will shew that they need not have been made, in which Case I doubt not you will excuse me. In all cases I hope the laws will be so framed as to enable Officers to execute them punctualy without embarrassment. and that that punctuality will be duly supported and encouraged. The coasting act I hope will present somthing to evince this notwithstanding the observation in your letter; for you know that if a faithfull discharge of the duties of Office and an unceasing attention to the interests of the revenue claim adequate compensations, those of my Colleagues, as you honour me by calling them, are not exceeded: and I hope you will have the pleasure to assure them that they are not neglected.

I fancy you anticipate the approaching recess with little less ardor than that of your family and friends to see you, for I think the marches and countermarches, to say no more, of the last Congressional Campaign must have so harrassed you as to make a domestic relaxation highly desirable.

ALS, Letters to Goodhue, NNS. Written from Salem, Massachusetts.

[1] Section 34 of the final act.
[2] Section 59 of the final act.
[3] Section 44 of the final act.

B. K. to Mr. Greenleaf

THE true reason of the *removal* of *Congress* from this city will be explained to the people in the course of a very few days. To the lasting disgrace of the majority in both houses it will be seen, that the Pennsylvania and Potowmack interests have been purchased with *twenty one and an half millions of dollars*, and that the good people of this state will have to pay about one eighth part of that enormous assumption, merely to remove Congress from their capital.

The debates upon the funding bill, as sent down by the Senate, will be well worth the attention of the citizens: it will be curious to see all the reasoning against the assumption done away: even the powers of Mr. M—n [*Madison*] are to be silent on the subject, but to preserve a consistency of character, he must vote against it, his mouth is to be shut, his silent negative is to satisfy his new friends, and he is to prove "that every man may be purchased, if his price is offered;" his price is the Potowmack; he has accepted, and, no doubt, he is a man of too much honor not to perform his part of the bargain. What inducement the members of this state can have to agree to the assumption are yet to be accounted for. Has the state any interest in such a measure? Has she not already paid [*the*] greatest part of her debt, and is the assumption to be agreed to, merely for the pleasure of paying over again? The people must, and will expect that their representatives will take so much care of their interests, as to use their endeavors to prevent the success of those disgraceful bargains. It is evident, that the present mode of bringing forward the assumption is to force the real friends of public credit into the measure, lest the interest of the union should suffer by a longer delay in funding the real debts of the United States.

If the assumption is a proper measure, why forever bring it forward with something else. Is it of such a nature that it cannot stand on its own merits, or has it so little merit of its own, that it must, of necessity, be introduced into the world in other company?

From the former proceedings upon this subject, we might have expected, that nothing more would have been said about assumption. But no sooner had the residence bill passed, than it is again brought forward. The M—l—d gentlemen, who live near the Potowmack, are now, by contract, to vote for it, I say by contract, and I defy them to shew any other reason for an alteration in their conduct, I would not suppose that they have speculated in state debts, and that motives, arising from those speculations, could influence their conduct. It would be an ungrateful supposition, especially as other causes are at hand. One thing is evident, that the interests of their state is not with the assumption.

NYJ, 27 July, edited by Thomas Greenleaf; reprinted at Hartford, Connecticut, and Baltimore. Greenleaf indicated that the piece arrived too late for the 23 July issue.

Letter from New York

You may ask when Congress will rise? If there is another session before the fourth of March, Congress will adjourn in the course of a fortnight—otherwise the session will be continued till September. The funding bill, which has taken up so much time, was returned yesterday from the Senate, with a number of amendments; among which was one for assuming 21 millions of dollars of the State debts, four millions of which are on account of Massachusetts. Some of the amendments have this day been agreed to in the House; but the most important, those respecting the assumption, and on which there will be the most debate, have not yet been considered. Two or three days will decide their fate and, I believe, the fate of the Bill for this session.

[Portland, Maine] *Cumberland Gazette*, 2 August. This is probably from a letter written by Thatcher to the newspaper's editor, Thomas B. Wait.

Other Documents

Benjamin Goodhue to Samuel Hodgdon. No copy known; acknowledged in Hodgdon to Goodhue, 26 July.

Christopher Gore to Rufus King. ALS, King Papers, NHi. Written from Boston.

King's brother (Cyrus) will leave for New York City by stage on Monday (26 July); "his conduct is such as will render both you & himself happy"; "We are constantly hearing strange stories about the acts of Congress relative to the public debt—and expresses are said to arrive here in ninety six hours from the seat of government—what will be the result no one is bold enough to divine."

Jeremiah Wadsworth to Harriet Wadsworth. ALS, Wadsworth Papers, CtHi. Addressed to Hartford, Connecticut; franked; postmarked.

Is anxious for an adjournment; "to return home is my ardent wish"; Elizabeth Laurance is a little better but still "dangerously ill."

Jeremiah Wadsworth to Harriet Wadsworth. ALS, Wadsworth Papers, CtHi. Addressed to Hartford, Connecticut; franked; postmarked.

(A second letter later that day) forwards an enclosure and reports that "this is the Hottest weather we have had—but a fine breeze from the Sea cools that part of the Town towards it" but their house in Maiden Lane is cut off by other houses and is "warm indeed."

Friday, 23 July 1790

John Bayard to Elias Boudinot

The present serves to enclose a Letter from my Dau[*g*]hter Jane to Miss Pintard,[1] wch. I shall be much obliged to you to forward—the Residence Bill I find is at last passed—I am sorry it took up so much of the time of Congress.

and that the most important Business, has been so long delayed—Be assured that Congress have lost the Confidence & Esteem of a very large proportion of their Fellow Citizens by their Conduct during their present Session—I have travelled lately through some of the principal Counties of Pennsylvania & have met with a general Murmur at the Expence, Congress were at, & the little Business they have done—I trust you do not mean to Rise, untill You have funded the Public Debt—Your Creditors have waited with unexampled Patience for Your Decissions, should you adjourn without granting them the long expected releif they are Justly entitled to, I fear the Consequences—be assured they are a Respectable & large body of the People—many of them, among the *most respectable* & Meritorious Citizens who from the most virtuous principles, performed services or loaned you money in the Hour of Danger & shall these be the only sufferrers at this Day?

Shall those who at that period w~~as~~ere either actualy opposed to us, or meanly skulked & witheld their Assistance now Riot in Affluence, while the poor public Creditor forgotten & neglected—forbid it Ye Patriots—speedily do Justice to this meritorious Class of your Fellow Citizens that the Blessings of thousands who are now in a perishing situation may descend upon your Heads—I am very sensible of your Exertions in this Virtuous Cause, & beleive you have nothing to answer for should—the Cries of the Widow & Fatherless & those that have been & are likely to be ruined by the faithless Conduct of our Rulers, bring down the Judgments of Heaven upon us—God is a God of Justice, He has declared himself—the Husband to the Widow, & the Father of Fatherless Children—How many & how excellent are the precepts that are contained in His Blessed Word, to inculcate public as well as private Justice—indeed I beleive a *real* Christian that studies well the Word of God, is the best qualified to perform the Duties of a good Representative of His Country, as well as that of a good Citizen—How much is it to be wished that the difft. states paid more respect to Moral Qualifications in the Choice of their Representatives in their Public Councils?

ALS, privately owned in 1980. Written from New Brunswick, New Jersey.

[1] Probably a daughter of John Marsden Pintard, the son of Boudinot's sister-in-law Susanna Stockton; Boudinot lived with the Pintards in New York City.

John Sherman to Roger Sherman

I transmit to you the ultimate Statement of my concerns unsettled with the United States in order to lay them before Congress for their consideration.[1] I wish to compleat the whole as soon as possible in order to git into business which will support a large Family, and do that Justice to the public which is the best I possibly can, four applications, one to Congress, three to the General Assembly when the Accts. were Stated and the whole of the Securities in my hands, I found them daily falling and no general Goverment established, which Induced me to take the measure I did, and by advice not from my friends who always held up an Idea of their being funded, but from other Gentlemen which promted me to the Action (It is done I cannot help it) having no resources at Command, I await the decission of Congress on the Subject. my person is subject to an Arrest tho they cannot command Gold nor Silver from me having none nor any Property, I will not attempt to Involve my friends as I never consulted them—my Accts. are fully Prepared for a Settlement I wish you to advise with Docr. Johnson who knows the circumstances of my first Application to Congress[2] likewise Colo. Wadsworth as to the State, and no further Intefere on my Acct. than you shall Judge necessary, I have Stated plain facts—& expect personally to be answerable.

ALS, Sherman Papers, DLC. Written from New Haven, Connecticut. Enclosure not found.

[1] John Sherman had been paymaster for several Continental Army regiments.
[2] For previous congressional action on Sherman's claim, see *JCC* 28:70–71.

George Walton to John Adams

By some intelligencies lately from Europe, it is said that Great Britain is zealously endeavoring to repossess the Floridas; and I have no doubt of the fact, because her interest is greatly concerned in the event, and in general she has seen it better than any other Nation. Her frozen possessions to the North are not calculated for Caribean Supplies. West-florida[1] is very much so; and the possession of the Navigation of the Mississippi would secure an exclusive right to the advantages of the immense agricultures of the west; and which would encrease by that event. The posts that Nation keeps contrary to her engagements with America, is the link which is intended to connect her power from the North to the South; and the Bourbon scheme, which aimed at deriving abundance from a wilderness, is now reviving with the felling axe and hoe. If care is not taken that enterprising and Commercial Nation will generate another Revolution in America. Independence west of the Mountains would draw one half of the Eastern Inhabitants. The result taken from the Union, and put in the scale of Great Britain, would greatly compensate her late losses. I take it for certain that an arrangement so fatal will be defeated, by alarming the Spanish Nation with the formidability of such a neighbor To me it appears one of the most important objects that Nation has latterly contemplated; And, success will be equally productive of

health, honor and revenge. As I shall be very much obliged to you for your opinion upon this subject, and of the detention of the Posts, I have taken the liberty of addressing this scrawl.
P. S. Mr. John Gibbons,[2] in point of character and ability, is qualified to be the Accountant [*commissioner for settling accounts*] in this State for the United States.

ALS, Adams Family Manuscript Trust, MHi. Written from Augusta, Georgia.

[1] In 1790 Spanish West Florida was bounded by the Gulf of Mexico on the south and the Chattahoochee and Mississippi rivers on the east and west respectively. Its northern border was claimed at thirty-one degrees by the United States and at thirty-two degrees twenty minutes by Spain.

[2] John Gibbons was appointed the first clerk of the city council and treasurer of Savannah, Georgia, in 1790.

Joseph Whipple to John Langdon

I have receivd your favor of the 7th instant by which I find that members of Congress are Still violent in opposing each other. We wish to see you—but dont hurry a way till the importat questions of assumption & funding are adopted or fairly rejected—fail in this & the most important object that has come before Congress in the Session is lost.

I have more money in my hands than you mention for which a draft in your favor will be pleasing to me—& which you can undoubtedly obtain unless it is otherways appropriated which will be known by your application to the Treasury for a draft on me.

You will please to recollect that I paid you last fall 500 Dollars for a bill drawn on me by the Secretary of the Treasury whose letter of Advice dated Nov. 1st. directed me to "transmit the bill to the Treasurer of the United States addressing my letter to the Treasurer under cover to the Secretary & that a regular warrant shoud be transmitted to me for the amount." I accordingly inclosed the bill in my letter to the Treasurer dated Nov. 11th. but have never receivd the Warrant—& agreeably to the mode which I conceivd to be proper omitted [*lined out*] to charge the amount till the warrant shoud appear & it still remains uncharged please to mention this matter to the Treasurer & request him to furnish me with the means of making & supporting a charge of this Sum.

***

In the Collection law [*HR-82*] now on the Carpet hope there will be some provision made for a just allowance to such of the Collrs. & other officers who are now unpaid for their Services—If this matter was left with the Secretary of the Treasury under proper restrictions it is more likely that justice woud be done more by any general establishment as he must be ~~more~~ a more competent judge of the Value of the Services than the Legislature can be. As to myself you will judge of my Situation when I tell you that my fees & Commissn. for a Year by an accurate calculation will be less than 240 Dollars allowing for a Clerk one half the time only The Secretary has a Statement of my emoluments for 6 Months with a Calculation for a year be pleased to represent the impossibility of the Collection's being conducted without an adequate Compensation.

ALS, Langdon Papers, NhPoA. Written from Portsmouth, New Hampshire. The omitted text asks Langdon to peruse some papers that Whipple has confided to Tobias Lear, regarding the improvement of Whipple's lands in New Hampshire, "making such use of them as may tend to obtain the end proposed."

Hugh Williamson to Thomas Ruston

Be advised not to meddle with any of the Certificates of N. Carolina issued in Pursuance of an Act of Decr. 1785.[1] Those Certificates were issued at Warrenton and signed by H[*enry*]. Montfort B[*enjamin*]. McCullock & J[*ohn*]. Mecon or by some two of them. They have some Value, i.e. some of them will prove good, but the Number of good ones in all probability so small that I repeat it, you had best not meddle with them. In the mean while you need not try to hurt the market. let the Paper circulate. Speculators ought occasionally to feel the Hook.

I dont know any Thing of any Bank Scheme, but am confident that no new Business will be taken up this Session, nor any other important Bills passed except the funding Bill which I fear may include the State Debts in Part, & the Bill for better collecting the Revenue [*HR-82*] & two or three others that have made some Progress. I had Thought of asking some friend in Philada. to take me a House by the 1st of Novr. but Mrs. [*Maria Apthorpe*] Williamson thinks it will be impossible for her to move before Winter. [*Son*] Charles was born on the 18th of Octr. and if he passes a year without a Rival it is as much as he can expect. To have voted for Philada. when I knew that I took the Risque of being obliged to part for six Months from a Woman whom I never did wish to leave for a single Hour & from one fine Boy ~~at least~~ was sacrificing private feelings to public Considerations.[2]

ALS, Coxe Papers, PHi. Addressed to Philadelphia; franked; postmarked 25 July.

---

[1] For additional information on so called "86ers" or certificates of 1786, see Williamson to Governor Alexander Martin, 6 March, volume 18.

[2] Like Williamson, Few also married the daughter of a prominent New Yorker while on public service at the seat of government. Catherine Few described Maria Apthorpe as a

genteel and accomplished young woman of twenty-five, towards whom Williamson acted like "a down right love sick swain." Playfully she complained that so many marriages to Southerners would lead Philadelphians to accuse their New York sisters of not being very particular (to William Few, 17 November, 13 December 1788, William and Catherine Few Papers, GU).

Z to the Honourable the Senate of the United States

On the proposition for lowering the rate of interest on indents, when funded, below the rate of interest on the principal.

SOME consideration ought ever to be allowed to a public error, if the idea of funding principal and interest on the same basis were such; but surely we ought to entertain a more favorable impression of this idea. These indents were issued by the former Congress, with an expectation that they would be received in taxes throughout the union some years since. That body did every thing to produce this effect that was possible for men to do; to accomplish this, they went to an almost unprecedented length: and shall we, acknowledging ourselves bound by the engagements of the confederation, refuse either to pay off or even fund those indents at what is professed to be the lowest rate of a just interest? I mean the terms of the principal. According to the change in the laws made by the new constitution, the holders of indents would simply have to expect that those indents should be received for every impost tax or excise laid by Congress; the very reading of the indents expresses nothing less; the words are these—"The bearer hereof is entitled to one dollar, which will be *received for taxes on any requisitions*, agreeably to the act of Congress of ." It is well known the requisitions mentioned then related to the several states; but by the new and more perfect union, all requisitions and taxes laid by Congress become transferred from states to individuals; therefore individuals would have a fair and just right to expect that these certificates should be received in every tax laid by Congress, for so the contract itself expresses. But the holders of certificates, generally speaking, are well informed men; they know that this would destroy all means of providing for the principal debt, they therefore do not expect it; they expect simply as great provision should be made for interest of the debt as the principal, though perhaps, in strict propriety, the interest should certainly have the preference.

In these sentiments they have the good fortune to be approved of by the sound argument of the Secretary of the Treasury, who, after a variety of close reasoning on this subject, concludes it as his opinion, that the arrears of interest have pretensions at least equal to those of the principal. It is a most extraordinary thing that this should be warranted by every resolve of the late Congress, approved by the best informed men of the House of

Representatives, and carried there by a large majority, yet, after an intervention of some months, a majority of the Senate would seem to possess sentiments so much in opposition: surely, it cannot be merely for the purpose of having it conceived that their discernment is so much greater than that of other men; I at the same time acknowledge it is great.

I have heard it alledged as a reason for this opposition, that interest, even funded at 3 per cent. would not subject the holders to much loss; but would it not be very hard indeed, if, in a general dispensation of favors, the holders of interest should alone be those who reaped no advantage? The state of North-Carolina has already shewn its sense of the justice of funding principal and interest in one sum and in one certificate, for long since the year 1783: these certificates bear interest, yet this case was very different from that of indents issued. By issuing indents we, to every intent and purpose, contracted a new debt, given for the payment of interest to the holders of the principal (who therefore could have no further demands for the same) with liberty to dispose thereof to new holders; and therefore it may be said, almost *ipso facto*, to have become principal, and that in strict justice Congress ought to pay interest from the very date of issue, as it was truly nothing else than a new loan, become intentionally separated by Congress from the original debt. For God's sake, gentlemen, would it be just reasoning, if that because I were unable to perform what by strict contract I were bound to fulfil, I should for that reason do much less than my ability would really permit? Changing the monosyllable, this I take to be the case respecting indents in other words.

I conceive gentlemen in favor of the assumption ought to consider well before they attempt such nice distinctions between the principal and interest of the United States debt. Certainly such distinctions cannot favor the assumption of the state debt, as there is certainly a greater distinction between the continental and state debts than there can be between the parts of which the continental is composed. I look upon the assumption as a politic measure, but I cannot help saying that this preference given to some part of the state debts over one part of the continental looks so very selfish, that I cannot help wishing the measure overthrown. I have since heard, to my great discontent, that your honourable house have passed the bill (after a motion of reconsideration) with the injurious parts of the bill I have stated still retained, which is now sent to the lower house for concurrence, who, according to the great confidence they have always possessed in the judgment of the Senate, will take it for granted that the amendment is right, and therefore we may with propriety presume it will pass into a law.

NYDG, 23 July. This concludes a piece that began in *NYDG* on 19 July and was continued on 20 and 21 July, above.

A Marylander to Mr. Hayes

I OBSERVE the Residence Bill has past through Congress, and received the approbation of the President; therefore, all chance of bringing Congress to Baltimore-town is now over. *It is provoking to reflect, that we have lost the residence by our own members, and should have been successful, had but Maryland been happily unrepresented both in the Senate and the House of Delegates.* The friends of one of our Senators [*Carroll*] even attempting to say, that he made a sacrifice of his own private interest in voting against Baltimore, and preferring the advantage of a corner of the state he represents, to that of a majority of the people in it, is really futile. Mr. *Stone* affected indifference, whether the residence was fixed at Baltimore, or on the Patowmack, which assertion is expressly contradicted by his conduct in the Susquehannah business last fall,[1] and when Baltimore was first proposed as the temporary residence. It is absolutely necessary, that every exertion should be made next October, to turn out Messrs. *D. Carroll, Contee, Gale,* and *Stone*; and as most of the able politicians throughout the state entertain strong prejudices against Baltimore-town, it cannot be done by address and management, but may be effected by open, manly and vigorous efforts. I could wish a town meeting to be called very soon, a committee of correspondence appointed, and directed to write to the different counties, requesting a convention of two deputies from each, to meet either at this town, or Annapolis, for the sole and express purpose of forming a ticket for Congress, of able men, who would consider the interest of a majority of the state, rather than a part of it—then let the ticket be recommended to the people, and the reasons assigned in an address. If Baltimore-town will but make the same exertions as in October, 1788,[2] Baltimore-county as in the contests between Messrs. *Ridgely* and *Deye,*[3] Harford and Cecil as when contending where their county courts should be held, and Anne-Arundel as at the convention election, we must be successful, so we are but unanimous, like Washington county, when our present Delegates in Congress were chosen. The Eastern-Shore will probably move pretty generally with us. It is necessary to take care, that one ticket shall be agreed on and supported, in order to prevent divisions among ourselves, while the Patowmack interest remains united as formerly. In 1788, Assemblymen were directed to vote for federalists as Senators. The government is now fixed, Mr. *Carroll*'s time, as a Senator, expires (I wish Mr. *Henry*'s did also) and our Assemblymen ought to be instructed to vote for no one as his successor, whom they could suppose capable of consulting the interest of a corner of the state in preference to that of the majority of the people. So worthy and able men are chosen, the most factious partisan cannot *now* pretend to say it makes any difference, whether they *originally* approved or not of the government.

I do not wish our four enemies to be turned out from motives of revenge, now it is impracticable to repair the mischief they have done us, but solely to shew our members hereafter, that they are not to run counter to the interest of a majority of the state with impunity. We know not what measures the next Congress may pursue, and dear-bought experience has proved the necessity of our being represented by even *timid friends*, rather than *inveterate enemies*. It is to be hoped Baltimore-town will not forget, how by their violent party election of October, 1788, and by being so much divided in chusing members of Congress, they were the lion and tiger in the fable, while the Patowmack interest (in consequence of their unanimity) like the fox, ran away with the spoil.[4] We should profit by our past errors, especially when we smart for them, and above all things be united. The Patowmack interest will probably try to revive the distinction of federal and anti; but I trust Baltimore-town will not again be thus bamboozled. We should fix upon the two Assemblymen, whose interest throughout the state would probably prove most efficacious in securing a *proper* successor to Mr. *Carroll*, without asking of what party they were two years ago. I was pleased to find both sides, last fall, so well disposed to conciliation and accommodation, as was exemplified by our present representation in Assembly, and surely we shall not now split among ourselves, when there is such a necessity for union and exertion. Two years ago every moderate person who advocated sending the ablest men into Congress, without respect to political sentiments, was branded with antifederalism, by violent and clamorous characters, who will now, it is to be hoped, freely confess they have been wrong, and not be so forward hereafter, to set up their own opinions as the models of perfection, and pronounce every man a fool or a rascal for presuming to differ from them on political questions. Let *such men* be termed *Carrollites*, and not federalists. It is really hard such a man as Mr. *Carroll* should be our enemy, when most of us were so extremely desirous of putting him into the Senate, little foreseeing how we should suffer by it. It shews how dangerous, in a republican government, may be the influence of a man, in whom are united talents, address, intrigue, integrity, and an overgrown fortune, added to an anxiety to encrease it.

[Baltimore] *Maryland Gazette*, 30 July; edited by John Hayes. Written from Baltimore. The 27 July issue noted that the piece had been received but was omitted for lack of room.

---

[1] The Seat of Government Bill [HR-25] would have placed the seat of federal government on the Susquehanna River in Pennsylvania.

[2] The closely contested and sometimes violent House of Delegates election in Baltimore in October was a continuation of the ratification debate between Federalists and Antifederalists (*DHFFE* 2:107).

[3] An apparent reference to the election of Baltimore County's delegates to the state's ratification convention in April 1788. Thomas C. Deye (1728–1807), a planter and longtime member of the state's House of Delegates (1777–92, including as speaker from 1781–88),

ran on a Federalist ticket, but withdrew during the acrimonious electioneering. Two Ridgeley cousins went on to be elected on an Antifederalist ticket: "Captain" Charles Ridgely, and Charles Ridgely "of William" (1749–1810), also a planter and longtime member of the House of Delegates (1781–86, 1788–96) (*DHFFE* 2:241; *AHR* 5[1899–1900]:41).

[4] An Aesop's fable describes how a lion kills an animal variously translated as a tiger, wolf, or ass, for challenging his claim to the "lion's share" of the spoils from a hunting party. A fox, also in the party, wisely learns his lesson from the tiger's imprudence and is amply rewarded.

Other Documents

Daniel W. Coxe to Tench Coxe. ALS, Coxe Papers, PHi. Written from Philadelphia. For the part of the letter concerning the federal government's move to Philadelphia, see Accommodations for Congress at Philadelphia in Correspondence: Third Session.

Relations between the Coxe and Wadsworth commercial firms; sends the maps T. Coxe purchased for the treasury department when he was in Philadelphia, Thomas (Lee) Shippen has rented a house supposedly for Smith (S.C.), for £200 a year.

Thomas Fitzsimons to Benjamin Rush. ALS, Gratz Collection, PHi. Addressed to Philadelphia; franked; postmarked.

Discusses the upcoming Pennsylvania gubernatorial election; F. A. Muhlenberg has written his friends of his intention not to be a candidate; "the Removal of Congress to Philadelphia renders his situation as Speaker so desireable, that there can be no doubt of the Sincerity of his Wishes indeed I had none before as I believe him a Very Candid Man"; the Opinion of some "is founded upon present Appearances & before Mr. Morris Name had been held Up"; "We shall Certainly be with You" at the state constitutional convention, "as our session is expected to Close that Week."

John Langdon to George Washington. ALS, Washington Papers, DLC. Glover had written Washington on 24 February seeking an appointment as an inspector of revenue under the Excise Act proposed by the secretary of the treasury in his report on public credit (*PGW* 5:173n).

"Inclosed is a letter which I Recd. ℘ post, from general [*John*] Glover; his Wishes are therein expressed; I have ever Esteemed him a worthy honest man, but you Sr. must be the best Judge of his Character. I hope I may be excused for the liberty I have taken."

From New York. [Boston] *Columbian Centinel*, 31 July; reprinted at Portland, Maine.

"A new *Collection Law* [*HR-82*] has passed the House, and will probably the Senate, in which many inconveniences are remedied. A new *Coasting*

Bill [*HR-89*] will probably pass before adjournment. A new *Impost Act* [*Ways and Means Act HR-83*] is also before the House, augmenting the duties, agreeably to what you see published in the papers; but I hardly think it will go through both Houses: If it should fail, it is uncertain what means may be adopted to supply."

Summary of a Letter from New York. [Winchester] *Willis's Virginia Gazette*, 7 August. The editors believe the letter was written by White.

Adjournment will "not take place so soon as was expected, as business of the most urgent nature was daily coming before them."

SATURDAY, 24 JULY 1790

James Burrill, Jr. to Theodore Foster

***

In Politics we have nothing. State Politics is now of little Consequence & you are at the fountain head of Continental. People in General are much dissatisfied at the long Sessions of Congress. And are much displeasd at the proposd removal. We have here a Picture of the Senate, the Majority in it are represented as carried on a Ladder by Mr. R. Morris & the minority as drawn after him by the nose.

He carries in one Hand the purse while with the other he draws the Senate along the road to Philadelphia. This picture was engravd in N. York & perhaps you have seen it. There was a Report here that you had voted against the Funding of the Debt of the U. States, or providing in any way for its Payment. This I stoutly contradicted, as I supposd such a Vote had not been taken since your arrival at Congress.

***

ALS, Foster Papers, RHi. Written from Providence, Rhode Island; received on the evening of 31 July. The omitted text acknowledges the receipt of a letter, discusses various business transactions, describes at length the destructiveness of a recent lightning storm, and mentions an enclosed letter from (Amasa?) Gray.

Roger Sherman to Simeon Baldwin

Enclosed is this days paper—The Senate have Agreed to Assume the State debts—In the house this day on the Question to disagree to that part of the amendment of the Senate it passed in the negative, then the house proceeded to the consideration of it and Some amendments were proposed, but none agreed to—I Suppose an amendment will be proposed and agreed to as to the rate of Interest on Monday next on which a conference will take place between the houses it cant be known what will be the final result.

ALS, Sherman Collection, CtY. Addressed to New Haven, Connecticut; franked; postmarked.

Letter from a Member of the House of Representatives to the Editor

Yesterday the *Funding-Bill* was taken up in the House, and some progress made in considering the amendments proposed to it by the Senate—One of them, proposing to fund 26 dollars at the end of ten years, was agreed to, with a further amendment, to fund 33 1/3 dollars, at the end of seven years.

Another amendment fixing the *Interest* of the loan of *Indents and Arrears of Interest* on the Debt of the Union at the rate of *three per cent.* was amended to *four per cent.* As both these alterations are favourable to the creditors and to justice, I trust the Senate will concur with them.

The Amendment of the Senate, providing for the ASSUMPTION of the State Debts was then debated; but the House adjourned without coming to a vote.

This morning the debate on the ASSUMPTION was resumed. On the opening of the debate, Mr. *Jackson* moved, *That the House* DISAGREE *to the Amendment of the Senate,* and so not assume the State Debts. The vote on this motion (this instant decided) is AYES 29—NOES 32—The Speaker, though he did not vote, is in opinion with the *latter.* So that the vote is, that the *House* AGREE *to the Amendment of the Senate for* ASSUMING THE STATE DEBTS: But this amendment is still open to amendments, which may delay the success, and embarrass the measure. However, it seems that it will prevail. It was then moved to strike out the preamble, which expresses, *that a provision for the debts of the States would contribute to an orderly, economical, and effectual arrangement of the publick finances.* This was negatived. It was then moved, to assume for *Massachusetts* no more than for *Pennsylvania*—Negatived. Mr. *Seney* then moved to raise *Maryland* from 800,000, to 1,000,000 dollars—Negatived. I do not suppose that we shall finish the business until Monday. It is three o'clock—Colonel [*Azor?*] ORNE is called for by the Master of the packet. I am sure this intelligence will give pleasure to the citizens of *Massachusetts.*

[Boston] *Columbian Centinel,* 28 July, edited by Benjamin Russell; reprinted at Portland, Maine; Exeter and Portsmouth, New Hampshire; and Northampton, Massachusetts.

Letter from Charleston, South Carolina to the Editor

I was much pleased on the whole with the observations on the English letter in your paper;[1] but I cannot say the pleasure was heightened by the reflection thrown out against the southern States. Tis true it would appear from the conduct of their representatives, (which, I think will not tend much to increase their popularity) that South Carolina and Georgia are violently opposed to restrictions on foreign navigation, but I believe, from the little information I have been able to gain, that the contrary is the case, particularly in this state, except amongst a *few* British merchants, who, though they enjoy all the privileges of American citizens, make it a point to injure our trade as much as possible. Every person must know it is the interest of the inhabitants at the *present moment* to export their produce in British bottoms—but they look forward—they are not so miserly short-sighted, as to lock up the penny to-day, which might produce them a shilling by to-morrow.

I think a writer who wishes to make the public wiser and better by his speculations, ought to be careful how he publishes any thing which may tend to keep alive vulgar local prejudices. It was the laying aside these prejudices that made us a nation—it was the revival of these prejudices that brought us to the brink of political ruin—it was the smothering of these prejudices again, that gave us a government. And, happy shall we be, if their re-animation does not bring us, not only to the precipice of ruin, but plunge us down, to rise no more.

GUS, 11 August, edited by John Fenno; reprinted at Philadelphia and Edenton, North Carolina.

---

[1] The observations appeared in *GUS*, 3 July; the undated letter, printed under May 1790 Undated, volume 19, appeared in *GUS*, 30 June.

Other Documents

Theodorus Bailey to Nathaniel Lawrence. ALS, Emmet Collection, NN. Written from Poughkeepsie, New York; place to which addressed not indicated.

Federalists can expect the federal government to flourish best in its "native City" (Philadelphia), and "there speedily attain the stature of a Giant under the Auspices of ~~the~~ it's immaculate God Fathers," James Wilson and Morris.

Pierce Butler to (Dorothea Butler) Fitzgerald. FC, Butler Letterbook, ScU. Sent to Castlebar, Ireland. The recipient (d. 1829) was the eldest daughter of Butler's deceased brother, Sir Thomas Butler. For the full text, see *Butler Letters*, pp. 54–55.

"Your aunt [*Mary Middleton*] Butler continues much indisposed She is now at the sea side bathing."

David Harris to George Washington. ALS, Washington Papers, DLC. Written from Baltimore; franked; postmarked 25 July. For the full text, see *PGW* 6:120–21.

Office seeking: commissioner of loans for Maryland; mentions Henry and Maclay as references.

Woodbury Langdon to John Langdon. ALS, Langdon Papers, NhPoA. Written from Portsmouth, New Hampshire.

Can procure masts and spars for Willing, Morris & Company.

James Madison to John Dawson. No copy known; acknowledged in Dawson to Madison, 1 August.

Edmund Randolph to an Unknown Recipient. Excerpt, *Henckels Catalog* 1272(1921):item 458. The ellipses are in the source.

"Before this day you must have heard of the resolution of Congress as to the seat of the federal government. . . . It may not be amiss to add, that even if the banks of the Potowmack should at last receive Congress, this [*New York City?*] is a theatre, on which real genius may always display itself."

Thomas B. Wait to George Thatcher. ALS, Chamberlain Collection, MB. Written from Portland, Maine; postmarked Portsmouth, New Hampshire, 26 July.

Fears he has contracted measles from his little daughter, Eliza; may not be able to write again until "the disease shall have left me. *Perhaps I may never write to you again!*"

SUNDAY, 25 JULY 1790

Fisher Ames to Thomas Dwight

***

Our politics have been critical the past week. the funding bill having passed the Senate with Amendments, on Friday the house took up the Amendments—and instead of funding 26 Dollars (on each hundred to be loaned) at the end of 10 Years, the house propose 33 1/3 at the end of 7 years. The Indents & Interest on the debt of the U.S. to be raised from 3 per Cent as proposed by the Senate, and funded at four per Cent—This being just I wish it may pass in the Senate. Three per Cent seems to be abandoning all pretence of paying the Creditors.

Yesterday, we renewed the battle for the assump[*tio*]n.—rather we began it on Friday. Mr. Jackson then made a speech which I will not say was loud enough for you to hear. It disturbed the Senate however & to keep out the din, they put down their windows. Mr. Smith (S.C.) followed him an hour. Yesterday Mr. Gerry delivered himself—Jackson rebellowed—The motion by Jackson being—That the house do disagree to the Amendment of the Senate Voted—in the negative, 32 not including the Speaker who is of our side agt. 29—Several Motions were made to alter the sums to be assumed from the states—but were negatived. Thus, my friend, we again stand on good ground—we shall finish the amendments I hope tomorrow—and as they are not likely to be founded on improper principles, I hope the Senate will concur—and relieve us from a state of solicitude which has been painful beyond any thing I ever suffered—I do not see how the Bill can be lost, as both houses have agreed to it's passage. and tho the Amendments may not suit both, I will not fear that they will be agreed to in some form—or other—we are impatient for the end of the session—should all go smoothly we shall sit till near the middle of August.

[*P. S.*] The Indian Chief, [*Alexander*] McGillivray is here He is decent & not very black.

ALS, Ames Papers, MDedHi. Addressed to Springfield, Massachusetts; franked; postmarked. The omitted text concerns their friends the Worthington family. For the full text, see *Ames*, pp. 86–87.

Pierce Butler to George Mason

***

We are here, my dear Sir, doing, I scarcely know what, for We do & undo. Passions, Prejudices, State Interest, toss us about so that I scarce know the object We aim at. Permanent & Temporary Residence; Funding system & Assumption all crowd at once, & almost overpower. I wish We may do justly, act wisely, and get well to the end of the session. We Potowmack Gentlemen are abused in the New York papers, yet none I think so much as myself, as You will see by the morning Post of Yesterday.[1] Why This unfounded abuse I know not, for my Enemys know I have been uniform and consistent, that I always declared that the permanent residence was my object; & that with me every thing consistent with Justice should yield to it:

and for this the New York Prints abuse me, & invent things that were not, nor are not—such is the tribute We pay for entering into publick life—Tho I have wished, and still do wish to see You on the floor of Sennate, I admire and applaud Your resolution in withstanding—I smile at the justness of Doctor Franklin's story of the Whistle—have You read it?[2]

May You long enjoy health & happiness to whistle at the follies of Mankind.

[*P. S.*] I was favored with your letter by Mr. Fenwick[3] to whom I shewed every attention.

FC, Butler Letterbook, ScU. The omitted text acknowledges Mason's letter of 9 July, promises to settle a bond despite Butler's "totally deranged" finances, and discusses news from France, where he "ardently" hopes the people "will accomplish their object." For the full text, see *Butler Letters*, pp. 55–56.

---

[1] The "Congressional Biography" on Butler in *NYMP*, 19 July, above.

[2] Written in 1779, Franklin's essay on the result of having paid too much for a whistle when he was a child offers reflections on the value of things.

[3] Joseph Fenwick, a partner in the Bordeaux based mercantile firm of Mason's son John, traveled overland from Virginia to New Hampshire between early June and late July, en route back to Europe (*PGM* 3:1200, 1205).

Solomon Drown to Theodore Foster

Your most agreable little Embassador was announced yesterday, and received with all that cordiality, to which your representative is ever so justly intitled. Your ideas of friendship and of the solace to be derived from a communication of thoughts by writing, most perfectly coincide with my own; and therefor I now attempt to [*lined out*] requite you for the pleasure & satisfaction your excellent letter afforded.

You observe that the fate of the two great questions before Congress is at present involved in uncertainty; and for my single self I could wish this might continue to be the case till the next or some future session: For if they should be decided in the negative much confusion if not even defection will ensue; and if, in the affirmative, great dissatisfaction in some of the states will be the consequence. These are some, in my opinion at present most devoutly to be deprecated.

*** I must now mention to you another Scheme which has lately occupied my thoughts. Philadelphia no doubt will be the seat of general Government for a long time to come; and tho' now, like London it may seem to be crowded with professional Characters, yet perhaps room may be found for another. Did not Collen & Hunter[1] go from a mean village one to Edinburgh, and ~~Hunter from~~ the other to London, and arrive at the highest degree of medical eminence in those Cities? I have consulted Mr. J—n F—o [*John Fenno*] on this subject, who thinks it adviseable to make the attempt, for he too, considers my prospect very unpromising here. If we should go, I should expect Mrs. Drown's Mamma[2] to go with us, who has been accustomed to board some of the Members of the Gen. Court, Massachusetts so I should have it in contemplation to board one or two Members of Congress, to help along at first. Perhaps too I might attend some of the Eastern Delegates in case of Sickness, &c.—Now what think you of this scheme; or can you propose a better?

You ask, what is said of Congress? Much blame is lavished on them for spending so long time about residence; and still more by some for going at last to Philadelphia, the scene of their former dishonour For it is thought strange they can so soon pocket their just resentment at the contempt, or pusillanimity discovered by those, who ought to have protected them from every insult. Congress also are blamed for determining to purchase a Library with the public money; I have thought of a plan that may obviate this last objection to their measures. Let each member subscribe one or two days pay, to be laid out in books; and every new member pay the same; by which means there will be a certain income, that perhaps will be adequate to collecting a sufficient number of Books Since I began to write we have had a tempest of rain & hail, with severe lightening. Mr. J. J. Clark's house was struck, and much shattered. 400 or 500 dollars at least will be required to repair the damage When you write again, do not forget the account of your visit to M. [*Louis Guillaume*] Otto; concerning [*Alexander*] McGillivray, &c. If you should have time to visit the Bookstores; and can find Mason's English Garden, a Poem in four Books by a Wm. Mason M.A. with a Commentary by Mr. [*William*] Burgh[3] you will oblige me by purchasing it for me; also a little pamphlet with this Title, Notes on Farming, printed in New York, printed in the Year 1787,[4] if there is not a later edition.

FC, Drown Collection, RPB. Written from Providence, Rhode Island. This letter may not have been sent. The omitted text concerns the health of friends.

[1] William Cullen (1710–90) taught medicine at Edinburgh from 1755. William Hunter (1718–83), one of his most famous students there, settled in London in 1740 and helped establish the practice of obstetrics.

[2] Elizabeth Russell (b. 1757) married Drown in 1777. She was the daughter of Thomas Russell of Boston and his second wife, Honora Loud.

[3] The edition Drown sought had been published at York, England, in 1783.

[4] Written by Charles Thomson, secretary of Congress from 1774 to 1789.

Thomas Fitzsimons to Benjamin Rush

We are about to do the Very thing you propose that is to pay 6 ℔ Ct. on $^2/_3$ of the debt & Suspend the other $^1/_3$ for 7 or 10 Years. so that we probably both mean the same thing—Indeed I do not think it imposssable. but 4 or $4^1/_2$ ℔ Ct. will yet be the Compromise—for the Whole—I am persuaded that would be more Advantagous to the Creditors. than any thing yet proposed—We have been these 2 days on the business in our house it is the only one that now Keeps us together—And I hope will determinate so as to Give pretty General satisfaction I have not the smallest Anxiety about Doctr. [*James*] Hutchinson & Co. but I feel extreamly When I find the Opinions of men Whose Judgement and Integrity stand high in my estimation differing from Me—I trust we shall as we go along find other Opinions as well as those of our Worthy Mayor [*Samuel Miles*] becomeing favorable—& I am not in the least discouraged at the Obstacles hitherto thrown in our Way—I think the present Week will Close our sessions—& Certainly will not pass thro Princeton without payg. My respects to Mrs. [*Julia Stockton*] Rush.

ALS, privately owned in 2008. Addressed to Philadelphia; franked; postmarked 26 July.

Nicholas Gilman to Governor John Sullivan

I am honored with your obliging favors of the 12th & 17th instant and am greatly obliged by the friendly part you have taken in what relates to my honor & interest—but be the event as it may I beg leave on this occasion to observe that my heart has never been much elated in consequence of public honors however desirable the possession may have been neither can my mind be depressed by the loss of them.

To my friends I feel a sense of obligation for their kind exertions—confiding always in the justice of their motives and most sincerely wishing—whenever they think they can serve the public better by promoting an other in my stead that they would withhold from me their individual suffrags—But when I consider the characters of those who I understand are to be my chief competitors I can draw no unfavorable conclusions from any Ideas that may be formed of their superior merit—Yet the enemies to the former revolution will push the interest of one of the most implacable of their party—The advotates of public fraud will perhaps be no less zealous to promote the interest of one of their chief partisans and a powerful junto occasionally formed by a coalition of parties from party views will I apprehend give my friends a very powerful, though I should hope not an insuperable, resistance.

Since the passage of the Residence bill which has given so much uneasiness throughout the Union the progress of business has been very considerable—the difficulties attending this affair which has so long agitated the public mind and has had so unfavorable an issue has been owing chiefly to an unreasonable desire in many of the Eastern people to continue Congress in this Eccentric position which subjected Some of the Southern members to a travel of more than a thousand miles; and as it was the wish of many of them to meet in Philadelphia a safe & more suitable place than this; I always considered it unwise and impolitic in the nothern people to oppose it—from this consideration and lest by endeavoring to continue here we should be carried further South, our Delegates in the old Congress were for assembling the new Congress in Philadelphia.[1] this being overruled has produced the effect they apprehended—but fortunately the time for removal to the Potomack is remote and I trust will not take place according to the Bill if the good of the Nation does not require it at the appointed time.

The Bill for funding the public debt is still before Congress—it came down from the Senate a few days ago with an amendment which comprehends the State debts to amount of 21,500,000 dollars To the general Idea of assumption—as containing a principle calculated to avert enumerable evils and to promote the general welfare I have ever lent a favorable ear In hopes that when the subject was generally understood that a plan (so modified as to relieve those States that feel most sensibly the weight of Debts incurred by their exertions during the war—without assuming the whole of their Debts and without laying an unjust burden upon other States) would meet with general approbation But the plan proposed by the Senate contains so large a Sum and the proportion to be assumed from each State so manifestly unjust that I have considered it my duty to disagree to the measure the Question (however) was carried yesterday in favor of the assumption and it is most probable the Bill will pass the House as it came from the Senate except some alterations in the rate of interest in which the concurrence of the Senate is doubtful But I hope this business will be determined within a few days or postponed to the next Session as the present is protracted to a most tedious & painful length.

ALS, New Hampshire Miscellany, DLC. Place to which addressed not indicated.

---

[1] Beginning on 2 July 1788 Congress debated the ordinance on when and where the FFC would meet. The disagreement over whether to remain in New York or move to Philadelphia delayed a decision until 13 September.

Benjamin Goodhue to Stephen Goodhue

Yours of 17th. I received, and find you expect me home sooner then you'l see me, for I do not think we shall more then get up by the last of next week, We have been for two or three days past upon the amendments to the funding bill as it came from Senate, and a motion was made and strenuously contended that we should reject that amendment of the Senate which includes the assumption, and just as we adjourn'd yesterday the vote was taken when 29 were for rejecting, and 32 against it, the question is yet to be taken whether We agree, We have said by the vote already taken that we would not reject it, but it does not follow in this critical bussines, that we shall accept and agree to it, therefore I yet consider the assumption as uncertain, tho' the vote yesterday has rendered it quite probable—I am glad to find you have a fruitfull season, please to tell your Printer[1] not to send me any more papers—I think you ought not to delay purchasing lumber and a large quantity.

ALS, Goodhue Family Papers, MSaE. Addressed to Salem, Massachusetts; franked; postmarked.

[1] Thomas C. Cushing, editor of the [Massachusetts] *Salem Gazette.*

Benjamin Goodhue to Insurance Offices

The bill for funding with the senates amendments thereto has been under consideration of the House for two or three days past, that one relating to the assumption has been violently opposed and a motion was made *that We disagree to that amendment.* just as We adjourned yesterday, the question was put on that motion when 29 were in favr. of it to 32 against it, the question for agreeing to the amendment yet remains to be taken, and tho' by the vote yesterday we said We would not disagree to it or reject it, it is by no means from thence certain that it will obtain, perhaps some who were in majority unless they can introduce an amendment into the measure or from other considerations may ultimately change their votes—however we flatter [*lined out*] ourselves it may eventualy be accomplish'd—the house have raised the 3 pr. Ct. interest on indents from 3 to 4 pr. Ct. and will probably do the same as to the 1/3 of the debt to be assumed, but its ~~whether~~ very doubtfull whether the Senate will acceed to that increase.

ALS, Goodhue Papers, NNS. Addressed to Salem, Massachusetts; franked; postmarked.

Christopher Gore to Rufus King

The people of this state own very large quantities of the debt of the U.S.—and in case of a funding system, on principles advantageous to the creditors and honorable to the government woud draw ve[*r*]y largely from its revenue—when I reflect on this, which is known to, & acknowledg'd by all our delegates, I am really at a loss to conjecture the motives, that have influenc'd the delegation from Massachusetts in acceding to a reduction of the interest.

I have known that a majority of them have advocated a less rate of interest than the proposal of the Secretary—the wisest and best men, in this quater of the country, have very explicitly declared to these gentlemen, their abhorrence of such reduction, as unjust & dishonorable.

***

ALS, King Papers, NHi. Written from Boston; carried by Cyrus King. The omitted text concerns Cyrus's accounts.

Thomas Jefferson to Thomas Mann Randolph, Sr.

*** I believe the assumption will take place in the form in which you now see it in the public papers. it has been so shaped, principally to quiet Massachusetts & S. Caroline the two states most in need of it, and Virginia the most opposed to it on account of the great progress she has made in paying her debt. the sum assumed for her will pay all her remaining debt, and it is exactly the quota she will have to contribute of the whole sum assumed. so that she will neither gain nor lose.

FC, letterpress copy, Jefferson Papers, DLC. For the full text, see *PTJ* 17:274–76. This letter was covered by one to Thomas Mann Randolph, Jr., in which Jefferson repeated some of his report on assumption and reported that "Congress will probably rise between the 6th and 13th of August."

Richard Henry Lee and John Walker to Governor Beverley Randolph

We have now the honor to acknowledge the receipt of your Excellency's letter with its enclosure respecting Lead mines and manufacture. The proposition came seasonably here when a Bill for augmenting the impost was under consideration.

We have the satisfaction to inform you that it was readily agreed to lay a duty of one cent pr. pound on all imported Lead, which we hope will be found a sufficient protection for our infant manufacture of this article. We are sorry to inform your Excellency that the assumption of the State debts into the funds of the U.S. is likely to succeed at last—The measure was brought on in Senate and carried by a small majority after having been twice or three times rejected in the H. of Representatives, where yesterday it was agreed to by a small majority. We have endeavored to render this business as little hurtful to our Country as possible, by pressing for as large an assumption for Virginia as could be obtained.

The Sum assumed for our State is 3,500,000 dollars, which being more than we owe, will serve to cover a part of the large ballance that we claim from the Union.

ALS, hand of Lee, Dreer Collection, PHi. Addressed to Richmond, Virginia; franked by Lee; postmarked 26 July. This letter is misidentified as Walker to Randolph, July undated, in *PTJ* 17:24n.

James Madison to James Monroe

After all the vicissitudes through which the assumption has passed, it seems at present in a fair way to succeed as part of the general plan for the public debt. The Senate have included it among their amendments to the funding bill, and a vote of yesterday in the House of Representatives indicates a small majority in favor of the measure. In its present form it will very little affect the interest of Virginia in either way. I have not been able to overcome my other objections, or even to forbear urging them. At the same time, I cannot deny that the crisis demands a spirit of accommodation to a certain extent. If the measure should be adopted, I shall wish it to be considered as an unavoidable evil, and *possibly* not the worst side of the dilemma.

PJM 13:282–83, from Madison, *Letters* 1:522. The letter was misdated 24 July by either Madison or the editors of the *Letters*.

George Thatcher to Sarah Thatcher

I beleive you begin to wish the post may pass without leaving you any Letter—This would be some encouragement for you to beleive I have left New-York; & am on my way home—I confess I am home-sick; and most heartily weary of all events as they turn up here—I long for some change of place—& to feel & smell the Country air.

For your and my consolation this I look upon the last Letter, or last but one you will receive from me at this place—We have nearly compleated our business—and I think before Saturday night we shall adjourn—or early the next week—And then I shall make all possible speed homewards—were it not that I must stop one day, at lest, in Boston. I would be but six days in passing from this to our dear home—provided I set out on monday.

My things saild this morning for Boston; should they arrive before I do, which I think they will not—I would have you open the box & take out the cloaths & then put it with the books & papers into the office.

ALS, Thatcher Family Papers, MHi. Place to which addressed not indicated.

George Thatcher to Thomas B. Wait

Last night I read yours of the 17th. inst. and laughed—because it was just such an one as I had been expecting for some weeks—Indeed I had begun to wonder you had not before ~~wrote me~~ expressed your grief in a Letter of Condolence.

It is four or five weeks since some of my friends have been hinting to me, in their Letters, that I must prepare for a political death—And it is curious to to observe with how much caution and delicacy this is done. They want I should know my approaching fate—and yet their feelings sympathise too much with me, ~~at~~ to permit them expressly to tell me what they apprehend will be painfull for me to hear, ~~to permit them expressly to tell me~~ Hence they conclude their dolefull sentence with an encouraging *but* or some words calculated to palliate the full force of what their fears have suggested—One sais, *"but I am not certain"* Another, *"but I beleive, on whole, you will succeed"*—a third—*nevertheless my feeble abilities, as well as my vote, shall be exerted in ~~my~~ your favour*—A fourth—*I beleive you may be elected if you choose it*—A fifth—*I yet hope the best*—A sixth—"the Candidates for the next federal election begin to ~~buz~~ buz about—And I assure you they are numerous, but—but what? but few will roll up Hill, for doziness will so seize their noddles, and then they must of course loose their way"—A seventh whose passions and affections are more lively and come nearer to friendship—*"It makes me angry while I sing"* of your fate[1] &c. &c. &c. &c.

Upon the whole I verily beleive I view the approaching election with less anxiety and concern than many of my friends—I have fewer passions, & those of a weaker kind, than what animate them, engaged in the business—To be at Congress is with me a secondary object, and rather a means to another, which I am led to think may now be effected at Biddeford or Portland [*Maine*] as well, and perhaps better than in any public employ—To lay your curiosity, and prevent its fixing on some less meritorious pursuit I will tell you what this is—It is the acquisition of knowledge—and the application of it to the happiness of my fellow creatures.

I shall be sorry to find, at the coming election, that friendship gives way to ambition—or that any means are made use of by the Candidates or their friends that are not agreeable to Truth, & consistant with the general peace and harmony of the people thro' the district. That these should be preferred as much as possible is what every one ought to aim at—And, I declare, I will take no step or speak one word that has a contrary tendency—And should any of my friends I shall certainly blaim them.

When 'tis objected against me that I am not a man of Religion, I would not wish my friends ever to deny the charge; because the people might thereby be led to imagine me religious after their own ideas of religion—which is not the fact. And as I said a few days since, in a letter to a friend;[2] "I had rather never be again noticed by the voice of my Country, than receive their unanimous vote on the ground of my holding to many things, which, I know, they look upon essential to a religious Character."

FC, Thatcher Family Papers, MHi.

[1] Wait himself, in his letter of 17 July, above.
[2] To Nathaniel Barrell, 21 July, above.

Letter from New York

The Bill for funding the Continental domestick debt was returned last week from the Senate, with a number of amendments: among which was one for assuming 21,500,000 dollars of the State debts. Those amendments were yesterday under consideration of the House, and some of them agreed to. A motion was made by the anti-assumptionists to disagree to the amendment containing the assumption; and on taking the question there were 29 for the motion and 32 against it. The anti-assumptionists then proposed amendments to the Senate's amendment, hoping no doubt to destroy the assumption by tacking to it some amendments that might induce the House or the Senate to reject the whole; but all their motions for this purpose were over ruled, and the House adjourned before they compleated the Senate's amendment. It is yet doubtful as to the event of the assumption; but a few days will decide that and put an end to this session.

[Portland, Maine] *Cumberland Gazette*, 2 August. This is probably from a letter written by Thatcher to the newspaper's editor, Thomas B. Wait.

Other Documents

John Adams to Henry Marchant. FC:lbk, Adams Family Manuscript Trust, MHi. Sent to Newport, Rhode Island.

Regarding the manner by which Marchant should signify his acceptance of federal office; Adams did not deliver Marchant's letter applying for the office because Marchant had been appointed before it arrived.

Elbridge Gerry to Samuel R. Gerry. ALS, Samuel R. Gerry Papers, MHi. Addressed to Marblehead, Massachusetts; franked; postmarked 26 July; answered 18 August.

Office seeking: has received Samuel's petition to the President to be made collector at Marblehead to replace Richard Harris, news of whose death "I received in the evening & it gave me such a shock as broke my rest thro the night"; "I fear a disappointment"; Knox, Hamilton, and Adams support Samuel's appointment "but the disposition of matters in other respects are against us."

Samuel R. Gerry to Elbridge Gerry. ALS, Gerry Papers, MHi. Written from Marblehead, Massachusetts.

Office seeking: hopes his brother has secured the Marblehead collectorship for him; "the Town in general appears to wish my having the office but suppose shortly shall know my fate."

John Jay to Robert Morris. No copy known; listed in *Ernest D. North Catalog* 20(1910):item 159.

"A. N. S. in the third person."

James Madison to Governor Beverley Randolph. No copy known; acknowledged in Randolph to Madison, 10 August.

Susan Stockton to Elias Boudinot. ALS, Boudinot Collection, NjP. Place from which written not indicated; carried by Abraham Van Bibber.

Introduces Van Bibber and asks Boudinot to pay him "some little attention."

James Sullivan to John Langdon. ALS, Langdon Papers, NhPoA. Written from Boston.

Encloses a letter to Langdon's care "for our good friend the Consul [*Philip Joseph De L'Etombe*] residing here it is on public business that concerns both Nations"; wishes to see Langdon in Boston; is pleased that "the Senate has done something decisive on the funding business for should Congress adjourn without doing any thing the Consequences would be very disagreeable"; thanks for the kind mention in Langdon's letter (unlocated) to a Mr. Russell.

George Thatcher to Henry Sewall. No copy known; acknowledged in Sewall to Thatcher, 21 January 1791.

Abishai Thomas to John Gray Blount. ALS, John Gray Blount Papers, Nc-Ar.
The opponents of assumption "have not given up the point, their hopes now consist in obtaining amendments [*to the Funding Act*] so as to give it such a questionable shape as finally to have it thrown out."

Jeremiah Wadsworth to Harriet Wadsworth. ALS, Wadsworth Papers, CtHi. Addressed to Hartford, Connecticut; franked; postmarked.
Hopes to return in two weeks, but is "tired of fixing a time we meet with so many delays"; rejoices at Daniel Wadsworth's recovery; Elizabeth Laurance was better on 23 July, but he has not heard more since then.

John Jeffries, Diary. Jeffries Family Papers, MHi.
Visited Adamses at "Richmond Hill" at noon; was "politely received" for afternoon tea at Dalton's, where they were joined by the Adamses and Ames, among others; in the evening, called on Wadsworth and left a card.

From New York. [Boston] *Columbian Centinel*, 31 July.
"The amendments to the amendments of the Senate, made by the House, will occasion a conference; and it is expected, points will *not* be earnestly contended. Besides, the Funding Bill, there are only four or five others to be finished—so that the recess may commence in ten or twelve days."

MONDAY, 26 JULY 1790

Nicholas Brown to Theodore Foster

As You was so friendly as to Mention me before you Went from this Town that You Should be glad to here from Your Old Friend Occationally I now take pen in hand Just to Shew You my Opinion in Sum late proceedings of Congress, which if not Attended to May prove Injurious to Your Pollittical Charactor here by way of Neglect or Inattention to the Interest of this State It is in This, I observe in the N. York papers is Mention'd the Report of a Comte. of the Sennett for the Sum each State is to have Assum'd of there Debts Sum of which Seems more & Sum less than what will be There due proportions of Debts, What method that Comte. went upon is Yet Unknown here without You have Wrote the reason to sum of your friends which have not Communicated it, I am well acquainted with Your Situation as to the Assumption, but You must Note That I go upon the Supposition that the assumption *will* take place at all events & Tho' You may Consider

Yourself Oblig'd to oppose it in every Stage Nevertheless this State who will probably pay by Impost &c. at least as much & I doubt not but more than her proportion into the Publick Chest and it was well known by the former Congress that this State Loand more money to Congress than Any State in the Union & had kept up there full Quota & will be found to have Advanc'd the full propor[*tio*]n. According to there Bigness This I have Often & very lately ben told by Our Members ~~of~~ of the former Congress has ben publickly Asserted on the floar of Congress & Could not be denied, but suppose we had done but little or Nothing as was the Case of Sum States why should not this State have her full proportion of the Sum Assum'd, as We must & Shall raise within this State Our proportion, of the Millions that Other Sta[*t*]es will have assum'd—This is a Matter that does not affect my Interest any further tha~~t~~n as a single Member that Must Suffer In proportion of what The state may Suffer by Not havg. our proporn. with other States, As the Over plus Sum That may not be subscribed for is to be paid into that State Treasurys & There to draw Interest till the State Accots. are Settled with Congress for we are morrally Sure this State will have a *Grait* Balance due to her, therefore as it may be a length of Time I feaer before those State Accots. are all clos'd—it is well known that Those who have Carried in there Secureties & taken the pappr mo[*ne*]y. when it was part of Time as much as 15 for 1, Under parr & those persons Generally, that Now hold the Goverment, will Not long sit & see those who Uniformly refused giving Up there Secureties for the paper Money & In Consequence of the assumption receive the Interest of the Same & principle Secur'd—But ~~there~~ will most Certainly have those payments Liquidated according to the Value of the paper when recd. towards sd. notes, This has you know ben don for the Invalleads, & will doubtless be Adjusted accordingly, as it is not to be suppos'd But people in Power will do as well for themselves as for the Invalleads, & those who have Complaind Agst. The Laws for forfitting there Secureties, as honest men Can but Joyn the majorety in doing Justice to the Widow orfans &c. so as to give those an eaqual Chance That Others have by the funding or assuming sd. debts—But in this Case where is the Means That is Necissary to pay of[*f*] Such Demands if we get no more of the Assumption than what will be Subscribed for; or Those Others who may have there Notes Consollidated, there will be Nothing to pay them with till the State receives it in a Bal[*anc*]e. from the Union.

Will not this Cause grait Complaints Agst. those who tamely Sit Still & forget (as may be said) there own States, *who have An eequal right to there full proportion*, I am told this State is graitly in Debt more than the Assum'd sum for this State, even on the suppossion, that all the Notes taken in for paper Mo[*ne*]y. will ever remain as Dischargd. This is a matter that will be as much agst. My Interest as My proportion of all those Secureties or other debts that may be so Setled but as An Honest Man & your friend I mention this Matter. I find the people Uneasy at puting the Interest so low & Espesially the Indents, & I think Publick Credit will not be fully established by the doings of Congress according as We here they will Most likely agree to Pay there Debts Contracted in The war—In a late Meeting of the Mudd [*River*] Massheen Company it was talked over as Exceeding injurous to said compy. if not Ruinous Not to have Liberty from Congress to Collect moneys from the Navigation to support the working of it to Clear out the Channel according to the Intention it is Now all done ready to begin in the Crook,[1] but Want of funds prevents, we hope You Will Attend to this matter & get it done before Congress rises. We Consider this as an Interesting matter to the Publick Advantage Greatly tend to Increase the Trade of the State Consequently will Increase the Publick Revenue.

Sum Other Things Should have mention'd but Time will not Permit My Compliments to Mr. Stanton.

ALS, Foster Papers, RHi. Written from Providence, Rhode Island, "Late" at night.

[1] The juncture of the Providence and Pawtucket rivers.

Elbridge Gerry to George Washington

I received a letter from Samuel Russel Gerry Esqr. to the Secretary of the Treasury, requesting to be nominated to the President of the United States for the office of collector for the Port of Marblehead [*Massachusetts*]. his application was made in this mode as he writes me, because not being informed on the subject he was doubtful whether candidates from a principle of attention & respect, with which in his opinion too great a degree of familiarity does not comport; should apply in any other mode than thro the head of the department. during the war he was requested by the General Court [*legislature*] to provide for troops stationed in that quarter, & gave such perfect satisfaction as to have been remarkable for the accuracy & justness of his accounts, in which he is compleat. he was on every occasion at the call of his country, being at the R. Island expedition & other places. he was appointed naval officer & having served one year resigned it in expectation of better office under the United States. his conduct there in was as satisfactory to the State as in the other instances mentioned, & he is now collector of excise for that place. The voluntary petition of the merchants & traders of that place, is an evidence that whilst his conduct in office has been ever approved by Government, it has not been less so by those over whom he has been placed, whose esteem by a mild & decent behaviour he possesses in a high degree. the subscribers to that petition, some of whom are the wealthiest citizens of the place, form as I conceive by far the greatest part of the commercial property thereof. if recommendations out of the town are necessary, to my knowledge he can procure them from the first characters of the State; but as circumstances may not admit of delay, I think it my duty sir, altho he is a brother, indeed the only one I have & for whom I have a tender regard, to say as I can with great Truth, that he is a man of strict honor, probity & assiduity, & in every respect equal to this office, & that sir his conduct therein I pledge myself to be responsible.

I have sir with reluctance troubled you on this occasion, but am sure your feeling heart will pardon these effusions of friendship, altho their object is the promotion of a brother as well as of the public service: & whatever may be your decision therein, You may be assured, that with the highest sentiments of respect & esteem I remain.

ALS, Washington Papers, DLC.

Samuel Hodgdon to Benjamin Goodhue

Your esteemed favour of the 22d instant came duly to my hand—I thank you for the delivery of my Letters—Pay Phillips small amount to Mr. George Clymer who is my particular friend—As yet I have not mentioned the purport of your letter to Mrs. [*Grace?*] Hastings—her house has no accomodations, and her infirm state induces me to think that yourself, and the Gentlemen you mention, can be better provided for elsewhere—and if you will permit *me* to make the arrangement, I will insure [*lined out*] suitable lodgings—all eastern Gentlemen are "*plain Men*" and it gives me pleasure to say that such "are most esteemed here, and consequently easier provided for"—We dine now at 1 oClock *never* to exceed two—*I think*, it will not under circumstances do for you, tho' Mrs. Hastings is as kind as ever but she is not able to do as formerly—I thought it best thus to write you—your next shall be my guide.

I hope a funding bill will be agreed on before you rise—if not much invective will break out, many are distress'd, yet hoping—you *must* contrive to Pay some *domestick interest*—salaries and Pensions dwell incessantly on the lips of the disafec[*ted*] and the distress'd *Whigs* begin to listen to the sound—not an *act* say some—appears, but a considerable part is taken up in creating new Officers, and determining their Pay—the present has been an ungracious session—but I will not torture *you* with complaints.

ALS, Letters to Goodhue, NNS. Written from Philadelphia.

Henry Marchant to Elbridge Gerry

I have the Pleasure of Yours of the 14th. Instant—I lament the unhappy Decissions, in your respectable Body; and I have for a considerable Time had anxious Moments, respecting the future, in Consequence of present Measures—You Sir have given Your faithful Testmony of Regard to the Peace and Prosperity of Your Country. your Efforts on a very late Occasion do you Honor—The more important Business, the Assumption, now before you, will call up every Exertion—And whither you succeed or not, you will be able to say: Tis not in Mortals to command Success but will do more, will deserve it—I cannot see the Pollicy of a partial Assumption—Great must be The Confusion, by the Interference of the States, and Difficulty of providing Means not incompattable with the Provision of the United States. Why will Congress have the Din & Noise of the publick Debt forever amongst the Body of the People, as it will be so long as the Individual States have any Thing to do with the Business: But I cannot add any Thing useful to you upon a Subject you are so thoroughly acquainted with.

Since my last I find by the Acts of Congress, the Chief Justice of the Supreme Court is to furnish a Seal for each of the *Circuit* Courts—I have written His Honor Judge Jay upon it, and mentioned I had requested You to procure me a Seal for the *District* Court. I wish the Word *Court* to be added round the Edge to the Words *Rhode Island District*, if not too late.

If You should see Judge Jay I wish You to mention the Device to Him, You may conclude upon.

ALS, formerly at ICarbS. Written from Newport, Rhode Island.

James Monroe to James Madison

Yours of the 4th of July was the last recd. acknowledging mine by Mr. [*Muscoe?*] Garnett. Those of earlier date were answer'd from Richmond. I find you have had before you two subjects only, of consequence latterly, that part of the revenue business wh. respects the assumpsion of the State debts, & the fixing on some places for the tempy. & permanent seats of Congress. The latter we hear has been finally adjusted in favor of Phila., & the headwaters of the Potow[*mac*]k. If this is the case, & the completion of the business committed in a sufficient manner, to the Executive department of the government, independantly of the further agency of Congress, it is certainly the wisest & happiest arrangment that can be made respecting it. A great question will be ended as it shod. be. But every thing will depend on its being completed, for if resort must be had hereafter to Congress, it will be found eventually as only the triumph of Phila. over New York, & at best not advancing a single step toward terminating the controversy or establishing a seat of permanent residence for the government. As I have not seen what shape it has ultimately recd., I can form no opinion on the subject, & only hope it has assum'd the proper one. On the other subject I took the liberty to make a few observations in my last. No proposition that I have seen removes my objections to it, for at best, if it does not compell the industrious & complying States to pay the debts, or a part of the debts, of those who have been less deserving, it prefers the exercise of taxation in the hands of the national to those of the State governments, wh. I cannot approve. And for wh. I can see no necessity, unless it shall be shewn me, that the national govt. is answerable for the debts of the individl. States, wh. of course I conclude they are not, till they assume them. I believe however, a satisfactory adjustment of the other business wod. make this more palatable here. we feel ourselves particularly oblig'd to you for yr. kindness in giving us intelligence from our friends. we never hear from them, except when you extract a line from them. It revives Mrs. M[*onroe'*]s. spirits,[1] wh. from her long absence are often depress'd. We hope to see you here in the course of autumn.

ALS, Madison Papers, DLC. Written from Charlottesville, Virginia; franked; postmarked Richmond, 30 July.

[1] Monroe's wife, Elizabeth Kortright, was a native of New York City.

A Citizen to J. L. E. B. and P. S. Esquires

Three of the Representatives in C—g—s for the State of N—w Y—k

THE Question of the ASSUMPTION is again come on in C–g—s, and to the no small surprise of a great number of your Constituents you again advocate it. Have we not already made sacrifices enough to the Union, and are now by your votes to be saddled with the enormous states of other debts? Are we tamely to put up with every insult, and must we now submit to the capricious whims of a Faction, without struggle at least on your part? In short, must we never have done doing more and more to satisfy our rapacious Brethren. For shame, GENTLEMEN, feel the sentiments of your injured Constituents, and with the manly spirit of American Senators, cease to give support to men, by whose intrigues you have already been duped.

☞ It is also time to have done legislating for *Speculators* and *Brokers.*

NYMP, 26 July. The New York Representatives were Laurance, Benson, and Silvester.

B. L. to the Printer

HAS the Legislature of the United States acted with that dignity which their station, or the interests of their constituents require? If this question can, with the voice of truth and candor be answered in the affirmative, with what pleasing sensations will each Member return to the bosom of his country; with what honest plaudits will he be received by his constituents. If, on the contrary, the very best friends of the two Houses should be obliged to give a negative to the question, what will—what ought to be their reception? What ought to be the kind of welcome they should receive at the hands of their injured fellow citizens? Should it be found on examination of their proceedings, that instead of attending seriously to the business of the union, and to the important interest of the people; they have spent nearly *eight months*, and about ONE HUNDRED and FIFTY THOUSAND DOLLARS, in the character of residence and insurance brokers?

Should it be found, that all this time and money have been spent merely to bring about one point, in itself uninteresting to the public; and another, ruinous to their interests, and that instead of bringing either of those forward on their own merits; the one has been basely sold to obtain the other. If these things should appear, where I ask, is the honor and dignity of that Legislature, which ought to be considered as the first in the universe? That these things do, and will more and more abundantly appear: I do most seriously aver, and nothing more than an attention to the proceedings of the two Houses is wanting to make clear as the noon-day. It may seem that the writer of this is displeased with the expected removal of the government; it will be no use, nor is it to his purpose to declare that he is not; he knows it will be put to that account, and he knows also that the arts of designing men have always placed the animadversions made upon their conduct to some personal motives; be this as it may, his wish and intention is to shew, that the *residence* is the price of the *assumption*; and that the *assumption* is the price of the *residence*; and in a future paper he will attempt to shew, that the *assumption* is manifestly unjust, ruinous to the credit of the Union, partial in its operation, and designed only to promote the interest of a certain class of people IN and OUT of Congress. Let the people of the United States look to the conduct of the opposers of the *assumption* at the beginning of the session, Examine their conduct and their arguments; compare that conduct, and those arguments with those of the present time; and if they can reconcile them upon any other ground, than that of a disgraceful and interested bargain, in which the public good had no concern; I will agree that I have abused the gentlemen and will most sincerely ask their pardon.

The Potowmack interest being satisfied, the great man from that State who formerly opposed the *assumption* with firmness and ability now comes forward: How? With the same firmness—with the same abilities—No! He now has but one objection—a small, a little objection—but he is one of those *sacred characters* whose consistency must be kept up: Mr. *White* and Mr. *Lee* may be inconsistent; but Mr. *Maddison* has a character to preserve; therefore he must *vote* as he did before, but not oppose as he did before. I ask these gentlemen, Is the *assumption* more just now than last spring? And I will ask the Maryland gentlemen who voted for it, what beauties they now see in it which were before hid from their eyes. Has the purling of the Conogocheque—the roaring of the majestic Potowmack, or the purchase of North-Carolina paper changed the scene; "circumstances alter cases," but is the face of the public affairs altered in favour of the measure? Or, have the gentlemen who met at Mr. Carrol's lodgings altered their circumstances? The proceedings of this junto shall in due time be laid before the public, nor shall the measures taken by some of them in consequence of the determination of that junto go unnoticed.

IG, 7 August, from non extant *NYMP*, 28 July; also reprinted at Providence, Rhode Island. Dated "Monday morning."

Other Documents

Elbridge Gerry to John Adams. ALS, Adams Family Manuscript Trust, MHi. Similar to Gerry's letter to Washington, above.

Office seeking: Samuel R. Gerry for collector at Marblehead, Massachusetts; "As you were so obliging on Saturday last as to inform me of your design to recommend my brother," thinks it necessary to inform Adams that Samuel has received three offices from the state, that the legislature found his accounts well vouched for, and that his popularity is manifested by the voluntary petition in his favor to the President from the merchants and traders of Marblehead.

William Heron to George Washington. ALS, Washington Papers, DLC. Written in the morning. For the full text, see *PGW* 6:125–29n.

Office seeking: any appointment; can be reached at Mr. Hall's, 190 Water Street, until the next day; thereafter, reply to be addressed to Sturges, who will forward it.

Thomas Jefferson to William Short. ALS, Short Papers, DLC. Place to which addressed not indicated; carried by Nathaniel Barrett; received 24 September. For the full text, see *PTJ* 17:277–81. In a second letter of this date, written in code, Jefferson informed Short that the Senate would sit only a few days longer (ALS, Jefferson-Short Correspondence, ViW; *PTJ* 17:282).

Congress is debating the Funding Bill; passage has been delayed over the question of assuming the states' war debts, but "a developement of circumstances & more mature consideration seem to have produced ~~a change~~ some change of opinion on the subject"; has reason to believe that a majority will vote for assuming up to a given amount; Congress will then adjourn probably between 6 and 13 August.

William Paterson to Euphemia Paterson. *Somerset County* [New Jersey] *Historical Quarterly* 2(1913):272. The funeral was held at Elizabethtown, New Jersey.

Has been invited to be a pall bearer at Governor William Livingston's funeral tomorrow at 3 P.M.; "shall set out in the morning and shall endeavour to return in the evening."

Theodore Sedgwick to Thomas Dwight. No copy known; acknowledged in Dwight to Sedgwick, 31 July.

John Jeffries, Diary. Jeffries Family Papers, MHi.

Attended Federal Hall to deliver letters to Wadsworth, and met Gerry and Otis there; heard Williamson, Smith (of "Georgia," probably meaning South Carolina), Madison, Gerry, Sherman, and Bloodworth speak on the assumption of the state debts.

TUESDAY, 27 JULY 1790

Abigail Adams to Mary Cranch

*** mr. Adams pines for relaxation, tho if one was to credit the Clamours of the Boston papers we should imagine that there was nothing going forward but dissipation, instead of which, there is nothing which wears the least appearance of it, unless they term the presidents Levee of a tuesday and mrs. Washingtons drawing of a fryday such, one last two & the other perhaps three hours She gives Tea Coffee Cake Lemonade & Ice creams in summer all other Ladies who have publick Evenings give Tea coffee Lemonade, but one only who introduces cards, and She is frequently put to difficulty to make up one table at whist, pray is not this better than resorting to Taverns, or even having supper partys. Some amusement from the Buisness of the day is necessary and can there be a more Innocent one than that of meeting at Gentlemens Houses and conversing together, but faction and Antifederalism may turn every Innocent action to evil.

We are all well you See my pens are bad beyond description, and dinner calls.

ALS, Abigail Adams Letters, MWA. Written from "Richmond Hill," outside New York City; addressed to Braintree, Massachusetts; carried by Mr. Codman.

Benjamin Goodhue to Insurance Offices

Yesterday the important question in the funding bill relative to the assumption was agreed to in our House 34 to 28—the bill is sent back to the Senate altering the interest on Indents &c. from 3 to 4 ℔ Ct. how far this may divide us I can't say, but I hope it may not be the occasion of loosing the bill after so long and painfull a struggle to obtain it—when this bill is finish'd whether the act for increasing the impost [*Ways and Means Act HR-83*], which has passed our house and is now before the Senate, or the excise act [*Duties on Distilled Spirits Bill HR-62*] which we some time past rejected, will be adopted, for the purpose of making provision is uncertain, but I think the latter the most probable.

ALS, Goodhue Papers, NNS. This letter was printed almost verbatim in the [Massachusetts] *Salem Gazette*, 3 August.

Benjamin Goodhue to Samuel Phillips, Jr.

With great pleasure I can acquaint you that yesterday, the amendment made by the Senate in the funding bill relative to the Assumption, was agreed to in our House by 34 to 28, we alter'd the rate of interest on the Indents and the 1/3 of the assumed debts from 3 to 4 pr. Cent, the bill is return'd back to the Senate with this amendment, how far we may divide on this is uncertain, their seems a pertinacity on both sides, but I ardently hope and expect it may not occasion the loss of a bill we have been so long painfully struggling to obtain—when this bill is finish'd whether we shall adopt the bill [*Ways and Means Act HR-83*] which some time ago pass'd our house and is now before the Senate, increasing the impost, or whether we shall revive the Excise Act [*Duties on Distilled Spirits Bill HR-62*] (which we have formerly rejected for the want of the assumption) for making further provision for the debt, is uncertain, but I think the latter more probable then the former—the Anti assumptionists say we have out general'd them—I am in hopes we may adjourn in a little time for I am weary beyond measure.

ALS, Phillips Family Papers, MHi. Place to which addressed not indicated.

Thomas Hartley to Jasper Yeates

The Assumption of the State Debts was Yesterday carried in our House, and they are now a Part of the Funding System I had some difficulties which I shall mention to you when I see you.

I presume our Session is near closing—we expect some Capers will be attempted to be plaid—however we shall strive to avoid them.

Mr. Blodworth gave us Notice Yesterday that he would this Day move to bring in a Bill to give a short Residence of Congress to New-York. a Curious Character—and I ought say rather an insignificant forlorn Hope.

ALS, Yeates Papers, PHi. Addressed to Lancaster, Pennsylvania; franked; postmarked.

Richard Henry Lee to [*Arthur*] Lee

I have this day received your two letters by ~~this~~ Post with the Certificates, which, tho I have not counted, I suppose to be right—The manœuvres concerning *funding* & *assumption* have been many and subtil—The latter had been frequently voted out in the H. of R. and a bill sent up for funding the Continental debts proper of the U.S. upon the 3 alternatives of the Secretarys report—The assumption having been voted against unanimously by our Representatives—In the Senate we rejected the Secretarys plan, funded the principal of Contl. debt 2 thirds immediately at 6 pr. Cent & the other third at same interest after 10 years—The whole Interest of this debt amounting to 13 Millions was to be at 3 pr. Cent immediately—And directed the Land to be kept a sacred deposit for sinking the principal—But—Upon this and in the same Bill, they the Senate assumed for State debts 21,500,000 dollars to be funded in fact on terms as good as the Continentals—This bill passed the Senate by a very small Majority—Say 2—It was generally supposed that the Assumption part of our Bill would be rejected by the H. R. but Mr. R. B. Lee & White from our Country [*Virginia*], with Gale & Dan. Carrol from Maryland, changing sides the Assumption was agreed to, and the Cont. interest upon interest raised to 4 pr. Cent—And 7 instead of 10 years proposed for funding the postponed third of the principal of the Continental debt at 6 pr. Cent—These latter amendments with respect to interest are now before the Senate—It seems probable that the whole will be agreed to because the contenders (some of them) for low interest, are still greater Contenders for the Assumption; so that 'tis probable they will take the increased interest rather than hazard the loss of Assumption—You contend for 15 shillings, if the debt is funded—Mr. Wm. Lee will take 12/—My idea is, altho I give all possible credit to the prevailing & powerful interest of Speculators, yet, with the Assumption of 21,500,000 for State debts, with the other Mass, that more is undertaken than can be accomplished—So that if the certificates were mine I would take 12/ and run no further risk—A large Seller in the Broker way, tells me that finals are now 10/ and that if the bill passes ~~that~~ they will be at 12/ but then they who purchase, will not allow any thing for interest, since the issuing of indents ceased—Or, since there was any provision for paying interest made by Congress—perhaps they may alter if the bill should pass giving 4 per Cent on *all* the interest presently—Thus I have told you all that I know about the matter and you will by return of post, give me your Ultimatum—Bank Stock I understand is not easily to be purchased here, the regularly paid quarterly interest being 7 pr. Cent—how it is at Phila. I do not know—I think it probable that we shall adjourn at the close of next week, i.e. the 6th. of August, so that I must hear from you before that time—I enclose you a letter for Capt. Chilton—whom I forgot, & who is certainly a very influential Man.

P. S. I have received 13 dollars for your cow & Calf—I shall presently pay for your Pork—the ballance ~~to~~ is ready for your order—The little Grocer in Queen Street ~~at~~ near the Corner Wall Street, says you paid him for a large Bottle of old F[*rench*]. Brandy that still remains with him—What is to be done with it? I have just now paid Mr. Henry Haydock 8¼ dollars for your Pork, the ballance in your favor for the Cow is 4¾ dollars which are at your command.

[*P. S.*] Will you be so good as attend a little to Cassius.[1]

ALS, Signers of the Declaration, NNPM. Place to which addressed not indicated. The recipient has often been identified as William Lee (*Lee* 2:535–37). The mention of William in the letter, the postscript indicating that the recipient was someone who had recently removed from New York (Arthur had served on the board of treasury since its creation in 1785), and the fact that the docket is in Arthur Lee's hand indicate that he, not brother William, was the recipient.

[1] Probably an enslaved person who may have carried the letter.

William Smith (S.C.) to Edward Rutledge

As no Vessel sails soon from this place, I write you a few words by Philada. to acquaint you with our proceedgs. The funding Bill having past the Senate with the Assumption annexed to it (on the terms mentioned in my last) we took it up last ~~friday~~ Thursday; we altered the terms of funding the domestic debt by [*increasing?*] the deferred third of the principal of the debt from 26 Dollars to 33 on every hundred, by altering the period of funding the deferred third from 10 to 7 years & by raising the Interest on Indents &

arrears of Interest from *3* to *4* per Cent: on friday came on the amendmt. of the Senate respecting the Assumption consisting of sundry Clauses; Jackson moved to disagree with the Senate in all their amendmts. relating to the Assumption; he made a long speech which you will see (with disgust) in the papers; I replied in one of equal length—we adjourned—Saturday, the debate was resumed—on taking the question, his motion was lost, ayes 29—noes 32. Sumpter voted against us, & Huger was absent, being very ill. We were [*torn*] Mr. White who voted with us having declared that altho he shod. Then vote against rejecting all the amendmts. of the Senate, yet that he should ultimately refuse to concur, unless some alterations took place—as we had to canvass the whole of the modification & there was considerable fear of our splitting when we came to adjust the proportions to be assumed from each State, I was very uneasy about the result; I therefore Monday morning prevailed on Huger, ill as he was, to attend the House & I employed all my rhetoric with Sumpter to change his vote—I stated to him the evil consequences which would flow from an apparent disunion among the members from our State on such a momentous question & one in which it was so much interested; that his constituents might sit uneasy under the measure by finding him persist in his opposition to it & that it would tend to sow the seeds of disunion in the different parts of the State—that he had acknowledged to me he thought the measure advantageous to us & as he found other States opposing it from local motives, he was justified in supporting it from similar motives—that he would not be charged with inconsistency in now voting for it, because he might alledge that he found his opposition ineffectual & that he thought it his duty to concur with the majority & that as he was now persuaded the measure would be carried, unanimity in our delegation would have a good effect on the State & would induce all parts to be pleased with it—I stated a number of other reasons & endeavoured to obviate all his objections. Whether my anxious ~~endeav~~ sollicitations ~~with him~~ had any effect or whether he thought the measure wod. be carried & that he had better concur in it & make his peace with his Country or that seeing Huger come from a sick bed to give his Vote & apprehending Some consequences from his Single negative from the State he was urged to a compliance, I will not say; but to the great astonishmt. of ~~the~~ both parties, he said Aye when he was expected to say no: we therefore, on the motion made by myself to concur with the amendmt. of the Senate, ~~we~~ carried it by a majority of *Six*. Mr. White had been gratified by the alterations made; we adhered to the proportions settled by the Senate, tho strong attempts were made by No. Cara. & Georgia to alter them—we had a majority of 3 on Saturday: Huger made 4—& Sumpter's change made 6. I am much pleased that he voted with us, tho the State are under no obligation to him for he has certainly done us all the injury possible in & out of the house: you will see ~~by~~ in Jackson's speech an assertion that the back country of So. Car. are against the assumption, because it will deprive them of State power & subjugate them ~~to Congress~~: these observations may do a great deal of mischief & would have done more had Sumpter persevered in his opposition to the last, for it would have countenanced the insinuations which I have no doubt came from Sr.—Jackson said in the house that he was informed the people's minds were much changed on the subject in So. Car. that the instructions were hurried thro without time to consider them & that such a measure would not pass at this time on a calm review of the subject. he must have had this from my worthy colleague—you may be sure I contradicted him on the spot. He said he was told the *good people* of So. Car. were against the measure—I answered I was sorry there were then so *few good* people in the State for I beleived 99 out of 100 were for it; that the [*state constitutional*] Convention of the people sat in May & might have given counter-instructions had the people disapproved it. I was the more anxious to have S.'s vote to do away these remarks & to satisfy our back country that S. had approv'd the measure on full consideration.

From the above account you may ~~well~~ have reason to suppose that the assumption is pretty secure; & yet would you beleive that it is still in Jeopardy & that a foolish difference of opinion about *3* and *4* percent maintained with shameless obstinacy by both parties is likely to mar all our schemes & set every thing a float? Some of the Senate are determined to postpone the whole business rather than agree to 3 per cent; others are resolved not to concur with our amendment for 4. the Same scandalous obstinacy prevails in our house, & the same disunion among members from the Same State; Ames & Gerry are for 4, Sedgwick for 3—Mr. Read (of the Senate from Delaware) agreed to vote for the Assumption provided the Indents should be funded at 3 per cent; Elsworth & Strong pledged themselves to stick to 3 to secure Read's vote for the Assumption—Schyler, Morris & King insist on 4 & will run all risques to carry it: the first told me just now he would himself move to postpone the whole funding Bill if the Senate would not consent to 4. what a cruel situation to be reduced to by a few *interested* individuals, who would involve the nation in ruin to gratify their inordinate avarice—Tho Mr. Izard & his connections are deeply interested in getting 4 rather than 3 pr. c., he has uniformly concurred in the latter for the sake of harmony & to secure the funding the public debt. This business comes on in the Senate this morning & I am full of anxiety about it.

The Assumption could never have been carried without the assistance of some new friends—Gilman & Livermore of New Hamp. have deserted us & Hartley of Pensylva.—In lieu of these we have gained [*Richard B.*] Lee & White of Virga. & Gale & [*Daniel*] Carrol of Maryd.—this acquisition is the result of the Patowmac scheme—it Seems there was an understanding between these gentlemen & some of the New Engd. Members that the latter would give no serious opposition to the residence bill if some of the Maryland & Virg. memrs. would vote for the assumption: New Engd. had it in her power to have defeated the Patowmac bill, by joining in the Baltimore Scheme, but the Massachtt. members of the Senate opposed it & by that means forwarded the residence bill; the consequence was that in the Senate Read & [*Charles*] Carrol who had been opposed to the assumption voted for it: thus, notwithstandg. the accession of No. Cara. & R. Island, two States bitterly opposed to the assumption, we have by dint of perseverance obtained a majority for it in both houses. It is laughable to find the same members who a few weeks ago insisted on the absolute necessity of detaching the assumption from the funding Bill & declared they never would vote for them united, now gravely voting for ~~it~~ an association because the residence bill is settled. Some danger might have been expected from the N. York membrs. but Hamilton has kept them with us.

July 25[27]th. P.M. The Senate have ordered our amendments to be printed & will I suppose take them into consideration in a day or two. The anti-assumpts. are busy in endeavouring to bring about ~~an assur~~ postponemt. to next Session; the 12 who are against the Assumption will Succeed if the 14 who are for it should divide on collateral points; one or two obstinate men in a moment of ill-humour & disappointmt. may defeat the whole business by joining the non-funders & the anti-assumpts. in a postponemt. to next Session. Schyler declares he will join them in this measure if the Senate should not consent to 4 per cent; this will divide the Senate equally; shod. Morris or King join him then the whole business will be blown up & we shall adjourn in great confusion. on the other side, Read, Elsworth, or Strong are equally obstinate. A few days will unfold this business—we shall then be in a flourishing or in a miserable Situation as the caprice of one or two individuals may direct.

The State of the votes for & against the Assumption in both houses is as follows.

Senate.				Representes.			
	For	*Against*			*For*	*agst.*	
[*N.H.*]	1.	1		N.H.	1	2	
[*Mass.*]	2.			Mass.	8.		
Con.	2			Connect.	5.		
R. Isld.		2		R.I.			
N. York	2		Vice President	N. York	3	3	
N. Jersey	2.		for it	N. Jersey	4.		Speaker
Pensya.	1	1.		Pensya.	3	4.	for it.
Delawe.	1.	1.		Delaw.	1.		

Maryd.	1	1.	Maryd.	2.	4	—one dead
Virga.		2	Virga.	2.	7.	
No. Cara.		2	No. Car.		5	
So. Cara.	2.		So. Car.	5		
Georga.		2	Georga.		3	
	14.	12		34	28	

I shall write you again in a few days.

P. S.

Your Son [*Henry*] is well—I saw him an hour ago.

The Committee on Gl. [*Nathanael*] Greene's business. sits tomorrow[1] I imagine we shall report favorably—we shall adjourn as soon as the fundg. bill passes.

ALS, Smith Papers, ScHi. Addressed to Charleston, South Carolina; franked. The letter is dated 25 July, but internal evidence indicates that it was written on 27 July.

[1] For background and documents on the petition of Catharine Greene, see *DHFFC* 7:493–542.

George Thatcher to James Sullivan

Yours of the 18th. inst. (penned, as we scripture-men say, when you were in a very singular state of mind) is now before me.

You tell me "the people thro' the eastern Counties [*Maine*], & N. Hampshire are universally dissatisfied with Congress"—I beleive you might have added, and thro all Massachusetts too, for the News-papers, which are the mouths of the people, are continually groaning with their complaints.

You say "we are divided into parties wherein the interest of the nation is but little concerned"—In this we only resemble the Christian world—they have been divided into angry parties for more than fourteen hundred years; and disputed with Gun, fire, & pamphlets about Dogmas of infinitely less consequence than the question of residence of Congress.

"No one cares where the Residence of Congress is to be"—so say all your representatives—yet it must be somewhere and tho we trouble ourselves but little about it; yet by others tis looked upon a matter of importance; and they make it a bone of hot contention, at which we grieve as much as the people of Massachusetts—but do not look upon ourselves the culpable cause of the dispute.

"But we all want a proper System of Finance"—so do your Representatives—and to obtain this, they have been, and still are labouring & toiling in the hot house of Division & contention, while you are heaping on them censure and black guard.

"But this system of finance must be on proper principles"—undoubtedly! who ever thought of a system of Finance upon any other—You dont mean by this, that they must be approved by every State County, Town & District in the Union—This would be giving them qualities which your Religion, tho of divine origin, does not possess—and ought not to be expected of any sytem or code prepared, by mere mortals, for the United States.

"And no one can wish the assumption of the State debts at the purchase of the integrity of the Country or upon principles that have long disgraced other Countries."

No one but a Boston man could have conceived such an idea! surely you did not pick this up in your eastern Tour—tis not of eastern Growth—to that country tis an exotic.

"If Justice dictates the assumption, the members ought to vote for it upon that idea"—precisely right—upon this idea, and no other, thirty two members voted for it on saturday—and thirty four, yesterday—The majority are always in the right.

"If Justice is not in favour of the assumption, he is a man of no principle" (you mean bad principle, because there are principles of Injustice as well as of Justice) "who will vote for it at any price, or upon any condition"—exactly right again—On Fryday when the Bill was before the House, and the motion was to agree to the amendment of the Senate which included the assumption of the State debts—a very, honest, upright and religious member [*Jackson*] rose, and after discanting three quarters of an hour upon Justice, honesty & integrity, declared, on his conscience, & his hand on his breast, his eyes uplifted to Heaven, that he did not see how any man in that House could consciencіously give his vote in favour of a measure so big with Iniquity—A pause ensued—I fell back in my chair and gave up the question as lost. What quoth I to myself, am I then, on the side of Iniquity, sin and injustice! and was just about whispering to my next neighbour, who appeared as much astonished as myself—when another member [*Smith (S.C.)*], equal to the former for his attachment to Justice, honesty and integrity, arose, & after some observations upon society & the social Compact, called God to witness that he wished nothing to take place but what was right and just, & for the good of the United States—and that nothing was more astonishing to him than to hear there was a single member in that House who laid the least claim to conscience, & could yet vote against the question! very well said I to my next man—the question, as it relates to conscience, is at lest doubtfull, and I shall be as safe in voting for it, as you will in voting against it—And on the whole I thought the members might as well have no conscience, as one that was at varience with every body's else—For it did not in this case appear to be a common rule by which all the members could regulate their conduct by. It really resembled much more thin woolen stocking that accommodated itself to every mans Leg.

"You will say I write like a man who is unacquainted with the world"—I say, in this Letter, you do not write like yourself; because you are accurately acquainted with the world, and have not wrote in conformity to the sentiments thereof.

"But let the practice in other Countries be what it may, I beleive this Country is not yet so destitute of virtue as not to be able to find a Congress who will act upon principles of virtue, Justice & honor."

In the course of ten or fifteen years past, I have frequently taken notice how readily people, on all occasions, lay hold of this climax of words—*virtue, justice* & *honor*—And some, whom I suspect much more, add *religion* too—Run over the whole science of politics and you will hardly meet with a word of so vague & equivocal meaning as virtue, justice and honor—They are a rule and standard to almost every man, if we pay any credit to what they say; and yet the conduct measured out thereby in different persons is more varient than their faces. In fact they are in politics what Conscience and faith are in religion—And every man is willing to measure the conduct and opinions of others by his own Rule—but not e converso.[1]

"I beleive there will be a great change at the next election"—so do I—because the Scripture saith—"Man in honor abideth not"—And experience proves, that every thing is changeable here below—and nothing more so than the opinions & sentiments of the people, in free governments, respecting their Legislators—All this is right; but I don't beleive the change will be much for the better—And to adopt your climax, I am persuaded the people of Massachusetts will not get men of more *justice, virtue* & *honor,* than their present Representatives—As to religion I shall be silent—it is founded on conscience, which, as before observed, in politics, is a very uncertain guide.

"[*William*] Lithgow, [*Daniel*] Davis & Josiah Thatcher are rivals to you"—For death political as well as death natural I am prepared—The latter is only a passage to joys celestial; and the former to joys domestic—and you as well as I can determine which are preferable—But for the present, give me the latter.

The assumption, I beleive, is now fixed—yesterday the amendment of the Senate to the bill for funding the continental debt, was agreed to in the House, by 34 against 28—with one or two small amendments—and these I am of opinion will be acceded to in the Senate.

As one of the people I have a right to declare my sentiments on the conduct of the representatives from Massachusetts—and it is this—they deserve great praise for their behaviour, & those may censure them that please,

I dont beleive the people could have elected a like number that would have more undeviatingly pursued what they really took for the general Good—or distinguished this *summum honour,*[2] with greater Judgment.

FC, Thatcher Family Papers, MHi.

[1] In return.
[2] Greatest honor.

Ebenezer Thompson to Theodore Foster

The inclosed letters have been wrote some days but No oppertunity Offering you will Receive them herewith—Our holders of Publick Securetyes of this State's have for sum days past been Clammerous About the Congress Not haveing Assumed our proportion of the State debt. they say that if the States Debts are Assumed our Senetors Aught to Exart themselves in order to get as large a proportion as possable, in case the Assumtion cannot be avoided I think it best to [*lined out*] have our full proportion—Our State in the time of the War maid as great or grater Exartions then aney in the Union and Our Advances will Appear to be larger then Aney when Ever Our State Acct. is Settled ~~and~~ I can Sea No Reason Why we should Not have our full proportion—By all Meanes Keep back the Assumtion if possable to the End of this ~~session~~ Congress which terminates in march and it will Never be dun afterwards—if the Assumtion takes place the Duties must be increased so much that their will be great fear of Clamour from the Marcantile Interest.

ALS, Foster Papers, RHi. Written from Providence, Rhode Island. Enclosures not found.

Thomas Tudor Tucker to St. George Tucker

Since I last wrote to you I have enquired of Mr. Page, who confirms me in the Opinion I before express'd, that Colo. Bland left no Will in this Place. His Information he had from Mr. Walker, & he was acquainted with the Circumstance of his having left every Thing to Mrs. [*Martha Dangerfield*] Bland. We have some time since pass'd a Law fixing the Seat of Government at Philadelphia for 10 Years, & afterwards on Potowmack River. I have no great Confidence in the Operation of that part which respects the Potowmack. The Assumption of the State Debts has pass'd in both Houses, but there remain some Differences between the two Houses respecting the funding System which will probably be reconciled in a Day or two. We expect to adjourn in the Course of a Week. It is probable that in about a Week more, I shall leave this place. I feel some Uneasiness at not being able to settle the Demands against Theodorick [*Bland Randolph*] & John [*Randolph of Roanoke*],[1] especially as our next Meeting (if any during my Service) will be in Philadelphia. ***

ALS, Tucker Coleman Papers, ViW. Addressed to Williamsburg, Virginia; franked; postmarked. The omitted text relates to family affairs.

[1] Probably debts that St. George's stepsons would have accrued while matriculating at New York's Columbia College.

Oliver Wolcott, Jr. to Oliver Wolcott, Sr.

I have recd. your favour of the 4th. instant—and am happy to hear of the health of my friends at Litchfield [*Connecticut*]. Betsy [*Elizabeth Stoughton Wolcott*] proceeded on her journy to Connecticut on Saturday and will continue with you for some time.

Yesterday the question for assuming the State Debts was carried in the House by a majority of six Votes—both houses having agreed on this question, it will probably be carried into effect.

No bill for ways and means has been settled, the house have passed a bill for extending the Impost [*Ways and Means Act HR-83*]—it is said that some considerable alterations will be made in the Senate—If they should propose what has been called an Excise a long debate will probably ensue—& if they agree to the bill of the House, they risque much upon the pacific temper of the Merchants and the vigilance of public Officers—I think that it is unfortunate, that they have so limited themselves with respect to a revenue system.

The House have disagreed to the amendments of the ~~House~~ Senate to the funding bill, by raising Indents to four ℔ Cent and engaging to fund the full remaining third of the principal of the debt after seven years, instead of ten years as was proposed by the Senate—On this question the Senate have not yet decided.

The system for funding the public debt is in my opinion too intricate—and the part which is to be funded at a future time will nourish improper speculations perpetuate the ideas of depreciation, and will be transferred to foriegners, at a low value—the Country will be charged with a heavy debt, & will receive but a small consideration.

These opinions however are not proper to come from me, considering my situation and I hope that experience will prove that they are fallacious.

The present is a very interesting period to this Country, the future state of society & the reputation of the government, will receive their direction from what shall happen in a few years.

I shall continually attend to every opportunity that offers to promote my brothers [*Frederick?*] wishes, & think that he may expect success.

Mr. [*Nicholas*] Eveligh the Comptroller is much out of health, as soon as he recovers I will come and make a visit to my friends.

ALS, Wolcott Papers, CtHi. Place to which addressed not indicated.

A Citizen of America to Mr. Greenleaf

I CAN bestow a smile of contempt on the little intrigues of a *book worm* [*Madison*]: I can bestow a *sigh* on the avarice of a *mercantile Senator* [*Morris*], who has distracted and convulsed the government of the union for his own *personal accommodation.* The duplicity and the avarice of these men, as *individuals*, may excite contempt—Charity may exercise a kind of *forgiveness*, which would hurt their feelings (if they have any) as the chiefs of a party, which have fabricated a law, which violates the constitution, and which contains an *insidious snare* for the virtue of the executive, by a *Grecian gift*;[1] they deserve my indignation—the peoples alarm, and a *parliamentary impeachment.*

The friends and the lovers of our good President, viewed the manœuvres of this faction with all the anxious solicitude of friendship and patriotism. If a faction can violate the constitution; this sacred charter of government, which they are sworn to support, may be considered as blank paper. The convention marked with precision the respective limits of the legislative and executive powers, and *concessions* and *encroachments* should be viewed with alarm. The government of this country will lose in future all steadiness, and will fluctuate with the versatile temper and interest of party.

The *residence bill* was a political trap, set for the integrity and popularity of the executive. This party was concealed in the ambuscade of hypocrisy, and waited with *malignant patience* the event of their poisonous *stratagems.* These *insidious* characters have succeeded, *and their crime resembles the guilt of the treacherous betrayer in the gospel* [*Judas*]. They have wounded the most responsible and popular part of the government, and may diffuse an *inauspicious discord* at the next election. *Division* will open a door to new competitions, and ambition is always a *self-flatterer.*

The tried virtue of the executive, is the sheet-anchor of the union—his deserved and virtuous popularity gives strength to a government founded on *hope* and *opinion.*

The hopes of the people may vanish, and the influence of opinion may be lost—if the virtue of this illustrious character is exposed to the wiles and intrigues of faction.

The friends to the union will despair, and will feel a prophetic gloom—Envy will feel a malignant pleasure, and the enemies of the union will rejoice in the prospect of its dissolution.

There is reason to suspect (as Virginia was active in this romantic business of a permanent residence on the wild and savage borders of the Potowmack) that she has other views. The enemies of the gospel, when it was first instituted, endeavored to injure it by tempting our *Saviour* into sin; the enemies to the new government mean to wound it, by leading our political saviour into error, and to destroy his popularity.

NYJ, 27 July, edited by Thomas Greenleaf.

[1] The Trojan horse; i.e., trickery.

John Steele to William B. Grove

THE assumption of the state debts passed yesterday—The yeas and nays on the question are inclosed—This event proves what can be effected by perseverance. In a good cause it is usually styled a virtue, but in this instance it deserves the appellation of obstinacy. The passage of the bill was effected by a change in the sentiments of General Sumpter, Mr. White, Mr. Carrol, Mr. Lee, and Mr. Gale. I have sent Dr. [*John*] Sibley by this conveyance the same information, and all the papers from the time you left this place until the present day, to which I refer you for the news.

[Fayetteville] *North Carolina Chronicle*, 27 December 1790. Addressed to Fayetteville; received ca. 16 August, according to Grove's affidavit printed with it.

Other Documents

Joseph Barrell to John Langdon. ALS, Langdon Papers, NhPoA. Written from Boston; "Answered."

Office seeking: their nephew Nathaniel Barrell, Jr., for consul at Martinus (Dutch West Indies); asks to mention him to "His Majesty the President"; if the Senate have altered the rate of Interest on Indents & assumed the State Debts, "I think they will reflect upon their conduct with more satisfaction than should they rise without."

John Elliot to John Woodworth. ALS, Betts Collection, CtY. Written from Killingworth, Connecticut; addressed to Albany, New York; received in August.

The people fret over assumption of the state's war debts, for which everyone looks impatiently to "the grand federal Head"; "The Clamour against Doctr. Johnson is very loud and he has almost wholly lost his Influence."

Royal Flint to Enos Hitchcock. ALS, Miscellaneous Collection, RHi. Place to which addresed not indicated.

The House agreed to assumption by a majority of six; the two houses may disagree about the House amendments to the Funding Bill, but "there is little probability they will let a small difference of opinion defeat the funding business"; "the most intelligent people here view the matter out of danger."

Thomas Hartley to Tench Coxe. AN, Coxe Papers, PHi.

Thirty day promissory note for $400 in specie.

John Langdon to Joshua Brackett. ALS, Sturgis Family Papers, MH. Addressed to Portsmouth, New Hampshire; franked; postmarked.

"The [*Creek*] Indian Chiefs have Just gone by."

William Short to Gouverneur Morris. ALS, G. Morris Papers, NNC. Written from Chateau de la Roche-Guyon, in Val-d'Oise, France; place to which addressed not indicated.

Imagines that Madison is the person most mentioned to succeed Jefferson as U.S. minister to France.

Thomas Upshaw to Thomas Jefferson. ALS, Washington Papers, DLC. Written from Essex County, Virginia. The writer was probably Thomas Upshaw (d. 1809), of St. Anne's Parish, Essex County, Virginia, who rose from ensign to captain in the Continental Army's Virginia line, 1777–78, before retiring in 1780 (Lenora H. Sweeny, "Upshaw Family of Essex," *WMQ*, 2nd series, vol. 18, 1[Jan. 1938]:79).

Office seeking: some "moderate post"; has written some time before to Page, soliciting an introduction to the President.

John Jeffries, Diary. Jeffries Family Papers, MHi.

Called on Gerry and left his card.

WEDNESDAY, 28 JULY 1790

John Carnes to George Thatcher

Not receiving is my Apology for not Writing, and how to account for it I dont know.

I write now at the desire of the Revd. Mr. Mansfield, requesting the favour that You will use your influence, in favour of his Petition, that he has sent on to Congress, for the recovery of Wages, while a Chaplin in the Army.[1] Pray Sir request the Assistance of all our Massachusetts Members. We still hope for the Assumption, & in a manner that will be agreeable to all good Men.

Our Papers furnish You with public News, so that it will be needless to mention any public matter. And as to private matters I have nothing very special.

We hope for your speedy return, but not till something is done to ease the Minds of the People, for at present there is a universal dissatisfaction.

P. S. I sent to Mr. Goodhue, Election Sermons for our Members, which hope you received.

ALS, Chamberlain Collection, MB. Written from Lynn, Massachusetts; franked; postmarked 29 July.

---

[1] Isaac Mansfield's petition was not presented to the House (by Gilman) until 16 December 1790. Referred to Secretary at War Knox the next day, it was never acted upon; see also *DHFFC* 7:577.

Robert Morris to Benjamin F. Bache

It will gratify me as much as it will You if I can be instrumental in promoting Your Views in regard to a share of the Public Printing business, but how to accomplish it is the difficulty for early as you think your application others have been before you. Mr. Jefferson has given to Mr. [*Andrew*] Brown the Printing of the Laws, Mr. Beckley Clerk of the House of Representatives employs Mr. [*John*] Fenno & so does Mr. Otis Secy. of the Senate, those Gentn. are authorized by the Two Houses to get the printing done which Consequently gives them the Choice of the Printer, Mr. Fenno Set up his press with the avowed intention of being always at the Seat of Government Consequently He will Remove to Philadelphia with Congress and claim the Continuance of that employ which he has already obtained I think however it may not be improper for you to make the Offer of your Services to the three Gentn. above Named as you are not to be supposed to have any knowledge of their engagements & the Removal of Congress gives every one in Philada. a justifiable pretension on which to ground Such an application. Some of your Friends here are rather Sorry for your intention of Printing a News Paper; there are already too Many of them Published in Philadelphia and in these days of Scurrility it is difficult for a press of such Reputation as you would choose yours to be, to maintain the Character of Freedom & impartiallity Connected with Purity, They Seem to entertain the opinion that you might be more Honorably & more lucratively employed by the Printing of Books, but of this you are the best judge, and I have only mentioned the Substance of a Conversation that arose upon my producing the prospectus of your intended News Paper.

ALS, Bache-Castle Collection, PPAmP. Addressed to Philadelphia. For background on the FFC's employment of public printers, see *DHFFC* 8:736–44.

Robert Morris to Walter Stewart

***

I expect Congress will adjourn next Week when we will add our mite of exertion into the Scale of such of our Fellow Citizens as wish Pensylvania to make in every way that Respectable & Important Figure in the Federal Eye, which from every Consideration She is entitled to. The Funding Bill comes again in Review of the Senate this day, I opposed it in all its parts when last before us because it was far short of that Justice which I think due to the Public Creditors; but I am now doing all in my power to get it through the Senate as amended in the House, because it is the best that can be obtained this Session and was it to be postponed to another, as many wish, perhaps Nothing might be done in it, whereas if the Funding is once begun and carried into execution, future applications of the Public Creditors may obtain from the Government that part of their dues which is now (under the plea of Necessity) witheld.

ALS, Barton Collection, MB. Addressed to Philadelphia. The conclusion of the letter was written on 29 July and is excerpted under that date, below.

Letter from Philadelphia

The Corporation of this city have it in contemplation to erect proper buildings for the accommodation of the President of the United States, of the Senate, and House of Representatives, on a plan equally superb and elegant with any that has hitherto been accomplished in America. As it would be inconvenient to crowd this august body into a circle of *Traders* and

Mechanics, it is proposed to erect the proper buildings above the upper end of Market-street, where they might hold their deliberations without being interrupted by the noise ever attending so busy a city as this. By placing these buildings in the situation above mentioned, not only great additions will be made to our city, but the idea of moving the seat of government to the Westward (alias Connogochegue) will be rendered truly ridiculous.

NYDA, 3 August. This is a brief summary of parts of A Citizen that appeared in *FG*, 26 July; the full text is printed with the documents related to Accommodations for Congress at Philadelphia in Correspondence: Third Session. The summary was reprinted at Exeter, New Hampshire; Boston and Worcester, Massachusetts; Providence, Rhode Island; Hartford, Litchfield, Middletown, and New Haven, Connecticut; New York City (*NYMP*, 3 August) and Poughkeepsie, New York; Philadelphia; Alexandria, Virginia; and Charleston, South Carolina.

Letter from a Member of Congress to Alexandria, Virginia

The assumption of the State debts had so many friends, that it appeared impracticable to go on with the government without it in some shape or other—I was therefore among those who agreed to it under certain modifications, which have either removed, or greatly lessened, my original objections—the State of Virginia in particular will not be injured; the sum assumed for her, 3,500,000 dollars, is more than her proportion of the whole sum 21,000,000—And if her creditors should not subscribe to the continental loan, the interest will be paid into her treasury—A bill has passed which I hope will prove effectual for the settlement of accounts soon after, or perhaps before, the assumption shall begin to operate—if inequalities appear in the sums assumed, it may then be remedied.

[Alexandria] *Virginia Gazette*, 5 August; reprinted at New York City (*NYDA*, 13 August); Baltimore; Edenton, North Carolina; and Charleston, South Carolina. The editors assume that R. B. Lee wrote this letter, probably to his brother Charles.

Other Documents

Samuel Clarkson to John Langdon. ALS, Langdon Papers, NhPoA. Written from Philadelphia; "Answered."

Has had difficulty procuring for Langdon "such lodging's as you told me you should want"; his enquiries have been impeded by Langdon's uncertainty as to whether he would attend Congress at Philadelphia; "if you can fix any thing certain" Clarkson will do "every thing I can for your agreeable fixture in this place."

Henry Latimer to George Read. No copy known; mentioned in Latimer to Richard Bassett, 29 July.

Seeking support for an appointment as commissioner of loans for Delaware.

William Nichols to George Washington. ALS, Washington Papers, DLC. Written from Philadelphia. For the full text, see *PGW* 6:132–33.

Office seeking: commissioner of loans for Pennsylvania; this letter will be delivered by Morris, whose "good nature" he relies upon as a reference.

John Jeffries, Diary. Jeffries Family Papers, MHi.

Called on Sedgwick and Ames, and there met Partridge, Benson, Dalton, and William Duer; took lodgings at Isaac Pollock's on "Gt. Dock St." with Sherman, Ellsworth, Baldwin, and Otis; attended Federal Hall where he was "politely noticed" by Adams.

THURSDAY, 29 JULY 1790

Thomas Fitzsimons to Benjamin Rush

I Approve extreamly of your Idea for extending the benefits of the College and will give every assistance in my power for Carrying it into effect—one thing more I wish you to Consider Whether it would not be practicable to Unite the University ~~to~~ with it[1]—Which would render One respectable & put an End to a division which Operates Injury to the city as well as the Cause of Science—in the present situation of Pensylva. there is a Necessity for Combineing the Whole Interest of the City to Counteract that of the Western part of the State—Which allready preponderates—if that is not done, or a Much more Weighty Representation is not Given to it in the state Legislature—great injury will result for some Years past the City interest has been preserved by the representation. Mr. McClays friendship will be Very Usefull—as his interest in the Country is said to be Considerable—I was not informed as to his opinion about Morris—but I expected from the oppys. he had of seeing his public Conduct that he would be in his favor—I Never heared of any design to oppose this Gent[*leman's*]. Election—nor of any disapprobation of his Conduct and the Report you allude to Must have been Raised to prejudice him—Indeed there is and has been Constantly A perfect harmony in the delegation—and I am persuaded their Efforts will be directed to one point, from the pains taken with [*Richard*] Butler & some other of the western people I have great hopes of our Succeeding in that part of the State—they Really Appeared Warm in the Cause, from Motives the

Most likely to influence them—a Strong Sense of the Advantage that would result to their Country—our business here is drawing to a close the funding bill is returned by the Senate to us without Agreeing to our Amendments—and I suppose we must Agree with them if so there is but one Thin bill of Conseqe. [*Ways and Means Act HR-83?*] to pass and that they have under Consideration I long extreamly to See my home & my friends [*torn*].

ALS, privately owned in 2008. Addressed to Philadelphia; franked; postmarked.

[1] The institution that became the Academy and College of Philadelphia was founded in 1749 under a constitution written by Benjamin Franklin, took in its first students in 1751, and graduated its first class in 1758. In 1779 the legislature chartered the separate University of the State of Pennsylvania, and in 1791 it issued a new charter uniting the two institutions as the University of Pennsylvania.

Robert Morris to Walter Stewart

This was too late for the Post office yesterday Morning & I have the Mortification to tell you that we could only Carry a small part of the Amendments made by the Representatives to the Funding Bill, it is gone back to them, but if they Stand fast & adhere to their Amendments I think we shall yet carry them

Mr. Bloodworth has laid a motion on the Table to Suspend the Removal of Congress from hence for Two Years—but—

ALS, Barton Collection, MB. Addressed to Philadelphia. This is a postscript to a letter begun on 28 July and printed under that date, above.

Samuel Phillips, Jr. to Benjamin Goodhue

I congratulate on the more favorable appearance which, according to the last accounts, the business of assumption put on; you have so far succeeded, that I think you have great encouragement still to persevere, tho' in this, as well as every case, prudence is requisite; by striving to reach beyond a certain point, we sometimes loose what we might have obtained—this point you will not exceed, and I am equally confident you will not suffer your impatience to close a tedious session, induce you to give up any thing important, which ~~upon~~ may be rationally presumed to be attainable: in a very short time, at the close of a session, more may be attained by well directed exertions, if circumstances favor in other respects as usual, than by long & tedious arguments at any other period; Decisions are then, generally prompt & ready, we ought however to be cautious of presuming too far: The *sedate & vigilant*, at *those periods, have greatly the advantage of the impetuous & impatient*:

May you have the full possession of every faculty, and, that which we need on every occasion, especially on the most important, the direction and blessing of *that Being who is wonderful in Counsel*: and may we ever remember, that without his benediction, our famed Republics will soon come to a period, and a period as disgraceful, as it's commencement was glorious.

I am particularly obliged for your kind Favor of the 17th. Instt. & others preceeding—altho' I am unfortunate in both the hands [*for guns*] which Mr. [*Samuel*] Hodgdon procured for me, I feel my obligation for the attempt to serve me; if another should come forward from Philada., I wish you to induce him to take up with as small a sum as you can for his expences, considering the risque of loosing the whole.

Hoping I shall have the pleasure of congratulating you, ere long, on the attainment of the object for which you have so faithfully contended, upon the best terms practicable.

[*P. S.*] Being unacquainted with Mr. Hodgdon's direction, will ask the favor of you to direct & forward the enclosed to him.

ALS, Letters to Goodhue, NNS. Written from Andover, Massachusetts.

George Thatcher to Nathaniel Wells

This is to inform you that the Bill for funding the domestic Debt of the United States, and assuming 21,500,000. Dolls. of the State Debts has passed the two houses, and I beleive is out of all danger.

The time consumed in the passage of this Bill is evidence of the many, & next to insurmountable difficulties its advocates have had to contend with.

I am not insensible, however, that this length of time is, by many construed into a different intention in the members, and made use of for very different purposes—But the reason of this construction is to be found in the misinformation, and mistaken ideas of those people themselves.

I need not observe to you, that the expectations people had formed of the benefits of the new Government were extravagant, but also fixed upon a time too short for them to take place, even if they were within the Limits of probability—That great good will result from the Constitution I have no doubt—but that a greater would not flow from a different administration of it I will not say—How far the present Congress have acted with wisdom and prudence, time & experience will determine—And how far different measures might have been productive of greater good to the United States, within any given period, must be left as a subject of every ones conjecture and reasoning—We Hope to rise soon.

FC, Thatcher Family Papers, MHi.

John Walker to James Brown

The Attorney General is now arrived, for whom alone Colo. Hamilton waited to settle your disagreable affair with Colo. [*William*] Heth. I spoke to them both yesterday on the Subject, & have no doubt but the ~~affair~~ Prosecution will be immediatly dismissed.[1] The Attorney makes no scruple of pronouncing your Innocency, & will I expect, speak to Hamilton on the subject to day: Should he neglect it, I shall jogg his Memory. My Family is in pretty good health, & Congress will probably rise in the course of next week. The Assumption is carried, tho' much against my Inclination.

ALS, Gratz Collection, PHi. Addressed to "Merchant," Richmond, Virginia; franked; postmarked.

[1] The reference is unclear. However, on 15 September, Hamilton wrote Heth a letter (unlocated), to which Heth replied on 10 November, exonerating a Mr. Brown from charges of deliberately falsifying a sworn oath about the foreign nationality of a shipmaster (*PAH* 7:146–47). A James Brown (1762–1841) emigrated from Scotland and in 1785 settled in Richmond as representative of a London mercantile firm (*John Marshall* 2:86n).

Hugh Williamson to John Gray Blount

The funding Bill passed this day—21 millions of the State Debts are to be assumed the Interest being also funded at an Interest of 3 ℔ Ct. By the reduction on this Head a saving is made equal to a Capital of 9 Millions nearly. All that we have gain'd by our Opposition is the partial instead of general Assumption A previous law securing the settlement of the Accots. and repayment to the Creditor States and the reduction of Interest.

State Securities are now here @ 8/ for the Principal and 6/6 for the Interest. Continentals are at 11/9. Cannot you use a little Industry and buy up a few State Securities not counterfeits. If you could change Paper into Specie it would be a good Business. If you could buy at 60 Days Credit and send me the Certificates I could sell them here immediately and give you Orders on some of the Collectors immediately in Payment, those Orders are to be bot. at the Treasury. If you can do any thing in that Way I will take half the Risque in the Speculation. I should think that Mr. [*Richard*] Blackledge who rides about very much might be able to buy up a good many. I believe I can sell 86ers[1] to a Man who knows that they are interdicted by the State. It is believed that the State will pay them as they were issued by proper Officers. Thus some speculators reason.

ALS, John Gray Blount Papers, Nc-Ar. Place to which addressed not indicated.

[1] See Williamson to Governor Alexander Martin, 6 March, volume 18, for information on these North Carolina certificates.

Paine Wingate to William Gardner

The Bill for funding the National debt has this day passed both houses of Congress & I conclude the President will approve. By this bill twenty one million & a half of dollars of the state debts are assumed according to certain quotas specified. Which quotas I conclude you have seen. The quota of N. Hampshire is 300,000 dollars—It is not my design in this letter to give you any opinion upon the justice or policy of this plan, which has not my concurrence; but only to inform you what has taken place. By this bill, the *principal* of the continental domestic debt, is, to those who subscribe within a year, two thirds of it to bear an interest of 6 pr. Cent. computed Jan. 1st. 1791. and the other third to be on the like interest after ten years. And the Interest of the continental debt, including Indents is to bear an interest of three pr. Cent. after Jan. 1. next. The above amount of State debts including Principal & interest as of equal~~ly to the~~ value computed to the end of the year 1791, is to bear an interest one third at the same rate as Interest of continental debt & the other two thirds at the same rates as the Principal of continental ~~securities~~ debt. The old emission money to be funded as principal at 200 for one. The Interest to be paid, in the respective states, quarter yearly and on the assumed debt not until 1792. This is the substance of the plan as near as I can give it you in a few words & in a great hurry. As the certificates I suppose are coming in dayly by taxes in New Hampshire I have thought whether it would not be expedient to put a stop to it for the present, if it could be done with propriety. The assumed debt of N.H. is compared with other states but small; & perhaps as things at present are managed, it will not be any advantage to the state to lessen the debt by paying in the taxes, unless our state debt including the Interest to the end of 1791, exceeds 300,000 dollars which I suppose it does not in proper state securities. No securities are to be received which are issued since last Jany. which should prevent further issuing either interest or principal. I have given you this early information as it may perhaps affect the welfare of the state. I shall be very much obliged to you if you would as soon as may be communicate this intelligence to the President of the State [*Josiah Bartlett*] as I cannot any other way so conveniently convey the intelligence to him. I desire my most respectful compliments to the President & hope very shortly to have the honor & pleasure of waiting upon him personally.

N. B. The principal & Interest of continental debt in the treasury may be funded for the benefit of the States.

ALS, Josiah Bartlett Papers, Rauner Special Collections Library, Dartmouth College, Hanover, New Hampshire. Place to which addressed not indicated. This letter was sent by Gardner to Governor Josiah Bartlett, 9 August, calendared below.

Henry Wynkoop to Reading Beatty

The funding Bill received the Sanction of both Houses this day between 3 & 4 oClock majority generally six, the Creditors will have two thirds of their principal funded at 6 ℔ Ct. the remaining third at the like Interest after the expiration of ten Years, & the Indents & back Interest up to the last day of december next at three ℔ Ct., this is doing less for them than what was agreable to the Wishes & Inclination of a Majority of the Representatives, but they were at length reduced to the Alternative of agreeing to this or loosing the Bill, the Representatives of Pensylvania to a Man prefer'd the former; The Ways & Means are yet with the Senate but hoping that will meet with little Difficulty conclude there is a fair Prospect of an adjournment being effected in the Course of next week, shall therefore order my light Wagon to meet me at Morton's on the evening of Saturday week, when I hope if not before to take a night Lodging with You.

Your Crop of Wheat is bad indeed, respecting the Cow, You may have her drove to Vreden's Berg & take one in return You & Mama [*Sarah Wynkoop*] shall agree upon, provided the one You send do not exceed nine Years old.

The State Debts are included in the funding [*lined out*] at 2 ℔ Ct. the Interest will not commence until the 1st. Jan. 1792, whereas that of the domestic Debt takes place Jan. 1791. so that the Interest thereon, which is to be paid quarterly will be discharged for the first time in the April following.

[*P. S.*] The Proposition laid on the table on tuesday last for the appointment of a Committee to bring in a Bill for repealing the fifth Section of the residence Bill, relating to the temporary Residence in Philadelphia, was this day withdrawn by the Mover, wether this ill natured thing will again make its appearance is uncertain, but should it, I do not conceive the least possibillity of its succeeding.[1]

ALS, Wynkoop Papers, PDoBHi.

[1] For House discussion of Bloodworth's motion, see *DHFFC* 13:1725, 1728–31, 1738–40.

N. E. [*Nicholas Eveleigh?*], Comptroller of the Kitchen to B. L.

YOUR scurrilous assassinating nonsensical attack upon Members of Congress who met at Mr. C*****'s [*Carroll*] lodgings, for the purpose of fair barter and exchange, shews you to be an enemy to all good brokerage government, and this public insult, which I hereby throw in your face, proves me to be a stout, bold, Beef eating Pimp in office, who am allowed TWO THOUSAND DOLLARS *per annum*, for what I do not do.

NYMP, 29 July. For B. L., see 26 July, above.

From New York

With pleasure I inform you, that the FUNDING-BILL, this day, hath passed both branches—the House receding from their amendments, 33 to 29. This Act, which embraces the *Assumption*, fixes the interest of the *Principal* of the *Domestick Debt* of the U.S. per cent. 66 and 2/3, at *six per cent per annum*—and 33 and 1/3 at the end of 10 years. at *six per cent.* The *Interest* of the debt to 1790, and *Indents*, at *three per cent.* The STATE DEBTS, *two thirds* of *two thirds*, at *six per cent.* and *one other third* of the *two thirds* at the end of 10 years also at *six per cent.* The remaining *one third* at *three per cent.*

The Bill for the temporary regulation of the *Post-Office* [*HR*-92], and

The Bill for compensating *Thomas Barclay*, both passed the House this day.

The Ship *Jay*, Capt. [*Thomas*] *Randal*, has arrived at the Hook, from Canton.

[Boston] *Columbian Centinel*, 4 August; reprinted at Portland, Maine; Exeter and Portsmouth, New Hampshire.

Letter from New York

This day the House completed the funding bill by agreeing to the amendments of the Senate—the assumption of twenty one million five hundred thousand dollars of state debt being included—four million for Massachusetts.

Paper is to be received in the loan at the following rate, viz. two thirds of the principal of the various kinds of continental debts at an interest of six per cent.—the other third in ten years at the same rate—the interest and indents at three per cent—old continental, considered as principal, at 100 for one—state securities, the principal and interest added, one third of which to bear interest at three per cent—one third of the remaining two thirds on interest after ten years—the remaining two thirds on interest at six per cent. The first quarter's interest on continental paper, to be paid the last of March next—on state paper, the March following. And where the amount of subscriptions in state paper may exceed the sum to be assumed in any state, the subscribers are to receive a proportion only.

[Worcester] *Massachusetts Spy*, 5 August; reprinted at Portland, Maine; Keene and Portsmouth, New Hampshire; Boston; and Providence, Rhode Island.

Letter from a Member of Congress to Alexandria, Virginia

We have this day completed the funding system; the out-lines of which are, the principal, which forms two-thirds of the continental debt, is funded, two thirds at an immediate interest of 6 per cent, and the other third at the same rate of interest at the expiration of ten years; the indents and interest due on the principal, which forms one third of the continental debt, are funded at the rate of an interest of 3 per cent. The assumed debt is funded, two thirds on the terms of the principal of the continental debt—and the other third on the terms of the indents.

This system seems to be satisfactory to the holders of the debt here: And has already produced a stagnation in the exchange of this kind of property. The principal of the continental debt is now at 12s. in the pound—State paper upwards of 8s.—and indents upwards of 7s.—and there is no doubt that the price will increase, and, in a short time, become stable.

There has been much difficulty in reconciling the various opinions on this subject—and some danger that nothing would have been done. The session will certainly close next week.

[Alexandria] *Virginia Gazette*, 12 August; reprinted at Baltimore. The editors assume R. B. Lee wrote this letter, probably to his brother Charles.

Other Documents

Jeremiah Allen to John Adams. ALS, Adams Family Manuscript Trust, MHi. Written from Boston.

Office seeking: consul for Russia, Sweden, and Denmark; recalls conversation at Jay's during which Adams observed "that every Man, who Wishd. an office, ought to apply"; encloses a list of Russian exports for 1786.

Daniel Carroll to Delegates and Inhabitants of Washington County, Maryland. No copy known; mentioned in D. Carroll to Washington County, 5 August, [Elizabethtown, Maryland] *Washington Spy*, 26 August. The 29 July letter was probably printed in a non extant issue of this newspaper.

George Rogers Clark to John Brown. [Kentucky] *Frankfort Commonwealth*, 25 July 1838, Draper Collection, WHi. For Clark's seventy-five page "pamphlet," see *PGM* 2:555–88.

Regarding the history of the Revolutionary War in the Northwest Territory that Brown (and Madison) wished Clark to write, progress is slow owing to the loss of papers; in the winter of 1779, Clark sent George Mason "a pamphlet" recounting events to that point, but Clark has not heard from Mason in response to a request for its return; asks Brown to "try and recover it for me."

Elbridge Gerry to Tench Coxe. AN, Coxe Papers, PHi.
Accepts Coxe's invitation for 3 August.

Henry Latimer to Richard Bassett. ALS, Washington Papers, DLC. Written from Newport, Delaware.
Office seeking: asks Bassett to mention him to the President for the office of commissioner of loans for Delaware; hears that James Tilton will probably be an applicant; asks if Bassett advises writing a letter of application to Washington; wrote to Read with the same request the day before, and "must confide in such representation as Mr. Read & You will make in my behalf."

George Hazard Peckham to George Washington. ALS, Miscellaneous Letters, Miscellaneous Correspondence, State Department Records, Record Group 59, DNA. Written from South Livingston, Washington County, Rhode Island.
Asks for loan of five hundred silver dollars for ten years without interest, to start a business; mentions T. Foster and Stanton as references.

William Shepard to George Washington. ALS, Washington Papers, DLC. For a partial text, see *PGW* 4:370.
Office seeking: loan office commissioner for North Carolina; is in New York City; mentions Johnston, Hawkins, Williamson, P. Muhlenberg, and Hiester as references.

Roger Sherman to Simeon Baldwin. ALS, Sherman Collection, CtY. Document torn.
Congress completed the Funding Act this day; the House consented to the Senate amendments "rather than lose the Bill"; the bill (Ways and Means Act HR-83) providing funds for it "passed the house and is now before the Senate."

Oliver Wolcott, Jr. to Elizabeth Stoddard Wolcott. *Wolcott* 1:50.
Langdon and their neighbors make jokes about Wolcott's bachelor existence; asks her to tell friends who inquire about politics that "Congress begin to proceed with success"; "they have assumed the state debts, and done a variety of good things to pacify the people who censure them."

John Jeffries, Diary. Jeffries Family Papers, MHi.
Met the Adamses over breakfast at Col. William Smith's; was visited by Ames and Sedgwick.

Letter from New York. *FG*, 29 July.
"Yesterday Mr. Bloodworth laid his motion for repealing the 5th section of the residence bill on the table, and this day, I suppose, it will be decided on. Mr. Lawrence seconded the motion."

FRIDAY, 30 JULY 1790

Pierce Butler to George Washington

I had the honor, last session, of transmitting to You a letter from Mr. [*John, Sr.*] Parker of So. Carolina—Permit me to bring Him once more before You—Mr. Parker is a Native of that Country; and Connected with some of the first Families in the state—When the War broke out He was possess'd of a Considerable Estate; By the Devastation of the British Army He is, with a large Family, reduced to slender Circumstances—He is a just Man; and if You shall think proper to notice Him, I have no doubt but He will discharge the trust with fidelity and honor—I am not Connected with Mr. Parker either by Blood or Marriage; Neither am I intimate with Him; yet I shall, as a Citizen of Carolina, feel myself much oblig'd by any attention that You may be pleased to shew to Him.

ALS, Washington Papers, DLC. A letterbook copy is dated 29 July (Butler Papers, ScU).

William Maclay to Benjamin Rush

Yesterday restored me to my family and I had the satisfaction to find Mrs. [*Mary Harris*] Maclay nearly recovered from her late perilous situation. could I entertain the most distant suspicion, That my presence in New York, had been necessary for a moment longer. I would now reject the information which hastened my departure, But I certainly left our affairs in perfect Safety.

As far as I have been able to observe I find, a full confidence and perfect acquiescence in the Measures of Government. The laus [*praises*] of the Country, are in a great Measure, confined to their farms. but what is remarkable, the removal of Congress to Philada. diffuses a Joy, which is not felt or at least not expressed, in the City.

A moderate Share of Prudence, will secure Us [*a*] degree of political happiness, unknown heretofo[*re*] in the annals of Pennsylvania, or perhaps in a[*ny*] other Country. I trust we shall not be wanting in that necessary Article.

I hope to see You als[*o*] in Town before the Convention rises. altho m[*y*] long absence, gives my family the Justest clai[*m*] on my company, during the Recess of Congress.

ALS, Rush Papers, DLC. Written from Sunbury, Pennsylvania; addressed to Philadelphia; carried by Col. Wilson.

William Smith (S.C.) to Edward Rutledge

After much toil & anxiety, I can at length, my dear friend, congratulate you & our whole State on the adoption of the assumption, which yesterday past both houses & is now part of the funding Bill. In my letter of the other day, sent by the way of Philada. I communicated to you the disagreement likely to take place between the two houses & which the enemies of the Assumption would avail themselves of to defeat the Bill; our house had raised the Interest on Indents of Interest & a third of the State debts from 3 to 4 per Cent & had made the deferred third of the debt payable in 7 years instead of 10: the Senate refused to concur in both these amendments & it was greatly apprehended by us that if our house insisted, the Senate would insist on their part & so the Bill be either lost or postpon'd to the next Session: some of our friends in both houses, from a rapacious disposition to get a little more on their Certificates were imprudent enough in their fits of anger to declare they would rather lose the Bill than yield; our enemies fomented these divisions & we have been for two days past in great trepidation: we however laboured to bring about an accomodation; when we found the Senate had by a majority of 16 to 8 rejected both our amendmts. our only prospect of carrying the Bill through was to recede; some of the Senate who were for 4 per Cent assured us that if we insisted their house would give up the point, while those who were for 3 per Cent warned us against the danger of letting the Bill get back to the Senate, as in Such case the consequences might be fatal: these embarassmts. were heightened by an alarm excited about a suspension of the residence bill, a measure artfully introduced by No. Cara. & Georgia to draw off the Virginia, Maryland, & Pensylva. members who had given their support to the Assumption in consequence of the residence bill having past. Yesterday the Senate sent us down the funding & assumption Bill with a message that they disagreed to our Amendts.: before we took it up, Vining moved to take up the motion respecting the Suspension of the residence Bill, in order to try Massachusts. & So. Cara. & to induce us to vote against it ~~in order~~ least we shod. disgust our new friends: our situation was an aukward one & we had no other recourse but in prevailing on Bloodworth to withdraw his motion for the Suspension for a day or two: we then took up the fundg. bill—it depended on us to see the assumption pass into a law in the course of a few minutes by receding from our amendmts. or by a pertinacious adherence risk the loss of the Bill & set every thing a float & involve the whole govt. in confusion & faction: notwithstg. the step to be taken appeared so obvious, some of our friends still persisted—our enemies rejoiced—it was an abominable folly on the part of the former—the latter had the prospect of a complete triumph: men, who ~~are~~ were in principle against funding at all & would ~~rejoice~~ be glad to spunge[1] out the whole debt, impudently affected to be the friends of the Creditors & the guardians of public faith; even Sumpter with the hope of damning the whole business, ~~insisted~~ voted for insisting, tho I urged every argument to prevail on him to recede: when I stated to him the danger of a postponemt. to the next Session he asked me what injury would result from such a measure? I got the rest of my colleagues to concur with me: I sent for Huger & I told every body the danger of insisting: after much debate we carried the question on both amendmts. & thus the Bill past, for which God be praised. Tho the business is not quite as well arranged as I could wish, yet on the whole I greatly rejoice—did you know the difficulties we have encountered, arising from jarring state-interests; private interest of holders of continental & State paper, speculators, men against any funding, you would be delighted at the reflection that we have been able to bring the funding & assumption to any thing like a point. The State debts are placed on this footing—every holder is to subscribe to the U.S. ~~as much~~ such proportion of his certificate as the debt assumed by the U.S. bears to the whole State debt; for instance—South Cara.—her debt—say 5,000,000 Doll. assumed—4,000,000 which is $^{4}/_{5}$ths—therefore if I go to the Treasury of the U.S. with a certificate of 500 Dollars; I get 400 funded & I must apply to So. Car. for the remainder: (that is in case no further assumption takes place, but we have always considered the present modification as a *good entering wedge* & when we find things will bear it, we shall push on for the whole) Suppose then my 400 Dollars funded by the U.S. they will be funded in the following manner, viz. $^{2}/_{3}$ds of 400 Dollars at 6 per Cent (on the Secretary's plan, which is $^{2}/_{3}$ds immedy. & the other third at the Expiration of 10 years) & the other third of 400 Dollars at 3 per Cent: as the Senate would not agree to fund the Indents of Interest of the continental debt at more than 3 per cent & as those Indents are about one third of the continl. debt, it was necessary (for the sake of uniformity) to have one third of the State debts funded also at 3 per Cent.

The whole operation will therefore be thus:

An Indent of So. Cara.—value 500 Dollars.
as 4,000,000 assumed is 4/5ths. of 5,000,000 State debt—then the U.S. fund—400 Doll.
2/3ds. of said 400: (viz. 266) is to be funded in this manner.

2/3ds. of said 266 immediately at 6 per Cent—viz. 178 D.	}	
1/3d of said 266 at the end of 10 years— viz. 88	}	266.
1/3 d. of said 400 (viz. 134) at 3 per Cent		134
		400

The *Continental* Debt is to be funded as follows:
2/3d. of the *principal* of the Debt immediately at 6 pr. Ct.
1/3d of do. at the end of 10 years—at do.
The *Interest* & *Indents* of Interest at 3 per Cent.
The State debts to be Subscribed indiscriminately, in principal & interest—

Give all my friends joy for me—my best respects to Mrs. R. [*Henrietta Middleton Rutledge*].
Henry [*Rutledge*] is well.
[*P. S.*] Your Brother [*John*] was taken with the Gout yesterday which prevented his dining with us; Mrs. R. & her daug[*hte*]rs. came & told us he had Suffered much pain from it: [*nephew*] John is hourly expected.[2]

ALS, Smith Papers, ScHi. Place to which addressed not indicated. The recipient's identity is based on internal evidence.

---

[1] To cancel or wipe out debt without payment.
[2] Supreme Court Justice John and Elizabeth Grimke (1744–92) Rutledge and their daughters Martha (1764–1816) and Eliza (1776–1842) expected the arrival of their son and brother, John, Jr., who had been in Europe since 1787.

Joseph Stanton to George Washington

I Received a Letter dated 17th Instant, from Mr. Job Compstalk [*Comstock*] of East Grinwich State Rhodisland, With his Thanks therein Contained for the Honor Confered on him, by your Nomination, & his Appointment to the Office of Surveyor for that port, Also a Letter to your Secretary Mr. [*Tobias*] Lear, Containing his Resignation, Permit me to Recomend Mr. Benjamin Howland to fill the Vacancy his Carractor is Unexceptionable, he Resides in the Compact part of the Town, Will Except, & Will be Acceptable to the major part of the Inhabitance, my Worthy Colleague Mr. Foster Joins in this Recomendation.

ALS, Washington Papers, DLC.

Caleb Strong to Samuel Phillips, Jr.

Yesterday the funding Bill was finished in the two Houses; by one part of the Bill State Debts to the amount of 21,500,000 Dollars are assumed of which 4,000,000 are of the Debts of Massachusetts, You can hardly conceive the Difficulties we have had in this Business the real Friends of the Assumption were perhaps a minor part in both Houses, but those who were anxious to fund the continental Debt separately found so many Obstructions to that Measure that they were constrained to join the Assumptionists, after all we could get but 14 in the Senate for assuming at any Rate or upon any Conditions whatever of these the Gentlemen from New York & Mr. Morris declared that if 6 ⅌ Cent was not promised upon the whole they would not assume, a still greater Number expressed a like Determination if the Interest was raised above 4 ⅌ Cent a Comittee was appointed to whom both the funding Bill & the Propositions for assuming which had been kept separate were committed, after every one had despaired of a Compromise it was said by one of the 6 ⅌ Cent Gentlemen, that if the other party would agree to fund the principal of the continental Debt to which the promise of Government as to ~~Interest~~ a Rate of Interest particularly attached upon Mr. Hamiltons third Alternative he would agree that the Interest now due and the Indents should be funded as the other Gentlemen wished, it was then proposed that the Principal should be funded upon that Alternative of Mr. Hamilton and the Interest & Indents at 3 ⅌ Cent this was agreed to by all except one of the Comittee, and you will see that we could not lose but one and even in that Case we must depend on the Vice President to turn the Vote; as the Interest of the continental Debt was one Third of the whole it was agreed that 1/3 of the State Debts should be funded as the Interest of the continental, and the other two thirds as the Principal—The comittee agreed to report this Arrangement and that the propositions for assuming should be made a part of the funding Bill, thus it passed the Senate the House proposed to raise the Interest and the 1/3d from 3 to 4 ⅌ Cent to increase the deferred part from 26 Dolrs. & 88 Cents to 33 & 1/3 & to [*lined out*] make the Interest on the deferred part payable in 7 Years instead of 10; with these Amendments it was returned to the Senate who agreed to increase the deferred part from 26 Dolrs. & 88 Cents to 33 Dolrs. and 1/3 but refused to agree to the other Amendments—Yesterday the House receded from their proposed Amendments & the Business was closed—If they had further insisted & sent back the Bill to the Senate, it is probable the whole would have been postponed to the next Session, for one of our Members who was against the Assumption told me to day that two who had been for the Assumption would have joined those who opposed it, and a postponement would have been the Consequence, this I was very apprehensive would be the Case, if it had been, the postponement would probably have been for a long Time for we should have broke up in very ill humour, ~~and~~ the eagerness of some Gentlemen for 6 ⅌ Cent. was so great that they declared most solemnly that they would prefer no funding at all to a less Rate of Rate of Interest than 6 ⅌ Cent—This Representation will enable you to account for the different Interest on the Principal & the Indents, those in the Senate who were for a high Interest were urged to accept of an immediate ~~& equal~~ Interest on the whole of four and an half ⅌ Cent. but they refused—Upon the Terms we have ~~agreed~~ proposed the Interest on the whole is reckoned ~~quite~~ as good ~~and perhaps a little better than~~ as 4 & 1/2 ⅌ Cent, perhaps it will be to the discerning, but the people in general will undervalue & be in danger of throwing away the deferred part and it would therefore I think have been better to have had the same Rate of Interest on the whole—whether the Interest is high enough or not I was early convinced that a higher could not be obtained in the Senate for if with the Aid of the Opposers of the Assumption a Vote had been carried to increase the Interest, some of its Friends would have joined its Enemies and postponed the whole however I believe we shall find Difficulty enough in providing the Means of paying even what we have promised—since the Matter is settled the Members in general are I think in better Humour than they have been these three Months some of the anti assumptionists themselves appear pleased that the Dispute is at an end, but there are others I confess who are somewhat sour—I doubt whether an Excise will take place at this Session, probably it might if the Measure was not unpopular at the Southward or the Election was more distant, perhaps there will be no other increase of the Revenue at present than additional Duties of Impost on some enumerated Articles [*Ways and Means Act HR-83*], if such shall be the determination I shall probably leave this place next Wednesday—and I hope Congress will soon after.

I have written to you frequently and have seldom received any Answers, but I am consoled with the Information Mr. Goodhue sometimes gives me, that I am mentioned in some of your Letters to him.

[*P. S.*] Upon looking over this Letter I was afraid you would suspect I wished to conceal my own Sentiments but I had no such Design—I thought 4 ⅌ Cent was as much as this Govt. could safely promise & that 19 in 20 of the Creditors when they considered the Circumstances of the Govt. and of the Debt for a number of years would & all ought to be satisfied, but to obtain the Assumption I was willing to agree to almost any Thing—Our Friend Mr. Goodhue is very much relieved, his Conduct deserves & I presume will meet with the Approbation of his Constituents.

ALS, Phillips Family Collection, MHi. Place to which addressed not indicated.

T. C.

Say virtuous Yorkites, freedoms firmest friends,
Whose glorious efforts, e'en each foe commends;
Who *Briton's* rage by soothing arts disarm'd,
And fiercest *Anties* as by magic charm'd;
By commerce *one*, by Fed'ral-Hall the *other*,
As firmly bound, as if each were thy brother;
Say when so long thy hospitable board,
Has Congress epicures with dainties stor'd;
Canst thou with patience see the ingrates spurn
At all thou'st done, and not with fury burn?
Oh call them ingrates, call them fools and knaves,
Call them of head-strong passion's wretched slaves,
Say that they must be brib'd by B—b's[1] long purse,
Say they deserve for that, Ernulphu's[2] curse;
Say that you hope a Philadelphia mob,
Will do at least for Southern States the job.
If well pav'd streets, and if a splendid hall,
With many a dinner and with each a ball;
If Circe's[3] charms shou'd not dissolve the league.
Establish'd here, by deep and black intrigue.
Then fear not what the impartial world shall say,
What tho' they cry, 'tis av'rice bears the sway;
What tho' through Southern States 'tis often told
You *Feds* became for sake of Congress' Gold.
This you avow with open manly face,
And surely think it can be no disgrace.
Fear nought, but boldly in each paper write,
And 'gainst each venal miscreant vent your spite;
Offending states with utmost freedom lash,
And call Virginia's polish'd members trash—
Let nought confine thy zeal and patriot rage,
Indulge thy fury, 'twill thy griefs assuage.

NYWM, 31 July.

[1] Bob, that is, Robert Morris.

[2] Readers would have been familiar with twelfth century Bishop Ernulph's excommunication curse from *Tristram Shandy*.

[3] The mythological sorceress known for her potions and spells.

OTHER DOCUMENTS

John Armstrong, Jr. to Horatio Gates. ALS, Gates Papers, NHi. Addressed to "Traveller's Rest," Berkeley County, West Virginia; enclosed in White to Gates, 1 August, below. "Bridewell" is a generic term for a prison, named for the London palace converted into a penitentiary for vagrants in the sixteenth century.

"*Society*" in New York City "will improve in a no small degree by the removal of Congress, which by the way contains a great many men whose manners & morals would dishonor a Bridewell."

Richard Bassett to William Jackson. AN, Washington Papers, DLC. Pearce's identity is uncertain. A Matthew Pearce (1764–1832) was a planter of Sassafras Neck, Cecil County, Maryland, whose estate neighbored Bassett's own holdings that straddled Maryland and New Castle County, Delaware. He married Read's only daughter, Mary Howell (1770–1816), in about 1787. Another, or possibly the same, Matthew Pearce was admitted to the bar in New Castle County in 1785 and became the first clerk of the federal District Court for Delaware from 1790 to 1792 (John Thomas Scharf, *History of Delaware, 1609–1888* [2 vols., Philadelphia, 1888], 1:526, 563).

Office seeking: asks Jackson to "Give the following Names to the President:" William Peery for one of the federal judges in the Southern Territory and Matthew Pearce for commissioner of loans for Delaware.

Lambert Cadwalader to George Mitchell. ALS, Mitchell Papers, NjR. Addressed to "Dagsbury," Sussex County, Delaware. A postscript dated 31 July is calendared below.

The Funding Bill has passed Congress; will send a copy if he can get one; "no doubt it will receive the Signature of the President."

William Constable to Gouverneur Morris. FC:lbk, Constable-Pierrepont Collection, NN. Sent by the ship *Nancy*; copy sent by the *Grange*.

Robert Morris has promised a copy of the Funding Act, which he will enclose.

Jedidiah Huntington to Jonathan Trumbull. ALS, Washington Papers, DLC. Written from New London, Connecticut; carried by Elisha Lathrop. For the full text, see *PGW* 6:132n.

Office seeking: Elisha Lothrop as consul at Demerara (Georgetown, Guyana).

Philip Schuyler to an Unknown Recipient. Listing of ALS, *Bangs Catalog*, 3 December 1874, item 79.

Theodore Sedgwick, Motion. Dft, Foster Papers, RHi. Sedgwick's motion began the process that resulted in the Navigation Act [HR-93]; see *DHFFC* 6:1523–25.

"That a committee be appointed to report a bill declaring the consent of congress, that the laws of the legislature of Rhode Island &   imposing duties on the tonage of ships & vessells, entering at providence in the said state, to be appropriated for the purpose of rendering more navigable providence river shall be valid."

David Sewall to George Thatcher. ALS, Foster Collection, MHi. Written from York, Maine; postmarked Portsmouth, New Hampshire.

Funding and assumption "are in so fair a Way that I presume they are effected and that We shall have the pleasure of seeing you soon."

John Jeffries, Diary. Jeffries Family Papers, MHi.

Breakfasted with Adams at "Richmond Hill," where he had a "pleasant & polite reception"; attended Martha Washington's levee, where Knox introduced him to "a number of *** Statesmen & Senators"; received a "Card of invitation" from Gerry.

Saturday, 31 July 1790

Samuel Dexter to Elbridge Gerry

Had the five articles of *charge* in my last letter been difficulties in my own mind, your observations and remarks upon them, in your favour of the 19th inst., would have fully cleared them up. The truth is, they were made partly in behalf of some honest people, of weak minds, with whom I had been disposed to converse, with a view to prepare them for the election in 8ber next, and in part to enable myself, from your answers, to furnish some influential persons with the means of enlightening men of the same description, with whom they might happen to be conversant. I was at Boston on Monday last, when I took your letter out of the office. Without mentioning anything about it, however, in that town, I had the pleasure to hear a number of gentlemen, respectable not merely for their property and the public characters they sustain, but for their good sense and judgment, speaking of several of the Massachusetts Delegates as the most fit to be sent in March next; and of yourself in the strongest terms of approbation and regard. One of them, in particular, upon my saying I hoped N. G. [*Nathaniel Gorham*] would not obtain a choice in Middlesex, joined zealously with me, and added that what influence he had in our district, should be employed against him, and in favour of the present member. Since my last I have heard of none who are busy in recommending G. except G. D—h,[1] of Hopkinton, formerly a member of the G. C. [*General Court, the state legislature*] from that town, one P—y [*Abel Perry?*], a petty fogging attorney, at Natick, and one or two others not a whit more reputable. But even men of such a character are sometimes attended to by the populace.

What "concealed writers" may throw out by and by, it is impossible to fore tell; but I know of no candidate whose reputation is less likely to be "the subject of reproach" in the papers than your's. Were it not for the great desire which the person above referred to has for a seat in Congress, or, in other words, for something to live upon, and the attachment which such men in this County as know least of mankind, have to him, I should not suspect that a single sentence would be either uttered or written against a reelection of the present member, inconsistent with candour and politeness. From what I have heard from several sensible men, whose professions call them much from hence, my fears of the C—n [*Charlestown*] man's success are considerably lessened since you heard from me before.

You [*lined out*] utterly [*paper cut*][2] some of your clerical friend [*paper cut*] I know. Divers of them I [*paper cut*]tre expression I used, that a few of them were needlessly cautious of giving their opinions in elections for the national government. When representative are to be chosen in their own towns, for our General Court, I think it prudent for them to be inactive—But no reasonable men can be offended for their acting with the same freedom as other electors, in regard to the choice of a member of Congress.

I think, Sir, with you, that democratic governments diverge from that denomination towards "aristocracy, monarchy, and even despotism" I think also, that a constitution is ever in danger from such men as you describe; and that the surest preservative of the liberties of a people is their having *wise, experienced,* and *incorrupt* representatives: And if such *could be* continued in place for a great length of time, so much the better. But you know, my dear Sir, that frequent elections have been always thought expedient to preserve, when it is needed, an undue influence from the executive. It would scarcely be worth while to purchase men whose period of duration in the legislature is short.

In G. Britain, you are sensible, a member of the House of Commons loses his seat on promotion. It is true that, through the influence of the Executive, he generally gets reelected—But the fault lies, in a great measure, in their Constitution, so far as it respects the popular branch of government. Could the people be as completely represented as they ought to be, and were their parliaments triennial, it might, perhaps, tend greatly to prevent the corruption both of the *electors* and the *elected.* After all, it must be acknowledged that *good men cannot be too long in place.* The difficulty is to get a House of Representatives "whose sense of honour and justice will guard them against undue influence." Were this feasible, it would be best they should continue *during life.* I entirely agree with you, that as the greatest part of such a body are generally of a different character, they should be put "above the reach of temptation by establishments that would effectually attach them to their constituents." You must know from this that I am not one of the grumbletonians, who drew up the 2d article in the indictment.[3]

The combinations that are formed to serve local interests were expected by all acquainted with mankind, and, consequently by yourself, and, though troublesome, cannot be surprizing to you. [*paper cut*] other States to combine to [*paper cut*] fortunate, however, if discussion [*paper cut*] them"—But parties there [*paper cut*]tions are not formed to oppose combinations, "public grievances and oppression" will be brought about by the first combiners.

I am extremely sorry to learn that your health is injured by your attendance upon public business; but I wish you not to be "weary of well doing." I cannot say that I am in raptures with the present prospect respecting *funding.* With the measures you have pursued, as to that matter, from first to last, I am however perfectly satisfied, as are all your constituents; and I think I can now convince ~~all~~ every gainsayer that has heretofore objected to the part you took in the Case of the compensations, of Baron Steuben, of the library, and of the application of the Officers of the Navy.[4]

I shall make a *prudent* and *friendly* use of the information and elucidations contained in your letter.

ALS, partly mutilated, Gerry Papers, DLC. Written from Weston, Massachusetts; answered 26 August.

[1] Gilbert Dench (1742–1807), a militia captain during the Revolutionary War, represented Hopkinton in the state House of Representatives, 1780–88 (except in 1784), and at the state convention, where he voted against ratification of the Constitution (*DHROC* 6:1186n, 1759n).

[2] A rectangular piece of the document was cut or broken out at this point.

[3] Dexter referred to the five "articles of charge" brought against Gerry by his political opponents; see Dexter to Gerry, 10 July, above.

[4] For more on the petitions of Frederick William von Steuben and of the Continental Navy Officers, seeking compensation for wartime service, see *DHFFC* 7:203–46 and 438–42, respectively. For more on Gerry's leading role in the efforts to establish a library for Congress in 1790, see *DHFFC* 8:653–60.

Thomas Dwight to Theodore Sedgwick

I am indebted to you for several kind favors of late—I have been journeying or should have written before—I have this minute received your's of the 26th. inst. in which you give me some very agreeable intelligence in regard to assumption—that your task in this business has been a very painful one—that your labors for the good of your constituents have been incessant I never have doubted—I am sorry that popular opinion is so much fixed against the present Congress, by the conduct of business in the present session but so it is—I am not without hopes that the assumption will in some measure lessen the severity of censure as well as the extravagance of prejudice—all divisions in Congress which appear to be grounded on local considerations or in which Southern men are generally opposed to Northern tend very much to create in the minds of the people a discrimination between one part of the union & another, a habit of considering the interests of each as very different which if supported, will certainly end in *disjunction* [*lined out*] and all the horrors of civil war.

Whether this letter will find you at N. York—I am in doubt—but will venture to forward it by the stage—In regard to our approaching elections no movements are made, from which I can form an opinion how the business is to be conducted—I will inform you from time to time as I acquire information on the subject.

ALS, Sedgwick Papers, MHi. Written from Springfield, Massachusetts; franked.

Governor Arthur Fenner to Theodore Foster

I recd. your letter of the 24th. Yesterday I am much obliged by the information I thereby recd. The Assumption of twenty one Millions of Dollars is not understood by any of us. some suppose it to be the whole that is intended to be assumed of the State Debts and of those are N[*icholas?*]. Brown J[*abez*]. Bowen &c. &ca. they complain very much at our 200,000 Dollars ~~whi~~ and say that our proportion is Double that amt. and we shall loose the remaing. part or sum and seem very willing to blame the Senators. I give them my Opinion in this way. That the Twenty one Millions is supposed by Congress to be the amount of the demands the States may have against the United States after deducting the several sums recd. by Particular States heretofore that after the settlements with the several States that State which is found to be in Advance or has demands more than their proportion of the sum assumed will have credit therefor.

That the reason why this State had not its full proportion or fiftee[*n*]th part was on Account of the large sums of Mony this State recd. in the time of War. They do not [*lined out*] seem to be willing to agree with me it seems they want to complain of your Conduct—whether I am right or they is for you to inform me (that I may fight as good a fight as I can) which I beg you to do as soon as Possible and let me into the whole plan and if you can get a larger sum added perhaps it may be no disadvantage especially if they are right & I am Wrong, but I cannot think they are right for what means the Assumption is it taking only part of the Debt, consider the confusion it would make in the several States among the State Creditors one to receive all and the other nothing.

I am exceeding Anxious that you should exert yourself in the appointment of the Excise officers if you can get Judge [*Ebenezer*] Thompson appointed he can make such under appointments we think best, next to him I beg you to remember Wm. Lyles Esq. who stands in need of help you are sensible he is qualified and I beleive will do as well as when employed by the State if any under appts. are made by Congress Remember Z[*achariah*]. Rhodes Alfred Arnold—The Country are so much engaged that I have not seen any of the leading men to converse with them but shall attend to what I think necessary for your Interest dont delay Writing to those you mention and if you know any in the County of Bristol and Newport think of them Mr. Stanton can inform you of the Newport County. I think you had better Write a short letter to Jonathan Gaston & Gideon Arnold both of Warwik.

I have heard but little said respecting our representative, but suppose Job [*Comstock*] to stand as fair as anyone—You must excuse this letter also for I have no time to correct or Copy the boat being ready to Sail and I had not timely information—my health is bad my Daughter Sally very poorly. the rest Well.

P. S. It is to be understood that if Judge Thompson gets the appointment he is to hold the Naval Office also. Remember John Wanton of Newport give my kind love to Mr. Stanton and he must receive this letter [*lined out*] in part with you I not having time to Write to both.

ALS, Foster Papers, RHi. Written from Providence, Rhode Island; delivered by Capt. John Tillinghast in the Senate lobby about 1 P.M., 9 August.

Benjamin Goodhue to Michael Hodge

Your kind favr. of 27th. has just reach'd me and I am to thank you for any favourable sentiments you and my friends may entertain of my political conduct, I am not sensible of having acted from views. distinct from the welfare of my Country. and the dignity and respectability of our infant Government, the funding in which I have always consider'd the assumption, as forming an essential and inseperable connection, has engross'd all my thoughts and exertions to accomplish, for without it, to me nothing appear'd worth preserving and I am happy beyond expression that we have at length effected it, and altho' it may not be in the shape the most pleasing to be wish'd for, it was the best we could attain—and to have hazzarded this bussines among so many enemies watching to destroy it, any longer, would have been playing too great a game, for had we lost this ground, to every appearance there could be little or no hope of ever regaining it—it would be folly to pretend, that its in human nature not to receive a pleasure, from the bestowment of public confidence, or pain at its being withdrawn, I feel myself under obligations for their good opinion, and I wish if by pursuing my duty I can preserve it—I was apprised before I came into the National legislature, that whoever had a share in carrying into operation in the first instance, the purposes for which the Government was instituted, must necessarily have to combat not only its avowed enemies, but the prejudices and unfounded expectations of many of ~~its~~ the friends of its adoption, and on that account be loaded over much, with the obliquy of ignorant and ill disposed characters—I am not therefore disappointed, and am prepared to meet any reproaches that do not arise in my own mind, from a neglect of duty, of which I feel myself perfectly acquited—I feel myself indebted for the good opinion of such respectable characters as you have named and hope to preserve it—as to my having a seat in the next legislature, (in as much as there is no probibility they will be in session more then 8 or 10 months during their appointment,) in a pecuniary view I consider it as no great object, but I will confess to you, if I should be dropt, it would imply a censure, that would at least for a while give me some inquietude—but should it so happen I suspect I shall have as much Philosophy as most others under like circumstances—We have nothing new since my last to Mr. [*William*] Coombs, excepting this a Committee of Senate ~~yesterday~~ today met a Committee of our House on the subject of the Impost bill [*Ways and Means Act HR-83*], which is now in Senate for encreasing the duties, as it went some time past from the House—I am informed they have agreed in conjunction with the Secry. of the Treasury, to a modification of that bill in such a manner as to do without any Excise till next session, what the modification is I have not heard, they will I suppose report to the Senate on monday, and if its tolerable I expect it will meet a speedy passage—it seems the general expectation that We shall adjourn this week or next, you will therefore not send me any more letters to this City—I hear the N. Yorkers and some others mean again to bring up the question of residence but I beleive the members are so perfectly weary of that contentious subject, that it will not receive much countenance.

ALS, Ebenezer Stone Papers, MSaE. Place to which addressed not indicated. Goodhue wrote "private" at the top of the first page.

John Hobby to George Thatcher

My House having been a perfect Hospital for a long time past, my attention has been too much engaged with my family to be able to attend to my other Objects which must be my apology for not answering your last to me before this. The two great, & I dare say to you very perplexing objects, viz. provision for the Domestic Debt, & the Residence of Congress being at last brot. to a conclusion, I can assure you is very pleasing to every individual that has capacity or inclination to acquaint themselves with what is passing in the Political world, & that almost universal complaint and disgust which evidently sat on the Brow of every class of Citizens, seems changing to a pleasing approbation, How you will get through with the unpleasing subject of the assumption is to us in this place a matter of much speculation, however of this you may rest asured, that among all the uneasiness, & hard speeches of Restless and Turbulent spirits, you have been attended with the best wishes of every well disposed mind, and all real friends to good government, in every stage of the trying difficulties attendant on your present Session. By the last N. York papers I find in the arangement of the Militia by Congress, the President has the appointment of an Inspector of them to each District, & as it seems to me probable some emolument will be attached to this office, I cou'd wish if agreeable to your feelings for your particular influence, as well as those of your friends who may be influential at Head Quarters for this appointment, which wou'd be flattering to my ambition, especially if attended with an income—It will I presume be a business in kind which after seven years Active service I shou'd feel myself equal to, however as fond as I still am of Military matters, I wou'd not be willing to sacrifice my time & exertions without being paid for it—upon the whole if you think it an object worthy of attention, I hope for your assistance as soon as may be, as I suppose many will be seeking for it, especially those who have been in our National service, & almost all of them are wishing for some of the Crumbs that are falling from her Table. as to News we have none in this quarter our shiping & navigation is daily encreasing, & in general good Voyages have been made from this Port—the season is beautifull, & our Farmers have the pleasing prospect of a bountifull Harvest of every thing excepting Hay, which has not recovered its last years Dearth & the destruction made by Inse[*c*]t.

ALS, Chamberlain Collection, MB. Written from Portland, Maine; franked.

David Humphreys to Thomas Jefferson

Upon finding that the Packet would sail sooner than I had expected, I hastened to make the necessary arrangements for my departure.[1] Apprehensive, however, that I may be too much pressed for time, to have opportunities of acquiring, in conversation, as much information as could have been desired on the different subjects which will claim attention, I shall be extremely happy to have the deficiency supplied by such written Notes as Mr. Madison, Mr. Brown & yourself may think proper to give. The best possible care will be taken of all secret papers, as well as of the Cyphers which shall be committed to me for my use, and for the Consul or Agent who may be employed in London. ***

ALS, Diplomatic Dispatches, Consular Correspondence, State Department Records, Record Group 59, DNA. Written from "Mrs. Haviland's Tavern," Rye, New York; received 5 August. For the full text, see *PTJ* 17:87–88. For Washington's report to the Senate on Humphreys's secret mission to Portugal and the official correspondence relating to it, see *DHFFC* 2:117–18, 469–73.

---

[1] Presumably Washington himself selected his aide for the secret mission to Europe that the President and secretary of state began to plan in the last weeks of July. In addition to delivering new instructions to U.S. diplomatic representatives abroad, Humphreys was to confer directly with foreign officials and to report back on European affairs. His itinerary, composed by Jefferson on 11 August, sent him first to London to meet with Gouverneur Morris and the recently appointed consul Joshua Johnson. From there Humphreys was to sail to Lisbon and meet with prime minister Pinto de Souza to discuss the grade of diplomats to be exchanged with Portugal (to which Humphreys would be appointed U.S. "minister resident" in February 1791). The most imperative and delicate errand of all was to the next destination, Madrid, where Humphreys delivered to the U.S. chargé d'affaires William Carmichael a cipher for secret communications and secret instructions that aimed to exploit the Nootka Sound Crisis and the prospect of an Anglo-Spanish war, by negotiating a concession of Spain's territorial claims in the American Southeast and the free navigation of the Mississippi River. The latter explains why Brown and Madison, both experts on the Mississippi question, were the only two members of Congress and the only other government officials in New York (besides Hamilton) to be informed of Humphreys's mission in advance. Its secrecy was further protected by furnishing Humphreys with letters of introduction implying that he traveled in a purely private capacity. After a final meeting with Washington on 30 August and two interviews with Hamilton later that day, Humphreys's departure was delayed three more days due to contrary winds, erasing the advantage he had hoped to gain by traveling on a privately owned ship rather than the British packet that did not arrive at New York until 2 September. He set sail from New York on 3 September and arrived in London on 14 October (*PGW* 6:217–20, 381–83).

William Jackson to George Washington

***

Mr. Otis, Secretary to the Senate, having signified his wish that he might receive an appointment in Massachusetts—several members of that body (among them Mr. Izard, Mr. Butler, Mr. Read, Mr. Bassett, Mr. Morris, Mr. Paterson, and Mr. Langdon) have spoken to me—and told me that in such an event I would probably be elected Secretary to the Senate.

Consulting only my own wishes on this occasion, as it respects the probability of my attaining a competency in life, and thereby being enabled to accomplish *the dearest of my expectations.*[1] I should entreat you, by every consideration that could move your consent to a compliance with Mr. Otis's request: but my wishes, I well know, are not alone to be consulted—and, if they were, I would never presume to bring them forward in any manner that might accuse either my duty or my delicacy towards you. No, Sir, I hold it proper, before you consent to such an appointment, that you should be informed of a consequence that will probably flow from it—which is, that it may introduce to the vacant office One, who has the honor to be near to your person; and who, whatever may be the sentiments of the Senate in his behalf, might probably, on that account, be considered as being peculiarly favored. To mention this to you, Sir, is a discharge of the duty which I owe to a generous Protector—and it [*is*] the part of delicacy that I should mention it without reserve—That being discharged, I am well assured that your goodness will allow me to state such other circumstances as may incline you, under a belief of its propriety, to comply with Mr. Otis's wish—in which, pardon the declaration, I feel myself deeply interested.

When Mr. Otis was elected to the office which he now fills, I was his competitor—a majority of the attending Senators decided in his favor. I mean not to disparage Mr. Otis when I say that the preference pained me. mr. Otis is acknowledged to be a good Man, and those who know him are agreed in his attention to his duty and his disposition to oblige—but a majority of the Senate (perhaps I am warranted to go farther) think that his talents are not adapted to the different duties of his immediate situation—this has led to a wish, on the part of many, that he might occupy a place more consonant to his abilities, and more congenial with his wishes—and on this head I am authorized to say so much by the opinions of his friends who advocate his present wish—those opinions, Sir, as they may be expressed by some of the Senators themselves would inform you how far they consider the business of their house connected with the wish to procure Mr. Otis another appointment—his own feelings and the happiness of his family are, I am informed, also concerned in the wish.

***

ALS, Washington Papers, DLC. The omitted text concerns Jackson's relationship with Washington. For the full text, see *PGW* 6:155–57.

[1] The last two paragraphs of the letter indicate that Jackson wished the Senate office so that he would have the financial security necessary to wed.

James Madison to James Madison, Sr.

***

The funding bill has at length passed the two Houses with a qualified assumption of the State debts. 2/3 of the federal debts are to bear an immediate interest of 6 per Ct. and the remaining 1/3 a like interest to commence in 1800 but in the mean time to be receivable for land. The indents & arrears of interest are funded at 3 per Cent.—of the State debts 2/3 are funded at 6 per Ct. & 1/3 at 3 Per Ct. The assumption was carried by a small majority in both Houses. Many who voted for it did so on a supposition that it was a lesser evil than to risk the effect of a rejection on the States which insisted on the increase. I could not bring myself to concur with them but am sensible that there was serious danger of a very unfavorable issue to the Session from a contrary decision and consider it as now incumbent on us all to [*lined out*] make the best of what is done. The truth is that in a pecuniary light, the assumption is no longer of much consequence to Virginia, the sum allotted to her being about her proportion of the whole & rather exceeding her present debt. She will consequently pay no more to the general Treasury than she now pays to the State Treasy. and perhaps in a mode which will be less disgreeable to the people, tho' not more favorable to their true interests.

The ways & means [*HR-83*] are now under consideration. The impost will be made equal to the federal debt. The provision for the State debts will be put off till the next session. It will be likely to consist chiefly of duties on rum distilled in the U.S. and on a few imported articles that will best bear a further augmentation.

We expect that an adjournment will take place in about a week. I shall set out for Virginia as soon thereafter as I can pack up my books papers &c. which will detain me here some days. Mr. Jefferson wishes me to wait for his setting out and as his company will be particularly grateful & also convenient I am not sure that I shall resist the invitation, if he finds that he can be ready for the Journey within a reasonable time. I shd. not hesitate if I did not wish to be in Orange by the election tho' as an attendance ~~would~~ can not be given at more than one of the 8 Counties it does not seem worth while to sacrifice much to that consideration.

ALS, signature clipped, Madison Papers, DLC. Place to which addressed not indicated. The omitted text discusses prices of household commodities and promises to forward a letter to Joseph Chew (ca. 1725–1798), a first cousin and intimate friend of Madison's father, who had emigrated as a loyalist probably around 1776.

Gouverneur Morris to Robert Morris

Your Letters of the fourth and sixteenth of June give me some Intelligence respecting public Affairs, and also of your family and my other friends. Accept my Thanks for that Attention, and make to them my affectionate Remembrances—Your Bill for establishing foreign Intercourse [*HR*-52] has it seems been lost by a Dispute between the two Houses. I cannot say that I am exactly of Opinion with either in that Dispute. Some Discretion should be left to the Executive on this Subject most clearly; but on the other hand, I do not think it consistent with the genius of our Constitution, to leave a very wide Space for the Exercise of discretionary Powers. While the present Magistrate exists, all would go right; but his Successors might much misuse the Authority: and altho' I have not the childish Apprehension of Tyranny from that Quarter, yet I think a Dependency of the diplomatic Servants might be rendered rather too great upon the Chief of the Republic, and thence perhaps Men might get into and continue in those Offices who are not duly fitted for them. I think also that it would have been well for the Representatives to have adopted an Amendment proposed to them for giving one Year's Salary as an Establishment to their Minister. I do not think a Gentleman can be suitably placed either in London or Paris for less than £2500 Sterling, and I suppose an Expence nearly as great must be incurred at the Hague or Lisbon or Madrid. There are not many of our Countrymen (suitable for the Office) whom it would suit to Make such an Advance upon it, more especially as they might be recalled in one or two Years, or be obliged by their own Affairs to return within that Period, and then the whole Sum almost would be lost. I am not surprized to find that the Idea you mention prevails, of having a Minister at only one Court, but sooner or later we must act like other People. That we may keep an Officer of higher Grade or superior Emolument at Paris is clear; perhaps we ought to do so, but we must take Care that in marking our Regard to one Power we do not insult another. Kings are proud, and if they were not nations are. Our real Interest therefore requires that we pay the due Respect to others. In fact this is required also by a due Respect for ourselves. I shall readily acknowlege that these national Attentions, like the interior Ceremonies of Good Breeding, do ~~not~~ in fact mean nothing, but in both Cases the omission means a great Deal. There is also in our Situation a strong Reason for having diplomatic Agents abroad, altho' from our Situation also we should endeavor to be as little connected as possible with the Politics of this Hemisphere. But the greater Powers of Europe have Dominions in our Neighbourhood, and the Incidents which must naturally arise from that Neighbourhood will require frequent Explanations to prevent serious quarrels. I might go farther were

I to consider America as a commercial Nation, but I stop short from the Recollection that many Truths, now familiar as Household Conversation, were once treated as the visionary Dreamings of a wild Imagination; and no Man has oftener than I have experienced that fate.

I must however give Utterance to one or two Sentiments on another political Topic: Indeed that was my Object in begining this Letter, tho' I was led into the other by replying to yours in the Order of their Dates. You acknowleged the Receipt of two Letters from me dated the 8th. of May 1789, but you have never said a Word to me of the Plan of finance which was enclosed in one of them,[1] from whence I conjecture that it was not well relished. I have seen much of the Debates on the subject of our Debts and finances, and observed with Concern that the Legislature have been divided by two opinions, against both of which solid Arguments have been adduced. Truth I still think lies in the middle. To assume the Payment of what the States owe, mearly because they owe it, seems to my Capacity not more rational than to assume the Debts of Corporations or of Individuals. To establish a Quota or Proportion of the whole, or of any Part, of the public Debt upon different Tracts of that great territory which composes the United States either according to past or present Population, seems to me not consistent with Justice. I say *the whole* or any Part, for I cannot help viewing Objects in a collective Capacity, and judging of them upon Principles. What is the Debt? the *public* Debt? the Answer is contained in a Definition of the Words. Sums *due*, by *United America*. What are the Sums? The Value of Monies advanced, Services rendered, and Supplies furnished to *America*; by any Individuals or Bodies corporate or politic. By whom should this Debt be paid? By existing Individuals or particular Corporations or Communities? No. It is to be paid by the Citizens of America at large; that is to say by their annual Contributions in Proportion (as nearly as may be) to their Wealth. He who purchases an acre of Land in America takes it, like other mortgaged Promises, subject to its just Proportion of the Debt; and he who without purchase becomes an Inhabitant of America, becomes thereby liable during his Continuance to pay his annual Contribution in common with his fellow Citizens. Take any different Doctrine, and try it's Truth by pushing it to the Extreme. Suppose the whole Debt were divided (by any Ratio whatever) among the different States. Rhodes Island and New York would each have their fixed Proportion. But in twenty Years the Population of New York must be more than double to what it is consequently each Man's Share of the Burthen would be but one Half whereas in Rhodes Island it must continue the same. Consequently the taxes there must be double, consequently the Inducement to quit it great, Consequently a Decrease of Inhabitants and thereby an Encrease of the Burthens; while from the same Depopulation the Value of Lands must be diminished. Now this is not right. And that which is not right cannot last. Justice is the great Support of Nations. What then does Justice require? The Answer it seems to me is clear. Pay to Individuals what is due to Individuals, and pay to Corporations and Communities what is due to them. If the Individual or Community be in Debt or not in Debt to others is a Circumstance which the Public, the Union, America in short, has nothing to do with. Having established thus the Totality of the public Debt, proceed next to make a Provision for the Payment ~~of the whole, the full Interest, is~~. And under this Chapter I must own that I differ from many of my worthy friends. I firmly beleive that the Payment of the whole, the full *Interest* is the best Mode. First I beleive so because it is right, and that is with me a sufficient Reason; but as in other Cases, where, Honesty is the best Policy. As to the Idea that the People cannot pay it, I look upon that not only to be weak, but a Contradiction in Terms. The People are not able to pay. What? What they owe to themselves. They are not able to bear the Burthen. What Burthen? That which is already on their Shoulders. But if they are not able to bear it how are they to be releived? By leaving them totally or partially as you found them.

Payment of the full Interest is most œconomical and here one Word on the Speculations of foreigners. So long as those who hold the Debt are in Want of Money, so long will they sell it for what they can get. The more valuable you render it, the more will it sell for, consequently as far as foreigners are concerned you will benefit by the Difference. But the Speculations of foreigners will alone enable you to reduce the Interest (in other Words the Debt) with Advantage. When it has been established for a little while, it will at six per Cent get above par, and of Course the Holders may be called in to reduce the Interest or to receive Payment. The Natives would incline to the latter, but foreigners would purchase of them to secure to themselves even the lower Interest, and thus Things would be brought to their natural Level, and thereby the Interest of Money in America would be lowered, a thing devoutly to be wished for but not to be effected by legislative Authority. The other Mode (pardon the Expression) is what the french call eating poor Corn in the Blade.[2] Let both be brought to the Test of plain Arithmetic, and admit that in any given Period (five years if you please) the Interest would of itself, get down to four per Cent, which seems to be the Basis adopted, and which therefore I shall not dispute. Take any Sum you please of foreign Money appropriated by the European Capitalists to speculation in our funds. I observe by the bye that this Sum is from the Nature of Things fixed to some certain Amount. ~~The Reasoning however will be equ~~ Altho' from the Nature of Things it is impossible to ascertain that Amount. The Reasoning however will be equally clear in any hypothetic Statement; we will therefore suppose Six Million of Dollars. One other Position remains to be established, which being a fact may perhaps admit of Dispute but you will find it on

Enquiry to be a fact viz. that the European Capitalists regulate their Purchases by the Amount of the Interest to be received. Suppose the Rate they fix on to be 10 ꝑ % for thier Investment, they must then purchase at sixty per Cent if the Interest of our Debt be six per Cent and consequently the Amount purchased will be ten Millions; whereas if the Interest be only four per Cent, they will give but forty per Cent and of Course the Sum purchased will be fifteen Millions. The Difference of five Millions is so much lost by the Bargain to America, and as in the admitted Case ~~that~~ Interest is within five Years to fall by natural Causes to four per Cent, which it certainly will if we do what is right, the foreigners would then receive a Revenue of only four hundred thousand from thier Capital invested, whereas in the Case of immediate Reduction they would receive six hundred thousand, not to mention the additional Capital. Indeed with Respect to the Capital it is a Thing of no Consequence, for whenever the Debt is properly funded, we shall find People as willing to accomodate us with Money as we can be to take it from them.

On the Subject of public Debts in general, I beleive it may be taken as a Maxim that whether foreign or domestic their Debt necessarily creates the Means for its Support. If domestic the Revenue derived from the People to pay the Expence is necessarily spent again among the People and creates in Advance in the Price of things just about equal to the Amount of the Tax. And if it be a foreign Debt, by means of the Commerce, it operates greatly to encrease the consumption of our Produce by ~~Means~~ our Creditor Nation. The striking fact to prove this Principle is in Holland. That Country was a great Manufactory, but in Proportion as it has lent Money to others the Manufacturing has so declined that they now take from their Debtor England the very Articles which formerly they supplied. But it is Time to stop, for I find that without being aware of it, I am converting my Letter into a Kind of political Essay.

FC, letterbook copy, Gouverneur Morris Papers, DLC. Written from London.

[1] For an abstract of G. Morris's "Plan of American Finance," see *DHFFC* 15:511–12. For the full text, see Jared Sparks, *The Life of Gouverneur Morris, with Selections from His . . . Papers* (3 vols., Boston, 1832), 3:469–78.

[2] Preventing things from reaching their natural level.

John Steele to George Washington

I am authorised to say that Colonel [*John*] Stokes will serve as Judge for the district of No. Carolina, if appointed. In a conversation on this subject with himself he expressed a wish that Colonel [*William R.*] Davie might hold that office in preference to any other man; but on condition that he declined offering, or refused to accept, he was not unwilling to be mentioned as a candidate.

That he wou'd perform the duties of this office with dignity, and give general satisfaction, I have not a doubt. His adjudications as additional judge of No. Ca. in several very weighty and intricate causes, have been highly approved. For other circumstances relative to this Gentleman, I beg leave to refer you to a former letter.

ALS, Washington Papers, DLC.

Ebenezer Thompson to Theodore Foster

My last was by Capt. Cuny which hope by this time is to hand, since which their has Nothing Occurd of any material consequence within the limits of our Circle this Way.

The speculators in Our State appear to be disturbed at congress Not having assumed a larger proportion of Our State Debts they Urge that our Senators should have been ernest for a larger Sum—I think their complaint is Nothing more than Parliamenttiariay—and to try if possable to Strengthen themselves in order to get in a senator of their own Kidney—but in this I think they must fail—however if their should happen to be any oppertunity I woud Advise to have the Sum increased as much as possable as No injury can Arrise to the state on that Score.

The Governor [*Arthur Fenner*] has just Shewn me your letter to him by Godfrey if their should be an opotunity to Accomplish what you hint at with regard to the office of the Excise [*?*] without giving Up to the ~~Office~~ Naval Office I should like it Much and it will Add to the many Obligations I am alread under to you—and as it is probable that the Sistem of the Excise may make it necessary to have a Number of Under Officers in Subbordination it may put in my power to help our Friend Tylor [*John Taylor?*] which I should Wish to Do if in my power—I must say that I have never Expereanced aney thing in him but what has been Manly and in Charracter—~~My~~ plese to present my most respetfull Compliments to Genl. Stanton.

ALS, Foster Papers, RHi. Written from Providence, Rhode Island; delivered by Capt. John Tillinghast (master of the sloop *Fanny*) in the Senate chamber on 9 August.

X to Mr. Brown

ALTHOUGH it must be considered as a painful duty to impose on our President, yet all federal citizens now look up to him for the exercise of that authority, with which he is invested by the constitution, to put an end to that shameful trifling which has so long disgraced our legislature, who, instead of making wholesome laws for the country they are deputed by, are contesting with all the heat and animosity of a Polish Diet,[1] where those laws shall be made. Sir, if Mr. Bloodworth should persist in his motion in expectation of having that clause[2] cancelled in a *thin* house, when the members, who supported that clause upon the fullest debate and most mature deliberation, have separated to their respective homes—I say, Sir, should even both houses, in their present mutilated state, agree to that motion, I conceive it will be one of those situations which calls loudly for the veto of the President—a motion which has been fully and amply discussed—which has shamefully lavished the time of both houses—which had roused the passions and resentments of sister states—and which have now happily subsided. The man, or the motion which tends to renew those evils, deserves, and I have no doubt, will meet the pointed disapprobation of our President.

FG, 31 July, edited by Andrew Brown; reprinted at New York City (*NYP*, 5 August).

---

[1] The Polish Diet or Sejm was a unicameral legislature composed exclusively of nobles, each of whom maintained practical sovereignty over his feudal holdings by an absolute veto over the proposal of any of his colleagues.

[2] The clause establishing Philadelphia as the temporary seat of government.

Newspaper Article

The Delegates, from this *State*, in the Congress of the United States, are intitled to every mark of the gratitude of their constituents, for their persevering firmness, and steady attention, to effect a measure, which justice, policy and the best interests of the Union, loudly called for. Without an eminent display of these qualifications, the *Assumption of the State Debt* must have been retarded for a long time; and this Commonwealth would still have groaned under the heavy burthen which her exertions in the COMMON CAUSE brought upon her. Their task has been arduous—and their conduct in it, open and magnanimous, though persevering and strenuous—and they can return to their constituents, happy in the consideration of having done their duty, and of having seen their labours crowned with merited success.

It is worthy of observation, that every subject debated in Congress which has been found fault with, the *Massachusetts* members, have, in general, strenuously opposed.

[Boston] *Columbian Centinel*, 31 July.

OTHER DOCUMENTS

Lambert Cadwalader to George Mitchell. ALS, Mitchell Papers, NjR. Addressed to "Dagsbury," Sussex County, Delaware. This is a postscript to a letter begun on 30 July, above.

Cannot get a copy of the Funding Bill to send; "you will receive one from Philada. as they will be printed there."

Henry Latimer to George Washington. ALS, Washington Papers, DLC. Written from Newport, Delaware.

Office seeking: commissioner of loans for Delaware; mentions the Delaware Senators as references.

James Madison to Benjamin Rush. ALS, Rush Papers, DLC. Place to which addressed not indicated. For the full text, see *PJM* 13:285–86.

Acknowledges receipt of Rush's *Eulogium on William Cullen* (Philadelphia, 1790; Evans 22862); encloses Jefferson's report on weights and measures (*DHFFC* 8:483–500), "which can not fail to please all those who set a due value on public reformations, and see the aids to be derived to them from a regard to philosophic principles."

Theodore Sedgwick to an Unknown Recipient. Listing of one page ALS, *Carnegie Book Shop Catalog* 277(1964):item 372.

Daniel Hiester, Account Book. PRHi. The date is supplied by the editors based on the assumption that the trip occurred on the weekend.

Shared a hack with Madison on the four mile circuit of Manhattan Island.

John Jeffries, Diary. Jeffries Family Papers, MHi.

Dined at "Richmond Hill" with the Adamses, Langdon, Dalton, Gerry, Trumbull, T. Foster, Strong, Jefferson, and John Trumbull (the painter).

JULY 1790 UNDATED

Letter from New York

The temporary and permanent residence of Congress is at length agreed upon—the former at Philadelphia, and the latter on the Potomak. Thus one great cause of delay in public business is now at an end; and it is probable that an adjournment will take place by the 1st of August. What will be the consequences of the law fixing the permanent seat of government so far south as the Potomak can only be conjectured; but some in the minority, as is usually the case when measures go against their wishes, have with freedom predicted, that when the ten years of temporary residence expire, Congress will either repeal or disregard the law altogether.

[Portland, Maine] *Cumberland Gazette*, 26 July. This is probably from a letter written by Thatcher to the newspaper's editor, Thomas B. Wait.

Letter from New York

No doubt you have heard, that the *Echo British sloop of war* lately arrived here. Her dispatches were for some little time kept a profound secret; but you may depend (*as I have good information*) that the British court has offered to open a free navigation of the Mississippi provided we allow them to hold the western posts and enjoy the fur trade—*Also a commercial treaty is now on the carpet.* A Spanish sloop of war has also arrived here a few days past; dispatches of consequence came in her—it has been whispered, that a free navigation of the Mississippi is granted to the Americans, and other important privileges. The court of Spain expects a perfect neutrality on the part of America if a war should take place between Spain and England—*I presume to say that in the present troubles, America will do well to milch the Cow.* I think in the present approaching storm, [*South*] Carolina and Georgia would do well to put their militia on a respectable footing as the *Don* [*the Spanish*] are near neighbours,[1] and already jealous of the growing power of America. I do not believe Congress will pass any bankruptcy law this session; I think it highly necessary for your state, as from what we hear, that the citizens of Carolina are in a deplorable situation—indeed the giving up of so many of your great men has struck us with horror.

[Charleston] *State Gazette of South Carolina*, 26 July; reprinted at Philadelphia, and Augusta and Savannah, Georgia.

[1] Spain gained East and West Florida from England in the Treaty of Paris of 1783.

Letter from Philadelphia

So many, and such curious reports circulate here respecting the removal and residence of Congress, that we know not what to believe; the Bostonians, we hear are for fixing their permanent seat in Heaven, but the majority think the way thither too intricate, the passage too confined, and the journey hazardous: therefore this being negatived, I think you cannot do *better* than remove to Philadelphia, where the *generous principle of Salvation to all men* now prevails.

NYDA, 31 July; reprinted at Exeter, New Hampshire; Worcester and Stockbridge, Massachusetts; Newport, Rhode Island; Norwich, Hartford, and New Haven, Connecticut; Poughkeepsie and New York (*NYMP*, 2 August), New York; Philadelphia; Baltimore; and Edenton, North Carolina.

August 1790

Sunday, 1 August 1790

Edward Carrington to James Madison

Having been for a considerable length of time out of the way of the post Office it is long since I received a letter from you. I am now on my way to Richmond where there are probably several lying for me. My tour upon the business of the Census is compleated except ~~that~~ as to that part which lay over the Allegany in the North West, where provision is made by sending Commissions to be delivered by a Friend for the Counties of Randolph Ohio Harrison & Monongalia. there exists throughout every part of the Country so favorable a disposition upon this subject that I am confident the business will be done with greater accuracy than any person at first expected; so far as political opinions have influence, federalist & antifederalist are alike desirous of a full & fair enumeration, some religious scruples exist with a few old people, but in these cases, the assistants who are truly respectable characters, will be able to come at the Numbers in a variety of ways so as to avoid any inconvenience in either hand.

I rejoice that the business of the residence of the Government is so fortunately got over, not only on account of the subject itself, ~~as~~ but of every other important one which requires, the consideration of Congress, as it must have hung with undue weight on all. I have been for several weeks out of the way of learning any thing worth communicating to you except that in every part of the Country great Crops of Wheat are made, and it is reaped in good order; should the price keep up, our planters will make considerable Strides ~~towards~~ in freeing themselves from Debt. p[*r*]esent me to your Worthy Colleagues.

ALS, Madison Papers, DLC. Written from Fredericksburg, Virginia.

John Dawson to James Madison

I am favoured with your letter of the 24 ulto. with a paper inclosed, for which I beg you'll accept my thanks.

I am sorry that the assumption business is again revived, altho in a less exceptionable shape than it at first appeared to my mind it is hideous in any form; & the zeal & perseverance of the eastern members discover how much that part of the continent is interested in its adoption. whatever will increase the continental debt must be injurious to the agricultural states; because, by the weight of taxes, you either force them to relinquish what reason points out to be their true interest, or they must pay an unequal proportion of the duties imposed for the discharge of that debt. this appears to be an objection against the very principle of the plan, nor can any modification take it away. the opposition of N.C. to the measure has always been unaccountable to me, & on the doctrine of chances it may be better to like a bad thing now than a worse hereafter.

The electioneering business is going on pretty warmly in several of the districts—especially in Caroline &c., where Mr. [*Francis*] Corbin has made uncommon exertions & many bows in opposition to Mr. Page. These aided by strong grogg & roasted piggs have had their weight, & if Mr. Page does not hurry in I realy believe that he will be left out—this you'll be so kind as to communicate to him. Docr. [*Arthur*] Lee opposes his namesake & kindsman—but I cant say with what prospect of success—Mr. Griffin's vote for receiving the old paper money at 75. for one is said to have done his business, & ensured Colo. [*Benjamin*] Harrison's election; & a quondam Parson will probably supply the place of Parker—We have not yet heard who is elected in the room of Colo. Bland, altho the election was on monday last.

If the three gentlemen, who have acted as commrs. [*for settling accounts between the states*] have done their duty I presume that they will be continued by the President; but as my name is now before him it must take its chance; especially as the Govr. [*Beverley Randolph*] & several other gentlemen have written to him on the subject—Shoud any new person be appointed, ~~the~~ & the state of the claims of Virga. does not form an objection. their assistance & yours will authorise an expectation that the application will not be unsuccessful.

I presume that you will have risen by the time you receive this letter, & that soon we shall have the pleasure of seeing you in Virga.

ALS, Madison Papers, DLC. Postmarked Fredericksburg, Virginia; franked.

Benjamin Goodhue to Stephen Goodhue

You must have hear'd before this of our finishing the funding bussines and happy am I that we have got through so troublesome a bussines—what remains is to pass a bill for encreasing the revenue and I understand the senate have been consulting some days on the subject, and mean to have some increase on impost and reserve the excise for a future session—I expect we shall be up this week or some time next, as soon as the above bill is through they will adjourn I hear they propose encreasing the duty on Salt to 12 cents, ***

ALS, Goodhue Papers, MSaE. Addressed to Salem, Massachusetts; franked; postmarked. The omitted text relates to their private commercial ventures, which are also the subject of an enclosed letter.

Thomas Hartley to Jasper Yeates

I date this Letter again from New York—you will say the Man is mad—why does he stay there—The Answer is he could not get away.

In solid Earnest the last week has been of immense Importance to this Country—The funding Bill has passed. not altogether to my wishes—but it was the best that could be obtained.

The ways and Means Bill [*HR-83*] is now before the Senate, and probably will be returned to us to Morrow. I understand (for there has been a Committee of both Houses) that no material Alterations will be made.

Ample Provision is in that Bill for paying the Debts of the union—and that the State Debts are assumed I believe they will not insist upon full Provision being made this Session—Indeed I had this Hint yesterday from Mr. Izard who is deeply interested.

An attempt will be made to the Residence [*Act*] within a few Days just before we rise—but I have some Condfidence—& I really believe we shall defeat our Enemies.

Do excuse me to my Friends as well as my Enemies—tho' I believe I have not many of the latter or at least I am not concious of deserving much Enmity from the world.

ALS, Yeates Papers, PHi. Addressed to Lancaster, Pennsylvania; franked; postmarked 2 August.

Robert Morris to Mary Morris

Sorry I am my Dear Molly to date a letter from this City in the Month of August, but so it is, and here we are, and here we must continue for another Week in order to finish the business of the Session with any tollerable degree of Reputation, therefore I shall expect to receive another letter from you before my Return home notwithstanding what you say on that point in your affectionate Epistle of the 29th. of July, Your letters afford me more pleasure & satisfaction than all the rest that I receive, and indeed more than I enjoy from any other Source. The litterary intercourse of those who are truely and Sincerely attached. to each other by Esteem Friendship and Affection is a never failing source of delight, the Receipt of a letter raises the Spirits and the reading of it Communicates Feelings similar to those under which it was written. If our Friend writes in good Spirits we enjoy them also, if otherwise we feel the Sympathy of misfortune, woe or Misery as the case may be. I am led accidentally into these Reflections, or else they are brought on by my present frame of Mind which is disturbed under the impression of some disputes with the Auditor that prevents the Closing of my Accounts with the Public[1] so far as depends on him for after he has done his part I have to go over them again with the Comptroller, but in the mean time the Auditor (who is a good Officer & a Sensible Man, but was not bred a Merchant) has taken up some Ideas that operate much against my Claims and being tenacious of his Opinions he gives me trouble & causes delay, Even after I have thought a disputed point was settled & done with it is brought up again & again untill I become so fretted and vexed as to be obliged to quit for a time to prevent me from giving Vent to improper expressions which as yet I have not been guilty off, indeed my Esteem for this Gentn. prevents it, for altho He wounds me, His intentions are pure and He desires to do justice to the Public & to me and all others as far as I can See, I am every day with him & still hope to finish with Him at least before I leave this.

This Moment I recive yours of the 29th by Mr. [*James*] Wilson who Sent his Servant with Toms [*Morris*] Bundle and I have Requested him to come & Breakfast with me which He will do and I shall soon have an opportunity to enquire what is passing in Philadelphia. I do not wonder that You grow impatient at my detention here, it is however flattering that you are So, and since I cannot help it, the best thing to be done is to indulge the agreable Sensations which that expression of your impatience gives rise to.

***

Tom is not Returned from Albany, his Bundle shall be delivered when he does come.

David Randolph (Polly[*'s*] David) is here and will either come to Philada. with or before me He wants to see the Hills.[2] Mr. [*William*] Constable & all his Family are gone to Philipsburg [*New York*] so that I am alone [*James*] La Caze & I have agreed to seek a dinner out of Town—perhaps Mr. Wilson will join us and may be Mr. Fitzsimmons Clymer & [*Samuel*] Meredith for I think the Pensylvanians are not so often engaged to dinners as they used to be.

I intend to ask the President & Mrs. [*Martha*] Washington to take their Quarters at our House as they pass through Philada. on the Way to Mount Vernon, but whether they will accept ~~or not~~ is very doubtfull I rather Suppose not, but if they do, I am Sure it will give you pleasure to Receive &

entertain them, as it will me—After writing the foregoing Mr. Wilson came & We have breakfasted together, He tells me that preparations for The President & for Congress are not pressed on with that Vigor & Spirit. we expected however He gives a satisfactory Reason in favr. of present delay and I hope that every thing will be done that can be reasonably expected of our State & City.

Mr. Edmd. Randolph is also here I dined in Company with him at Colo. Griffin's on Friday. He is much pleased with Mr. Dunlap[3] & also with his House.

I wish every body that are to fix in Philada. in Consequence of the Removal of Congress may be equally pleased.

Fare you Well my Dear untill we Meet & I devoutly join you in praying that we may soon meet, not to part again during Life for where you are there is my Heart & Happiness.

P. S.

I believe Mr. Clymer is gone Home, Mr. Wilson thinks He met him in the Stage, I wish He had stayed to the end of the Session.

ALS, Morris Papers, CSmH. Addressed to Philadelphia. The omitted text discusses family friends.

---

[1] When the former board of treasury's authority ceased in 1789, Auditor of the Treasury Nicholas Eveleigh and Comptroller Oliver Wolcott, Jr. assumed direction over the settlement of Morris's unadjusted accounts as chairman of the Continental Congress's secret committees on trade and secret correspondence (1775–77). For background on this and on Congress's reexamination of Morris's accounts as superintendent of finance from 1781 to 1784, which was being conducted simultaneously, see *DHFFC* 8:663–75.

[2] "The Hills" was a country estate acquired by Morris in 1770, located on the Schuylkill River in present-day Fairmount Park, Philadelphia.

[3] Randolph stopped in Philadelphia en route to New York in mid July, by which time he would have been aware of the passage of the Residence Act and the need to arrange accommodations for himself for the third session. In 1789 the publisher John Dunlap bought the entire block between Eleventh and Twelfth streets, on the south side of Market, and built a house that he rented to Randolph in 1790–92 (*PTJ* 17:211; Henry A. Boorse, "Barralet's: 'The Dunlap House, 1807,' and its Associations," *PMHB* 99:[April 1975]:131–55).

William Paterson to Euphemia Paterson

Mr. Cole called on me this Morning, and informed me, that you were well—I suppose Cornelia [*Paterson*] has returned by this Time, and hope that the Jaunt may prove useful to her—Congress will rise towards the latter End of the Week; but I am notwithstanding apprehensive, that the Senate will be obliged to continue longer owing [*to*] the Treaty now on Foot between the [*Creek*] Indians and the United States—[*Alexander*] McGillvary has been indisposed for several Days, which has of Course obstructed the Progress of the Treaty. Mr. [*Senator*] & Mrs. Walker will pass a few Days with you on their Return to Virginia.

***

If you want any Articles from this Place, please to let me know in a Day or two.

Colo. [*John*] Bayard, at the Request of some Gent. at Brunswick and in West Jersey, spoke to me about being set up for the Government of New Jersey.[1] Several Gent. in East Jersey, and particularly Judge [*John*] Chetwood, have also addressed me on the same Subject. The Answer I gave was, that I would do whatever my Friends thought I ought to do—Publick Life has always been disagreeable to me; I would much rather pursue the Line of my Profession than be placed in any official Station, especially if it should be an high and important one. I suppose there will be several Competitors for the Office, and I really do not want to enter into the List; it will create Strife and Contention, to which my Soul is utterly opposed—I hope, that the Legislature, when they meet, will turn their Attention to some Person better qualified to fill the Office than I am, and to whom it will be more convenient and acceptable.

The Congress will meet at Philada. some Time in December; much important Business will be laid over. The next Session will *complete the System of Finance*; and I hope give Stability and Efficacy to the Government, and shape it's future Progress and Operations. Much remains to be done; new Sources of Revenue are to be opened and applied to the Support of national Credit, and the honorable Fulfilment of Contracts. We are laying the Foundation of a great Empire; the Prospect widens and brightens as we proceed; and to every enlarged Mind must give the highest Pleasure.

ALS, Paterson Papers, NjR. Place to which addressed not indicated. The omitted text relates to household management.

[1] William Livingston, governor of New Jersey since 1776, had died on 25 July.

William Smith (Md.) to Otho H. Williams

A few days past, I had the pleasure of receiving your letters dated the 3d. & 7th ulto., *at the Warm & Sweet Springs* [*Virginia*], & of hearing you were all well. Mr. Dell, I am informed reports, that, you & Peggy, are perfectly restored to good health & Spirits; These good effects, I presume are not to be altogether attributed to the Waters, but rather to the pure air of those high mountains wh. you describe.[1]

I wrote you some time ago, that the permanent residence of Congress, was fixed by Law, on the Banks of Potowmac, betwixt the Eastern branch,

& mouth of Canogocheauge, *at the Option of the President,* Since which, a law has passed both houses for funding the Public debt, in which is included 21,500,000 Drs. of What is commonly called the State debts. This assumption tis said is given, in consequence of a bargain for the temporary & permanent residence, which produced a coalition of two or three different parties, & *interests.*

A new collection law [*HR-82*] has passed, providing for many of the inconveniences of the first; it is very long & minute. I can therefore only say at present, that so far as it immediately concerns your interest, The commissions, for collecting are raised to, *one* ℔ *Cent.* the fees of enterance and clearance, I believe are the same as heretofore, & to be divided betwixt the Collr. & Naval officer the Collr. to hire offices &ca. & the Naval officer to pay one third of Office rent, Stationary &ca.—I expect the Session will close the last of this, or begining of next week, you will no doubt agree with me in opininion, that it has proved much too long, for the Services rendered to the public; I am most heartily tired of my Situation & wish to be at home, where I hope to meet all my children, & friends, *early in Septemr.*, in good health & Spirits.

***

We have no certain information, on the Subject of War, *between Great Britain & Spain,* the accots. are various from different ports in Europe, some say the dispute is Settled & the Spaniard has agreed to pay an indemnification, for the Captures she [*h*]as made, and a Sum of money to defray the expences, incured by the British, in fitting out her fleets &ca. whilst other accots. Say hostilleties are commenced—however, on the whole, it is generaly expected here, a peace will take place.

ALS, Williams Papers, MdHi. Addressed to "the Warm or Sweet Springs," Virginia. The omitted text discusses family health and rumors of bankruptcy by over extended wheat exporters.

---

[1] Williams and his family were at the medicinal Sweet Springs, Virginia, for health reasons, from early June until their return to Baltimore on 25 September (Williams to Henry Knox, 26 September 1790, Knox Papers, Gilder Lehrman Collection, NHi). The family at this time included Margaret ("Peggy," d. 1842), Smith's daughter and Williams's sister-in-law, who would marry Baltimore merchant Robert Smith (1757–1842) on 7 December 1790.

James Sullivan to George Thatcher

The last evenings post gave me an opportunity of reading your favour of the 27th Ult. in answer to mine of the 18th. I readily own that I was in "a singular state of mind," when I wrote it for I viewed Congress as about to rise without making any provision for the Creditors of the Nation, or without affecting those great measures which appear to me to be necessary to our national Existence. I considered them as other people did, as having set since the Constitution took place for thirteen months to very little purpose but since you are in a fair way of answering the expectations of the people & am releived and of course shall recover from *my singular State of mind.* When Hamiltons plan came out it was nearly treason in this part of the union to raise an objection to it, and it was criminal to acknowledge that we did not understand it. but there seems now to be no feature of it remaining.

You write with great address & propriety upon the uncertainty and indeterminate meaning of the words Justice Virtue & Integrity, and I am quite convinced that they have ~~not~~ been rendered very vauge in their use amongst men, but it does not follow that these principles do not exist; Truth and reason Exist, but yet there are more who apply them to falshood and folly a man may think that he acts according to truth Justice &c. and may be mistaken.

I beleive no one doubts but that the Jarring members on each side of the questions ~~of~~ which have been agitated in your assembly are honest men, but it is very uncommon that a small Majority should decide every question of every kind. Some men doubt whether the nature of business admits of questions being so frequently determined in this way.

I have heard no particular censure on the members from this State. it is generally agreed that many Speeches are calculated for the Gallery and the Gazette. indeed some of them appear to me to be a Satire upon Congress, and upon the Country. When Cicero declaimed to 20,000 of the rude Citizens of the roman republic it was necessary that he should be very minute ~~in~~ in his statements that he Should detail the first rudiments of civil policy and teach them the nature & propriety of Government but it would have been a waste of Time and an imposition for him to have done it in the Senate.

The greatest complaint arises from an apprehension that there is not a temper of compromise Exhibited in questions which might be Settled in either way proposed consistantly with the public good but this is not a charge particularly against the Representatives of Massachusetts.

You say you are prepared for death natural or political, that the one will introduce you to Joys celestial, and the other to Joys domestic. You are indeed then very happy & I congratulate you but I do not wish you to try the Experiment on either at present.

It appears to some who are said to be men of much understanding that some of your warmest debates have been on questions which might have been indifferently Settled in either way as if the question was whether the standard of measure called a Yard should be thirty or thirty six Inches but I have not discovered this myself. I am glad for my Countrys sake that you are in a likely way to affect important measures.

ALS, Chamberlain Collection, MB. Written from Boston.

Alexander White to Horatio Gates

The enclosed was just handed to me by a Servant of General Armstrong[1]—I have only time to congratulate you and my Country on the conclusion of two important Objects—The fixing the Seat of Goverment, and providing for the Debts of the Union—The latter is not on principles intirely to my wish, but it is the best that could be obtained, and to have risen without accomplishing that business might have given a shock to the Union.
P. S.
I hope the present Week will put an end to the Session.

ALS, Gates Papers, NHi. Place to which addressed not indicated.

[1] John Armstrong, Jr. to Horatio Gates, 31 July, above.

Letter from New York

I hope to have the pleasure of taking you by the hand in a few days, as we have now little business to do but the bill for raising an additional revenue, and that we expect from the Senate tomorrow. You have no doubt seen our plan for funding the debt, which tho' on the face of it may appear somewhat complex, is upon the whole a good provision. {Some of our public creditors will probably find fault with our conduct, but the good effects of the system already appear. I am told public securities are now selling here at 13/4, and real estates it is expected will rise in proportion.}[1] The whole sum to be raised annually is less than 3,400,000 dollars, which can be done by adding a few pence per lb. on tea and something more on spirits and wine, not a shilling on lands or houses; on the contrary, we have rendered it unnecessary for the states to lay any such taxes, as we have taken the burthen of debt off their shoulders. Pennsylvania besides being relieved from two millions of dollars of her debt, will be entitled to receive from the treasury of the United States interest on three millions, which may be employed in improving her roads and navigation, while the property of her citizens in the funds to the amount of 7 or 8 millions will be greatly enhanced. Add to this the benefit that will accrue from the temporary residence of Congress, &c. and you must allow that our time here however usefully [*uselessly?*] employed as to ourselves, has not been so as it respects the State.

FG, 5 August; reprinted at Winchester and Richmond, Virginia. The editors believe this is all or part of the letter from Fitzsimons to Benjamin Rush listed in *Parke-Bernet Catalog* 499(1944):item 120 and described as "pertains to civic affairs; also relates to the removal of the seat of government from New York to Philadelphia." The present location of the ALS is unknown; it was most recently listed for sale in *The Collector* 64(1951):item W816.

[1] According to the quotation in *The Collector*, the manuscript version of the text in wavy brackets reads, "I expect the Execrations of some of our Avaricious public Creditors—but the good Effects of our System already appears—Public Securitys are now Selling here at 13/4 in the £—and before the End of the Year I have no doubt will be at 16/6."

Original Communications

CONGRESS, it is thought, will adjourn in all next week. The Senate have several Bills to decide upon, which may soon be dispatched. It is expected the WAYS and MEANS [*HR-83*] will be sent down to-morrow; and as there has been a conference, it is supposed the Amendments of the *Senate* will meet with no opposition.

The motion to bring in a Bill or Resolution to suspend going to *Philadelphia* for two years—will probably be renewed. The prospect of success is, however, very faint.

The FUNDING-BILL being passed, it should seem, that the *Ways and Means* should face [i.e., *cover*] it.

The ASSUMPTION being obtained, the way is plain before the *General Government*; for of all rivalries, that of Revenue is the most to be deprecated—it cannot be exercised by two Powers, in the same place, without intolerable oppression to the people—and the final subversion of their freedom, or the destruction of the Constitution—which is the same thing.

The *Assumption* may be justly considered as a glorious federal achievement—and will in the issue develope the *General Government* to the view of the people in such manner as to convince them, that for those great purposes of political association—security of person and property—freedom and publick happiness, they must look to the LEGISLATURE OF THE UNION.

[Boston] *Columbian Centinel*, 7 August; reprinted at Portland, Maine.

OTHER DOCUMENTS

Thomas Fitzsimons to Benjamin Rush. See Letter from New York, under this date, above.

Thomas Jefferson to William Blount. FC, PCC, item 120, v. 4:177, DNA. For the full text, see *PTJ* 17:292.

Having been informed by Williamson that Blount does not have copies of the acts establishing the western territories, Jefferson encloses the Northwest Ordinance of 1787, the Northwest Territory Act [HR-14], and the Southern Territory Act.

Winthrop Sargent to George Washington. ALS, Territorial Papers, State Department Records, Record Group 59, DNA. For the full text, see *PGW* 6:172–73.

Additional background to Sargent's petition to Congress; see *DHFFC* 8:134–37.

Daniel Hiester, Account Book. PRHi. (The date is supplied by the editors based on the assumption that it was a weekend.)

Shared a hack with Morris and Fitzsimons and dined at Gray's.

John Jeffries, Diary. Jeffries Family Papers, MHi.

Breakfasted with Trumbull, Tench Coxe, and John Trumbull; accompanied the latter "to the Conference Room, Federal Hall, where he is Painting, the President for the City—a very fine Picture whole length as large as the life, attitude of leaning on the left holster of his Horse—the small Picture at present the best likeness—each of them very perfect in his great characteristical Trait of a cool busily occupied reflecting mind—together with a most complacent, peculiarly commanding dignity—saw there likewise ~~a~~ very fine Pictures of the Pre[*se*]nt King & Queen of France [*Louis XVI and Marie Antoinette*], delicate Pictures, with superb & exquisitely finished drapery, and both verry good likenesses, particularly that beautiful part of the Queen, her inchanting Arm & hand—indeed her whole likeness very like as I saw her in January. Febuary March 1785—& etc. the King"; dined with the Gerrys; met Burke and Coles.

Monday, 2 August 1790

Abigail Adams to Cotton Tufts

*** Congress are not yet up, they hope to rise in a few days. you have no doubt seen the funding, & Assumption Bills ~~the last~~ they are not what was wisht by many members of each House, but the danger of finally loosing the Bill was so great, that it was consented to by both houses as an anchor that it would not do to quit, least the whole should go to Ship wreck the my dear sir August 2d. 1790 N york

Commencement being finishd. some of your cares for my family will be lessned. I esteem it amongst my blessings that my young family have all past through Colledge with so much reputation, and that in scenes strewd thick with dangers, they have escaped so well. I hope their future progress through Life may be equally pure. I feel myself indebted to many of my friends for the kind care they have excercised towards my sons in the almost constant absence of their parents. and particularly so to you sir whose attention has been truly parental I hope they will ever mantain towards you a gratefull sense of your kindness.

Mr Adams proposes that Thomas should come on here as soon as may be. I hardly know what studies to advise him too, for some time he appeard inclined to merchandize. but without stock, there is but a poor prospect, and I do not think that scholors ever make very good merchants, Mr Adams remitted a bill of 500 dollars to you which I presume was duly received. but immediatly after this he heard of the arrival of 2 casks of wine which we suppose will more than swallow up the surplus. his intention is to send on 40 or 50 dollars more by Dr Jeffries who will leave this City in the course of the week. Congress are not yet up. they hope to rise in a few days. you have no doubt seen the funding & assumption bills they are not what was wisht by many members of each House, but the danger of finally loosing the Bill was so great, that it was consented to by both Houses as an anchor that it would not do to quit, least the whole should go to shipwreck

Abigail Adams to Cotton Tufts, 2 August, ALS, p. 2. Abigail's letters to Tufts, who managed the Adams family's finances in Massachusetts, furnish congressional news from someone "in the know." This excerpt discusses members' attitudes toward the Funding Act, as well as Abigail's own investments in Continental securities. (Courtesy of the New-York Historical Society.)

Abigail Adams, by Mather Brown, 1761–1831, oil on canvas, 1785. Brown painted this portrait of Abigail shortly after John Adams assumed his duties as ambassador to Great Britain. Their daughter Abigail ("Nabby"), who resided with them in London, considered it an accurate likeness (Andrew Oliver, *Portraits of John and Abigail Adams* [Cambridge, Mass., 1967]), pp. 46–54). (Courtesy of the Fenimore Art Museum, Cooperstown, New York.)

funding the whole debt at once, at an interest of four pr. cent and placing the indents upon the same footing, was what was most earnestly wishd for by many, but the states who were opposed to it Clamourd so loudly that the best, is done that could be affected the House are now upon ways and means designing that the first Quarters interest shall be paid on the first of April next, I will thank you sir to let me know by my son Thomas the amount of the little interst I have in your Hands and what proportion is State, & what continental. and whether you cannot find it in your own Name, giving me some memorandum that you hold in your Hands Such an interest belonging to me which may serve in case of accident.

The wine which I suppose is in Mr. [*John*] Codmans store we should be glad to have sent round by [*Capt. Thomas*] Barnard our present intention being, not to remove this winter, but when Congress set Mr. Adams designs to go & tarry only during the session, which he flatters himself, will be a short one.

***

ALS, Miscellaneous Manuscripts, NHi. Place to which addressed not indicated. The omitted text relates to family news and finances.

Obadiah Brown to Theodore Foster

I am requested by the River Machine Company of this Town, to advise you of the unprosperous State of our Affairs, and to solicit the Favr. of your Attention, in procuring us the Earliest releif from the Congress of the United States.

You well know, that a Number of the Merchants of this Town, finding that the [*Providence*] River Shoaled perceivably every year or two; and that it had been several feet deeper within the memory of man than at present; procured a Charter from the Legislature of this State, incorporating them into a Body politic, for the purpose of deepning the River; and were allowed by them a Revenue of two Cents ℔ Ton, for all Vessels entering the harbour, of Sixty tons and above.

The Company after advancing a Considerable Sum, in procuring the Machine & Scow to be Built, find that from their otherwise agreeable agreeable Situation in the Union, their whole design lays dormant: and must be intirely frustrated unless Congress do Confirm their Charter, or grant then one Simular.

There are now three horses Subsisted at the Companies Expence.[1]

The Machine and Scow now lay Idle in this very wormy river, while this and the month following, are the Extent of the Season for Working: the whole Fall Season afterwards being generally too boisterous.

The Company were in hopes of having a a Number more of Subscribers, but the present State of our affairs, as it has already abated the Ardency of the first promoters, will if it Continues put an Effectual Bar to the Increasing the Number of Shares in the Company; and of Course to the Increase of Stock, which is much wanted particularly for Building more Scows.

These, and more Inconveniencies we suffer, wholly for the want of a Confirmation of the Revenue by Congress.

You are aware that all large Vessels are obliged to unload part of their Cargo at the Crook, which in the Icy Season is dangerous: the Scows sometimes taking in Water to the Damage of the Goods, and sometimes Sinking with the whole property on Board.

That there are a greater Number of Vessels belonging to this port, than belong to New York.

And that it is a place of more Navigation, than any of its Size in the Union.

Perhaps it need not be mentioned to you, that this port will probably afford a greater Revenue than this whole State besides, and it is really no Chimera, that the Exertions of Art Excepted the time is fast approaching when Providence can be a port no longer.

The Company when met this afternoon, was very desirous of hearing what was done, & what it was likely might be done for their Assistance.

Their Letter to you, and your Colleague, ~~inclosing~~ inclosing an official Copy of their Charter; they had not much doubt was received.

A Line from you, or even an Intimation through some of your Friends, would greatly oblige.

Your Early attention to this Affair, will greatly increase the Regard of the members of the River Machine Company.

ALS, Foster Papers, RHi. Written from Providence, Rhode Island. Brown signed as "Secy. to the Company."

---

[1] Horses powered the dredging machines which were in operation by 1792 but accomplished little by the time operations ceased permanently in 1796 (Joseph S. Davis, *Essays in the Earlier History of American Corporations* [1917; reprint, 2 vols., New York, 1965], 2:284–85).

Michael Jenifer Stone to Walter Stone

Your Letter of July 21st. Came to Hand with the inclosure just now. I shall take Special care of it—I believe the British Packett has not Sailed—But it appears to me that it would go Safest by an American vessell—I will however send it that via that will be Safest.

I presume all our Friends are well.

If the people of Baltimore would be pleased to Exercise their reason they would not be displeased with any of the representatives But if they have even more Candour they Cannot blame me—Because I gave Baltimore Every fair Chance. And always voted for it—untill by the proceedings of the Senate that there was no chance of its Success. If those *who have been on the Spot* will tell the truth they must own "That Baltimore could not have succeeded unless the Maryland Delegates had *Bargained* for 4 years residence in N. Yorke and the Assumpsion." This Bargain was *offered thro' one of our* representatives and rejected by all the rest—Mr. Smith was the Gentleman who tho' he voted against the assumption was willing to have adopted it if Baltimore could by that means have gained the Seat of Congress—In the whole business I have been cool and impartial—and a reveiw of my Conduct in Every Step gives me pleasure.
[*P. S.*] We shall probably get up in 10 Days—I believe I shall not come Directly Home but travel somewhere for confirmation of my Health.

ALS, Stone Family Papers, DLC. Place to which addressed not indicated.

William Tyler to Theodore Foster

I had the Honour of Peruseing your last Letter to His Excellency Our Governor [*Arthur Fenner*], as [*lined out*] well as all Your former Letter to him & Judge [*Ebenezer*] Thompson, & Should have wrote to you before this, could I have given you any more inteligence concerning matters &c. &c., than you Recd. in their Several Answers, as you well know our Sentiments Unite upon the true Republican Principles.

I have the Hapiness to inform you that I have Conversed with many Leading Carricters in our Party respecting your re-Election as a Senator who, one & All say, they are Perfectly Satisfyed, and approve of your Conduct, & will Exert themselves in ~~in~~ your Intrest, So long as you remain a friend to the Rights of the People at Large, and it is my Candid Oppinion, by the Exertions of your Friends, *your* ~~Ellection~~ *Election will be sure?* [*lined out*] You may Depend on Every Exertion in my power in your favour, and I shall be as Anxious ~~for~~ to succeed as I was in your first Appointment, ~~&~~ so that you may Depend on My Might.

I Observed you mentioned in your last Letter to His Excellency, [*lined out*] "Now the Assumption had taken place, there would be an Excise & of Course be Several Vacancies for Appointments and it would be in your Power to Serve any of his frie[*n*]ds." I include myself in that number, & hope you do also, & hope you think at least I am one of your fast frieds, tho I am not mentioned particular, & Judge Thompson is, the Judge is Provided for, I am not, half the Exertions I should think mad[*e*] by you & my Friend Genl.

Stanton that [*lined out*] you made for Judge Thompson (which god knows I am happy in his Appointment) will secure me of Success, but However you are on the ground, & know the Recommendations, that I have had from the Govr. &c. also from Govr. [*Jabez*] Bowen to the President, &c. &c.

Sir if you will but be kind enough to Exert your self half so much in secureing an appointment for me, That I have & shall for you, I make no dout of Success.

[*lined out*] Sir youl Pardon my importunity [*lined out*] & anxiety, when you Reflect of my being out of Business and a Family to Support, a Son at Colledge, & business Much Duller than when you left here.

Sir Perhaps you have not heard who is in Nomination for a Fœderal Representative to Congress Job Comstock Esqr. is Much in Vouge in our Party, it Mortifies the Great Brige to the Soul, which Spurs us on & from the best information I can gett from Different Quarters of the State, he will Succeed.[1]

Sir Please to give My Best Respects to Genl. Stanton & beg his Assistance in any Appointment you Shall think Proper to ask for me I saw Mrs. [*Lydia Fenner*] Foster & Datia [*daughter Theodosia*] yesterday & they were very well but want to see you Very Much.

ALS, Foster Papers, RHi. Written from Providence, Rhode Island; received from Captain John Tillinghast in the lobby of the Senate chamber in New York 9 August.

[1] For more on Rhode Island's first federal election, see *DHFFE* 4:436–46.

Paine Wingate to Timothy Pickering

I am told by Major [*Samuel*] Hodgdon that you are expected at Philadelphia this week, and as in the course of the week it is probable that Congress will adjourn; I have now improved the opportunity of writing to you before I shall leave this city. We have at last finished (I trust) two tedious subjects, those of Residence & the funding system—Whether well done or not time must determine. There may perhaps yet be an attempt to keep congress here two years longer; but I think with very little prospect of obtaining it. I expect, if nothing extraordinary should prevent, to be at Philadelphia next December and should be very happy to have the opportunity of seeing you there, more especially if you had some agreeable appointment in the government & was removed there. It is said that Mr. [*Samuel*] Osgood will resign his place when Congress shall remove. If his place would be agreeable to you it is my wish you might obtain it—As the post office bill is only continued until the next session of congress I suppose no new Post master general will be now appointed but if he should resign (which I hardly think likely) before the next meeting of congress the President would appoint one to succeed. I should think the business might not be disagreeable though the emoluments are not very tempting. I think you will probably see the President at Philadelphia & may it not be worth while for you to let him know your sentiments respecting the appointment. I know that it is not your disposition to court favours or to urge any thing from interested views; but you will judge what is proper and act accordingly. It would be a gratification to many of your friends to see you in office. The assumption of the state debts & the terms of funding you will be informed of in the news papers; I shall therefore add no information respecting them. It is proposed to lay some additional duties of impost & it is likely there will be no excise take place in the present session. In that case a few days more will close our business. I have not heard from my family since the middle of July; nor have I had any late letters from Salem [*Massachusetts*] I expect to meet my wife [*Eunice Pickering Wingate*] there on my return & hope then to see all our friends well. If you should have an opportunity of writing to me by the middle of this week I should be very glad to hear from you. I do not recollect any thing remarkable to mention to you.

ALS, Pickering Papers, MHi. Addressed to Wilkes-Barre, Pennsylvania; franked.

Newspaper Article

A Correspondent cannot but observe the many fulsome remarks in favor of "Mr. Am*s, a Representative from the District," in the [*Columbian*] Centinel. Whether the Editor feels himself under peculiar *obligations* to this gentleman, it is not necessary to say; but unless he does, it must appear such a gross reflection on the other Members from this State, as cannot be accounted for. It would puzzle the Editor or any other person to say wherein "Mr. Am*s, a Representative from this District," has excell'd his colleagues; unless lengthy, tedious speeches fraught with sentiments that which had *over and over* been advanc'd by Mr. G—r—y, a Representative from the district of Middlesex: and others; together with tautologies; redundancies—unmeaning figures—undigested ideas—are consider'd as the criterion of diction and sentiment. Mr. Am*s, Representative as aforesaid, has made a figure in this line, but for any *original plans* or *systemized measures* the district of S—ff—lk, cannot claim pre eminence, from their member—This district it is true has the mortification of originating a motion which was contrary to the express declaration of the state Convention respecting representation;[1] this must be acknowledged an *enterprizing stroke*, for a Representative to endeavour to carry a vote in opposition to the most serious injunctions of his constituents. If therefore this gentleman is to be PUFF'D, at the expence of every other member, let the Centinel inform the PEOPLE of this State, Why Mr Am*s, Representative as aforesaid DARE make a proposition to supercede a measure which he knew was SOLEMNLY BINDING on him to maintain. The motion alluded to is that made by Mr. Am*s for one Representative for 40,000 instead of 30,000 *inhabitants*; this last number is sacredly imposed on our members to get effected, and yet this man who is the idol of a *party*, endeavour'd to carry a point in violation of such instructions. These measures may possibly please certain individuals in office, who care for nothing but their own emolument, but the free citizens of this commonwealth will look well to their own privileges, however disgusting it may be, to those who are within the focus of public favour.

Boston Gazette, 2 August.

[1] The Massachusetts ratifying convention proposed an amendment to the Constitution guaranteeing one Representative for every thirty thousand persons. On 14 August 1789, having failed in an attempt to raise the number to forty thousand during the debate on Amendments to the Constitution, Ames proposed a complicated alternative that would gradually raise the number to fifty thousand. See *DHFFC* 4:14, 27.

OTHER DOCUMENTS

Samuel Hopkins to Roger Sherman. ALS, Roger Sherman Addition, CtY. Written from Newport, Rhode Island.

Continues their discussion on self love and Christian morality.

John Irwin to William Paterson. ALS, Paterson Papers, DLC. Written from Philadelphia; franked; postmarked 3 August. Irwin, the son of Paterson's sister Frances, emigrated from Ireland to Pennsylvania in 1762.

Thanks Paterson for paying two of Irwin's accounts which adds to his "numerous obligations" to Paterson who has been his "best—indeed I might say my only friend" since his father departed; encloses letter for forwarding to Gen. Irwin (William Irvine); asks advice on where to set up medical practice; it is generally believed in Philadelphia that Paterson will succeed William Livingston as governor of New Jersey.

Abishai Thomas to John Gray Blount. ALS, John Gray Blount Papers, Nc-Ar. Addressed to Washington, North Carolina; postmarked.

The Funding Act will probably be presented to the President today.

Thomas Tudor Tucker to St. George Tucker. ALS, Tucker-Coleman Papers, ViW. Place to which addressed not indicated.

Has made enquiries on rates of exchange for St. George; "We expect to adjourn in the course of a few days"; may stay another two weeks, or a few days, rather than leave the (college) accounts of "the Boys" (John Randolph "of Roanoke" and Theodorick Bland Randolph) unsettled.

Paine Wingate to Samuel Hodgdon. ALS, Pickering Papers, MHi. Addressed to Philadelphia; franked; postmarked 4 August; received 14 August. For the full text, see *Wingate* 2:376–77.

Acknowledges Hodgdon's letter of 13 July; encloses letter to Timothy Pickering; Congress has finished "the great businesses" of residence, assumption, and funding; expects they will adjourn in a few days; refers to newspapers for details; wishes success to Hodgdon's efforts for (Pickering's) appointment (as postmaster general); "I shall be ready to add my endeavours"; hopes to see Hodgdon in Philadelphia in December.

Daniel Hiester, Account Book. PRHi.

Attended the last "Monday Club" or Mess Day with the Pennsylvania delegation at Fraunces Tavern.

John Jeffries, Diary. Jeffries Family Papers, MHi.

Strong, A. (?) Foster, and Knox visited; "nothing particular."

Certificate of John Vining. ANS (by Bassett, co-signed by Read), Records of the Supreme Court, DNA. Bassett and Read provided this document to Vining, who filed it in support of his application to be admitted as a counselor to the bar of the Supreme Court on this date. For the full text, see *DHSCUS* 1:545.

Certifies that Vining had practiced law in Delaware since his admission to the bar in 1783.

GUS, 4 August.

Bassett and Vining were admitted as counselors to the Supreme Court of the United States.

TUESDAY, 3 AUGUST 1790

Peter Allaire, Occurrences

Congress have passed the following Tonage Bill, Viz.
All American Built Vessells owned by subjects of the United States to pay Six Cents ℔ Ton.
All American Built Vessells owned in part, or wholly by any other Person or Persons then subjects of the United States Thirty Cents ℔ ton.

All Foreign Vessells owned by Subjects of the United States or Foreigners to pay fifty Cents ℔ ton.

N.B. a Cent is about a half penny Sterling.

[*Alexander*] McGillivray the Indian Cheif of Several of the Southern Tribes of Indians arrived here the 24 Ulto. accompanied by Twenty Nine Kings, Cheifs & head Men of different Nations to fix on the boundaries between them and the United States, they are much caressed and great attention is paid them, when any treaty is formed Your Agent in Canada shall have timely notice that he may Order goods out Accordingly, or remove where he thinks it may be most for the Interest of the concerned.

***

Congress have adjourned to meet next December at Philadelphia, a party was formed and they carried the Question by four, however there will be no difference with Respect to any Engagements, With regard to commerce but what your house will know just as soon as if they remained here, as the same business will be carried on and the Packets Sailing from New York no one can have sooner Intelligence, the post Arriving daily from Philadelphia at this place, and as New York has layd out About 40 thousand pounds in buildings for their Accomodation, they make no doubt of their Returning, Philadelphia having no place fit for their Reception.

Congress proposes adjourning the 6 Instant if they can finish this business, but the place where to meet is again to be debated.

Your favor of the 3d June I have safe in Answer thereto, we are to poor to partake of your Offer nor is it a time *for them* to Enter into disputes with foreign Powers, having almost as much to do as the French national Assembly: we are far from being a Setled Nation at present the Southern Members forming one the Northern Members another party in both Houses, their chief aim is setling the Individual States debts to be paid by the Union—*a mere flea bite* but yet it has occupied their Attention for Months & created great ill will amongst them.

But with your permission I will inform you what I think may be done with certainty—from 5[000] to 7000 Men may be had from the Western Country that would Assist any Nation to take the Floridas from the Spaniards on Condition they the Western Territory should have a free Navigation of the Mississipi.

It is now in your power, (If a War with Spain is Actually begun tho by recent Accounts they have asked Pardon) to bind us in Adamantine Chains of Friendship & Alliance with You—take the Floridas, Open a free Navigation of the Mississipi for the Western Inhabitants, and you bind that Country & its inhabitants for Ever in spite of Congress or all the world, for without the Missisipi, its fruitfullness is useless, a few frigates & 2000 Men would Retake it in three Weeks & if proper means were made use of I would Engage for a Sufficient Number to Assist, those People are not as yet Subject to the Laws of the Union, they are at present a large body of People, governed by local Laws of their own forming, and propose being part of the Union on certain Conditions, as a proof of which they undertake Expiditions against the Indians, destroy them and add their Lands to their possessions, they have drove away two Spanish posts of 30 & 25 Men, & have demanded & Obtained a free Navigation for their produce, this has been done contrary to the Express Orders of Congress, if therefore a proper mode is made use of, which I will communicate If you order it, nothing so Easely done as your Regaining the Floridas, your Answr. to this, must be in the Mercantile Stile, which I shall fully comprehend.

A due consideration of the above, may lead to matters of the greatest Importance to both parties, for they are Men desperate in principal & fortune, and would almost undertake impossibilities to Acquire a few thousand Spanish Dollars.

You may Rest Assured nothing can be done with this Government at present, no Offer would tempt them at present to Enter into a War, nor is the Animosity of the leading Men Yet so intirely forgot against the English as to induce them to join in a War with them, we are a Strange Nation English principals & Roman Ideas, every Man of £100 a year is a Souverain Prince, every Mechanick a Man of an Independant principal, there is no distinction amongst us today Speaker of the Assembly or President of the Senate tomorrow the same Men, one a Carpenter the Other a Grocer, thus we jog on.

***

ALS, Foreign Office 4/7, pp. 569–82, PRO. The omitted text reports on legislation and discusses land grants in Canada. The Occurrences were dispatches written for the British Foreign Office through intermediary Sir George Yonge in England. For more on Allaire's dispatches, see *PTJ* 17:91n.

Richard Henry Lee to Arthur Lee

The enclosed letter sealed with black was this day given to me at the Levy[1] by a Gentn. just arrived from Engd. who said Lord Lansdown [*William Petty, earl of Shelburne*] desired him to deliver it to you—the other letter was given me by I know not whom at present—You desire information how our representatives voted, last year, on the question of instructions—I have enquired, but cannot learn—do you not think however, that in Canvasses like yours,[2] it will be well to apply the Law Maxim—That claim should be founded upon the strength of your own Title not on the weakness of your Adversary's—It seems to me that this will be the most successful method, and certainly the least exceptionable. You will receive enclosed the

Secretarys estimate of the sufficiency of the funds for paying the interest of the foreign & domestic debts if the Ways & Means bill now under consideration passes,[3] which will probably be the case—provision for paying the interest of the 21,500,000 assumed for State debts will not be made until the next Session—The present being to end the last of this, or the middle of next Week.

I have not received any answer yet from you to my last stating the present price of finals & of their interest, and desiring to know your Ultimatum on the subject of selling or funding yours. A Broker told me yesterday that finals now sold, principal for 12/3 and the interest for 7/6 or 8/ I forget which—but then they allowed nothing for interest since the Old Congress ceased to make provision for paying interest—A bad reason, since the present Congress provides for all the interest, but at 3 pr. Cent. only—I have shipt your demy John of french brandy to Mr. [*John*] Brent at Norfolk desiring him to send it to Alexandria to you—I hope to see you in a fortnight.

[*P. S.*] No Spanish War the 8 June, but likely to be.

ALS, American Manuscripts, CSmH. Place to which addressed not indicated.

---

[1] The weekly levee hosted on Tuesday evenings at Lady Temple's, wife of the British consul Sir John Temple.

[2] Arthur Lee was running against R. B. Lee in the second congressional election and sought information on how the incumbent had voted on 15 August 1789 on a proposal to add the people's right to instruct their Representatives to the Amendments to the Constitution under consideration.

[3] Hamilton's estimate was presented to the Senate committee on the Ways and Means Act, of which Lee was chair, on 2 August; see *DHFFC* 6:2053.

William Smith (S.C.) to Gabriel Manigault

I have pleasure in congratulating you on the Assumption, a measure not only beneficial to the U.S. and to So. Car. particularly, but to yourself personally, a circumstance which adds much to the satisfaction I have felt. Although we have not assumed to the full amount of each debt and have not funded the Debt at a full six per cent, yet, considering the very violent opposition to the measure we must be satisfied for the present with what has been done: at the next session in December we shall probably do more.

We shall adjourn in the course of a few days, as soon as we have past a Bill [*Ways and Means Act HR-83*] raising a revenue for the continental debt; this is intended to be by an addition to the impost; the Excise will be reserved for the State debts, the Interest on which will commence 1st Jany. 1792, a year after the other.

AHR 14(1908–9):778–79.

George Thatcher to John Fox

Yours of the 27th. June came to hand in due season.

I am sorry to inform to, that nothing can be done this session touching the Light-House on Portland head—This is owing to the Cession of the Light-houses by the Legislature of Massachusetts not being forwarded to Congress—at this we are much at a loss to know the reason; & began to apprehend the Bill, for that purpose, had never passed into a Law, till Mr. [*Nathaniel*] Gorham, who arrived here on sunday, assured us to the contrary.

The inclosed Bill[1] is now before the Senate; it is their amendment to a Bill sent them by the House some time ago, a copy of which I then transmitted to Captain [*Thomas*] Robison—and if I mistake not, has been published in the Cumberland Gazette.

The one I now send you, I beleive will pass into a Law—perhaps, there may be some few amendments—And as soon as this is thro, Congress will adjourn—I hope by saturday, or monday—The inclosed estimate will afford you some idea of the existing duties—also the proposed increase—And the purposes to which they are to be applied—I ought to observe, there is a mistake of an hundred & fifty thousand Dollars which ought to be added to the amount of the Duties; & will make the whole to 2,770,000 Dollors.

FC, Thatcher Family Papers, MHi.

[1] The Senate's amendatory Ways and Means Act [HR-83], presented and ordered printed on 2 August, and the accompanying estimate which Thatcher also enclosed, are printed in *DHFFC* 6:2045–53.

Newspaper Article

IF the [*Columbian*] Centinel, says a correspondent, does pay the tribute of applause, to the merits of the Hon. Mr. AMES; the Gazette, on the other hand, is continually heaping upon him the most undeserved scurrility and abuse. Now the public will judge, which line of conduct is most deserving applause. It is a pity, when, owing to the unwearied endeavours of the Senators and Representatives of this State, a measure has been brought to a successful issue, which will relieve it from a most oppressive burthen, that illiberal detraction, should be the reward of one, whose exertions to effect that end, have been exceeded by none; and whose independence and industry are the theme of universal applause, at the seat of the general government.

[Boston] *Herald of Freedom*, 3 August. The measure in question was federal assumption of the Revolutionary War debt of the states.

OTHER DOCUMENTS

Samuel Meredith [?], Accounts with Fitzsimons and Clymer. Ms., Meredith Papers, University of Delaware, Newark.

John Montgomery to Benjamin Rush. ALS, Rush Papers, PPL at PHi. Written from Carlisle, Pennsylvania; addressed to Philadelphia.

Two things prejudice voters against Morris's candidacy for governor of Pennsylvania: the supposed arrearage in his unsettled public accounts, and his motion to strike the Susquehannah River in favor of Germantown, Pennsylvania, in the Residence Act (Seat of Government Bill HR-25); "the next Election will be very important"; "if Mr. MaClay woud serve [*again*] I think that you Cant get a better man Mr. Heartly for a Delagate will run high with us and genl. [*William*] Irvine if he will Consent to Same and mr. [*William*] Findly who ~~is~~ are mentioned with you or will you Send the same again that has Sarved you we ought in Justice have three Delagats on this Side of the river Susquhana."

Hugh Williamson to John Gray Blount. ALS, John Gray Blount Papers, Nc-Ar. Addressed to Washington, North Carolina; franked; postmarked 6 August. For the full text, see *Blount* 2:92.

Reports on the profitability of North Carolina certificates; describes effort to sell subscriptions to and publish a map of the state's western lands (Tennessee); believes he could sell no more than eight in New York; "McGillivray is here & lives with the Secretary at War; his Indians at a public House 2 Miles out of Town on the North River. I presume the Treaty [*of New York with the Creeks*] is progressing but know not any particulars. I think Congress will adjourn in 8 days or less from this date. Letters to me ⅌ Consequence from distant Posts will be charged with Postage if they come by Post."

John Jeffries, Diary. Jeffries Family Papers, MHi.

Knox believes that if Jeffries moved to Philadelphia, he could probably expect patronage from the Adamses, Izard, Smith (S.C.), and others.

NYDA, 3 August.

Advertisement for recovery of White's runaway slave, Jim.

Wednesday, 4 August 1790

Gouverneur Morris to Robert Morris

***

Before I close this Letter I must notice what you say respecting the Unhealthiness of New York. You speak so seriously that I suppose you beleive it, and I am not surprized because Circumstances frequently predispose the Mind to adopt a particular Creed. it would however be a little whimsical if Congress should leave the Hudson in the Hope of finding Health on the Susquehanna or Potowmack. Having said thus much, I shall admit that the Climate of New York is less favorable to pulmonary Complaints than that of Philadelphia the orators in Congress therefore will I hope be able to entertain both themselves and their Audience next Session with less Danger to their Lungs And if half a dozen or half a Score of them should be confined by an Intermittent that is no Reason why the Business of the Union should intermit but may in the Course of divine Providence be the Reason of more rapid Progress.

FC:lbk, Gouverneur Morris Papers, DLC. Written from London. The omitted text relates to European investments in R. Morris's Delaware River water works and various land speculations, the sales of which "will certainly be promoted so far as the Distress and Confusion of France and Flanders can promote them."

Louis Guillaume Otto to Comte de Montmorin

Upon arriving yesterday at the public audience of the President of the United States, I was surprised by the First Magistrate's asking me "if I wanted to see the key of the Bastille."[1] One of his secretaries instantly showed me a big key, which had been sent to the American President by the marquis de LaFayette through a young American [*John Rutledge, Jr.*] just arrived from France. I hid my astonishment by making an observation to the President, "that the time had not yet come in America to study the example that he had before him." The Americans who were present looked at the key more or less with indifference. They even looked like they were asking themselves why it had been sent! But the serene forehead of the President indicated that he considered this gift an homage from the French nation. I turned the conversation toward the news brought by the same boat, announcing a perfect peace in the [*French*] Kingdom. The President and all Americans still evince the greatest interest in our revolution and they are convinced that the future of Europe depends on it. It seems that a similarity in political principles would favor and increase the direct links between the two countries, but based on previous parallels, the Americans are wrong when flattering themselves that, under the new regime, trade with the French Antilles will be freer than it has been in the past; however, that is the consequence that they like to draw from the changes that have taken place in France. I can not help but believe that His Majesty's Council had granted to our planters and to the United States all that was possible to grant, and that it had found the right place to stop so as not to injure the commerce and manufactures in the Kingdom. The English Parliament has been much stricter than we regarding this clause, without meeting with the disapproval of the British nation. For a long time it will be impossible to combine the interests of the Kingdom with the pretenses of the free Americans who, as seafarers, enjoy too many advantages to compete with ours and who will soon be visiting the Pacific islands, Nootka Bay, and all the parts of India with as much ease as Europe and the Antilles. Even now, there is a native here from the Society Islands,[2] brought by an American ship whose owners want to establish a trading post there. With the exception of the Mediterranean, where Corsairs [*Barbary pirates*] are impeding the commerce of the United States, the American flag is seen everywhere and is well received. One can consider the Americans as the most formidable rivals to any nation who wants to keep or increase its navigation; and under that point of view, France has no motive for extending the privileges granted to the United States in its colonies. I have already had the honor of pointing out to you elsewhere, Sir, that Congress does not offer any example of that moderation and liberality that its members preach to others. Invariably mindful of the interests of their constituents, it throws upon foreigners all the burdens they can carry without being completely discouraged or angered. Without blaming its conduct, which answers its needs, I throw back its own rules of conduct to those Americans who protest against a [*French*] monopoly of trade in the Antilles. I have not found any better way to silence them. They are only contending for the theory since the practical aspect is presently as favorable to them as they could wish it. Even their flour and biscuits are allowed and the violent upheavals that have agitated our colonies have facilitated their capability to export our sugar. But it is right that the French nation should be able to impose limits on that freedom when she judges it proper, and when her interests require it, in spite of all the arguments by Mr. Jefferson and his compatriots. Then they will realize that the key of the Bastille, which they now have in their possession, will not indistinctly open to them the doors of the French colonies, and that these doors can be closed with better locks.

Copy, in French, Henry Adams Transcripts, DLC. Place to which addressed not indicated; received 25 September. Otto's letters included in *DHFFC* were usually written over the course of days, and even weeks, following the day they were begun.

[1] Paris's infamous prison was a symbol of absolutism, arbitrary punishment, and terror from the fourteenth century until it was stormed by a mob on 14 July 1789, when it instantly became the symbol of liberation from the ancien regime. The main key was turned over to the marquis de LaFayette, then commander of the French National Guard, who entrusted Thomas Paine to present it to Washington under a cover letter dated 17 March 1790 and enclosed with it a drawing of the prison-fortress in the process of demolition. Paine forwarded the letter, the key, and the drawing to America under the care of John Rutledge, Jr. (see Rutledge to William Short, 9 August, below), and the two relics remain to this day in a place of honor at Washington's Mount Vernon estate (*PGW* 5:241–43n).

[2] Tahiti is the most famous of the South Pacific's Society Islands, administered today as French Polynesia. The "native" was probably brought by the ship *America*, which had just concluded a celebrated voyage from Canton to New York.

A Correspondent Says

It is to the reputation of the worthy Representative of this district [*Ames*], that his eulogium is sung by those who have been eye and ear witnesses to his merit—and it is equally to his credit, that he is the constant theme of the detraction of those, who, guided by no principle, have continued since his appointment to a seat in the Supreme Councils of America, that same species of abuse they so liberally bestowed on him, before his election. But, the publick know, that such abuse betokens merit in the abused.

Nothing can exceed the ignorance and illiberality of the correspondents of the Gazette, in fulminating every species of unmerited detraction against a man, whose unceasing endeavours, and steady attention to promote the interest of Massachusetts, as well as that of the Union, in common with his colleagues, have deserved well of his constituents. But from past experience, he must know, that such detraction is merely the ebulitions of a few envious, intriguing demagogues, whose sole delight is in striving to injure the government—to excite murmurs and discontent—and to restore those days of confusion, imbecility and anarchy, which not long since, had well nigh involved our country in ruin—and is highly discountenanced by the community at large.

Not less unmanly and disingenious is the *feeble* attack of the Gazette,[1] on the Hon. Mr. AMES, than its unfairness is conspicuous in its misrepresentation of the CENTINEL, in charging it with neglect in noticing the merits of the several delegates from this State—when, in the very last Centinel the tribute of merited gratitude was paid them ALL for their steady, persevering and successful efforts to relieve this Commonwealth from the *unequal* burdens, which her exertions in the "*times that tried men's souls*" laid upon her.[2]

And we venture to pronounce, that in thus paying the tribute of gratitude, we are joined by every patriot—every friend to justice and equity—and every well wisher to the best interest of the United States, in general, and this Commonwealth, in particular. In no instance has the Centinel neglected to "render to merit, merit's due"—and notwithstanding the suggestions of the Gazette to the contrary, we are happy in the reflection, that the firmness, impartiality, and persevering industry of the Hon. Mr. GERRY, have been the subject of repeated eulogiums in the Centinel.

[Boston] *Columbian Centinel*, 4 August.

[1] Newspaper Article, *Boston Gazette*, 2 August, printed above.
[2] From Thomas Paine's first *American Crisis* paper (1776).

A New Song

THE Congress have spent many a day,
In hopes for to find out the way:
At last its found and pointed at;
When they go there they'll lose their fat.
  The road to Philadelphia has cost cash.
R[*obert*]. M[*orris*]. its said, that leads them all,
And by such routs I think they'll fall.
It happen'd once upon a time,
They stuck to other like bird lime.
  The time of the war.
Soldiers and sailors, wet and cold,
Stuck to their colors stout and bold;
But should it be the case again,
Where purses sway, its all in vain.
  So strange and not old times.

Two verses of an old Scots Song

ROB MORRIS who ploughs in the haugh o'the glen,
Tho King of the beggars, and leader of men,
He's got a string of them fast by the nose,
He'll twig them up tightly you all may suppose.
  So fast he's got them.
When he's got them upon his dunghill,
The sight of the market their bellies must fill;
For fish and for lobsters, you all know it well,
They need not use jaws, but suck thro' a quill
  So tender they are.

Compos'd on board the Federal ship,
As they go round I hope they'll dip;
She's now moor'd in the Bowling Green,[1]
Better she had ne'er been seen.
Columbus was the man, as we have been,
But now no more he can be seen:
This poor man he is now forgot,
While we are feasting on the spot.
The vision thereof.

NYMP, 4 August.

[1] After its appearance in the 23 July 1788 New York City parade to celebrate ratification of the Constitution, the thirty foot long "Federal Ship Hamilton" was deposited on Bowling Green.

Other Documents

Edward Rutledge to Pierce Butler. ALS, Wayne Papers, MiU-C. Place from which written not indicated.

Sorry to have received no reply to his last two letters; is told that Butler's lands in Georgia are to be attached later that month and sold for what they would bring.

William Shute to George Washington. ALS, Washington Papers, DLC. Written from Elizabethtown, New Jersey.

Office seeking: loan office commissioner for New Jersey; Paterson informed him this day that applications for office ought to be made to the President.

John Jeffries, Diary. Jeffries Family Papers, MHi.

Breakfasted with Adams, Col. William Smith, and Jonathan Mason at "Richmond Hill," "after which much confidential political conversation passed in my presence—the Vice P. boldly & openly avowing the propriety for punctually & fully fulfilling all contracts & Payments and establishing Impost, Excise, Stamp Duty & Land Tax for the Ways & Means of discharging it—and unequivocally for a supreme effective Government, and not thirteen distinct petty republicks or governments—exclaimed with justice & propriety against the political sentiments of Hon. S[*amuel*]. Adams Esqr.—and those lesser echoing Politicians like him"; dined at Sir John Temple's, with P. Muhlenberg, Strong, Partridge, Clymer, Benson, Ames, Madison, Page, Leonard, and many others.

THURSDAY, 5 AUGUST 1790

Benjamin Rush to Thomas Fitzsimons

I cannot view the effects of your funding System in the same light that you do. It is to me a Monster—calculated to sow the Seeds of every Vice & calamity in our Country. The high price of wheat during the last year has kept our people from attending to it—But they will awaken to its danger, especially as they will soon be drained of all their certificates at *half price* by the numerous emissaries from the Brokers who now Swarm thro' every County of the state. The Spanish cruelties in America & the English cruelties in the East Indies in my opinion do not stain human Nature with a blacker hue than the conduct of the present Congress towards the Army that established our Independence and New goverment. I grant that you have lessned the evils of your injustice, by dividing the Certificates—But the mass of iniquity is the same. The whole profits of the War will soon center in the hands of american tories—Amsterdam Jews & London Brokers—while the brave Men who deserved them, will end their lives in goals [*jails*], & hospitals, or beg their bread from door to door. Pardon me for introducing the Subject again. I never think of it, without lamenting that I am an American. Virtuous Britain! How differently has she treated her Loyalists from the Manner in which America has treated the Men who [*lined out*] saved us from Destruction.

Real property has taken a start in our city—& back lands sell & settle rapidly—what then? This is only the preternatural Strength of a Convulsion in our Country. Our Vitals are unsound—& we must finally perish under the weight of Mr. Hamilton's "public blessing" which you have imposed upon our Country.

Your funding law would never have been passed, had Congress sat in Philada.

I have heard nothing lately respecting Mr. Morris [*for governor*], except that Geo. Ross is his decided, but timid friend.

I shall be glad to welcome you to Philada. After your Adjourment—Under every variety & difference of Opinion upon public questions be assured my dear Sir that I am ever yours.

P. S. you will probably meet Mrs. [*Julia Stockton*] Rush at Elizth. town [*New Jersey*].

ALS, Dickinson College, Carlisle, Pennsylvania. Written from Philadelphia.

James Schureman to George Washington

Mr. James Ewing. having suggested his intention of applying to be appointed Commissioner of loans for the State of New Jersey and requested my interference in his favor My duty to my Constituents will apologize for my troubling your excellency with a statement of some facts which I made to him as objections to his claim.

The supplies from the state of New Jersey to the late Army from the combination of several circumstances are supposed to have been furnished, in much greater proportions from the eastern than the western parts. The bulk of The public debt in the State is consequently in the hands of Inhabitants of the middle and eastern counties.

From the arrangement made by the act providing for the debt of the U. States The Citizens of that State will I presume have it in Their power to subscribe their loans at the Offices of New York or Philidelphia.

The intercourse of the five Counties below Trenton is almost exclusively with ~~Philadelphia~~ the latter City a large majority of the Inhabitants of those counties to transact business at Trenton pass through Philadelphia It is therefore presumeable that they will prefer receiving the interest on their stock at the *Treasury* in Philadelphia even if the office for New Jersey should be established at Trenton.

The same observations will be applicable to the county of Bergen & part of the counties of Essex & Monmouth with regard to the loan office of N. York if that should be permanently established in the City of New York.

The remaining Counties then of Hunterdon Sussex Morris Somerset & Middlesex with part of Essex & Monmouth will principally depend on the loan Office of the State for their accommodation.

Mr. Ewing if appointed would no doubt expect to ~~transact the~~ keep his office at Trenton. This I need not observe would be an extreme excentric situation for the counties last mentioned and an inconvenient one for the holders of the debt in the State at large.

To Mr. Ewing I trust I shall be understood to have no personal Objection I beleive him to be qualified for the office; but as I am sensible the place of his residence will not be convenient for the people of the State whose accommodation should be a primary motive. I have thought it my duty to submit these circumstances to your excellency's consideration, An attachment to the part of the State in which I reside may present them partially to my view, Your Excellency will judge without prejudice.

Some of my Colleagues have been consulted who concur in sentiment.

Should your Excellency see any weight in the observations I have made. I trust it will not be deemed presuming to call to your recollection Col. John Neilson as a fit person for the appointment.

ALS, Washington Papers, DLC.

Samuel Street to Jeremiah Wadsworth

Colo. [*Alexander*] McGilvray having recover'd for the Creek Nation, the Teritory granted by the Governor of Georgia, to some of the Citizens of that State, in Consequence of his application upon the grounds of the 4th. Section of the Act for regulating Trade and intercourse with the Indn. Tribes, proves a disposition in the President to Justify the Indians in their rights, as well as a power to redress their grievances; which induces me to hope he will accede to the first part of my Requisition in behalf of the five Nations.

I observe in the Same Act that the President is vested with power to make such order respecting the Indian Tribes which are surrounded in their Settlements by the Citizens of the United States, as he may Deem proper, which enables him to answer the Second part of my requisitions, and the third part is so obvious that I presume no difficulty will arise, unless with respect to the mode of doing it, previous to their making such appointment; and that may be obviated by an assurance that when such appointment shall be properly made and Authenticated, it shall be attended to.

Altho an accomodation with the five Nations may be considered of much less Importance, than with the Creeks, to the United States, Yet as it woud be paving the Way for a Similar Settlement with the Shawanes &c. who are in Confederacy with them, it would make the Inhabitants of the Frontiers feel Secure and easy in their Settlements, and be important to them; and the Object would be in a great measure gain'd of Pleasing the Indians, and Securing their Confidence without the expence of a Treaty.

I wish Something could Conveniently be done soon, as I have been a Considerable time attending to their business, at my own expence, and what is worse, I do not see how they Can repay me, Since they are disappointed in doing it, as they intended, out of the Mony they Claim'd from the State of New York, which fell so far Short of their expectation that they really had it not in their power to spare it.

If you will have the goodness to intimate my desire to return, in some manner that it may reach the Presidents Ear, you will do a favor to the five Nations of Indians.

ALS, Knox Papers, The Gilder Lehrman Collection, on Deposit at the New York Historical Society, New York. [GLC 2437.04670]. Wadsworth's role as intermediary was probably limited to forwarding the (unlocated) "Requisition" either to Knox or directly to Washington, who then forwarded it to Knox. Street had been authorized in April by the Five Nations

(Iroquois) to ask the federal government to intervene in their relations with New York State; for more, see George Beckwith, *Conversations with Different Persons*," n. 1, August 1790 Undated, below. Despite assurances to the contrary, Knox ultimately informed Street that Washington would not interfere in New York's Indian affairs, and recommended instead petitioning the state legislature. According to Beckwith, Street then resolved to return to Niagara in late August (Lord Dorchester to Lord Grenville, 25 September, in Douglas Brymner, ed., *Report on Canadian Archives, 1890* [Ottawa, Canada, 1891], pp. 153–54). Members of the Iroquois' Seneca tribe subsequently suspected Street of secretly serving as agent for Oliver Phelps in the Genessee Purchase and disavowed his authority to act further on their behalf (*PGW* 7:10–11, 15n, 122–23).

George Thatcher to John Fox

Very contrary to my apprehensions when I wrote you on the 3d inst. I have now the pleasure of informing you, that after my last was closed & sent to the Post-Office, a Boston paper came to hand, which [*lined out*] contained the ~~Law~~ act of the Legislature of Massachusetts, ceeding the Light-houses of that State to the U. States—And yesterday I gave notice to the House that I should to day move a Resolution Authorising the Secretary of the Treasury to finish the Light-House on Portland head [*Maine*]—Accordingly a Bill was this day brought in for that purpose—it has had two readings, & will be read the third time on the morrow—A sum not exceeding fifteen hundred Dollors is appropriated to defray the expence; I followed your Judgment with regard to the sum; and if this should prove insufficient I shall be sorry; because I could have had eighteen hundred, or two thousand appropriated as well as not.

The [*Ways and Means*] bill, inclosed in my last, has passed the Senate with a few alterations—I beleive the duty on unwrought Hemp is ~~lowered~~ reduced, & that on cordage & cables raised—I think it will pass our house tomorrow.

FC, Thatcher Family Papers, MHi.

George Thatcher to Thomas B. Wait

I hope you will write me many, many times yet; but if yours of the 24th. July is the last, & the meazels close your eyes to be opened no more in this world—I claim the right of being husband to your widow, son to your mother, & father to your lovely children; and so bid you adieu till we meet at the general Resurrection.

You know I dont beleive in the existence of a soul independent of the body—If I did I should recommend you to some of my friends in Hades—more particularly to my father and mother[1]—However if I am mistaken on this point; and souls do actually exist in a sensible state between death and the resurrection, you may inform my friends there how it is with me—That all things considered I have no reason to complain of my allotment in Life.

As to my father, I dont know but a little before he died, & in a conversation we held upon my future destination in life, he was led to beleive I should turn preacher—I know it was his wish. & if I recollect, I did not possitively assure him to the contrary—You will therefore inform him of my situation and prospects—where I live—of my family—what are my religious sentiments &c. &c. that many people deem me a monster in wickedness—but making reason & revelation my guide; & thinking my own understanding a better guard against error, than the Dogmas of those who censure me; I trust I shall do very well here, & finally meet him in a world more favourable to virtue* & happiness than this.

The inclosed Bill[2] has this moment come from the press; & 'tis of great importance that it be known thro the United States as soon as possible, I therefore send you the only copy I have—And once more subscribe your friend if you are alive—& if not a certain friend to your mother, widow & children.

*P. S. This sentence needs some explanation; but time will not admit—to give you directions what to say to my dear honored Mother—only that our Language does not afford words sufficiently expressive of the lively sense I ever shall retain of her affection for poor George.

FC, Thatcher Family Papers, MHi.

[1] Peter (1712–75) and Anne (Lewis) Thatcher (1716–84) married in 1734.

[2] Presumably the Funding Act, which Wynkoop indicated he had in hand the next morning (to Beatty, 6 August, below), although the act had only been signed by Washington on 4 August.

[*Daniel Carroll*] to the Delegates and Inhabitants of Washington County, Maryland

I did myself the honor to address a few lines to you on the 29th ult. inclosing the Funding Bill. There was a small mistake which you will observe on comparing it with that published.

If this system has been concluded in a manner which appears exceptionable, it may be well to consider some of the difficulties attending it. There was certainly in each House a respectable Majority for Funding, but not so exclusively of the state debts. There were some averse to any funding system. The first mentioned differed widely in opinion on the terms. It will be readily conceived that the non-funding party, under such circumstances, though comparatively small, must of course had considerable weight. Considering the subject in this point of view, and the variety of clashing interests, which were connected with it, I am more surprized, that any system took place, than at what has been done to parts of which perhaps there may be well founded objections. I had indeed serious apprehensions that we should return after a long and expensive session, without accomplishing some of the great objects for which we were appointed, viz. the restoration of public and private credit; objects too much connected with the safety of the government, and the relief of the community to have been left undone, as far as it was possible to be accomplished.

With respect to the state debts so much has been said and published on that subject, I cannot add further information. Among the objections I had to the Assumption as it was proposed were, 1st. Because it was general and unlimited; consequently the extent not known. 2d. The want of cautionary provisions, in which the state of Maryland was particularly interested. 3d. I considered part of the Secretary's report, page 10, as having a very injurious tendency against the interests of Maryland: Speaking of the justice of having all expenditures brought into a common mass, he proceeds to say, "This plan seems to be susceptible of no objection which does not belong to every other, that proceeds on the idea of a final adjustment of accounts. The difficulty of settling a ratio is common to all. This must probably either be sought for in the *proportions of the requisitions* DURING THE WAR, or in the decision of Commissioners appointed with plenary power. The rule prescribed in the Constitution with regard to representation and direct taxes, would evidently not be applicable to the situation of parties during the period in question."

It will be obvious that the idea suggested by the Secretary might place Maryland in a very disagreeable situation on a settlement of accounts, viz. *the proportions of the requisitions during the war* as the rule. It appeared to me essential that this evil should be avoided, and the weight and authority of the Secretary's suggestion done away by a positive act. A law has passed for the settlement of the public accounts [*HR*-77], by which the ratio is to be in proportion to numbers, as shall be returned by the Census to be taken. The other difficulties are removed. I had some not mentioned, but on the removal of what I have stated, it appeared to me to be for the interest and security of the Union to accede to a qualified assumption, rather than risk the whole of the Funding System. These my sentiments have been known for a considerable time past, before the subject of the residence of Congress and seat of Government were in contemplation. As I cannot have the satisfaction of seeing many of my Constituents, I have thought it proper to say this much, not on personal considerations, any further than my character may be concerned, but as information which may be due at least to my more immediate Constituents.

[Elizabeth-Town (present-day Hagerstown), Maryland] *Washington Spy*, 26 August.

Other Documents

Judith Sargent Murray to Mary Turner Sargent. Ms., Murray Papers, Ms-Ar. For the full text, see *Murray*, pp. 228–29.

"The weather is intensely hot *** in this crouded City [*New York*], not a breath of air can we obtain, and the noise, and tumult is greatly annoying"; (husband) John Murray has gone to see if any letters have come for them in care of Goodhue, whose (franked) covers have saved them a small fortune; Goodhue will leave early in the next week.

Item 187, p. 83, PCC, RG 360, DNA.

Boudinot returns General Washington's "Sentiments on a Peace Establishment," dated 2 May 1783 to records of the Confederation Congress. (For the sentiments, see John C. Fitzpatrick, ed., *Writings of George Washington* [39 vols., Washington, D.C., 1931–44], 26:374–98.)

[Boston] *Independent Chronicle*, 5 August; reprinted at Northampton, Massachusetts; Hartford, New Haven, and Norwich, Connecticut; New York City (*NYDG*, 12 August); and Philadelphia.

The funding system is so complicated that "seven-eights of the community are unable to fathom its principles"; such an "excentric plan may suit a M-rr-s [*Morris*]."

[Stockbridge, Massachusetts] *Western Star*, 10 August.

Sedgwick arrived home.

[Connecticut] *Litchfield Monitor*, 30 August, from the non extant [Petersburg] *Virginia Gazette*, 5 August.

Giles elected to serve out the remainder of Bland's term.

Friday, 6 August 1790

Members of the New Jersey Delegation to Alexander Hamilton

Col. [*John*] Conway I understand is making application to be appointed to the command of one of the revenue boats. From my knowledge of his conduct when Sheriff of the County of Middlesex I have no scruple to recommend him as a fit person to be employed in the above Service.

Should his application be successful, as I hope it will, his general character affords reason to expect a faithful and diligent execution of the trust.

Js. Schureman

The Subscriber certifies, that Colo. Conway is an active honest Man; was brought up to the Sea, and is well acquainted with the Jersey coast.

Wm. Paterson

From the personal knowledge I have of Col. Conway & his general character in the State of New Jersey I take the liberty to recommend him as a suitable person to command one of the Boats to be employed in Securing the collection of the Revenue of the United States.

Jonathn. Elmer

Colonel John Conway being desirous of an appointment to the Command of one of the revenue Cutters: We recommend him as an active Honest Man, who was brought up to the Sea and is well acquainted with the Coast of New Jersey. Should he be appointed to that trust we think he will execute it with industry and Integrity.

Thos. Sinnickson
Lambt. Cadwalader

Ms. copies, Washington Papers, DLC. Elmer's and Paterson's testimonials are transcribed on the same sheet of paper.

Henry Wynkoop to Reading Beatty

Notwithstanding the confident Expectations of being at Your House tomorrow evening, it is now tollerably well ascertained that I am to be disappointed, for the revenue [*Ways and Means*] Bill was not return'd from the Senate until yesterday about two oClock it is so amended as to alter its Complection much & adds greatly to the uncertainty of the time it will yet consume, so that should Mama [*Sarah Newkirk Wynkoop*] be at Your House she must return without me & I must get home as soon & as well as I can.

Conceiving You must be anctious to see the funding Bill, I send it enclosed, as also some of the Caricaturas sold about the Streets expressive of the Spleen of the Cittizens on account of the Removal of Congress; You probably must have heard of the Motion for repealing part of the residence Bill, this was brought forward yesterday & rejected by a Majority of 12, so that I hope we shall not hear any more of it; The Rabble here are very free in bawling out some one or other of the dirty expressions you will see in the Labels, when they perceive a Pensylvania Delegate passing the Streets, from which You may judge somewhat of the agreableness of our Continuance here, but be that as it may, I beleive not a man of us will leave the place until all is over & safe, which probably will be by tuesday or wednesday next; ***

ALS, Wynkoop Papers, PDoBHi. Written in the morning; place to which addressed not indicated. The omitted text relates to family news.

Disinterestedness

IF the Corporation are solicitous for the fame of disinterestedness, and have a right to squander the city treasure for the purpose of disinterested flattery; we would advise them exhibit the portraits of Mr. M—s [*Morris*], in the Senate chamber, & the miniature of the modest V—n [*Vining*], in the chamber of __. This would show the world, that resentments have no hostile abode in the passive breasts of the wise & honorable fathers of the city, & that they acquiesce in the national policy and necessity of a removal, and in the c—l [*constitutional*] agency of the executive in adjournments.

S.

NYJ, 6 August.

The Philadelphia Fever

THE notice of Mr. Bloodworth, of his intention to bring forward a motion for the *suspension* of that part of the *residence bill* which respects the *temporary* residence of Congress, says a correspondent, has so agitated the minds of those of the citizens of Philadelphia as were interested in the event, that the healths of many were considerably endangered—it having produced all the symptoms of the late sweeping *influenza*. Our correspondent further observes, that the faculty are exceedingly enlightened by the circumstance, as it has clearly pointed out the *causes* of that alarming disorder (for the discovery of which large premiums have been offered) viz.—*anxiety*, DISGUST, ANGER, *RAGE*!

NYJ, 6 August. This piece was followed by "Antidote for the Philadelphia Fever," a summary of the House proceedings of 5 August on Bloodworth's motion; see *DHFFC* 3:550–51.

Newspaper Article

We learn from Philadelphia, that the corporation of that city have already debated upon the *means* necessary for rendering the residence of Congress *tolerable* in that city—and that they have postponed the fixing upon a *spot* or *plan*, until the meeting of the legislature of that state. *Query*—Have the CITIZENS of Philadelphia less patriotism than those of *New-York*, that they should wait for the STATE LEGISLATURE to grant the *ponidustum!*

NYJ, 6 August; reprinted at Philadelphia and Winchester, Virginia.

To John Laurance, Rufus King, Elbridge Gerry, and Fisher Ames, Esquires

WE esteem you as good men, for your manly, upright, and judicious conduct in certain cases interesting to your Constituents, for which we return you, in the name of 15,000 of our Countrymen, our most hearty thanks, and assure you, the period, (not very far remote) shall arrive, that six of our own family will leave us, we will, as we heretofore have done, sacrifice our lives, our property, and all that is dear to us, to perpetuate our freedom, and will avail ourselves of the opportunity to do ample justice, seeing you have none to help you to afford it as under the present scheme; so we will acquit ourselves like men, and if our families must perish with us, it shall be in an honorable cause, but it will fix a stigma of Contempt on a certain Legislative Body to ALL ETERNITY.

The 52 Representatives of the 15,000 Veterans, East of Philadelphia
J. COBOT, & CO.

NYMP, 6 August.

Letter from a Member of Congress to Hartford, Connecticut

An adjournment of Congress is expected to take place in a day or two; the necessary business of the session being nearly closed, and the members as impatient to return home as their constituents probably are to have them.

About fifty acts have been passed in the course of the session, and altho' unanimity has not been attainable with respect to all of them, the session will nevertheless end in harmony and with better prospects than it commenced.

The [*Funding*] act proposing a new loan for the domestic debt, which you will have seen, has taken up more time than any other, and may be the subject of more animadversion. To embrace every description of creditors who had contributed to the general defence, and not to swell the public burthen to a forbiding size, were among the objects necessary to be regarded in framing the act; and an accommodating spirit on the part of the creditors will be necessary to give it effect.

With regard to the annual revenue which will be requisite for the proposed loan, together with the foreign debt and civil list, it must amount to 3,200,000. For 2,600,000 of this sum funds are already provided, by the impost and tonnage acts. For the remaining 600,000, which will not be wanted till January 1792, funds will be provided the next session; and may probably consist of inland duties of different descriptions. Direct taxation will not be resorted to but in case of a deficiency of other resources, which it is presumed will not happen, and at any rate cannot be large.

The interest on the foreign debt has this year been paid, and there will remain in the Treasury at end of the year a sum which, employed in a bank operation, may be very convenient in facilitating at once the payment of the duties and a prompt discharge of the quarterly interest.

It is sincerely to be regretted that so much of the public paper has heretofore been trifled away for the want of a criterion to ascertain its value, or indeed evidence that it would continue to be of any value at all. There are now data for calculation, which men of forecast will regard, and which, after a few payments of interest shall have been made all will attend to. The stock created by the new loan will average a profit of about four and an half per cent. which is more than real estate produces, and which in a shorter period of time probably than is generally imagined, will be near the rate which money in this country ought to produce in deposits unaccompanied with trouble and risk.

[Hartford] *Connecticut Courant*, 16 August; reprinted at Portland, Maine; Salem and Boston, Massachusetts; Newport, Rhode Island (partial); and New Haven, Connecticut.

Other Documents

Catharine Greene to George Washington. ALS, Washington Papers, DLC. For the full text, see *PGW* 4:74–75n.

Office seeking: her younger brother, William Littlefield, for loan officer or some other office; mentions Wadsworth as having a good opinion of him.

Governor Beverley Randolph to Frederick A. Muhlenberg. FC, Executive Letterbook, Vi. Written from Richmond, Virginia.

Cover letter to Giles's credentials as Bland's successor.

[Edenton] *State Gazette of North Carolina*, 6 August.

"We can assure our readers, from good authority," that the funding bill, including assumption, passed the Senate, 14 to 11; that "there is the greatest probability of its passing" the House.

SATURDAY, 7 AUGUST 1790

Timothy Bloodworth to George Washington

In compliance to repeated applications, I beg leave to Mention to the President of The United States som Carecters who are Candidates for the Commissioner of Loans, in the state of North Carolina, Viz. Mr. Abisha Thomas, now agent for setling accounts with the United States, the abilities of thiss Gentleman is generally Acknowledged. Mr. [*Stephen*] Moore from North Carolina, whose Carrecter & Abilities are also unquestionable. Mr. Binford [*John M. Binsford*] with whome my acquaintance is but superficial but am inform'd he is a Carrecter of know Abilities. these Gentlemen have made aplication for recommendation. Mr. [*William*] Barrey Grove of Fayette have signified in conversation his wilingness to accept the appointment, thiss Gentlemans Fortune, & Carrecter, are favourable to the appointment. his situation is at the present seat of Government [*Fayetteville*], in that state. Hope You will pardon my freedom in Mentioning Mr. Samuel Ashe Junr. son of Judge [*Samuel*] Ashe, whose Carrecter I will venture to affirm are inferior to non[*e*] in that State, who suffered in defence of his Country at the Capture of Charls Town,[1] with a degree of fortitude that does him honour, & I flatter my self he would fill with dignity any appointment.

ALS, Washington Papers, DLC.

[1] After a siege of almost five weeks, approximately 2500 Continental and militia forces as well as one thousand civilian combatants surrendered to 17,000 British army and navy forces at Charleston, South Carolina, on 12 May 1780.

Tristram Dalton to Nathaniel Appleton

With great satisfaction, My Dear Sir, I embrace the first post to advise You that your appointment as Commissioner of Loans for Massachusetts was this day made—on which I sincerely congratulate you.

You had a very busy competitor on the ground whose endeavors to obtain the place were not, in my opinion, founded either in policy or justice.

The two houses having finished the Bill providing ways and means, Congress will adjourn early in the next week.

I hope soon to have the pleasure of taking you by the hand.

ALS, Colburn Autograph Collection, Bostonian Society, MHi. Addressed to Boston; franked; postmarked 8 August.

Joseph Stanton to George Washington

I Observed the State of Rhodisland was Left a Blank, in your Excellencys Nomination of yesterday for Commissioners.

I beg Leave to Recomend Mr. James Sheldon, a Gentleman of Probity Industry and Sensibility, ready at the Cost of Intrest as I have frequently Been with him on Committees of the Assembly, Is now a member from the town of Richmond, and hath Been to the Best of my Recolection, from the Commencement of Our Contest with Britain, In which dispute he took an Active part in favour of his much Loved Country, My Colleagu [*T. Foster*] only regrets his not Living in Newport or providence, I prefer him on that Very Acount, Because it must be Acknowledged Every Attention hath Been paid those two towns. Not to mention particular Families.

ALS, Washington Papers, DLC.

Hugh Williamson to John Gray Blount

Congress is to adjourn on the 10th Inst. I am informed by good Authority that the Treaty with [*Alexander*] McGillivray & [*Creek*] Indians goes on very well, of this the Govr. [*William Blount*] of new ceded govt. must be glad; for it will greatly relieve his Labours.

Certificates of N. Carola. have been sold here at 8/ on their Face, no allowance made for Interest. They are rather falling as are all other Securities. Finals have fallen from 13/3 to 11/3 in six days arising from the great Quantity thrown into the Market. And the Dutch Agents combining probably not to buy, in order to keep down the Price. Doubtless our Certificates will prove worth 8/ Specie & if you could buy for that Price in Paper you would make a good Speculation. I would be glad to have £1000 on such Terms. Strange Opinions prevail here respecting our 86 Certificates. Some People think that the State will infallibly be compelled to pay them and are buying them up accordingly. I therefore repeat the former advice viz. If any of your Acquaintance have of those Certificates, if they will send them on I will probably be able to sell them, provided they cannot sell them in the State to Speculators.

The Accots. of our State which I am to enter upon as soon as Congress rises are to be absolutely new modelled, it is a herculean Labour.

***

ALS, John Gray Blount Papers, Nc-Ar. Addressed to Washington, North Carolina; franked; postmarked 9 August. The omitted postscript concerns a private business transaction.

Paine Wingate to [*John Pickering (of Salem, Massachusetts)*]

A resolution has passed both houses of Congress to adjourn on next Tuesday and the public acts, which were in contemplation for this session, have passed—A few other acts which are of no great consequence & are chiefly for appropriation of money to individuals are yet to pass the house of Representatives & may be easily dispatched on monday next; But the secretary of the treasury, for reasons which [*lined out*] I will not now trouble you with relating, has proposed this day some new business which may possibly work some delay[1]—We shall I fear be always cursed with a number of men who like Gerry would be glad to sit continually & care for no expence if it conduces to their own advantage. Whether we shall rise on the day fixed I can not say; but I am determined with a number of others to leave this place on that day unless there is an absolute necessity of tarrying. I have engaged a passage in a packet to Providence [*Rhode Island*] with Mr. Goodhue & several others to sail on that day if the weather will permit I hope to be at Boston on Friday or Saturday at furthest. If you should not receive a letter from me by the next post after this, you may depend upon it that I have left N. York at the time mentioned, & you will probably see me at Salem on Saturday or as soon as I can get from Boston after that day. I think it likely that my wife will be at Salem before that time, & she may then expect me. I will enclose to you the funding bill & the new impost [*Ways and Means*] law which are now passed. I will add no remarks, every one must form an opinion of his own respecting them. The Secretary of the treasury has stated that there will be in the treasury about a million of dollars before any will be wanted to pay the Interest of the funded debt; & proposed that commissionners be appointed & empowered to buy up the Securities at the market price. I suspect that it may be a plan to raise the price of securities which ~~should~~ would suit speculators very well & afford employ to some who want employment. I may be mistaken in my conjecture, But I think it is a little extraordinary to throw in such a proposition just at the close of a session when the members are impatient to get away & some gone already. Mr. Langdon Mr. Strong & several others have got leave to go home; & we shall soon have a thin Congress & there will be an opportunity of Smuggling business ~~business~~ through which would not otherwise pass, unless we should rise immediately—I will not now spend any time in writing to you about Congressional matters, I hope to have the pleasure very shortly of seeing you & all friends well.

ALS, Putnam-Jackson-Lowell Papers, MHi. Place to which addressed not indicated. The recipient was identified by internal references to Salem, Massachusetts, and the letter's address to the "Hon. Mr. Pickering."

[1] The secretary of the treasury's report of this date resulted in the Sinking Fund Act [HR-101] and the Special Appropriations Act [HR-100].

An American to Mr. Russell

"ALMIGHTY TRUTH WILL PREVAIL"[1]

THE Funding Bill, is the important subject of discussion; the earnest inquiry of everyone is, "What reason can Congress give for depreciating the interest of the debt below the principal, contrary to the opinion and practice of all honest men in all countries?" The answer to this question from some of the Representatives, is, "The Senate were obstinate and would pass no Bill unless the House would agree to this unjust clause." The reason offered by the Senators in favour of the Bill, is, "the nation is bound by *express promise*, to pay six per cent. interest on the principal of the debt, but there was no such promise to pay the same per cent. on the Certificates given for the interest; it is only by *implication*, not *express* and *literal*—and as we must make a saving somewhere, this was thought to be the best mode." Thus we have the *reasons* on which Congress found their discrimination between interest and principal; but it may be doubted whether one person, *out of Congress*, will be found to subscribe to this clause. It is a dangerous experiment to violate the principles of equity in which all the honest part of mankind have been agreed for ages—it appears to be a *sacrifice of character* without a prospect of even a temporary benefit—For we may be assured the creditors will not be silly enough to be caught in such a trap; but they will tell the *wise Senators* who say "there were no literal promise to fund the interest equal to the principal," that there is a *literal promise to* PAY *the interest*, and PAYMENT they demand! For they will not loan their money lower than is given to others—and *this demand* being founded in the principles of national faith, and eternal equity, it must be complied with—The fair fame of our rising NATION must never be clouded with such a foul stain; honest men will arise with efficient energy to overturn every system of iniquity. GERRY! and AMES! we hail thee as the guardians of our country's honour! While time remains we will remember your energy in support of TRUTH.

[Boston] *Columbian Centinel*, 7 August; reprinted at Dover, New Hampshire. Benjamin Russell was the editor.

[1] From Robert Dodsley's *Preceptor* (2 vols., London, 1747), on the education of youth.

A Million—surplus

The *Secretary of the Treasury* this day reported, that there was a *Million of Dollars*, in specie, of the collections of the last year, in the Treasury of the United States, which was not appropriated—and submits to the consideration of the House, the propriety of appropriating it to the purchasing such part of the debt of the Union as will be most to the advantage of the government.

A Committee was immediately appointed to bring in a Bill [*Sinking Fund HR-101*] for this purpose—and it is supposed, that it will retard the rising of Congress, two or three days. I think the bill will pass. You will recollect, that the interest on the domestick debt, does not begin until 1791.

Though the *Funding-Bill* appears complex, at first, yet it is, upon the whole, a good provision—and one of the effects of it is a rise of Publick Securities, so high as 13/4 on the pound—which is a certain indication that real estates will raise in the same proportion.

[Boston] *Columbian Centinel*; reprinted at Portland, Maine, and Portsmouth, New Hampshire.

OTHER DOCUMENTS

William Barton to Thomas Jefferson. ALS, Washington Papers, DLC. Written from Philadelphia. For a partial text, see *PTJ* 17:350n.

Office seeking: for the state department's second chief clerkship, vacated by Roger Alden; mentions the Speaker and most of the Pennsylvania "delegates," as well as Page, Madison, and Boudinot, as references.

William Cushing to John Adams. ALS, Adams Family Manuscript Trust, MHi. Written from Middletown, Connecticut, in the evening. For a partial text, see *DHSCUS* 2:84–86.

Had made plans to pay his respects to Adams before leaving New York City, but the hack he hired failed to appear before he was supposed to sail to New Haven, Connecticut; there was some discussion what route their next circuit court should take; "it being the general opinion that a rotation was not necessary in the Contemplation of law," he and Jay will begin in Albany, New York, in October and end in Providence, Rhode Island, at the beginning of December; hopes they meet if Adams travels eastward.

Thomas Fitzsimons to an Unknown Recipient. Listing of ALS, *Carnegie Book Shop Catalog* 207(1956):item 74 and 225(1958):item 123. The editors believe that this may be a mistranscription of the date of Letter from New York (Fitzsimons to Benjamin Rush), 1 August, above.

Ebenezer Hazard to Jeremy Belknap. ALS, Belknap Papers, MHi. Place to which addressed not indicated. For background on Congress's purchase of the 1617 acre tract at West Point, New York, see *DHFFC* 7:110–17.

Congress is about to adjourn, having done more business in the preceding month than in all the rest of the session; Hazard may find it easier to win a seat in Congress at some later election; has recently served on the commission to appraise the value of the land at West Point which Congress is about to buy.

Philip Schuyler to Henry Knox. ALS, Knox Papers, Gilder Lehrman Collection, NHi. Printed in *DHFFC* 7:265–66.

Requests list of invalid pensioners, and arrearages due to them and to pensioned widows and orphans (for the Senate committee on the Stirling Act).

Caleb Strong to Nathaniel Appleton. Summary of ALS, *Julia Sweet Newman Catalog* 218(1967):item 205, 228(1968):item 193, 242(1970):item 187, and 248(1971):item 154.

Regarding the Senate confirmation of Washington's nomination of Appleton as loan commissioner for Massachusetts.

Jeremiah Wadsworth to George Washington. ALS, Washington Papers, DLC. The enclosure, to Wadsworth from Samuel Dana, et al., is calendared under 20 May, volume 19.

"I should have presented the inclosed sooner—but as I knew of no Vacancy I have kept it. I wish Mr. [*William Walter*] Parsons may be numbered among the Candidates for Office."

John Jeffries, Diary. Jeffries Family Papers, MHi.

Dined with the Adamses at "Richmond Hill."

SUNDAY, 8 AUGUST 1790

Fisher Ames to Thomas Dwight

I have not replied to your friendly letters, because I have hoped to give you absolute assurance that I should quit this place next Wednesday. A bill

[*Sinking Fund Act HR-101*] is ordered to be reported, and will be to-morrow, for employing a million of dollars which we have to spare, for buying up the debt. This will restore a great sum to circulation; raise credit and the price of paper; make foreigners pay dear for what they may buy, or stop their buying; produce good humor among the creditors, and among the people, too, when they see the debt melting away; create a sinking fund of near eighty thousand dollars yearly, and, by a little management, of upwards of one hundred thousand. Objects so great and so popular carry away every personal consideration. I think such an act of vigor and policy would restore all the credit and regard that the government has lost. This bill may, and I fear will, detain us two days longer, but no new business will be touched. Wherefore I think that on Monday week at the latest, and perhaps on Friday next, I shall reach Springfield [*Massachusetts*], and help you help our fair friends [*the Worthingtons*] keep house. I despise politics, when I think of this office. I shall forget, though you hint at it, that I am a candidate, and am to be gibbeted in Edes's newspaper.[1] I am in haste, and why should I write a great deal, and spoil my pleasant task of telling you all I know?

Ames 1:88.

[1] Benjamin Edes (1732–1803) was the Antifederalist editor of the *Boston Gazette*, 1755–98.

John Crawford to William Irvine

Since your departure some changes has taken place—a Report from the Secretary of Finance to the House of Representatives suggestion to the house that 1,000,000 of dollars appropriated as soon as possible to purchase at market part of the debt; would be very advantageous to the Union as well as to the holders of Certificates. the report was read on Saturday morning Certs. then @ 11/. in the evening of the same day 12/3 Cash; such has been the affect of this Report.

A motion was made in the Senate to suspend a part of the Bill fixing the permanent and Temporary residence, there was but 5 members in support thereof—this motion has been now negatived by large majorities in both houses & any further attempts ~~will be~~ for a suspension bill will be fruitless—The Bill for Appointing two Commissioners to the Board was negativ'd by a large majority in the Senate. There has no nomination of Commissioners for the Board taken place yet, that I can learn—Thos. Smith esquire is Appointed Commissioner for the State of Pennsylvania—Congress [*torn*] to adjourn on tuesday—Finals 12/3 Indents 6/5—State debt 8 pr. for your satisfaction I have quoted you the best prices of [*illegible*].

ALS, Irvine Papers, PHi. Place to which addressed not indicated. The letter is misdated 8 May and is filed under that date at PHi.

John T. Gilman to William Irvine

Nothing further has transpired Respecting the appointment of Commissrs. for settling accounts—it was fully Expected a Nomination would have been made Yesterday, but it was not done.

Some Say that a Certain party will petition against the appointment of some of us, others that they will protest against our Settling accounts &c.

As Congress will Rise on Tuesday a determination must soon take place—if a Nomination, altogether new, should be hazarded, (which I cannot believe) it is probable the Senate may Negative it, but (as Dr. Doughty said) all things are Uncertain, and their is no knowing what a day may bring forth.

I understand that it is Expected their will be near One Million Dollars in the Treasy. by last of Decr. over and above Govermental Expences & it is probable an act [*Sinking Fund Act HR-101*] will *now* pass to apply it in purchasing securities which Suppose will Cause a Rise in Stocks.

ALS, Irvine Papers, PHi. Place to which addressed not indicated.

Benjamin Hawkins to William Blount

I have two long letters from yo[*u*] the one of July the 10th. I am surprised you did [*not*] sooner receive my letters written in the Senate Chamber, as I went to the post-office and put it in the hands of the post-master, myself, immediately after it was written. [*Alexander*] McGillevray is here, and there is no doubt every thing will be amicably settled with him and his people, he has been unwell and is, now, and has been pretty much confined. I have waited for some time with the expectation of being able to send you the treaty But, it will not be ready till tuesday; Georgia will complain tho' to the extent of the wishes of her citizens they will be gratified in the Oconee lands. These Indians being friendly, will greatly conduce to keeping the other tribes quiet, and of course ease you of many anixious [*illegible*] for the situation of the people of your Governm[*ent*].

General Sevier wishes that you may not go out till he returns home a[*nd*] is fearful you will not be treated with [*the?*] respect he wishes, He and his acquain[*tances*] think [*Landon*] Carter should have been the [*torn*] and you may be insulted by some who [*are?*] not respectable. The sooner you go the better—yet I wish I may be in Warren [*North Carolina*] first and that you would make my house in your way. The Civil list are paid punctually quarterly. I shall set out for home on Wednesday, we expect to adjourn on tuesday to meet the first monday in december.

Your Statement relating to [*Joseph*] Martin I have communicated, You stand well with the Executive. I suspect that Martin himself and by Mr. [*Patrick?*] Henry, endeavoured to bring you in [*?*] as perfectly acquiescing in the report [*torn*] not being the author in toto, to the end that he might be screened [*?*]. The whole of the land business and the parties, their views &ca. are known to a few here.[1]

AL, William Blount Papers, DLC. Addressed to Washington, North Carolina; postmarked 9 August.

[1] The editors believe this last paragraph relates to the Yazoo companies' investments in Georgia's far western territory; Patrick Henry was a principal investor in the Virginia Yazoo Company.

Richard Henry Lee to William Lee

*** This tedious Session is to end on the 10th. ~~August~~ instant, so that I hope to be at home before the end of the month—The State debts are assumed to the amount of 21,500,000 dollars, to be funded as is the domestic debt of the U.S.—Two thirds of the principal of the domestic debt to be funded immediately at 6 pr. Cent & the remaining third after 10 years at same interest—All the interest of this debt to be funded presently at 3 pr. Cent—The fund for paying this is the former impost increased—provision for paying the interest of the State debts assumed will not be made until next Session, which is to meet the first Monday in december at Philadelphia.

The compass of a letter does not permit me to be so particular (as you might wish) on so complex a subject as the funding system. To conversation this must be left, for I hope to see you in the Northern Neck in course of next fall. You may conclude from the interest being funded at 3 pr. Cent, that this will not sell for so much as the principal. N. York Bank Stock is not easily to be had, the divident of 7 pr. Cent being paid quarterly.

ALS, Lee Family Papers, ViHi. Addressed to "Green Spring," near Williamsburg, Virginia. For the full text, see *Lee* 2:538–39. The omitted text discusses linen, bedding, and rum purchased by R. H. Lee, either for trade or for personal use.

Robert Morris to Gouverneur Morris

I spoke with Mr. Jay on Friday about your appointment, He has not heard any Thing on that Subject latterly but seems to think you are [*lined out*] intended for the court of London and that the Disposition of that Court

is not (now) favorable to the Reception of a Minister. I told him that you preferred the Court of France; he ~~said Spain~~ says Mr. Jefferson has never said any Thing to him on your Subject but the President has and before Mr. Jefferson's Arrival (he knows that) he thought of you for one or other of the two Courts, indeed ~~Misster~~ Mr. Jay considered it as a fixed Point. I fear Mr. Jefferson thinks of Madison for France but I have never opened my Lips on this Subject to Either the President or him although the first has shewn me your correspondence respecting the unfulfilled articles of the treaty.[1] I think it best to be silent altho very impatient for the Event. But never mind, if you can sell Land, That is a much better Employment.
P. S. You will hear more on this Subject soon & I hope to your satisfaction.

Copy, hand of G. Morris, from unlocated original in cipher, Gouverneur Morris Papers, NNC. With this manuscript is a loose piece of paper, on which G. Morris wrote, "~~im~~ impatient, because I consider your appointment to the Court of France or London as certain, but nothing will be done until he comes." The editors assume this is a decoding of an earlier R. Morris to G. Morris letter and that the "he" referred to is Jefferson; if so, it might have been included in one of the letters dated 17 February or 3 March.

---

[1] For G. Morris's correspondence with Washington on secret negotiations with Great Britain, see *DHFFC* 2:451–67.

John Page to St. George Tucker

Mrs. [*Elizabeth Moore*] Walker informs me that Col. Bland left no Will amongst his Papers *here.* I ought to have told you this in my last—but [*lined out*] the Business of Congress; the Business of removing to my new Quarters, & the old Business of ceremonious Visits left me no Time for Recollection what to write—We are now moved to Mrs. [*Elizabeth*] McEuen's into the Rooms which Mr. Rogers & his Lady lately occupied opposite (#) to that in which your Brother [*Tucker*] Lodges. I have two large Rooms & 2 large Closets—Your Brother & Huger hold those which are opposite & correspond to mine; Col. R. H. Lee & Mr. Patterson of the Senate have 2 others in another Wing of the House over the 2 Rooms which Mr. & Mrs. [*Elizabeth Moore*] Walker occupy—I moved into this cool large House to be better accommodated than we could be in the hot Weather in Mr. [*William*] Lowthers small House whith the large Family he had Mrs. Dawson's & Mrs. [*seal*] being added to his—I should not have moved however, if I had not found that in this House I should be amongst valuable Friends—for Mr. & Mrs. [*Barbara Gregory*] Lowther are as good People as I would wish to live with—She is one of the best Women in the World with the sweetest Temper & he a plain honest Scotchman—free from Affectation or Meanness. I had written as far as this Mark (#) & was interrupted & till this Day the 8th.

of August have not had Leisure to sit down at my Table where I had locked it up—I have been ever since scribbling to my Constituents except when I made up two little Packets for you, or wrote to my Children or scribbled Rhymes to burle[*s*]que the potionate petulant Fools of N. York—one of my little Pieces is inclosed a second is in the Hands of [*John*] Fenno—which ought to have been in his yesterday's Paper[1] I have not Leisure to say any thing respecting your *Corrections*—but hope in a few Weeks now to discuss that Subject at Rosewell—for we shall set out probably on Thursday next in Carey's Norfolk Packet, ~~he~~ Carey is a clever Fellow & she a fine Vessel—Mrs. [*Barbara Lowther*] McLaine accompanies her Sister [*Margaret Lowther Page*]—Mrs. [*Catherine Thompson*] Coles & Mrs. [*Eliza Montfort*] Ashe with their Husbands & Col. Parker will be our fellow Passengers—I had added a little to Dodsley before I had Time to make your Corrections & I have had the few Copies which were left bound up the same stupid Fellow who printed the Collection was for Cautions Sake entrusted to bind them & he has done this like his other work witness the inclosed—Mrs. Page desires to be remembered by you.
[*P. S.*] Give a Copy to W[*illiam*]. N[*elson*]. with my Love to him—you see him every day I suppose.

ALS, Tucker-Coleman Papers, ViW. Place to which addressed not indicated. Enclosure not found. The first part of this letter was written on 12 July, but it is printed here to help the reader understand Page's comment about where he stopped writing on that date.

[1] See [*John Page,*] Consistency, 11 August, below.

Josiah Parker to Thomas Jefferson

Mr. John Cowper junior of Portsmouth [*Virginia*] requested me to name him as a candidate for a Consulship at either the ports of London—Bristol. Lisbon, or Bilboa—I therefore take the liberty of giveing a Sketch of his pretensions by ~~giveing~~ informing of his progress in life—Mr. Cowper after receiveing a more than common Education, was sent to Liverpoole to obtain a Mercantile education, he there served in the House of Crosbie & Greenwood five years—returnd to Virginia and conducted the Mercantile concerns of his Father Mr. Wills Cowper of Portsmouth, untill last Spring but one when he went to Bourdeaux and remaind there some time—long enough to acquire a tolerable knowledge of the French language and their mode of conducting Mercantile concerns—he would have preferd Burdeaux to any other place, but as a Consul is appointed for that port he does not presume to offer for it.

Mr. Cowper is a Young Gentleman of address & abilities & supports a very good Character, Mr. William Stokes of Virginia wishes allso to be appointed consul at a port in St. Domingo or at Bristol. Mr. Stokes is an industrious but has been an unfortunate merchant. but amongst his misfortunes he has conducted himself in such a manner as to support an unblemishd Character—both these Gentlemen are attached to their Country & the present Government of it.

If Mr. Cowper in particular should be honord with an appointment I am fully convinced that the information he may give to the Executive of the United states will be proper; and his attention to the mercantile Interest will do him credit.

You will please to name those Gentlemen to the PRESIDENT. should they or either of them be fortunate enough to receive an appointment. I am fully persuaded they will answer the purpose for which they may be employed.

ALS, Washington Papers, DLC. *PTJ* 17:326 points out that the state department acknowledged receipt of this letter on 7 August and suggests Parker may have been mistaken in the date.

James Seagrove to Pierce Butler

When at St. Mary's[1] about three weeks past, I receivd. your t[*w*]o favours of the 8th. & 15th June and pay all due regard to the Contents. It gives real concern to find my good friend Mrs. [*Mary Middleton*] Butler continues unwell—I wish it was in my power to relieve and restore her to health, it should speedily be done.

Capt. [*Roger Parker*] Saunders was at St. Mary's with me; I believe he is much pleased with the Country—Indeed no one can dislike it—however there is a great barr to its becoming a Country of consequence whilst the Spanish Govmt. continue to encourage & protect our slaves. There is a new Governor[2] arrived at Augustine who affords them every protection, and has been very abusive to some people who have followed their Slaves into Augustine—A Mr. Jones of North Carolina who was with a vessel about ten days past at St. Mary's, had two of his Negro's run away, and took the boat from his Vessel, with which they escaped to the Spanish post at Amelia [*Island*]—he persued—and landed a few Minutes after them—and demanded his Negro's and property from the Spanish Commandant at that Post who positively and insolently refused either Boat or Negro's—The Negro's were then forwarded in a spanish Boat to St. Augustine—Mr. Jones followed and arrived as soon as they—Jones waited on the New Governor who in the most arbitrary insulting tone, asked Jones "do not you know sir, that as soon as a Negro enters his Spanish Majesty's Dominions in Florida that he is free" Jones answered in the Negative "then sir say the Don, I tell you they are and as such they shall be protected—How came you here sir—begon instantly or the Castle[3] will be your portion—and do you hear sir, do not let me see or hear that any more of your Country Men come on such errand—or they shall find difficulty in returning"—Thus treated the poor Man was glad to git off and is now here ready to attest to every word I have related—But should the President, or Congress, wish further information the Bearer Lieutenant [*John*] Pierce of the Continental Troops at St. Mary's, will fully acquaint them. Is not this horrid—I would not by any means advise your moving your Negro's to the Southward unless something is done in this business. I expect retaliation will soon take place, and so on from one Step to another, until a General business is made of it.

You will see by the inclosed [*grand jury*] presentments of the County of Camden in what a serious light they view it. I wish to god you would make some stir in this business. I wrote the secretary [*Hamilton*] some months past, and recommended an armed boat Stationed at St. Mary's directly opposite to the Spanish post—which would in my opinion answer a valuable purpose as well to the revenue as towards preserving the property of the Good Citizens of the United States—and prevent those insults we dayly receive—He wrote me he had laid my Letter before Congress,[4] but I have heard no more of it. I suppose our Eastern friend would be glad every Negro in Georgia & the Carolinas woud do as poor Jones's has done. With a proper boat, and 12 Good Men, I will engage to put an effectual stop to this business—and I would chearfully undertake it.

***

I am realy sorry to find Congress going to Phila.—I despise the place and 99 out of a hundred of it's inhabitants. *** An Indian has lately been killed by a White Villan of the Name of Martin Johnson, without the smallest provocation—another had an arm broak—this was done within four miles of the Continental Post ~~on~~ at the Rock landing—our Governor [*Edward Telfair*] has issued his Proclamation offering £100 for Johnson—The Indians have demanded Satisfaction, and have given Two moons for it to be done in. what the consequence will be if Johnson can not be found is very clear—some inocent will suffer. ***

ALS, Butler Papers, PHi. Written from Savannah, Georgia; enclosed in Seagrove to Butler, 9 August, below. The omitted text discusses lawsuits in which Butler was concerned, the local harvest, and Seagrove's recent contracts for provisioning the federal army with, among other things, "a large supply of very fine Beef cattle from the Creek Nation." Seagrove also related having sent Butler a dozen watermelons three weeks earlier.

[1] The St. Marys River marked the border between Georgia to the north and Spain's colony of East Florida to the south.

[2] Jean Nepomucano de Quesada became governor of Spanish East Florida, based in St. Augustine, in July 1790 (*McGillivray*, p. 276).

[3] St. Augustine's Castillo de San Marcos was a fortress used as both protection and a prison.

[4] Neither Seagrove's letter to Hamilton nor the latter's reply has been located. On 23 April 1790 Hamilton had recommended improvements to the first Collection Act [HR-11], including the commissioning of revenue cutters armed with swivel guns, one of which would patrol Georgia's coastline. Hamilton may have submitted Seagrove's letter to the same committee to which this report had been referred and which reported the Collection Act [HR-82] on 8 July. Seagrove's letter may also have been shared with the Senate committee whose amendment furnished the final language of the relevant section of the act (*DHFFC* 4:429–30, 443–44, 460).

William Smith (S.C.) to Edward Rutledge

I have read with much pleasure, My dear Sir, your very agreable Letter by [*William*] Elliott; your observations on the conduct of Congress & on the merits of our new [*state*] Constitution accord perfectly with mine; I am much flattered in finding that I had anticipated in public debate & private conversation the Strictures & animadversions which you have made on the subject of *Residence*; the conduct of the Majority in both Houses entitles them to every severity which honest & independt. Men can inflict. Do not however attribute too much to Morris's influence; he possesses I admit, more than he ought; he has weight with the Pensylva. Delegn. & that Delegn. has too much influence in our House; their centricity places on many occasions the Ballance in their Hands & they never fail to avail themselves of their advantageous Situation to make a good Bargain. On this occasion a combination of circumstances lent their aid to the promotion of the Philada. Scheme. The State of Pensylv. being supposed averse to the Assumption, their Delegs. had a good plea to withhold their assent—they saw the extreme eagerness of Massachtts., Connecticut & So. Cara. ~~for the Assumpn.~~ & it rested with them to turn the scale; those Delegas. from Maryld. & Virga. who had most violently opposed the Assumtn. promised their consent if the Patowmac shod. be made the permant. residence—neither Pensylva. nor New York wod. agree to this immedy.—it was therefore necessary to combine interests; a strong association of Penya. Virg. & Maryd. was the result, & it was understood that Massa. & Connect. would not oppose the measure, provided enough members could be draughted from Peny. Virg. & Maryd. to carry the assumption. The New Engd. States could at any time have overset the whole Scheme but they had too much at stake—they flattered themselves that Congress would never go beyond Philada. to which place they had no considerable objections—indeed some of them thought a great point was secured by fixing the Govt. down in that city for 10 years certain, as the prospect of going to the Potowmac in a few years was ~~more probable~~ greater at New York, which is confessedly an eccentric Situation: Georgia & No.

Cara. who were bitter against the assumption were compleatly duped by their elder Sister Virga. & the cunning Philadns.—they voted for the Scheme under the pretence of a Southern position ten years hence; in fact many of them had a predilection for Philada. & held up the Potowmac as a bait to their constituents. When they found the Assumption follow, they began to repent of their folly, but were ashamed to retract. South Cara. was divided—in the Senate, Mr. Z. [*Izard*] stood firm & made a manly opposition, his Colleague [*Butler*], after taking a great deal of pains to counteract Morris by bringing in a Bill to establish the permanent reside. on the Potowmac, suffered that very bill to be made the Instrument of Morris's projects & under color of the Potowmac was completely gulled into a vote which carried the Bill thro the Senate; had he voted against it, the Senate would have been equally divided & it is known that the [*Vice*] President would have rejected it. such an instance of versatility I scarce remember; whether he thought the New York Senators had not paid him Sufficient respect, or wished to shew his power or his independe. in differing from his Colleague is uncertain but it is most certain that his conduct has occasioned general disgust here—the New Yorkers reprobate his procedure & the Philda. say they have made him fall into the pit he dug for them & laugh at him accordingly. In the Repres[*entative*]s. Sumpter as usual followed the wrong road—it was sufficient for him that he voted with Virginia, whose Represen[*tativ*]e. he shews himself on all occasions: Tucker seemed sunk in an ~~apathy~~ indifference proceeding from ill-humour—he was dissatisfied with every thing (as he gener[*all*]y. is)—he hated the Assumption, but was obliged to vote for it—he didn't like the Residence bill much better; he ~~therefore~~ disliked the govt. itself & was not therefore sorry to see it become contemptible—he accordy. took no part, but allowed things to take their own course. Huger was sick, which was unfortunate, for I prefer him to all the rest of them; he votes right & behaves like a gentleman: Burke behaved very well & took an active part. I was invited into the Scheme by frequent hints, but I set my face against it & I even attempted to excite some indignation in the breasts of the Mass. & Conn. members against it, but in vain: they contented themselves with voting against the Bill, but threw cold water on every project which had a tendency to defeat it. After this famous Bill had passed, the funding Bill was taken up in the Senate & to the great surprize of those who were not in the Secret, the Assumption was immedy. engrafted on it, by the accession of [*Charles*] Carrol & Read & Elmer, who had before violently opposed it: they counted off enough to carry it without resorting to Adams's vote, which would not have looked so well; when the bill with the Senate's Amendmt. came to us, Pensylva. promised 3 votes, Maryd. 2 & Virga. 2. which upon calculation were deemed sufficient: there was however a corps de reserve, Hartley from Pen. would vote for it, *after a conference* with the Senate, but his *conscience* would not allow him to consent to so material an alteration, ~~before~~ *without one*: [*Richard B.*] Lee & White from Virga. who had reprobated the Assumption on any terms or conditions, declared that their objections were removed by the Bill for the Settlemt. of accots. [*HR*-77] having past, & by the limitation of the debts assumed; & Gale & [*Daniel*] Carrol, who had been equally bitter against it, did not think it worth their while even to assign a Reason for such an astonishing conversion & were as anxious for the measure as they ~~were~~ had been to defeat it a month before. North Carolina, seeing the turn things were taking, tried to get more of their debt assumed, but the House were afraid of deranging the proportions least the whole shod. be set afloat: some indeed wished to punish that State for her misconduct; all our members however voted for the motion to add 600,000 Dollrs. for No. Car. & I was not sorry that we lost the question, for they have behaved shamef[*ull*]y. Georgia made an attempt also, but failed. none of the proportions were touched. A few days after the [*Funding*] Bill had passed, Jackson had the modesty to ask leave to bring in a Bill making a further assumpn. for Georgia of 300,000 Dollars, & tho' he prefaced his motion with some illiberal remarks on the 4 mill. of So. Cara. I found Tucker, Burke & Sumpter voting for his motion—which was carried; the New-Engld. Memrs. consented to it with a view of quieting that State; I represented to them the impolicy of gratifying ~~them~~ Georgians now, for we should hereafter lose their aid when a general assumption ~~was~~ shod. be attempted & they would be as violent as ever agst. it, but all in vain, they let the Bill go to a second readg. when No. Cara. tried to get a further Sum, but failed—New York the same—I then mentioned that if the Bill past in its present form Georgia wod. have $^{6}/_{7}$ths. of her debt assumed, & that So. Cara. was entitled to the same benefit & therefore ought to have at least another half million, & that from the message of the Govr. of Georgia to his Legislature,[1] it appeared She had in her Treasury bonds to the amount of £200,000 beyond her debt & required conseq[*uentl*]y. no assumption at all, but I was unsupported—I therefore opposed the [*Georgia*] Bill—the No. Caras. & New Yorkers got displeased, & on putting the question for the passing of the Bill, it was fortunately *rejected* by a majority of *one*; it had however the votes of my three Colleagues. I have observed that Sumpter regularly votes for any thing required by Georgia or Virga. Burke is also a great friend to that State, notwithstandg. her Members execrate us & do us all the Injury they can. The No. Caras. are now keen for a general assumption; Massachtts. also wishes it & we shall probably now have the aid of Georgia, which we were about to lose. there only remain now unassumed about four or five Millions, of which one fifth is thrown upon us, which is unequal as we are only about $^{1}/_{14}$th. or 15th. of the Union—Jackson has behaved thro this whole business in a manner which has excited the greatest indignation in my breast: so much rancour agst. our State, all proceeding from a mean Envy & a desire to see her sink under the pressure of her debt!! I told Williamsen that it was thought by some persons in So. Cara. that one cause of opposition to the assumpt. on the part of his State was an apprehension that we shod. flourish too rapidly when releived from our burdens: he seemed to feel a conscious Shame.

[*John*] Trumbull is painting a magnificent Picture of the President; the figure 7 foot high—a great likeness—it is for the Corporation of New York who are to give a hundred Guineas for it—I saw it yesterday & I felt fired with desire to have such a one in Charleston—can't our Corporation do the same? would the Citizens of Charleston contribute to such a gratification with less Zeal than those of New York? I think not—Suppose then you feel the pulse of the Corporn.; if they are not warmed with the bare mention of it, say no more to them, but inquire whether a hundred Guineas cannot be presently raised by Subscription for the purpose, & put my name immediately after yours for the same sum you subscribe; or let the Expence be divided equally among all the Subscribers; Such an opportunity may never offer again—if I receive your orders, I will prevail on Trumbull (with whom I am very intimate) to send you a Peice of Painting for the decoration of our new State house which will delight your eyes all the rest of your Life.

I received by [*William*] Elliott a Letter from one Thomas White, who requires my assistance in some business he wishes to be done here & who informs me that he writes to me under your auspices; you said nothing about him in your last: who is he? he has written me a long detail of grievances but does not explicitly inform me what he wants done.

Your answer to the various objections against our new [*state*] Constitution has afforded me much satisfaction; it will assist me in removing those objections when I hear them re-iterated; I beleive they sprang from inattention to ~~those~~ considerations which should always be taken into View in forming an opinion of a governmt. calculated for a particular State; general principles won't always apply: a citizen from a compact Eastern State, like Connecticut, will require a frame of govt. which would be altogether disgustful ~~for~~ to a state thinly settled, with an extensive back-country: accordingly old Roger Sherman thought we might have made a better constitution; but when I entered into the explanation necessary to make him relish it, he thought better of it. For my part, I am very well satisfied & consider myself, as a citizen of So. Cara., under very great obligations of gratitude to you & your friends, whose Labors obtained such advantages for the low Country & established a constitution which I believe will promote the tranquillity & welfare of the State in general.

The President has concluded a Treaty with [*Alexander*] McGillivray & the Creeks: it is now before the Senate for their consent. I was present at the Talk delivered by General Knox ~~to the Creeks~~ on the occasion & at the signing of the Treaty: your nephew John [*Rutledge*], Harry Izard & my brother [*Joseph Allen Smith*] ~~were~~ signed as witnesses to it. The boundary Line is settled & proper arrangemts. adopted to ensure amity hereafter between the U.S. & Creeks. The Georgians will however, I fear, be much dissatisfied with it, as it takes from them some Lands which they claim & will deprive their Land-speculators of further opportunities of taking possession of Lands to which they never had any claim. I had some conversation with McG. just before the Treaty was signed; on my expressing a satisfaction that matters were brought to a happy issue, he replied that his Nation had been always much pleased with the conduct of So. Cara. & had been well treated by us, that the direct contrary was the Case with Georgia whose citizens thought too highly of their own power & too meanly of that of his Nation; that he had given the Georgians in the present Treaty a line more favorable than they had any right to expect, ~~but that~~ because he was disposed to make great concessions for the sake of peace. He & his friends are much gratified by the kind treatment they have met with; they Could not have fallen into better hands than the President, & Knox, who vie with each other in acts of friendship. McGillivray lives with Knox, at whose house I am very intimate; they pass this Evening & sup with us: McG. says that his life has been a constant scene either of actual warfare or preparation for it, ever since he has had the command of the Nation, & he now anticipates with pleasure the tranquil enjoyments of peace. They return shortly by water, but have not yet determined at what port they shall land, If in Charleston, I hope their favorable impressions will be justified by the reception they will meet.

The Law for the Settlement of accounts between the Un. States & the individual States [*HR*-77] has passed. The Commissioners are not yet appointed; the Virginians tried hard to have two additional Commrs. beleiving that one would be from their State, but the Senate would not concur: after the Law had past, they manœvered so effectually as to get a supplementary bill [*HR*-95] ~~pa~~ thro' our house, but it was immedy. rejected by the Senate: Some time ago the Virgns., beleiving that their Claims were very enormous, joined in a motion, directing the Commrs. to lay before the House the amot. of the Claims of the several States, & to state~~ing~~ the grounds & principles on which the various claims were founded: this was accordingly done, & the Commrs. reported that those ~~Claims~~ of Virginia were brought forward in so confused & indigested a shape that they could not make head or tail of them, that they were at a loss by what rule to ascertain the specie value of the several charges some of which were beyond all calculation & they instanced a horse which was charged at *400,000 dollars*, & which at the continental scale of 40 for 1. would make the *specie* charge of *10,000 dollars* for *a horse*: the rest of the regiment was charged at nearly the same value. This report was taken in high Dudgeon by the antient dominion who complained sadly of partiality & prejudging, when in fact the Commrs. had done nothing more than they were directed by the Virginns. themselves to do.[2] They now affect to predict an unfair settlement & that their State will not have justice; the fact is that every honest man would cut off at least half their claim; this they are aware of & now want to impute such curtailment to undue biass. The President has (I suspect) been made acquainted with the uneasiness of that State, for he kept back the Bill for settling the accots. until the Supplem[*entar*]y. bill had been agreed to; he then signed it (on the last day) beleiving the supplemy. bill would pass & I imagine he would have sent it back with objections had the supplemy. bill not passed our house: they are however all much disappointed at the rejection in the Senate. The President is now embarassed about the appointment of the Commrs. the Virginns. complain of the late Commrs. & the President is afraid of giving offence if he shod. appoint others. I beleive [*John*] Kean will be re appointed; I hear him gener[*all*]y. spoken well of; his abilities & integrity give much confidence; ~~at~~ I have a particular regard for him, [*lined out*] because I have had proof of his worth.

It is now necessary, my dr. Sir, that some immediate steps shod. be taken for the Exhibition of our claims; our ~~Del~~ Senators have recd. a~~n answer~~ Letter from the Governor in answer to one written to urge him to an attention to this important business; in his Letter he informs them that he & the Council were of opinion that Congress would send some Commrs. into the State, & that it would be adviseable to wait the meeting of the Legislature; no Commissr. is to be Sent & even were one Sent it would not be his duty to gather up our scattered claims, he would only receive & examine them when tendered to him by the state agent. A State agent must at all events be appointed & the sooner the better: I had much trouble in obtaining further time to 1st. July next; the Eastern members were for allowing but a few months, & it would be provoking that with these advantages all our claims should not be brought forward. The Govr. & Council should in my opinion proceed without further delay to appoint an agent for the purpose of collecting & transmitg. our Claims with the necessary Vouchers: If they won't undertake to make the appointmt. let it be done the momt. the Legislature meets: at my request Kean has drawn up the form of the act, with a specification of the proper evidence necessary to substantiate the claims: I thought, from his experience of this business he could best point out the species of evidence which would be admissible, & that his ideas ~~on the subject~~ might tend to throw light on the subject & facilitate the arrangements. I enclose you his observations (with a draught of the Act [*HR*-77]): if you mean to make use of them, they shod. first be copied, as from prudential reasons, his hand-writing ought not to appear.

ALS, Smith Papers, ScHi. Place to which addressed not indicated. Continuations of this letter, dated 13 and 16 August, are calendared under those dates, below.

[1] See Governor Edward Telfair, Debt Held in Georgia, 7 June, volume 19.
[2] See Report of the Commissioners for Settling Accounts, 8 May, volume 19.

Henry Wynkoop to Reading Beatty

Yesterday the Senate concurr'd with the House of Representatives in the Resolution for Adjourning on twesday, think therefore may now without Danger of Disappointment, make Disposal for getting Home; Therefore request You if convenient to give Notice to my family to send a Light Waggon to be at Morton's by sunrise on Thurdsday morning next, or if You can not conveniently give that Notice, then to send some Vehicle to Morton's by that time to take me & my Baggage; Writing this at Doctor Elmers, who is just going off, is the Reason I send You no papers, but in a few days You shall have all the News.

ALS, Wynkoop Papers, PDoBHi. Place to which addressed not indicated.

Other Documents

Robert Morris to Gouverneur Morris. LS, Gouverneur Morris Papers, NNC. Place to which addressed not indicated. An inserted sheet depicts a map drawn by R. Morris of the Genessee tract.

"Yesterday I made a bargain which if properly improved will I expect, not only be the means of extricating me from all the embarrassments in which I have been involved, but also the means of making your Fortune and mine"; describes his purchase of the Genessee tract from Nathaniel Gorham and Oliver Phelps and solicits Gouverneur to serve as agent for its resale, upon the same general terms as Joel Barlow's Scioto Company sales; sends a copy of the Naturalization Act [HR-40], and suggests appealing for buyers in the Austrian Netherlands (Belgium), where revolution must have created "such a scene of anarchy and distress that I do suppose there are thousands of those People of good circumstances that would be glad to seek an Asylum in such a Country as this."

Robert Morris to Walter Stone. ALS, Stone Family Papers, DLC. Addressed to Port Tobacco, Maryland; franked; postmarked.

Joshua Johnson "is appointed Consul at London, His long standing there gave him the preference, otherwise you would have had it, I offered to give for you any Security, that might be Required, but that was not deemed Necessary."

Monday, 9 August 1790

Ignatius Geoghegan to Pierce Butler

I arrived here well after a tedious passage of 20 dys, Mr. [*John*] McQueen was just setting off for the Southard so that I had but time to forward your letter to him. *** The People to the Southward are exceedingly exasperated against the new Spanish Governor of Florida [*Juan de Quesada*] who not only openly protects the runaway Neg[*roe*]s. but has treated their masters (who have gone in search of them) with the greatest insolence I have not a doubt from the present disposition of the people that some violence will be committed. When I last had the pleasure of seeing you, You were pleased to enquire if my brother Domnick was determined on settling at the Aux Cayes [*present-day Les Cayes, Haiti*]. not knowing at that time his fixed determination I was unable to answer, I now take the liberty of informing you he is; & at the same time I beg leave to request that in the nomination of Consuls, (shou'd such a thing take place) for these places his name may be mentioned. His knowledge of the French language, & usages, wou'd justify the appointment. His misfortunes render him the object. Shou'd he, through your means obtain some appointment of this nature I'll venture to answer for his ever retaining the most lively sense of gratitude.

ALS, Butler Papers, PHi. Written from Savannah, Georgia; carried by "Capt." (Lieutenant) John Pierce. The omitted text relates to Georgia state judicial proceedings.

Daniel Hiester to Clement Biddle

I have reeceived Your Polite favour some days ago, and hope on Doctor [*James*] Hutchinsons shewing you my letter,[1] You have not understood it as if I doubted Your attention to the business in question, I do assure you I did not, the subject struck me whilst I was writing, and ~~was~~ I intended simply to express a wish to know what was done, and ~~I~~ am much obliged to you for the information You gave me on that head—Colo. [*William Stephens*] Smith hearing that I had a copy of your instructions to your assistants, asked the loan of it yesterday.

In a Conversation a few days ago on the subject of taking the Census, Alderman [*Daniel*] McCormick of this place told me, that, in lately going through this City to take the Constitutional State Census he found *even here* considerable difficulties, in many families in obtaining a true account of their number merely from a fear that Government might have some improper intentions. Upon this Permit me [*to*] suggest whether it would be well to throw something into the Public Papers explanatory of the true intention of the law previous to entering on the execution of it. It is certain enough that in some parts of Europe, Enumerations of the people have preceeded (and paved the way for) the blackest designs of despots, the knowledge of which, and a consequent fear, no doubt, still rests on the minds of some. and others may, from a natural distrust, be disposed to with hold the information.

This day, A Bill [*Sinking Fund Act HR-101*] will be brought into the House of Representatives, to authorise the Secretary of the Treasury to lay out the Surplus of money, that may at the end of the year, be in the Treasury, after the appropriations are satisfied, in Purchasing Stock in the Market. This surplusage It is supposed will be a million of drs. If this and some other matters reported by the Secretary, does not extend the Session, the Adjournmt. will take place to morrow, Agreeably to the resolution of both Houses.

ALS, Washington-Biddle Correspondence, PHi. Addressed to Philadelphia; franked.

[1] Neither Hiester's letter to Hutchinson, nor the letter from Biddle that it prompted, has been located; they almost certainly dealt with census taking under the Enumeration Act, a responsibility of federal marshals like Biddle and William Stephens Smith.

William Samuel Johnson and Oliver Ellsworth to Governor Samuel Huntington

In obedience to the Resolution of the General Assembly transmitted to us by your Excellency,[1] we immediately executed a Deed of Session, to the United States of the Light House & its appendages, at New London.

Your Letter naming a person for Consular appointment to Demerara [*Surinam*], unfortunately was received one Day too late.

An adjournment of Congress is expected to take place in a day or two; the necessary business of the Session being nearly closed, & the Members as impatient to return home, as their Constituents probably are to have them.

About fifty Acts have been passed in the course of the session; & altho' unanimity has not been attainable with respect to all of them the Session will nevertheless end in harmony & with better prospects than it commenced.

The Act, proposing a new loan of the domestick debt, which we herewith inclose, has taken up more time, than any other; & may be the subject of more animadversion—To embrace evry description of Creditors, who had contributed to the general defence, & yet not to swell the publick burdthen to a forbiding size, were among the objects necessary to be regarded, in forming the Act; & an accomodating spirit on the part of the Creditors will be necessary to give it effect.

As to Revenue, the most difficult acquisition in all Governments, 3,200,000 Dollars pr. ann. will be requisite for the Civil List, Foreign debt & the new proposed Loan. For 2,600,000 Dollars of which, funds, are already established by the Impost & Tonnage Acts, for the remaining 600,000 which will not be wanted till January 1792 funds will be provided the next Session, and may probably consist of inland duties of different descriptions—Direct taxation will not be resorted to, but in case of a deficiency of other resources, which it is presumed will not happen, & at any rate cannot be large.

The interest on the foreign debt, has this year been paid. and there will remain in the Treasury, at the end of the year, a sum, which employed in a Bank operation, may be very convenient in facilitating at once, the payment of the duties, & a prompt discharge of quarterly interest.

A Treaty, is now concluding, with the Cheifs of the Creek Indians, who were induced to come here for that purpose. This Treaty, together with an Act that has passed to regulate trade & intercourse with the Indian Tribes, & the establishment of a few Military Posts along the frontiers, for the purpose of mutual protection; give us a right to hope for lasting peace with the Indian Nations—And it is with pleasure we add, that from the present aspect of their affairs, the United States have a right to look for peace, & respect from all Nations.

LS, Connecticut Miscellany, DLC. Place to which addressed not indicated.

[1] The act was enclosed in Huntington's letter of 18 June, volume 19.

Richard Henry Lee and John Walker to [*Thomas Mathews*], Speaker of the Virginia House of Delegates

In conformity with the directions that we received from the General Assembly, we had the honor of presenting their Address to the President of the United States. The answer that he was pleased to make, we immediately transmitted to the Governor, who will, we doubt not, lay it before the Legislature.[1] We have not failed, Sir, in conformity with another direction of our Constituents, to propose to the Senate of the United States in the name of the General Assembly of Virginia, that the doors of the Senate should be open when that Body were engaged in Legislative discussions; to the end that their debates might be heard by the Citizens of the United States. As we were not favored with the reasons that produced a negative on the proposition, we are not able, even to guess at the principles that influenced the refusal of what appears to us a reasonable request, and coming moreover from a source so respectable.[2]

The many Laws that have been passed this session of Congress, it is not necessary for us to recapitulate, as they will be transmitted to the Executive by the proper Officer of the United States.

The most important of these Acts are those for funding and providing means of paying the debts proper of the United States, and for assuming the debts of the individual States. The latter of these measures we could not approve, as being premature, and properly to follow a fair and just settlement of accounts between the United States and the individual States. And because it appeared to be unjust with respect to those States, and particularly our Commonwealth, that had by heavy taxes already paid a large portion of public debt. Should we have erred in this opinion, it will be imputed, we hope, to mistaken judgment; and we shall be happy to find that in the ultimate issue, general good, not partial evil shall be the result. The laws for the above purposes we have the honor to enclose together with an estimate shewing the funds for paying interest on the foreign and domestic debt, and for defraying the expenses of the civil List.[3] The Law for fixing the permanent Seat of the Government of the United States on Potowmac, by it's tendency to encrease the commerce of Chesapeake Bay and its dependencies, seems likely to produce good to our Country. The final accomplishment of this will depend greatly upon the completion of the generous offer made by our Legislature to join Maryland in a contribution for defraying the expenses of the Fœderal Buildings &c.

An enclosed certified paper will shew the progress made in the proffered Amendments of last Session to the Constitution of the United States.[4] The Assent of our Commonwealth may, we humbly conceive, secure the establishment of principles, that, by being fixed on the minds of the People, will be conducive hereafter to arrest the progress of power, should it be disposed to exert itself in future times to the injury of public liberty.

LS, Executive Communications, Vi. Enclosures are in the same location. Place to which addressed not indicated. This letter was first printed in the [Richmond] *Virginia Gazette and Public Advertiser*, 11 December (not extant) and reprinted in four of Philadelphia's newspapers between 21 December 1790 and 5 January 1791.

---

[1] R. H. Lee and Walker forwarded the reply to Governor Beverley Randolph on 28 April; it is printed in volume 19.

[2] The Virginia Senators made the motion to open the Senate doors on 29 April. It was defeated when only Maclay voted with Lee and Walker.

[3] The enclosed estimate, in the hand of a House clerk, was submitted by Hamilton to the Senate committee on the Ways and Means Act [HR-83], which Lee chaired; it is printed in *DHFFC* 6:2053.

[4] The enclosed paper is a certified copy, in a House clerk's hand, of the report of the committee chaired by Steele, dated 29 July, on the status of state ratification of the Amendments to the Constitution proposed by Congress in September 1789; see *DHFFC* 8:472–73. In an

additional notation, dated 12 August, Beckley certified the ratification of the Amendments by New Jersey, as transmitted to the House on 6 August.

John Rutledge, Jr. to William Short

***

I am sorry to tell you that on my arrival here I found things in a very unpleasant situation in consequence of Congress's resolve to move to Philada. those who had been active in effecting this change in the seat of government are much more abused (& quite as publickly) by those who were opposed to the measure than the most highflying Aristocrats were when I was in france by the most sound [?] democrats—this [*illegible*] has been gone into by the ladies as well as the Gentlemen & these Amazons have not been less active than their lords I have not myself seen any Caps pulled—but have heard of the renting of gauzes tearing of laces breaking of Plumes &c. &c. &c.

***

Make my Comps. to the Marquis de la Fayette & say to him that the day after my arrival & at a crowded drawing [*levee*] where amongst other great folk there were 30 Kings Princes warriors & Sachems I presented to our great & good Presidt. the Key & drawing of the Bastille.

***

AL, Short Papers, DLC. Place to which addressed not indicated. The omitted text makes excuses for not writing at greater length and conveys New York City gossip.

James Seagrove to Pierce Butler

I did myself the pleasure of filling a sheet of paper to You under date of yesterday, which accompany's this. Last Evening [*Cornelius*] Schermerhorns Vessel got in, and brought me another proof of your friendship, dated the 29th. June. I fear it may prove unfortunate that this Letter was so long by the way, as perhaps the appointment for Havana may have taken place ere this, in favour of some other.

In case of a War between Britain and Spain, there is nothing on Earth I would so much desire as being enabled to go to Havana in Character of Consul from the United States. *** My dear friend I hope you will not loose a Moment in your endeavouring to procure me the appointment. I fear R. Morris will push a very worthless fellow of the name of *Oliver Pollock* whom he once before had appointed—and who the Spanish Govmt. would not receive from his infamous and well known Character—having for years been Confined by them for Counterband and other breaches of their Laws.

*** This Man & his transactions was the principal cause of all the bad treatment the Americans receivd. at Havana. I believe he is well know[*n*] to Congress for his good actions on the Missasipee—and his demands on them & the State of Virginia.

***

I want words to express my gratitude for your offer of protection, under your roof at this moment it is impossible—as Tomorrow I am obliged to Sail for St. Mary's with Supplies for the Troops and some other business which cannot be done without my presence—but in case I am appointed, and you think it necessary, I will come on at all events. I have reason to think [*William?*] Constable will assist me all in his power—but I am not affraid of obtaining an extensive Credit, if we can arrang matters otherwise. I have not a doubt my friend if we can bring these matters about—that I can relieve my self from debt in a Short time, and better your Situation very much. It will rest with yourself in what light you wish to be placed with respect to all future concerns. ***

I have the Vanity to think that no person who could be sent [*to Havana*] would be more agreeable to the people there then I should—And as a proof of it I now inclose you the Intendant Generals Letter to me on my quiting Havana in 1784[1]—which in my Opinion might not be amiss to let the President see when you speak to him for me. For Gods sake take care of the Original, as it will be well for me to have it, in case of going there. I have sent you my translation which I believe was unnecessary, as I think you read Spanish.

In case I get the Consulship at Havana, the Collectors place at St. Mary's will becom vacant—and tho' it is of little consequence at present I could wish as my Brother Robert Lives there, and is well acquainted with the Business—having been my Deputy since I have had the office you would use your influence with the President to have him Appointed in my room. The Bearer Capt. [*Lt. John*] Pierce is on the point of departing, so that I have not time to say more.

[*P. S.*] If it is not dissagreeable to you, I could wish you would call on Secty. Howard[2] as by introduction from me—It will have a good effect—and I am of opinion he will give a favourable Character of me to the President if necessary.

ALS, Butler Papers, PHi. Written from Savannah, Georgia.

[1] The original AL of Juan Ignacio de Urriza to Seagrove, Havana, 29 July 1784, is accompanied by an English translation in Seagrove's hand.

[2] The Spanish army captain Don Carlos Howard, provisional secretary to Governor Quesada of Spanish East Florida, took a sick leave from the capital, St. Augustine, in order

to advise Alexander McGillivray during the Creek Treaty negotiations in New York City (*McGillivray*, pp. 43, 270, 276).

Michael Jenifer Stone to Tobias Lear

I have inquired and can only recollect two Gentlemen who would answer the purpose of Surveyor at Llewellensburg—Col. Jeremiah Jordan—and Charles Llewellin—of those Jordan is I believe the fitest But I really cannot tell if either will accept—Their conditions are rather above it—But it might not be Materially inconvenient to them—Jordan keeps a Store at the Spot—and I think it would be [*most*] probable that he would serve.

ALS, Washington Papers, DLC.

Hugh Williamson to Governor Alexander Martin

Inclosed is the copy of a late Act of Congress for setling the accounts of the States and paying the ballances to such as may be Creditors [*Settlement of Accounts Act HR-77*]. By this setling Act you will observe that the powers of the Commissioners are greatly enlarged They are authorized to determine all claims of any State that are made or shall be made before the first of July next according to the principles of general Equity whether the expenditures were made for the *general* or *particular defence* during the late War. This naturally includes *all* our Indian expeditions our Sea Coast defence The Vessels we sunk the Cannon we bought, and sundry other charges some of which have hitherto been doubtful and others exceptionable.

One indisputable Principle of equity is that we shall be paid for all services their full value. Our Militia services as you know form a large sum on our public accounts. Those services have been strangely setled in depreciated paper. The Commissioners alledge that they are not intelligeble. This I hold to be a fortunate circumstance, for they must be stated again, and Col. [*Abishai*] Thomas and myself propose immediately to enter upon that work. We shall take the whole Militia Service from the begining and charge every days service of officer or Private according to the Specie price originally paid by the State. Our Militia Pay was a little more than Continental Allowance but this will naturally come under the Head of bounty as some of the States have charged Bounties for all the Militia they ever mustered. By this new settlement of our Accounts we shall gain at least one Million of Dollars In all other cases where we can prove what was the article furnished we shall think ourselves at liberty to charge the true Value of that Article regardless of the Scale by which it was paid. I think the State will also authorise us to charg all the Land promised and paid to Privates as Bounty in the Continental line of the Army. You observe that an arduous Task presents itself I hope we shall acquit ourselves to the advantage and approbation of the State but I belive it will be necessary to submit some of the cases mentioned to the consideration of the State in order that we may be enabled to make the charges under the instructions of the State. Having examined the charges of the other States I think North Carolina must be a Creditor State to the amount of two millions of Dollars. Virga. Maryd. N. Jersey N. York & Connecticut and Newhamshire will probably be the greatest Debtors. Massachusets will hardly be above par and her members have indicated no great desire to promote the Settlement of Accounts. If the law could have been passed for Assuming the State debts before the other Law had passed for setling the accots. of the States and if the whole debts had been assumed I think a Settlement would have been prevented which must hav[*e*] made a difference of some Millions against our State. North Carolina is now secure in being repaid her liberal advances during the War This is the object I have had so much at heart from the begining you will probably be informed that I have not been deficient in my assistance to secure this Law and in so doing I believe that I have been serving the State very essentially. All objections being removed to the admission of every proper claim I shall now betake myself wholly to the arrangement of our Accounts and hope we shall make them unexceptionable in form & respectable in size I believe it will be necessary that either Col. Thomas or myself should attend at the sitting of the Assembly that we may be enabled fully to explain such legislative aid as we may need towards the support of new charges.

Copy, Governors' Letterbook, Nc-Ar.

A Poem

Addressed to the writer of those Essays
published in the Connecticut Journal, signed "A Republican"

And dost thou write to get some votes thyself,
To go to Congress, and encrease thy pelf?
Or dost thy eager Master pat thy head,
And say "Good fellow, here's a bit of bread?"
Snarl the old members out, if thou art able,
And thou shalt eat the crumbs beneathe his table.

[Hartford, Connecticut] *American Mercury*, 9 August; reprinted at Litchfield, Connecticut.

Newspaper Article

The Correspondent in your last paper, who is so highly censured in the Centinel for observing on the fulsom "puffs" which appear in behalf of Mr. Ames, renews his request, to be informed why this "Guardian of our Country's Honor" should presume to originate a motion contrary to the most positive instructions of the State Convention?[1] Let the writers in the Centinel answer this question, and not content themselves with blazing away on his *pretty sounding Speeches*, but let them satisfy his CONSTITUENTS why he dare violate their most serious and solemn injunctions.

Boston Gazette, 9 August.

[1] See Newspaper Article, *Boston Gazette*, 2 August, above.

Newspaper Article

EITHER the Demon of Discord, or the Philadelphia INFLUENZA, has already led the sociable Citizens of New-York by the ears—Every man who owes *six-pence* is sued by his neighbour—say the evil spirits, "you should secure yourself, least your Debtor go to Philadelphia with Congress." For shame, ye Yorkers—have more confidence in each other and be not afraid of Elopements, because one Taylor and one Shoemaker attempted to desert you. Courage boys, we are still here.

A correspondent who has read [*John*] FENNO's Assumption paragraphs supposes that he was aided by an Aristocratic Member from the same state that sends the Republican B**ke [*Burke*]—How amazingly different are the colleagues of some States! Depreciating the state of Georgia, has become a species of Entertainment for the purse-proud abettors of the Murderers of innocent Women and Children.

NA BACKLISH!!!

NYMP, 9 August. "Na backlish" may be a variant of the Scottish "Na backling," or "never backwards."

OTHER DOCUMENTS

William Gardner to Governor Josiah Bartlett. ALS, Bartlett Papers, NhD. Written from Exeter, New Hampshire; addressed to Kingston, New Hampshire.

Covers letter (Wingate to Gardner, 29 July) and its enclosed copy of the Funding Act, which Wingate asked to be forwarded.

Tobias Lear to Richard Nestor. FC:dft, Miscellaneous Letters, Miscellaneous Correspondence, State Department Records, Record Group 59, DNA. Addressed to Portsmouth, Virginia. For background on the petition of Sarah Nestor of Tuam, County Galway, Ireland, to George Washington, which sought information about her son Richard, who had emigrated from Ireland by 1780, see Lear's letter to her of this date, *PGW* 6:226–27n. An unlocated enclosure to Lear's letter included information that Washington had solicited of a gentleman from Portsmouth, whom the editors of *PGW* identify as Parker.

Forwards by Parker the enclosed petition from Sarah Nestor.

George Washington to Clement Biddle. LS, Washington-Biddle Correspondence, PHi. Addressed to Philadelphia. For a partial text, see *PGW* 6:11n.

Forwards Martha Dangerfield Bland's "application" for documentation regarding some of her husband's unsettled public accounts.

[Charleston, South Carolina] *City Gazette*, 11 August.

The ship *York* arrived from New York with news that Izard had introduced a bill to continue three more years residence in New York City.

John Jeffries, Diary. Jeffries Family Papers, MHi.

Breakfasted with the Adamses at "Richmond Hill."

Tuesday, 10 August 1790

Henry Knox to Theodore Foster

I am sorry that I happened to be engaged when you did me the honor of calling upon me.

The reason Major [*William*] Allen and his officers are unpaid at this time is that he and they declined taking warants on the receiver of continental taxes in the state of Rhode Island which was the only mode the treasury could adopt to pay him and the other troops peculiarly circumstanced with him & his officers.

But provision has now been made for the purpose, the amount due to him and each of his officers will be paid at the pay office in this city on their orders respectively—If you have the said orders I will issue my warrant for their payments.

ALS, Foster Papers, RHi. Written from the "War office."

Governor Beverley Randolph to James Madison

I am much obliged by your Favour of the 25th. of July. I am sorry that your efforts to obtain an Augmentation of the number of commissioners [*for settling accounts*] have been unsuccessful. The executive, immediately upon receiving notice of the Form in which the new Law for settling accounts [*HR*-77] stood, thought themselves bound to declare a want of confidence in two of the commissrs. & forwarded to the President an extract from their report with copies of Colo. [*William*] Davis's reply & correspondence upon that Subject.[1] Should these Papers reach New York Time enough they may perhaps be thought sufficient ground for filling up the appointments with new men. But should they have arrived after the appointments were made, the Presidents Discretion will prevent their having an bad Effect.

We are impatient [*lined out*] for the funding Law. If any Thing should have delayed its passage till this reaches you I will beg the Favour of you to forward me a copy of it as soon as it has all the Sanctions necessary to give it Force.

The Assumption Business as it is now modified will I beleive be more favourably received than it would have been in it's original Dress, but never will become a favourite in Virginia.

LS, Madison Papers, DLC. Written from Richmond, Virginia.

[1] See Report of the Commissioners for Settling Accounts, 8 May, volume 19.

John Steele to William Blount

I expect to be in No. Ca. in a few days, and will thank you to inform me by the 1st. Oppty., when and by what route you will go to the Western territ[*or*]y.

In your letter of instructions from the President,[1] the goods stored at Swannanno [*Swannanoa, North Carolina*] will be noticed, pray inform me immediately, to whom, and when they shall be delivered—I wish to deliver them before I return to Philada. and to be present myself at the delivery.

ALS, John Gray Blount Papers, Nc-Ar. Addressed to Washington, North Carolina; franked.

[1] Washington's instructions of 27 August to Blount, the newly appointed governor of the Southwest Territory, have not been located (*PGW* 7:537n). The "goods" probably referred to the large number of gifts kept on hand for any official meetings with Native American treaty negotiators.

[*Philip Freneau,*] The Removal

FROM Hudson's banks, in proud array,
(Too mean to claim a longer stay)
Their *new ideas* to improve,
Behold the great *Sanhedrim*[1] move!

Such thankless usage much we fear'd,
When Robert's [*Morris*] coach stood ready geer'd,
And he, the foremost on the floor,
Sat pointing to the Quaker shore.

So long confin'd to little things,
They now shall meet where *Bavius*[2] sings;
Where Mammon[3] builds his walls in style,
And B—h—'s *bawdy* seasons smile.[4]

The Yorker asks, but asks in vain,
"What Demon bids them move again!"
The house that moves must suffer loss,
And rolling stones attract no moss.

Have we not to our utmost strove,
For fear the Congress should remove?
At dull debates no silence broke,
And walk'd on tiptoe while they spoke?

Have we not paid for Chaplain's prayers,
That Heav'n might smile on state affairs?
Put some things up, pull'd others down,
And rais'd our streets through half the town?

Have we not toil'd through cold and heat,
To make the FED'RAL HALL complete?
Thrown down our fort[5] to give them air,
And mov'd our guns, the Lord knows where?

Times change! But memory still recalls
The day when ruffians scal'd their walls,
When sovereigns bow'd to black-guard men,
Mere *prisoners in the town of Penn*!

Can they forget, when, half afraid,
The timorous COUNCIL lent no aid;
But left them to the rogues that rob—
The tender mercies of the mob?[6]

Why, if they can, their lot is cast—
One hundred miles shall soon be pass'd.
This day the FEDERAL HALL is clear'd,
To *Pawles Hook*[7] their barge is steer'd,
Where Robert's coach stands ready geer'd.

NYDG, 10 August; printed in *NYJ* the same day and reprinted at Charleston, South Carolina. The fact that each New York paper claimed the poem was written for it, while the Charleston version includes an entire stanza and other textual variations not in either of the other two, suggests Freneau may have sent copies to each newspaper independently. The *City Gazette*'s acknowledgment of Freneau as the "supposed" author is confirmed by the poem's inclusion in his *Poems written between the years 1768 & 1794* (Philadelphia, 1795).

---

[1] The administrative and judicial council of the Jews before and during the time of Jesus.

[2] The reference denotes "inferior" and comes from Virgil's mocking a minor poet and literary critic by that name (Eclogue 3:9).

[3] The evil spirit that personifies greed, riches, avarice, and miserliness.

[4] The *City Gazette* version supplies the name "Bingham" for "B—h—" in this line (a reference to William Bingham) and adds a new fourth stanza at this point:

New chaplains now shall stretch their jaws,
New pensions grease their sacred paws,
Some reverend dunce, that turtle carves
Shall fatten—while the soldier starves.

[5] Fort George.

[6] A reference to the mutiny of the Continental Army and military demonstration at the Pennsylvania State House, the building in which Congress met, on 21 June 1783. "Tender mercies" is from Psalm 25:6.

[7] Paulus Hook had been since 1764 the New Jersey terminus of the post road ferry to New York City.

Newspaper Article

☞THIS DAY *both Houses of the Hon. the* CONGRESS *of the* UNITED STATES, *agreeably to their Resolutions of Yesterday, and their Message to the* PRESIDENT *of the* UNITED STATES, WILL ADJOURN—*to meet in the City of* PHILADELPHIA *on the first Tuesday of* DECEMBER *next. At this Juncture the* EDITOR *takes occasion to express his Gratitude to his Patrons in general for their generous Support of his Journal and Register—and to assure them, that, let the* Congress *of the* United States *reside at a greater or less Remove from this City, the* NEW-YORK JOURNAL, *and* PATRIOTIC REGISTER, *shall contain faithful* Sketches *of the* PROCEEDINGS *of that honorable Body—with such of the* DEBATES, *which may occur on the most important Subject of Legislation, as may be generally Interesting: These will constantly be Supplied by a* PHILADELPHIA CORRESPONDENT.

NYJ, 10 August. On this day, Congress postponed its adjournment to 12 August.

Other Documents

John Brown to Benjamin Logan. No copy known; acknowledged in Logan to Brown, 27 September.

Daniel Carroll to Governor John Eager Howard. ALS, Autograph Collection, Wayne State University, Detroit, Michigan. Place to which addressed not indicated.

> "Your favor of the 2d Ulto. came to hand. ~~An Accident~~ Having sufferd by a fall prevented me from giveing all that attention to it, which I shou'd otherwise have done—I put it into the hands of some of my Coleagues; & believe nothing cou'd be attempted this session with a favorable prospect."

Gouverneur Morris to William Short. ALS, Short Papers, DLC. Written from London; place to which addressed not indicated.

> Thinks that the appointment of Madison as U.S. minister to France would be "not quite constitutional" (under Article I, section 6); "If that Objection does not occur I think it highly probable that he will be the man."

John Page to St. George Tucker. ALS, Tucker-Coleman Papers, ViW. Place to which addressed not indicated.

> Encloses poetry "which [*John*] Fenno refused to publish"; in addition to the two copies of "our Dodsley" sent with his last, he encloses another with Margaret Lowther Page's "Journal" prefixed, which he entrusts "only to particular Friends"; requests Tucker's corrections of "the vile Typographical Errors"; "we sail the Day after tomorrow."

John Pintard to Elisha Boudinot. ALS, Boudinot-Pintard Papers, NHi. Addressed to Newark, New Jersey; carried by Mr. Burnet.

> Congress has adopted Hamilton's proposal for a sinking fund; "now is the time therefore if ever to prove whether any dependance can be put on a Courtier"; advises Boudinot to come to New York City; "yr. brother [*Elias*] thinks your personal renewal of this business may prove effectual."

John Jeffries, Diary. Jeffries Family Papers, MHi.

> Departed from New York aboard the packet to Providence, Rhode Island, at 4 P.M. with Wingate, Trumbull, Partridge, Goodhue, Leonard, A. Foster, and several others.

[New Hampshire] *Concord Herald*, 10 August.

The congressional delegation is expected home the last of this week or the beginning of next, since Congress was determined to adjourn by the first of August.

Letter from New York to Philadelphia. *IG*, 21 August; reprinted at Exeter and Portsmouth, New Hampshire; Boston; and New York City (*NYDG*, 25 August; *NYP*, 26 August; *NYJ*, 31 August).

"This day the meeting place of Congress in this city [*Federal Hall*] will fall to its proper owners. May it never be occupied again by a set of ungrateful men, who think that expending 26,000l. for their convenience is a *triffle*—Men of such sentiments will be a curse instead of a blessing to America."

WEDNESDAY, 11 AUGUST 1790

John Brown to James Brown

Congress adjourns this day to meet again on the 1st. Decr. in Philada. you will readily conceive how desirable a relaxation must be after Seven Months constant attention to Business—I enclose you a list of the Acts pass'd this Session—when printed I shall take the earliest oppy. to forward both them & the Journals to you—The inclosed Gazette contains the Act funding the public Debt—the assumption of 21,500,000 Dolls. of the State debts was carried by a small majority & was effected by a Bargain three or four Members agreeing to Vote for the measure provided the permanent seat of the Government was established on the Potowmack R. Bland Lee & White of our State were of the Number I will trouble you with no observations upon this subject as the Gazettes heretofore sent you contained so fully the arguments on both sides of the question—I send you an Estimate of Annual Interest on the Original debt with the Ways & means[1]—It is expected a [*?*] Revenue sufficiant for the payment of the Interest can be raised, without having recourse to direct Taxes—An act [*Sinking Fund Act HR-101*] has passed appropriating one Million of Dolls. now in the public Treasury for the purchase of Cert[*ificat*]es. in the market & the President is authorised to borrow two million more to be applied to the same purpose—The design of this measure is not only to reduce the Capital of the Debt but also to raise Securities to their full value & thereby put a stop to the purchase of them by Foreigners at a great discount—The proceeds of the sales which shall be made of the western Lands are also to be appropriated towards sinking the public Debt. An Act opening a Land Office will I expect be one of the first passed at next Session.

We have not as yet any further information relative to the expected War between Engd. & Spain ~~except~~ than contained in my last letter, except that very great preparations are making by both & that both discover a strong disposition for war.

The British Packet has been expected for some time past by her we ~~expect~~ shall probably have decisive information—The President considers this as a favorable moment to urge our claim to the Right of Navigating the Mississipi & has in the most explicit terms declared his determination to take the most effectual measures for obtaining that important object & for perpetuating the Union between this & the Western Country—I am sorry that I cannot be more explicit in my communications to you upon this subject None but Mr. Jefferson—a Gentn. [*David Humphreys*] who proceeds immediately to Madrid & myself have been admitted to confer with the President on this head—all therefore I am now at liberty to say is that should the plan proposed succeed the result must prove highly satisfactory to the Western People.

A Treaty was this day concluded with McGilvery & the Creek Chiefs—it has not as yet been published & some of the Articles [*I*] am told are to be kept secret I am informd by the Secretary of War that it is as advantageous as could be desired.

I do not now expect to return to Kentucke before March next the time between this & the next Session being too short to admit of my making a stay in that Country so long as to compensate for the fatigue & risk of the Journey I therefore shall take this leisure time to Visit such parts of the States as I have not yet seen & expect to set out in about an hours time with one or two very agreeable friends for Albany & shall proceed from thence into Vermont & perhaps into Canada—should I not go into Canada my return will be in three or four weeks & in that case perhaps I may visit my Virga. Relations—However write to me as frequently as usual & inclose them to Sam. [*Brown*] in Staunton [*Virginia*] I will give him directions how to forward them to me I will write you as frequently as private oppys. of Conveyance offer—as my priviledge of franking ceases after to day—I wish you would let me know what necessaries you may want as I can get them so much cheaper & better for you in Philada. than they can be had in Kentucke & will have an oppy. of sending them to you this fall I shall also have Cash to spare & if my affairs in Kentucke or yours require a remitance from me I beg you to let me know it—Let me know what A[*lexander*]. Breckenridge has done about the Lands I purchasd from Quick—I also wish you to make some enquiry about my Military Locations on the Continental [*lined out*] Line[2]—if you find the Land has been taken by a prior Entry—get Colo. [*Abraham*] Buford & Colo. [*Richard*] Taylor to assign the Warrants to me & get them located between the Sciota & Miami [*rivers*].

I write this in my place in the House amidst that confusion which always preceeds an adjournment therefore need make no other appology—I am in good health.

ALS, Liberty Hall, Frankfort, Kentucky. Place to which addressed not indicated. Brown may have written this letter on 12 August.

[1] For Hamilton's estimate, dated 2 August, see *DHFFC* 6:2053.
[2] A reference to Brown's military bounty lands.

Pierce Butler and Ralph Izard to Governor Charles Pinckney

By Captain [*William*] Elliott We had the Honour to receive Your Letter of the 20th of July[1] acknowledging the receipt of the President's Answer to the Address of the Citizens of So. Carolina—Also the Sundry Bonds of Commodore Gillon delivered to Us by Mr. Jefferson.[2]

We are led to believe, from what Your Excellency is pleased to remark in Your Letter respecting further Claims by the state against the United states, that the Nature and importance of the business, and of early bringing forward those Claims have not made the same impression on Your Excellency, and the Council, that they have on Us—You have been some time since informed that most, if not all, of the other states have presented new statements of Claims for all the Expenses incurr'd in defending their individual State Vidzt. for Fortifications, for Arm'd Vessels, built or bought for defence—for Water Obstructions, for State Troops, for Indian Affairs—for Cloathing and Provision, furnished either to Continental or state Troops from 1775 to 1782—for Militia Call'd out under any Resolve of Congress, or by Order of any Continental Genl. for Pensions to Invalid Militia disabled in service, or to the widows or Children of such as fell in the service—for Militia brought into the Field, though unauthorized by any Act of Congress, but drawn out for Actual defence—for Bounties—Debts Assumed from, or rather to Individuals, for Supplies furnished to the Continental Army—And in short for every Expence Actualy incurr'd during the war—We repeat the observation that the other states have brought forward Charges for every hoeful of Earth throun up for defence during the war—for every Expense incurr'd.

We Conceive it will not only be more Regular but more promising of Success to present the Claims here to the Commissioner's that are appointed for the purpose of adjusting the Claims of Individual States against the United states; and to send them by a State Agent capable of Explaining them; who may also from time to time Examine the Credits given to the state by the Commissioners; and where they appear short to remonstrate against the statement, in order to get it adjusted—For this purpose most of the states keep Intelligent Agents on the spot; and it appears to Us that it woud be beneficial to so. Carolina to do the same—we are very apprehensive that if not done immediately the state will be shut out from making any further Claims—We feel it Our duty to be thus particular knowing of how much importance the subject is to so. Carolina.

ALS, hand of Butler, Lafayette Manuscripts, Lilly Library, Indiana University, Bloomington; FC, Butler Letterbooks, PHi; copy, U.S. Relations, Sc. Place to which addressed not indicated. The letter was submitted to the South Carolina legislature on 18 January 1791.

[1] Letter not found. For further comment on its contents, see Smith (S.C.) to Edward Rutledge, 8 August, above.

[2] While stationed in Paris in the summer of 1789, Jefferson was empowered to receive the canceled bonds originally passed by Alexander Gillon, as South Carolina's agent, to the state's Dutch creditors, the Van Staphorsts (*PTJ* 15:257–58, 16:324–25n). Jefferson turned the bonds over to Butler and Izard immediately upon his arrival in New York in March 1790; for the Senators' signed receipt, see 23 March, volume 19.

John Brown Cutting to John Adams

If ever there was a time when the volunteer exertions of a citizen of America became a duty incumbent upon him in a foreign realm—that period has existed here.

For many weeks past I have not been absent a single day from the Admiralty—sundays only excepted. It is not for me to say how efficacious in resisting individual oppression or national mischief this unintermitting attention has proved.

I have not yet leisure to transmit either to Yourself or to Mr. Jefferson a full detail of facts. By the inclosed papers however You will obtain some information.

The press notwithstanding pacific appearances in the newspapers yet continues, throughout the british ports: but whether the british fleet is rendering thus formidable for warlike enterprize or only politic intimidation, the best informed people here can only conjuecture.

***

[*Enclosure*]

Copy of a

Letter from Mr. Hugh Purdie—a native of Virginia—dated on board the Crescent, a british ship of war at Torbay [*England*] and superscribed to his Excellency John Adams—in his absence to his successor: erroneously brought by the post-man—to Mr. Cutting and by him honsetly open'd and answer'd on the 27 July 1790

"Sir,

You will find I am a native of Virginia by a certificate in my possession; but am deprived of my liberty by being imprss'd into the service of his britannic majesty. My late father bore considerable posts under the constitution during the late war He was printer to the public and post master general to the state of Virginia; but by too great faith in the paper currency of the state reduced those of his family who survived the fatigues of the war to servile employments for their subsistence. I have urged the faith of treaties and the consequence of a violation in vain. I must therefore humbly solicit your protection or assistance in procuring my discharge.

I have already acquainted Mr. Ebenezer Hazard, a friend of mine in New York of my being impress'd, and doubt not he will make use of his influence in that quarter for my discharge Shou'd your Excellency be refused that power, I doubt not your Excellency will release me as soon as possible.

P. S. At the time of my discharge I think it but reasonable they shou'd find me a passage from some port from whence I may get home with payment for my detention—Shou'd it be requisite I can get some in London to prove with my own oath I never was in England before—and ever denied any allegiance to its government."

N. B. I stated in reply the absence of Mr. Adams or any person invested with the public authority of the United States—recommended to Mr. Purdie a declaration of certain facts in writing—and a reference for corroborative testimony to some person in London—promising on my part the most strenuous application at the Admiralty and a zealous perseverance in every measure in the power of an individual to use with ~~the best~~ any probability of success, for his relief.

ALS, Adams Family Manuscript Trust, MHi. Written from London. The omitted text reports on diplomatic affairs in Continental Europe. The author and subject of the enclosure (Copy, hand of Cutting) was Hugh Purdie (b. 1767), son of the noted revolutionary newspaper editor Alexander Purdie (d. 1779) and a native of Williamsburg, Virginia, who signed onto the crew of an American merchant ship bound from Norfolk to London in August 1789. After a second brief tour on a British West Indian merchant ship, he returned to London on 5 June 1790 and was immediately pressed into service in the British navy, despite producing a birth certificate signed by Williamsburg's Anglican minister. The case was not unusual: during the intensive mobilization undertaken in response to the Nootka Sound crisis with Spain, the British navy relied heavily on impressment, or the forcible drafting—almost kidnaping—of able bodied merchant mariners picked up from the streets and taverns of English harbors. Cutting later estimated that 13,000 sailors were impressed by the British navy in 1790 alone, and that no fewer than 2,000 of these were United States citizens—roughly half the number of American seamen who sailed into London every year. Within weeks of the "hot press" that began on 4 May, Gouverneur Morris complained to the Duke of Leeds, who was routinely amenable to correcting such abuses when they could be proved. Purdie first presented his particular case in the enclosed letter to John Adams "or his successor." In the absence of any American consul in London, Cutting, who had been Adams's secretary there in 1787–88 and had just been employed as an agent by American sea captains to protest impressment of their seamen, immediately assumed responsibility for Purdie's appeal. In addition to the enclosure printed here, Cutting probably enclosed his copy of Purdie's letter of 30 July, responding to Cutting's request for more information on 27 July. (For a partial text, see *PTJ* 18:318.) This second account of Purdie's impressment includes the hope that Cutting would "not omit laying my case before Congress. My father was well known to that honourable body, as his son is to the members for Virginia," and he concludes by adding that Representative Parker "is my particular friend and acquaintance." (A third enclosure may have been Cutting's copy of his letter to Jefferson dated 18 July, also in the Adams Family Manuscript Trust, which dealt specifically with the case of several American seamen impressed on 15 July; for the full text, see *PTJ* 18:324–29.) Despite the successful issue of Cutting's personal interview with William Pitt "The Younger" about Purdie's case in mid-August, the Admiralty's discharge orders were not acted upon until 17 September, two days after his ship returned to port and Purdie himself had been flogged for insubordination (over an unrelated matter). Secretary of State Jefferson would use Purdie's overt mistreatment as a test case to seek broader assurances against future impressment of documented U.S. citizens, as well as indemnification when they were impressed. Unfortunately, the Washington administration chose a poor example of justified American outrage; after Purdie alienated both Cutting and the newly appointed U.S. consul in London, Jefferson let the matter drop. The unlawful impressment of American seamen remained a major point of contention that was addressed, but never adequately resolved, in the negotiations leading up to Jay's Treaty of 1794. For extensive background and additional documents, see *PTJ* 18:310–42.

[*John Page,*] Consistency

THE great, the learned Dr. H[*ugh*]—
Wrote a long Essay for to shew
   Th'nonsense of Greek and Latin;[1]
Then in the House, both hands in's breeches,
With twisted phiz,[2] he lards his speeches,
   With scraps *lugg'd smoothly* pat in.
Thus have I heard a patriot bawl,
And on the very building call,
   To witness to his zeal, sir;
But yet relentless doom to toil,
His fellow men in bondage vile,
   With bosom cas'd with steel, sir.

GUS, 11 August; reprinted at Boston.

[1] Hugh Williamson's widely reprinted essay of 14 September 1789 (see *DHFFC* 17:1549) was quoted and critiqued by Mirifica, 30 October 1789, volume 18, and by L, March 1790 Undated, volume 19.

[2] Physiognomy, or face.

Other Documents

John Brown to Benjamin Logan. No copy known; acknowledged in Logan to Brown, 27 September.

Daniel Hiester to William Irvine. ALS, Irvine Papers, PHi. Addressed to Irvine "In [*Pennsylvania's state constitutional*] Convention [*torn*]"; franked; postmarked 12 August.

"[*torn*] paper containing y[*our ap*]pointment I take Ple[*asur*]e in Transmitting it the H[*o*]use meet tomorrow 9 oclock to receive such laws as the President shall send—then will adjourn to the 6th Decr. next to meet at Philada. we were told Gerry meant to give further uneasiness but this day shew'd he will not."

Jeremiah Wadsworth to Royal Flint. ALS, Wadsworth Papers, CtHi. Place to which addressed not indicated. (Accompanies a receipt in Hamilton's hand, for the "within mentioned sum," dated 15 September.)

When reimbursed expenditures for the capture of the public securities counterfeiters (Francis and Adonijah Crane), Flint is to repay Hamilton the $561 loaned on that account.

GUS, 11 August.

"We hear that the Senate have, in Committee, agreed to the bill for reducing the public debt [*Sinking Fund Act*] by a large majority."

[Springfield, Massachusetts] *Hampshire Chronicle*, 18 August.

Livermore passed through Springfield.

[Northampton, Massachusetts] *Hampshire Gazette*, 18 August.

Strong arrived at Northampton.

Thursday, 12 August 1790

Elbridge Gerry to Samuel Hodgdon

I think it will be best under all circumstances to take at Miss Dally's[1] the Chamber which Governeur Morris had, untill a party is formed & secure in a House that will be agreable to me—I am yours in Haste.

ALS, Gerry Papers, MHi. Place to which addressed not indicated.

[1] With her sister Mrs. Clarke, Miss Dalley kept a boardinghouse on Second Street, Philadelphia, where members of the Massachusetts delegation frequently resided during the Second Continental Congress. She may have been involved with Gerry and other delegates in currency speculation in 1781 (*LDC* 10:344n, 16:727n).

Louis Guillaume Otto to Comte de Montmorin

***

The session which has just been terminated, My Lord, has been much more difficult than the first in that its object was to fund the public debt and consequently to satisfy the impatience of a large number of public creditors without overburdening the people less disposed in America than anywhere else to provide for the needs of the government. Several states having contracted considerable debts during the war in order to carry the Revolution to success and finding themselves consequently creditors of Congress make the greatest efforts to engage the general government to take upon itself directly the reimbursement of these debts. Some other states pretend to consider these debts as foreign to Congress and to complain about the apparent injustice that there was in making their citizens support the losses of their co-states. A great deal of skill, conciliation and intrigue was necessary to make a measure of this importance succeed, and they could attain that end only by presenting this transaction as the condition *sine qua non*[1] to fund the public debt of Congress. The debates and indecisions have lasted nearly five months and the decision of an accessory question, which was the one about the residence of Congress, has been the only means of winning a small majority. Independently of the interests of a few states, creditors of the general government, this measure favors more than any other the final consolidation of the American Government in that it no longer leaves to the particular legislatures the right to tax their citizens to pay debts which from now on will have to be paid exclusively by Congress. That was the real aim of the Secretary of the Treasury who had proposed this operation. Fortunately the legislatures which had the greatest expenses to pay desired themselves to get rid of this burden, although their own importance depended in great part on it. The principal advantage which it could be hoped to draw from a law to fund the public debt consisted in the reduction of the interest which was six per cent. This reduction will not be forced but it will depend on the choice of the creditors, with this difference only, that those who would choose to convert their bonds into new bills bearing four per cent will be paid sooner than the others. To facilitate this operation, the President of the United States is authorized to borrow about 60,000,000 tournois either in public stocks or in cash. This loan will probably serve in part to refund the credits of Europe which are above four per cent and it is very probable that it will soon be realized through the confidence which this government has inspired abroad, especially in Holland where the capitalists are more numerous and more anxious to invest their money in a secure way. Besides the ordinary expenses of the government, the Treasury of the United States has had this year a surplus of 5,000,000 tournois which by order of Congress will be used to redeem public bonds while they are still at low price. This operation seems so advantageous that the President of the United States is authorized to borrow 10,000,000 more for the same purpose so that at an average rate these 15,000,000 will redeem a capital of about 26,000,000 which carried an interest of six per cent. One can only applaud measures so clearly advantageous to the public. They are due to the excellent administration which these states enjoy and which, by reason of the President's responsibility and good judgment, is one of the most virtuous and most active which has perhaps ever existed. It is not the same with the legislature which, not being responsible for anything, always includes a large number of intriguers or mediocre persons. But the play of different interests and the constant surveillance of the public prevent the majority of this assembly from sacrificing the public good to private considerations. The very slowness of its deliberations which gives the public time to speak out on the most difficult questions serves as a check on the petulance or the speculation of some of its members. This slowness also gives to the ablest and most respectable deputies the means to persuade and to bring back those who have been misled. From this point of view only, I have had good reason to become convinced during this last session of Congress that the delays occasioned by the debates of *two* legislative chambers have been useful to the United States by leaving to equity and to reason the time to rectify ideas and to crush cabals.

After having consolidated the public debt and charged the general government with the particular debts of the individual states contracted during the war, Congress has given its sanction to forty-seven laws which concern only the domestic policy and which can interest you, My Lord, only as far as they have relation to commerce and navigation. The duties on imports which form the only revenue of Congress have been increased by one third, with the exception of dry goods which are not of daily consumption. There is in the tariff no exemption in favor of French commodities although the Americans enjoy in many respects great prerogatives in France. The committee charged with the drawing up of this law has taken into consideration only the immediate interests of its constituents. The new tonnage duty [*Tonnage Act HR-78*] imposed on foreign ships without excepting from it the French vessels derives from the same principle, although it appears to be contrary to our treaty of commerce. The House of Representatives had, it is true, proposed an exception in favor of *allied nations* but the Senate has peremptorily refused to admit this clause. I await your orders, My Lord, to demand officially an exemption which I have been able to uphold until now only in private considerations. This case is entirely similar to the one of 1786 in which by order of the Court I demanded and obtained the revocation of the laws of New Hampshire and of Massachusetts which imposed an extraordinary tonnage duty on foreign ships.[2]

As for the American public, My Lord, it seems that it is generally content with the last session of its legislature and that its confidence in the new government increases daily. The slight animosity of the city of New York at having lost the residence of this government hardly deserves to be noted. It is too local to affect the general interests and the arrangements of the union.

As affairs no longer require the presence of the head of the confederation, the President is going to leave in a few days to go to Rhode Island which since its adherence to the new Constitution has appeared to deserve this visit, which is regarded here as bringing much honor. He will be back in about fifteen days to prepare to return to his plantations in Virginia from where he will go to establish himself in Philadelphia. All the public officers are going to leave New York within a few months to be at the meeting place which is set for next December. Until that time the United States will probably offer no interesting events. I await your orders, My Lord, or the instructions from my Chief to follow the government to Philadelphia; but if before the stated time I do not receive any direct news, I hope that you will approve if I go from time to time to the residence which Congress has chosen in order to pay my respects to the President and to follow more closely the measures of the government and the deliberations of the legislature.

***

O'Dwyer, pp. 441–44. Received 26 September. Otto's letters were usually written over the course of days and even weeks following the day they were begun. The omitted text relates to French immigration to the West.

---

[1] Necessary.

[2] French merchants protested that the laws violated the Franco-American Treaty of Amity and Commerce of 1778 and Secretary of Foreign Affairs Jay agreed (*JCC* 29:817–20). New Hampshire suspended its 1785 act in February 1786, until the other New England states and New York imposed similar tonnage duties. For the Massachusetts act, see John Adams to Thomas Crafts, 25 May, n. 2, volume 19.

William Paterson, Accounts

	Drs.
The Honl. Wm. Patterson	
To Elizabeth McEwen	
To your Board from 27th. Apl. to 12th. Augt.	
is 15 Weeks & 3 Days @ 40/6	£30.17. 3
To Wood had	9. 6
To your proportion of Club Acct.	12. 6.11
	£43.13. 8
Cr. To 2 Weeks & 2 Days you whare [*were*] absent	2. 5. 8
	£41. 8. 0

New York 12th. Augt. 1790

Recd. payment In full
Elizabeth McEwen

Ms., Paterson Papers, NjR.

Roger Sherman to Governor Samuel Huntington

The Congress have this day adjourned to the first Monday in December next to meet at Philadelphia. The session has been long, and tedious for the members, tho' I hope a beneficial one for the public. I have enclosed a printed paper containing the titles of the Several Acts and Laws that have been passed. this session Some of them are of great magnitude & importance and required much time to accommodate them to the different interests of the union, & opinions of the members.

I dont know how far the provision for funding the domestic debt, will be Acceptable to the Creditors, or the Community—it was the only one that could be agreed on by the two Houses, tho' I believe the modification of it in all its parts is not perfectly agreable to the mind of any member of either House.

The Interest on the Several parts will be about equivalent to four *per cent per annum* on the whole.

If interest on the whole had been fixed at one rate to commence at one time, it would have been more agreable to my mind.

The assumption of the State debts, will ease all the States of a burthen of direct taxation, and put the other branches of revenue under one direction.

The law for Settling the accounts of the united States, with the individual States [*HR*-77], was an interesting Subject which took up considerable time.

The provision for the defence of the frontiers, for regulating trade &

intercourse with the Indians Occasioned considerable debate; but I hope matters are So arranged as to prevent future troubles from those Savages.

A Bill [*Sinking Fund Act*] originated and passed near the close of the session for reducing the principal of the public debt, whether it originated from a view to personal conveniency or public good, I am not able to determine, it was but a Short time under consideration, but did not meet my Approbation.

There are Some matters unprovided for, which it was Supposed required another session at So early a period. To make a further provision for paying the Interest on the State debts. And. for providing for the public defence by regulating the Militia. Establishing a Land office & other matters. And the two Houses have not been able to agree this session on a Law to establish & regulate the Post Office. There are about 30 Indian Chiefs from the Creek tribes, now in this City, negociating a Treaty with the united States, which is nearly compleated, they appear to be well disposed for peace.

The enclosed News papers contain the evidence on which Baron Steuben's claim[1] was founded. your Excellency will be able to Judge how well it is Supported.

ALS, The Gilder Lehrman Collection, on Deposit at the New York Historical Society, New York. [GLC 5282] Place to which addressed not indicated.

[1] For more on Frederick William Steuben's petition for military service compensation, see *DHFFC* 7:201–46.

Thomas Lee Shippen to William Shippen

I had scarcely time yesterday to tell you that I was in a hurry—and it was because some gentlemen who were engaged to breakfast with me at the Vice President's were then waiting for me. I told you therefore nothing of the President, nothing of Congress and indeed hardly any thing of myself. On Sunday afternoon I went into the Country with Mr. Madison & the Attorney [*General Edmund*] Randolph and met at a tea house in the neighbourhood with [*William*] Jackson and [*David*] Humphreys—They proposed to me drinking tea with the President—I went accordingly and found the family en famille—remained nearly two hours had a good deal of conversation with the good man and was more than a little pleased with him and it. I have not seen him look so well since my return to this Country. The appropriation of an undisposed of million in the Treasury of the U.S. (rare circumstance you'll allow in this Country) has protracted until now the adjournment of Congress—At length they have determined to purchase a million's worth of the *debt* at the Market price, to vest in the President the power of borrowing two millions more and with the whole to establish a sinking fund—a most glorious circumstance you must allow—How different this from bankruptcy and want! Today the Congress adjourn—nothing remains to be done but that the Senate ratify the Creek Treaty—A propos—Do you know that I had the honor of assisting at this Treaty? that in a room at Gen. Knox's where thirty kings & chiefs headed by McGillivray were assembled to form the league Gen. Knox with his interpreter on his right hand addressed himself to them and having read the Treaty which he had formed and called upon them to sign it—[*John, Jr.*] Rutledge [*Joseph Allen*] Smith & myself signed as witnesses.

***

ALS, Shippen Family Papers, DLC. Addressed to Philadelphia. Postmarked; franked by Hartley. The omitted text concerns family affairs and the New York lottery.

Joseph Stanton, Jr. and Theodore Foster to Governor Arthur Fenner

The Honorable Legislature of the State were pleased, on the 12th. Day of June last to confer upon us the distinguished Honor of serving them in Congress. We repaired to this City, the Seat of the National Government, as soon afterwards as it was in our Power; and on the 25th. Day of that Month We were admitted and sworn as Senators of the United States. And supposing that it will be agreeable to your Excellency and the Honble. the General Assembly, to receive Information relative to our Conduct in the National Legislature, and of the Grounds and Motives of the most important Measures adopted by Congress we shall, from Time to Time, as occasion shall offer, write to your Excellency communicating the Information that shall appear to us necessary, or such matters as are most interesting to the State, avoiding on the one Hand the Tediousness of Prolixity, and on the other that dissatisfactory Brevity which may have the appearance of Careless Inattention. Our Situation will enable us to give Information which can be obtained from no other Quarter and we shall endeavour to improve all the Opportunities presented us of Serving our Constituents to the utmost of our Abilities, as well by communicating useful and necessary Information relative to their Federal and National Concerns, as by our active and unremitted Exertions in the National Legislature for promoting the Prosperity, Honor and Happiness of the State.

We arrived in this City at an unpropitious Time. It was a Matter generally determined on, that the Temporary Residence of Congress must be either in New-York or Philadelphia. These Two Cities seemed to divide the Nation nearly equally under their respective Banners. The Question of Residence being one of those Matters which from various Considerations of Interest, Prejudice, local Attachments, and personal Friendships engages the Passions and interests the Feelings more than the common Affairs of Legislation, it blended itself with almost every other Matter that came before Congress, so as to arrest the Progress of the Public Business and to prevent any thing of Consequence being done until that was decided. The Assumption of the Debts of the Several States which had accrued on account of the War and the Funding the whole of the National Debt were great and important Questions also pending at the same Time and remained undetermined, as was supposed, because the Residence of the Government was not established. Things being in this Situation a Bill was brought forward in the Senate for establishing the temporary Residence for Ten Years at Philadelphia, and the Permanent Seat of the Government after that Time within the State of Maryland, on the Eastern Side of the River Pawtomack between the Mouths of the Eastern Branch of that River, and Connogochegue. We acted and voted against this Bill, because we supposed it unadvisable to remove the Temporary Residence of Congress from New York, and improper at present to establish the permanent Residence at any Place, especially at a Station so far Southward, and so long before the Time proposed for removing to it. The Bill however was passed by a Majority of Two in the Senate and was concurred with by a Majority of Three in the House of Representatives.

After passing the Bill for Establishing the Seat of the Government of the United States—A Bill was brought forward entituled "An Act making Provision for the Debt of the United States." By this Bill the whole Debt of the Nation Foreign and Domestick was proposed to be funded, on the Revenue of the Country, provided and to be provided for the Purpose and a Loan proposed to the Amount of the whole Domestick Debt, including also therewith Twenty One Millions and Five Hundred Thousand Dollars assumed from the Several States, as having accrued on Account of the War, in the General Defence. As the Convention of the State which we have the Honor to serve, when they adopted the Constitution had, "in the Name and Behalf of the People of the State of Rhode Island injoined it upon the Senators and Representatives of the State in Congress, to exert all their Influence, and to use all reasonable Means that Congress should not directly, or indirectly, either by themselves or through their Judiciary, interfere with any one of the States, in the Redemption of paper Money already emitted, and now in Circulation, or in liquidating or discharging the Public Securities of any one of the States. But That each and every State should have the exclusive Right of making such Laws and Regulations for the before mentioned Purposes, as they should think proper." We supposed ourselves therefore, as Servants of the State, bound to observe those Instructions and to oppose the Assumption of the State Debts, and We acted according to our Instructions. The Bill however was passed by the same Majority as the Residence Bill—Assuming from the State of Rhode Island only Two Hundred Thousand Dollars—We remonstrated against the Injustice done the State of Rhode Island, in not assuming a larger Sum in Case the Debts of the other States were assumed, and the Absurdity and Impropriety of assuming only so small a Part of our State's Debt, which had accrued in Consequence of the War, when much larger Apportionments in Proportion to Numbers and Wealth had been made to some of the other States, who had not State Debts existing against them to the Amount of the Sums respectively assumed from them. To which it was replied that this was all that could be done for us at present. That other States were in the same Predicament with Rhode Island in not having a greater Proportion of their State Debts assumed than Rhode Island had—That Justice would hereafter be done either by a further Assumption of the whole of the State Debts remaining unassumed, or in the Settlement of the Accounts of the United States with the Individual States. This Bill also passed the Lower House by a Small Majority.

Another Act was finished the 5th Day of this Month particularly interesting to the State of Rhode Island. It is entituled "An Act to provide more effectually for the Settlement of the Accounts ~~of~~ between the United States and the Individual States" {*HR*-77}. This Act establishes a Board of Three Commissioners who are "to receive and examine all Claims which shall be exhibited to them before the First Day of July A.D. 1791, and to determine on all such as have accrued for the General or particular Defence during the War and on the Evidence thereof, according to the Principles of general Equity (although such Claims may not be sanctioned by the Resolves of Congress or Supported by Regular Vouchers) so as to provide for the final Settlement of all Accounts between the United States and Individual States," as directed by this Act. As the Enemy with a large Army were Three Years in Possession of the Capital of the State:[1] As the State notwithstanding kept so large a Proportion of Troops constantly in the Continental Army; As the Militia of the State were so constantly upon Duty; As the Specific Advances made by the State were greater in Proportion than those of any of the other States, and the Exertions and Advances of the State were constant and unremitted from the Commencment to the Close of the War, there can be no Doubt but that there is a large Balance in Justice and Equity due to the State, on a Settlement of the National Accounts, upon the Principles proposed in this Bill. Your Excellency and the Honble. the General Assembly will therefore permit us to suggest the Propriety of appointing a Person, or Persons, in Behalf of the State seasonably to exhibit, State, vindicate, and Support the Accounts and Claims of the State of Rhode Island against the United States. The Accounts of the States in the Southern part of the Union are in such a Situation that they must be Settled more by Compromise, Negociation, and Agreement than by any certain established Rules—which is an additional Argument for bringing forward the Accounts and Claims of our own State on the same Grounds as they are brought forward in the Southern States, and for appointing a Suitable person or Persons to Support them accordingly, in order that the Burthen incurred by the War may be equalized on the same Principles in every Part of the Union.

A Treaty has this Day been concluded between the United States and the Creek Nation of Indians. And Forty Seven Acts have been passed by both Houses of Congress and approved by the President at the Present Session. Copies of the whole of which we will endeavou[*r*] to procure and lay before your Excellency and the Legislature. Congress have this Day adjourned to the First Monday of December then to meet in Philadelphia.

In all our Conduct we have endeavoured to comply with the Sentiments and Wishes of our Constituents so far as we knew the General Sense of the State. Our best Services are due to the Public. Happy indeed should we be if those Services should answer the Expectations of our Constituents, or our own Wishes. But we can only assure your Excellency and the Honble. Legislature, of the deep Sense of Gratitude we feel for the Honor conferred upon us, and the Confidence placed in us, and that it will be at all Times our Study to promote the best Interests of the States by all the Means in our Power.

Fervently beseeching the omnipotent Ruler of the Universe that the Counsels of the State and of the National Legislatures, may be so directed as shall be most conducive to the General Prosperity and Happiness of the People, and that your Excellency and every Member of both Houses of the Legislature may experience and enjoy all the Blessings of Life, in their utmost Extent, which Heaven can bestow, We are with the highest Sentiments of Respect for your Excellency and the Legislature of the State, Your Excellency's most Obedient and humble Servants.

P. S. Inclosed herewith is an Extract from the Journal of the Senate shewing the Classes in which we were respectively placed, by Lot, and the Terms we are respectively to serve previous to a new Election.[2]

ALS, hand of Stanton, Letters to the Governor, R-Ar. Place to which addressed not indicated. The enclosed excerpt is from the Senate Legislative Journal; see *DHFFC* 1:372.

[1] Newport, joint state capital with Providence until 1900, was occupied by the British from 1776 to 1779.

[2] Foster drew a term that concluded with the FFC. Stanton's term ended with the Second Congress.

Hugh Williamson and Abishai Thomas to Governor Alexander Martin

You will observe that the three Commissioners appointed by the former Congress for settling the accounts of the several States with the United States were not furnished with power either to do complete Justice or to make a final Settlement, they were not authorized to admit claims for the particular defence of a State, and in many cases they could not determine whether the charges of a State, of our State in particular were for Continental or State services, all such doubtful claims must in consequence have been rejected. when the Accounts should have been settled the Commissioners had no rule for fixing the quota of any State, and therefore never could have struck a balance, hence it would follow that nothing could have been paid to the most deserving State. An Act [*Settlement of Accounts Act HR-77*] is now passed to remedy those several defects, and the three Commissioners are re-appointed. The whole system now wears a new face. Our State will now be enabled to support her old claims and to raise some new charges which ought to be allowed. We therefore propose immediately to begin with the Militia charges and re-state them in such form as we shall find most advantageous to the State, We have not yet found it necessary to employ a Clerk, and our joint Labour we hope will continue to be equal to the necessary dispatch— You was pleased to ask our opinion respecting certain final settlements now in the Treasury of the State, by the late Acts of Congress you will percieve that all payments which have been or shall be made by any State except those which are subject to reduction by a Scale are equal to payments in Specie, and we think that the State had best retain those securities, or any other public securities she may have on hand. On this and sundry other interesting subjects we shall be enabled to explain ourselves more fully by the time the legislature is in session.

We enclose the [*Funding*] Act of Congress making provision for the debt of the United States.

ALS, hand of Thomas, Governors' Papers, Nc-Ar. Place to which addressed not indicated; carried by Steele.

Letter from New York

CONGRESS rose this day at noon, to meet at *Philadelphia*, on the first Monday of *December* next. All the publick business is completed—and when it is viewed in the gross, it will be seen that our Rulers have been far from idle.

I am told, that there are agents from Houses in Europe, here, who stand ready to loan immediately the *Two Millions* of Dollars, which the *Sinking Fund*

Bill impowers THE PRESIDENT to borrow. With this sum near Four Millions of the debt will be bought in—consequently two Millions will be sunk.

There are persons here, who do not scruple to bet any sum, that within a year the funded Continental paper will be at par.

The PRESIDENT proposes a visit to the State of Rhode-Island.

[Boston] *Columbian Centinel*, 18 August; reprinted at Portland, Maine; Keene, New Hampshire; Salem, Massachusetts (in part); and Providence, Rhode Island.

Letter from New York

I have seen in some of the Boston papers, several ungenerous insinuations, and electioneering slander against Mr. *Ames*; you may depend, that he does not merit them. I have not the honor of an acquaintance with the gentleman—but I have been an eye and ear witness, the principal part of this session, to his patriotism, abilities, and perseverance. His consistency is spoken of by every one; And all the measures, which I see by the papers, are not well received in Massachusetts, he has *invariably* opposed; He opposed the introduction of the business respecting the slave trade; alledging that it would create ill blood and disunion, when temperance and union, were so necessary; and when the yeas and nays were called for, he voted as well as spoke against the admission of the report on the journals. You can judge how far his predictions have been verified. He has uniformly opposed the introduction of the business of residence—and the odious business of discrimination. On the subject of assumption, his industry, together with that of Mr. *Gerry*, has been unremitting. Early and late, in and out of the House, he has endeavoured, by a just and fair examination of documents, to convince those who were opposed to the measure, of its justice and policy. On the subject of funding, the same consistency has been observed; and the discrimination respecting indents, which I see occasions much clamour, was zealously opposed by him. A reference to the proceedings of Congress, will convince any one of his merit and independence; as I am told he is not in the least, concerned in the funds—a charge made against many of the Members. No man in Congress possesses more influence; and I never knew him to speak, but upon the important subjects. I mention this, because I see, he has been censured for long speeches. But his speech on the assumption[1] will be celebrated for its elegance, show of ideas, facts, and genuine principles, while they can command celebrity.

[Boston] *Independent Chronicle*, 19 August. J. W., who submitted the piece to the editor, noted that it was received on the evening of 10 August.

[1] For Ames's famous speech of 25 May, see *DHFFC* 13:1432–46.

OTHER DOCUMENTS

Thomas Jefferson to William Barton. FC, letterpress copy, Jefferson Papers, DLC. For the full text, see *PTJ* 17:347–48.

Congress allowed him to appoint two chief clerks, because the two incumbents (Roger Alden and Henry Remsen) were so well acquainted with the public papers in their respective areas that they were "necessary to me as indexes"; Congress had received his request "with some jealousy, lest it might be intended to bring forward again the plan of two departments" (home and foreign affairs), a proposition that had been disapproved by a considerable majority of the previous session.

Josiah Parker to Governor Alexander Martin. Copy, Governors' Papers, Nc-Ar. Printed in *DHFFC* 8:694–95.

Relates to federal and state support for the Pasquotank (Dismal Swamp) Canal.

Melancton Smith to John Langdon. ALS, Langdon Papers, NhPoA. Addressed to Portsmouth, New Hampshire.

Explains delayed payment of a bill of credit he owed to Langdon, to be drawn on the collector at Portsmouth, and describes his mortification when he went to deliver it and Ebenezer Hazard informed him that Langdon had already left town.

FRIDAY, 13 AUGUST 1790

William Paterson, Accounts

Honorable Wllm. Paterson
1790

To Michl. Huck

To Your board & Lodgings from 7th. Jany. to 28th April @ 46/ Week		£38. 8
To 16 Weeks Wood & Candles	@ 8/.	6. 8
To 28 dinners	—3/	4. 8
To Coach Hire at different Times		.16
To Your Club for Wine Spirits & bitters		12.16
To Cash pd. the barber		.16
		£63.12
	By Cash	10.10
	Ballance	£53. 2

Receivd. 16th June from the Honble. Mr. Paterson Sixty Dollrs. on acct. of the Above

Michl. Huck

Paid on the above 50 Ds.

Recd. the above in full of all Accts. 13th. Augt. 1790

Michl. Huck

Ms., Paterson Papers, NjR.

William Smith (S.C.) to Edward Rutledge

The adjournt. took place yesterday, to meet the first Monday in Decr. at Philada. The Treaty with the Creeks recd. yesterday the assent of the Senate, dissentg. Butler, Walker, Gunn & Few. It is to be ratified with great solemnity this morning in the great Hall of the Representatives by the President & such memrs. of Congress as remain, with [*Alexander*] McG. & all the Chiefs &c. &c. The three former Commissrs. [*for settling accounts between the United States and the individual states*] [*John*] Kean, [*John T.*] Gilman & [*William*] Irvine are re-appointed; there is now a prospect of this great Settlemt. being accomplished. Mr. Izard's family, with Mrs. S. [*Charlotte Smith*] are going in a few days to Lebanon Springs near Albany: I ~~am going to~~ shall make a Tour into Connecticut & the back parts of Massa. & this State & Vermont & then ~~shall~~ meet the Lebanon party—we shall return here about the middle of Sepr. & leave this City for Philad. the end of Octor.

The President Sets off in a fortnight for Virginia, he says he has not Sufficient time to go to So. Car. & Georgia this year, but proposes to make his grand Tour in the Spring, shod. Congress be in recess. I shall make my Visit to my friends at the Same time.

The Creeks Sail soon for Georgia, they are to go as far up the Altamah. [*Altamaha River*] as they can.

Mrs. Smith requests her best respects to Mrs. [*Henriette*] Rutledge, who I am happy to hear has much improved in her health. Please to add my Respects. Henry [*Rutledge*] is well. Continue to direct to me here.

ALS, Smith Papers, ScHi. Place to which addressed not indicated. This letter continues one begun on 8 August, printed under that date, above, and is followed by a postscript calendared under 16 August, below.

[*Josiah Parker?*] The Great Dismal

THIS Swamp called the GREAT DISMAL lies within the northern limits of North Carolina, the latitude of the middle of it about 36°, 20′, and the eastern edge of it bordering on the waters of Currituck Sound. This is the principal of all those dreadful places, called swamps, only to be met with in America, for there is nothing of the kind to be found in all Europe, Asia, or Africa. This swamp is in the form of a vast oval, thirty miles in breadth, and fifty in length, with a lake nearly in the center, seven miles diameter and twenty miles in circumference, abounding in fish. From this lake there is no outlet or running water to any other place; nor can there be said to be any descent throughout all this immense swamp, except a little without its outer circumference; all within being in a manner entirely covered with water, out of which innumerable quantities of large, straight and lofty cypress trees are growing in almost impenetrable closeness to each other throughout the whole extent; betwixt these trees infinite numbers of that strange production, cypress knees, rise above the water from three to fifteen inches, almost as close as they can stand together.

Throughout the whole of this truly *dismal* place, there is scarcely the least appearance of any kind of soil; for even where there is no water nothing can be discovered but cypress knees, closely intermixed with a matted body of strong fibrous roots, vines, and vegetative productions every where, in a dark and dreary shade altogether impervious to the rays of the sun. The trees &c. growing so thick, close, and lofty, that one person will lose another therein, at ten yards distance; and afterwards, if they wander a few hundred yards asunder, no noise, clamour, or hallooing, from either of them, can be heard by the other; for the woods are so close as to prevent the vibration of the air for any distance through them; even the report of fire arms is smothered.

The only way of hearing any sound, for the least distance, is by laying one's ear close to the ground, by which means one can hear six times as far as any other way.

There is a kind of ridges running throughout this swamp, from fifty yards to a quarter of a mile, and upwards, across, and one, two, four, and sometimes six miles asunder.

These ridges are without water, although no earth or soil can be seen, but all between them is covered with water, from two to five and six feet deep. On these ridges are astonishing numbers of bears, wolves, panthers, wild cats, opossums, raccoons, snakes, some deer, and almost every kind of wild beast; between them are vast numbers of otters, musk rats, beavers, and all kinds of amphibious animals.

In very dry summers some of these ridges have been accidentally set on fire, and caused most dreadful conflagrations, the flames consuming all before them, burning into the earth for a vast depth, and overspreading the whole country around with a thick smoke. Those places are soon afterwards filled with water, and become small lakes.

There was some years ago, one fire in the Great Dismal particularly horrid and tremendous. It happened on an extraordinary dry summer, and burnt with irresistible fury for many weeks, spreading terror and destruction all round.

The wild beasts were so frightened, that prodigious numbers of them of all kinds forsook the swamp, over-running the plantations for many miles distance, and the whole country was perpetually enveloped in thick smoke, during many weeks, for ninety miles round.

The effect of this horrid conflagration formed a lake, a mile and a half in breadth, and about three miles long from four to eight, ten and even twelve feet in depth.

It is supposed that the Great Lake in the centre was formed by some ancient dreadful conflagration far beyond human memory; as burnt wood is frequently found in the bottom of it, even near the middle, and in the deepest places throughout.

This swamp belongs to a company of proprietors, who have begun to render it of advantage and profit to themselves. They commenced with getting lumber, cypress shingles and boards, and with incredible labor they have now formed several plantations therein, which produce immense crops of Indian corn.

They have also cut a navigable canal, nine miles in length, from the Great Lake, for the conveyance of their lumber and produce, as near to the edge of the Great Swamp as possible, and they have formed a causeway of timber, as a road through it, from the end of the canal. The land all around it is somewhat higher than it is within it, and is flat, sandy, wet and barren. It is a safe harbor and place of perfect security for all kinds of wild beasts, as well as stray horses, cattle, hogs and run-away negroes, many of whom live here to be old, without the least danger of being discovered; in short, this is the general asylum for every thing that flies from mankind and society.

NYDA, 13 August; reprinted at Philadelphia. The editors are printing this piece because of the strong likelihood that Parker was the author. Parker's August motion in the House that North Carolina and Virginia be permitted "to enter into a compact for the purpose of opening a navigable canal between the waters of the Pasquotank river in North Carolina and those of the south branch of the Elizabeth river in Virginia" was referred to a committee to prepare a bill. See *DHFFC* 8:694–95.

Other Documents

James Madison to Various Friends. FC, Madison Papers, DLC. The letter relates to the Second Federal Election and will be printed in that section of Correspondence: Third Session. For the full text, see *PJM* 13:293–94.

Encloses a list of acts passed in the second session and explains his inability to be in the district for the election.

William Samuel Johnson, Diary. Johnson Papers, CtHi.
"Indian Treaty publickly Ratified by President in the Hall."

William Smith (S.C.), Travel Journal. PPRF.
Washington resolved that morning to travel to Rhode Island in recognition of its ratification of the Constitution (on 29 May), and invited Smith to join the travel party; "I could not decline so acceptable an invitation."

[Rhode Island] *Providence Gazette*, 14 August.
A. Foster, Goodhue, Leonard, Partridge, and Wingate arrived on board the *Aurora*.

[Springfield, Massachusetts] *Hampshire Chronicle*, 18 August.
Thatcher passed through Springfield.

[New London] *Connecticut Gazette*, 20 August.
Trumbull passed through town en route to Lebanon, Connecticut.

Treaty of New York with the Creeks

The Treaty of New York was the first treaty negotiated and ratified under the Constitution.[1] Although the treaty proved immediately controversial and many of its provisions were never executed, contemporaries agreed on its significant impact on federalism and states rights, federal Indian policy, westward expansion, the United States' relations with Spain, and the balance of power in the Mississippi Valley generally. Documents illuminating the Treaty's background, evolution, and aftermath will appear under a more substantive headnote with Correspondence: Third Session.[2]

Printed below are the only known eyewitness accounts of the ceremony in which Washington and Jefferson ratified the Senate's "advice and consent" to the Treaty of New York by adding their signatures. Secretary of War Henry Knox, the Creek Indian leader Alexander McGillivray, and twenty-three other Creek headmen had signed the Treaty on 7 August. Eight others signed as witnesses, including four young men who happened to be in New York City at the time and were evidently invited to be signatories in deference to their near relations: three important members of Congress (Smith of South Carolina and Senators Izard and Lee), and a Supreme Court Justice (John Rutledge). The Senate ratified the Treaty on 12 August, immediately before adjourning for the session. The ceremony that took place in the House chamber at noon the next day was the federal government's last official function in Federal Hall.

The evening preceding the ceremony, Jefferson asked Knox if the official representatives of Spain, France, and The Netherlands might bring "respectable strangers of their nation with or without limitation," including ladies. "The ladies by all means," Knox hastened to reply. "The president proposes to have it informally notified to the Senators and representatives in Town and who may find it convenient to attend," Knox added, along with the suggestion that he and Jefferson meet at 7:30 the next morning "to decide upon the particular arrangements." Beyond the official protocol arranged by the two secretaries, Washington made a personal present to Alexander McGillivray of "elegantly gilt bound Books" as well as a pair of gold epaulettes that he had worn during the Revolutionary War.[3]

[1] The first treaty ratified—but not negotiated—under the federal government had been concluded between Governor Arthur St. Clair and various nations of the Northwest Territory at Fort Harmar on 9 January 1789. On 17 September of that year, Washington asked the Senate whether it would advise and consent to his executing the treaty, or whether it was "perfect and obligatory in its present state." Although a committee reported the next day that the Senate's advice and consent was "not expedient or necessary" in the case of Indian treaties, the Senate ultimately did advise and consent to its ratification on 22 September (*DHFFC* 2:41, 42, 43).

[2] For the full text of the Treaty, including the secret articles, see *DHFFC* 2:241-50.

[3] *PTJ* 17:340–41n; John Pope, *A Tour through the Southern and Western Territories of the United States* (1792, reprinted, Gainesville, Fla., 1979), p. 51. McGillivray, who would later show off the epaulettes as a gift from his "adopted Father," supposedly gave them in turn to his brother-in-law Louis Milford, who, less sentimentally, exchanged them for a less old fashioned pair sometime after his return to Paris in 1795 (John Francis McDermott, ed., *Memoirs or A Cursory Glance at My Different Travels & My Sojourn in the Creek Nation by Louis LeClerc de Milford* (Chicago, 1956), p. 104. Under the Treaty's second secret article, several Creek and Seminole chiefs were to be given a peace medal. Although there is no other evidence that these traditional tokens were bestowed on the Creeks in New York, peace medals that had been struck in 1789 may have been distributed (Francis Paul Prucha, *Indian Peace Medals in American History* [Norman, Okla., 1994], pp. 5–6, 73–75).

Judith Sargent Murray to Winthrop and Judith Sargent, 14 August

*** We proceeded from this scene to another of more radical, and general importance—The illustrious object of our veneration [*Washington*] was to take part in a most interesting transaction—The Indian treaty was to be publickly ratified, and we took our seats in that superb Hall, where the delegates of the United States, so lately convened in council—Behold then the galleries filled by a respectable, curious, and highly gratified populace—Males, and Females, are indiscriminately seated—Gentlemen of the first rank, are ranged in the body of the room, appropriated to the representatives of the people—The handsome and commodious seats without the pales, are occupied by a brilliant circle of Ladies, richly habited, and displaying some of the most beautiful faces, which nature when bounteously indulgent, hath to bestow—Mrs. [*Martha*] Washington, with dignified ease takes her seat—elegant Women compose her train, and, upon either hand, are seated her grandson [*George Washington Parke Custis*], and daughter [*Eleanor Parke Custis*]—The Chair of State is empty—a number of Chairs upon the left, are also vacant, and the Vice President takes his seat upon the right—Suddenly rude, and tumultuous sounds are heard—frightfully terrific they vibrate tremendously upon the ear Now the most dreadful shrieks wear the semblance of horrid yells, and now they characterize ceaseless riot, and unlicensed mirth—"What sounds are these?"—Every eye seems to ask—It is the song of praise as sung by the Kings, Chiefs, and Warriors, of the Creek Nation, and now having entered the edifice [*sounding*] their untutored joy—They fill the vacant seats—They are in a complete uniform of blue, faced with red, and McGillivray takes the lead—The heads are bound about by a handkerchief, others are ornamented with feathers—wreaths &c. &c. and all are fancifully painted, and decorated with earrings, and Nose jewels. Thus is the Assembly disposed, when the Illustrious President of the United States appears. He is followed by his su[*i*]te—he is habited in Vestments of rich purple satin—Every eye is upon him, while his benign regards, equally distributed, he bends with inimitable grace to surrounding spectators—He ascends the Chair, a reverential silence pervades, and the articles of the treaty are distinctly read by the Secretary [*Tobias Lear*]—They are fourteen and they commence with a stipulation of perpetual peace, and amity! They acknowledge the Sovereignity and protection of the United States; they demand the emancipation of prisoners, they describe the boundaries of the two Nations—they guarantee possessions, they proceed to the adjustment of a variety of particulars, they grant to the Creeks, an annual subsidy, of one thousand, five hundred dollars, they stipulate many other immunities, they promise an oblivion of resentments, and, upon the whole they look with a very benign aspect upon the interests of Concord—The treaty being read, our august Leader, rising from his seat of eminence, delivers, in his accustomed elegant, energetic and animated style, his sentiments to the assembled Citizens, and to the Kings, Chiefs, and Warriors of the Creek Nation—He observed, that as far as he was capable of judging, the Treaty was mutually beneficial, he recommended a spirit of Amity, and he added, that a studious cultivation of unanimity was expected—He enjoined it upon the Indians to interpose with their good offices, so far as their power extended, to endeavour to annihilate animosities, and to conciliate the Nations, with which they might stand connected—and he supplicated the great Spirit, the Master of breath, to forbid an infringement of a Contract, formed under such happy auspices. The address was solemn, and proper, and it was delivered in sentences, which thus detached, were communicated by a sworn Interpreter to the Indians. The Creeks, in their own manner, audibly assented to each proposition, and the signing of the treaty succeeded—The President presented to Col. [*Alexander*] McGillivray—as a token of perpetual peace a string of beads, with a paper of tobacca, to supply the Calumet of friendship—McGillivray, who is invested with the Indian Sovereignty, received the tokens, returned a short speech, and complimented the President with the Wampum—and now the Kings, Chiefs, and Warriors one by one advance—they approach Majestically, with native elevation, and they join hands in peace, and with unusual warmth, McGillivray follows the accustomed Mode, a few indians are influenced by his example but the majority, seizing the President by the elbow entwined their arms with his, thus ardently expressing their satisfaction, and a second song of peace, by the indians concluded this affecting, important, and dignified transaction—Thus have I endeavoured to sketch for my beloved parents, as concisely as possible, a scene of which I was a spectator, which highly interested my feelings—and which, perhaps, succeeding Centuries may not repeat. ***

Copy, Murray Papers, Ms-Ar. For the full text, see *Murray*, pp. 256–57. Although the amount of original detail in this letter proves that Murray was an eyewitness to the events it describes, the question of her letters' authenticity and plagiarism still remains; note, for example, her liberal paraphrasing of *GUS*'s account of the signing ceremony (printed below). For more, see Murray to Winthrop and Judith Sargent, 29 May, location note, volume 19.

Louis Guillaume Otto to Comte de Montmorin, 14 August

The Secretary of War having been named by the President as commissioner plenipotentiary to negotiate with the Creek ambassadors, of whom I have had the honor of announcing to you the arrival in my Dispatch no. 35, the negotiations have lasted only a few days, a spirit of accommodation between the two sides has leveled the difficulties, and the treaty has been signed. As there remains only the ratification by the President of the United States, that officer has taken on the responsibility of making that ceremony as solemn as possible in order to leave a strong impression on the minds of those Indian ambassadors.

Yesterday morning the President of the United States, accompanied by the Secretaries of the Government, went to the great hall [*House chamber*] of Congress where the Creeks had already assembled to attend the ratification. The Secretaries, the Representatives [*members of Congress*], all the officers of the Government and the ambassadors of foreign courts, who had been formally invited there by Mr. Jefferson, were seated according to their rank. The foreign ambassadors sat to the right of the Vice President, whose seat was placed immediately below that of the President. The treaty was read in a

This day there will be a review of the uniform companies of the New-York Militia at Mr. Rutger's ground.

It is expected that the President of the United States, Gen. Knox, and several of the pricipal Executive officers will be present, and that Col. M'Glilivray, with all the Chiefs and Warriors of the Creek Nation, now on a visit here, will appear dressed in cloathes made in the present fashion.

Names of the Chiefs, of the Creek Nation now in this City.

Colonel Alexander M'Gillivray.

Tuskenaiah, or *big lieutenant*; Homatah, or *leader*; Chickwockly Mico; Mico Nomalthle—4 Coweta Chiefs—*and two young Warriors.*

Fuskuche Mico, or *bird tail King*; Fusikiah Mico, or *Warrior King*; Nealthlock, or *second Man*; Tuskeegie Tuftunegie, or *big fear*; Halleremathle, or *blue giver*—5 Cushtah Chiefs.

Opay Mico, or *the Singer*; Totkeshajou-Sainonia—2 Chiefs from Litle Tallasee.

Stimalejie, or *Menkiller*—Albama Chief.

Stimasutchkee, or *good humor*, *and four other Warriors*—From the Coosades.

Chinabie, or *the great Notchee Warrior*, *and three young Warriors*—From the Notches.

Ochee Hajou, or Aleck Cornel; Soholoffe, or *young second Man*—2 Chiefs from Tuskabatchy.

Tallissee King, and Holatah, or *the blue*—Tallissee Chiefs—*and two Tallissee Warriors.*

David Francis, *a young half breed, Kinsman to Col.* M'Gillivray.

David Tate, *Nephew to Col.* M'Gillivray.

Mr. Cornel, *the Interpreter.*

Names of the "chiefs," or headmen, of the Creek Nation in New York City to negotiate a treaty with the United States. The President's signing of the Treaty of New York on 13 August was the federal government's last official function in Federal Hall. (New-York Daily Gazette, 27 July)

Stimafutchkee, by John Trumbull, 1756–1843, pencil on paper, 1790. Also known as "Good Humour," this signatory to the Treaty of New York represented the Coosades—a tribe closely allied with the neighboring Creeks. (John Trumbull, *Autobiography* [New Haven, Conn., 1841], p. 165.)

loud voice by a Secretary who, having declared the words of the ratification, presented it to the President for his signature. The latter summoned the interpreter, and rose to deliver an address to the Creeks that was simple yet forceful, explaining the importance of the treaty that they came to conclude, and making them foresee the danger of violating its articles. At the end of each sentence, the interpreter explained the sense of it to the Indians, who responded with a cry of approbation. The discourse concluded, [*Alexander*] MacGillivray, head chief of the Creek Nation, approached the President to assure him that he would do all in his power to maintain the good harmony and abide by the letter of the articles agreed upon. After which the Indians, embracing the President in their manner, strongly clasped his right arm. The President signed, and after expressing again his satisfaction with the happy event that had pacified the two Nations, he was requested by one of the Creek chiefs to listen to a song of peace that they intended to sing. That Indian music ended the ceremony and added to it a new feature both singular and bizarre. The twenty-six Creeks who were present all wore American uniforms, that they changed into from time to time. Their figures painted in all sorts of colors, their strange hairstyles with feathers, their ears covered and stretched, the thousand fantastic ornaments that they had overloaded themselves with, not even omitting a huge wig, their legs half covered and the Chinese fans which they used, contrasted utterly with the ceremony's solemnity. MacGillivray had accepted from the President a brigadier general's uniform, and the other chiefs had those of colonels. After the ratification the President invited us to take punch at his house. I interpreted this invitation as an indirect way of having us present our felicitations and I complimented him as a result. He seemed very satisfied at having avoided at such little expense a war that would be very inconvenient for the United States. I was invited once more to a grand dinner that the Government gave for the Indians. There we found several other Indians from Canada[1] and a young man just recently arrived by an American vessel from the island of Owhyhee [*Hawa'ii*], where Captain [*James*] Cook was assassinated.[2] It is difficult, Sir, to see a society more uniquely composed; besides the Americans that one sees, foreigners from all European nations who mingle among the Indians had good reason to believe that they were much more cultivated than one would have thought at first. National songs and dances ended the celebration and the Creeks showed such satisfaction and attachment to the United States that it was almost impossible not to believe their sincerity.

The articles of the treaty, Sir, do honor to the moderation and wisdom of the President of the United States. Far from availing himself of the advantage that MacGillivray's presence gave him over that chief, he committed himself to stipulating only mutually favorable conditions. Here are the principal ones:

1. The Creeks submit to the protection of the United States and disavow that of all other powers whatever.

2. They will restore prisoners both White and Black.

3. They will recover possession of the greater part of lands invaded and usurped by the Georgians.

4. The Creeks will receive annually a subsidy of $1,500 (7875 tournois) in compensation for the lands they lose by the new running of boundary lines.

5. The United States guarantee the Creeks all their possessions.

6. The Creeks can punish any American that settles on their lands or hunts there.

7. On their side, they promise to extradite from their Nation whoever commits some crime against the United States.

8. To spread and perfect the Civilization of the Creeks, the United States commits to furnishing *gratis* livestock and instruments of husbandry. To that end, they will send them three or four commissioners to receive from the Creeks some land for their subsistence, but who will not be able to engage in trading.

The only article to face some difficulty, Sir, is that which grants a subsidy of $1,500. The Senate, whose consent is necessary to give validity to the treaty, along with the President, has objected from the beginning that the dignity of the United States would be compromised if they lowered themselves to purchase the friendship of a savage Nation, and that they would prefer to make an honorable war than to subscribe to a rather humiliating peace. The Secretary of War consequently was charged with estimating expenses for a military campaign. That estimate amounts to more than a million tournois. The sum of $1,500 seemed so moderate that it put an end to the opposition and the article passed unanimously.

The agents of European powers had been invited to the treaty's ratification by the Secretary of foreign affairs; but Spain's Chargé des Affaires [*José Ignacio Viar*] did not attend; it is not difficult to guess the reason, seeing that, by the treaty, MacGillivray formally renounces all his connections with Spain.

Copy, in French, Henry Adams Transcripts, DLC. Otto's letters were usually written over the course of days and even weeks following the day they were begun.

[1] Four or five Caughnawaga (Kahnawake) Indians from Canada's St. Lawrence River valley were in New York City at this time seeking compensation for services provided to Continental Army officers imprisoned in Canada during the war. Catholic converts also known as "French Mohawks," they had been alienated from the rest of the Six Nations for almost a century until 1775 when they formed a league of defensive neutrality with the Oneida, whom they frequently accompanied on friendly missions to the United States (George Beck-

with's Conversation with Samuel Street, [August 1790], Colonial Office 42/69 p. 41, PRO; Joseph T. Glatthaar and James Kirby Martin, *Forgotten Allies: The Oneida Indians and the American Revolution* [New York, 2006], pp. 96–97, 112, 279–80).

[2] In a letter of 4 August (above), Otto mentions the presence of a native recently brought to New York from the South Pacific's Society Islands; here, Otto may be confusing those islands with the Sandwich Islands, or Hawai'i (Owhyhee), where the British naval captain and explorer James Cook was killed by native peoples in 1779. Capt. Robert Gray's ship *Columbia* had just completed a three year circumnavigation of the globe that took him to China by way of Hawai'i, where he remained for twenty-four days in the late summer of 1789 and where a young native boy joined the voyage ([Boston] *Columbian Centinel*, 11 August). But the ship's celebrated arrival in its home port of Boston on 9 August would hardly have left the youth sufficient time to be properly fêted before being conducted to New York by 13 August.

Newspaper Article, 14 August

Yesterday the treaty of peace and friendship between the United States and the Creek nation was solemnly ratified by the contracting parties, in Federal Hall, in presence of a large assembly of citizens. The Vice-President of the United States—the great officers of State—his Excellency the Governor [*George Clinton*]—and of several members of both Houses of Congress.

At 12 o'clock the President of the United States, and his suite—General Knox, the commissioner; the clerks of the department of the Secretary at war; Col. [*Alexander*] M'Gillivray, the Kings, Chiefs, and warriors of the Creek nation being assembled, the treaty was read by the Secretary of the president of the United States [*Tobias Lear*].

The President then addressed Col. M'Gillivray, the Kings, Chiefs and warriors; he said that he thought the treaty just and equal; and stated the mutual duties of the contracting parties, which address was communicated sentence after sentence, by Mr. [*Joseph*] Cornell sworn interpreter; to all of which the Creeks gave an audible assent.

The President then signed the treaty—after which he presented a string of beads as a token of perpetual peace; and paper of tobacco to smoke in remembrance of it; Mr. M'Gillivray rose, made a short reply to the President, and received the tokens.

This was succeeded by the shake of peace, every one of the Creeks passing this friendly salute with the President; a song of peace performed by the Creeks concluded this highly interesting, solemn and dignified transaction.[1]

GUS, 14 August; reprinted or paraphrased by more than two dozen newspapers at Exeter, Keene, and Portsmouth, New Hampshire; Bennington, Vermont; Salem, Boston, Worcester, Northampton, and Stockbridge, Massachusetts; Newport and Providence, Rhode Island; Elizabethtown and Burlington, New Jersey; Philadelphia and York, Pennsylvania;

Baltimore; Fredericksburg, Richmond, and Winchester, Virginia; Edenton and Fayetteville, North Carolina; and Charleston, South Carolina.

[1] The brief summary in *NYDA*, 14 August, noted that "the highest degree of satisfaction was expressed on the part of the Indians."

SATURDAY, 14 AUGUST 1790

Thomas Jefferson to Thomas Mann Randolph, Jr.

*** we have just concluded a treaty with the Creeks, which is important, as drawing a line between them & Georgia, and enabling the government to do, as it will do, justice against either party offending. Congress separated the day before yesterday, having in the latter part of their session reacquired the harmony which had always distinguished their proceedings, till the two disagreeable subjects of the assumption and residence were introduced. These really threatened, at one time, a separation of the legislature *sine die.* They saw the necessity of suspending almost all business for some time; and, when they resumed it, of some mutual sacrifices of opinion. It is not foreseen that any thing so generative of dissension can arise again, & therefore the friends of the government hope that, this difficulty once surmounted in the states, every thing will work well. I am principally afraid that commerce will be overloaded by the assumption, believing it would be better that property should be duly taxed.

ALS, Jefferson Papers, DLC. For the full text, see *PTJ* 17:390–91.

Newspaper Article

This day the Editor concludes the history of the proceedings of the second session of Congress. It affords him singular pleasure to find that his vigilent attention to this department of his paper has been crowned with the entire approbation of every citizen. He studies to be impartial—to be useful; his object is to please—to inform.

To abate of DILIGENCE is to solicit *ruin*; for the Editor is confident that his very uncommon success, and the FIRM ESTABLISHMENT of the FEDERAL GAZETTE, have been owing to *superior effort*, and a disposition in an enlightened discerning public to encourage an individual evidently laboring for the good of society.

This paper has been the first to *inform*, and its intelligence has been invariably *authentic*—these are facts which cannot be disputed.

The Editor, in his future selections for this paper, and in the history of every future session of the Federal Legislature, will study to preserve the same DECENCY and consistency of conduct, and never relax from the most prudent as well as the most vigorous endeavours.

The Representatives of this state, in both houses of Congress, are now about to return home. They doubtless will be most cordially and affectionately received by their fellow citizens. The people are sensible that they have done their duty, and they have gratitude enough to acknowledge it.

Respecting the RESIDENCE of Congress, that business being settled, even the opposers of the bill acquiesce in the decision, and the people of New-York, on this occasion, have acted like friends of good government. They have received, and they were most certainly entitled to, the thanks of the Federal Representatives in Congress assembled.

Murmurings against any part of the public proceedings will shortly be done away, when the delegates shall have returned to their respective states, and the people are fully informed of the motives which actuated their conduct.

"All public bodies, whose duty it is to deliberate, will move slow, and every nation has more to fear from passion and enthusiasm hurrying their representatives into errors, than from ever-caution which will waste only time. Ask a party-man why has Congress been so long occupied in funding the debt. Perhaps he will say, because the state debts were crowded in. Ask another, he will say, because opposition was made to assuming the state debts. A moderate man of no party will answer, that business was delayed, because the members could not agree how it should be done. If the advocates for the state debts would have joined the opponents of the measure, they might have finished the whole in a week. The like would have happened if all the members had agreed to the assumption. But did the members use more argument for and against the measure, and did they persevere in the support of their respective opinions with more zeal and industry than the different classes of the citizens desired, and had a just right to require of them? The public has been divided as well and perhaps as much as the members. Each man seems to have become angry because others who opposed his opinions would not yield, and not because his representative persevered in trying to persuade him to do it. He would have been more displeased had he found no support, or a faint one given in Congress to the great measures which have called up all his patriotism. The session has not been a period of leisure. As the great subjects of contention are now settled, and a foundation is laid for union, energy, and public credit, there will be less reason for delay in future. We are just beginning to act as a nation. Business will soon wear itself a channel, and flow as fast as it ought."

"The business of Congress has been in the highest degree difficult. The entire business of a distressing war has been to settle. A great debt existing in various intricate forms, has been new modified, and the terms of a new loan agreed upon. Extensive funds have been provided. The public anxiety has proved the difficulty and importance of this part of their labor. Provision has been made for settling the accounts between the United States and the individual states. It was foreseen that this would prove an embarrassing subject, and those who know how much jealousy was entertained on this account, and how many well-informed persons have despaired of its being done at all, will wonder that it has been accomplished. Tho' Congress is charged with fostering faction; the progress and success of this great operation is evidence that the spirit of conciliation is not absolutely banished from the Federal Hall. The controversies about the state debts, the quaker memorial, and the seat of government have been carried on with acrimony. However, it is in the highest degree pleasing to see the appearance of harmony, which seems to have returned at the end of the session. Many apprehended that it would never return. Perhaps business never proceeded in Congress more smoothly than it has of late. Altho the very difficult affairs of this session, the most important in the civil history of the Union, have not been transacted at this time, nor in the manner many earnestly desired, it is to be hoped that the public apprehensions and jealousies will subside, and that all good men will cultivate that national spirit which diffused such a lustre over the first session. This country wants nothing but a wise and energetic administration of its government, to become the happiest in the world. But the happiness we have just cause to expect as a people, will be hastened in its progress and encreased in degree by cherishing that love for the Union, and that mutual good will which made us a nation. Those who are industrious to sow discord ought to be discountenanced."

FG, 14 August; reprinted at Boston and Northampton, Massachusetts.

A Friend to Two Branches of the Legislature

A CORRESPONDENT Who read a rhapsodical kind of a speech delivered in a certain house on *the subject of residence*, hopes and believes the public will not be duped by such absurd reasons as the advocate for Philadelphia has employed, nor be imposed upon by the slender artifices of *self-interest*. When a man has so little regard for the public good as to neglect the public business altogether in matters of *an important and general nature*, and to spend his time in private chat in committee rooms, or in lounging about the streets while he is paid for attending to the affairs of his constituents, we can give him but little credit for his assertions of disinterestedness and patriotism, when we find him blowing up the flame of discord, sowing the seeds of disunion between the two branches of the legislature, insulting a respectable part of the government in gross and indecent terms, and wasting the time of C—ng—s in reiterated motions on a subject of little concern to the public at large[1]—Is it expected that the citizens of America are to be cajoled by the verbose prating of these interested and factious disturbers of the public tranquility, and that they will impute all the disturbance and mischief which have been excited on a late occasion to pure patriotism? The expectation, if it exists, is a shocking insult to the people of these states.

When the momentous subjects of funding the domestic debt, assuming the state debts, organizing the judiciary, vesting the President with the power of removal, settling the terms of naturalization, proposing amendments to the constitution, and establishing the principles of a settlement of accounts between the states were on the tapis, the patriotic feelings of some persons were asleep, their passions were not moved, and the vacancy of their chairs indicated the attention they bestowed on such important concerns; their tongues instead of finding employment in promoting the general welfare, were only active in obscene dialogues, or in regaling themselves with apples in the lobby or molasses in the committee chamber. But when Philadelphia was the subject of discussion, then the *laudable zeal*, the *independence of spirit of the honest representative of a free people* bursts forth, and his duty to his constituents stimulated by a consciousness of the rectitude of his intentions hurries him on, in defiance of all order, decorum or moderation to urge an instantaneous removal from this unfortunate city.

Such very extraordinary petulance and zeal denote something more than a sense of duty—private motives sufficiently shew themselves thro' the thin veil of pretended patriotism, and the people must be blind indeed not to see thro' it. Is the scene of __ become insipid? Does it require a change to stimulate the glutted appetite? Are new objects wanted to gratify inordinate desires? Or does a sense of shame render unpleasing to the sight the theatre of detection and exposure? The indecent and gross invectives against a respectable body display a littleness of character—to speak ill of a man in private life in his absence is always dishonorable—to insult a whole body when they could not be heard was taking an ungenerous advantage—to traduce them because they exercised a constitutional right—to calumniate them and apply to them terms of reproach and derision because they pursued independently the dictates of their own judgment, and did not follow the views of a faction, manifested in the calumniator a want of that very independence for which they were censured; to take advantage of a crouded audience to vilify and degrade a part of the government and diminish its respectability was treason against the constitution and calls for the reproof of every honest citizen.

What becomes of the constitution and of those checks so wisely established if it is in the power of any rash partizan or demagogue publicly to animadvert in scurrilous language on the proceedings of the other, and attempt to excite by unfair methods the popular hatred against it for no other cause but a difference in sentiment? If the conduct of the other branch is censurable, the public will censure it and the public require not the aid of virulent scurrillity—the manly language of firmness and moderation will make itself heard—tho' their doors are not open, their journals are published, and every citizen may know and judge of their proceedings. Such conduct must therefore be always disgusting to the moderate and to those who wish the preservation of the government. When the two branches of the legislature differ, decency and fair argument should regulate the debates of both—a proper deference should be paid to the opinions of each other, and the same politeness should manifest itself as takes place between well bred gentlemen who in their intercourse with each other frequently differ on political topics. Acrimony and rudeness on such occasions indicate the pride of a self opinionative coxcomb and the vulgar manners of a clown; and the judicious part of the community will always impute these intemperate attacks to a want of education, ungovernable passions, and the obstinate pertinacity of ignorance.

NYDA, 16 August; reprinted at New York City (*NYP*, 17 August).

---

[1]The editors have identified the member as Parker, based on his motions to remove to Philadelphia, debated between 8 and 11 June, and his speech of 10 June, which advocated adjourning to Philadelphia, attacked the Senate's obstructionism, and elicited several calls to order (*DHFFC* 13:1559–61).

Letter from Philadelphia

Some of the blessings anticipated in the removal of Congress to this place are already beginning to take effect. Rents of houses have already risen, and I fear will continue to rise in a shameful proportion. Even in the outskirts of the city rents have lately been increased from 14, 16, and 18l. to 25, 28, and 30l. This is oppressive. Our markets, it is expected, will also be dearer than heretofore. Whether the advantages we shall enjoy in the removal of Congress will be equivalent to these advances upon the inhabitants, time alone will determine. I am convinced, however, if things go on in this manner a very great majority of our city will have good reason to wish them well settled at Connogochegue, long before our *ten years* are expired.

NYDA, 17 August; reprinted at Portland, Maine; Keene and Portsmouth, New Hampshire; Bennington, Vermont; Boston and Northampton, Massachusetts; New Haven, Connecticut; New York City (*NYDG*, 18 August); Philadelphia and York, Pennsylvania; and Baltimore.

Other Documents

James Madison to James Madison, Sr. ALS, Madison Papers, DLC. Place to which addressed not indicated. The letter relates to the Second Federal Election and will be printed in that section with Correspondence: Third Session. For the full text, see *PJM* 13:292–93.

The weather and his health prevent his return home before the election; encloses several copies of a letter to friends in each of the district's counties.

Thomas Tudor Tucker to St. George Tucker. ALS, Tucker-Coleman Papers, ViW. Addressed to Williamsburg, Virginia; carried by Page.

Laments he cannot afford to visit St. George "and the rest of my very dear Friends"; Page "is gone this moment and I must follow or send After him."

Boston Gazette, 16 August.

Goodhue and Thatcher arrived at Boston.

[Rhode Island] *Newport Mercury*, 16 August.

Stanton arrived in town with news that the President was coming.

[Worcester] *Massachusetts Spy*, 19 August.

Langdon and Thatcher passed through Worcester.

Sunday, 15 August 1790

Hugh Williamson to John Gray Blount

This goes by Water to Edenton and in future I shall generally to thin Postage, embrace some such Conveyance. I have forwarded to Capt. [*Josiah*] Collins a Copy of the Treaty [*of New York*] with McGillivry, it certainly gives the Indians as much Territory as they could have expected and cuts in very much on the Georgia People in the southern Part of that State. Those People growl exceedingly, I mean their Senators & Reps. but all other People seem to think the Treaty well made. In fact the Idea of buying Land to be jobbed away by Georgia Speck[*ulator*]s is not accordant with the feelings of the Nation.

I have some Suspicions that the Treaty to be made with the Cherokees will not be very palatable to some of our french broaders & others in that Part of the new Govt.[1] I have three Alternatives to propose to your Consideration and to that of other holders of Western Lands that may be [*by*] Treaty be confirmed to the Indians. The State has sold those Lands and received

Certificates for them. It has given the country to congress our Claims being reserved. If we had our Certificates they ought to be funded. Not having the Certificates we ought to be possessed of the Value. I would exchange those Lands with the United States for other Lands which they have purchased from the Indians, or I would surrender them to the U.S. for what they cost in Certificates or I would surrender those Lands to the State of N.C. in Exchange for the very Certificates I paid. The State ought not to hold the Payment for Property she does not defend & whenever the Lands are purchased of the Indians they will by such Commutation belong to the State. This last alternative I prefer as being the most probable in Point of Success. If you and other Purchasers are of same Opinion Application should be made to next Assembly, that so we may be enabled to fund the Certificates returned us, or in Case of Refusal by the Assembly may be enabled to apply in due Time to Congress for Redress. Be so good as think seriously of this matter, for myself I should greatly prefer the Certificates to the meer Chance of getting the Land within any reasonable Time.

ALS, John Gray Blount Papers, Nc-Ar. Addressed to Washington, North Carolina.

---

[1] On 11 August, the Senate gave Washington its advice and consent to renegotiate the Cherokee cession boundaries stipulated in the Hopewell Treaty of 1785 (see *DHFFC* 2:169–74), which had proven unpopular and difficult to enforce among the residents of the Southern Territory, especially those living on the French Broad River ("our french broaders"). The resulting treaty, which Governor William Blount was authorized to conclude in mid-March 1791, was signed at Holston (present-day Tennessee) on 2 July (*DHFFC* 2:95–96; *PGW* 7:564, 8:224n).

Other Documents

Silvanus Bourn to John Adams. ALS, Adams Family Manuscript Trust, MHi. Written from Boston.

Office seeking: Mr. (Joseph?) Woodward as agent for purchasing part of the public debt; is at a loss to know what has happened to the Consuls and Vice Consuls Bill.

Silvanus Bourn to Thomas Jefferson. ALS, Washington Papers, DLC. Written from Boston.

Thatcher has informed him that the Senate has assigned the Consuls and Vice Consuls Bill over to the next session.

William Smith (S.C.), Travel Journal. PPRF.

Sailed in the morning for Newport on the Rhode Island packet, as part of Washington's travel party, with Governor George Clinton, Justice John Blair, Jefferson, (T.) Foster, and Gilman.

Monday, 16 August 1790

Malachi Treat to John Nicholson

***

I give you Joy, on your geting Congress to reside in yr. City, I hope they will give more Satisfaction in future than they have done heretofore, if you build a House for them, make no Galleries—they will do more Business if they hear themselves speak only—fine fellows speak to fine Ladies in the Gallery.

We have not a Word of news. the City as quiet as a Village since the Departure of the Congress. ***

ALS, Gratz Collection, PHi. Written from New York; received 20 August.

[*David Daggett,*] A Republican to Messrs. Printers, No. 9

It is said by men experienced in building, that it is a much cheaper mode of doing the business, to hire workmen *by the jobb.* They are far more industrious, and, of course, accomplish the work with far greater expedition, than when they are employed *by the day.*

A gentleman of veracity tells me, that he once attempted to complete a house, which was already framed and raised, by employing a company of workmen *by the day*, but, to his great surprize, found it impracticable. He says the labourers were sure never to begin their work till 11 or 12 o'clock, and always to quit by three in the afternoon, and that the whole of Saturday they appropriated to themselves. That they had frequent holy-days, in which they were perfectly at leisure, and totally neglected the building. He tells me, that directly after they began their labour, they fell into a great dispute, whither those who were to perform the more curious part of the work, such as making the door-pannels, the window sashes, &c. should not receive greater wages than those who attended the rough parts. That they frequently got together and spent *hours* and *days* in disputing, whether they should *board* and *lodge, for the present*, at the *north* or *south* house of their employer, tho those houses were at equal distances from the frame—They would, almost every day, be engaged in discussing a question which arose about purchasing a small spot of land, on which they might erect buildings for their *residence*, till the house should be finished, and finally, before they had put on a single board, or shingle, they choose a *swamp* about a mile distant, which they voted should be their permanent abode. It was not uncommon to see them, in the most violent contention about things totally foreign to their undertaking, such as whither they might not, one and all, join and attempt to relieve some of their brother carpenters, who were sold in slavery to a cruel master and, by him, compelled to labour in servitude—whither it would not be expedient to furnish themselves with a complete set of *joiners tools*, at the expence of their employer—and whither the *tenders* who furnished them with *brick, stone* and *mortar*, should make a low bow every time they entered their presence. Indeed the workmen were so exceedingly dilatory, that their employer beheld with indignation, his elegant frame, which, for want of covering and properly attending to, was surpizingly *weather-beaten* and really worse than when it was first erected, it having stood almost two years in that situation.

It is matter of great surprize to many, that the session of Congress has been protracted till this time, and so little business of importance effected; the reason is, we pay Congress *by the day*, and the more days, the more *six dollars*. It will be found, by calculation, that if Congress meet again on the first Monday of December, and sit till the 4th of March, (which is the present plan) that each of the members from Connecticut will receive about 3520 dollars for his services the two years, and, in that period, may have been at home almost seven months or one third of his time. And will the members wish to curtail the session, when they acquire property so rapidly? Is not 17 or 1800 dollars per annum worth obtaining? And can either of our representatives, (one [*Wadsworth*] only excepted) earn half that sum at home? Ought not Congress to blush at such salaries or compensations as these? It is a pitiful excuse for any gentleman to alledge (as one from Connecticut has done) to vindicate his conduct to his constituents, *that he was not present when the bill passed ascertaining the pay of the officers of government*. Such pretences will not screne any one from the odium justly cast upon Congress, especially if it can be proved, that this same gentleman never opposed the law, and particularly insisted that the *representatives* should have their present compensations. If any member disliked the salaries, &c. he was bound, in conscience, to oppose them—and 'tis ridiculous, to advocate a measure, with great vehemence, till the question is about to be taken, and than desert the house, lest the public should know who have sported with their money. Viewing the subject of the pay of Congress, 'tis suggested to my mind, if it would not be prudent in future, to hire Congress by the *jobb*—Let us engage to pay them such a sum for every public act, having regard to its importance—for instance—for hearing, granting and enacting upon *Nathaniel Twining's memorial*, I would willingly allow them 2000 dollars—for determining the place of residence 5000, and for a *trifling act*, such as funding the national debt, 300 dollars.

[New Haven] *Connecticut Journal*, 25 August; reprinted at Portsmouth, New Hampshire, and New York City (*NYJ*, 3 September). For information on this series and its authorship, see the location note to A Republican to Messrs. Printers, No. 1, 15 May, volume 19. The issues being satirized include salary discrimination between the House and Senate, the temporary and permanent residences of Congress, the Quaker antislavery petitions, a library for Congress, and the general issue of deference.

OTHER DOCUMENTS

Clement Biddle to George Washington. FC, Biddle Letterbook, PHi. Written from Philadelphia. For a partial text, see *PGW* 6:11–12n.

Reports in reply to Martha Dangerfield Bland's inquiries, forwarded by Washington, regarding her deceased husband's unsettled accounts from the Revolutionary War.

Catherine Hite to Hannah Nicholson. ALS, Gallatin Papers, NHi. Written from Philadelphia.

Overtook Stone at Woodbridge and (R. B.) Lee and Henry at Brunswick, New Jersey, "and all [*blot*] together made a very respectable Cavalcade Mr. Lee and Mr. Stone took seats in our stage and our servants to their Horse and Cain Betty Sally Mr. Stone and myself sung for the entertainment of Mr. Lee"; "please to direct your letters [*to me*] to Mr. White."

John Hoomes to George Washington. ALS, Miscellaneous Letters, Miscellaneous Correspondence, State Department Records, Record Group 59, DNA. Written from Bowling Green, Virginia. For the full text, see *PGW* 6:263–64.

Defends himself against complaints of irregularities in the delivery of public mail along his stagecoach line from Alexandria to Hampton, Virginia; Parker can testify that the mail sometimes arrives early at the next stop, Norfolk.

Thomas Lea to Jeremiah Wadsworth. ALS, Wadsworth Papers, CtHi. Written from Philadelphia; addressed to Hartford, Connecticut.

"Altho you have voted against coming to See Philadelphia, you will not be the less Wellcome to many here."

William Smith (S.C.) to Edward Rutledge. ALS, Smith Papers, ScHi. Place to which addressed not indicated. This is a postscript to a letter written on 8 and 13 August and printed under those dates, above.

"The President having done me the Honor to invite me to be of his Party to Rhode Island, I have so far altered my plan as to visit that State before I go to Connecticut—we set off this morning & I shall either return here with the President or proceed on from Providence to Hartford &c. Mr. Izards family & Mrs. S. [*Charlotte Izard Smith*] set off day after tomorrow."

FG, 16 August.
Upwards of twenty members have arrived in Philadelphia since the adjournment of Congress.

[Springfield, Massachusetts] *Hampshire Chronicle*, 18 August.
Ames arrived at Springfield.

NYDA, 19 August.
Elizabeth Laurance died after a long illness.

Tuesday, 17 August 1790

Jonathan Dayton to William Paterson

As it is unquestionably matter of some moment, so it has been subject of great enquiry as to the person who shall fill the vacancy occasioned by the death of Governor [*William*] Livingston. Several names have been mentioned & some tickets for the approaching state elections seem already to have been concerted with a direct view to that appointment.

Unaccustomed to flatter, I trust I shall not be suspected when I assure you that at the instant in which the death of the Governor was made known, my mind designated you as his fittest successor: I trust also that my sincerity will not be questioned when I declare that it is my very earnest wish that that important appointment should be given you. As there are those who have not hesitated to say openly that you will decline the office, and no one yet appears who is authorized to contradict it, I have thought it proper to write to you upon the subject in order that I may know & communicate to others in this quarter of the state your inclination or decision. If there has been any foundation for the saying that it is your intention to withhold your name from the list of Candidates, let me join my entreaty to others of your friends that you would think better of it & take a different resolution. I know no one who would be so much approved of by the people of the state—Allow me to add that I know no one who better deserves to be so; My wishes as well as those of my particular friends & connections are that you would permit us to speak of you as a Candidate & to exert the little influence we possess, if it should be needed, in your behalf, not only for your appointment to the government in the first instance, but for your continuance in it.

Be so good as to write to me by the Mail unreservedly in this matter.

ALS, Paterson Papers, NjR. Written from Elizabethtown, New Jersey; addressed to New Brunswick, New Jersey.

William Few to Governor Edward Telfair

Congress has finished the business of the Session, we Adjourned on ~~Saturday~~ Thursday last, after having passed forty eight Acts, which I imagine will, by this opportunity, be transmitted to you by the Secretary of State, whose duty it is, Some of them you will perceive are important and very interesting to the States and I am sorry to observe that those Acts which are of the highest importance were the most controverted, and are the least approved of. The [*Funding*] Act for making provision for the National debt and assuming of the States Debts was more than six Months on its passage through Congress, and in its progress assumed various shapes, and was opposed on various principles. Some were for Assuming of all the State Debts and funding of the whole National Debt at an annual Interest of six per cent—which would probably have swelled the Debt of the United States to more than 80 Millions of Dollars; and the yearly interest of this Debt it was contended the United States could pay with ease, if proper principles of taxation were established—Others were of opinion that policy forbid the United States involving of themselves in a greater debt than would be accumulated by funding of the Debt of the United States only at an Interest of four per cent, and some indeed were opposed to assuming, or funding on any principle. These clashing opinions were agitated in both Houses of Congress, until by a kind of compromise they produced the Act in its present form, with the assent of only a small Majority of Congress. How far it will meet the approbation of the people of the States, a little time will discover.

Agreeable to this Act the Debt of the United States, the ensuing year will be 2,660,861 Dollars including the interest of the foreign Debt, and the Expenses of Government. This sum it is estimated can be raised from the duties on imports and tonage, but when the Interest becomes due on the assumed Debt, some other mode of taxation must unavoidably be adopted, and I find that some of our Statesmen are of opinion that it will be advisable to levy a direct tax either on the lands or poles of the Citizens; but the most prevailing opinion is that Congress will at their next Session pass a general Excise act and perhaps a Stamp Act—You see these measures all tend to a high toned Government, and it is easy to perceive that there are powerfull individuals that are Strenuous advocates for it, and I must confess to you, that I have my apprehensions that Congress ~~will~~ will be disposed to run into that extreme; perhaps it is a natural consequence after the feeble Government ~~that~~ as we have had for sometime past; but I trust the minds of the Americans are sufficiently enlightened to investigate the principles of there Government, and clearly ascertain their invaluable rights, and timely pursue with firmness such Constitutional measures as will best secure them.

You will see that by the Act for Settling the Accounts & claims of the different States against the United States, the Commissioners are vested with full powers to Judge and finally determine on the legality and equity of every claim, according to their understanding of the matter; and to ascertain on certain principles what may be due, to, and from each of the States. And it also allows farther time for the States exhibiting accounts and evidence. I have no doubt but you will see the indispenable necessity of our States attending to this interesting business, otherwise we shall be loaded with an enormous debt when perhaps if timely exertions are made to collect and transmit the accounts and claims of every nature against the United States, with the best vouchers and evidence in support of them that the Nature of the case will admit, we should on principles of Justice be entitled to receive a balance from the United States.

The enclosed paper contains the treaty of the United States with the Creek Indians, and notwithstanding one of its objects was to secure peace to the State of Georgia I am apprehensive that the terms will be very offensive to the Citizens of that State; for it is too obvious, that the third and fourth Articles Are injurious and dishonourable to them. I will not here animadvert on the Constitutionality, of, or the consequenses that treaty may produce, but assure you that every possible exertion was made by the Senators of Georgia in every stage of the business to prevent its origin and adoption on those principles and on the question in Senate to consent and advise the President to ratify the Treaty we made every effort to have those two articles passed over in order to introduce an article to revise and explain them, so as to have secured our territory and a return of the property that has been taken by the Indians, and when that could not be effected we remonstrated in the most pointed terms against the Constitutionality, the Justice, and policy of the measure and have marked the question with our negative—Genl. Jackson and Colo. Gunn are going on to Georgia and inform me they will both attend the Assembly at Augusta in Novr. Next and to them I must refer you for further information relative to this negociation, and proceedings of Congress.

ALS, Cuyler Collection, GU. Mentioned as read in Executive Council on 10 September (Executive Council Journal, G-Ar).

The Residence

VIRGINIA TO MASSACHUSETTS

Dear S—gw—k [*Sedgwick*] give over the making a pother
About the Potowmack, about the Potowmack.
We speak not in fun, 'tis as sure as a gun,
You there shall smoke shoemack, you there shall smoke shoemack.[1]

And you, Mr. G—y [*Gerry*], be not quite so merry
About Connogocheque, about Connogocheque[2]
For your dull punning jeers, your mobs and your fears,
We care not one fig, we care not one fig.
It is, Sir, at Georgetown, that you shall be set down,
In spite of your canting, in spite of your canting:
When there we'll ensure you, of hectic to cure you:
No more of your ranting, no more of your ranting.
Ye grave learned asses, so fond of molasses,
You're fairly out-witted, you're fairly out-witted,
With this Georgetown motion: O Lord, what a potion!
In the teeth you'll be twitted, in the teeth you'll be twitted.
You talk of your dying, with sobs and with sighing,
If you go to Potowmack, if you go to Potowmack:
But we'll send you home sound, and your wives all quite round,
And you shall smoke shoemack, and you shall smoke shoemack.

NYDG, 17 August; reprinted at Boston; Philadelphia; Baltimore; Winchester, Virginia; and Augusta and Savannah, Georgia.

---

[1] Sumac leaves, used as a substitute for tobacco.
[2] The confluence of Conococheague Creek and the Potomac River at Williamsport, Maryland, south of Hagerstown, was the western limit set by Congress for the seat of federal government.

Other Documents

Pierce Butler to Edward Rutledge. FC, Butler Letterbook, ScU. Sent to Charleston, South Carolina; carried by Capt. William Elliot; copy sent by way of Philadelphia. For the full text, see *Butler Letters*, pp. 57–58.

Has received Rutledge's letter of 4 August minutes earlier; regrets Rutledge did not receive his letter of 4 July or the duplicate of it sent by way of Philadelphia; "some dishonorable person must possess great curiosity in intercepting so many of my letters"; generally sends duplicates "which in time of Peace is seldom done"; "Who can the person be that has such an avidity to read my letters! My feelings could not let me be wanting to a person so friendly & attentive to me"; would come to South Carolina to resolve his financial problems but Mary Middleton Butler's health "is such that I can not leave her one day."

John Fitch to Robert Morris. FC:dft, Fitch Papers, DLC. Written from Philadelphia.

Thanks Morris for the "Princely Generosity" of his $50 subscription for the steamboat; the "money has been applied to the Good of our Empire and the World of mankind in General"; will make the steamboat available to Morris and his friends any day, time, and place "you shall direct."

William Smith (S.C.), Travel Journal. PPRF.
Arrived in the morning at Newport, Rhode Island; toured and dined with the President's party.

[Portsmouth] *New Hampshire Spy*, 18 August.
Langdon arrived at Portsmouth.

[Philadelphia] *Pennsylvania Mercury*, 24 August.
Wynkoop's daughter Anna married James Raguet.

WEDNESDAY, 18 AUGUST 1790

The Residence

(*Answer to the lines in yesterday's Gazette*)
MASSACHUSETTS TO VIRGINIA

YE noddies, how noozled, perplex'd and bamboozled,
Are ye of Potowmack, are ye of Potowmack;
Ye had better been found at your homes, safe and sound,
A smoking of shoemack, a smoking of shoemack.
The union you'd sever, for sake of your river,
And give up assumption, and give up assumption:
There's White and there's Lee, and there's Maryland G[*ale*].
Wise men all of gumption, wise men all of gumption.
Then there's Daniel C—l [*Carroll*], who looks like a barrel
Of Catholic faith, sir, of Catholic faith, sir,
He swore, he was true, but the boog, sir, it flew,
And went off in a breath, sir, and went off in a breath, sir.
Virginia, give over the making a pother
About the Potowmack, about the Potowmack;
For altho' you have got it, assumption shall rot it,
And smoke you like shoemack, and smoke you like shoemack.

NYDG, 18 August; reprinted at Boston; Philadelphia; Baltimore; Winchester, Virginia; and Augusta and Savannah, Georgia. White and Lee of Virginia and Gale and D. Carroll of Maryland were the four Representatives who switched from opposing to supporting assumption as part of the Compromise of 1790.

OTHER DOCUMENTS

George Clymer to Tax Commissioners of Bedford County, Pennsylvania. Summary of one page ALS, *Doris Harris Catalog* 24(ca. 1979):item 15.
"Details about payment of his taxes. His absence in New York caused the delay in sending payment."

Andrew Craigie to Samuel Rogers. FC:dft, Craigie Papers, MWA.
Craigie "was more perhaps than almost any other person a believer in" assumption; it "appeared at times to be very much at hazard & [*lined out*] continued so till the Compromise took place."

Richard Curson to Horatio Gates. ALS, Gates Papers, NHi. Written from Baltimore; place to which addressed not indicated.
Smith (Md.) returned to Baltimore last Saturday (14 August).

William Smith (S.C.), Travel Journal. PPRF.
Breakfasted with the President's party in Newport, Rhode Island, and embarked together on a seven hour "tedious passage" to Providence; the President paraded through town with (T.) Foster at his side, followed in order by (George) Clinton, Jefferson, (John) Blair, and Smith; dined and toured together.

[Springfield, Massachusetts] *Hampshire Chronicle*, 18 August.
Strong passed through Springfield last week enroute to Northampton.

[Providence, Rhode Island] *United States Chronicle*, 19 August.
T. Foster, Gilman, and Smith (S.C.), accompanying the President and his suite, arrived in town on board the packet *Hancock* at about 4 P.M.; a procession including the congressmen escorted the President to his lodgings.

[Springfield, Massachusetts] *Hampshire Chronicle*, 25 August.
Dalton, Grout, and Livermore passed through Springfield.

THURSDAY, 19 AUGUST 1790

Richard Bland Lee to Thomas Jefferson

You may recollect that I mentioned Mr. Daniel Brent to you as a young gentleman of merit who would be happy to be employed in some of the public offices as a clerk. If any vacancy should happen in your department in consequence of the removal to Philadelphia—your patronage of this gentleman would be useful to him, and I flatter myself without injury to you or the Public.

The assumption will probably endanger my election. I shall be a willing victim—if the government should be established and prosper.

Richard Bland Lee to Thomas Jefferson. ALS, Washington Papers, DLC. Written from Alexandria, Virginia.

Letter from Philadelphia

You desire to know whether we are really building a Federal Hall, &c. for the accommodation of Congress. Be assured the report is unfounded. We Philadelphians have not studied Poor Richard's Almanack (formerly published by Dr. Franklin) to no purpose. In that almanack much sage advice is given, which you New-Yorkers ought betimes, like good boys, to have attended to. One saying of Poor Richard's, particularly has impressed itself upon our understanding, relative to this matter, viz. *Look before you leap*, also, *Old birds are not to be caught with chaff.* Be assured we mean to build no halls of any kind, for the purpose above mentioned, unless there should be a certainty of a permanent residence. In that case, something of the sort, after a while may possibly be done. The character of Congress was never more respectable than in the time of the late war. Our state house held them comfortably *then*, and, with some few alterations and improvements, it is thought it may do so again, even with the additional branch. Farewell, and remember that we hold *two and thirty thousand pounds* an object too considerable to be trifled with.

NYDA, 1 September; reprinted at Portland, Maine; Portsmouth, Concord, and Exeter, New Hampshire; Windsor, Vermont; Boston; Hartford, Connecticut; New York City (*NYP*, 2 September); New Brunswick, New Jersey; Philadelphia; and Baltimore and Easton, Maryland.

Other Documents

William Smith (S.C.), Travel Journal. PPRF.

Dined and toured Providence, Rhode Island, with the President's party; left the party and took a chaise for Norwich, Connecticut.

An Old Soldier. [Boston] *Independent Chronicle*, 19 August. For the petition, see *DHFFC* 7:176–78.

Asks why the petition "from the officers and soldiers of the late army *** was not presented when it was received by *the Member* from this district, the 10th of July last."

[Portland, Maine] *Cumberland Gazette*, 23 August.
Thatcher arrived safe at Biddeford.

Letter from New York. [Boston] *Columbian Centinel*, 25 August; reprinted at Portland, Maine; and Exeter and Keene, New Hampshire.

"What, with the adjournment of Congress, and the absence of The President, this city looks very dull. There is nothing new stirring, and our gallery-loungers wander about like the Jews in the wilderness."

FRIDAY, 20 AUGUST 1790

Thomas Fitzsimons to Tench Coxe

I am not more Obliged for the usefull information you have taken the trouble to give me than for the friendly terms in which it is Conceived. if Mankind generally had the disposition to benefit each other even where it could be done without injury to the person Conferring how much Smoother would the difficultys of this world be Made—your information may be Important to me but whether or not the Obligation is Equally great While the Provision for the Public debt was undecided upon—and I had an Agency in the Measures that was to make the provision I Scrupulously avoided any Kind of Speculation ~~to~~ in it—at present I think it as fairly Open to Members of the Legislature as to any other persons tho I do not beleive it would be proper to Appear Remarkable in that Species of traffick neither My Resources or inclination would render it proper for me to become so but I have no objection to being concerned as farr as these Circumstances will warrant. I never shall intentionally Require of any official Character information inconsistent with their honor or their duty if—I was unguarded Eno. to make the Request I have no doubt I should be denyd it.

The Aspect of things here at present as they Relate to our state governmt. is farr from being flattering. a total inattention in the people of the City [*Philadelphia*] leaves little room to hope for any well Concerted plan while some busy spirits from the Country are forming such as is [*if*] Effected Must prove highly injurious. I have endeavoured to procure a Meeting but after several Efforts it Could not be Effected Earlier than tomorrow. If I can depend upon Report, the Western people [*lined out*] Mean to Carry things with a high hand and Endeavor to get both a Governor & representation to ensure the Removal of the State Government. Nothing less than a total Change of the Present Representation in Congress, and that in future the City shall have but one Representative—I do not give intire Credit to all this nor do I believe if there are such designs that they could be Effected the report however proves the intention. after tomorrow I shall be able to give you more Certain Information—as I shall do from time to time—it is unfortunate that the Republican interest in the present assembly—tho Considerable in point of Nos. should in every other Respect be Very Weak.

It is so much of that Complexion that in a Crisis of difficulty I think them lost—I have advised them to deferr every important business till the New legislature Meets. Merely from an apprehension that if they attempted any they wd. be Over Reached—by their Opponents who tho not Much Stronger within—have Arguments Suggested from Without—which they have docility Enough to Conform to & Support. Among other things the Appointment of a Senator in the Room of Mr. McClay was intended. and if his Reelection could be secured I should heartily Concurr in it but Genl. [*Peter*] Muhlenberg. has been Canvassing for himself and endeavoring to Compromise for Finlays [*William Findley*] Election in Congress provided he was appointed in the place of McClay—this is all dirty business but will have the Effect of divideing I hope and beleive the speaker [*F. A. Muhlenberg*] has had no hand in it.

I have written to the Secy. [*Hamilton*] about our friend Rush's house you can so well describe it to him that I have Referred him to you on that Score I think the rent high yet in the present temper see no prospect of getting a Suitable one Cheaper—I hope Mrs. Coxe & your son are in good health.[1] Mrs. F.[2] is farr from being so she is at present in the Country and a Little better than when I returnd I am obliged to Conclude Abrubtly.

ALS, Coxe Papers, PHi. Written from Philadelphia. The editors believe that a shorter letter from Fitzsimons to Coxe dated 20 August was actually written on 21 August; see below.

[1] Rebecca Coxe (1763–1806), whom Coxe married in 1782, had just given birth to their fourth child, Alexander Sidney (d. 1821).

[2] Catherine Meade (ca. 1740–1810), sister of George Meade, married Thomas Fitzsimons in 1763 (*American Catholic Historical Researches* 5(1888):4, 25).

William Paterson to Jonathan Dayton

Your very polite and friendly letter of the 17th. of this month reached me yesterday. Gentlemen, in different parts of the state, have made the same enquiry as you have done, and wished to know, whether, if elected, I would accept the office now vacant by the death of Governor [*William*] Livingston. My answer has invariably been, that if under all circumstances, my friends think it proper, that I should accept, I would. It is easy to discern, that I had at first considerable difficulty to ~~encounter~~ surmount. The uncertain tenure of the office, although it may be ~~very~~ highly proper and guarded as it respects the publick, would naturally excite doubts, and create apprehensions in the mind of a person situated as I have been in the line of my profession, to which, after the next session of Congress, I had fully determined to return. Besides, a publick life is liable to a thousand casualties, from which a private is entirely exempt. Permit me to observe, that your opinion adds weight to that of my other friends, who have spoken to me on the subject, and to whom I have uniformly given the answer already mentioned. the result is, that, if appointed, I look upon myself bound to serve. Your sentiments and assurances on this occasion are expressed in language the most kind and unequivocal, and merit my most grateful acknowlegements.

FC:dft, Paterson Papers, NjR. Written from New Brunswick, New Jersey.

Other Documents

Samuel Anderson to Samuel Meredith. ALS, Meredith Papers, University of Delaware, Newark. Addressed to Philadelphia.

Is enclosing this letter to Clymer so Meredith does not have to pay postage.

John Hay to James Iredell. ALS, Charles E. Johnson Collection, Nc-Ar. Written from Fayetteville, North Carolina; addressed to No. 63 Wall Street, New York.

The opposition of the North Carolina members to the assumption and funding "will be very grateful to their constituents"; if Congress resorts to excises, land taxes, and capitation taxes, they "will not be acquiesced under by the people of the southern States in which event I feel much for the safety of the Union"; residents of Fayetteville lament the federal district court not meeting there alternately with New Bern, but hope for success of (William Barry) Grove's efforts to get the state legislature to petition Congress (to amend the relevant portion of the North Carolina Judiciary Act [HR-68]); asks Iredell to obtain for him a bound set of the acts passed in the second session of FFC and to ask Johnston if he would send it under cover of his frank.

Benjamin Rush to George Clymer. [Philadelphia] *Columbian Magazine* 5(August 1790):67–74; reprinted in newspapers at Portland, Maine; Boston and Northampton, Massachusetts; and Philadelphia and Carlisle, Pennsylvania.

An essay, in the form of a letter, entitled, "Thoughts upon the Amusements and Punishments which are Proper for Schools."

William Smith (S.C.), Travel Journal. PPRF.

Toured Norwich, Connecticut, with Huntington; passed the night as a guest of Trumbull at Lebanon, Connecticut.

Ohio Company Advertisement. [Rhode Island] *Providence Gazette*, 21 August.

Whereas a committee of the proprietors of the Ohio Company was appointed on 31 July to write to T. Foster at New York to request him to ask the treasurer of the company to furnish "a true statement of their Affairs," and Foster having returned to Providence, the proprietors will meet to hear the information obtained.

[Springfield, Massachusetts] *Hampshire Chronicle*, 25 August.

Otis passed through Springfield.

Saturday, 21 August 1790

Hugh Williamson to [*Henry Knox*]

With this I have taken the Liberty of sending you a Map of the ceded Part of North Carolina ~~for~~ that I had nearly prepared for engraving. This Map will help to explain some Observations that seem to present themselves from the Hopewell Treaty.[1]

By the Treaties made with the Chickasaws and Cherokees you will observe that the Southern Bounds of Settlement, for our Citizens, is the Ridge of Hills, beginning on the Ohio, that divides the River Cumberland from the Tenessee. It follows that Ridge to the Eastward until is [*it*] comes to a Point nearly South of Nash Ville. thence running North East it strikes Cumberland River 40 Miles above Nash Ville near Bartons Creek or Cedar Creek. It continues up Cumberland River to the great Cumberland Mountain. Be pleased to observe that

1. The Tract of Land reserved by North Carolina for her Officers and Soldiers of the continental Line begins on the Virga. Line near the Mouth of Rock Castle River thence running due South strikes the Cumberland Mountain, thence running West on the South Side of the Twin Mountains it strikes the Tenessee about 20 Miles South of the Mouth of Duck River. It is bounded on the West by the Tenessee.

2. Genl. [*Nathanael*] Green's Land, a fine Tract of 20,000 Acres (I think, that is the Quantity) is without the military Reservation, opposite Lick Creek on the South Side of Duck River.

3 The greater Part of Sumner County falls in the Indian Country.

4 The new Road which is said to be very convenient and was laid out at the public Expence from the Mouth of French Broad & crossing Cumberland Mountain opposite the Mouth of Clinch River and running from the Mountain NW to the Mouth of Lick Creek where it crossess Cumberland River and thence runs down on the North Side of that River, The greater Part of this Road lyes as you see within the Indian Reservation. The Communication is extremely difficult, between the Holston Settlement and that on Cumberland River about Nash Ville, except by this new Road.

You will be pleased to observe there is a Ridge of high ground that divides the Waters of Elk River above the Muscle Shoals from those of Duck River. Perhaps this Ridge might be taken for a Boundary begining on the River Tenessee at Rains Creek about the Lat. 35.° 20′ thence running Eastward between the Waters of Duck & Elk Rivers to the Cumberland Mountain thence cross the Mountain to the Mouth of Clinch River, thence up the Holston Branch to the Mouth of ~~the Ten~~ Little River between the Tenessee and French Broad.

In this Case the new Road would be clear from any Danger.

The S[*e*]ttlements from Nash Ville would extend to the Foot of Cumberland Mountain.

In this Case too the Western Settlement including the Waters of Duck River would be about 70 Miles broad. Such a Settlement might have Strength and respectability else it must remain weak & exposed to Insult for on the North there is a great Barren that cannot be settled. I have said Nothing of the Loss that must be sustaind by those Officers who have located their Lands as they had a Right to do on or near the Mouth of Duck River nor of the Loss to be sistain'd by Genl. Green's Family.

The Lands that have been survey'd to the Westward of the Tenessee and are granted by the State to Citizens of North Carolina may probably be surrendered by the Patentees or exchanged for other Lands, as the Chickasaws are very solicitous to preserve those Lands.

ALS, J. S. H. Fogg Autograph Collection, MeHi. The recipient was identified by his handwriting on the docket. On 26 August the two men conversed about the subject of this letter and Knox took notes, which are printed below under that date.

---

[1] The Hopewell Treaties with the Cherokees and Chickasaws in November 1785 and January 1786, respectively, are printed in *DHFFC* 2:169–74, 177–80.

The Valedictory

(*Spoken by a* Fisherman *at* Paules Hook.)
Addressed to the *Pennsylvania* Members,

FAREWELL stupid *Wynkoop*, *Peet Mull* [*Peter Muhlenberg*] and *George Clymer*,
To salute you at parting, 'tis meet I turn rhymer;
Sneering *Tom* [*Fitzsimons*], whose nose led thee with the great giant S***t [*Scott*],
And blundering *Hartley*—ye will all go to pot.

Bawdy *Bob* [*Morris*] may support ye a while d'ye see,
But at last you'l be bit by the biter, old *Lee* [*R. H., i.e., Virginia*]:
Neither *Madison*'s Caution, nor *Page*'s great Sense,
Will ever stop *Bobby* from fobbing the Pence.

Yet had not *Fitzsimons* supported the scheme,
The whole would have ended in smoke like a dream;
For *Fitz* has more influ'nce whenever he wills;
Then staggering *Bob* with his *noted* long bills:

Mark this Philadelphia; *Fitz* alone was the Man
Who bit *Sedgwick* and *Lawrance* [*Laurance*] in th' Residence plan.
'Tis to *Fitz* ye should pay the debt of thanks due,
For *Fitz* was the man that sent Congress to you.

Fred Augustus [*Muhlenberg*], God bless his red nose and fat Head,
Has little more influ'nce than a Speaker of Lead;
And now sister *Phila*, we return you your Clowns,
Transform'd into shapes like Men bred in Towns.

When some of them first made their 'pearance in *York*,
They scarcely knew how to hold a knife or fork,
But by living some time 'mongst People well bred
They've learned to walk and to hold up a head.

Our *Taylors* and *Barbers* have learn'd them some taste,
Yet these wandering Members have departed in haste:
Farewel silly Congress—and repent all your Lives,
For following the Devil wherever he drives.

NYMP, 21 August. On 10 August *NYJ* refused to print a piece titled "Farewell" on the ground that it was "too gross"; this may have been that piece.

Other Documents

Thomas Fitzsimons to Tench Coxe. ALS, Coxe Papers, PHi. Written from Philadelphia. Although the letter is dated 20 August, the editors believe it was written on 21 August as Fitzsimons stated in his 22 August letter to Coxe. The existence of another 20 August letter from Fitzsimons to Coxe supports this conclusion.

Requests Coxe to inquire of the secretary of the treasury as to the status of certain Rhode Island public securities Fitzsimons has been offered as payment for a debt.

[Worcester] *Massachusetts Spy*, 26 August.

Grout arrived home at Petersham, Massachusetts.

Sunday, 22 August 1790

Pierce Butler to John Langdon

I hope this letter will find You well at Home, recruited from the fatigues of the Campaign, that is the long Session, and from the Journey & that You found Mrs. [*Elizabeth*] and Miss [*Elizabeth*] Langdon well.

***

We have had some warm weather since You left this place. We Closed the Session with a Treaty of peace with the Creek Indians. the disposition of One Million of Unappropriated Dollars [*Sinking Fund Act HR-101*] You have been informed of—what think You of it? The President returned last night from Rhode Island.

ALS, Langdon Papers, NhPoS. Place to which addressed not indicated. The omitted text introduces three young South Carolinians on a tour of the New England states.

Thomas Fitzsimons to Tench Coxe

I wrote you a short letter by a Gent. that went from hence Yesterday upon a Subject Interesting to me as Indeed upon it may depend the Security of a Sum Little less than £1000. this I hope will apologise for my giveing you the trouble I would have taken the liberty to write Imm[*ediatel*]y. to the Secy. [*Hamilton*] but it would give him the trouble of writeing the an Answer—and I knew how Much his mind and time must be Occupyd by Public Objects—My Apprehension is that the State of Rhode Island by some Acts has Annulled the Certificates Granted formerly by their treasurer if not exchanged—and the offer made to me Confirms my suspicion: [*lined out?*] it might Indeed become a Question how farr the State has a Right to Annull its own Obligations—& whether the holders of such Securities Would not be intitled to subscribe them on the terms proposed by the U.S. or could not even have a Remedy Against the State—What information you can obtain upon this Subject will be Very thankfully Recd. I would only add that probably the Laws of that state Which Respect this business will be found in the office of the Secy. of State a transcript of them would on this Occasion be Very desireable.

Our [*state constitutional*] Convention propose breaking up on Tuesday without haveing made any Important alteration in the Constitution as first proposed—the People are either ~~so~~ well satisfyd with it or so much Engaged in other pursuits as to pay no attention to it I am sorry to add that the Affairs of the State generally appear to be left intirely in the hands of a few and that not the least exertion is Makeing to adjust Matters for our Election. I have myself been obliged to attend to some private affairs which so long an Absence has rendered Necessary to which has been Added the Care of a Wife [*Catherine Meade Fitzsimons*] in a Very delicate state of health—rendered much More so by want of Air & Exercise—and an Anxiety Occasioned by my being so long from home I shall however Make an Exertion to get a Meeting between some of the principle Members of the Convention & a Number of our Citizens ~~that~~ in hopes that Measures may be fallen upon to promote the Interest of the State I shall not fail to inform You What Our prospects are.

ALS, Coxe Papers, PHi. Written from Philadelphia.

Robert Morris to Tench Coxe

You have conferred a favour by the transmission of the Map[1] which accompanied your letter of the 14th Inst. and by the Remarks and information Contained in that letter for which I return my Sincere thanks.

I propose to have this & Mr. [*Nathaniel*] Gorhams maps Copied & to obtain the others you mention so as to have the whole laid down together (and give a just View of that uncultivated part of the States of Pensylva. & New York) which shall be transmitted to Europe and when I have the pleasure to see you we will if you please have some Conversation Respecting those Lands which you mention as offered for Sale at 1/ ℔ Acre. I suppose it will not be long before you pay a visit to Philadelphia.

ALS, Coxe Papers, PHi. Written from Philadelphia.

[1] This may have been the manuscript map sent by a British consul to the foreign office in 1790 (Foreign Office 4/8 p. 878, PRO); it is published in Edmund B. O'Callaghan, *Documentary History of the State of New York* (4 vols., Albany, N.Y., 1850–57), 2:645.

Philip Schuyler to Thomas Jefferson

Being on the point of embarking for this place, when I was honored with your note, of the 14th. inst., and much engaged, I neglected to send you all the memorandums, I had made when perusing your report.[1]

The novelty of the Subject, the ingenuity Evinced in its discussion, the pleasure it afforded, added to a sence of duty, induced me to examine the principles, and make the calculations, the former appeared to me demonstratively Just, the latter, thro' error of the press, or mistake in Notation, I found, somewhat incorrect, but in so triffling a degree, that I should neither have noticed, or mentioned them to you, If I had not been perswaded, that perfection is your aim, as far as it is attainable, in whatever you offer to the public.

The length of a Pendulum, which shall vibrate Seconds in the latitude of 45 degrees, and the Rod thence deduced, as a Standard of measure, being 58.72368 inches, English, this Rod divided into five equal parts, to be called feet, each foot will then be 11.744736 Inches English, which Cubed, will produce 1620.05506862 (the Cubic inches English, in the Standard foot,) now as 1000 ounces av~~oi~~erdupoise, of pure rain water, will Exactly fill a Cubic foot English, or 1728 Cubic inches English. and as the Standard foot contains, only 1620.05506862 Cubic Inches English, it is evident, that if the water, which will exactly fill this Cube, be divided into 1000 Equal parts, Each of the parts, will be less in bulk, and consequently less in weight, than the former, in the ratio of 1728. to 1620.05506862, therefore, we shall have as 1728 (the Cubic inches English in a Cubic foot English) to 1620.05506862 (The Cubic Inches English in the New Standard Cubic foot) so is 437.5 (The grains Troy in an ounce av~~oi~~erdupoise) to 410.17019243 the grains Troy, in the new or Standard Ounce, $^{11}/_{12}$ths of which, is the pure Silver in the Unit, or dollar, that is 375.989343 Grains Troy, and hence the Expression of the Unit, or dollar, when the Avoirdupoise ounce shall consist of only 18 penny weights, or 432 Grains Troy, will be found by the following proportion, as 437.5, to 432. so 375.989343, to 371.2626277 the Expression of the pure Silver in the Unit.

If my Calculation ~~is~~ be founded, then the report will require the following amendments.

Page 37.	Line 9th.	dele.	376.02985	Substitute	375.989343
	18th.	ditto	371.30261.	ditto	371.2626277
Page 41.	line 6th.	ditto	1620.23	ditto	1620.05506862
do. 42.	last line	ditto	376.02985	ditto	375.989343
do. 43.	line 2d.	ditto	.38985	ditto	.349343

And le~~a~~st the English foot, Inch, &c. Should be taken for the Standard foot, Inch, &c. Perhaps the following amendments might also be proper.

Page 40. line 2d. Page 41. last line before "foot" insert *Standard*
do. 40. 20th. between "100" and "feet" insert *Standard*
do. 41. line 5th. & 15th. Page 42. line 5th. & 6th. & Page 43 line 5th. before "Cubic" insert *Standard*
do. 41. line 6th. before "Bushel" insert *Standard*
do. 42. do. 3d. 6th. & 18th. & Page 43 line 5th. dele. "an" Substitute *a Standard*
do. 42 7th. dele. "the" Substitute *this*

Your observation, page 40. that, ~~that~~ "It may be better generally to retain the name of the nearest present measure," has led me to enquire, if it was not possible to find Standards for measures, weights, and Coins, which while unchangeable in their nature, should be of such determined length, Capacity, and Weight, as that the New, or Standard *Unit* in each may not only retain the name, but as often as may be, coincide in length, Capacity and Weight, with those now in use within the united States, and that where they do not so coincide, the proportional numbers, for converting the expression of the one, into that of the other, may be composed altogether of pure Integral whole numbers, or pure terminated decimals; Probably this may be affected, in a great degree, by means of your Standard Rod of 58.72368 Inches English, for If it be increased, by some Equal part of its own length, it will still be an invariable, unchangeable *Standard.*

Let us then increase the Rod, by one forty sixth part of its own length, and it will become 60.0002817 Inches English, and as the fraction above 60. is so extre~~a~~mely small, that it may safely be rejected, in all the computations which are the subject of your report, let us state the length of the *Standard,* at 60 Inches English, let it be divided into five Equal parts, let each part be called a Standard foot, which will be the same, as an English foot. let the Standard foot be divided into 10 Standard Inches, each standard inch will then be Equal to 1.2 Inches English, and then we may have the following Series as in your report,

A Point.
10 Points a Line
10. Lines an Inch
10. Inches, a Standard foot
10. Feet, a Decad

10. Decads, a Rood
10. Roods, a Furlong
10. Furlongs, a Mile
Then the Standard Mile will consist of 1. Mile 3. Quarter 1. furlong 32 Yards & 44/100 English, and the former will be to the latter as 10000. to 5280.

SUPERFICIAL MEASURE

Superficial Measures have been Estimated, and so may continue to be, in Squares of the measure of length (A) Except in the Case of Lands, which have been Estimated by Squares called Roods and Acres.

Let the chain be of 100 links, each link of 6 Inches & 6 lines Standard, then the chain will be 66. Standard feet, but 66 Standard feet are the same as 66 English feet, hence the Standard chain, will be the same as Gunters chain.[2] Each link 6.6. Standard Inches, is equal to 7.92 English Inches, which is the length of a link in Gunters chain, hence the area of a Survey, whether made by the Standard, or Gunters chain, may be computed in the manner now in use, and the Areas will coincide, and be expressed, as now, in Acres, Roods &c.

MEASURE OF CAPACITY

Let the measure of Capacity, be the Standard Cubic foot, to be called a Standard Bushel, It will contain 1000. Standard Cubic Inches. be very nearly 1/5. less than the Winchester Bushel,[3] of 8 Gallons Corn measure English, and 1¼ Standard Bushel will be only, 8 Cubic Standard Inches more, than the Winchester bushel, and then we may have the following Series as in your report,

A Metre, the least measure which will be of a Cubic Standard Inch
10. Metres, a Demi-pint.
10. Demi-pints, a Pottle.
10. Pottles, a Standard Bushel (B.)
10. Bushels, a Standard Quarter (C.)
10. Quarters, a Last or double Ton

The measures for use being four Sided, and the Sides and bottoms rectangular, the Standard bushel will be a Standard Cubic foot.

The Pottle 5 Standard Inches square, and four deep.

The Demi-pint 2 Standard Inches square, and 2½ deep, hence any person, with a Standard foot Rule, divided into Standard Inches, may readily determine if his measures of capacity be true or otherwise.

WEIGHTS

Let the weight of a Standard Cubic Inch of rain water, or the thousandth part, of a Standard Cubic foot, be called a Standard ounce, then this ounce will be precisely of the same weight, as the avoirdupoise ~~weight~~ ounce, now in use, and then we may have the following Series as in the report.

A Mite, the least Nominal weight

10. Mites, a minim or demi-grain
10. Minims, a Carat
10. Carats, a double Scruple
10. double Scruples, an Ounce (D.)
10. Ounces, a pound (E)
10. Pounds a Stone. (F)
10. Stone a Kental (G)
10. Kentals a hogshead (H)

Coins

Let the money Unit be a dollar, and let its weight be Equal to a Standard Cubic Inch of rain water, that is equal to an avoirdupoise Ounce, or 437.5 grains troy, ~~and~~ now the pure Silver in a dollar, was by the Act of the late congress of the 8th. of August 1786.[4] to be 375.64 Grains Troy, and 34.15 grains Troy of alloy, making together 409.79. Grains Troy. If then the standard dollar be of 437.5 Grains, there must be more Alloy, and as this encrease of Alloy is of some value, there must consequently be an equivalent value of the Silver less, in the Standard dollar, than in the dollar of 1786; Supposing the Alloy to be worth about 11 Cents Pr. pound Avoirdupoise, the Encrease of Alloy will be equal to very nearly 0.64 grains, or $^{64}/_{100}$th of a grain Troy of Silver equal in value to 1$^{7}/_{10}$ Mill, and this deducted from 375.64 grains troy the weight of the Silver in the dollar of 1786, there will remain the weight of the Silver in the Standard dollar Equal to 375. Grains Troy, the difference between this, and 437.5 Grains, is the Alloy, for the Standard dollar, and is 62.5 grains Troy, or $^{1}/_{7}$ part of the whole, hence the Standard Dollar will consist of 6 parts pure Silver, and one part Alloy, and now we may have the following Series.

A Mite, the least Weight Equal to 0.04375. Grains Troy
10. Mites, a Minim, or demi-grain, or 0.4375 ditto
10. Minims, a Carat, or 4.375 ditto
10. Carats, a double Scruple, or 43.75. ditto
10. double Scruples, an Ounce, or 437.5 ditto (I.)
10. Ounces, a Pound, or 4375. ditto

[*footnotes*]

(A) If the Sides of a Superficies [*surface*] be given, in entire Standard feet, the Area will be the same, and Expressed in like manner, as if the Sides had been given in English feet.

If the sides of a Superficies be given in Standard feet & Inches, Lines, & Points, the feet in the product, will be indifferently Either Standard, or English feet, and the decimal parts of the product, will consist of Standard Inches, lines, & points, which may be converted into English Inches, Quarters, &c. by the usual mode of Converting decimal, to Vulgar Fractions.

If the Sides of a Superficies be given in Standard Inches Lines, & points, the product will be Standard, and will be to the English as 100. to 144.
(B) The Standard Bushell will be to the Winchester bushell as 17280. to 21504.
(C) The Standard quarter will be only 64 Cubic Standard Inches, or 64 Metres, more than the English quarter, of 8 Winchester bushels, the Standard Quarter is, to the English Quarter, as 17280. to 21504.
(D) The Standard Ounce, is ~~the~~ of Equal weight with the av~~oi~~erdupoise ounce, and also of a Standard Cubic Inch of rain water, and also of a Metre of rain water.
(E) The Standard Pound is equal to 5/8th. of an Av~~oi~~erdupoise Pound, also Equal to a Standard demi-pint of rain water, the Standard pound, is to the av~~oi~~erdupoise pound, as 10 to 16.
(F) The Standard Stone, is Equal to 6¼ pounds av~~oi~~erdupoise, also Equal to a Standard pottle of rain water;
(G.) The Standard Kental is Equal to 62.5 Pounds Av~~oi~~erdupoise, also equal to a Standard or english Cubic foot of rain water, and Equal to a Standard bushel of rain water.
(H) The Standard Hogshead is Equal to 625. Pounds Av~~oi~~erdupoise, also equal to 10. Cubic Standard feet, also Equal to 10. Standard Bushels of rain water in weight,
(I.) The Standard ounce, is equal to the Av~~oi~~erdupoise ounce, also equal to a Cubic Inch of water, also equal to a Metre of rain water
(K) From thise coincidence, between Weights, and Measures of Capacity, it is Evident that Either, might be applied as a Substitute for the other.

Thus if I wanted to weigh, a Kental of Wool, and have no Standard weights, but ha~~d~~ve a standard bushel, place the empty bushel in one scale, counterpoise it by something in the other, then fill the bushel with water and Counterpoise the whole by Wool on the other Scale, and so of the others.

No Standard, other than that which is derived from yours, has hitherto occurred to me, that will combine an equal number of advantages, should I discover any, I will with great pleasure communicate it, if what I have detailed on the Subject can be improved to any public advantage you are perfectly at liberty to make what use of it you may think proper.

LS, Jefferson Papers, DLC. Written from Albany, New York. A FC:dft (John Williams Papers, N), dated 19 August and in Schuyler's hand, corresponds to the LS except for its slightly different concluding paragraph. Schuyler's undated draft of the substitute paragraph, as well as undated drafts of calculations and tables, are in the Hamilton Papers, DLC. In an undated memo to Jefferson, evidently written immediately upon receipt of Jefferson's (unlocated) note of 14 August, Schuyler excuses himself for sending only a rough copy of some calculations, as he was at that moment on the point of embarking for Albany (*PTJ* 17:409n). For background on Jefferson's report, see *DHFFC* 8:482–83 and *PTJ* 16:602–17.

[1] Jefferson's Report on Coins, Weights, and Measures, dated 4 July, is printed in *DHFFC* 8:484–500.

[2] Gunter's chain, also known as a surveyor's chain, was developed by the early seventeenth century British mathematician Edmund Gunter and designated by the Confederation Congress as the standard unit of terrestrial measurement for the western surveys conducted under the Ordinance of 1785.

[3] A standard unit for measuring dry volumes, used in British trade for centuries before being legally defined in 1696 as 2150.42 cubic inches, or the volume of a cylinder eighteen and a half inches in diameter and eight inches high. It was named for the ancient English capital and trading center.

[4] *JCC* 31:503–4.

Hugh Williamson to John Gray Blount

[*Alexander*] McGillevray and his [*Creek*] Indians saild two days ago for St. Mary's [*Georgia*]. He has left a Nephew [*David Tate*] a Boy about 10 under Care of Genl. Knox for Education. One of the Clerks [*Caleb Swan*] out of Genl. Knox's office is gone with him. The Presidt. saild for Rd. Island last Monday, is expected back to day. I understand from Genl. Knox that as soon as the President returns Instructions are to be prepared & forwarded to Govr. [*William*] Blount. I presume they may be finished by this day Week & I presume they will be sent by Express from some Office on the Post Road, say from Richmond. For I take it as granted that they will be sent to the Halston [*Holston River*] Settlement say to Washington Court House, for from a Question asked of me about the best mode of sending a Packet, it seems to have been taken for granted that the Governour is to be found by a Messenger in his Government. Governor [*Arthur*] St. Clair arrived here some days ago. I do not learn what is his Business but have heard from an Authentic Quarter that the Wabash Indians must ~~of~~ certainly be corrected. McGillevray has promised to use his Influence with a leading Cherokee Chief to make Peace &c. I have Reasons for believing that Difficulties arise about the Hopewel Treaty. I have on the new Map lain down the new Road from the Mouth of Fr. Broad [*French Broad River*] to the crossing of Cumberland River & shewn that the whole of the Road is in the Indian Country according to the Hopewel Treaty also that the only communication between the strong Settlement about Halston & that about Davidson Co. is by the new Road unless the Traveler chuses to go into Virga. The People on the south side of fr. Broad must be quieted & perhaps a Ridge of Hills between Fr. Broad and little River may be the proper Boundary. I have alledged that a Line from the Junction of Halston with the Tenessee extending Westwards across the Cumb. Mountain might be proper to ask of the Indians because it would leave the new Road on our Side. But where is that Line to terminate or how far South is it to point? This is a difficult Question. I think it not improbable that the Indians would allow us to run along the Ridge that divides the Waters of Elk from those of Duck Rivers. I have been asked whether I did not think that Duck River itself would be a proper Boundary to be proposed. Doubtless I would prefer it to the romantic Idea of running up Cumberland River. On the whole I suppose the Governor [*William Blount*] will be asked to manage that Matter as well as he can. Too much will not be insisted on but it seems almost necessary that some thing in addition to the Hopwel Cession must be made. The Spirit of the Creek Treaty shews that the Idea of pressing hard on the Indians is not embraced. I need hardly ask you to send the Govr. this Letter if he has not departed for his Government. ***

ALS, John Gray Blount Papers, Nc-Ar. Addressed to Washington, North Carolina; postmarked. The omitted text concerns private business.

Other Documents

Michael Jenifer Stone to Walter Stone. ALS, Stone Papers, DLC. Written from Frederick, Maryland; addressed to Charles County, Maryland, in care of Mr. Underwood. A portion of this letter is excerpted with documents relating to Maryland's Second Federal Election in Correspondence: Third Session.

"I have only time to inform you that I am here and in tolerable health— but intend to go on to Bath [*Berkeley Springs, West Virginia*] by way of invigoration My constitution has been so broken up that I must give it some rest."

William Smith (S.C.), Travel Journal. PPRF.

Attended Congregational worship in the morning with Wadsworth and family in Hartford, Connecticut.

Boston Gazette, 23 August.

Otis arrived on the New York stage coach.

Monday, 23 August 1790

William Paterson to George Washington

By the death of Mr. [*David*] Brearley the office of district Judge for New Jersey has become vacant; and I have been informed, that the friends of Mr. [*Robert*] Morris have mentioned or intend to mention him as a proper person for his successor. As, perhaps, you have not, sir, any or but little personal acquaintance with Mr. Morris, I have been requested to communicate my sentiments respecting him. I know him well and have known him long. Mr. Morris took an early and decided part in the revolution of this country; he was a disinterested and persevering patriot to the very last; and was a friend to America as well in the gloom of adversity as in the sunshine of prosperity. In the winter or early in the spring of 1777, the legislature of this State appointed him to the office of Chief-Justice; he accepted the appointment. At this period it was not a little difficult to procure a proper person to occupy this important station; the time stamped a value upon his acceptance and shed a Lustre on his political reputation. Mr. Morris resigned in the summer of 1779; it had been always his intention to continue in office no longer than till the legislature could find a fit person to act in his place. At this time Mr. Brearley was proposed, agreed to serve, and was elected. About two years since the peace, Mr. Morris removed to the city of New York; he has returned to this State, in which he continued his practice, and has taken up his abode in this place.

Mr. Morris is a sound, well-read and judicious Lawyer, and fully competent to the office in view; his integrity is unquestionable and I believe, that his appointment to the office of district judge will be grateful, and give satisfaction to the people of this State.

ALS, Washington Papers, DLC. Written from New Brunswick, New Jersey.

Jonathan Trumbull to John Trumbull

Notwithstandg. a Head Wind the first Night after leaving N. York—yet I had a pretty good passage to N. London [*Connecticut*], arriving there in about 45 Hours—& Home in about 50 hours. ***

[*lined out*] Last Week I was at Hartford—& find that Wadsworth had much longer & much worse time [*traveling*] Home than I had, the weather—was extremely hot—& his Horses failed at N. Haven—which gave him trouble & fatigue—The family there were very Well except Daniel, whose health is mending.

Mr. Smith of S.C., was here last Week—having left the President & Suite in Providence [*Rhode Island*]—he came by Way of Norwich [*Connecticut*], & is gone on to Hartford—much pleased with what he had seen of our Country.

Wadsworth tells me, the Corporation [*Hartford*] had concluded they must have the portrait of their Govr. ***

Special Collections, Charles Roberts Autograph Letters Collection, PHC. Written from Lebanon, Connecticut; addressed to 31 Maiden Lane, New York; carried by Capt. Niles; answered 30 August by Niles, with the painting. The omitted text concerns family matters and John's portrait of their father, Governor Jonathan Trumbull, Sr. Jonathan reminds John to "make my Bow to all our good friends for me, on my sudden departure," particularly to the Tench Coxes.

Other Documents

William Smith (S.C.), Travel Journal. PPRF.
Toured Wethersfield, Connecticut, with Wadsworth.

[Springfield, Massachusetts] *Hampshire Chronicle*, 25 August.
Ames left town (after spending a week with his fiancé).

Tuesday, 24 August 1790

David Mead to William Maclay

Inclosed I have sent an Application to Congress for the Establishment of a post in this Settlement. I am totally unacquainted with matters of Form in such cases, But if any thing is improper in the Address or Otherwise I must Beg you to make the Necessary Appologies, and bring the matter to a Decision as soon as Possible.

I apprehend when you take the matter into Consideration you will in a moment deside that many great advantages from the removal, of the Troops at Fort Franklin[1] and Establishing a post at Cussewauga (or fixing a post there at any Rate) will arrise to the Publick and Also to the Safety and increase of the Settlement—a Short explanation of the situation of the present post is set fourth in the Petition your Brother Samuel & Other Commissioners[2] were lately at my House who can give you a more perticular Description of the Country.

However you will find it a Fact, that not more than three or four Plantations can ever be within several Miles of Fort Franklin for Mountains and Barrans, which is generally the case near the Allegany River—But about Eight or Ten Miles up French Creek the good Land Begins and is Extensive Indeed at present almost unknown, that a post near the heart of this Fertile Country would help to Encourage the Settlement that in a Short time it may be Compart to Prisquisle [*Presque Isle*]. In case this post succeeds (for the Immediate Accomodation of the Troops) a subscription of about one hundred Days works of the Inhabitants is already subscribed over & above the Boards & Team work mentioned in the Petition.

Upon the whole the Garrison in its present situation appears to me of Little Consequence I found it the Other day without one pound of meet and had then been eight Days without & but one Keg of Flower on hand, this

Information I Recd. from the Commanding Officer, who said he had given timely Notice to the Contractors. in this Situation was it in the settlement and in Dainger of Invation an Immediate supply of Provision could be had from the Inhabitants.

[*enclosure*]

To His Excellency the President, the Members of the Senate and Representatives of the United States in Congress Assembled at Philadelphia

The Memorial and Petition of a Committee of the Inhabitance of Cussewauga on French Creek Respectfully Sheweth—

That a Settlement is formed on French Creek about Thurty Miles up from the Mouth[3] and from the Post called Fort Franklin, in The Heart of an Extensive Country of Excellent Lands capable of being a Compact Settlement the whole way to Lake Erie—That the situation of Fort Franklin is near the Mouth of French Creek surrounded with mountains & Barrans so that no Settlement of any Consequence ever can be near it—That your Memoralists are under Apprehensions of Dainger from a Nation of Indians called Chipeways who have lately Thretned Distruction to the Garrison, and Settlement Both, That the remote Situation of the Post and Settlement from each Other makes it Impracticable for the one to afford any Assistance to the Other in case of Necessity—Whereas if this post was Established in or near the Settlement, they Apprehend Many Advantages would Arrise to the Publick as well as the safety of the People, that in case of Invasion, Both would Opperate on the Defensive together—and a Supply of Provisions could be had from the Inhabitance for the Garrison, and the settlement of this part of the Country would be so much more Incouraged, that in a Short Period the Expence of any Post we Beg leave to Suggest will be Unnecessary, and Also we are Authorised to engage that in case a post is Established here that for the Immediate Accomodation of the Troops, a number of Teams shall be furnished, and as many Boards as are Necessary to Accomodate the Garrison will be Advanced all Gratis.

Therefore your Petitioners Request that the Honourable Congress will be pleased to Order a post Established in or near the said Settlement and they as in Duty Bound will ever Pray.

ALS, Miscellaneous Letters, Miscellaneous Correspondence, State Department Records, Record Group 59, DNA. Written from Cussewauga, north of present-day Meadville, Pennsylvania. The petition was signed by John Brown, Robet fitz Randolph, John Gregg, David Mead, Joseph Dickson, Thomas [*illegible*], John Mead, Matthew Vigon, and Robert Hillson; it was not submitted to Congress.

---

[1] Fort Franklin was located about a thousand yards up French Creek from the place where it enters the Allegheny River in northwestern Pennsylvania.

[2]In 1790 Pennsylvania appointed Samuel Maclay, John Adlum, and Timothy Matlack as commissioners to study potential water transportation routes in the northwestern part of the state.

[3]Cussewauga was founded by David Mead and his brothers in 1788 at the junction of Cussewago and French creeks.

John Page to St. George Tucker

Come as soon as possible & let me tell you a thousand Things, of your Brother [*Representative Tucker*]; of myself; of Congress, &c. & let me introduce you to my dear Peggy [*Margaret Lowther Page*] & shew you how happy we are.

P. S. I found yours of the 22d. stuck in my Glass today when I arrived—if any Thing can induce me to go so far from Home as you propose, it will be the hope of enjoying your Company—I have a Letter for you from yr. Brother the Dr. he was to sail on Tuesday last—we sailed the Saturday before.[1]

ALS, Tucker-Coleman Papers, ViW. Written from "Rosewell," Gloucester County, Virginia; place to which addressed not indicated.

---

[1]Page returned to Virginia on the New York packet (*PTJ* 17:310n).

Lies of the Day

LAST Tuesday, about dusk, a large body of people collected, within the city of Philadelphia, and raised every stone which had been planted a few days before as a foundation for a (*temporary*) CONGRESSIONAL EDIFICE, *in that city!*

FROM THE COUNTRY

The day on which Congress adjourned, the enraged citizens of New-York assembled at the *Federal-Hall*, and attacked that honorable body in so unmerciful a manner, that many of them were killed, and several wounded in a dangerous manner!

OBSERVATION

The two preceding paragraphs are of the same species of many others which still find a welcome residence among the credulous—it affords a particular satisfaction to be able to observe, that neither New-York nor Philadelphia have been so lost to decency and good government as is depicted in these sentences.

NYJ, 24 August.

Newspaper Article

It must give sincere pleasure to every one who wishes well to his country, to reflect on the happy issue of the late session of Congress. The business they had to accomplish was arduous—the obstacles to be removed almost insurmountable. The wisdom of our rulers, their industry and perseverance, have attained the objects of their patriotick wishes. They were called by the election of their fellow-citizens, to administer an unorganized government, that last hope of America; to provide for the support of publick credit; to restore the wounded name of their country to the esteem of the world; to relieve the industrious farmer and mechanick from the pressure of enormous burdens,† which had produced almost intolerable distress; to provide for the regular and impartial administration of justice; to discharge large anticipations, which, from the imbecility of the former government, had become unavoidable; to establish administrations for the colonial governments in the Western Territory; and to propose the necessary taxes to effect all these important operations. All these things, in two sessions of the National Legislature, have been performed; although in every step of their progress, the inveterate prejudices of some were to be encountered, and local, jaring, and opposing interests to be reconciled. They have done more; they have provided effectually the means of lessening considerably the principal of the national debt. And in all this, the malign predictions of the enemies of the government have not been verified—no tax has been imposed on the people at large. Congress finding one million of dollars in the Treasury, have providently directed that sum, together with two million more to be obtained on loan, to be employed in purchasing the debt, while it remains below par. By this measure, many important, valuable effects will be produced. The money will, instead of remaining useless, be again carried into circulation; the publick burdens alleviated, and the people convinced that the national faculties are equal to all its necessities. This will remove all those apprehensions of oppression, which the arts of some have disseminated, and the fears of others entertained.

It must be confessed, that it is to be lamented, that in some instances, the allowances and grants which have been made, are beyond the expectations of the people, in this part of the United States. It will, however, give pleasure to the citizens of this Commonwealth to reflect, that this exorbitancy met a manly and determined opposition from their Representatives; and the good people will, with that moderation which ever distinguishes their conduct, consider this as the effect of the difference of habits prevailing in the several parts of the nation; and that what here would be considered as profusion, would in other places be termed parsimony. Though in this instance, respecting allowances and grants, the Representatives of this State were in a minority,* yet it has been their singular good fortune, and highly honourable to the people they represent, that in no other measure of importance was that the case.

NOTES

†*No measures can possibly contribute more to effect this desirable purpose, than the assumption of the State debt; by the General Government, as an heavy debt will now be discharged by impost, tonnage and excise duties, which, in case of a non assumption, must have been principally discharged by large land taxes, so grievous and oppressive to the agricultural interest. In mentioning this, we cannot but observe, that while the delegates from this and some other states spared no pains to effect the assumption of the State Debts, the unwearied and persevering attention and patriotick exertions of the Hon. Member from this District* [Sedgwick], *contributed not a little to the accomplishment of the measure.*

**To their honour is this circumstance mentioned.*

[Stockbridge, Massachusetts] *Western Star*, 24 August; reprinted in whole or in part at Portland, Maine; Portsmouth, New Hampshire; Boston; Philadelphia; Wilmington, Delaware; Winchester, Virginia; and Charleston, South Carolina.

Other Documents

Thomas Fitzsimons to Thomas Sumter. No copy known; acknowledged in Sumter to Fitzsimons, 15 November.

Memorandum Book of the Department of State. Item 187, p. 88, PCC, DNA.
Gerry was given a copy of Jefferson's letter to Massachusetts Governor John Hancock, dated 24 August and related to fisheries (see *PTJ* 17: 419–20).

William Smith (S.C.), Travel Diary. PPRF.
Toured the Hartford area and dined at Wadsworth's.

[New Hampshire] *Concord Herald*, 24 August.
A. Foster and Gilman arrived home last week; Livermore expected on 24 August, en route to Holderness (New Hampshire).

[Worcester] *Massachusetts Spy*, 26 August.
Ames passed through Worcester.

[Winchester] *Willis's Virginia Gazette*, 28 August.
White arrived at his home.

Wednesday, 25 August 1790

William Paterson to George Washington

Mr. Samuel W. Stockton, the bearer of this letter, intends to make application for the office now vacant by the death of Mr. [*David*] Brearley. Mr. Stockton is a gentleman of the law, and as such has been in practice for many years; he resides at Trenton; is prothonotary for the county of Hunterdon, and one of the masters in Chancery in this state; he was secretary to the commissioner of Congress to the courts of Berlin and Vienna during the course of the late war [*William Lee*]; his character, both as to politicks and morals, is extremely good, and highly respectable.

ALS, Washington Papers, DLC; FC:dft, Paterson Papers, NjR. Written from New Brunswick, New Jersey; place to which addressed not indicated.

Other Documents

Thomas Russell to John Langdon. ALS, Langdon Papers, NhPoA. Written from Boston.

Was looking forward to a visit during Langdon's return home, until (Henry?) Jackson told him he'd already left Boston for Portsmouth; invites Langdon family to stay during the fall.

Stephen Sayre to Thomas Jefferson. ALS, Washington Papers, DLC. Written from Havre de Grace, France.

Office seeking: some diplomatic post in Europe; mentions Izard and Floyd as references.

George Washington to Martha Dangerfield Bland. FC:lbk, Washington Papers, DLC. For the full text, see *PGW* 6:12–13n.

Apologizes for the delayed response to her inquiries regarding Theodorick Bland's unsettled public accounts from the Revolutionary War, due to the unusual press of public business at the close of the session.

Moses Young to John Langdon. ALS, Langdon Papers, NhPoA. Written from Trinidad; addressed to New Hampshire.

Acquaints Langdon with prospects of American trade with Trinidad, the expected poor harvests of cotton, and the more promising experiments with cane sugar and coffee.

William Smith (S.C.), Travel Journal. PPRF.

Breakfasted with Ellsworth at Windsor, Connecticut.

A Friend to Humanity. [Providence, Rhode Island] *United States Chronicle*, 26 August. Written from Gloucester, Rhode Island. For the full text, see *DHFFE* 4:439.

Claims Foster and Stanton are members of the Rhode Island Abolition Society.

[Winchester] *Willis's Virginia Gazette*, 26 August.

White arrived at his home.

Thursday, 26 August 1790

Pierce Butler to Roger Parker Saunders

*** I defered latterly writing to You, being in daily expectation of having it in my power to inform You of Your Uncle's [*John Parker, Sr.*] appointment. I applied both by letter and in person, & had reason to hope if the President had had any appointments to make Your Uncle would have been of the number. If the Excise law had taken place last session I believe I should have succeeded for Your Uncle—The only appointments the President had during the session was commissioner of Loans, and to this he felt a necessity of naming the same persons who formerly acted—I refused making application for others that I might reserve the whole of my little Interest for Your Uncle. To evince my attention I trouble You with a copy of my letter to the President before I waited on him to apply in person. I never can be unmindful of the friendship I owe and feel for You. You have my dear Sir, by Your most friendly, generous, and disinterested attention to me, made such a lasting impression on me, as can only be obliterated when I cease to exist. I am grateful for the fresh instance of attention in saving my Island[1] I wish You cou'd find out the name of the person who meant to attach it. *** —I agree with You that it would not do to settle the Island 'till there is some understanding with the Spaniards. I have repeatedly pressed this business, of the Spaniards, on the President: it will in time be adjusted.

*** My dear Mrs. [*Mary Middleton*] Butler's present ill health, being confined to her room, renders it impossible for me to go to Carolina during the recess; indeed I scarce ever put my foot out of the house, I have therefore wrote to the Commodore [*Alexander Gillon*] to send me an intelligent Clerk that may take the troublesome part of my business, ***

You have before this heard of the Treaty with the Creeks. It was not satisfactory to the Georgia Members. I think the article of the Treaty that regards the Negroes taken from the Georgians is vague and Weakly worded. I wanted the restoration of the Negroe Property an express condition of the future payment of the money that the Indians are to receive: losing this in Sennate I would not advise & consent, as the Constitution expresses it to the ratification: yet, between You & me, I should have been very sorry to have seen it broke off. Genl. Knox had it in his power to [*demand the?*] restoration of the Negroes taken. I blame him for not doing so—Gun is loud against him: they must quarrel. Gunn is really a good Member.

FC, Butler Letterbook, ScU. Sent to Charleston, South Carolina, by way of Philadelphia. The omitted text relates to additional private business and the management of Butler's estates. For the full text, see *Butler Letters*, pp. 59–61.

[1] Butler's Island, a rice plantation in the Altamaha delta, opposite Darien, Georgia. Butler acquired it sometime before 1784, probably through the estate of his brother-in-law William Middleton, and was able to keep it by a timely loan from Saunders at this time (*Butler*, pp. 117–20, 543).

John Chaloner to Jeremiah Wadsworth

By the removal of Congress to this place property between the improved part of the City & Broad Street is enhanced in value & is beginning to be enquired for—I am of opinion that this rise has taken place in consequence of some talk of building a house for the President & for Congress in Broad Street near Markett Street— *** Nothing is yet determined respecting those buildings—and altho the wish & expectation of many is that they will be erected w[*h*]ere I have described say 2 squares west of your ground yet there are many opposed to it & think the buildings ought to be in the improved part of the City.

ALS, Wadsworth Papers, CtHi. Written from Philadelphia; postmarked. The omitted text discusses the possible terms of sale of Wadsworth's lots in Philadelphia.

Hugh Williamson, Observations Respecting the North Carolina Cession

Minutes respecting the North Carolina Cession, accepted—2 April 1790

John Armstrongs office	4,000,000.
Genl. [*Nathanael*] G[*r*]eenes—	25,000.

//

some of the enteries in John Armstrongs office have been located in the Country South and west of the Tennassee, and on the Mississippi r. the chief [*illegible*] country, and the patents returned in the secretarys office.

//

A. goes to the entry takers office ~~& makes the location~~ what is called making his location and deposits his money according [*to*] the price fixed by law, which is £10 ⅌ hundred acres, and you obtain a certification from his office, had you hence deposited the money and a description of the Land—This is taken to the surveyor—of the District who makes the survey & returns the platt thereof according to the scale fixed by Law—This Survey is returned to the office of the Secretary of the state who issues the patent with the Governors signature where completes the title.
N. B. In all the descriptions of the Land in the western count[*r*]y the description was understood to be ~~ob~~ Vague—But in the surveyors return the land became sufficiently described wch. prevented interferences In order to remedy this interference, A law passed rendering it proper for any person who located upon a previous [*?*] survey upon the discovery [*thereof?*] to remove his location to another place unappropriated.

The whole Cession may be estimated at 21,000,000 ~~Acre~~ about 8,000,000 of which has been granted by North Carolina.
In the rights sold by the State of North Carolina it is understood that the State is to extinguish the Indian Title when the same shall be convenient—without any further expence to the individual, & that the individual, n[*o*]t to take possession untill the Indian Title should be extinguished.

Ms., hand of Henry Knox, Knox Papers, The Gilder Lehrman Collection, on Deposit at the New York Historical Society, New York. [GLC 2437.04574] Knox evidently recorded these observations, which he docketed as "Minutes . . . taken from Dr. H. Williamson," during a conversation with the congressman.

Other Documents

Samuel Bard to George Washington. ALS, Washington Papers, DLC.
Office seeking: his brother John Bard for excise officer in New York City; mentions Laurance and Benson as references.

Thomas Jefferson to Henry Knox. ALS, Knox Papers, Gilder Lehrman Collection, NHi. For the full text, see *PTJ* 17:430–31.
Expresses his opinion as to whether there is a conflict between the Treaty of Hopewell with the Cherokees and the North Carolina cession as accepted by Congress; concludes that "the act of cession of N. Carolina only ~~confirms the~~ preserves the rights of it's citizens, in the same state as they would have been, *had the act never been passed* *** Congress, by their act accept on these conditions"; admits it would have been desirable to settle the issues involved and purchase the right of occupation from the Cherokees.

Hext McCall to Pierce Butler. ALS, Butler Papers, PHi. Written from Charleston, South Carolina; postmarked Philadelphia, 5 September.

Asks Butler to use his "very great Influence" with the back country members of the state legislature to secure McCall's appointment as sheriff of Charleston District.

John Wallace to John Gray Blount. ALS, John Gray Blount Papers, Nc-Ar. Written from "Shell's Castle," North Carolina; addressed to Washington, North Carolina; carried by Capt. (Nathan?) Horton. For the full text, see *Blount* 2:97–99. Wallace (1758–1810) was a chandler and tavern keeper on the twenty-five acre Shell Castle Island, also known as Beacon Island, located just inside Ocracoke Inlet to Pamlico Sound; all but a quarter acre is now submerged (2006).

Senator and Mrs. (Frances Cathcart) Johnston have arrived.

[Portsmouth] *New Hampshire Gazette*, 26 August.

Wingate arrived at Stratham, New Hampshire, "since our last [*19 August*]."

Friday, 27 August 1790

Pierce Butler to Tench Coxe

Mr. Butler presents His Compliments to Mr. Cox, and returns Him many thanks for His Observations on the Trade of Pensylvania,[1] which Mr. B. has read with much Satisfaction. It is no Compliment to say, that the Observations are not only clear and well Conceived, but they Shew an intimate knowledge of the true Interests of the Union—Assuredly the Government of the United States ought to be more than ordinarily Cautious in the Restrictions they lay on the Carrying Trade. Circumstanced as the States are, with a large Uncultivated Territory, Every means ought to be fallen on to Encourage Cultivation of the Soil, which is the truest Source of Wealth—The greater the Competition for the Carrying Trade, the greater the demand for the produce of the Land. The European Carriers are generaly purchasers on the Spot Rather than Return Empty they will even give something more than a saving price.

It is ardently to be wished that We had similar Statements from the other States—We shoud then be no longer at a loss for a Correct knowledge of the Resource of the United states But We are not to expect to find in every State a person so qualified or that has given the same attention to the Subject.

Mr. Butler requests to know if the Book No. 6 is the only Copy Mr. Cox has left—If it is not Mr. B. will thank Him to let it remain with Him; but if it is the only Copy it shall be Retrieved this Morning.

AN, Coxe Papers, PHi.

---

[1] "The state of Pennsylvania," an eight page essay on the state's natural resources and commercial potential attributed to Tench Coxe (*Coxe*, p. 216n), appeared in Philadelphia's *American Museum* vol. 7, no. 6 (June 1790). The "Book No. 6" that Butler asks Coxe's permission to retain evidently refers to this issue of the monthly magazine.

Other Documents

John Codman, Jr. to John Adams. ALS, Adams Family Manuscript Trust, MHi. Written from Boston.

Office seeking: his brother Richard for consul at Cadiz, Spain; understands that the disproportionate number of appointments from Massachusetts might prevent the appointment, although education in commerce is more attended to in that state; asks who else ought to be solicited for letters of recommendation.

George Washington to John Adams. LS, hand of Tobias Lear, Adams Family Manuscript Trust, MHi. This letter enclosed queries, also in Lear's hand, regarding the administration's response in the event that the Nootka Sound crisis led British troops to launch an attack from U.S. territory against Spanish outposts on the Mississippi River; for the full text of both documents, see *PGW* 6:343–44. The same queries, under substantially the same cover letters, were sent to Jefferson, Hamilton, Knox, and Jay.

Is desirous of Adams's opinion, in writing, on the subject of the enclosed queries.

Saturday, 28 August 1790

William Constable to Robert Morris. FC:lbk, Constable-Pierrepont Collection, NN.

"My family return you thanks for the polite termes in which You are pleased to acknowledge the trifling Attentions paid You while here be Assured the pleasure of your society made us ample Amends for the very little trouble wh. You gave & if it were not for detaining you from Mrs. [*Mary*] Morris & the Enjoyments of your dear family We shoud have rejoiced to have kept you at New York much longer."

Thomas Hartley to Tench Coxe. ALS, Coxe Papers, PHi. Written from York, Pennsylvania.

Personal finances between them.

Edward Jones to Governor William Blount. ALS, John Gray Blount Papers, Nc-Ar. Written from Fayetteville, North Carolina; place to which addressed not indicated. For the full text, see *Blount* 2:101.

Office seeking: federal attorney for the Southern Territory; asks Blount to use his influence with Hawkins.

William Smith (Md.) to Tench Coxe. ALS, Coxe Papers, PHi. Written from Baltimore; postmarked 29 August.

Requests information regarding payment of certificates issued by Quartermaster Timothy Pickering dated after 1782; Smith has a few and will send them to Coxe if they can be paid in specie at the treasury department.

Z. [Boston] *Columbian Centinel*, 28 August. For An Old Soldier, see 19 August, above. For the petition, see *DHFFC* 7:176–78.

Regrets that the "*Old Soldier*" had not inquired about the petition of some of the officers of the late army with "the persons who best could have answered him"; the insinuation (against Ames) "must be intended only for electioneering purposes."

SUNDAY, 29 AUGUST 1790

Bossinger Foster, Jr. to Andrew Craigie

***

In every question of importance that has been discussed in Congress—& in which Mr. Ames has taken a part he appears to have discovered ~~the~~ a laudable independence of sentiment—the features of an improved understanding & Strong indications of a rising Character. tis true his opportunities of improvement in the Science of Politicks have not hitherto been many—but such as he has enjoyed, have been well attended to.

As for Mr. Gerry I take him to be a much older man his frequent introductions to political Life & popular assemblies undoubtedly gives him some advantages that *Ames* cannot of course possess—I am unacquainted with the Man—I only know his Character is fair & his reputation is increasing—he is certainly a Man of abilities & his integrity seems to be unimpeached.

***

ALS, Craigie Papers, MWA. Written from Boston.

Jeremiah Wadsworth to Tench Coxe

Your favor of the 14th should have been sooner noticed—but my long absence had so d[*e*]ranged my affairs that I have been constantly occupied in restoreing them to order.

I believe your plan of purchaseing the debt to be a good one and I earnestly wish it were begun as their is yet much speculation on the holders of paper—and it is selling greatly under its Value. I have prevented all who come for advise to me from selling—but too many are yet doubtfull & become a prey to their own fears which are artfully increased by those who are eager to purchase—"*the timid & needy*" who [*illegible*] are every day selling—I pray you present me respectfull to Mrs. [*Rebecca*] Cox with my family who are all acquainted with her and long to see her.

ALS, Coxe Papers, PHi.

Other Documents

Abigail Adams to Mary Cranch. ALS, Abigail Adams Letters, MWA. Addressed to Braintree, Massachusetts; written in the evening. For the full text, see *Abigail Adams*, pp. 57–59.

Intends to visit Martha Washington later that day, before her departure for Mount Vernon; she regrets their parting, since "we have lived in habits of intimacy and Friendship," and the departure of her and other "principal connections" makes New York City, "delightful as it is, much less pleasant than it has been"; John Adams intends to go to Philadelphia to search for a house, suspecting that he would be miserable in lodgings; presumes that letters to the Vice President will continue to be franked under the current post office establishment, as they would have been under the proposed Post Office Bill [*HR-74*] if it had passed.

John Adams to George Washington. ALS, Washington Papers, DLC; FC:dft, dated 28 August, Adams Family Manuscript Trust, MHi. For the full text, see *PGW* 6:358–60.

Does not doubt the probability or the consequences to American tranquility of British military operations against Spain in the Mississippi valley; the response of the United States should be neutrality, since the government has neither the popular support nor the resources for a war; the administration should withhold approval if Britain asks permission to march its troops across U.S. territory, and negotiate with Britain if its troops march without permission; the continuing absence of any ambassadors between the two countries at such a critical moment would present difficulties; laments the absence of suitable ministers to any European court generally, and Congress's reluctance to provide a suitable establishment for such a system.

Samuel Anderson to Samuel Meredith. ALS, Meredith Papers, DeU. Addressed to Philadelphia.

Acknowledges receipt of Fitzsimons' note which Anderson delivered to William Seton and it was discounted; regards to Fitzsimons and Clymer.

James Madison to Edward Carrington. No copy known; acknowledged in Carrington to Madison, 24 December.

William Smith (S.C.) to Jeremiah Wadsworth. ALS, Wadsworth Papers, CtHi. Written from New Lebanon, New York; place to which addressed not indicated.

Asks Wadsworth to pay a note until Smith's return to New York in about a month; arrived the night before, over an "infernal road" from Springfield (Massachusetts), and intends to go by horseback to Bennington (Vermont).

Monday, 30 August 1790

[*Simeon Baldwin,*] Gallio to the Republican [*David Daggett*]

With a great deal of avidity, I have read your numerous publications on the subject of Congress and our new government. Those stubborn facts, and that fair and candid representation of them must assuredly strike conviction into every mind that attends to them, that all things are not right, and that somebody wants to go to Congress.

It is a matter of great importance in every free government, that the conduct of Rulers should be scanned, and be held up to the public eye; *fairly* if it can be, but at any rate let them be scanned—and in this country which overflows with Liberty, as ancient countries did, with milk and honey, it matters not how, or by whom, or for what motives, provided, they be but scan'd.

In this view I was happy to see you oppose opposition in the bud. A man has a much better opportunity to do justice to his cause, by keeping the field alone, than when he is obliged to turn aside and contend with facts and oppose arguments. 'Twas right therefore to answer the fool according to his folly, and to ward off the blows of your opponent by your armour of brass.

I am happy on another ground, that you did not encourage an opponent. You know between you and I that some facts might have been represented a little different from your representation, and by different accounts from unknown sources, the ignorant vulgar would not have known which to have believed; but from your happy talent at communication, and a very prolific pen to aid your lively imagination, and a great facility in applying texts of scripture, and pertinent parables to the subject before you, whether that be the residence of Congress, or [*Frederick*] Stuben's memorial, from all this without opposition, nobody can be at a loss.

We readily assent to the cream of your essays—that all things are not right, and somebody else must go to Congress. Your elaborate performances have convinced us that a very thorough reform is necessary. I have been anxiously expecting your proposals for alteration: as they have not yet appeared, it may be of some advantage to you in making them, to receive communications from your friends in different quarters. I have therefore taken the liberty to make mine.

It appears to me impossible that so many evil streams should flow from a pure fountain. The Constitution must be radically defective. I would therefore propose the following:

FURTHER AMENDMENTS TO THE CONSTITUTION.

1. Clashing interests and local policy or prejudice shall no longer exist in the minds of the Members of Congress; and,

2. To prevent a mispense of time in unnecessary debate, two thirds of each house shall always agree in every bill or resolve, before it shall be proposed.

3. To convince the other third, and keep up the perfect freedom of debate, five speakers on each side shall be allowed to debate in speeches five minutes long.

4. All resolves shall be like those of the Medes and Persians, unalterable, unamendable,[1] for that would imply mutability, and occasion loss of time and money.

5. The fees of all officers, door-keepers not excepted, shall be regulated by those of the state Government of Connecticut.

6. The residence of Congress shall not be in an Indian wigwam, nor in the howling wilderness.

7. The petitions of Baron Stuben and Nathaniel Twining,[2] shall be negatived, without being read.

These amendments will, I think, comprehend most of our sources of uneasiness, and I am surprized that the wise framers of our new Constitution had not the sagacity to insert them. 'Twould have saved you a world of trouble and perplexity. But, somebody wants to go to Congress, fairly if it can be, but at any rate must go to Congress. There must be a change of members. Can you name the man or men? I dare say you have them in your eye—Men who fear GOD, and hate covetousness. Men who have grown grey in the political employments of their country, and therefore they better understand them. Men who known the worth of money, and therefore will work cheap. Men who cannot talk, and therefore will not spend time in idle debate. Men whose characters are known, and who will therefore have influence. To raise such men it would be a trifle in the politics of this state, to sacrifice only five argolic lives on the altar of jealousy or ambition; especially as their remove would make promotion for younger folks. Do be so good as to publish your list, and oblige your friend.

[New Haven] *Connecticut Journal*, 1 September; reprinted at Boston. Daggett responded on 6 September, below. For information on this series, see the location note to A Republican, No. 1, 15 May, volume 19. Junius Annaeus Gallio (d. 65) was a Roman proconsul who dismissed the charges brought against Paul by the Jews (Acts 18:14–16). While the internal date of this piece in the newspaper is 30 August, a draft in the hand of Simeon Baldwin, signed "Anonimous," rather than "Gallio," is dated 20 August (Ms., Simeon Baldwin Papers, CtY).

[1] Daniel 6:8.

[2] For the petitions of Frederick William Steuben and Nathaniel Tracy, see *DHFFC* 7:201–33, 8:241–44.

OTHER DOCUMENTS

Thomas Jefferson to Alexander Hamilton. FC, Jefferson Papers, DLC. For the full text, see *PTJ* 17:474–75.

Asks Hamilton to frank the collection of acts of the second session that will be sent to each member of Congress during Jefferson's absence from the seat of government.

[New York] *Poughkeepsie Journal*, 4 September.

Benson arrived at Poughkeepsie.

TUESDAY, 31 AUGUST 1790

Dorothy Elsworth, Mr. Madison's Bill

1790		Mr. Madesan Bill	
Augt.	12	Ballence on A bill delever	£ 34 19 1
	20	Cash Gave Mrs. H.	1 15
		do. for Calleco	4
		pd. Makeing Gound	0 4 6

	27 pd. Mrs. Brower	1 18 11
	tea	1 5
	Cash to Mrs. Harmon	1
	Shew maker	1 4 0
Augt.	13 to 31 to board	7 4 0
	Servent—do.	3
	wine & porter	2 4 4
		£ 58 16 10

186 doulers
is £ 74-8
58-16
15:12

Ms., Madison Papers, DLC. Elsworth signed the bill and indicated that she had "Recd. payment."

August 1790 Undated

George Beckwith, *Conversations with Different Persons*

***

[*Ames*] We understand Lord D. means to pass through the States on his way to Europe, and had hopes to have had the pleasure of seeing His Lordship this Autumn.

[*Beckwith*] Lord Dorchester had applied for leave of absence, and did purpose to pass this way, but the appearances of War [*between England and Spain*] have put a stop to it for the present.

[*Ames*] In the formation of our present government we have copied greatly from Yours; there is indeed a material distinction, we have no hereditary Sovereignty, nor a hereditary Aristocracy, but we have endeavoured to form something as nearly resembling those, as circumstances rendered practicable. In every regulation introduced the strictest attention has been paid to Your conduct in similar instances, and wherever Your system applied, it has been invariably adopted. It is glorious for Great Britain, that all the polished nations in the world are endeavouring to introduce her form of government in some shape or other, and that France notwithstanding all her present struggles may fail in attaining it.

I look forward with pleasure to an end of all our remaining differences, those violent personal animosities, which are so disgraceful to any people, who harbour them, are now done away, and I hope we shall shortly connect the two countries by Treaties to the advantage of each. The markets of Great Britain are the best for the raw materials of the States; Your manufactures are the best adapted to our tastes; the encouragement of the domestic manufacture in the States I dont conceive to be prejudicial to Your interests, we shall become richer by it, our luxuries will encrease with our wealth, and our consumption of all finer articles will follow, we shall also pay better than at present. The enthusiasm of a dreamer cannot lead to the supposition of Great Britain's aiming at territorial superiority in this country; on that score therefore there is no room for jealousy, and I wish that You may in some shape or other judge it expedient to relax some of Your Navigating Acts, which have a tendency to prevent the formation of a durable connexion between us.

[*Beckwith*] I hope we may come to a perfect good understanding, but you must be sensible how important those Acts are to us, which secure our naval power.

[*Johnson*] Our Session has been a long one, and it has lowered the Congress greatly in the public opinion, the length of time wasted in the residence bill, the debates upon it, and the bargains, which connected this subject with the Assumption of the State debts, have got abroad, and have created doubts in the wisdom and in the character of the Legislators, which must produce much censure and some reproach. The conduct of the Connecticut delegation has been uniform and rational, they laid a regular plan at the commencement of the Session, and have abided by it; they wished to secure six or seven years residence in favor of New York, and to have given the permanency to Baltimore; they proposed this to the Maryland gentlemen, but these had entered into previous engagements with the Virginia and Pennsylvania delegates for Philadelphia and the river Potowmac, which they were the means of carrying to the injury of Maryland, as it respected the residence, and they stipulated to vote for the assumption of the State debts, which is a measure contrary to their local interests; they have therefore acted weakly, and I really believe these gentlemen will not be well received on their return. The increase of the duty on Salt will likewise be very unpopular and create disgust. The Elections are at hand, and I am persuaded many alterations will take place in the Representative Body. As to Potowmac I have no idea, that the Government will ever go there; once fixed at Philadelphia the Eastern Members will all vote against going further south. The treaty between us and the Creek Indians is nearly completed. If Georgia has encroached on their territories, justice ought to be done them. I have always been of opinion, that the State of New York has acted unwarrantably towards the Indians of the six nations.[1]

Had any accident happened to the President Mr. Adams would have expected to succeed him, but I doubt greatly, whether he would have been chosen, he is by no means popular in the Southern States, and I think Mr. John Jay would have been preferred; he possesses a smoothness of manners, a moderation a conciliation in his general language, which render him better liked than the other, and cover a warmth of temper, accompanied by a sullenness of disposition, from which the Chief Justice is far from being exempt.

Mr. Maddison's bill for the discrimination of duties cannot be brought forward this Session, however earnest he may be about it; the Committee has been called on repeatedly by the party in the senate, who are anxious to promote this measure, but without success; there are not more than seven or eight members in that house of this way of thinking, and Mr. Langden of New Hampshire, who is a man of a fair private character is one of the principal ones; there is no convincing him, but that You have laid a deep concerted plan to recover the Sovereignty of the States, and that Your whole conduct at present leads to this point; other gentlemen think such ideas quite visionary, and that if even they were prevalent here, the British Nation would not listen to them: It is certain, that, whether Your views go to this or not, the formation of a Treaty of Commerce, and afterwards of a Treaty of Alliance, lead as well to this object, as to the establishment of National friendship.

[*R. H. Lee*] I doubt we shall have no war between Great Britain and Spain.

[*Scott*] I doubt so too, but for very different reasons, and mine are these: If Great Britain had possession of the opening of the Mississippi, her commercial enterprize would give us a fair and liberal market for our various exports, which is not now the case, it would tend to people our country, in consequence to give us more weight in the general scale, we should grow wealthy and powerful; in these ideas all the people upon the western waters are united.

[*R. H. Lee*] You would injure us greatly were this to happen (meaning the Atlantic States) You would undersell us fifty per cent in every article, for although Your distances to New Orleans may be great, the transport down the streams is so easy and expeditious, that the price of the Articles would not be enhanced in any great degree.

[*Beckwith*] How would you go home again?

[*Scott*] We must return by the Atlantic States.

[*Beckwith*] Then you would lay out Your money there, in European, and in East and West India commodities, and the Exports of the Western waters, or their value, would center ultimately in the Atlantic Cities.

[*Scott*] Partly, but not altogether; we should carry some of the money over the mountains to pay labourers, and to improve our lands,[2] and the gentlemen in Virginia for instance are greatly alarmed, they have already tracts of old lands, without cultivators, in consequence of Western emigrations; such are the advantages of a better climate, and being lords of the soil.

[*Beckwith*] I also doubt our having a Spanish War, but from motives widely different from either Yours or [*R. H. Lee*]; his he has told me proceed from his hope, that such a contest will raise the price of wheat, and thereby afford encouragement to Agriculture.

***

Ms., Colonial Office, 42/69, pp. 34–38, PRO. These conversations are part of a compilation received by Lord Dorchester at Quebec on 11 September and forwarded to Lord Grenville in London on 25 September 1790. Their dating is based on references to the approaching end of the session and the pending completion of the treaty with the Creeks. Beckwith identified his interviewees by a numbered code, the key to which was provided in a separate document. Johnson was "No. 1," Ames was "No. 17," R. H. Lee was "No. 18," and Scott was "No. 14." For an exhaustive treatment of Beckwith's role in the FFC, see Julian P. Boyd, *Number 7: Alexander Hamilton's Secret Attempts to Control American Foreign Policy* (Princeton, 1964).

[1] By the Treaty of Fort Herkimer (1785) and the Treaty of Fort Schuyler (1788), negotiated while the Articles of Confederation limited Congress's authority over the matter, Governor George Clinton secured over five and a half million acres of land in central New York State, ceded primarily by Oneida Indians. The latter treaty was particularly controversial among the Oneidas' fellow tribes of the Six Nations, owing to the questioned authority of the Indian signatories and their mistaking the promised annuities for rent payments only (J. David Lehman, "The End of the Iroquois Mystique: The Oneida Land Cession Treaties of the 1780s," *WMQ* 47, 4[October 1990]:523–47; Alan Taylor, *The Divided Ground: Indians, Settlers, and the Northern Borderland of the American Revolution* [New York, 2006], pp. 162–66, 179–85).

[2] At this point Beckwith indicated that Lee left the conversation.

Thomas Fitzsimons, Remarks on Proposed National Bank

Mr. Fitzsimons—

Mr. F. seems to think, that it would be most eligible that any Bank in the United states, with which Government might chuse to connect its affairs, should stand upon independent ground as to its direction, operations &ca.—that the Bank should on each occasion, when government contemplates an important operation in finance, treat with you for the terms on which they would execute the proposition—that the Bank of England[1] conducts itself thus f with the government. (1) that he does not immediately see the benefit that the Bank of N. America could derive from the Connexion with government upon other terms than those exemplified in the case of the Bank of England (2)—that he is not certain it would be beneficial or eligible in the opinion of the Bank that the United States should become stockholders—that he has no appre[*he*]nsions that any of the depositors (or customers) in the Bank would leave it should a connexion in any form with Government take place—that an election [*lined out*] must as he conceives, be given to every *stockholder* either to receive his Stock or embrace the new plan, yet he does not think more would be inclined to leave it than could find ready purchasers of their Shares—that no Bank can hold to any advantage or for any time any considerable portion of the public Monies unless it be at the seat of Congress—that he will converse on the Subject with Mr. Morris & Mr. Clymer, and that he has no Objection to throwing his thoughts on this subject upon paper, which I expressed a wish that he would do.

He observed further that he could not immediately see the occasion government would have for loans of any consequence or any such Measures as would render a national bank, connected with their debts, an object—that all that was requisite in that kind of business would be comprehended in the funding System.

Note (1)

The renewal of the Charter in England including the Monopoly rests entirely with the Government & gives them a weight in these negociations, which can in no such way be derived to our Government in their treaties with the Bank of N. A. nor indeed with either of the three now instituted,[2] nor with any other Bank that may be hereafter established *under the Laws of any State.* A Question of consequence here presents itself whether the Legislature of the United States are vested by the Constitution with a power to grant charters of Incorporation.

Note (2)

The circulation of their Notes as an Universal Medium & their operating upon the Basis of their paper Capital, which to a certain length they manifestly might do—and their securing ~~to them~~ these benefits from going in to the aid & promotion of any other institution—the reputation at home & abroad of their being the great national reservoir are some of the Advantages.

Ms., hand of Tench Coxe, Coxe Papers, PHi. Coxe indicated at a later date that the conversation occurred in "July & Augt. 1790."

---

[1] A company of merchants chartered by Parliament in 1694 to loan money and make cash advances to the government in exchange for certain privileges, including the issuance of bank notes.

[2] The Bank of North America was chartered by the Confederation Congress in 1781; the Pennsylvania legislature incorporated it in 1782, and several other states granted it a temporary charter for wartime purposes. These soon expired, and Pennsylvania also repealed its state charter in 1785, although it rechartered the bank two years later. The remaining two banks in the United States in 1790 were the Massachusetts Bank, chartered in 1784, and the bank of New York, which began business in 1784 but was not chartered until March 1791.

James Madison, Advice on Executing the Residence Act

"The act for establishing the temporary and permanent seats of the Government of the U. States" requires the following steps for carrying the latter into effect.

1. The appointment of three Commissioners
of sufficient respectability
having good will to the general object without any particular bias of private interest*
residing (a majority at least) so conveniently to the scene of business as to be able to attend [*lined out*] readily & gratis
Should it be adviseable after securing a majority near at hand to make an appointment with a view to attach particular parts of the Union to the object, N. England, particularly Massachusetts, first occurs—and next, S. Carolina & Georgia.

Mr. [*Andrew*] Ellicott
Mr. [*William*] Fitzhugh (of Chatham)
Mr. Loyd [*Edward Lloyd*] (of Annapolis)
Mr. Gorum [*Nathaniel Gorham*]
Mr. O[*liver Jr*]. Wolcott
Mr. of Rd. Isd. [*Rhode Island*]
Mr. [*John?*] Bull
Mr. [*Thomas Tudor*] Tucker
Mr. [*Abraham*] Baldwin
Revd. R. Lee Massey

2. That the President inform himself ~~himself of~~ of the several rival positions; leaving among them inducements to bid against each other in offers of land or money. As the location when compleated by the survey will not be mutable by the President, it may be well to have the offers so framed as to become ipso facto absolute in favor of the U.S. on the event ~~of the~~ which they solicit.

3. That the President direct the survey of the District which he shall ultimately elect. It seems essential that the District should comprehend the river water adjoining the establishment, and eligible that it should comprehend the oppos[*ite*] shore. The legality of this seems to be decided by the clause confining the purchase or acceptance of land for the use of the U.S. "to the East side of the river within the said district" which ~~would be~~ imply that the *whole* district was not *necessarily* to be on *that* side. Quer: whether it will not be convenient to accept in the first instance so much less than 10 miles square as will allow places to be afterwards taken in, which may not now be attainable, or it may not be prudent now to accept.

*Quer. if local situation or interest be an objection [*lined out*] outweighing the advantage of proximity and zeal for the object, as the President is to prescribe the place & the Comisrs. only to define the district, and as the subsequent discretion in the Comissrs. will give no opportunity of sacrificing their trust to [*lined out*] local consideration. The essential point seems to be that the Commission sd. be filled by men who prefer any place on the Potowmac to any place elsewhere. On this supposition, it may be easy to find men who would suit.

4. The district being defined & the requisite quantity of ground secured, the next step must be to fix the site for the public buildings—and provide for the establishment or enlargement of a town within the district. As no special authority is given for the later purpose the consent of proprietors will be necessary: but as they will have a common interest with the public, voluntary arrangements between them and the Commissioners may be readily procured in favor of any plan which the President may patronize. Should any difficulties be apprehended on this point they can be guarded agst. in the negociations preliminary to the actual location of the district.
5. The plan for the public buildings is to be approved by the President. The Commissioners will no doubt submit different ones formed by themselves, or obtained from ingenious Architects. Should it be thought proper to excite emulation by a premium for the best, the expence is authorized, as an incident to that of the buildings.
6. The completion of the work will depend on a supply of the means. These must consist either of future grants of money by Congress which it would not be prudent to count upon—of State Grants—of private grants—or the conversion into money of lands ceded for public use which it is conceived the latitude of the term "Use" & the spirit & scope of the act will justify.

Ms., Madison Papers, DLC. The dating of the document is based on the fact that it preceded actions by Jefferson, Madison, and Washington after their visit to the Georgetown, Maryland, area in mid September. It was probably prepared for a meeting with the President at New York City, perhaps as early as the last two weeks of July. For Jefferson's advice on the same issue, see *PTJ* 17:460–61.

Other Documents

Tench Coxe to John Adams. ALS, Adams Family Manuscript Trust, MHi. It is possible that this letter was written as late as the first week of September.

Encloses a letter "received from Mr. Fitzsimons by this days mail" regarding a potential house near Philadelphia for Adams and his family; describes the property.

Daniel Hiester, Account Book. PRHi.

Paid John Fenno for seven months of *GUS*.

[Hagerstown, Maryland] *Maryland Spy*, 2 September.

Last week Stone passed through Hagerstown "in a bad state of health" en route to Bath [*Berkeley Springs, West Virginia*]."

September 1790

Wednesday, 1 September 1790

Pierce Butler to Rev. Weeden Butler

I am not very equal to the writing of a letter at present. Yet I must thank You for Your favour of the 1st. of June, which I received in August. The critical situation of Mrs. [*Mary Middleton*] Butler's health affects both my mind and health—She is as helpless as an infant and reduced to a shadow. She is in the hand of the Lord it is my duty to submit to His Sovereign Will—I will try to do so properly; yet the Conflict is great.

My former letters will acknowledge the receipt of the Thermometer, with thanks—The money that my attentive good Sister [*Frances Butler*] may Remitt to You please to pass to my Boy's [*Thomas Butler*] Acct.—I have not heard from Her for near twelve Months.

I sincerely hope Your good Lady's health is quite reestablishd—We are yet ignorant here whether You are in Peace or at War. We have, thank God, closed Our session well, after making provision for the Expences of the War and well Establishing the Credit of the Country. All the Members have left new York but myself. We meet in Philadelphia the first week in December—I shall Embrace the first good Conveyance to send You Our Journalls.

Are the poor Brabanters to return to their Slavery?[1] if so, they had been happier not to have had their Chains loosen'd—their situation shoud be a Caution to the French to Guard against Counter Revolution I hope We shall have nothing more to do with the Wars of Europe than to soften the rigors of them, by supplying all parties with bread, and an Assylum in Our Ports. I have suffered so greatly by War that I shall the rest of my days pray for peace on Earth.

I conclude from a letter I had from Our friend Doctor [*Thomas*] Spence, that He is now trying Native Air. I ardently wish He may return to London with the health of a Young Highlander.

I have drawn on You in favour of my Son for a Crown I hope He continues to deserve Your Esteem—If He ever forfeits it He will make me miserable—yet My Dear Sir, let not this anxiety of mine prevent Your giving me freely Your opinion of Him in every stage—It is essential that I shoud know him thoroughly my dependence is on You for that knowledge—I have my apprehensions that so long a Separation may weaken His affection for His Mother and myself—filial affection is not only the surest but most pleasing tie to hold him by—to direct and influence his Actions hereafter—On that account I wish to be nearer Him yet I can not make it convenient—I place all my Confidence in Your keeping the Spark alive till I can make it convenient to Visit Europe.

[*P. S.*] In future direct, if you please, State instead of Province the Name is Changed by an Act of Parliament—for Representative [*torn*] [*Sena*]tor.[2]

ALS, Butler Papers, Uk. Addressed to Cheyne Walk Chelsea near London; postmarked twice; answered in October.

[1] A reference to the suppression of the Brabant Revolution in the Austrian Netherlands (present-day Belgium and Luxembourg).

[2] Weedon Butler had apparently addressed his letter to Representative Pierce Butler, Province of New York. The reference to Parliament refers to its recognition of American independence.

Abishai Thomas to John Gray Blount

*** When the question of assumption was about to be carried our H. W. [*Williamson*] in order to obtain as large a portion as possible for N.C. made and exhibited calculations by which it appeared that the debt thereof was much larger than it really is, now sir as the purchasers have not faith that the State will make good that part which is not assumed so they make their calculations & contracts accordingly, but as I know they reason from false data, so I also know how to set them right & have most of the materials in my possession which I will make use of the moment I find it my interest so to do & this I hope will soon happen, I confide that you will keep this information to yourself & if you can benefit by it I shall be happy.

***

ALS, John Gray Blount Papers, Nc-Ar. Place to which addressed not indicated.

Other Documents

Phineas Bond to Francis Osborne, Duke of Leeds. ALS, Foreign Office 4/8 p. 323, PRO. Written from Philadelphia; place to which addressed not indicated.

It is supposed that Congress will resume the tonnage (Trade and Navigation) bill in the next session.

John Gladstone to John Langdon. ALS, Langdon Papers, NhPoA. Written from Salem, Massachusetts; addressed to Portsmouth, New Hampshire.

Will be happy to furnish Langdon with any information respecting the trade of Liverpool, England.

Alexander Hamilton to Thomas Fitzsimons. ALS, Hamilton Papers, NNC. Addressed to Philadelphia. For the full text, see *PAH* 7:5.

Regarding rental of a house for Hamilton.

David Humphreys to George Washington. ALS, Washington Papers, DLC. For the full text, see *PGW* 6:381–82. Humphreys refers to Cutting's letter of 3 June as being dated 15 June, the date the mail packet left England.

Adams read to Humphreys, on the night of 29 August, the letter he had received from John Brown Cutting dated 3 June (printed in volume 19), regarding U.S. relations with Great Britain given the probability of an Anglo-Spanish war.

Richard Henry Lee to Corbin Washington. ALS, Peyton Family Papers, ViHi. Written from "Chantilly"; addressed to "Walnut Farm," both in Westmoreland County, Virginia. For the full text, see *Magazine of American History* 22(1889):507.

"I arrived here monday afternoon pretty much fatigued with my Journey."

[Savannah] *Georgia Gazette*, 2 September.

Gunn and his wife arrived from New York in a sloop bound for Charleston, South Carolina; Jackson arrived on a sloop by way of Charleston.

NYDA, 13 September, reprinting a Charleston, South Carolina, source.

Jackson arrived there on the *Exchange* six days after leaving New York.

Thursday, 2 September 1790

Theodore Foster to Dwight Foster

*** You was indebted I believe to Me more than one Letter in Case we ~~we~~ should go in the Grou[*n*]d of Debtor & Creditor in epistolary Correspondence—It was matter of some Regret to Me that so much Time had elapsed since I Recd. a Line from ~~you~~ a Brother for whose good Opinion and Friendship I have so high a Value—I frequently thought of the pleasure it would give Me to receive a Letter from you while attending on Congress at New York and more than once determ[*in*]ed to write you from thence:

But the very important Business of the Nation on which I was constantly involved while there prevented the pleasing Satisfaction I should have taken in writing you from thence.

***

I will with great Pleasure comply with the Request in your Letter of informing you respecting the Characters Abilities &c. of my Fellow Senators so far as I can inform and Judge of them from the Little Opportunity I have had—But I must postpone the Matter 'till I have a Little more Leisure which I expect will be after the Rising of the Legislature of this State the Next Week—It will be an important Week to Me since I expect the Senator for this State will then be chosen to serve for the next Six Years after the Term which I was chosen for expires which will be in March next—I expect to be in Nomination—No Doubt others will also be in Nomination. My Prospect is I believe good at present as all the same Members will have a Voice next Week who gave Me my present Appointment. But you know in popular Governments depending on the Opinion of the Day Elections are uncertain. The Governor [*Arthur Fenner*] and a Number of other Gentlemen have promised Me all the Support and Assistance in their Power.

Tuesday last came on the Election for a Representative from this State in Congress—Benjamin Bourne Esqr. of this Town Job Comstock Esq. of East Greenwich and James Sheldon Esq. of Richmond have had the Greatest part of the Votes which have been given in. The Two First have much the greatest Part of the Votes—But it is uncertain whether there is an Election as the Law makes it necessary that the person chosen shoud have a Majority of all the Votes Given in—The Numbers betwen Mr. Bourne and Mr. Comstock are nearly equal. 300 Votes were given in this Town for Bourne & 20 for Comstock But the Country have more generally voted for Comstock.[1]

ALS, Dwight Foster Papers, MHi. Written from Providence, Rhode Island, at 11 A.M.; addressed to Brookfield, Massachusetts; carried by their brother, Peregrine Foster (b. 1759). The omitted text concerns reflections on youth and mentions forwarded newspapers.

---

[1] For documents relating to the election of a Representative for Rhode Island, see *DHFFE* 4:436–46.

Other Documents

Samuel Adams to John Adams. LS, Adams Family Manuscript Trust, MHi. Written from Boston.

Office seeking: Nathaniel Byfield Lyde to command a revenue cutter; "have not written a single line to any friend in, or out of Congress during the late session."

William Samuel Johnson to Jeremiah Wadsworth. One page ALS, *Libbie Catalog* 6 January 1891, item 22155.

The President has set out for Mount Vernon.

Nathaniel Byfield Lyde to John Adams. ALS, Adams Family Manuscript Trust, MHi. Place from which written not indicated; answered 12 September. The letter is undated and was likely enclosed with Samuel Adams's letter of this date.

Office seeking: commander of a revenue cutter.

George R. Minot to George Thatcher. ALS, *The Collector*, July 1949, item I1308.

"On financial matters."

[Worcester] *Massachusetts Spy*, 2 September; reprinted at Portland, Maine; Exeter, New Hampshire; and Newport, Rhode Island.

"Great preparations are said to be making in Philadelphia for the reception of Congress; and if we may judge from the accounts given us of the rise of provisions, houserent, &c. &c. a federal Representative will be able to live in a tolerably decent style at about eight or ten dollars per day."

[Charleston, South Carolina] *City Gazette*, 3 September.

Burke arrived from New York on the *Delaware*.

Saturday, 4 September 1790

Newspaper Article

The citizens of Philadelphia have ever been remarkable for their public spirited undertakings; and we cannot doubt that they will continue to exert themselves on all occasions, in procuring every accommodation for themselves and for those strangers who may visit them. Of this kind are an Exchange and an Assembly room. An exchange has long been talked of, and its utility universally acknowledged; but no exertions have been made towards carrying this idea into execution, As our commerce extends it will become more and more necessary. The rooms hitherto used for our assemblies have been too small to accommodate those who attended; and they will in future be still more inconvenient, as the presence of Congress will bring hither a number of strangers, who will wish to frequent these places of amusement, and this perhaps will induce more of our citizens to attend. It seems therefore necessary to erect an assembly room. Some subscriptions were formerly collected for this purpose, but not sufficient to defray the expence. A meeting of the subscribers, and of other persons disposed to encourage the undertaking is announced for monday next. A correspondent wishes to suggest the expediency of combining an exchange and a ball room. An elegant building might be erected, containing ample accommodations for both purposes, at much less expence than separate buildings; and many more persons might be induced to subscribe, if the objects were united, than if they were separated. In addition to convenience, such a building, if planned and executed with taste, would be no small ornament to our city.

FG, 4 September; reprinted at New York City (*NYP*, 9 September) and Winchester, Virginia.

For the Independent Gazetteer

THE conduct of our Representatives in Congress has been repeatedly and with some severity inquired into in various points of view—There is one part of it which I have often heard noticed in conversation—seldom seen in print—I mean the indelicate extension of their authority and emolument. In all other respects, and in this too, they may have been honest—in other respects they may have been useful—In this (to say the least) they have not been delicate. Was it delicate when their number was so greatly increased, when they stood not as the Representatives of separate sovereignties, but of economical individuals; at a time too when it was their duty to make the government as light and pleasing as possible? Was it delicate to appoint for themselves wages to the utmost extent that the former practice in this state with a less number of Representatives would possibly admit? Was it delicate, having resolved to receive as high wages as possible, afterwards to resolve that it should be constitutionally unlawful to lessen these wages while they were in office? Having thus appointed and secured to themselves the highest practicable wages while they should serve, Was it delicate to resolve that they should serve and be paid as long as by a very forced and inconvenient construction indeed they possibly could? These things if not *crimes* appear at least *transgressions* in political morality. What part in these proceedings our immediate Representatives[1] may have taken I do not know, but I presume there are many of their constituents who will be desirous to inquire—and whose votes the issue of this inquiry will probably regulate.

IG, 4 September.

[1] This is probably a reference to Clymer and Fitzsimons.

OTHER DOCUMENTS

Elbridge Gerry to Henry Knox. ALS, Knox Papers, Gilder Lehrman Collection, NHi.

Leaves for Massachusetts by packet in a day or two; since Knox will not have time to obtain subscribers to the publication of Mercy Otis Warren's poems, requests the list be sent to Gerry by the bearer and he will deliver it to Boston.

William Knox to Henry Knox. ALS, Knox Papers, Gilder Lehrman Collection, NHi. Place from which written not indicated.

Relates to sale of lands that Henry owns, with Schuyler and Morris, along the St. Lawrence River.

John Page for Francis Bright. Ms, hand of Page, Washington Papers, DLC. Written from "Rosewell," Gloucester County, Virginia. For the full text, see *PGW* 6:497n.

Office seeking: letter of introduction and recommendation for Bright, who gave the first notice of British Admiral Richard Howe's fleet entering Chesapeake Bay in 1777.

William Smith (S.C.), Diary. PPRF.

Traveled with Henry Izard from Lebanon Springs, New York, to Stockbridge, Massachusetts, where they spent the night with the Sedgwicks.

An American. [Boston] *Columbian Centinel*, 4 September.

"the people of Massachusetts will never forget the assiduous services of an AMES, a GERRY, a SEDGWICK, and a GOODHUE, in effecting the assumption of the State debts."

SUNDAY, 5 SEPTEMBER 1790

Pierce Butler to Peter Spence

*** The friendship that has long, and so uniformly subsisted between us will not let me be an unconcerned Spectator where You are concerned. I look not again to form any such attachment, it is not only too late in the day, but the disposition ceases; & the more intimately I read my fellow-creature Man, the less credulous I am, & the more inclined to believe that We are not the best of God's Works.

***

My dear Mrs. [*Mary Middleton*] Butler continues much indisposed. I really thought last Thursday that she would have taken a most painful departure. I am confined to the house by her indisposition. I am not prepared for such a shock. My mind, as You well know, has been much broke in on during & since the war—it is ill prepared indeed for such a shock. ***

Every thing is tranquil & orderly in Our Government. I mean the Federal, & the states are rapidly progressing to consequence & to an eminent station among the Nations of the Earth. We have I trust taken effectual measures to establish the credit of the U.S. & to provide for the expences of the late War. I sincerely wish for a good understanding between this Country & England. In my small Walk as an individual who has a voice in the ratifying of treaties I shall do all in my power to promote it. ***

FC, Butler Letterbook, ScU. The omitted text discusses their friendship and Butler's financial situation. For the full text, see *Butler Letters*, pp. 62–64.

Other Documents

Abigail Adams to John Quincy Adams. ALS, Adams Family Manuscript Trust, MHi. Place to which addressed not indicated. "Bush Hill" was a large three story mansion built ca. 1740 by the noted lawyer Andrew Hamilton (ca. 1676–1741). In 1767 his grandson William (1749–1813) vacated the then-suburban estate located north of present-day Vine Street between 12th and 13th streets, and it was demolished in 1871.

John Adams sets out for Philadelphia the next day to find a house; they are considering taking "Bush Hill," belonging to William Hamilton, "uncle of my favorite Nancy [*Ann Hamilton*]."

John Fenno to Samuel A. Otis. ALS, Records of the Secretary: Concerning Publications, Senate Records, DNA. For the full text, see *DHFFC* 8:601.

Binding the printed Senate journals; the President arrived at Philadelphia on Wednesday; rents there have risen one hundred percent.

John Page to Francis Bright. ALS, Washington Papers, DLC. Written from "Rosewell," Gloucester County, Virginia.

Office seeking: encloses letter of introduction and recommendation dated 4 September, above; also encloses a letter to be delivered to his wife's mother (at New York?).

William Smith (S.C.), Diary. PPRF.

Smith and Henry Izard breakfasted with the Sedgwicks.

Monday, 6 September 1790

Abigail Adams to Thomas Brand-Hollis

***

I have a situation here, which, for natural beauty may vie with the most delicious spot I ever saw. It is a mile and a half distant from the city of New York. The house is situated upon an eminence; at an agreeable distance flows the noble Hudson, bearing upon its bosom the fruitful productions of the adjacent country. On my right hand, are fields beautifully variegated with grass and grain, to a great extent, like the valley of Honiton in Devonshire. Upon my left, the city opens to view, intercepted, here and there, by a rising ground, and an ancient oak. In front, beyond the Hudson, the Jersey shores present the exuberance of a rich, well-cultivated soil. The venerable oaks and broken ground, covered with wild shrubs, which surround me, give a natural beauty to the spot, which is truly enchanting. A lovely variety of birds serenade me morning and evening, rejoicing in their liberty and security; for I have, as much as possible, prohibited the grounds from invasion, and sometimes almost wished for game laws, when my orders have not been sufficiently regarded. The partridge, the woodcock, and the pigeon are too great temptations to the sportsmen to withstand. ***

Mr. Adams is absent upon a journey, or he would have written you a letter of a later date than that which Mr. [*William*] Knox is the bearer of. This gentleman is a brother of our Secretary of War, and is appointed consul to Dublin. He is intelligent, and can answer you any question respecting our government and politics, which you may wish to ask; but, if he should not see you, I know it will give you pleasure to learn that our union is complete, by the accession of Rhode Island; that our government acquires strength, confidence, and stability daily; that peace is in our borders, and plenty in our dwellings; and we earnestly pray, that the kindling flames of war, which appear to be bursting out in Europe, may by no means be extended to this rising nation. We enjoy freedom in as great a latitude as is consistent with our security and happiness. God grant that we may rightly estimate our blessings.

Charles Francis Adams, *Letters of Mrs. Adams* (Boston, 1841), pp. 204–6. The omitted text discusses their friendship and relates family news.

Abigail Adams to Cotton Tufts

Mr. Adams received your Letter dated August 31. he sat of[f] that morning for Philadelphia *** where is Thomas [*Boylston Adams*] we have been daily expecting him for near a month, and Mr. Adams delay'd going his journey a week expecting him here *** Mr. Adams had thoughts of going to Braintree [*Massachusetts*], but his journey to Philadelphia will prevent it as I suppose if he can get a House there, we must remove next month. ***

How will Elections go? are they still in a rage for Rotations in Massachusets? or does the Clamour rise from a few wrestless spirits who have no other importance, if they change mr. Gerry for mr. any body else, they will lose one of the firmest men they have as independant a man, and as honest a one. in the first session, his mind was irritated & he was hurt, his speaches were misrepresented, and his conduct misconstrued, but through the whole of this last session no man has exerted himself more for the honour and Reputation of the Nation, nor more firmly gaurded the constitution against innovation. I most sincerely hope he will be reelected.

*** All Letters addressed to the v. president are franked in the post office, so that you may write by that conveyance when you please.

Will you be so good as to tell mr. [*John*] Codman that as the president and Secretary of State are both absent, there cannot any application be made at present in favour of his Brother [*Richard Codman*]. that on a former occasion when Mr. A. named a gentleman to the president as proper for consul, he replied that he had no other objection than that a much greater number had been appointed from N. England than from any other of the States and that his object had been to distribute offices as equally as possible. Mr. A. will however communicate to Mr. [*Tobias*] Lear the contents of the Letter.

ALS, Miscellaneous Manuscripts Boxes, NHi. Place to which addressed not indicated.

Ralph Izard to Tench Coxe

Mr. [*Thomas Lee*] Shippen has informed me that I can not have Mr. Edward Shippen's House in Philadelphia, as he has let it to his Son in Law, & has offered to endeavour to procure me another. I have written to Mr. Shippen that you knew of a House to be let that you thought would suit me, till I should have time to get a better. If you would take the trouble of writing to Mr. Shippen on the subject I should be obliged to you. I hope the House has a Coach House, & Stables to it, as it is very inconvenient to have them at a distance: it is a circumstance, of which Servants always take advantage, & pretend to be there whenever they are wanted. Mr. Smith [*S.C.*], & my Daughter [*Charlotte Izard Smith*] leave this place for New York tomorrow by way of Albany: in about three Weeks I expect to follow them.

ALS, Coxe Papers, PHi. Written from Lebanon Springs, New York.

Letter from Philadelphia

Mercy on us, what dreadful doings are there like to be here! I have a whole budget of news for you—frightful news, diabolical news—melancholy news, and, in short every kind of news that is miserable and lamentable! It is discovered by some nice noses resident among us that the drains of Still Houses and Breweries will be injurious to the future health of Congress—Ergo, either Congress or the Brewhouses and Distilleries must be planted in the fields—Is not this terrible news, Messieurs Printers? Do not also the butchers, the tanners, skinners, curriers, chandlers, all send forth disagreeable smells and unsavoury vapours? Probably they will in a short time be told to make way and remove home, as the health and benefit of the citizens will require it! We shall then have the town filled with men of science, leisure, and refinement, such as have been accustomed to sit upon their broad bottoms at home to enjoy a free and pure country air. So say some—The improvements for Congress in New-York, and those in consequence of their residing there, were generally made on vacant lots. Hence it was that your mechanics viewed them as a blessing. So will ours, if we pursue the same measure: but on the contrary if they are thrust into the heart of the city by any ill advised step of the Legislature or corporation, this useful class of citizens, who are now looking forward with expectation of benefit from the measure, will, from the raising of rents and other causes, curse the day they came amongst us, and *the men* who were the means of bringing them hither.

NYDA, 8 September; reprinted at Charleston, South Carolina.

[*David Daggett,*] A Republican to Gallio

HAVING finished my observations about Congress and their measures, for the present; nothing but your *severe, pointed* and *masterly* attack would have induced me to resume my pen.

Your proposed amendments, as I have altered and enlarged them below, are already become part of the constitution, by the conduct of Congress.

1. Clashing interest and local policy or prejudice *shall* exist in the minds of the members of Congress; and,

2. To *increase* a mispence of time in unnecessary debate, two thirds of the house *shall* never agree in *any* bill or resolve, *till it hath been discussed two days.*

3. *Not* to convince the other third, *nor* to keep up the freedom of debate, *but to puff themselves off as actors, thirty* speakers, on each side shall be admitted to debate in speeches of *three hours* long.

4. All resolves shall be like *childrens play-things, alterable, amendable*, for that occasions loss of time, *and produces more six dollars.*

5. The fees of all officers, door-keepers not excepted, shall be regulated *as tho our land overflowed with money, "as antient countries did with milk and honey."*

6. The residence of Congress *may* be in an Indian wigwam, or howling wilderness, *provided there is a play-house* [*theater*] *at hand, and the hon.* R. M—s [*Robert Morris*] *thinks such plan best.*

7. The petition of Baron Steuben, Nathaniel Twining, or *Pitman Collins,*[1] *may be debated six days, if any member of Congress, or his friends are interested in the issue, otherwise they shall be negatived without reading.*

8. The rights of the people may be sold and bartered by Congress, at any time—as for instance—the northern members may barter away the residence of Congress, for the assumption of the state debts, and so *vice versa*; in which case, it shall be lawful for the anti-assumptionists to be entirely silent when the question is debated.

9. No change of representatives shall ever take place, lest "argolic" or Grecian "lives should be sacrificed,"[2] and,

10. Lest such sacrifice should be made, each representative, for the time being, shall be, and he is hereby authorized, to protract the session of Congress till his pay shall amount to 2000 dollars per annum, and till, by some *funding bill,* he can double or treble his fortune, so that the *young Grecians of his family,* may not be injured by such sacrifice.[3]

[New Haven] *Connecticut Journal,* 8 September. This is a response to [*Simeon Baldwin,*] Gallio to the Republican [*David Daggett*], 30 August, above.

---

[1] The inclusion here of Collins's petition, which was not mentioned by Gallio, is an attack on Sherman, who presented it.

[2] From Plutarch's life of Aristides; referring to a defeated representative's political demise.

[3] Three of Sherman's sons suffered serious financial problems involving the federal government. William died during the first session, bankrupt and suspected of embezzling from the army. Isaac unsuccessfully sought compensation as a government surveyor before ultimately securing a clerkship in the treasury department. John was never able to settle his accounts as a regimental paymaster for the Continental Army.

Other Documents

Governor William Blount to Daniel Smith. ALS, James Robertson Papers, Tennessee State Library and Archives, Nashville. Written from "Governor [*Alexander*] Martin's" (Danbury, North Carolina).

Has obtained information that requires him to meet with the President immediately; reminds Smith that laws of North Carolina "will go on in the same Manner as if no Cession had been made or accepted"; thanks Smith for his "friendly recommendation of me to your Congress Friends to the Appointment of Governor" of the Southern Territory.

George Clymer to [*Samuel Meredith*]. ALS, Dreer Collection, PHi. Places from and to which written not indicated; written in the morning. The recipient's identity is based on internal evidence.

"To day I shall have all the Virginians in town [*Philadelphia*] at dinner."

Thomas Jefferson to William Short. ALS, Short Papers, ViW. Written from Philadelphia; place to which addressed not indicated. For the full text, see *PTJ* 17:496–97.

The governorship of Pennsylvania was to have been contested between Morris and Thomas Mifflin, but Morris has declined.

John Laurance to Jeremiah Wadsworth. ALS, Wadsworth Papers, CtHi. Addressed to Hartford, Connecticut; postmarked.

Laurance and daughter Polly will visit Wadsworth in about two weeks.

TUESDAY, 7 SEPTEMBER 1790

Pierce Butler to Joseph Habersham

Your two favours of the 10th. & 18th. of August did not reach my hand 'till a day or two ago Congress had been some time adjourned. Believe me there is not a Man on Earth bears You a sincerer friendship than I do; or woud have more satisfaction in evincing it. There will next session I believe be some respectable appointments in the Excise. If You approve, I recommend Your writing a short letter to the President & enclose it to Mr. Baldwin or me, or both of us, & I will deliver it in person; & do every thing that friendship can dictate. I mention a written application because I know this mode is not only best—but is expected.

You have heard before this day of the peace with the Creeks. I disapproved much of the wording of that Article that respects the Negroes taken by the Indians from the Citizens of Georgia. It is studiedly vague & delusive I was displeased at the intended deception & was against ratifying that part of the Treaty so worded—Colonel Gunn behaved vastly well & with judgment on the occasion.

FC, Butler Letterbook, ScU. Sent to Georgia.

OTHER DOCUMENTS

GUS, 15 September.

Williamson arrived in Boston.

Wednesday, 8 September 1790

Pierce Butler to Peter William Van Lankern

***

As I know You correspond with Itally I beg the favor of You to write to some of your most confidential & Esteemed correspondents there to inform themselves fully whether or not the U.S. of America, on securing the payment of the Interest beyond a doubt, could negociate a Loan of Money in Genoa, Venice, or any other part of Itally; & to what amt. in one year, & on what terms; that is at what rate of Interest & what expence would attend the making a Loan—Be so good to request of them to inform themselves fully. and I will esteem it a favor if You will prevail on them to write me on the subject as soon as possible. You can tell them how to write to me. I wish this to be Entre Nous. Beg of them to send duplicates of their letters & write as soon as possible. Congress have sent an Agent to Amsterdam to try to Negociate a Loan of Money there. I know nothing of his abilities in that way. The Gentleman is Mr. [*William*] Short, who is at present Our Charge d'Affaires in Paris—If You can early inform yourself of his success or his prospects You will oblige me by communicating them to me. I request You will lose no time in writing to Itally for me. The President & Sennate would not consent to appoint any Consul, at present to Genoa as We have no Trade to that City. If a Loan cou'd be made there on reasonable terms I could get it thrown into your friends' hands if they are of such consideration that You could recommend them.

Our Congress adjourned last month to meet in the City of Philadelphia in December—I wish Europe enjoyed the tranquility that We do at present. I feel for the Belgic States.[1] I think it is a critical situation: if they accomplish their views it may have a good effect in time on your Country.

FC, Butler Letterbook, ScU. Sent to Amsterdam. The omitted text relates to private business transactions Butler was managing for Van Lankern and mentions an enclosed letter for Mr. Berghause. For the full text, see *Butler Letters*, pp. 66–68.

[1] A reference to the imminent collapse of the United States of Belgium and its potential impact on ongoing turmoil in the neighboring Dutch Republic between the executive (Stadtholder William V) and the legislature (estates-general).

Pierce Butler to Nicholas and Jacob Van Staphorst and Nicholas Hubbard

It is a long time since I have had tha letter from You. By the time this reaches You You will have heard that the President has authorised Mr.

[*William*] Short, now at Paris, to negociate a Loan of 12 million of Dollars for the states, conformable to an Act of the Legislature passed last Session.[1] On this subject I fully informed Mr. Cazneuve [*Theophile Cazenove*] & he has written to You or your connections largely on it. If You attend to the contents of his letter you will not do rong. I have a right to say so much, because Mr. [*Jacob?*] Le Roy, by following my advice has saved You thousands in regard to purchases. I will do him the Justice to say that he attended to it, & often called on me for it. Mr. Short is an entire stranger to me—What his abilities are I know not. I have good reason to believe that an Offer will be made to your house to take a concern in a Speculation on the Debt of the U.S. to France. It will in the end be found by You more advisable to decline it. If you attend to Mr. Cazneuve's letter You will assure to your Connections strong friends here.

I will thank You to give me the very earliest information of Mr. Short's success, & if he does succeed the terms of the Loan. There is one thing more will you give me such authentick information of the lowest terms on which You and your Connections will undertake a Loan for the U.S. & the amt. yearly as will authorise me to rise in sennate & say that my friends will do so and so. I depend on your advising me from time to time on this business by the earliest opportunities.

***

FC, Butler Letterbook, ScU. Sent to Amsterdam. The omitted text relates to a private financial transaction. For the full text, see *Butler Letters*, pp. 68–69.

[1] Section 2 of the Funding Act [HR-63].

Other Documents

Pierce Butler to David Olyphant. FC:lbk, Butler Papers, PHi. Written to Newport, Rhode Island.

Did not reply sooner to Oliphant's last letter, because he had planned to see him in person during a visit to Rhode Island with Mary Middleton Butler; because of her illness, she could not bear to be moved and he has given up the plan.

[Boston] *Columbian Centinel*, 8 September; reprinted at Portland, Maine; Exeter and Portsmouth, New Hampshire; Georgetown, Maryland (present-day Washington, D.C.); and Winchester, Virginia. The speech alluded to was probably that given on 1 April; see *DHFFC* 13:948–56.

Attacks Representatives who base their bids for reelection on their opposition to Assumption; the arguments in its favor have never been controverted; "See the masculine speech of the Hon. Mr. *Gerry*, on the subject."

Mirrour III. [Springfield, Massachusetts] *Hampshire Chronicle*, 8 September.
Enquires into the conduct of Massachusetts' representatives in promoting the "standing instructions from the people, to use their utmost endeavours to procure the adoption" of the amendments proposed by the state's ratification convention; finds that only one received Congress's assent and "others are expressly superseded and dispensed with."

NYDA, 11 September.
Adams arrived in Philadelphia to locate a house for his family.

GUS, 18 September.
Boudinot and Ellsworth were awarded honorary doctor of laws degrees by Yale.

THURSDAY, 9 SEPTEMBER 1790

Rusticus to Mr. Adams

***

But it has been repeatedly said, that our own members in this Commonwealth, have resisted this torrent of dissipation, extravagance and inconsistency, with becoming spirit. This I deny; and I now call upon the friends and advocates of these gentlemen, to prove the fact. The truth is, this circumstance has been strangely misrepresented to the public. In no instance, saving that of the compensations, and even in that, some of them finally voted for the bill, even after the pay of the senatorial branch had been raised beyond the original report, did they make the least, or if any, but a very feeble opposition; as if, saving appearances, had been their only object.

***

[Boston] *Independent Chronicle*, 9 September; edited by Thomas Adams. The omitted text criticizes the aristocratic tendencies of Congress's excessive expenditures and argues for a rotation of the state's delegation. "Rusticus" is Latin for farmer, rural, and unsophisticated.

OTHER DOCUMENTS

William Constable to Robert Morris. FC:lbk, Constable-Pierrepoint Collection, NN. On Humphreys's mission, see *DHFFC* 2:117–18, 469–73.
David Humphreys has gone "in cog[*nito*]." to London; it is speculated he goes as ambassador; "I wish you Joy of your neighbours as I understand the President is to have your House."

William Short to Thomas Jefferson. ALS, Jefferson Papers, DLC. Written from Paris; marked private; received 11 January. For the full text, see *PTJ* 17:505–8.

Butler is talked of as the American consul or minister at The Hague.

FRIDAY, 10 SEPTEMBER 1790

William Constable to Gouverneur Morris. FC:lbk, Constable-Pierrepoint Collection, NN.

David Humphreys carries William Short's commission to negotiate a $2,000,000 loan.

Tench Coxe to Benjamin Rush. ALS, Rush Papers, PPL at PHi. Addressed to Philadelphia.

Asks Rush to inform Fitzsimons that Hamilton received Fitzsimons' letter and will rent Rush's house; Hamilton "is not an ostentatious man, that he desires comfort, and decency and cares not about shew—This Gentleman, be assured, has many virtues, and many talents. He is a man of great constant industry and immense occasional exertions—of a very firm mind with a great deal of caution & prudence—His table, his person and his wife and children are not ever ornamented or costly."

Alexander Hamilton to Nicholas Gilman. ALS, privately owned in 1979. Places to and from which written not indicated; marked "Private." For the full text, see *PAH* 26:554.

Office seeking: requests, for the President, names of persons in Portsmouth, New Hampshire, who are best qualified and willing to serve as officers on a revenue boat "on your Eastern Coast."

FG, 10 September.

Adams left Philadelphia for New York this morning; has chosen William Hamilton's "elegant mansion" at Bush Hill as a residence for his family, who will return with him to Philadelphia in a month.

[Connecticut] *Norwich Packet*, 10 September; reprinted at Stockbridge, Massachusetts, and Newport, Rhode Island.

"*A large superb Hall with other preparations in point both of propriety and elegance are making in Philadelphia for the accomodation of Congress.*"

Saturday, 11 September 1790

William Smith (Md.) to Tench Coxe. ALS, Coxe Papers, PHi. Written from Baltimore; postmarked 12 September.

Asks him to obtain immediate payment of the enclosed certificate; offers to render Coxe any services he needs at Baltimore.

[Boston] *Columbian Centinel*, 11 September.

The Gerry family has arrived at Cambridge, Massachusetts.

[Rhode Island] *Providence Gazette*, 11 September.

Bourn elected Representative.

Sunday, 12 September 1790

James Wilkinson to John Brown

Last Evening recd. your Letter of the 12th. July, the first I have recd. from you, since you left the District—I thank you for the Contents, they interest the Union generally, & no Man in it more than myself—I am happy to find that the Atlantic People think justly on the Subject of the British possessing themselves of Louisiana, we have unfortunately too many Blockheads in this Country who wish for this Event, for should it take place the dismemberment of the Union will speedily follow, this is one setled principle of their Policy, digested more than three Years since—I shall write you more fully on these Matters by the next conveyance, about the 20th. Inst. *** I do not think it of importance that you should come to the District before the Spring, but you must then make it a Point to spend a couple of Months among us—in the mean time you must not be so [*eastern?*] in your Correspondence, send your Letters into every quarter of the District, dont write as I do now a great deal about nothing, tickle the self love of every babling Puppy you can recollect, above all things I would have you write to John Hawkins, & Isaac Morrison, to make Friends of them, old [*Samuel*] Scott absolutely deserves yo[*ur*] thanks. [*George*] Nicholas & [*Harry*] Innes are different Characters—Your Friend Gerard [*James Gerrard*] has become a Zealot, & you can promise yourself little else but Prayers from him hereafter—if he did you no harm, he did little good on the late occasion—write to [*John*] Edwards, to Marker [*?*], Parson [*William*] Wood, also to Col. Ricd. Taylor, to whom you gave just cause offence by Nominating [*Peyton*] Short before him for the Collectorship, Taylor is your Enemy, Short is his *own Friend.* you do not calculate well—you know I suppose that you are held responsable for every appointment in this Country & for every Act of Congress respecting it—your past arrangements cannot be defended—the fœderal [*district*] Court at Harrods Burgh was a most damnable faux pas—Danville was the only place where you could fix it without exciting clamorous discontent, for there you had the Wisdom & Justice of the Legislature to direct & support you—You must write to Old Payne (Edward) & Thos. Lewis, they are my best Friends & both voted for you—they are zealous wherever they takes & of course are valuable Friends & dangerous Enemies—I will excuse you from writing to Old Muter[1] again, but what do [*you*] think of droping Old [*Thomas*] Marshall a few lines, indeed I would do it—I send this by James Parker who waits for it, under cover to Col. [*Clement*] Biddle, who will take care of it.

[*P. S.*] N. B. I realy have much to say of the depen[*d*]ing Expedition against the Savages & of the Spanish War, but I have not time, nor am I in time for a solid [*illegible*] Subject—suppose I should make up a Party of 500 or 1000 Men, & go down to the assistance of the Don [*Spanish*]?, what would the Congress Say? tell me explicitly.

ALS, Brown Collection, CtY. Written from Lexington, Kentucky. Place to which addressed not indicated. The omitted text relates to the Second Federal Election and is printed in Correspondence: Third Session.

[1] George Muter (d. 1811) of Mercer County was chief justice of Kentucky and a member of the district's "court party," which supported statehood and opposed ratification of the U.S. Constitution.

Other Documents

Abigail Adams to John Quincy Adams. ALS, Adams Family Manuscript Trust, MHi. Addressed to Boston.

Laurance's reelection is proof that New Yorkers, "being sensible when they have good & able men," can resist the cry for rotation in office; Adams has just returned from Philadelphia; presumes the family will move there next month.

John Adams to John Quincy Adams. ALS, Adams Family Manuscript Trust, MHi. Addressed to Boston; franked. The letter is undated but postmarked 12 September.

Advises about social and professional life; in political life, "never loose sight of Decorum. assume a Dignity above all Personal Reflections: and avoid as much as possible a Party Spirit"; looks forward to receiving his letters on political subjects.

John Adams to Samuel Adams. ALS, Letters of John and John Quincy Adams, NN. Addressed to Boston; postmarked and franked. For the full text, see *John Adams* 6:411–12.

Office seeking: will give Samuel's letter of 2 September and that of Nathaniel Byfield Lyde, to the secretary of the treasury; officers who served in the navy during the Revolutionary War will likely have preference, but Lyde nevertheless has a fair chance; Adams's family is in "as good Spirits as the prospect of a troublesome removal will admit"; discusses the possibility of political change worldwide; "your Boston Town Meetings, and our Harvard Colledge have Sett the Universe in motion."

John Adams to Nathaniel Byfield Lyde. FC:lbk, Adams Family Manuscript Trust, MHi. Sent to Boston.

Office seeking: just returned from Philadelphia that morning; will forward Lyde's job application to the secretary of the treasury.

Monday, 13 September 1790

John Adams to John Quincy Adams. ALS, Adams Family Manuscript Trust, MHi. Place to which addressed not indicated.

Has just returned from his trip seeking lodgings in Philadelphia; advises him to avoid "like a Pestilence" James Sullivan, while respecting his office and rank at the bar; "A more false and faithless Character is scarcely to be found. His pretended friendship and secret Envies [*?*] to me, of both of which I have sufficient Evidence, I equally despise"; "This must go no further than you and me, at present."

John Adams to Thomas Welsh. FC:lbk, Adams Family Manuscript Trust, MHi. Sent to Boston. For the full text, see *John Adams* 9:571–72.

Acknowledges letter (unlocated) received before Adams's departure for Philadelphia; "It is not probable that any special Agents will be employed in the business you had in contemplation"; the loan officers or collectors will be assigned those additional duties, "without any other reward than the honor of it, as I suppose"; is happy that John Quincy Adams resides with Welsh, whose example will teach him not to let politics interfere with one's profession; "If a Fathers partiality has not deceived me very much, John [*Quincy*] is as great a Schollar as this Country has produced at his age."

William Robinson to John Langdon. ALS, Langdon Papers, NhPoA. Written from Philadelphia; place to which addressed not indicated.

Encloses a correct copy of the new constitution of Pennsylvania.

Benjamin Rush to Tench Coxe. ALS, Coxe Papers, PHi. Written from Philadelphia; postmarked.

Will turn the key to his house over to Fitzsimons to give to Hamilton; "it is said" Charles Biddle has assured P. Muhlenberg of Maclay's Senate seat "if he will assist" in Thomas Mifflin's election as governor of Pennsylvania; laments that Morris "yielded to the fears of a few of his friends in declining" to run for governor.

Tuesday, 14 September 1790

Samuel Griffin to George Washington

As my friend Corbin Braxton has resignd his Office of Surveyor of the District of Richmond and Manchester, I do myself the Honor to enclose you a letter from a Mr. [*Zachariah*] Rowland, who has requestd of me to make known to you his wishes to fill up the Vacancy he is at present employd by Colo. [*Edward*] Carrington, to take the enumeration for the County of Henrico and City of Richmond, he is reputed to be a Sober Industrious Man, well acquaintd with arithmetick.

I must at the same time take the liberty of recommending Mr. John Hague, who lives on the Spot for that Office—he was formerly Searcher at Rockets landing, he recd. his Appointment from Mr. Edmund Randolph while Governor of this State, I am informd by some of the Council that he filld that Station with great propriety, and his conduct was much approved of by the Executive he prays that Mr. Randolph may be applyd to [*as*] to his Character & abilities—[*Alexander*] McRoberts & [*David*] Lambert, have both declined making Application.

ALS, Washington Papers, DLC. Written from Richmond, Virginia.

Letter from Prince George County, Virginia, to Boston

*** I hope Mr. *Gerry* will be re-elected with you, for I think him one of the most useful men in Congress, and is highly respected, I find, by the Members from this State.

The grant of 2500 dollars per annum, to the Baron Stuban, gives great disgust here; the people of this part of Virginia who have served under him, will allow him no great merit as an officer, nor can they conceive what has entitled him to that enormous grant.[1] Can you explain to me the grant made to the Widow of Lord Sterling?[2]

Will not the support of the civil list—the grants made to Congress—support of the troops—presents to Indians, &c. &c. swallow up the revenue of the United States, almost entirely, even with the additional duties, to take place in January next? What then becomes of the debt? I full well know that the duties are as high as they can be carried: What remains but a poll and land tax? I also know that these will be very unpopular.

[Boston] *Independent Chronicle*, 14 October; reprinted at New Haven and Litchfield, Connecticut, and New York City (*NYP*, 23 October).

[1] For more on Frederick William Steuben's petition for military service compensation and the resulting annuity granted under the Steuben Act, see *DHFFC* 7:201–46.

[2] For Sarah Stirling's successful petition for her husband's half pay, granted under the Stirling Act, see *DHFFC* 7:261–70.

Wednesday, 15 September 1790

Samuel A. Otis to John Langdon

I presume on the friendship you have honored me with to forward the Journal of Senate for the [*New Hampshire*] Govr. President of Senate & Speaker which I beg you to be so obliging as to forward—I send you for your own use,

A Journal of Senate,

Same of the House of Reps.

" and a sett of the Laws; also a package for Mr. Wingate to your care.

I came home very sick, but by good nursing, air and exercise I am restored, and shall in a few days, return to new York; where, & at all times you may command Your most huml. Sert.

ALS, Langdon Papers, NhPoS. Written from Boston; place to which addressed not indicated.

Thomas Lee Shippen to William Shippen

*** My journey was a delightful one from Chester town [*Maryland*] to George town—whether spoken of for the excellence of ~~my~~ the society, my fare, the weather or the roads. For I overtook as I told you I expected I should, my two valuable friends Messrs. Jefferson & Madison—At Rock Hall 12

miles from Chester town we waited all that day for want of a vessel to take us over, and I never knew two men more agreable than they were—We talked and dined, and strolled, and rowed ourselves in boats, and feasted upon delicious crabs. A six hours passage over the bay for us, and one of eighteen for my poor [*servant?*] Baptist—I had made him go with my horses and carriage in a~~nother~~ different boat from that we went in, as there was not room for all and wonderful to tell, although at one time they had got before us on the passage, we arrived 12 hours before them at Annapolis. There I saw my dear friend Shaaff and found him the same thing I had ever known him—He was overjoyed to see me and we were constantly together—I introduced him to my fellow travellers and he became our Ciceroni.[1] We passed 3 hours on the top of the State House steeple from which place you descry the finest prospect in the world, if extent, variety Wood & Water in all their happiest forms can make one so. My good friend Shaaff was not displeased at my comparing him to the Diable Boiteux[2] whose office he seemed to fill in opening the roofs of the houses and telling us the history of each family who lived in them. Mann's Inn at Anna[*poli*]s. is certainly to be placed among the most excellent in the world. I never saw so fine a turtle or so well dressed a dish as he gave us the second day for dinner—Every thing was of a piece—Old Madeira £80 a pipe to season it. He has made two additions to his house both very handsome one of them magnificent—But enough of Annapolis. After the Turtle feast we proceeded as far as Queen Anne's a dirty village 13 miles from Annapolis—Here a most perfect contrast to Mann's—Musquitos gnats flees & bugs contended with each other for preference, and we had nothing decent to eat or drink You may imagine how much we slept—from the company we were in—breakfasted next morning at Bladensbgh. with an old black woman who keeps the best house in the town and calls herself Mrs. Margaret Adams—She diverted us with an account of the resentment which discovered itself towards her because the President & his family had preferred her house to lodge at as he passed through Bladensburgh. After trying every other expedient to distress her, they pulled down her temple of Cloacina[3] and there was the demolished building when we arrived, a monument at the same time of the envy of her fellow citizens & her own triumph. Dined at George Town—were waited upon after dinner by Col. [*Uriah*] Forrest, Mr. Dan. Carrol,[4] Colo. Dickens [*Francis William Deakins*], Mr. [*Benjamin*] Stodart &c. &c. who reside in the town—They proposed our setting off in the early morning of the next day to view [*the falls?*] & fine prospects which the vicinity of G[*eorge*]. T[*own*]. [*affords?*]. We acceded to their proposal—breakfasted in the [*morning?*] at a beautiful seat of Mr. Notley Young[5] who a[*mong*] other gracious things told me that he had gone to school with you 30 or 40 years ago—We traversed the whole country were joined by the different gentlemen who lived upon the confines and had at last a cavalcade of thirteen: dined at Forrest's and after dinner went in a boat to the falls 4 miles above the town[6]—romantic scene—at 1/4 past 7 at night I left my companions who accompanied me in the boat to this side of the Potowmac—they returned to George town— ***

ALS, Shippen Family Papers, DLC. Written from Alexandria, Virginia; addressed to Fourth Street, Philadelphia. For the full text, see *PJT* 17:464–65. All places mentioned were in Maryland.

---

[1] The Italian name for the Roman orator Cicero. The word is used to describe a person who can elegantly inform others about the art, culture, and curiosities of a place, hence a guide. The man who served in this role for Shippen was probably the prominent Annapolis lawyer, Arthur Shaaff.

[2] Alan-René Lesage's *Le Diable Boiteux*, first published in 1707 and put in final form in 1725, was based on a Spanish story about a demon who removes the roofs of the houses of Madrid to expose the private lives inside.

[3] Cloacina was the Roman goddess of sewers; hence a privy.

[4] Probably Daniel Carroll of Duddington, not Representative Carroll.

[5] Young's four hundred acre "Turkey Buzzard Plantation" on the then banks of the Potomac River constituted most of what is now Southwest Washington, D.C.

[6] The Little Falls of the Potomac, not Great Falls.

Other Documents

Joshua Barney to George Washington. ALS, Washington Papers, DLC. Written from Baltimore; addressed to Mount Vernon, Fairfax County, Virginia; franked; postmarked. For the full text, see *PGW* 6:437–38.

Has been informed by Smith (Md.) that, during the President's tour through Baltimore, Washington had enquired whether Barney had decided to accept command of revenue cutters for Chesapeake Bay, which Barney declines.

George Clymer to Samuel Meredith. ALS, Dreer Collection, PHi. Places to and from which written not indicated. The public letter in support of St. Clair appeared without signatures in *FG*, 13 September; *PG*, 15 September, included the signatures.

Has told Fitzsimons in a note how disturbed Meredith was about his own situation with the Bank of New York and why Fitzsimons must give Meredith immediate relief; "I now hope and from the latter part of it for once *believe* he will not disappoint You"; a letter supporting Arthur St. Clair for governor of Pennsylvania is printed in the newspapers with Morris, (F. A.) Muhlenberg, Fitzsimons, and himself among the signers; it will "excite a flame against the signers. be it so, for me I am indifferent about it."

Alexander Hamilton to Thomas Fitzsimons. ALS, privately owned in 1963. Addressed to Philadelphia. For the full text, see *PAH* 7:34–35.

Thanks Fitzsimons for his assistance in providing Hamilton with a house in Philadelphia; encloses the first year's rent.

Judith Sargent Murray to Mary Turner Sargent. Ms., Murray Papers, Ms-Ar. For the full text, see *Murray*, pp. 290–93.

A short undated letter from Mary to Judith had been enclosed in one to Goodhue at New York; preferring an "abode with a member of Congress *** it contrived to conceal itself among that gentleman's papers, and being conveyed therewith to the state of Massachusetts, its retreat was not discovered, until it reached the good town of Salem."

GUS, 15 September; reprinted at Edenton, North Carolina. New Hampshire's second federal election for Representatives took place on 30 August.

Disagrees that the low voter turnout in New Hampshire's second federal election was due to distrust of elected representatives; praises the "candid, open and liberal plan" that marked the commencement of the United States government; "The freedom of the press was very early an object of attention to both Houses of Congress—not an individual of either was ever known to utter a sentiment hostile to the freest discussion of every political subject: The publication of the debates of the House of Representatives was encouraged, and the papers, containing those debates, circulated by the members to all parts of the United States"; cites the importance of representation as "an infallible remedy for our political disorders."

[Boston] *Columbian Centinel*, 22 September.

Ellsworth has arrived in Boston "since our last."

[Springfield, Massachusetts] *Hampshire Chronicle*, 22 September.

Ellsworth and Sherman, with their wives, passed through Springfield en route to Boston.

Thursday, 16 September 1790

Thomas Fitzsimons to Samuel Meredith

I will Place to the Credit of the treasurer of the U.S. in the bank of No. America on the 29th. inst. $3100 ***

I have to thank you too for your Answer to my query about the purchase of Certificates—which to be sure I wished to Know no More of—than was Consistant with your official duty—You Cannot be uninformed—of the great dissatisfaction expressed by people here on the Management of that business because being in Every bodys Mouth—it is of public Notoriety—they Judge only by the event without (probably) seeing the Motives—and I suppose some are Very much disappointed the price of Contl. Certificates here is I am told under 12/.

ALS, Dreer Collection, PHi. Written from Philadelphia. Place to which addressed not indicated.

Other Documents

Thomas Lee Shippen to William Shippen. Copy, Lee Family Papers, ViHi. Written from Mount Vernon, Fairfax County, Virginia; addressed to Fourth Street, Philadelphia.

His decision to travel to Mount Vernon with "those charming men Jefferson and Madison, though it gave me infinite pleasure cost me money."

Federal Government to Mr. Adams. [Boston] *Independent Chronicle*, 16 September; edited by Thomas Adams.

The length and proliferation of law processes under the federal judiciary system "plainly proves, that the *present Members* have fully provided for their *own profession*; and established an inexhaustible source of business for themselves, and posterity."

Friday, 17 September 1790

Joseph Manigault to Gabriel Manigault

***

This is a fine City, and fully answers my Expectations, in point of Regularity & size, but this uniformity soon tires; and I could reside in New-York with all its angles and curves, with much more pleasure than here. The country about New York is allso much more delightful; I can imagine nothing finer than the views up the North [*Hudson*]-River; excepting the Glacieres of Savoy from Geneva [*Switzerland*]. There are two ~~thin~~ Pleasures worth enjoying here, one is being at the City Tavern[1] where they serve you most elegantly; with all the niceties of the country; and the other to walk in Grey's Gardens, which are laid out I think with a good deal of Taste. Mr.

[*William*] Bingham's House is more handsomely finished than ~~any I have seen in America~~ I supposed; though I had heard you speak much of it. Many people think it too much ornamented, but it does not strike me in that light; I think it proves him to be a man of Taste.

The Inhabitants of Philadelphia are extremely pleased, with the exception of having congress here; House rent is raised 100 pr. Cent in consequence of it. Mr. Morris has given up his house to the President; but he will not by any means be so handsomely lodged as at New-York. ***

ALS, Manigault Family Papers, ScU. Written from Philadelphia; addressed to Charleston, South Carolina.

---

[1] Philadelphia's premier tavern, built in 1773 at the busy intersection of Second, Walnut, and Dock streets. This popular gathering place and accommodation for congressmen starting in 1774 was managed by Gifford Dalley before his appointment as House doorkeeper (1789–94).

Picture of New-York—August 1790

THE observations is not new,
But still tho ancient, not less true,
That where men cluster thick together,
(Like cackling geese in stormy weather)
Amidst the din of news and noise,
Some wond'rous theme each tongue employs;
Some one great subject thro the town,
Runs all inferior topics down.
As for example look at London,
Great Britain's heir by debt is undone;
Then poor Mad Peg, with carving knife,
Aims at great George's—*coat*—or *life*[1]—
***
—Thus in all places some great matter,
Is found for universal chatter—
Assumption, Residence, [*Alexander*] M'Gillivray,
Treaties, trainings of Artillery,
Coweta's, Cussitahs, and Choctaws,
Tuskabatchees, and other Crackjaws.[2]

When Congress wish'd to go away,
Thus said our cit[*izen*]s—or seem'd to say,

"Ungrateful men, and will ye go,
"And can ye—dare ye—leave us so?
"After we've turn'd Old City Hall,
"Into fam'd Mansion Federal;
"After dismissing all our *pavers*,‡
"Worne smooth by trampling sweeps and shavers;
"Those venerably ancient stones,
"That bore our great forefathers' bones;
"That made the ploughman, when at work,
"Remember, he had seen New-York,
"And limping, tell his neighbour Clods,
"That city streets a'n't pav'd with sods.
"After new mod'ling all our matters,
"And treating ye, as if our betters;
"And see! The lofty fort [*George*] is down,
"The *harmless* guardian of our town;
"All open to the bay and seas,
"T'invite—for you—the summer breeze;
"And see yon tow'ring pile arise,[3]
"A Babel! threatening the skies;
"Rising—oh! most unapt allusion,
"I *do not* mean to our confusion:
"And can ye so ungrateful be,
"From such kind patriots e'er to flee?
"Where will the soft, sweet, southern manners,
"So soon allure to pleasure's banners?
"So soon convince the artless maid,
"That love at best is but a trade;
"Beauty, a saleable commodity,
"Marriage, a stale old fashion'd oddity;
"For which free joys may be exchang'd,
"In case affairs should be *derang'd*;
"But otherwise a girl of *merit*,
"Should manage matters with more *spirit*;
"Taste uncontroul'd the joys of love,
"For ever? that is—till ye move.
"Oh think, and think, and think again,
"Our thick, deep, complicated pain;
"How much we wish, and wish, to keep ye,
"Altho long speeches make us sleepy;

"Remember all our anxious toil,
"The Philadelphians arts to foil;
"That we to keep ye—glad and willing,
"Gave six pence, hoping for a shilling."

Thus rav'd the wise ones of our city,
Some *swore* t'was shame; some *said* t'was pity;
When suddenly this topic dies,
And all the rage is *blank and prize*!
No longer bluster, bounce and zounds,
But ev'ry thought—*three thousand pounds*:
From National Assembly prancing,
They seek th' Assembly Room for dancing:§
No longer loiter, nod and slumber,
But watch the wheel, and catch the number;
No longer, peeping thro the grates,
See Senators desert their seats,
And walking forth as if for air,
Strait to the anti-room repair,ß
View TRUMBULL's forms sublimely blaze,
And *feel* the paint—with wondering gaze.
Justly admire the glowing work,
A lasting honor to New-York;
An honor to our corporation,
A future honor to our nation.
Blest Lottery! Blest thirst of gain!
That makes us lose all sense of pain:
While our grave citizens were watching,
And every rumour's rumour catching,
Of who is blank, and who is prize,
Mine is four pounds young Noddy cries—
I'll not put up with it, not I,
But oft to Roosevelts'[4] and buy—
Four pounds! Why tis'n't worth a thank—
D—n it, I'd rather have a blank.

While thus all ranks were deep engag'd,
And various war with fortune wag'd;
Congress perceiv'd the lucky minute,
Slipt off—left us—*to bear and grin it.*
"Slipt off! but pray what did they do,
"By way of recompence to you?

"You! who in pure good natur'd pity,
"Granted them house-room in your city;
"And gave them beef, and fish, and mutton,
"And genteel Congress coats to put on;
"Their horses, cows, and goats, found hay for,
"And ev'ry thing—that they could PAY for?"
What did they do? Why Sir, I'll tell,
They gave what we deserv'd full well—
They met in form—good Heaven guard us,
Resolv'd *nem. con.*[5] they *would* reward us;
Voted for great Potowmac's banks,
And gave us—"What?"—They gave us—THANKS.

*** ‡*Stones for paving.* §*The Lottery it is well known was drawn in the Dancing Assembly Room.* ß*The Room adjoining the Senate Chamber, where Mr.* [*John*] *Trumbull paints his truly historical portraits of The President, and Governor* [*George*] *Clinton.*

GUS, September 22.

---

[1] In August 1786, a disgruntled petitioner named Margaret Nicholson attempted to stab George III as he walked on the grounds of Windsor Castle. She was subsequently declared insane.

[2] The Coweta, Cusatees or Kasitah, and Tukabahchees were tribes of the Creek Confederacy; the Choctaws were an independent tribe based further to the west, along the present-day Alabama-Mississippi border. "Crackjaws" are unpronounceable names.

[3] Government House, intended as the President's residence.

[4] Any of several New York City merchants of that clan.

[5] Nemine contradicente, i.e., with no one dissenting.

OTHER DOCUMENTS

Thaddeus Burr to Jeremiah Wadsworth. ALS, Wadsworth Papers, CtHi. Written from Fairfield, Connecticut; addressed to Hartford, Connecticut.

Office seeking: Jonathan Maltbie to command a revenue cutter; Burr has written Ellsworth, Johnson, and Sturges on the matter.

Samuel Hodgdon to Henry Knox. ALS, Knox Papers, Gilder Lehrman Collection, NHi. Written from Philadelphia. Place to which addressed not indicated.

Discusses "this general rage for rents" in Philadelphia; "I have several other Gentlemen in Public Character to provide houses for—and I wish I may be able to accomodate all to their liking."

Saturday, 18 September 1790

Samuel Johnston to Robert Ferrier

*** being about to remove myself and Family to the Northward for some time for the Benefit of ~~my h~~ our health, in order to that purpose—I resigned my Office of first Magistrate of this State and accepted of a Seat in the Senate of the United States, ~~wh~~ the duties of which I attended during the last Winter & Summer at New York, but without reaping the benefits, which I promised myself from the change of situation, having been much indisposed during ~~par~~ the greatest part of the time, I am here only for a short time to see a little into my Affairs and shall shortly set out for Philadelphia to prepare for the sitting of Congress which is to meet ~~there at that place~~ in that City on the first monday in December next. from that place I will do myself the pleasure of forwarding to you the News and such other publications as I shall judge will be acceptable to you, I am very thankfull to you for the Books & papers which you mention [*lined out*] in your Letter to have been forwarded to ~~you~~ me by your order, tho they have not yet come to hand, I had the pleasure of perusing your Brothers book[1] which I found in the publick Library at New York, I think it does great Honor to his Abilities as an Author, but hope for the honor of human Nature that the sketch he has given of the temper & manners of the ~~Port~~ people of Portugal ~~will admit of much~~ is rather a Characature than a perfect~~ly true~~ likeness.

***

My two Boys are at School on Long Island near N. York,[2] my eldest daughter was married last January[3] and is now in the house with me in good health, my second [*Frances*] I left in N. York with my Sister Mrs. [*Hannah*] Iredell, Mr. [*James*] Iredell is appointed one of the Judges of the Supreme Federal Court and will of course reside ~~at~~ with his Family at the seat of the Federal Govt. my Youngest daughter [*Helen*] only 3 yrs. old is with me laboring under a severe indisposition—she is almost reduced to a Skeleton and her recovery very uncertain— ***

FC:dft, Hayes Papers, NcU. Written from Edenton, North Carolina; place to which addressed not indicated. The recipient was the widower of Johnston's deceased aunt Elizabeth, whose estate was still involved in a legal dispute for a share of the unpaid salary due to her brother, North Carolina's former royal governor Gabriel Johnston (ca. 1698–1752), which had been left to her as a legacy in his will and was probably the indemnification referred to below. The omitted text relates to European immigration to the South; a business transaction with Henry Laurens, about which he has written to Laurens "a great number of Letters," and which Johnston hopes "some of my South Carolina friends in Congress" can help resolve; Johnston's hope that Ferrier would have "before this" been indemnified by the British government "but as the Acts of Publick Bodies are more under the influence of favor than Justice," Johnston suggests Ferrier's success will depend on the "number and weight of your Friends at Court."

---

[1] *Mémoires historiques, politiques et géographiques des voyages* of Louis François, comte de Ferrières-Sauveboeuf (1750–1814), describing the author's travels through the eastern Mediterranean from 1782 to 1789, was published in two volumes in Holland in 1790 and is still among the holdings of the New-York Society Library.

[2] Samuel and James Cathcart Johnston attended Erasmus Hall in Flatbush, Brooklyn.

[3] Penelope Johnston married John Swann on 4 January. Swann (1760–93), a planter of Pasquotank County, North Carolina, filled Ashe's resigned seat in the Confederation Congress in 1788 and attended the state's second convention, where he voted to ratify the Constitution (*DHFFE* 4:363n).

Other Documents

William Constable to Governeur Morris. FC:lbk, Constable-Pierrepont Collection, NN.

Robert Morris writes to ask for £2500 sterling, "or He will be ruined."

Francis Taylor, Diary. NcU.

Madison and Jefferson arrived at the Orange County, Virginia, courthouse at noon, en route home from New York.

A Customer. *IG*, 18 September; reprinted at New York City (*NYDG*, 22 September).

A poem, signed "P," making fun of Morris, Clymer, Fitzsimons, and F. A. Muhlenberg for signing the Address in support of Arthur St. Clair for Pennsylvania governor that appeared in *PG* on 15 September.

Monday, 20 September 1790

John Fitch to Robert Morris. FC:dft, Fitch Papers, DLC. Places to and from which written not indicated; addressed to "Worthy honored Sir." An earlier version of the letter dated 11 September is in the same collection, as is a draft of this version of it.

Acknowledges the enemies of his steamboat navigation schemes, but feels himself "perfectly easy whilst I know the candour and abilities of Mr. Morris"; proposes that Morris patronize a trading company at New Orleans that would employ steamboats to convey upriver those who had come down river with goods; such a plan would finally make New Orleans the wealthy city it should be, "probably cause a revolution in the Western World, more astonishing than the introduction of Arts" into Russia by Peter the Great, and give Morris the "same secreet pleasure and reward, as Great Peter of Muscova had in rendering real service to his Country";

if Morris cannot "engage in this business," perhaps he could recommend it to his acquaintances or give his opinion of its defects and advice on how to pursue it.

Thomas Jefferson to James Madison. FC, letterpress copy, Coolidge Collection, MHi. Written from Monticello, Albemarle County, Virginia; place to which addressed not indicated. For the full text, see *PJM* 13:298–99.

Suggests a third party set the price for a horse Jefferson wishes to purchase from Madison; knows nobody whom he is as likely to disagree with as Madison, as shown by the disputes over money during their journey from New York to Virginia.

James Sullivan to John Langdon. ALS, Langdon Papers, NhPoA. Written from Boston; addressed to Portsmouth, New Hampshire.

Wife Martha (Langdon's sister) forgives Langdon for his not stopping by en route home; looks forward to their visit the next month on the way through Boston.

Tuesday, 21 September 1790

[*Otho H. Williams,*] General Remarks

THE United States are happy to have in the House of Representatives Gentlemen who are intimately acquainted with the commerce, and all the different interests of the rising empire; they reason closely, in a language distinguished by its purity and elegance. They do not obtrude their speeches upon us—They observe Horace's rule, *Ne deus intersit nisi modus sit numine dignus*[1]—But Gentlemen of narrow conceptions, who are affected by local prejudices, and interested views—who but superficially understand the general interests—they, by their frequent talk and unseasonable motions, made on purpose to delay and embarrass, have greatly prolonged the session; but, considering the temper which often prevailed in the House, we have reason to congratulate ourselves that it ended so much to the advantage of the nation.

It was observed, that a bill was before the House some time ago, that might properly be called the navigation-act: It does more honour to the House than any thing that came before them this session: It discovers a proper spirit, shows the world that they understand their interest and will pursue it: It will command respect from foreign nations: It was distressing to the friends of government, to see how heavily it was carried on.

As a coward is more liable to be insulted than a man of spirit, so will a timid state, that has not spirit to demand a reciprocity.

Mr. Livermore tells us of a river that runs two hundred miles up the country, and asks what advantage that would be to Congress; only to facilitate sending their acts to the foot of the Allegany Mountain! Does Mr. Livermore imagine that the advantage of Congress is to be solely consulted in fixing the seat of government? He will please to be informed, that his fellow-citizens are of opinion that the mileage and six dollars a day are a sufficient compensation for his services; and he knows well, that sum is more than the Governor of New-Hampshire has for his salary. He is likewise to be informed, that the general advantage and convenience of the United States, are principally to be consulted in fixing the seat of government; and that there are a body of brave people on the western waters,[2] who, in spite of the united ferocity of Indian nations, and in defiance of all the British troops at the different posts on the lakes, supported by the Canadians at those posts, established themselves in a remote wilderness, at the expense of a great deal of blood, and many valuable lives—They are now three times as numerous as the inhabitants of New-Hampshire; and does he not think it reasonable that the interests of that growing people should be consulted, as far as is consistent with that of the other states?

Mr. Gerry asserts, that, taking so southern a situation as Patowmac, will amount to the total disqualification of many of the northern members—That speech[3] does not Indicate the modesty which might have been expected from a Gentleman of Mr. Gerry's politeness. To be a member of the legislative body of a great and rising empire, is one of the greatest honours that a citizen can aspire to. He likewise declares, that Patowmac is more eccentric for the seat of government than New-York. The census now in agitation will shortly prove that assertion ill-founded.

As to disqualification—greater than now exists is entirely unnecessary; and it is earnestly recommended to the electors in the different states, to examine the qualifications of the different candidates—to inquire how far they understand the interests of the state they are desirous to represent—whether they know the course of their trade—whether any measures can be taken to facilitate the sale of their commodities at the markets they go to—whether they have an idea of the general interest of the United States; and are of so liberal principles, that they can easily divest themselves of interested views—If possessed of these qualifications, they will be useful and worthy members of the legislature—If it is otherwise, they had better stay at home; they will be an incumbrance, a mere dead weight, upon the Gentlemen who understand and do the business of the nation.

[Baltimore] *Maryland Journal*, 21 September. The piece was concluded on 24 September, below. The writer's defense of the Conococheague, at the mouth of which sat Williamsport, Maryland, and the detail on the Revolutionary War in South Carolina where Williams served as an officer in the Continental Army point to him as the author of this piece.

[1] Let God not intervene unless the need is worthy of him (or, do not use strong remedies for trifles), from Book I of Horace's *Ars Poetica*.

[2] In this context, the "western waters" refers to the entire Ohio-Mississippi watershed.

[3] Gerry's speech of 7 July (*DHFFC* 13:1675).

Other Documents

Thomas Fosdick to John Langdon. ALS, Langdon Papers, NhPoA. Written from Portland, Maine; sent to Portsmouth, New Hampshire. (The author was probably Major Thomas Fosdick of Portland, Maine [ca. 1756–1801]).

Office seeking: excise inspector in "this district."

Thomas Welsh to John Adams. ALS, Adams Family Manuscript Trust, MHi. Written from Boston.

Inquires when the sinking fund commissioners (of which Adams was one of five) planned to make another purchase of public debt certificates.

Wednesday, 22 September 1790

Newspaper Article

The approaching arrival of Congress ought to induce the citizens of Philadelphia to make such exertions, consistent with prudence, as a sense of the advantages to be derived from their residence may require. The temporary alterations of the County Hall, while it subjects the judicial department to some inconvenience, renders it necessary that the City Hall should be compleated with the utmost expedition. Public spirit will therefore dictate the propriety of compleating the sale of the remaining tickets in the lottery, for it will be no small deduction from the profit—if, as is reported, there are a considerable number left on hand, the risk of which should be borne by the city. When we consider what has been done at New-York, we ought not, individually, to hesitate at this kind of subscription, in which there is a chance of receiving material benefit in the very act of contributing to public utility.

FG, 22 September; reprinted at New York City (*NYP*, 25 September; *NYJ*, 28 September) and Charleston, South Carolina.

OTHER DOCUMENTS

John Rutledge, Jr. to William Short. ALS, Short Papers, DLC. Addressed to Paris.

"The rising of Congress has made this city a very sad & solitary place *** there does not remain even the vibration of a former Society"; Madison "is to be appointed Minister to France & will embark in the spring."

THURSDAY, 23 SEPTEMBER 1790

John Dawson to Tench Coxe. ALS, Coxe Papers, PHi. Written from Fredericksburg, Virginia; place to which addressed not indicated; marked "private."

"it is thought that Mr. Walker will not be continued as a Senator by the legislature."

Thomas Jefferson to James Madison. ALS, Madison Papers, DLC. Written from Monticello, Albemarle County, Virginia; signed "yours affectionately"; place to which addressed not indicated. For the full text, see *PJM* 13:299.

Sends for the horse he is buying from Madison; suspects Madison would undervalue the horse, so suggests a third party estimate; proposes to pay in Philadelphia; hopes to host Madison during the county court session (14 October), when they would plan their return (to the seat of government).

Junius to Mr. Adams. [Boston] *Independent Chronicle*, 23 September; edited by Thomas Adams.

Is alarmed that so many members of Congress are sworn in as attorneys before the Supreme Court, and questions whether it may lead to laws being passed that "depend on the particular causes such individuals may have to manage in the judiciary."

FRIDAY, 24 SEPTEMBER 1790

[*Otho H. Williams,*] General Remarks

MR. Burke's ostensible reason for voting for Baltimore, was, that he would rather have the seat of government in a thriving city, than in a wilderness—The industrious commercial people of Baltimore merit all encouragement that can be given them; and, had the temper of the times admitted, it was, without doubt, the proper place for the temporary residence: It is too remote from the western settlements for the permanent residence—besides, it may be expected that the jealousy of foreign powers, or the imprudent conduct of the United States, will engage us in war some time or other, the later the better. In time of war, the Congress, the Officers of State, the Treasury, will be an object; an enterprising partizan would easily captivate or disperse them at Baltimore; and it might as easily be done anywhere on tidewater on Patowmac. It is not necessary to have the seat of government at a seaport, more than it is necessary to remove the seat of the Spanish government from Madrid to Cadiz.

By moving further up Patowmac, that thoroughfare to the western regions, the situation will become more healthy; it will add to the cultivation of an extensive, fertile, and populous country, and it will be more accommodated to our fellow citizens west of the mountains, and more so to almost one half of Pennsylvania, than if the seat of government was at Philadelphia.

The more Congress are by themselves, the better they will mind the business of the nation—the less liable they will be to be teased by applications, or seduced by the assiduity of interested designing men.

The political Dutch preferred the village of the Hague for the seat of government, to the great commercial city of Amsterdam.

Mr. Burke is requested to attend to a sketch of the country, which he designates a wilderness. Within four or five miles of Conochocheague, is Hager's-Town [*Maryland*], with twelve or eighteen stores in it, and some manufactures; within ten miles down the river, is Shepherd's-Town [*West Virginia*] and Sharpsburg [*Maryland*], with as many stores; within twelve miles further southwest, is Martinsburg [*West Virginia*], with ten stores in it; within twenty-four miles north-east, is Chambers'-Town [*Chambersburg, Pennsylvania*], the capital of Franklin county; within thirty-four miles southwest is Winchester [*Virginia*], in which is sold about £80,000 sterling worth of goods annually.

Within fourteen miles of Conococheague, there are upwards of thirty pair of bur mill-stones employed in manufacturing wheat; within the same distance there are four furnaces, and three forges for making iron.

It is believed, that the true reason of Mr. Burke's voting for Baltimore, was to defeat the bill, because the House of Representatives would not agree, right or wrong, to assume the state debts of South-Carolina, at the time and in the manner he proposed.

There was not a single member against doing all the justice to the state of South-Carolina, that in reason could be demanded—The people of that state were unhappy in attempting to defend the city [*Charleston*] against an army so well appointed, when the safety of the country was the object—They had examples before them, of the evacuation of New-York and

Philadelphia—This capital and fatal blunder cost the United States very dear—The contrary conduct would have saved an army, the military stores, and immense property, and a great number of valuable lives of citizens, murdered by the friends of the British government.

However, the people of South-Carolina have the satisfaction to reflect, that by the strenuous exertions of Sumpter and [*Francis*] Marion, two of their own valuable fellow-citizens, a remnant was saved, until another army was assembled.

The frontiers of that state were settled by emigrants chiefly from Virginia, and including the loss of these valuable citizens, Virginia lost more natives in the defence of that state, than Carolina did.

After these considerations, that the delegates from South-Carolina should divide, on a great national question, from the delegates of Virginia, is unaccountable, especially as the difference between Baltimore and Patowmac, was no more to them, than the difference 'twixt Tweedledum and Tweedledee.

Mr. Burke is pleased to give an eulogium on the state of Pennsylvania. It is very just and well placed. Had that Gentleman address to import into South-Carolina a dozen of men of the abilities and disposition of Tench Cox, Esq.; South-Carolina would soon rise superior to Pennsylvania, or any state in the union; the natural advantages of that state so greatly exceed them. Their staple commodities are more valuable and more numerous—they have no winter to interrupt the business of the field—their port is always open, and in the space of an hour you may be from the wharf into the ocean. There are many respectable characters, and men of abilities in South-Carolina, but there is a certain genius and turn of mind wanting, which insensibly leads the common people to pursue their real interests, and consequently that of the state.

[Baltimore] *Maryland Journal*, 24 September. This is the conclusion of a piece that began in the 21 September issue of the same newspaper, above, where the editors explain the attribution to Williams.

Letter from Philadelphia

We have seen with an eye of admiration, which even the rage of rivalship could not obscure, the noble edifice that was raised by the citizens of a sister state for the accomodation of the federal legislature. We have traced the extensive foundations of a fabric which their provident zeal had designed for the future residence of our illustrious President, and every district from Georgia to New-Hampshire, resounds with just encomiums of the respectful and hospitable treatment which the representatives of the union have individually experienced, during their attendance at the seat of government.

An equal degree of attention should therefore be paid on the part of Pennsylvania to these objects, and what New-York has done in the hope of retaining her guests, we are certainly bound to do, in acknowledgement of their removal. The spirit of individuals, however, seems to be almost evaporated in respect to a subscription for the proposed new buildings; and it is to be lamented, that so far from joining in a spontaneous overture to defray the expence of erecting them, the landlords have in general, shewn a disposition to extort exorbitant compensations, for the use of the old. Our streets are daily traversed in vain, by the members and officers of Congress in search of habitations; those gentlemen are disappointed in the number of houses which were reported to be vacant, and they are disgusted with the amount of the rents, which were declared to be reasonable. In short their plans are frustrated; their reliance on the liberality of Pennsylvania is impaired, and the rapacity of a few persons, may, at their first entrance into our city, lay the foundation of a lasting discontent.

NYDA, 27 September.

Other Documents

John Dawson to Otho H. Williams. ALS, Williams Papers, MdHi. Written from Fredericksburg, Virginia; place to which addressed not indicated.

"Bland you know is gone to that country where I hope that his opposition to the present government, & his other good acts will be amply rewarded."

Thomas Fitzsimons to Samuel Meredith. ALS, Dreer Collection, PHi. Written from Philadelphia; postmarked 27 September.

Has not written often to save Meredith the expense of postage; Philadelphia's public security dealers are dissatisfied with the methods hitherto pursued by the federal government in purchasing certificates as it confines the advantages to people living in New York City; if like methods are pursued after the removal to Philadelphia "they will then have a like advantage and this expectation I suppose prevents their being Clamorous"; "We are going on with our preparations for Your Reception" despite the "Multiplicity of Works going on"; discusses opposition to Thomas Mifflin in Pennsylvania's gubernatorial election.

Thomas Fitzsimons to Jeremiah Wadsworth. ALS, Wadsworth Papers, CtHi. Written from Philadelphia; addressed to Hartford, Connecticut; postmarked 27 September.

Reminds Wadsworth of his promise to furnish him with a list of the prices at which provisions were furnished to the French Army during the

Revolutionary War; "it would be extreamly important to [*John*] Holker to have such a list."

James Madison to Thomas Jefferson. ALS, Madison Papers, DLC. Places to and from which written not indicated; signed "yours most affectionately"; received 24 September. For the full text, see *PJM* 13:300.

The bearer delivers the horse Jefferson is purchasing, which Madison will consult others in order to set a price on; "I consider this credit as a necessary set off agst. advances which you will have made for me in France"; hopes to visit him at Monticello.

Saturday, 25 September 1790

Tristram Dalton to Rufus King

I was this week informed in Boston that Mr. [*Samuel*] Osgood, not inclining to remove to Philadelphia, had determined to resign the Office of Post Master General—and that [*Nathan*] Dane was looking after it.

Should Mr. Osgood give up his place, it appears to me, on a sudden reflection, worthy my notice—and that the duties of it would be as agreeable to my disposition as any I could obtain—The Salary, it's true, is moderate at 1600 dollars, but it will not lessen—and the advantages Mr. [*Lewis*] Deblois might reap, by my being so near him, might counterbalance it.[1]

The Office not having been created—nor the emoluments increased, *since* my Election, I can apprehend no difficulty on account of the last Clause of the 6th sect. in 1st Article of the Constitution—On this point, however, I will rely upon your better Judgment—If there can be no objection on this head it would be fortunate, as almost every other Office has been created since I have acted as a Senator—If this desired event should take place at the Commencement of the session, a resignation of my Seat would, on *no* account, be disagreeable to me—the new elected Member [*George Cabot*] being, without a doubt, ready to attend, if the Executive shd. think proper to appoint him.

I have, by this post, written, confidentially to Mr. [*Tobias*] Lear, on this occasion—and wish you to discourse with him freely thereon.

If Osgoods intentions can be known, I shall be much obliged by your attention to the affair, as circumstances shall turn up.

Mr. Lear knows my general wishes—Should this opening present, & my application prove successful, it would be peculiarly fortunate so soon to be ascertained of my future fate.

I will thank you for your free advice and opinion, as to the importance,

& suitableness of the place, for me—the constitutionality of my being appointed—and the best mode of conducting toward the attainment of it.

Many, no doubt, will apply for it—I should suppose I might rely upon the Senate's consenting if the President should think proper to nominate me.

I have inclosed to Mr. Lear a letter to the President, to be delivered—or kept back—as you & He shall think but—after weighing all circumstances.[2]

Would our friend Hamilton favor my Wishes? You can judge.

I could fill the remainder of the Sheet with the most sincere regards of my whole Family to every branch of yours—their affections are warm and substantial.

The subject matter of this Letter will remain solely in your & Mr. Lears bosom.

ALS, King Papers, NHi. Written from Newburyport, Massachusetts.

[1] Lewis Deblois, a Boston merchant who moved to Philadelphia, married Dalton's daughter Ruth on 21 July 1789.
[2] The letter was apparently not delivered.

Joseph Ward to Elbridge Gerry

I this day examined the Acts & Resolves of Congress of the 18 March 1780,[1] relative to the new Bills then issued, & from a view of the whole proceeding, it appears to contain an explicit obligation on the part of the United States to pay the holder of the Bills the nominal sum of interest & principal, in case of any failure or neglect of the State which issues it; but I may mistake, & therefore wish for information. As you had time yesterday only to read part of the proceedings relative to these Bills, if you should find leisure to review the whole & would be pleased to favour me with your *private tho'ts*, I will keep them private, and feel an additional obligation to those already received.

P. S.

It may be necessary to apologize for troubling you with this request. I am greatly interested in the fate of these Bills, & as I lately suffered much for want of proper information, by exchanging a large sum of Loan Office Certificates for Indents just before the funding Bill passed, in full confidence that (according to the first draft of the Bill) no difference would be made between interest & principal.

ALS, formerly on deposit at ICarbS. Written from Boston; addressed to Cambridge, Massachusetts; answered 6 October.

[1] *JCC* 16:262–66.

Other Documents

William Paterson to Samuel A. Otis. ALS, Records of the Secretary: Concerning printing, Senate Records, DNA. For the full text, see *DHFFC* 8:747.
Recommends a stationer in Philadelphia.

Monday, 27 September 1790

Benjamin Logan to John Brown

This day I received Yours dated the 11th of August. I confess it gives me pleasure to hear of the welfare of every State in the Union & much more so to hear that Kentuckey should have the Countenance of Goverment & the smiels of Good & great men I am also hapy to hear a peace have taken place with the creeck Indiens perhaps, it may discourage the Chekimagies [*Chickamaugas*] from part of there Hostile intentions before this will come to your hand I am satisfied you will have repeated infirmations of the depredations of differrent Indien tribes on our frontiers & also Cumberland[1] A Campaign has taken place by the Order of Governor Sinkler [*Arthur St. Clair*] on the north west side of Ohio the Militia from Jefferson Nelson & Lincoln is Ordered to the post the Militia from the other [*Kentucky*] Counties is ordered to the Mouth of Licking [*River, Kentucky*] both parties have Marched the Horses called in to public service from the Counties of Mercer & Lincoln on the 16th 17th of August is to cross the Ohio in a few days upwards of forty Militia have deserted from that place this I have heard last evening from good Athurity who came from there Camps I confess my Abilities are too weak to Judge in to the Conduct of such great & good Officers as those imployed in this importent Buisness but was I in there situation at present I could not promise my self success it is the Opinion of our best men this Campaign could have been carried on by by the Kentuckyens them selves with a great deal less expence to the Union to mention any further pertickelers on this subject would be too teadious As to the difference between Inglind & spain is a subject Most seriously draws the intention of the western ~~World~~ People & from my Aquantenc on the Missisepia in the Province of Spain I am lead to beleave nearly all the Amiricans wishes would be that, Ingland had that Country in Possesion for the that [*illegible*] are Citizeens at that place when it was formerly in the British possesion say the never have had so good a trade since & the think with out a free-trade with all Nations the could not be in so good a situation for says they if the United States had the Navegation of the River it is of no use to us the do not want our Produce & with out A Commerciel treaty with some Power that wants our produce we can not Exist &c. we know of none suiets us but the Inglish. (This Languish [*language*] held out to so many of our Kentuckey People that have latly gone down to Orlens & finding no demand for there produce only that part that is taken for duty I think the Opinion of the ~~citizens Americans in of the province of Spain is growing fast~~ [*lined out*] Western People in General will soon follow the opinion of the Americans in the province of Spain & Sir as you have intemated to me for my sentements & information I most seriously tell you that if the British gets in possesion of Missisepia & holds out ~~a~~ flatering view in the Comerciel line to the people of Kentuckey & Cumberland the great Bul~~e~~k of them will depart from the Union nothing in my Opinion will prevent such a Measure only the exertions of Goverment taking up the Buisness in proper time in procureing the right of Navegating the River Missipia & a trade with some Power who wants the Produce of the Western Contry I have not spent my Opinion on this importent subject untill I have done it now with my pen) you will find the last Convention[2] determined on a seperation this Buisness you will be informed of in course You got all the Votes in Madeson Mercer & Jefferson but two in each County Mr. James Marshel got & his intrust was but half as good in Lincoln as either of those Counties for he got but one vote in Lincoln which was his Uncle Billey [*William Marshall*].

[*P. S.*] N. B. when I was in new Orlans the market was Gluted with the produce of Kentuckey I had secret promises that if I would return it would be to my advantage if your intrust &c. my small [*rest of letter torn off*].

ALS, John Brown Collection, CtY. Written from Lincoln County, Kentucky; place to which addressed not indicated.

---

[1] The settlements on the Cumberland River in middle Tennessee, including Nashville (founded 1784), had about seven thousand residents in 1790.

[2] On 26 July, Kentucky's ninth statehood convention agreed to the terms for separation contained in Virginia's fourth Act of Separation of 18 December 1789 and set 1 June 1792 as the date for assuming statehood.

Other Documents

Thomas Fitzsimons to William Paterson. ALS, Paterson Papers, NjR. Written from Philadelphia; addressed to Brunswick, New Jersey. The Donaldson referred to may be John Donaldson (1754–1831), a prominent Federalist merchant and insurance broker of Philadelphia, who served as Pennsylvania's register general from 1789 to 1794 (John H. Campbell, *History of the Friendly Sons of St. Patrick* [Philadelphia, 1892], pp. 108–9).

Regarding personal financial transaction between Paterson and Donaldson.

Tench Francis to [*Samuel Meredith*]. ALS, Meredith Papers, DeU.
Has just discussed with Clymer whether Fitzsimons "had paid into [*the*] Bank for you as Treasurer."

Tuesday, 28 September 1790

Louis Guillaume Otto to Comte de Montmorin

***

The moving of all the offices of Congress to Philadelphia has temporarily dispersed all the Heads of Departments, who will come together again and resume their duties around the same time that you ordered me, Sir, to take steps to obtain the modification of the law that places conditions to the high tonnage on foreign ships, which would be fruitless without the act of the Legislature that is supposed to convene in December. The absence, at this time, of Mr. Jefferson and of the members of the new Administration delay the result of this negotiation, which I attend to with all the zeal I am capable of, although I cannot conceal from myself the difficulties that it will necessarily meet. I would not have even waited for any particular orders on this issue if an important consideration had not stopped me at the time. It is based on the results of a similar case that occurred in 1785–86. The states of New Hampshire and Massachusetts had imposed a high tonnage on all foreign ships so that they could overcome the stronger rivalry of English merchant ships. I received the order to object to these laws as contrary to our Treaty of Commerce;[1] I addressed the Congress and the Governors of these two states. That of New Hampshire did his utmost to obtain from the Legislature a simple exemption in favor of the French, but the merchants, who are nearly all bound to England, being too strong, it was necessary to either revoke the law or leave it intact. The same debates took place in Massachusetts and since we feared to let remain a law that is contrary to our Treaty and that the merchants do not allow to be modified or revoked, I was thanked by the English consul for the service I did his nation. This experience, Sir, led me to be very reserved on the commercial advantages we could ask from the Congress and, limiting myself to simple conversations with some influential members, I thought it was my duty not to take any official step without being specially authorized. I will attend the first moment of the meeting of the Government in Philadelphia to present the just complaint that you ordered me to make and that, beyond its immediate goal, could be very useful later in making the Congress feel that, despite the change that occurred in the American Constitution, His Majesty [*Louis XVI*] does not lose sight of the privileges and the rights that were stipulated in a Treaty signed under the old regime.

During the long debates on tonnage [*Trade and Navigation Bill HR-66*], I had the honor to inform you, Sir, that the Southern Party proposed, as an amendment, to offer an exemption in favor of *allied Powers*, and that this amendment had been passed by the House of Representatives. I have since heard that the motives of this amendment were none other than to have the bill fail, since they were convinced that the Senate would not agree. The Senate did indeed reject the amendment, and the bill being again presented to the House of Representatives, they managed to persuade the Southern Party that it was better to have the Allies pay the tonnage than to lose this branch of the revenue.[2] The few who sincerely wanted to favor the French navigation were disturbed by the consideration that, by the terms of the Treaty, the Dutch, Prussians, and Swedish would share the advantages that are granted to us, and since it is difficult to be more dispassionate towards these nations than people are here, where one is regarded as a rival as to shipping and the others as to producers, a little eloquence is necessary to influence our supporters.

It is noticeable, Sir, that in the course of the conversation, the movers of an exemption in favor of the allied nations never cited our Treaty of Commerce. I pointed out the fact to one of them, who replied that the exemption on French ships, being only founded on a fair interpretation of Article 5 of our Treaty and not on express terms, could not be defended favorably in a Legislature especially since the preamble of the Treaty gave explicitly each contracting party the power to follow at home the rules of commerce and navigation that are the most favorable to them. I replied that this very preamble also established *as a basis of the Treaty complete equality and reciprocal advantages* and that this reciprocity happened to be subverted by this new law on tonnage; that it was necessary to consider the *spirit* as much as the *terms* of the Treaty and that the power granted to the United States by the 5th Article, to tax coastal navigation, sufficiently proved the exclusion of all other tonnage duties, by reason that the clause would have been useless if the King had acknowledged the power of the United States to lay a duty on French tonnage. The Representative agreed that the interpretation of the Treaty with us was totally in our favor but that it would be better to discuss it with the Secretary of State than in the House of Representatives, because according to the Constitution the interpretation of treaties is assigned to the Judiciary Department, which ought to decide according to equity. "We have continued to be very hampered in our ability to raise a revenue. Direct taxation has so far been prohibited, we have no other resource than the duties on imports and tonnage. The shipping states passionately urge us to raise the tonnage on foreigners to reduce competition from the British in our ports; we would like to make an exception in favor of the French, but the merchants connected with England prevent us and their influence is great. They tell us that the Dutch, the Swedes, and even the Prussians will partake of the advantages accorded to the French, inasmuch as Article 2 of your Treaty, which alone can shelter their claims (A), has been omitted from other treaties. The desire to be recognized in Europe made our former Congress much too eager to conclude treaties. One can still excuse those that were made during the war, because it was necessary to find friends at any price, but there was no reason in 1786 to add Prussia to the number of favored Powers. Before even knowing our ability, our resources, and our relations with other countries, we tied our hands forever. For wishing to be friends with the whole world, we became friends with none. If our ministers had not been restrained, we would have made treaties with the entire universe. Some grounds of interest and reciprocal usefulness dictated our first treaty with France; since then the same advantages have been agreed to with three other nations and as our people are not [*illegible*] disposed to favor them, it follows that we are not according those same favors to France, and that in all our commercial regulations we will only consult our own interests. As to England, we are fully convinced that the competition from our shipping reduces amazingly the number of their seamen and that at the first war she will find it very difficult to fill her crews. In that sense we will perhaps render service to France, despite the violation of her Treaty of commerce, which I am far from wishing to justify. It is only in raising the tonnage duties that we are able successfully to reduce British shipping with which we are, at the very moment, the most active and dangerous rivals. All the commercial laws of that Session aim at that interesting object, and in less than a year we will perceive the success of our policy."

The House of Representatives, Sir, is really the voice of the people of the United States, and a great majority of that chamber has from the beginning voted for the exemption of allied nations. The Senate on the contrary represents the states or the legislature of the states, which all seated in the commercial towns receiving their impetus from the merchants and [*illegible*] of their English agents, means, Sir, that we have more partisans in the House of Representatives than in the Senate, or rather that the members of the two chambers conduct themselves according to the passions of their constituents.

Reading through the correspondence of Monsieur [*Eleanor-François Elie*] le comte de Moustier and the reports I have had the honor to submit to you, Sir, since his departure, you have undoubtedly noticed, that there is toward us a sensible difference between the legislature and the Administration of the United States. Members of the Legislature, as long as they do not lose themselves in particular intrigues, have no other object, with a few exceptions, than to preserve their popularity and to relieve their people at the expense of foreigners. The Administration or the Executive power, on the contrary, has views more noble, more vast, and less personal, but the Executive's hands are tied and their good intentions are almost null as to their effect. Its conduct is very gratifying but fruitless. However, the affairs of little significance that entirely rest upon the Executive are easily and quickly disposed of and from what it accomplishes on a small scale we can conclude that its grand measures would be excellent, if it were allowed to take them. Members of the Administration sincerely want to favor France but they can only do what the law allows them to. Several members of the Legislature want it as well, but they only say and do what could please the party they belong to, or what at first sight could relieve the people who employ them. Measures that maintain good relations abroad demand a much too complicated thought process for the people to understand, who ordinarily feel and desire only what is immediately useful to them without having any wider views on the results than involve an apparent momentary benefit. Several members without talent or merit sit in the Legislature only because they blindly oppose all expenses that are to be imposed. Among themselves the states do not treat each other more gently than they treat foreigners. They compete to tax their neighbors higher. The strong have the weak pay and the Northern States have for long been in a position to have the burden of public taxation carried by the Southern ones. The tonnage law is a very recent proof of this situation. People of the South are not seafarers, and having goods of great volume, it is important to them to attract indiscriminately to their harbors vessels of any nation in order to have commercial freight, but the commercial polity of the majority of Congress will force them to hire vessels from New England, whose shipowners will impose their rules and triumph over the commerce of European nations. Tobacco and rice will mainly transfer through them and considering the activity, the intelligence, and the great good economic sense of these Northern seafarers, those products are already as cheap in Boston as in Carolina and Virginia. The shipowners of Massachusetts and New Hampshire want to become the Dutchmen of this continent. It is at their demand that the new tonnage has been asked and gained. Their political skills, their solidarity, and the perseverance of their Representatives ensure them a long predominance in Congress.

Since the adjournment of this Assembly, Sir, the United States has not offered anything of interest. The President is in Virginia. Mr. Jefferson has likewise gone to his plantations; the other officers of the Administration are busy with the transfer of their offices to Philadelphia. Peace and public confidence give new impetus to industry. The Antifederalists are, or pretend to be, tranquil. Elections to the new Congress will take place without turmoil and almost two thirds of the former members being reelected, one can conclude that people are satisfied with the Government's operations.

I just learned, Sir, that the Commissioners of the state of New York and Vermont have finally agreed amicably on the conditions under which the latter will be emancipated and will achieve a complete independence. At present it concerns nothing more than its admission to the Union—a measure that will probably meet with some difficulties in the Congress and from the people of Vermont themselves. The founding of a new northern state will be negatively accepted by the Southern States because it increases the power and influence that it will give to the adverse party. It will be the occasion to promote the case of Kentucky and to restore balance by the creation of a new state in the South. In addition, the people of Vermont, having usurped to a large extent lands that belong to private owners from New York, fear the law suits that may be brought before the federal courts. The accession of this new state will probably be determined in the next session of the Congress.

Mr. {*David*} Humphreys, former Secretary to the legation in France, and enjoying the special trust of the President, is secretly gone to Europe. We believe it is in order to negotiate several loans to reimburse some of the foreign and domestic debts whose interest are above 4%, loans that the President has been authorized to contract for the legislature. Others think it is in order to demand England's return of the forts along the Great Lakes. The first conjecture seems to me more probable. Besides this mission, it is likely that Mr. Humphreys, a favorite of the President and friend of Mr. Jefferson, will ultimately be offered a diplomatic mission in Europe. As a man of culture, he has often proved in public his affection for France but he unfortunately has not many friends in this country.

***

(A) In virtue of that Article, the *conditional* favors cannot be claimed by other nations except by means of a parallel compensation. Mr. {*John*} Adams no doubt had his reasons for omitting that article in the treaty with Holland. It was put back by Mr. {*Benjamin*} Franklin in that of Sweden.

Copy, in French, Henry Adams Transcripts, DLC. Translated by Christophe Loman and the editors. Otto's letters included in *DHFFC* were usually written over the course of days, and even weeks, following the day they were begun.

---

[1] For France's Treaty of Amity and Commerce with the United States (1778), see *DHFFC* 2:389–408.

[2] At this point Otto is reporting what occurred in the first session debate on the Tonnage Act {HR-5}.

Cotton Tufts to Abigail Adams

***

Gen. [*Benjamin*] Lincoln mentioned to me the 16th. Inst. Dr. Williamsons Wish to exchange some Bank Notes for the Value to be received in New York;[1] to oblige the Dr. I consented to Gen. Lincoln endorsing my order on Mr. Adams, it was accordingly delivered to the Dr. of which I gave information by Letter, which I hope reached Mr. Adams timely enough to prevent his sending forward the order proposed.

I have enclosed a List of the public Securities, you requested, if it is not descriptive enough, Youll let me know.

***

Pray what will the Commissioners ~~allow~~ employed to purchase Continental Securities, allow, or how will they conduct their Business? State Securities are sold at 8/ ℔ £ Continental @ 12/2d. Indents from 6/6 to 7/—Will it best to sell or best to buy.

***

ALS, Adams Family Manuscript Trust, MHi. Written from Weymouth, Massachusetts; place to which addressed not indicated. The omitted text relates to Tufts's management of the Adamses' affairs in Massachusetts, and his thoughts on funding. Part of the letter and a postscript dated 6 October are printed in the Second Federal Election section with Correspondence: Third Session.

[1] Williamson arrived in Boston on 7 September.

An Elector to Mr. Printer

***

It is observable, that those gentlemen who have not paid the printers for publishing their speeches, have more influence (by their *short remarks*) than those who have filled columns in our papers. Influence, as it respects Mr. AMES and Mr. GOODHUE, is vastly in favour of the latter. Mr. SHERMAN and other gentlemen, can be mentioned in proof of the remark, that *verbocity* and *loquacing* [*?*], do not constitute the essential qualifications for a member of Congress; for if they did, Parrots, Magpies, and JACK-DAWS,[1] would be our most influential Representatives.

[Boston] *Herald of Freedom*, 28 September; edited by Edmund Freeman. The omitted text criticizes the prejudice for "speechifying lawyers" as candidates for Congress.

[1] One of the smallest species of crows and ravens, known for its voluble cackling.

Other Documents

[Massachusetts] *Salem Gazette*, 28 September.
Sherman visited Salem last week.

Wednesday, 29 September 1790

William Few to Governor Edward Telfair

***

Since the recess of Congress we have had but little political News from any quarter. Nothing decissive has yet transpired Relative to the Negociation of England and Spain, it is still thought by some that War and destruction must terminate the business, and it is the opinion of others that it will be compromised in an amicable manner, but I will confess that I have not yet found any ground on which to form an opinion as to what may be the event, and shall therefore wait for time to develope the matter.

I was desireous of returning to Georgia this Autumn but the very short recess of Congress has prevented me, and as the next Session of Congress cannot continue longer than the first of March, I flatter myself with the expectation of seeing my friends in Georgia before the first of May.

I am much pleased with a paragraph in your letter which mentions the probability of pointing out funds to the next Legislature to discharge the arrears due to the Delegates of the former Congress if the business should succeed it will be very acceptable to me and I believe it will be equally so, to the others that are concerned in the event.

ALS, Telfair Papers, GHi. Place to which addressed not indicated. Newspapers enclosed. The omitted text reports on a business transaction between them.

Richard Henry Lee to George Washington

A long and severe visitation of intermitting fever since I returned from Congress, has placed me in a very low and reduced situation. But unfit as I now am for writing, I cannot with hold my testimony when it is requested, in favor of a very deserving young Man who wishes an appointment to the command of one of the Cutters to be equipped under the late Act of Congress "providing more effectually for the Collection of the duties &c." Mr. John Parker who will have the honor of delivering you this letter, is a trained Seaman, and well acquainted with this [*Chesapeake*] Bay—he is a Man of honor & spirit, and a fifth brother of that brave and persevering family of brothers that served, three of them in the Continental Army, and one in our State

Navy during the late war. His eldest brother fell at Charles Town, and the two next served under your command from the beginning to the end of the war, and as I have been informed, with honor to themselves and usefulness to their country.

Since the peace, this young gentleman has been diligently fitting himself for Sea service, by voyaging to Europe and the W. Indies, and by the command of Vessels in the Bay trade. It is my opinion Sir, that if you shall be pleased to appoint Mr. Parker, he will prove an useful Officer in his Line, and I am sure he will always retain a grateful remembrance of his Benefactor.

ALS, Washington Papers, DLC. Written from "Chantilly," Westmoreland County, Virginia; carried by John Parker.

Samuel Meredith to Thomas Fitzsimons

Your favour of the 24th Inst. I recd. last Night & am much obliged by the communication of the 3100 D. being lodged in the Bank—it has relieved me extreemly, from reflextions I think very unbecoming, & which were not warranted, but these are a tax we pay in passing thro the world, & the less we think of them, the happier we are ***

I shall appear in the Market again the first of the Month, which by some Means or other the People here have arrived at the knowledge of, I am sure it has not been from any communication of mine which I have studiously avoided & should not now have mentioned but that is known—this has given a rise to Certificates they are now from 12/4½ to 12/5 each & will I suppose waver from that to 12/6 the price I the last time gave, and at which I think there is a chance of their remaining till foreigners appear in the Market which I think they cannot do in any numbers before two Months or more, the necessitous here have been obliged to sell this with the influx from other parts has served to reduce them, another sweep may take off from some of the most needy that remain, & will no doubt fix them at, from 12/4 to 12/6—I have understood from [*William*] Duer that the North Carolina Debt is not actually near so much as their Members would have it believed, & that the sum assumed will cover all, if this should be the case, it certainly would be the best speculation as the average Interest is 7 Years, & the Debt 9/2 to 9/3, if there was a certainty of not buying bad ones, (to avoid which great Caution ought to be used, as there are Many of the kind passing here).

***

As I am not much Skilled in these matters, little relyance is to be placed in my opinion.

ALS, Gratz Collection, PHi. Addressed to Philadelphia; received 2 October. The omitted text relates to the election of Thomas Mifflin as governor of Pennsylvania and reports the prices of various certificates.

Letter from Philadelphia

On the building to be appropriated to the use of the House of Representatives in this city, it was thought by some artists, that a dome covered with strong glass ought to be raised in imitation of the dome Cupola in your Federal Hall at New-York. One of the projectors, being asked his real reason for wishing to put the city to this extraordinary and, apparently, useless expence, answered that his whole view in proposing it, was, that it might *throw a better light upon their proceedings.*

NYDA, 4 October; reprinted at Portland, Maine; Portsmouth and Exeter, New Hampshire; Boston, Salem, and Worcester, Massachusetts; Poughkeepsie, New York; Burlington, New Jersey; Philadelphia; and Charleston, South Carolina.

Other Documents

William Constable to Robert Morris. FC:lbk, Constable-Pierrepont Collection, NN.

Suggests that Morris raise the money he has asked to borrow by selling $30,000 worth of South Carolina military certificates that Constable can send him.

Alexander Hamilton to George Washington. Copy, Washington Papers, DLC.

Smith (S.C.) recommends William Hall to command a revenue cutter out of Charleston, South Carolina; "but on information, not on personal knowledge."

Thomas Lee Shippen to William Shippen. Copy, Lee Family Papers, ViHi. Written from "Menokin," Francis Lightfoot Lee's estate in Richmond County, Virginia; addressed to Fourth Street, Philadelphia.

Describes a visit to "Chantilly" (R. H. Lee's estate in Westmoreland County, Virginia), where no one except Lee's daughter Sally (Sarah Caldwell Lee [1775–1837]) was "perfectly well."

Voters to the Inhabitants of Plymouth and Barnstable District. [Boston] *Columbian Centinel*, 29 September. Portions of this piece are excerpted with documents relating to the Second Federal Election in Massachusetts in Correspondence: Third Session.

Argues the advantages of electing Representatives with landed property, who share the inconvenience of tax burdens; "Too many gentlemen who have no such property are already in Congress."

[Exeter] *New Hampshire Gazetteer*, 1 October. The crime referred to occurred on 6 October 1789; Planteum, who took clothing and furniture, was immediately captured and confined at Portsmouth, New Hampshire, on the brig *Standfast* ([Exeter] *New Hampshire Gazetteer*, 10 October 1789).

A jury found Anthony Planteum, a Frenchman, not guilty of burglary but guilty of stealing from Wingate's house; sentenced to double damages and twenty stripes "which were immediately applied to his deserved back."

Thursday, 30 September 1790

Thomas Jefferson to William Short

*** I think it possible that it will be established into a maxim of the new government to discontinue it's foreign servants after a certain time of absence from their own country, because they lose in time that sufficient degree of intimacy with it's circumstances which alone can enable them to know & pursue it's interests. seven years have been talked of. be assured it is for your happiness & success to return. every day increases your attachment to Europe & renders your future reconcilement to your own country more desperate: and you must run the career of public office here if you mean to stand on high & firm ground hereafter. were you here now, you would be put into the Senate of Congress in the place of Grayson whose successor is to be chosen next month. (for the late appointment was only for the fragment of his time which remained.) there would scarcely be a dissenting voice, to your appointment. but it is too late for that. Monroe will be pressed into the service, really against his will. but, two years hence will come on another election in the place of R. H. L[*ee*]. who will unquestionably be dropped. if you were to be here a few months before, I would forfeit every thing if you were not elected. it will be for six. years, and is the most honorable & independent station in our government, one where you can peculiarly raise yourself in the public estimation. ***

ALS, Jefferson-Short Papers, ViW. Written from Monticello, Albemarle County, Virginia. For the full text, see *PTJ* 17:543–46.

Other Documents

Pierce Butler to Messrs. Simpson and Davisson. FC:lbk, Butler Papers, PHi. The "measure" Butler refers to is Georgia's sale of its western lands to the Yazoo companies.

Expects the United States will observe a strict neutrality between Spain and Great Britain if war breaks out, unless there is an interference with American vessels as carriers; state debts have been assumed "and things are going on as well as coud be wished to restore the credit of the Union. The conduct of Georgia is justly reprehensible. I am of opinion that the general government must interfer and prevent such a measure"; has lost £1000 by failures in South Carolina since the FFC began; had the pleasure of Davisson's visit in New York en route to Nova Scotia; has not left his home for three days because of heavy rain; his mind is distressed by daily dread of losing his "dangerously indisposed" wife (Mary Middleton Butler).

Hugh Williamson and Abishai Thomas to Governor Alexander Martin. Dft, hand of Thomas, Governors' Papers, Nc-Ar.

They are unable to settle an account for the purchase of leather deerskins at the request of Congress in 1777 because the treasury department has packed the relevant documents to be moved to Philadelphia.

September 1790 Undated

Letter from Boston

*** As to the Assumption of the State Debts, so much used as a motive to re-elect the old Representatives—They perhaps might be much interested in that event; besides it is wholly problematical with me whether it proves so very beneficial as some think, unless it be to speculators—be that as it may, the Representative from your district [*Sedgwick*] can't claim but small share of the credit of the success of a measure that had well nigh been defeated by his intemperate zeal. ***

[Northampton, Massachusetts] *Hampshire Gazette*, 29 September.

Other Documents

Pierce Butler to Tench Coxe. ANS, Coxe Papers, PHi. Dated "Tuesday morning." This note is undated and could have been sent as early as July or as late as October, when Coxe left New York. The editors believe September is most likely.

Thanks Coxe for sending him the plan of a house in Philadelphia; the absence of out buildings to accommodate "Servants and Horses" makes it "inellegible for so large a Family" as Butler's.

Robert Morris to Tobias Lear. No copy known; mentioned in Lear to Washington, 20 September (Washington Papers, DLC)

Thinks it best that the President's furniture should not be removed from New York sooner than 1 October.

Letter from East Hampton, Long Island. *NYDA*, 2 October. Floyd lost his bid for reelection in April 1790, but James Townsend, the winner, died within a month of the election. A special election was held in April 1791, but Floyd did not run.

"We are looking out for *** a representative, who will make us appear respectable to the world, and convince the folks abroad that we not only have such an one about us, but have likewise discernment enough to elect him."

October 1790

Friday, 1 October 1790

George Beckwith to William Samuel Johnson. AN, Johnson Correspondence (BK 811.J633BZ), NNC. Written from 15 Wall Street, at noon.
Acknowledges gift of cheese from Mrs. (Anne Beach) Johnson; jokes about Johnson's partiality to all things English; presents him with a book.

Samuel Tucker to John Adams. ALS, Adams Family Manuscript Trust, MHi. Written from Boston; delivered by Henry Knox (Tucker to Alexander Hamilton, 10 November, FC, Tucker Papers, MH). Tucker addressed this subject in a second letter to Adams, also dated 10 November (FC, Tucker Papers, MH), but internal evidence indicates it was intended only as a supporting document to be enclosed in Tucker's letter to Hamilton, 10 November (to be calendared in volume 21).
Office seeking: command of a federal revenue cutter.

Yankee Doodle. [Boston] *Columbian Centinel*, 2 October. Written from "West-Boston."
Folly despises "the powerful effects of the eloquence of an AMES, and a GERRY, those great ornaments of this Commonwealth in Congress."

Saturday, 2 October 1790

Nathaniel Appleton to Jabez Bowen. FC:dft, Appleton Papers, MHi. Written from Boston; place to which addressed not indicated.
Thinks all the loan officers should discuss the issue of their pay and expenses with the members of Congress from their states before they return to Congress.

A Correspondent. [Boston] *Columbian Centinel*, 2 October.
Is confident that Gerry will be reelected; "Good sense, abilities, integrity, industry, and patriotism will not be deserted."

SUNDAY, 3 OCTOBER 1790

Abigail Adams to Mary Cranch

Do you not pitty me my dear sister to be so soon all in a Bustle, and weary of removing again, as much Boxing and casing as if we were removing to Europe. our furniture may well be stiled *movables.* the expence attending the various removals would very handsomely furnish one House. I feel low Spirited and Heartless. I am going amongst an other new set of company, to form new acquaintances, to make and receive a hundred ceremonious visits, not one of ten from which I shall derive any pleasure or satisfaction, obliged to leave Mrs. [*Abigail Adams*] Smith behind, and the Children to whom I am much attached, and many other things I have upon my mind and spirits which I cannot communicate by Letter. I live however upon the Hope that I shall come and see you next Summer: I hope congress will not set out the Month of April.

***

ALS, Abigail Adams Letters, MWA. Addressed to Braintree, Massachusetts.

Abigail Adams to Cotton Tufts

*** Dr. Williamson calld last week and received his money delivering your order. ***

Do you not pitty me my dear Sir, that I have again to pack up and remove. and that at a greater expence than when I removed from Braintree. from a hundred and twenty to a hundred and sixty dollars, is the lowest we can get a vessel to take our things for. 400 dollars we are obliged to give for a House out of the City near 2 miles. not a Garden spot upon it, a House Large and convenient enough; but by no means equal to this which we now occupy. I should like Sir to get my Salted Beaf from Boston put up by Baldwin. Beaf is a very dear article in Philadelphia 56 shillings pr. hundred upon the Hoof. 3 Barrels of Beaf such as you procured for me last year would be a sufficient winter stock if you could send it round early in the winter and 2 kegs of Tongues I still have some of the Beaf which you sent me, and it is very good. I wish you would be so good as to let me know whether there is a probality of getting it for me. ***

ALS, Miscellaneous Manuscripts, NHi. Addressed to Weymouth, Massachusetts. Adams's brief remarks on the Virginia and Massachusetts Second Federal Election are calendared with that section in Correspondence: Third Session.

MONDAY, 4 OCTOBER 1790

John Adams to John Quincy Adams. ALS, Adams Family Manuscript Trust, MHi. Place to which addressed not indicated.

Advises to neither admire nor despise either political party in Boston; longs to visit him in Boston, "but the Care of a troublesome Removal to Philadelphia, will prevent me till next year"; asks him to write as often as possible.

Samuel Adams to John Adams. FC:dft, Samuel Adams Originals, NN. Written from Boston. For the full text, see *John Adams* 6:412–14.

Responds to letter of 12 September and speculation about the dawn of the millennium; former political principles have led to contention and disorder by the blind prejudice of philosophers' disciples; liberty is lost by passion controlling reason, without regard to checks and balances; the renovation of the age depends on educating youth in Christian virtues and the love of God and country; if there is need of any government during the millennium, hopes it is republican or something better.

John Laurance to Jeremiah Wadsworth. ALS, Wadsworth Papers, CtHi. Written from Newport, Rhode Island; addressed to Hartford, Connecticut.

Two of Laurance's children will visit the Wadsworths for two weeks.

TUESDAY, 5 OCTOBER 1790

Melatiah Jordan to George Thatcher. ALS, Chamberlain Collection, MB. Written from Union River, Maine; addressed to Biddeford, Maine.

Office seeking: "any Post of Profit" in the area; reports town of Trenton (Maine) voted unanimously for Thatcher as Representative on 4 October.

John Langdon to Tobias Lear. No copy known; acknowledged in Lear to Langdon, 14 October.

WEDNESDAY, 6 OCTOBER 1790

Pierce Butler to Weeden Butler

***

It is impossible my Dear Sir, to convey to You the feelings of my mind at the moment I write this. My Dearest Wife [*Mary Middleton Butler*], the friend of my bosom, the partner of my sufferings and losses in a long Civil War, is in that painful state as to make me, *even me* almost wish the last scene over—When I call to mind Her many Virtues I cling to Her! I fondly wish to hold Her back! when I behold Her sufferings I feel my selfishness, and am ready to wish Her released from them—Great God! how shall I bear the Separation! I need the hand of friendship to pour balm in to my Afflicted breast—where can I find that friendship here, unless in my Children, who are equaly Afflicted with myself! willingly woud I take the wings of the morning and holding fast to them, flee to thee my friend, and to my Old and well tried friend Docter [*Thomas*] Spence to comfort me by Your friendly Council but that can not be—My own health is greatly impaird by the anxiety of my mind and my Constant watching shoud I follow, my Children may truly be Stiled Orphans—Not One Relative in America! Not One on Earth but my Sister Frances [*Butler*], with whom they coud be desirably placed—She also is infirm and Advanced in Years—what will become of my innocent for they are truly so helpless Girls! the thought is too Excrusiating and shakes the firmness of my Soul—My poor Boy [*Thomas*] I Commit to Your friendship—I beseech You to take Him under Your Sole Guardian Ship—let this Instrument, in Case I shoud never write another, be kept to testify this disposition I make of my Dear Son—had I not lived in boisterous times he woud have had a very Considerable Estate; or even if I had not by a kind principle been led into suretyships for Others he woud, notwithstanding the ravages of War, had a handsome Estate—As it is, He will have an Indep[*end*]ence with the Aid of some honorable profession which I entreat he may adopt & follow.

My Estate to this hour groans under suretyships—Since I left Carolina to attend Congress, I have lost Nine Thousand pds. Sterling by failures in Carolina; Debts I considered as good—the Men are Bankrupts and by being absent I get nothing—the more pressing Creditors swept all—such are Our laws.

If I can get any Indemnification from those I am Security for, I will Change the Scene and see You—I am not Justified to myself in leaving America 'till I I do all in my power to accomplish it—Pardon my troubling You with so much on my own Affairs—In case anything shoud happen to me It is right You shoud know them.

***

ALS, Butler Papers, Uk. Addressed to Cheyne Walk, Chelsea near London; postmarked; received 18 November; answered 27 November.

Daniel Cony to George Thatcher

The River St. Croix which forms the Eastern boundary of the United States has become a Subject of dispute between the Our Citizens, & the

Subjects of the British government—As the Subject Matter thereof has been transmited to Congress—As the United States are Concerned—And this Commonwealth deeply interested, and will be materially affected in the issue of the dispute, I doubt not that as you are the most Eastern Representative—that you will pay such attention to that business as the importance of the Subject may require—There are a Considerable number of papers in the Secretaries office[1] at Boston touching the Merits of the dispute—Also a Mr. [*James*] Boyd of Boston who is interested in the disputed Lands has in his poss[*ess*]ion Some papers that will give light on the Subject—permit me Sir to request that you will Examine the papers referrd to, as you pass thro' Boston to Congress—as I am Sure you will be better able to judge of the merits of the dispute.

I call'd to See you on that Subject on my return from Boston but had not the pleasure to find you at home.

[*P. S.*] I can't guess whether you have half the vote in this quarter or not.

ALS, Chamberlain Collection, MB. Written from Hallowell, Maine; addressed to Biddeford, Maine. For documents relating to the Northeast Boundary Dispute with Great Britain, see *DHFFC* 2:359–87.

[1] Massachusetts Secretary of State John Avery, Jr.

Joshua Lathrop to Elias Boudinot

***

I am very Sorry Congress is removed from N. York and the more So, as I fear it will be the means of depriving my Daughter of so good & agreable a Neighbour[1] But truly this is not of So much importance. *if there* the great Good, of the united States can be better conducted, I am very glad that in the last Session you were able So well to git through the adoption of the State Debt we find *in this* as well as in many other instances that perseverence will affect great things.

I heartily wish that hereafter there may be a more happy Union, & that the great & important Interest of the united States may be promoted. that there may be a desirable union & agreement between Rulers & ru[*led*] in consequence of which may Justice & Judgment run d[*own?*] our Streets as a river & Riteousness as an over flowing Stream, & we be that happy People whose God is the Lord. ***

ALS, formerly at PPRF. Written from Norwich, Connecticut; place to which addressed not indicated. The omitted text includes regrets that "any important Business should intervene" to have prevented a visit by Boudinot and his wife to Norwich.

[1] Lydia Lathrop Austin (1764–1818) married Rev. David Austin of Elizabethtown, New Jersey, in 1782.

Robert Morris to John Langdon

I had the pleasure to receive your letter of the 16th. [?] ulto. in due course and immediately set on foot an enquiry after such Lodgings as you describe but not meeting with any place so suitable as the House of Mr. Hunter I have agreed with him on the terms expressed in the enclosed Memorandum. The price is dearer than I could have wished, but I think you will like the House & its situation And Mr. Hunter insists that He cannot afford to take less. You will have to provide your own Table and I think that mode will be found Cheapest & most agreable. Mrs. [*Mary*] Morris joins me in Compliments to Mrs. [*Elizabeth*] & Miss [*Elizabeth*] Langdon and Yourself, wishing you all a pleasant Journey and safe arrival, and when that happens pray drive to our House & We will shew you the way to your Domicile.

[*Enclosure*]

Philadelphia October 5th. 1790. Memorandum of an Agreement between William Hunter and Robert Morris made this day.

Mr. Morris on behalf of The honble. John Langdon Esqr. agrees to rent [*from*] Mr. Hunter the following Rooms in his house to be ~~rent~~ occupied [*by*] Mr. Langdon and his Family from the time of his arrival in [*th*]is City untill his departure after the next Session of Congress is [*fi*]nished.

The Front Parlour on the first Floor
The drawing Room & Chamber up one pair of Stairs
One Chamber up two pair of Stairs—
Garretts for Servants Lodgings
The use of the Kitchen for Cooking &c.
Stables for his horses, and a place under cover for his Carriage.

The whole to be decently furnished—For which the said Jno. Langdon is to pay at the rate of Twelve Dollars ℔ week.

ALS, enclosure in the hand of a clerk, Langdon Papers, NhPoS. Written from Philadelphia; addressed to Portsmouth, New Hampshire; postmarked New York; answered. According to the 1791 Philadelphia Directory, a coach maker named William Hunter resided at 319 Market Street.

Other Documents

[Springfield, Massachusetts] *Hampshire Chronicle*, 6 October.

Sedgwick and Strong were co-counsels for the defense in a state supreme court arson case; during the hearing the defendant escaped.

GA, 8 October.

Princeton awarded Ellsworth an honorary doctor of laws degree.

[Connecticut] *Norwich Packet*, 8 October.

Anne Huntington, "Consort of the Honorable Benjamin Huntington," died of consumption at Norwich, Connecticut.

Letter from Boston. *NYJ*, 15 October.

If elected (over Ames) to the Second Congress, Benjamin Austin "would have manfully combatted for the PEOPLES RIGHTS, as *Gerry* has done."

THURSDAY, 7 OCTOBER 1790

GUS, 13 October.

Benson, as a commissioner appointed by the New York legislature, signed the document granting New York's consent to the formation of the state of Vermont.

FRIDAY, 8 OCTOBER 1790

Thomas Fitzsimons to Tench Coxe. ALS, Coxe Papers, PHi. Written from Philadelphia; postmarked.

Office seeking: his neighbor Hugh Montgomery for command of a revenue cutter; finds it "difficult to resist these kind of Applications and unpleasant to trespass on the time & patience of the Gent. who have the disposal of such appointments"; asks Coxe to mention Montgomery to the secretary of the treasury.

Philip Theobald to George Thatcher. ALS, Chamberlain Collection, MB. Written from Pownalborough, Maine; addressed to New York. The remainder of the letter relates to the Second Federal Election in Maine and is excerpted with those documents in Correspondence: Third Session.

Thanks Thatcher for offer to recover money due him in Philadelphia; cannot expect "to see a farthing of it without your influence."

SATURDAY, 9 OCTOBER 1790

Thomas Fitzsimons to Thomas Sumter. No copy known; acknowledged in Sumter to Fitzsimons, 15 November.

SUNDAY, 10 OCTOBER 1790

Abigail Adams to Mary Cranch

*** we have begun to pack up our furniture, and expect to get it on Board by the 20th perhaps we may make it later. but I hope not as the weather will every day become more & more uncomfortable. the Idea of going so much further from you is painfull to me, and would be more so if I did not hope to spend the next summer with you. at present you have your Family with and near you. but it is my destiny to have mine scatered and scarcly to keep one with us. my seperation from mrs. [*Abigail Adams*] Smith is painfull to me on many accounts. there is at present no prospect of their going with us. and if their prospects here were as fair as they ought to be, I should be less solicitous for them. ***

ALS, Abigail Adams Letters, MWA. Addressed to Braintree, Massachusetts. For the full text, see *Abigail Adams*, pp. 60–61.

OTHER DOCUMENTS

John Adams to John Codman. FC:lbk, Adams Family Manuscript Trust, MHi. Addressed to Boston.

Preparations for the move to Philadelphia consume all his time; thinks there would be opposition to or censure for the appointment of too many consuls from one state (Massachusetts), but will support Codman's brother [*Richard*] nevertheless; if supporting documents were sent, he would deliver them to the President.

John Adams to Cotton Tufts. FC:lbk, Adams Family Manuscript Trust, MHi.

Asks Tufts to subscribe all of Adams's paper securities in his hands, both state and federal, to the new federal loan; the Adamses will move to "Bush Hill," about two miles outside Philadelphia, in about ten days.

John Adams to Thomas Welsh. FC:lbk, Adams Family Manuscript Trust, MHi.

Would be happy to do the favor Welsh requested, "but I am not at Liberty to communicate the most distant hint to any one relative to the subject"; "I am afraid all my friends will find as long as I live, that my friendship is not worth a groat."

Maxey Ewell to Thomas Jefferson. ALS, Jefferson Papers, DLC. Written from Charlottesville, Virginia; addressed to Monticello; received 16 October. For the full text, see *PTJ* 17:584–85.

Asks him to inform Madison that Ewell had not received his pay as commissary at the Albemarle (Virginia) barracks during the Revolutionary War.

Monday, 11 October 1790

Paine Wingate to John Langdon

I am told that Mr. Nathl. Gilman has declined his late appointment, on account of the emoluments not being equal, in his opinion, to the trouble & responsibility of the office. You will recollect that I mentioned to you at New York Colo. Nathl. Rogers as a person, who I thought would discharge that office with fidelity & ability; but as Mr. Gilman had been the former loan officer, & had discharged that trust unexceptionably well, it was supposed that he would be the most suitable person for a reappointment. You observed that you wished to befriend Colo. Rogers when there should be a proper opening, and as Mr. Gilman has declined serving, I should be very glad, if it should meet with your approbation & concurrence, to joyn with you in recommending to the President of the United States Colo. Rogers for the commissioner of loans in New Hampshire. I conclude that it will be necessary that an officer in that place should be appointed soon, before the meeting of Congress. You know Colo. Rogers perfectly well & I know that you are a friend to him. He would be willing to serve for the present emoluments, & I think there is no doubt but he would make a faithful officer and give good satisfaction. There would be an additional pleasure, to other considerations in his appointment, that he would thereby be enabled ~~be~~ to provide for a very *numerous* family of likely children in a manner more agreeable to his wishes than he might otherwise do. I have taken the liberty to make the proposal to you, and will thank you to favour me with your sentiments respecting the matter by the bearer of this, or by some other opportunity. I suppose that whatever is done must be done pretty soon.

I thank you for the Packet you took the trouble of for me, & was very sorry that I had not the pleasure of waiting on you, on your late return from Exeter [*New Hampshire*]. That afternoon I had engaged to spend in company with a brother & sister in law from Salem [*Massachusetts*] at my daughter [*Mary*] Wiggin's & could not dispence with my engagement. I hope to have the pleasure of seeing you before you set out on your journey for Philadelphia.

ALS, Etting Collection, PHi. Written from Stratham, New Hampshire; addressed to Portsmouth, New Hampshire.

Letter from Philadelphia

The great increase of rents in this city is an evil that presses peculiarly hard upon such of the inhabitants as have no emoluments to expect from the Congressional sessions. What think you of one hundred dollars advance upon rents in such parts of the city as may in any degree be called central; yet this is common, and I wish I could say it was the most that has been demanded. This evil, however, will I doubt not, in time, work its own remedy. Induced by the present exorbitant rents our moneyed people are building daily upon vacant lots, and erecting large edifices in the room of old ones of a smaller size; which must have the two-fold effect of lowering rents, and enlarging this city far beyond its old bounds, in a short time—And as Penn's plan of extending the city westward does not seem to be a prevailing idea at present, the consequence will be, that Kensington will soon be lost in the bosom of Philadelphia, and we shall advance rapidly up the Delaware, whose various commercial advantages will ever claim a preference over Schuylkill, where it is hoped our poets and poetesses will wander as usual, for centuries to come, and enjoy the grassy meads and cool shades of the evening, without being interrupted by the vulgarity of sailors and draymen, or that strong scent of tar, pitch and sulphur (ever execrated by the muses) and which are too apt to banish every idea of Parnassus from the taste of refinement and elegance.

NYDA, 13 October; reprinted at Philadelphia and Baltimore.

Other Documents

Jeremiah Barker to George Thatcher. ALS, Chamberlain Collection, MB. Written from Falmouth, Maine; addressed to Biddeford, Maine. The entire letter will be printed with documents relating to Maine's Second Federal Election in the Correspondence: Third Session volumes.

In Gorham, Maine, on election day (4 October), he heard Stephen Hall argue in favor of rotation in office; the principle "was viewed as a matter of such importance by many *great men*, that Mr. Page of Virginia, had publickly declared that he did not wish to arrive to greater honor in this world, than to have it recorded upon his Tomb Stone, that he voted against Genl. Warshington at his second election! upon no other principle than, the expediency of *Rotation*."

Nicholas and Jacob Van Staphorst and Nicholas Hubbard to John Adams. LS, Adams Family Manuscript Trust, MHi. Written from Amsterdam. An identical letter was written the same day to Jefferson. (Giuseppe Ceracchi [1751–1801] sculpted busts of many public figures during his visit to the United States in 1791–92.)

Introduces the bearer, Joseph Ceracchi, an eminent Roman sculptor, and requests on his behalf every civility in Adams's power.

Daniel Wood to George Thatcher. ALS, Thatcher Papers, MeHi. Written from Berwick, Maine; addressed to Biddeford, Maine. Portions of the letter concerning the Second Federal Election are printed with Correspondence: Third Session.

Office seeking: some "imploy" that is active and profitable; had hoped Thatcher would have found him something by now.

Tuesday, 12 October 1790

Samuel A. Otis to Silvanus Bourn. ALS, Bourn Papers, DLC. Addressed to Boston. For the Convention, see *DHFFC* 2:346–51.

As requested, encloses a copy of the "Consular Bill" [HR-86] and the Consular Convention with France; wishes to have this "communication considered as confidential."

Samuel A. Otis to Jeremiah Wadsworth. ALS, Wadsworth Papers, CtHi. Addressed to Hartford, Connecticut.

Forwards to Wadsworth's care a package for the governor of Connecticut; respects to the Wadsworth family.

Thomas Russell to John Langdon. ALS, Langdon Papers, NhPoA. Written from Boston.

Is told that Mrs. Elizabeth Langdon and daughter "Betsy" go to Philadelphia with him; hopes they will visit en route.

Governor Arthur St. Clair to Thomas Fitzsimons. ALS, Gratz Collection, PHi. Written from Fort Washington (Cincinnati), Ohio; addressed to Philadelphia; received 26 November.

General Josiah Harmar marched with 1300–1400 men on 30 September; Major John F. Hamtramck went from St. Vincennes (Indiana) on about 25 September.

WEDNESDAY, 13 OCTOBER 1790

Louis Guillaume Otto to Comte de Montmorin

The total stagnation of public business since the adjournment of Congress furnishes no nourishment for a purely political correspondence. Not only the members of the legislature but also the officers of the executive branch have abandoned New York, the one to confer with their constituents and the other to establish their offices at Philadelphia. It is now indeed occupied only by speculators, who, given the revolution in finances occasioned by the fiscal laws of Congress, have never shown more activity than at this moment. Confidence in the government seems perfectly reestablished, industry resumes all its vigor; the fisheries and navigation increase in proportion to the capital that the measures taken by Congress have almost doubled in the hands of merchants. There remain meanwhile some signs of dissatisfaction in some of the states that ratified the Constitution only by the smallest of majorities, and that pass over no opportunity to attack the weak flank of the administration.

Among those defiant states, Virginia holds first place by the great influence that Patrick Henry, the declared enemy of Congress, continues to exercise. That man, who unites much skill with an energetic and irresistible eloquence, has controlled the Virginia legislature for many years. He is always forcefully rising up against the federal government, and one perceives that he is now working to have his state protest the financial measures recently taken by Congress. General [Horatio] Gates, who knows him personally, assures me that the President could easily win him over by giving him a lucrative office under the general government; it is to be regretted that such a step has not been taken to quiet one of the most dangerous and restless men in the union. One must dread his influence not only in Virginia but in Maryland, since that latter state commonly adopts the opinions of the former, of which it used to be a part. North Carolina is equally prone to follow Virginia's lead, and the opposition of those three states often hampers Congress. What makes Patrick Henry's intrigues more astonishing is that Virginia's members in Congress themselves have consented to the measures taken, and that it will be very strange to see the *legislature of Virginia* oppose (as is expected) what has been done by the *Representatives of the people of Virginia*—a paradox that must necessarily be the consequence of the Sovereignty that the federal Constitution has left to the individual states. One also hears of some agitation in Georgia's legislature to disapprove of the treaty *of New York* concluded by the President with the Creek Nation.

It is surprising at first glance, Sir, to see the opposition to the laws and measures of Congress always come from the southern states, the weakest and least enterprising of the union, while those of the north submit with complete resignation to the will of Congress. It is easy to account for the causes of this difference. The northern states completely control the operations of Congress and adopt by acclamation the laws that their Members draw up after the instructions they constantly receive from their constituents; but the southerners, frequently finding themselves in the minority, have no other recourse than protests and remonstrances. It commonly happens that the southern Members are divided among themselves over the question under debate, so that they are defeated separately by their opponents—always partisan, much more diligent, and more adroit than the others. Boston, formerly the center of the Revolution, today is again the center of political America. Everything comports to the interests of that town and the state of which it is the capital, and as she always has on her side the other three New England states, it is easy for her to maintain in Congress the majority that she has had since the beginning of the war. An ineffectual jealousy and some expressions of discontent are the only weapons that the southerners can avail themselves of.

Copy, in French, Henry Adams Transcripts, DLC. Received 18 March 1791.

Thursday, 14 October 1790

Tobias Lear to John Langdon

I had just now the honor to receive your letter of the 5th Inst. which was forwarded to me from New York.

As soon as the Secretary of the Treasury was informed of Mr. [*Nathaniel*] Gilman's resignation he called upon me to know what Candidate there was for that office who would probably accept it to reside in Portsmouth and enter upon the duties of it immediately. I mentioned your brother [*Woodbury Langdon*] as having been named to the President for that purpose, and I presumed upon his acceptance from the circumstances which you had mentioned to me. The President was accordingly written to on the subject; and by this time the appointment of Judge Langdon to that office is undoubtedly on the Road.

Should Mr. John Taylor Gilman resign his Office,[1] or from indisposition be incapable of discharging the duties thereof; I know of no person who could fill the place to more acceptance than Judge Langdon. I had mentioned him to the President for that purpose when the Commissioners were about to be nominated, and have no doubt but he would have been appointed if any change had taken place in the Commission. In case of Mr. Gilman's resignation I think he will come in.

As Judge Langdon is undoubtedly appointed Commissioner of Loans I can say nothing, at present, respecting Mr. [*Keith*] Spence for that Office. It requires an accurate & able man to execute it; and if circumstances should render Judge Langdon's resignation necessary, we must then think of some other person in Portsmouth to fill it.

P. S.

Mrs. [*Mary Long*] Lear & myself arrived in this city yesterday, and are happy to hear that You intend to bring Mrs. [*Elizabeth*] Langdon & Miss Eliza—to whom you will please to present our respects as well as to all our friends & relations.

ALS, Langdon-Elwyn Family Papers, NhHi. Written from Philadelphia. Place to which addressed not indicated.

[1] Gilman was a commissioner for settling accounts between the United States and the individual states.

Other Documents

Pierce Butler to Edward Rutledge. FC, Butler Letterbook, ScU. The letter is incomplete and may not have been sent. For the full text, see *Butler Letters*, pp. 71–73.

Acknowledges undated letter; regrets the recent "reserve" shown by (Charles C.) Pinckney, "for whom indeed I have long had a real friendship"; Mrs. (Mary Middleton) Butler "lies just as she was. I thank God she does not lose ground, but she does not gain. I have tried to persuade her to try native [*South Carolina*] air but her dread of the sea" is too great.

Ralph Izard to Tench Coxe. ALS, Coxe Papers, PHi.

Is interested in renting [*Matthew?*] Clarkson's house on Spruce Street which has a coach house and stables; asks Coxe what he thinks of it.

Henry Knox to Jeremiah Wadsworth. ALS, Wadsworth Papers, CtHi. Written from Boston; addressed to Hartford, Connecticut; franked; postmarked.

Leaving Boston for Hartford, the Knoxes' carriage overturned; it was damaged and the Knoxes badly bruised; will not be in Hartford until the beginning of next week.

NYDA, 15 October.

Maria Apthorpe Williamson, wife of the North Carolina Representative, died at New York City.

FRIDAY, 15 OCTOBER 1790

William C. Claiborne to John Robinson. ALS, Moncure Robinson Papers, ViW. Written from Philadelphia; addressed to Richmond, Virginia.

"The little Quaker Girls in this City, are so very beautiful"; Beckley left that morning for New York City, for his marriage to Miss (Maria) Prince the next evening; "the Buildings for the accommodation of Congress are going on with great rapidity."

Stephen Sayre to George Washington. ALS, Miscellaneous Letters, Miscellaneous Correspondence, State Department Records, Record Group 59, DNA. Written from Paris. For the full text, see *PGW* 6:559–63.

Office seeking: consul general in France, Holland, Sweden, or England, minister to any secondary court, or consul at Havre de Grace; refer to Izard and Floyd for further information on Sayre's contributions during the Revolutionary War.

Abel Whitney to Theodore Sedgwick. ALS, Sedgwick Papers, MHi. Written from Westfield, Massachusetts; addressed to Stockbridge, Massachusetts; by post. A portion of this letter is excerpted with the Second Federal Election documents in Correspondence: Third Session.

Office seeking: excise collector, as they discussed when last together; asks for advice how to proceed with the application; Strong will be "busy" promoting (Samuel) Hinckley, as "he never fails to push his particular friends into every place where their own merit, or his influence can carry them"; asks Sedgwick to keep silent about the matter, as disappointment "is always attended with a degree of ridicule."

SATURDAY, 16 OCTOBER 1790

Paine Wingate to George Washington

I am informed that Mr. [*Nathaniel*] Gilman, who was lately appointed Commissioner of loans for the State of New Hampshire, has declined accepting his appointment; And concluding that it will be requisite that some other person should soon be appointed in his room, I beg leave to recommend Colonel Nathaniel Rogers as a suitable person for that office. He is a Gentleman well qualified to discharge such a trust. He is much esteemed for his integrity and fair character. Has had a good education, and particularly is well accomplished as an accomptant—Has been habituated to business—Has been improved in several honorable stations in the State, in which he has acquitted himself with reputation and good acceptance, particularly as a member of our late State [*ratification*] Convention, and repeatedly as a Representative, and as a Senator in our legislature, which last office he now sustains. May I add—that, though he is not destitute of property yet having a very *numerous* and promising family to provide for, the emoluments of the office, in this part of the Union, which would not be an object with some, might to him afford very valuable assistance.

Should you be pleased to appoint him, I have leave from him to say, that he will very gratefully accept the office, and exert his utmost ability to discharge his duty. As he had not the honor of being personally known by you, he proposed that a direct application of his own would be of no consequence; but wished that his desire might be expressed, and such recommendation of him might be given as the disinterested might think fit. I can pledge myself for his fidelity, and have no doubt but he would give general satisfaction to the publick, should he be fortunate enough to have the *nomination* and appointment of the President of the united States.

ALS, Washington Papers, DLC. Written from Stratham, New Hampshire; place to which addressed not indicated.

Other Documents

John Adams to William Temple Franklin. FC:lbk, Adams Family Manuscript Trust, MHi.

Advises early publication of Benjamin Franklin's papers; will remove to Philadelphia as soon as Mrs. (Abigail) Adams recovers from a fever which has kept her in bed.

Thomas Jefferson to Maxey Ewell. FC, letterpress copy, Jefferson Papers, MHi. Written from Monticello, Albemarle County, Virginia. For the full text, see *PTJ* 17:599.

Spoke with Madison about Ewell's Revolutionary War pay; Madison suggests that Ewell forward his papers to Madison at Philadelphia.

Elizabeth Smith Shaw to Abigail Smith Adams. ALS, Adams Family Manuscript Trust, MHi. Written from Haverhill, Massachusetts; carried by the Daltons. This is a postscript to a letter begun on 28 September.

The Daltons plan to leave "for the Southward" at the end of October; Ruth Hooper Dalton is "a fine woman, & an excellent Mother"; Mrs. Dalton and daughter (also Ruth) will probably inform Abigail of her son John Quincy's social life; congratulations on birth of the Adamses' third grandchild (Thomas Hollis Smith); "there will be statesmen in plenty, if Mrs. [*Abigail Adams*] Smith goes on from year to year in this way."

Isaac Sherman to Alexander Hamilton. ALS, Hamilton Papers, DLC. For the full text, see *PAH* 7:117–18.

If Isaac can continue to study law in Hamilton's office after the government moves to Philadelphia, he will be able to pay with assistance given by his father, Roger Sherman, who "directs me in a letter which I received yesterday, to present his respectful compliments."

NYDA, 18 October.

Beckley and Maria Prince of New York City were married in the evening in that city by Rev. William Linn.

Sunday, 17 October 1790

George Beckwith, *A Conversation with Alexander Hamilton*

Mr. [*Hamilton*] I have read the determination of the National Assembly of France of the 25th. of August respecting the Family compact,[1] their cordial support of Spain seems at present very questionable.

I cannot help thinking that the friendship of this Country is not unimportant to you even at present, and it will become infinitely more so; the resources of France and of Spain if well administered are very great, and the securing the good will and affection of the States may have political weight; I speak with great delicacy certainly of what ought to be your policy with regard to us from my natural bias in favor of this country, but I am inclined to believe that it might be an advantageous measure for you to open your West India islands to us under certain limitations at the commencement of a War; it would afford you a cheap and a very plentiful supply: I only throw out this idea as it strikes me and it might take place for a short time as a mere matter of experiment.

Major Beckwith. I imagine the possession of New-Orleans would be of great importance to you?

Mr. [*Hamilton*] The Rapid increase of our Western Country is such, that we must possess this outlet in a very short space of time, whatever individual interests may be opposed to it; the general advantage of the States points it out most evidently.[2]

Major Beckwith. I cannot help thinking that it would be greatly for the benefit of your western territory if you were to conclude a just and honorable peace with the Savages within your limits, in a contest between you and them, I am inclined to believe you have more to lose than they have?

Mr. [*Hamilton*] It is consistent with our system to terminate Indian differences by accommodation, in the present instance General [*Arthur*] St.

Clair the Governor of our Western Country had made many arrangements, and matters had gone such a length that we could not put a negative upon this business[3] without disobliging our Western people; one tribe has some causes of complaint, the others have not; it is somewhat late in the Season and possibly the present expeditions will have no great effect, but they will mark the disposition of our government; exclusive of the regular troops the Militia is numerous, and the prospect of an early Campaign next year may make some impression. General [*George Rogers*] Clark (of Virginia) tells me the Indians in that part of the world [*Northwest Territory*] are in the practice of burying their grain to conceal it from an enemy and that they effect this with much address, consequently very usually with success.

Major Beckwith. We have now a probability of a Spanish war, and a possibility of a French one, I trust it will not interrupt our tranquility with you?

Mr. [*Hamilton*] It is the determination of all the gentlemen who take a leading Part in the affairs of this country to preserve an honorable attention to their engagements with foreign powers, I speak to you on this head merely the opinions of an individual; it does not appear to me from the present condition of things, that we shall consider it to be encumbent upon us to take any part with France in a contest in which she is altogether an auxiliary, on the contrary, as the matter strikes me at present, it will be for our consideration whether we ought not to avail ourselves of the period in which Spain shall be involved in a war, to secure those points which are in contest between us and that power; things may change, but as they are circumstanced at present, we are in my opinion perfectly at liberty to follow up our own interest and certain Matters have occurred since the peace, which leave us altogether free with respect to France, *even if she should go to war as a principal*; I think it proper also on this occasion to declare positively and directly, that no treaty, stipulation, or agreement of any sort subsists between us and France, excepting the public printed treaty universally known.[4]

Major Beckwith. I trust the judicial branch of your Government will apply an effectual remedy to those complaints made by our Merchants against the laws passed since the peace, especially in the southern States, which impede the ordinary course of justice between Debtors and Creditors?[5]

Mr. [*Hamilton*] I have the most perfect confidence that this will be the case; by our constitution treaties with foreign powers are to be considered by our Courts of justice as the law of the land; the judges in general are men whose opinions on this subject are perfectly well ascertained, and nothing but an insurrection in opposition to their decisions can in future prevent the regular and usual course of justice; I admit that individual losses have arisen from the delays hitherto too often practiced, these are not to the extent commonly represented, taken in the general, however prejudicial to individuals, and such proceedings are by no means defensible.

By various communications made to me as well from the Eastern as from the Southern States, our government acquires daily strength and consistence in the public Mind, it is found to produce many beneficial effects to the Nation at large; I am persuaded when our Census is completed we shall have at least three Millions and a half of people; at this time we are making considerable exertions even Maritime ones, if from circumstances it became a measure of government to encourage them, and I must beg leave to repeat, its being my opinion, that looking forward particularly to what may be the expected condition of this Country in a few years, it would be an Act of wisdom in the Minister of Great Britain to attach and connect the States upon political as well as commercial considerations.

It seems proper to mention to you at this time, that last Summer it was intended to have written to Lord Dorchester on the subject of our Eastern boundary with your provinces for which purpose directions had been given to the Secretary of State, but the matter was put off, from the expectation that his Lordship would have been here before this time.[6]

Major Beckwith. You are going to remove in a few days to Philadelphia; if any thing should happen that I might wish to communicate to you, can you point out a mode of my doing it by letter?

Mr. [*Hamilton*] That would be precarious, there seems a necessity for my seeing you.

Ms., Colonial Office 42/21 pp. 300–304, PRO. Beckwith identified the person with whom he was talking as "7," his code number for Hamilton.

---

[1] In the spring of 1790 the French national assembly cancelled this alliance that had existed between the Bourbon monarchs of France and Spain since 1733. In August 1790, in the midst of the Nootka Sound crisis, the French National Assembly offered to negotiate a new treaty of alliance with Spain.

[2] The eastern half of the Mississippi River from its source to a point just above present-day Vicksburg, Mississippi, fell under American jurisdiction. From that point south to the thirty-first parallel, jurisdiction was claimed by both Spain and the United States under each country's respective peace treaty with Great Britain in 1783. The lower almost one hundred miles of river (from the thirty-first parallel southward, and including Baton Rouge and New Orleans) lay in undisputed Spanish territory. The American demand for free navigation of the Mississippi River primarily meant access to its mouth and the port facilities of New Orleans. The issue had been a sectionally divisive one in federal politics since 1784 when Spain first closed the mouth of the river to American commerce. In the Treaty of San Lorenzo in 1795, Spain recognized the United States' southern boundary as the thirty-first parallel, the right of Americans to navigate the Mississippi south of that point, the use of New Orleans for three years, and the use of some other port to be designated after that time. In 1803, as part of the Louisiana Purchase, the United States acquired the western half of the Mississippi River and New Orleans from the French, who had acquired it from the Spanish three years earlier. While most Federalists opposed Jefferson's Louisiana Purchase, Hamilton was a vocal supporter.

[3] Gen. Josiah Harmar's punitive expedition against the Native Americans of the Northwest Territory was ordered in June, organized throughout the summer, and carried out in October 1790.

[4] The Treaty of Amity and Commerce (1778), printed in *DHFFC* 2:389–408.

[5] A large proportion of the debt due British citizens was owed by southerners. During and after the Revolutionary War the American states passed laws inhibiting the payment of pre-war debts to British citizens. For example, Maryland and Virginia laws during the war allowed citizens indebted to British citizens to obtain a certificate from the state declaring the debt paid simply by giving the state treasury continental or state currency worth far less than their debts; at the end of the war Maryland passed an act closing its courts to British creditors. Beckwith knew the federal judiciary had the authority after 1789 to enforce the provisions of the Treaty of Paris that required the United States to recognize all pre-war debts.

[6] Soon after the Treaty of Paris of 1783 that ended the Revolutionary War, a disagreement arose between the United States and Great Britain over the boundary between Maine (then part of Massachusetts), and New Brunswick, a Canadian province separated from Nova Scotia in 1784. The question was which of three rivers that flowed into the Bay of Fundy was the river identified by the treaty as the St. Croix. The American claim extended northeast from the present boundary to a point opposite Saint John; the British claim extended southwest as far as the south shore of Passamaquoddy Bay.

In January 1784 the Confederation Congress asked Massachusetts to make an inquiry as to whether the British were encroaching on its northern boundary. The matter had not been resolved by the time the Constitution became effective in 1789, and Massachusetts referred the matter back to the federal government. The Senate resolved on 24 March 1790 that measures should be taken to settle the dispute. Although the Jay Treaty of 1794 between the two nations established an International Boundary Commission to settle the issue, it was not resolved until the Webster-Ashburton Treaty of 1842. (For documents relating to the Northeast Boundary Dispute with Great Britain, see *DHFFC* 2:359–87.)

Other Documents

John Quincy Adams to Abigail Adams. ALS, Adams Family Manuscript Trust, MHi. Written from Boston; addressed to "Richmond Hill," outside New York City. A portion of this letter will be excerpted with Massachusetts' Second Federal Election documents in Correspondence: Third Session.

Asks to be informed of John Adams's opinion on the likely success of William Short's negotiation of a European loan, as the value of securities will depend on it.

Jeremiah Wadsworth to Thomas Fitzsimons. Copy, Wadsworth Papers, CtHi. Written from Hartford, Connecticut; place to which addressed not indicated.

Encloses a list of prices of provisions charged the French Army in 1780 and 1781.

MONDAY, 18 OCTOBER 1790

John Adams to Samuel Adams. ALS, Letters of John and John Quincy Adams, 1776–97, NN. Addressed to Boston; franked; postmarked 24 October. For the full text, see *John Adams* 6:414–20.

Acknowledges Samuel's letter of 4 October, and shares pessimism about political development of Europe; despairing of sufficient benevolence among men, he seeks institutions that will supply its deficiency; is often disappointed with opinions of David Hume, but agrees with Hume that governments relying on "extraordinary degrees of Virtue are evidently chimerical"; thinks any good government must be "Republican," but "there is not in Lexicography, a more fraudulent Word"; any meaning of the word inconsistent with "a mixture of three Powers forming a mutual ballance" threatens to make it detestable to Americans; comments on politics and history; hopes to do justice to nobles, for there are nobles "in Boston as well as Madrid"; "It is time that you and I should have some Sweet Communion together" and does not believe that, having preserved an "uninterupted Friendship" for more than thirty years, they "are now so far asunder in sentiment as some People pretend."

Benjamin Hawkins to John Gray Blount. ALS, John Gray Blount Papers, Nc-Ar. Written from Warren, North Carolina; addressed to Washington, North Carolina; carried by John Seagrove. For the full text, see *Blount* 2:126–27.

Will set out for Philadelphia so as to arrive the last week in November; offers to assist Blount with any demands he might have there.

Cotton Tufts to John Adams. ALS, Adams Family Manuscript Trust, MHi. Written from Weymouth, Massachusetts.

Discusses Adams's business affairs at home; enclosed in his last to Abigail Adams a list of John's public securities; sympathizes with their having to remove from such a delightful spot as New York City; thinks that if Adams had traveled less, he would have enjoyed better health.

Jeremiah Wadsworth to John Faxon. FC:lbk, Wadsworth Papers, CtHi. Written from Hartford, Connecticut.

Expects the next session of Congress will enable him to pay all of Nathanael Greene's bonds.

Letter from Philadelphia. *NYDA*, 21 October; reprinted at Philadelphia. The letter is undated, but *NYDA* indicated that it had arrived in New York on 20 October.

"So great is the disappointment" with the expected election of Thomas Mifflin as governor of Pennsylvania "to a certain *hitherto influential junto*, that is thought they will now lay plans either to remove C——ss, soon after the next session, to Connogocheque, or back again to the Federal Hall, in New-York."

Tuesday, 19 October 1790

Pierce Butler, Receipt book. Butler Papers, PHi.

To Robert Waln for rent (in Philadelphia), £120.

Wednesday, 20 October 1790

James Brown to John Brown

Before this, my Letter committed to the care of Mr. [*Harry*] Innes has reached you. Since that time nothing of a public nature, which deserves your notice has occurred A total cessation of hostilities on the part of the Indians, partly owing to the Expedition[1] partly to the late Treaty with the Creek Nation has taken place. This circumstance, so favorable to Emigrants, has led us to hope that our Country would, this Fall, receive a considerable increase of Inhabitants. Our expectations, on that score have not yet been gratified. Few Boats—very few indeed have yet landed; and accounts from the Eastward do not encourage us to hope for many more. This circumstance so truly discouraging to the Settlers of Kentucky, is imputed to the ready sale of produce in the Settlements, and to the exagerated accounts of Indian depredations which have been industriously diffused throughout the Union.

***

In some of my late letters I was presuming enough to hazard some remarks on the means which appeared to me the best calculated to continue and extend your Influence in this Country. Amongst others I mentioned that of writing frequently to our most influential Characters. I know not whether you will approve of the liberty which I have taken. It was suggested by a motive of a nature very different from that pride which we feel on seeing our friends in possession of honorable stations. It was dictated by an affection, the warmth of which, no change of circumstances can abate. You have not intimated that you were displeased with my freedom. I shall mention the Names of those who were most active at your late Election, and appear to have it more extensively in their power to serve you. In this [*Lincoln*] County you cannot hesitate on whom to bestow your most particular attentions. Mr. Innes your heart will say must not be neglected Colo. [*George*] Nicholas is really a valuable man. I admire his understanding and venerate him on account of his integrity. He is a man of uncommon firmness and inflexible perseverance. In the course of our practice he has treated me with a degree of friendship which shall ever command my most sincere acknowledgements. He is becoming extremely popular; and his exertions at the late Election were such as discovered him to be a warm friend on whom you may safely rely. [*Samuel*] McDowell's and [*Christopher*] Greenup you may view in the same light as formerly In Madison Irwin [*William Irvin*], Millar [*John Miller*], [*Samuel*] Barnett, [*James*] French, & Kennedy.[2] A joint Letter, inclosing a Journal or a few News papers will do.

In Fayette Genl. [*James*] Wilkinson still continues to possess the confidence of the people and convinced me, by his successful exertions on your behalf that he is much the most influential character in that County. You must feel happy in corresponding with a man of his abilities: and you have discernment enough to accomodate your stile to his disposition. [*Edward*] Payne together with his relations and religious connections, forms a very powerful and respectable party. You ought to secure them. The Todd's [*Robert and Richard*] and [*James*] Trotter together with [*Robert*] Patterson should be attended to. Their long residence in this Country has acquired to them some influence. In Nelson [*John*] Caldwell, [*Matthew*] Walton, [*Andrew*] Hynes & [*John Hardin*] Harding—In Jefferson you have a warm friend where you did not expect one In Colo. John Campbell.[3] He is an intelligent old fellow—and very fond of your humble servant—Colo. [*Richard*] Taylor, Rob Breckinridge & Willm. Shannon must be remembered. In Mason [*Henry*] Lee, [*Alexander*] Orr, [*George*] Lewis and Warrins [*Thomas Waring*]—Do not forget Colo. Lyne—he is really a valuable man—Expend a few pounds in Newspapers and Journals—Do not sicken at the means which ambition prescribes—You must bid Adieu to that squeamish refinement—that sickly delicacy, which is disgusted at compliancy with the humors of the Vulgar. Fortune, just to your deserts, has taken you by the Hand and raised you on your feet. But she has left to walk without her further assistance—and, trust me, the staff of Caution is necessary to support you. In a World Ignorant and Wicked, Merit is but a frail and unsubstantial prop. Designing weakness and Artful Villainy can readily undermine it—You are prudent; but unfortunately you feel all the stubborn, uncomplying pride of conscious Merit and Conscious Virtue—I am affraid your continuance in office will be precarious—And still more do I fear that you are too much attached to your present situation to resign it without concern.

I just now heard that Mr. Lee Pauw had arrived and that he had a [*letter*] directed to You. I ordered my Horse—rode out with the greatest impatience, but did not see him—He had rode out. Your Letter was given me It informs Me that you are well, and returned to Philadelphia. I am sorry that your trip to Vermont did not answer your expectations. However I flatter myself that the pleasures of the gay and populous City where you now are, will make you ample amends for the past fatigues and disappointments.

Mr. Birney has just returned from Philadelphia. Letters from you sent by the way of Pittsburgh are coming on in his Waggons. I intended to have made this Letter longer but will wait the arrival of those Letters tog[*ether*] with the one promised in your last, and then shall write you fully. Writing to you is not one of my tasks—It is one of my most refined—most exquisite pleasures, a pleasure my Dear Brother which can only be surpassed by that which I derive from the perusal of your Letters. ***

ALS, John Brown Collection, CtY. Written from Danville, Kentucky; place to which addressed not indicated. The omitted text concerns court business, James's study of law, and sends compliments to a Mr. Bayard in Philadelphia.

[1] Following orders dating to the early summer, Brig. Gen. Josiah Harmar set out from Fort Washington (present-day Cincinnati, Ohio) on 26 September with a 1,500 member force of regular army and militia on a punitive expedition against the Miami and Shawnee of the Northwest Territory. After penetrating 170 miles and destroying several Indian towns, on 21 October Harmar began the two week long return march, during which his forces suffered several devastating ambushes. News of Harmar's pyrrhic victory preceded the official reports to the Washington administration in mid-December (Richard H. Kohn, *Eagle and Sword* [New York, 1975], pp.102–7; *PGW* 6:364n).

[2] Either Joseph (1760–1844) or Thomas (ca. 1760–1839), both of whom served in the Revolutionary War and became involved in the Kentucky statehood movement.

[3] Although there were many men of this name associated with the early history of Kentucky, Brown most likely refers to the John Campbell (ca. 1735–99) who was born in Ireland and became a trader on the disputed Virginia-Pennsylvania frontier by the mid-1760s. In 1773 he purchased a half share in the four thousand acre tract that would include Louisville, the seat of Jefferson County, and settled there as a merchant and ferry master shortly after the Revolutionary War, during which he had served as a colonel in the Virginia militia (Jim Reis, *Pieces of the Past* [Covington, Ky., 1988], vol. 1).

James Monroe to Thomas Jefferson

After the most mature reflection I have at length yielded to my inclinations to ~~be named~~ suffer my name to be mention'd for a publick appointment [*to the Senate*]. If it takes place, unless some unpleasant reflections on probable future events shod. press on me, it will contribute greatly to my own & the gratification of Mrs. M. [*Elizabeth Kortright Monroe*]—as it will place us both with & nearer our friends. But to be candid there is not that certainty in the event we seem'd to suppose. Mr. [*John*] Harvie, Mann Page, Walker & Govr. [*Benjamin*] Harrison are in or rather will be in the nomination, and as some of them are active in their own behalf it is extremely doubtful how it will terminate. Colo. [*Henry*] Lee & Mr. [*John*] Marshall are for others—How a particular character [*Patrick Henry?*] of whom we spoke is dispos'd, I know not, but other circumstances have interven'd to make his inclination in my favor more questionable. There are but few men of any weight in the house & I really know none ~~with~~ on whom I can rely with certainty—I have reason however to believe that with the body of the house I stand well. but the body if well dispos'd requires a head to keep it in a proper direction.

ALS, Jefferson Papers, DLC. Written from Richmond, Virginia; received 27 October.

Other Documents

Governor William Blount to John Gray Blount. ALS, John Gray Blount Papers, Nc-Ar. For the full text, see *Blount* 2:126–28. Written from "William Cobb's Washington County"; addressed to Washington, North Carolina; postmarked Richmond, Virginia, 6 December. Cobb (ca. 1735–1803) migrated from Virginia to present-day Piney Flats, Tennessee, where he built "Rocky Mount" at the confluence of the Holston and Watauga rivers. The house served as Blount's territorial capitol until 1792. On 11 August the Senate authorized Washington to renegotiate the boundary line with the Cherokee established by the Treaty of Hopewell (1785), which forbad white settlement along Tennessee's French Broad River (*DHFFC* 2:95–96, 170). The line was ultimately redrawn well south of the river under Blount's Treaty of Holston in July 1791.

Discusses his public support as territorial governor; "Sevier is open and clear in his Declarations in my favour"; as soon as he is done organizing the governments of the four established counties in the Southern Territory, he will lay out a new county on the south side of the French Broad River, because Sevier informed him that the Senate decided in favor of those settlers.

Charles Carroll to Joshua Johnson. FC, Carroll Letterbook, 1771–1833, Arents Collection, NN. Written from Annapolis, Maryland; sent to London.

Acknowledges receipt, while at New York, of eight volumes of Frederick the Great's posthumous works (*Oeuvres* [Berlin, 1788]) and the continuation of Edward Gibbon's history (*Decline and Fall of the Roman Empire*).

William Smith (S.C.) to Tench Coxe. ALS, Coxe Papers, PHi. Addressed to Chestnut Street (Philadelphia).

Requests that Coxe assist the bearer, who "accompanies my furniture," in conveying it to the house.

Letter from Lexington, Kentucky, to Philadelphia. *PP*, 23 November (the date on which members of Congress would have seen it); reprinted at Lexington, Kentucky.

Reports on the colony he is about to help establish on the South Carolina Yazoo Company lands (in present-day central Mississippi); soldiers recruited for the purpose include one thousand, with their families, to arrive by Christmas under Gen. James Wilkinson, "and General [*John*] Savier [*Sevier*] will take down a similar number."

THURSDAY, 21 OCTOBER 1790

Newspaper Article

The Hon. Mr. Parker of Virginia (says a Correspondent) was the first Gentleman who, to his immortal Honour, introduced a Motion in Congress to discourage the "disgraceful Slave-Trade,"[1]—it appears, that the same worthy Gentleman is again elected one of the National Representatives, a Testimony at once expressive of his Merit and the perfect Approbation with which his Constituents view his laudable Endeavours to check the odious Commerce. Lord Penryn[2] (continues our correspondent) one of the most violent Opposers of the Abolition of the Slave-Trade in England, has lost his Election, as Member of Parliament for Liverpool, while Mr. [*William*] Wilberforce, the excellent advocate of the glorious Cause of Freedom and Humanity, is re-elected Member of Yorkshire. These auspicious Indications of the public Opinion must add new Energy to the Efforts of the respectable society in Great-Britain, to "wipe that foul blot from their national Character;" and surely the Friends of Liberty in this enlightened Country, have the most animating Motives to "*press forward*," with unremitting Zeal and unshaken Perseverance, until they fully accomplish the important and benevolent Objects of their joint Exertions: Exertions, which Heaven will no doubt ultimately crown with complete Success.

[Providence, Rhode Island] *United States Chronicle*, 21 October; reprinted at Philadelphia.

---

[1] On 13 May 1789 Parker, seconded by Scott, moved to insert an impost duty of ten dollars on each slave. The motion was withdrawn and on 18 May Parker was appointed chair of a committee to bring in a slave trade bill. The bill was reported on 19 September and postponed until the second session. It was not taken up again and no copies of the bill are known.

[2] Richard Pennant, Baron Penrhyn of Penrhyn (ca. 1737–1808), a wealthy Liverpool merchant who made his fortune in the slave trade, represented that city in the House of Commons from 1768–80 and 1785–90.

Other Documents

Charles Adams to John Quincy Adams. ALS, Adams Family Manuscript Trust, MHi. Place to which addressed not indicated. Portions of this letter relating to the Second Federal Election in Massachusetts and Virginia are printed with that section in Correspondence: Third Session.

Had a talk with their father that evening about John Quincy's lack of public speaking skills; is not concerned about postage, as he intends to spend the three winter months in Philadelphia studying law with Laurance; hopes New York City will awake from the lethargy and torpor it fell into following Congress's removal; perhaps no place in the world cares less about politics.

Elbridge Gerry to an Unknown Recipient. Listing of ALS, *George A. Van Nosdall Catalog* 734(1940):item 7.

Friday, 22 October 1790

James Monroe to Thomas Jefferson

I wrote you a few days past in great hurry by the Albemarle [*Virginia*] post which I presume has been received. You have been able to collect from that communication, that my services will be offer'd for the Senate, unless upon the information of my friends it shall appear probable they will be rejected. I gave you there a detail of circumstances relative to that business, & can only now add that as far as I know it will equally suit their present situation; unless indeed the activity of some gentn. professedly candidates for that station shod. have occasion'd a change: one additional competitor only excepted, Colo. [*Henry*] Lee. You will observe that I only give you what I hear for I know nothing of myself. It is propos'd by some to continue the present Gentn. [*Walker*] ~~for the~~ untill march. I have determin'd [*lined out*] in great measure in case of my election [*lined out*] to abandon my profession. You find ~~I~~ my letters contain [*lined out*] little foreign intelligence; that I engross the whole to myself. I may probably be up at the county court.

P. S. It is also said that Mr. [*Thomas*] Matthews the Speaker will be nominated & the chair has latterly been [*lined out*] a step to other offices.

ALS, Jefferson Papers, DLC. Written from Richmond, Virginia; received 25 October.

Theodore Foster to the Candid and Impartial Public

AFTER I arrived in Providence from New-York, in August last, I was informed that a report had been circulated, "*that in apportioning the sums to be assumed from the several States, the Senators of this State had the offer of having one hundred thousand dollars more of the debt of this State assumed, to be paid by the United States, than was assumed by the funding act, and that they declined the offer.*" The report in itself was so absurd, and so highly improbable, being without the least colour of foundation, that I thought it impossible it could gain credit, and I then took but little notice of it. But I am informed that the same report is now unjustly used to injure my political character, and to answer the purposes of *electioneering* against me; I am therefore in this public manner necessitated to declare, that it is FALSE and ENTIRELY GROUNDLESS.

I know of no circumstance that could give rise to such a report; it is matter of astonishment to me that it has originated from any quarter, and more so that gentlemen who have the strongest reasons to suppose it *false*, should so *ungenerously* countenance and make use of it to my disadvantage. As soon as it became certain that the assumption would take place, my colleague (the Hon. General Stanton) and myself, did what was in our power to obtain a larger sum to be assumed from this State than the sum of two hundred thousand dollars, mentioned in the funding act. But circumstances were such, at that time, that no greater sum could then be obtained. We were told that justice would hereafter be done to the State, either by a further assumption of the remainder of the State debts that accrued on account of the war (which it is probable will take place, in case the States heretofore opposed to the measure shall consent to and support it) or in the settlement of the accounts of the United States with the individual States.

The assumption of the State debts has much engaged the attention of the public mind. Much has been said, and probably will be said, respecting it; and as various opinions have been entertained on this great national measure, in which the voice of my country called me to act, at a critical period, in an honourable and conspicuous station, and as misrepresentations have been made, I am induced, on the present occasion, further to remark, that the Convention of this State, when they adopted the national Constitution, gave INSTRUCTIONS on this subject to their Senators and Representatives in Congress, in the following emphatic language.

> "The Convention do, in the name and behalf of the people of the State of Rhode-Island and Providence Plantations, ENJOIN it upon their Senators and Representative or Representatives in Congress, who may be elected to represent this State in Congress, *to exert all their influence, and to use all reasonable means*, to obtain a ratification of the following amendments of the said Constitution, in the manner prescribed therein; and in

all laws to be passed by the Congress in the mean time, to conform to the spirit of the said amendments, as far as the Constitution will admit."

AMENDMENT III

"*Congress shall not, directly or indirectly, either by themselves or through the judiciary, interfere with any one of the States in the redemption of paper money already emitted, and now in circulation, or in* LIQUIDATING OR DISCHARGING THE PUBLIC SECURITIES *of any one State: But that each and every State shall have the exclusive right of making such laws and regulations for the before mentioned purposes as they shall think proper.*"

This must be considered as a solemn, public, declared adjudication of the State at that time; and so long as the same general circumstances remained as when the instructions or directions it contains were given, and so long as they appeared to be agreeable to *the general sense* of the State, unaltered by any act or declaration of the Legislature, so long they must be considered as of force, and binding on the public servants of the State in Congress. Any vote therefore given in conformity to these instructions, so far from operating to the prejudice of the person thus called upon to act agreeably thereto, ought to be considered rather as operating in favour of his general political character, and as evidencing a desire to conform to this great republican principle, that *the general sense* of his constituents, *when duly expressed and known, should have its proper weight, and that the voice of the majority should govern*—a principle in republican governments, on which "*the greatest happiness of the greatest number of the people*" more essentially depends, than many of aristocratic or monarchical sentiments are willing to admit. I have had the honour to serve my country in various public capacities—as a member of the General Assembly of this State, during the arduous war with Great-Britain, in its most gloomy and difficult periods—one year as a member of the Upper House of the Legislature, and lately as a Senator of the United States; and I feel thankful to my fellow-citizens for the confidence with which they have so repeatedly honoured me; and thankful to Almighty God for a consciousness of integrity in the whole of my political conduct; and that I have in no instance within my recollection, in any public capacity, swerved from conscientiously acting agreeably to the dictates of my best judgment, in promoting the interest, honour, liberty and happiness of my country, on every occasion—and that I possess a disposition which causes me to be most happy, when most sensible that I am usefully employed in advancing the public good—the good of my country, that serves to make a people happy. I therefore feel a confidence in the candour and justice of my fellow-citizens, and that they will not readily give credit *to groundless and improbable reports*, propagated for the purposes of *electioneering*, to the disadvantage of my private or political reputation, without a due examination into their truth and probability.

With the highest veneration for the general good opinion of the public, I beg leave to subscribe myself their obliged and obedient servant.

[Rhode Island] *Providence Gazette*, 23 October. Foster may have decided to publish this letter, a week before the Rhode Island Assembly was to vote on whether to reelect him to the Senate, in response to an 18 October article in the *Newport Mercury*, advocating an unnamed candidate: "the Affections of the People of this Part of the State are set on a Man *** above all sordid and selfish Motives, who, tho' he has always declined, is not unexperienced in political Business."

Saturday, 23 October 1790

John Adams to John Quincy Adams. ALS, Adams Family Manuscript Trust, MHi. Addressed to Court Street, Boston; franked.

Professional advice; Abigail Adams is recovered from a "Severe ill turn," and they expect to move to Philadelphia the next week; laments lack of John Quincy's company and despairs of ever living with his family all together; the public in every state rejoices at Ames's and Gerry's reelection, but there is some anxiety over a restless party spirit in Boston.

Governor Samuel Huntington to Oliver Ellsworth. FC:dft, Lane Collection, CtY.

Informs Ellsworth of his reelection to the Senate.

William Smith (S.C.) to Edward Rutledge. ALS, Pinckney Family Papers, DLC. Addressed to Charleston, South Carolina.

"My furniture & Servants being shipped to Philada. we are on a Visit to Mr. Izard for a few days, while in transition."

Michael Jenifer Stone to Walter Stone. ALS, Stone Family Papers, DLC. Written from Annapolis, Maryland; addressed to Charles County, Maryland. Portions of this letter concern the Second Federal Election and are printed with Correspondence: Third Session.

Hopes to be home (Charles County, Maryland) in five or six days; fears his nieces, whom Stone had invited to reside with him at Philadelphia during the third session of the FFC, "will not know exactly how to Strike the line in their preparations—Let them be Liberal to Stay—And not too much to go. Go pretty boldly up to the Scheme of going to Phila. but not Compleatly through it—If they should want anything it will be to go there cheaper quicker and better."

Monday, 25 October 1790

Alexander Moultrie to Thomas Fitzsimons

Your Favour of the 9th. Instant, was safely handed to me, a few Days past: the Assembly of Georgia Legislature meet on Monday next, & the Grant[1] will, no doubt, Issue forth in a Week after. after which, I will communicate to you, something *more extensive*, which will take it's Birth I hope at the same time,[2] & in which, you may have some Participation, if you please. I daily expect Accounts, of *Importance*, from [*New*] Orleans: 'tis our Interest to cultivate & improve, a rich, & Substantial Friendship, with the Spaniards. the Choctaws are *firm* to our Interest also. I received a Letter from [*Alexander*] McGillivray a few Weeks past, from St. Mary's [*Georgia*], dated 11th. Septr.—I shall soon have an Interview with him, & a few more of my Friends. as soon as the [*state*] Legislature does our Business, in which, an immunity from Taxation for a few Years will be no bad political Stroke, much more will be then to be done—*Many, many* of our Friends of Georgia the Carolina's, & *Franklin* [*Tennessee*] & *Kentucky*, are waiting in Swarms to decamp & join our Advanced Settlers: in Bahamas I have now above two Hundred Families waiting; & I am looking out for Proper Persons to send to the French [*West Indies*] Islands. in Ireland I have secured the Means to do much. Organization on Principles of Jurisprudence & Justice must be carefully attended to. Population & System are the two Cardinal Objects.

*** I hope soon to *unfold*, many things to you. I hope America will keep clear of War; a little Spanish Plata [*money*], with Yazoo Lands, will do very well together. in the Mercantile Line, several are booking Ships, to an Affrican, & Fur & Peltry Trade.

***

ALS, Miscellaneous Manuscripts, NN. Written from Charleston, South Carolina. Place to which addressed not indicated.

---

[1] To the South Carolina Yazoo Company, of which Moultrie was one of the four initial investors.

[2] Probably a reference to the secret Combined Society, organized in the summer of 1790, by Yazoo investors among others, to lobby Georgia for unclaimed bounty lands reserved for veterans within an eight million acre tract between the Oconee and Chattahoochee rivers. The society's articles of association were "exposed" in the press and made the subject of official state enquiry and censure, although its full membership roster was never revealed before its demise sometime shortly thereafter (Lamplugh, pp. 74–75).

OTHER DOCUMENTS

Abigail Adams to Mary Cranch. ALS, Abigail Adams Letters, MWA. Addressed to Braintree, Massachusetts. For the full text, see *Abigail Adams*, pp. 63–64.

Details her illness, treatment, and restoration of health; "but I have a journey before me which appears like a mountain & three Ferries to cross. very fortunate for me the winds have kept back the vessel from returning from Philadelphia" that was to have taken "our furniture" on 20 October; acknowledges the two casks delivered to Charles Adams at Laurance's office; John Brisler would like his money sent with Ames when the latter comes to Philadelphia.

TUESDAY, 26 OCTOBER 1790

Ralph Izard to Tench Coxe

I have received your favour of 23d., & find that you have taken Mrs. Harper's House for me. The situation is not such as I could have wished, but I am as much obliged to you for the trouble you have taken as if it was. It may possibly happen that you may be able, before my arrival in Philadelphia, to exchange with somebody who has a situation more agreeable to me, upon my paying a valuable consideration. This I should be glad to do, but I fear there is no probability of it. About the middle of next Month I expect to send my furniture from hence, & shall take the liberty you have given me of addressing it to your care. As Mrs. Harper is to build a Coach House, & Stables, I hope it will not be inconvenient to her to have the first large enough to hold my Coach, Post Chaise, & one horse Chair; & there should be a door to communicate between the yard, & the Stable.

ALS, Coxe Papers, PHi. Addressed to Philadelphia; postmarked New York, 27 October.

OTHER DOCUMENTS

Royal Flint to John Chaloner. ALS, Chaloner and White Papers, PHi. Addressed to Philadelphia; carried by John Fenno.

Introduces Fenno, who intends to publish *GUS* at Philadelphia, and asks Chaloner to assist Fenno; "He is a worthy, honest man."

Alexander Hamilton to John Langdon. ALS, Langdon Papers, NhPoS. Written from Philadelphia; marked "Private."

Office seeking: a day or two before leaving New York, received Langdon's letter recommending Keith Spence for New Hampshire's commissioner of loans and intimating that Langdon's brother, Woodbury, would not accept the post; the President has however chosen to nominate Woodbury Langdon and Hamilton, who had recommended him to the President, will forward a letter from the President to Woodbury notifying him of this nomination; understands Spence is insolvent, a condition weighing against his appointment.

GA, 1 November.

Paterson unanimously elected governor of New Jersey.

WEDNESDAY, 27 OCTOBER 1790

William Constable to Thomas Fitzsimons. FC:lbk, Constable-Pierrepont Collection, NN. Under the Impost Act, duties "secured to be paid" on imported wines subsequently exported within one year qualified for a "drawback" or rebate of all but one percent (*DHFFC* 5:942).

Offers Fitzsimons a share in purchasing a recent shipment of Madeira wine and directs its being re-casked for resale abroad; "tho' all will be entitled to the Drawback, yet unless the Proprietors have an understanding with the Collector the duty will fall due long before the [*qualifying*] Certificate can be returned, & as they must be started into other Casks they will not be strictly according to Law—be so good as to have this well understood."

Thomas Jefferson to George Washington. ALS, Miscellaneous Letters, Miscellaneous Correspondence, State Department Records, Record Group 59, DNA. Written from Monticello, Albemarle County, Virginia. For the full text, see *PTJ* 17:643–45.

Is delaying his return to Philadelphia so that he can travel with Madison who cannot leave for some days; he and Madison have urged some members of the state House of Delegates to support Virginia's building ten houses each year for ten years in the Federal City; candidates for U.S. Senator from Virginia are Thomas Mathews, Benjamin Harrison, Henry Lee, and Walker, but many think Monroe will be "impressed into the service" and he has agreed to serve if elected.

George Thatcher to Philip Theobald. FC, Thatcher Family Papers, MHi. Written from Biddeford, Maine; sent to Pownalborough, Maine. A paragraph relating to the Second Federal Election is printed with Correspondence: Third Session.

Acknowledges letters of 24 August (forwarded from New York, to which it was addressed) and of 8 October, which arrived "this morning"; will set out for Philadelphia in about twelve days and will investigate the status of money privately owed to Theobald.

THURSDAY, 28 OCTOBER 1790

Characteristic Sketch of a New Yorker and a Philadelphian

NO sooner is the dusk of the evening come on than a Philadelphian bars up his door and shuts out all the world for the remainder of that night, unless requested to open it by particular desire.

In New-York, on the contrary, the street door stands most hospitably open till nine or ten o'clock—if shut, you may conclude some of the family are sick, dead, or dying.

If in passing through a street in Philadelphia, you see any person at his door with whom you have a moderate acquaintance, you may talk with him an hour on his own steps before he will ask you to walk in and sit down.

In New-York, the inhabitant upon ever such slight business or conversation with you, commonly asks you into his parlour or back room.

A Philadelphian cannot endure any kind of bench or conveniency for sociably sitting down at his front door—A New-Yorker, on the other hand, would part with every thing rather than his *stoop*—It is here he sits and smokes—here he reflects upon the past, observes what is present, or meditates upon what is to come—Here also he entertains such persons with his morning or afternoon discourse, as do not choose to accept his invitation to walk in.

When a Captain of a vessel arrives at Philadelphia, his owner invites him to dine once or twice at his house while in port, and that always on a Sunday—In New-York a master of a vessel has a general invitation from every one concerned, and is desired to consider himself as one of the family.

In Philadelphia you will have a hundred invitations to breakfast or drink tea where you have one to dine—The reason is this, it is necessary sometimes to pay a compliment, but the inhabitant wishes to do it as cheaply as possible—In New-York, nobody thinks of paying a friendly compliment of this kind at a less expence than a dinner.

Angry party men (of which Philadelphia is full) in that city are rarely or never upon speaking terms. This silly resentment is even communicated to their wives, children and domestics. When a party man is walking the streets of Philadelphia, and sees a noted man of an opposite party coming at a distance on the same side of the way he instantly crosses the street to avoid him—In New-York party men are upon good terms with each other in every respect except politics, and can even walk side and side without growling at each other, provided it be not election time.

If a man steps into a shop in Philadelphia, and happens to loll a little upon a counter, where, strictly speaking, he has no business, ten to one if he does not see himself advertised the next day in one or more of the public papers for a *lounger*—In New-York, upon a very slight acquaintance with the man behind the counter, you may walk in, warm yourself, and even pilfer a few raisins or drink off a glass of gin, in an honest way, without danger of seeing yourself held up to the world as a nuisance.

In Philadelphia, the city tavern or coffee house is the receptacle of dullness and despondency—you will now and then see a melancholly ghost of a politician stalking through it, very much upon the reserve and inclined to converse with no one—In New-York the coffee house is a scene of sociability, intelligence and good humor, from seven in the morning, till ten at night.

A Philadelphian ever more makes his supper upon a dish of tea and a biscuit just after sun-set—the New-Yorker takes care about nine o'clock every night to line his inside with some good beef steak, lobsters, oysters or cold ham.

A Philadelphian is fond of adapting every thing to public conveniency, and what he builds, he builds to endure for ages—the New-Yorker is satisfied if any thing of this sort will last his own time—and as to posterity he leaves it to take care for itself.

The New-Yorker pays a considerable annual tax to convey the filth of his family into one or the other of his large adjacent rivers—the Philadelphian (like the Cat) buries it in the ground, altho' certain it will more or less infect the springs that supply him with drink. By these means, the digested animal and vegetable substances are kept in constant circulation, and as Solomon says, *nothing is lost.*

NYDA, 28 October; reprinted at Salem and Boston, Massachusetts; Newport, Rhode Island; Hartford, Connecticut; New York City (*NYJ*, 8 November); and Philadelphia (*PP*, 1 November).

Other Documents

Ralph Izard to Gabriel Manigault. ALS, Izard Papers, ScU. Addressed to Charleston, South Carolina.

Informed Baron von Steuben of the "unhealthiness" of the Baron's (New York state) land grants; (son) "Harry" leaves for Charleston, South Carolina, in a few days, "attended by his Boy Joe"; hopes Harry will prove a good lawyer, "which will be the surest means of making him respectable, & useful"; asserts "there is no foundation" for the opinion, which was rumored to be circulating in Charleston, that "money lent to the State was not intended by the [*Funding*] Law to be assumed"; has spoken on the subject with Hamilton, who has written to (John) Neufville (commissioner of loans for South Carolina).

Robert Morris to William Temple Franklin. Duplicate, Gouverneur Morris Papers, NNC. Written from Philadelphia. An appended list of enclosed papers indicated that a copy of the Naturalization Act [HR-40] was included.

Instructions for the sale in Europe of land that he has purchased on Oliver Phelps's and Nathaniel Gorham's Genessee tract in New York State.

[Portsmouth] *New Hampshire Spy*, 3 November.

Langdon, Mrs. Elizabeth Langdon, and daughter "Betsy" left in their carriage for the third session of Congress at Philadelphia.

FRIDAY, 29 OCTOBER 1790

Oliver Ellsworth to Governor Samuel Huntington. ALS, Dreer Collection, PHi. Written from Windsor, Connecticut; place to which addressed not indicated.

Accepts reelection as Senator.

John Sitgreaves to John Gray Blount. ALS, John Gray Blount Papers, Nc-Ar. Written from New Bern, North Carolina; addressed to Washington, North Carolina. For the full text, see *Blount* 2:129.

Office seeking: the death of (John) Stokes renders necessary the appointment of a new federal district judge for North Carolina; Sitgreaves will seek the position and believes recommendations from one or two Representatives and a Senator would have due weight; believes Williamson will support him and asks Blount to write Williamson on his behalf.

SATURDAY, 30 OCTOBER 1790

Newspaper Article

The exertions of our citizens to accommodate Congress in a decent and republican manner deserve the highest praise. The county court house is nearly completed for the temporary reception of the Senate and House of Representatives. The hon. Robert Morris, Esq. has politely given up his elegant dwelling house, in Market-street, for the accommodation of the

President of the United States. The sacrifice of this worthy citizen, upon this occasion, is a fresh proof of the disinterested patriotism which has always guided his conduct in public, and the generosity which has equally marked it in private life.

FG, 30 October; reprinted at New York City (*NYDA*, 5 November).

SUNDAY, 31 OCTOBER 1790

Pierce Butler to Thomas Butler

My mind is so greatly afflicted at this time that I am incompetent to write to You as I wish to do; yet I must acknowledge the receipt of Your letter No. 8 which I received by the last Packett. Your Dear and Excellent Mother [*Mary Middleton Butler*] lies at this time dangerously indisposed. Her life hangs by a very slender thread—If it shall be the will of God to take Her hence how severe will be the Stroak to me, to You and to Your Sisters! Great will be Our loss! In Her You had a tender fond Parent—She woud have been to You an Excellent Monitor and Adviser as You grew up—Alas! my Son I fear You are doomed thus early to lose this best of Counsellors! She loved You almost to excess—If the Lord thinks proper to deprive Us of so great a Treasure, We must try to submit to His Sovereign Will; and Study through life to render Ourselves worthy to meet Her in those blessed Mansions where all tears shall be wiped away—Determine then my Dear Child, from this instant, to be virtuous, just and good that as You are thus early ~~in life~~ deprived of the best of Mothers in this life You may fit Yourself for Her Society in that which is to come—May God, Almighty God take You under His holy keeping prays Yr. greatly Afflicted Father.

***

ALS, Butler Papers, Uk. Addressed to Revd. Mr. Butler's, Cheyne Walk, Chelsea near London; postmarked Portsmouth Ship Line; received 13 December; answered 3 January 1791.

Robert Morris to Gouverneur Morris

I have already told you, that, if time permitted, you should have a separate answer to your letter of the thirty-first of July, and if I confine myself merely to the contents of that letter, a very few lines will suffice, because we are agreed in sentiment on every point touched in that letter; so much so, that I could not help telling Colonel Hamilton, who dined with me yesterday, that I had just received a letter from you, offering to my consideration some of the very arguments, which I had used upon the floor of the Senate Chamber, in favor of the public credits.

I reprobated, as you do, the assertion so generally made use of, that America cannot now pay, and for the same reason, viz. that America *has* paid, and I insisted, that the contest *now* is only, whether the *whole* shall reimburse the *few*, who sustain the advance. I urged repeatedly, that the cheapest thing America could do was to pay six per cent, to fund it well, and pay punctually; that being the only means to prevent foreigners from making the enormous profits, which they do make out of our public debt, and insisting that all they make is lost to America. These, and many other arguments, I urged and repeated, until I was almost alone in these sentiments; and finding I could do nothing else, I filled the journals with yeas and nays upon all the questions, that related to this important business.

It is wonderful, you will say, that amongst such a collection of sensible men as compose the Senate, there should not be found a majority in favor of propositions so just and self-evident; but the wonder ceases, when the word *popularity* is suggested. There are but too many, who sacrifice to that deity, and my belief is, that the public credit and creditors have been sacrificed to that idol. But it may be asked, why is such conduct popular? The answer is plain; because the many are to pay the few, and the many do not see in what their real interest consists, consequently those, who wish to please for the moment, indulge their vice and ignorance, so that whilst the multitude shall think it better not to pay, than to pay, the Legislature will be too apt to act in conformity with such opinions.

I have made it a point to urge and encourage the public creditors to subscribe to the new loans, but to come forward at every session with petitions or memorials, until they shall obtain further provision, equal to their just claims, and in the end this will, I expect, be obtained, but not until our country shall have lost greatly from its not having been done at first.

I cannot account for the non-appointment of diplomatic officers, in any other way, than by supposing that the Chief Magistrate is influenced by the general expression of sentiment against such appointments, made in both Houses at the time of debating the bill for establishing intercourse with foreign nations. He is now at Mount Vernon [*Virginia*], and is expected back the latter end of this month, by which time my house will be ready for his reception. I now live in the corner house, next door to my former residence, and refer you to Mr. [*William Temple*] Franklin for all that respects my having given up my house to accommodate the President. I consider this amongst the sacrifices I have made, both of interest and convenience, and I think there is no other man for whom I would have done it. It will have the effect of keeping me at a greater distance from him, although I shall live next door. I have nothing to ask of him for myself. He cannot render me a service, and if I am seen much there it will create envy, jealousy, and malice, and I do not see why I should expose myself to be the object of such passions. I have suffered, most undeservedly, by them too often already.

You, my dear friend, must have discovered in the course of our acquaintance, that I have no real attachment to public life, although, from the share I have had in it, most people suppose otherwise. After my return from New York, I contrived to get clear of the intended contest, by declaring off from being a candidate for the government [*governor*]. Some blame me for it, because they wished to turn out [*Thomas*] Mifflin, and they thought I was the only person that could do it; but perhaps those very men would have served me, as they have served General [*Arthur*] St. Clair, whose name they gave out, promising to support him, but never gave themselves any farther trouble; and, therefore, Mifflin's industry and promises carried him almost unanimously. I feel that I was right, and have such calls on my time, that I am sure it would have been wrong to take any part of it from my private affairs. Nay, I would now resign the Senatorship, if I could do it consistently.

Jared Sparks, *Life of Gouverneur Morris* (3 vols., Boston, 1832), 3:17–19. Written from Philadelphia.

Other Documents

Pierce Butler to Thomas Cobham. FC, Butler Letterbook, ScU. Sent to Greenwich Hospital near London. For the full text, see *Butler Letters*, pp. 74–75.

Little hope exists for Mrs. (Mary Middleton) Butler's recovery; "You who know her worth You who know how dear She is, to me, how happy We lived together can judge of my affliction! Were it not for my Children I should pray to go into the grave with her. How slender Our tie on Earthly bliss!"; explains his financial difficulties and consequent inability to pay his debt to Cobham; "my only Brother was not nearer my breast than Docter Cobham."

Pierce Butler to Edward Rutledge. FC, Butler Letterbook, ScU. Sent to Charleston, South Carolina; carried by Mr. (T. B.?) Ernst. For the full text, see *Butler Letters*, pp. 75–76.

Blames his (Middleton) inlaws for withdrawing their security during his financial problems, "but I am at peace with mankind & I forgive them"; is "sorely afflicted by the painful state the friend of my bosom is in: her sufferings indeed are too great for human nature to bear. I even almost wish her released by death. yet when I call to mind her many virtues, I cling to her; I hold her fast, & can not agree to part with her. The conflict is great. I pray to God to strengthen me to bear it as a Christian ought to do."

James Jackson to Governor Edward Telfair. No copy known; mentioned in Executive Council Journal, G-Ar, as read and filed on 5 November.

October 1790 Undated

Letter from Philadelphia

Before Congress had determined to remove hither, an argument much insisted upon, to the prejudice of Philadelphia was our having no lobsters wherewith to entertain the members of that august body. That objection is now in a great measure taken away. Since the boatmen have found the way to Amboy and the mouth of the Raritan river with their cargoes of lobsters, we can be supplied with that delicious shell fish great part of the year (nearly at as cheap a rate as the people of New-York) by the way of Burlington and Cooper's Ferry,[1] a distance of about seventy miles. If the lobster men would take the pains to bring their lobsters by water to the Egg Harbour forks (which would be a very easy matter with good sailing smacks[2]) the whole distance then, by land, to Philadelphia would not be more than 40 miles, a distance easily travelled in half a day. The demand for lobsters in this city will always be an object worth the serious attention of those who depend for a livelihood upon the marketing this species of fish.

NYDA, 6 October. The places named are all in New Jersey.

[1] The principal and most direct ferry access to Philadelphia from New Jersey; the site of present-day Camden.

[2] A sailing ship used mostly in coasting and fishing.

Other Documents

Pierce Butler to Mr. (T. B.?) Ernst. FC, Butler Letterbook, ScU. Sent to Charleston. For the full text, see *Butler Letters*, pp. 76–77, where the editors have identified the recipient as the T. B. Ernst who appears as one of Butler's correspondents in another letterbook.

Engages Ernst to assist in the settlement of his accounts with anyone in South Carolina and Georgia, including arrears of dues to the South Carolina Agricultural Society and to the Society for the relief of clergies' families; as he will be absent from South Carolina for some time, directs that his name be taken off the membership list of the latter.

Robert Morris to William Constable. Listing of one page ALS, *Parke-Bernet Catalog* 611(1944):item 331.

Roger Sherman to Samuel Hopkins. FC, Sherman Collection, CtY. Written from New Haven, Connecticut; place to which addressed not indicated.
Acknowledges letter of 2 August; continues their discussion of love, self love, and various theological issues.

FG, 29 October.
The Delaware legislature met last week (20–26 October) and unanimously reelected Read to the Senate.

[Providence, Rhode Island] *United States Chronicle*, 4 November.
Last week T. Foster was reelected to the Senate.

Residences of Members

Second Session

The following is a list of known or likely residences. The street addresses are taken from the *New York Directory and Register for the Year 1789* (Evans 22021), and their approximate location is indicated on the map found at *DHFFC* 17:1743. The residences are numbered according to the key used for that map; an asterisk (*) indicates addresses that do not appear there. Some members changed residences at least once during the session; 1 May, for example, was "a day of General moving," noted Maclay, "being the day on which their leases chiefly expire." (*DHFFC* 9:257) Antifederalist members appear in *italics*; state names appear in parentheses.

1. Mary Dobiney's, 15 Wall Street[1]
   Cadwalader (N.J.)
2. Vandine Elsworth's, 19 Maiden Lane[2]
   Hartley (Pa.)
   White (Va.)
4. Philip Mathers's (?), 47 Broad Street[3]
   Thatcher (Mass.)
5. Michael Huck's, 81 Wall Street[4]
   Tucker (S.C.), until at least May
6. Mrs. Van Cortland's, 52 Smith Street[5]
   C. Carroll (Md.)
8. Isaac Polluck's, 37 Broad Street[6]
   Baldwin (Ga.)
   Ellsworth (Conn.), after May
   Gilman (N.H.)
   Sherman (Conn.)
16. Rev. John C. Kunze, 24 Chatham Street[7]
   Maclay (Pa.)
   F. A. Muhlenberg (Pa.)
   Peter Muhlenberg (Pa.)
23. John Marsden Pintard, 12 Wall Street[8]
   Boudinot (N.J.)

27. John Alsop, 38 Smith Street[9]
King (N.Y.)
28. Corner of Thames and Broadway[10]
Gerry (Mass.)
30. William Constable, 39 Great Dock Street[11]
Morris (Pa.)
31. Mr. Anderson, Pearl Street[12]
Clymer (Pa.)
Fitzsimons (Pa.)
* Widow McEuen's, 32 Broad Street[13]
Bland (Va.)
Brown (Va.)
Hiester (Pa.)
Huger (S.C.)
R. H. Lee (Va.)
Madison (Va.)
Page (Va.), after his marriage in March
Paterson (N.J.)
Tucker (S.C.), after at least July
Walker (Va.) (Political affiliation undetermined)
* 14 Wall Street[14]
Laurance (N.Y.)
* Marketfield Street[15]
Ashe (N.C.)
* Mr. Hall, 190 Water Street[16]
Sturges (Conn.)
* Peter Wynkoop (?), Bowery Lane[17]
Wynkoop (Pa.)
* 98 Broadway[18]
Schuyler (N.Y.), until at least May, when his six month lease with T. Ellison expired
* 69 Courtland Street[19]
Williamson (N.C.), through at least April
Seth Harding's, 59 Water Street[20]
Huntington (Conn.)

---

[1] Fitzsimons to Samuel Meredith, 18 March.
[2] New York City *Directory* (1789), and probably still at that address in 1790.
[3] Thatcher to John D. Bourne, 13 April.
[4] Tucker to St. George Tucker, 24 April.
[5] C. Carroll to Mary Caton, 11 July.
[6] Strong to Nathan Dane, 13 March; John Jeffries Diary, 28 July.

[7] Maclay Diary, 4–5 January, *DHFFC* 9:178.

[8] Lewis Pintard to Boudinot, 2 June.

[9] William A. Duer, *New York As It Was* (New York, 1849), p. 9n.

[10] New York City *Directory* (1789), and probably still at that address in 1790.

[11] Morris to Mary Morris, 19 June.

[12] Clymer to Samuel Meredith, calendared in November 1790 Undated, Correspondence: Third Session

[13] Thomas Lee Shippen to William Shippen, 12 April; Page to St. George Tucker, 12 July.

[14] New York City *Directory* (1789).

[15] Thomas Blount to John Gray Blount, 1 June.

[16] William Heron to Washington, 26 July, *PGW* 6:127.

[17] Wynkoop to Reading Beatty, 21 January.

[18] *NYP*, 27 March.

[19] *NYDA*, 7 April.

[20] Benjamin to Anne Huntington, 6 March.

New York City Weather Charts

Archibald McLean published monthly weather charts during the second session of the First Federal Congress. He indicated that the thermometer on which the charts were based "is constantly in the open air, though guarded from the influence both of the sun and wind." On 8 June, *NYDG* stated: "HAVING hitherto published Meteorological Observations *monthly*, at the request of several Subscribers we shall for the future insert them *weekly*."

Meteorological Observations, December

Day of Mon.	Degrees of Heat. by Farenheit's The. A.M. 8	P.M. 2	P.M. 8	Prevailing Winds. A.M. 8	P.M. 2	P.M. 8	Change & Full of Moon.	WEATHER, &c.
1	36	40	35	NW	W	W	Full	Clear—clear—clear
2	32	40	37	W	NW	W		Ditto—ditto—ditto
3	33	43	36	SW	NW	W		Cloudy—clear—clear
4	36	44	40	SW	SW	SW		Clear—cloudy—clear
5	33	37	37	SW	SW	SW		Cloudy—snow—cloudy
6	36	43	40	SW	SW	SW		Cloudy and foggy—clear—clear
7	46	55	53	S	SW	NW		Cloudy—clear—rain and squally
8	38	41	31	W	NW	NW		Clear—clear—clear
9	33	40	35	NW	W	W		Ditto—ditto—ditto
10	38	45	44	S	S	S		Ditto—ditto—ditto
11	40	45	40	NE	NE	NE		Cloudy—rain—rain
12	38	36	28	W	NW	NW		Cloudy—clear—clear
13	24	27	24	NW	NW	NW		Clear—cloudy—clear
14	24	28	17	N	N	NE		Clear—clear—clear
15	29	40	38	N	S	S		Dull—cloudy—cloudy
16	40	46	44	E	S	E	New	Dull—cloudy and windy—rain
17	44	45	43	NE	NE	NE		Dull—dull—dull

18	43	47	40	N	NW	NW		Drizling—dull—clear
19	35	32	37	NW	NW	NW		Clear—clear—clear
20	21	30	29	NW	SW	NW		Ditto—ditto—cloudy
21	30	35	35	NE	NE	NE		Cloudy—cloudy—cloudy
22	33	35	34	N	N	N		Ditto—ditto—clear
23	31	35	35	S	S	S		Cloudy—cloudy—cloudy
24	34	37	35	SW	SW	S		Snow—light snow—cloudy
25	32	36	33	NW	NW	NW		Clear—clear—clear
26	31	37	35	SW	SW	S		Ditto—ditto—cloudy
27	38	41	40	SE	N	N		Rain—rain—rain
28	39	41	40	NE	NE	NE		Ditto—ditto—ditto
29	38	37	34	NE	N	N		Rain—snow—clear
30	34	37	33	W	S	S		Clear—clear—misty
31	40	48	49	SE	SE	S		Dull—rain—rain

NYDG, 4 January.

Meteorological Observations, January

Day of Mon.	Degrees of Heat. by Farenheit's The. A.M. 8	P.M. 2	P.M. 8	Prevailing Winds. A.M. 8	P.M. 2	P.M. 8	Change & Full of Moon.	WEATHER, &c.
1	37	42	35	W	W	W	Full	Clear—clear—clear
2	37	42	38	SW	SW	SW		Ditto—ditto—ditto
3	36	45	41	SW	SW	SW		Ditto—ditto—ditto
4	42	54	44	SW	SW	NW		Clear—clear—cloudy
5	35	30	25	N	NW	NW		Cloudy—clear—clear
6	20	24	27	NW	SW	S		Clear—clear—cloudy
7	35	42	37	SW	SW	W		Cloudy—cloudy—clear
8	34	37	38	SW	S	SW		Cloudy—cloudy—cloudy
9	34	37	34	NW	W	W		Cloudy—clear—clear
10	26	26	24	NW	NW	NW		Clear—clear—clear
11	23	36	24	SW	S	SW		Cloudy—dull—light snow—rain
12	32	33	30	W	W	NW		Clear—clear—clear
13	27	33	36	NE	E	E		Cloudy—dull—rain
14	35	40	37	SW	SW	W		Cloudy—cloudy—clear
15	35	36	33	NE	NE	E	New	Cloudy—snow—clear
16	35	37	38	N	SW	SW		Rain—dull—dull
17	35	38	35	N	SW	SW		Dull—clear—clear

18	31	37	37	N	SE	SE		Clear—clear—cloudy
19	39	41	40	SE	SE	S		Dull—foggy—dull—rain
20	23	25	28	NW	NW	W		Clear—clear—clear
21	21	24	27	NW	W	W		Ditto—ditto—ditto
22	25	37	37	W	W	W		Ditto—ditto—ditto
23	32	36	35	SW	SW	SW		Clear—cloudy—cloudy
24	33	35	33	NE	NE	NE		Dull—sleet—snow
25	25	31	29	NW	NW	NW		Clear—clear—clear
26	26	39	39	N	N	S		Cloudy—dull—dull
27	37	34	31	NW	NW	NW		Sleet—snow—cloudy
28	24	30	30	NW	S	NW		Foggy—dull—clear
29	25	29	28	SW	SW	SW		Clear—clear—clear
30	28	34	28	SW	SW	SW	Full	Clear—cloudy—clear
31	26	34	32	NW	SW	S		Ditto—ditto—ditto

NYDG, 4 February.

Meteorological Observations, February

Day of Mon.	Degrees of Heat. by Farenheit's The. A.M. 8	P.M. 2	P.M. 8	Prevailing Winds. A.M. 8	P.M. 2	P.M. 8	Change & Full of Moon.	WEATHER, &c.
1	33	37	38	NE	NE	SW		Cloudy—cloudy—cloudy
2	32	33	30	NW	N	N		Cloudy—clear—clear
3	17	25	25	NW	NW	N		Clear—clear—clear
4	29	35	34	NE	NE	SW		Rain—cloudy—cloudy
5	27	31	22	W	W	NW		Clear—high wind—clear
6	16	19	19	NW	NW	NW		Clear—clear—clear
7	20	29	32	SSW	SSW	SSW		Cloudy—dull—cloudy
8	33	29	22	NW	NW	NW		Clear—clear—clear
9	15	18	16	NW	NW	NW		Ditto—ditto—ditto
10	9	14	13	NW	NW	W		Ditto—ditto—ditto
11	12	19	18	W	W	NW		Ditto—ditto—ditto
12	13	18	18	NW	NW	NW		Ditto—ditto—ditto
13	12	21	21	NW	SW	SW	New	Ditto—ditto—ditto
14	21	26	26	S	S	W		Snow—dull—cloudy
15	29	38	36	SW	SSW	S		Clear—clear—-rain
16	36	42	38	SW	W	SE		Dull—drizzling—rain
17	35	38	38	SW	SW	S		Dull—drizzling—cloudy
18	36	38	36	NE	NE	N		Dull—cloudy—cloudy
19	36	45	42	NW	NW	SW		Clear—clear—cloudy

20	39	40	36	NE	NE	NE		Cloudy—dull—rain
21	34	36	34	NE	NE	NE		Dull—dull—dull
22	35	36	36	NE	NE	NE		Dull—dull—hazy
23	36	36	36	NE	NE	NE		Hazy—sleet—drizzling
24	36	37	45	NE	NE	NE		Drizzling—dull—clear
25	39	42	37	W	NW	NW		Cloudy—clear—clear
26	34	42	38	W	SW	W		Cloudy—clear—clear
27	37	42	40	W	W	W		Clear—clear—clear
28	34	46	42	SW	SW	NW		Clear—clear—clear

NYDG, 3 March.

Meteorological Observations, March

Day of Mon.	Degrees of Heat. by Farenheit's The. A.M. 8	P.M. 2	P.M. 8	Prevailing Winds. A.M. 8	P.M. 2	P.M. 8	Change & Full of Moon.	WEATHER, &c.
1	29	30	36	NE	E	SE	Full	Clear—cloudy—rain
2	36	42	42	NW	SW	SW		Dull—clear—clear
3	44	36	24	W	NW	NW		Clear—clear—clear
4	17	25	24	NW	NW	NW		Ditto—ditto—ditto
5	23	32	36	W	SW	SE		Ditto—ditto—cloudy
6	41	51	38	SE	SW	SW		Dull and rain—cloudy—clear
7	38	42	37	W	W	SW		Clear—cloudy—cloudy
8	22	27	20	NW	SW	NW		Clear—heavy gale—cloudy
9	6	18	20	NW	NW	NW		Very heavy gale—clear–clear
10	18	20	25	NW	W	SW		Cloudy—cloudy—deep snow
11	32	32	32	N	NE	W		Snow—dull—clear
12	30	36	34	NW	W	SW		Clear—clear—clear
13	34	40	35	S	S	W		Dull—dull—clear
14	36	41	37	SW	SW	SW		Cloudy—rain—clear
15	35	44	41	NW	NW	W	New	Clear—clear—clear
16	35	38	39	E	SE	SE		Cloudy—dull—rain
17	39	55	51	SE	SW	SW		Cloudy—dull—dull
18	44	43	33	NW	N	NW		cloudy—cloudy—clear
19	28	35	39	NW	NW	SE		Clear—clear—clear
20	36	40	38	SE	SE	S		Cloudy—cloudy—clear

21	40	54	46	SW	SW	SW		Dull—clear—clear
22	45	55	42	NE	N	NE		Clear—clear—dull
23	40	45	40	NE	N	E		Dull—cloudy—cloudy
24	39	40	38	NE	NE	E		Dull—drizzling—rain
25	40	51	43	E	S	S		Clear—clear—clear
26	43	43	40	NE	NE	NE		Rain—rain—drizzling
27	41	47	51	NE	NE	SE		Dull—cloudy—clear
28	45	50	46	W	W	SW		Clear—cloudy—clear
29	40	45	41	NE	NE	SE		Ditto—ditto—ditto
30	36	45	40	NW	NW	NW	Full	Clear—clear—clear
31	35	45	40	NW	S	S		Ditto—ditto—ditto

NYDG, 12 April.

Meteorological Observations, April

Day of Mon.	Degrees of Heat. by Farenheit's The. A.M. 8	P.M. 2	P.M. 8	Prevailing Winds. A.M. 8	P.M. 2	P.M. 8	Change & Full of Moon.	WEATHER, &c.
1	40	45	44	S	S	S	Full	Clear—clear—clear
2	45	46	45	SE	SE	SE		Dull—rain—rain
3	48	55	53	NW	NW	W		Clear—clear—clear
4	52	65	60	SW	S	S		Ditto—ditto—ditto
5	54	65	62	NW	NE	S		Ditto—ditto—ditto
6	45	46	43	E	E	N		Rain—rain—rain
7	33	40	37	NW	NW	NW		Clear—clear—clear
8	38	43	41	SW	SW	S		Dull—dull—rain
9	43	55	42	NE	S	S		Clear—clear—clear
10	50	52	52	SE	SE	SE		Clear—cloudy—rain
11	47	51	48	N	N	NW		Cloudy—cloudy—clear
12	46	61	57	NW	NW	NW		Ditto—ditto—ditto
13	43	57	51	NW	SE	SE		Ditto—ditto—ditto
14	44	43	41	NW	SE	SE	New	Ditto—cloudy—rain
15	42	48	40	N	NE	NE		Cloudy—dull—drizzling
16	38	40	42	N	NE	SE		Clear—ditto—ditto
17	39	45	40	N	NE	E		Ditto—cloudy—cloudy
18	34	42	40	NE	NE	E		Snow—rain—heavy gale
19	38	44	40	W	W	NW		Dull—cloudy—clear
20	40	42	38	NE	NE	E		Cloudy—rain—heavy gale—rain
21	44	55	47	W	W	W		Clear—ditto—ditto

22	46	53	50	SW	SW	W		Ditto—cloudy—clear
23	46	56	51	NW	NW	NW		Ditto—ditto—ditto
24	48	49	50	NW	NW	NW		Ditto—cloudy—clear
25	42	45	44	NE	NE	NE		Cloudy—ditto—ditto
26	40	50	48	NW	S	S		Ditto—clear—clear
27	36	40	35	NW	NW	N		Snow—cloudy—rain
28	34	40	40	N	NW	N		Uncommon snow—cloudy—cloudy
29	40	45	43	W	SW	S	Full	Clear—squally—cloudy
30	42	54	50	NW	NW	NW		Clear—clear—clear

NYDG, 3 June.

Meteorological Observations, May

Day of Mon.	Degrees of Heat. by Farenheit's The. A.M. 8	P.M. 2	P.M. 8	Prevailing Winds. A.M. 8	P.M. 2	P.M. 8	Change & Full of Moon.	WEATHER, &c.
1	45	60	55	NW	S	S	Full	Clear—clear—clear
2	49	62	55	SE	SE	S		Clear—clear—cloudy
3	55	68	64	S	S	S		Cloudy—dull—clear
4	58	60	58	NW	NW	SW		Cloudy—cloudy—cloudy
5	52	56	53	E	E	E		Dull—ditto—ditto
6	51	57	51	NE	NE	NE		Dull—cloudy—dull
7	46	56	53	NW	N	S		Clear—clear—clear
8	50	55	55	SE	SE	S		Ditto—ditto—ditto
9	53	57	55	SE	S	S		Cloudy—clear—clear
10	55	68	66	S	SW	SW		Clear—ditto—ditto
11	61	63	60	N	SE	N		Ditto—ditto—ditto
12	58	73	65	S	S	NE		Ditto—ditto—ditto
13	58	65	62	NW	S	NE	New	Cloudy—clear—clear
14	55	66	63	NW	NW	N		Ditto—ditto—ditto
15								
16	53	66	50	NW	S	S		Ditto—ditto—ditto
17	58	60	58	N	SE	SE		Ditto—ditto—ditto
18	56	63	58	NW	S	S		Ditto—ditto—ditto
19	55	63	59	N	SE	SE		Ditto—ditto—cloudy
20	58	58	58	SE	SE	NE		Rain—rain—dull
21	58	65	64	N	N	S		Cloudy—fair—fair
22	58	65	63	NW	NW	NW		Clear—clear—clear
23	62	72	63	NW	NW	NW		Ditto—ditto—ditto

24	62	74	68	S	W	W		Ditto—ditto—ditto
25	59	66	62	NE	SE	SE		Dull—clear—cloudy
26	58	67	64	SE	SE	S		Cloudy—clear—clear—thunder and rain in the night.
27	62	65	60	NE	NE	NE		Dull—rain—dull
28	56	62	57	NE	NE	S	Full	Dull—dull—clear
29	56	60	59	NW	SE	SE		Clear—dull—dull
30	57	63	58	SE	SE	SE		Dull—clear—dull
31	60	70	55	SW	SW	SW		Drizzling—clear—cloudy

NYDG, 4 June.

Meteorological Observations, June

	HEAT			PREV. WINDS			
	a.m	p.m.	p.m.	a.m.	p.m.	p.m.	WEATHER.
	8	2	8	8	2	8	
1	65	68	63	SW	SW	NE	Clear—clear—cloudy
2	62	68	60	NE	S	S	Cloudy—clear—clear
3	60	68	58	SW	S	S	Clear—clear—cloudy
4	60	64	63	SE	SE	S	Misty—cloudy—dull
5	64	75	70	S	S	S	Dull—clear—clear
6	68	75	69	N	S	S	Clear—clear—cloudy
7	70	73	69	S	SE	S	Cloudy—rain—clear
8	69	75	68	SW	W	W	Clear—clear—clear
9	58	68	65	NW	NW	NW	Clear—clear—clear
10	60	61	60	NE	NE	N	Cloudy—rain—clear
11	57	70	66	NW	SW	SW	Clear—clear—cloudy
12	62	60	60	S	SE	SE	Rain—rain—dull—New Moon
13	65	67	68	S	N	SW	Dull—rain—clear
14	65	73	70	SW	SW	SW	Clear—clear—clear
15	69	75	71	N	S	S	Ditto—ditto—ditto
16	70	75	70	S	S	S	Ditto—ditto—ditto
17	70	80	74	S	S	S	Ditto—ditto—ditto
18	71	73	70	NE	SE	E	Clear—cloudy—cloudy
19	68	72	65	NW	NW	NW	Clear—cloudy—clear
20	64	72	68	W	NW	S	Clear—clear—clear
21	65	72	69	NW	S	S	Ditto—ditto—ditto
22	67	76	72	S	W	W	Ditto—ditto—ditto
23	68	72	69	S	NW	N	Dull—a hard shower—clear
24	69	70	69	N	S	S	Clear—cloudy—cloudy

25	69	65	64	SE	SE	SE	Rain—rain—rain—Full Moon
26	69	69	68	SE	SE	SE	Dull—dull—clear
27	68	75	71	SE	SE	S	Cloudy—clear—clear
28	71	75	73	S	SW	S	Cloudy—clear—clear
29	65	71	64	N	W	SW	Clear—cloudy—cloudy
30	68	73	67	W	W	NE	Clear—clear—clear

NYDG, 8, 15, 23, 29 June, 7 July.

Meteorological Observations, July

	HEAT			PREV. WINDS			
	a.m	p.m.	p.m.	a.m.	p.m.	p.m.	WEATHER.
	8	2	8	8	2	8	
1	64	73	68	N	NW	NW	Cloudy—clear—cloudy
2	66	77	74	W	SW	SW	Clear—clear—cloudy
3	69	76	70	SW	W	SW	Clear—cloudy—clear
4	69	76	73	SW	SW	SW	Cloudy—cloudy—clear
5	72	81	76	W	SW	W	Clear—clear—clear
6	75	78	74	SW	SW	SW	Clear—cloudy—clear
7	73	79	75	SW	W	N	Cloudy—cloudy—clear
8	67	74	69	NW	NW	NW	Ditto—ditto—ditto
9	64	76	69	N	S	S	Ditto—ditto—ditto
10	67	72	68	SW	S	S	Ditto—ditto—ditto
11	66	72	69	SW	S	S	Cloudy—cloudy—cloudy
12	69	75	69	SW	S	S	Cloudy—clear—clear—New Moon.
13	68	74	70	NE	SW	E	Dull—clear—clear
14	69	76	71	S	S	S	Fair—fair—fair
15	70	76	72	S	S	S	Hazy—cloudy—cloudy
16	72	78	72	S	S	S	Clear—clear—cloudy
17	71	78	70	NW	NE	NE	Clear—clear—clear
18	70	70	70	NE	SE	SE	Cloudy—dull—rain—Moon first quarter.
19	68	72	69	NE	E	NE	Rain—dull—dull
20	67	72	69	N	SE	S	Cloudy—cloudy—cloudy
21	68	76	74	NW	S	S	Clear—clear—clear
22	72	79	73	W	W	S	Ditto—ditto—ditto
23	75	79	76	SW	S	S	Cloudy—cloudy—clear
24	75	80	76	W	SE	N	Cloudy—clear—rain
25	74	76	71	NW	NW	NW	Clear—clear—clear—Moon full
26	66	76	72	NW	NW	S	Ditto—ditto—ditto
27	71	76	74	S	S	SE	Cloudy—clear—cloudy

28	75	77	73	NW	NW	W	Cloudy—clear—clear
29	68	75	73	NW	S	S	Clear—clear—clear
30	70	76	74	SW	S	S	Ditto—ditto—ditto
31	72	80	74	S	SW	S	Ditto—ditto—ditto

NYDG, 7, 13, 21, 28 July, 5 August.

Meteorological Observations, August

	HEAT			PREV. WINDS			
	a.m	p.m.	p.m.	a.m.	p.m.	p.m.	WEATHER.
	8	2	8	8	2	8	
1	68	74	68	N	NE	SE	Dull—clear—clear
2	67	74	70	N	SE	E	Cloudy—cloudy–cloudy—Moon last quarter
3	69	69	67	NE	NE	E	Dull—dull—cloudy
4	67	75	72	SE	S	S	Dull—clear—clear
5	72	80	77	SW	S	S	Cloudy—clear—clear
6	75	82	77	S	S	SE	Clear—clear—dull
7	75	77	75	N	SE	SE	Cloudy—dull—rain
8	73	76	74	NE	S	E	Clear—a shower—clear
9	72	74	72	E	S	E	Rain—rain—rain
10	74	79	75	SW	SW	NW	Dull—clear—clear—New Moon
11	72	76	74	NE	SE	S	Dull—cloudy—clear
12	75	81	78	S	S	S	Cloudy—clear—clear
13	76	84	82	W	SW	S	Clear—clear—clear
14	78	85	79	SW	SW	SW	Ditto—a shower—clear

NYDG, 11, 18 August.

BIOGRAPHICAL GAZETTEER

The following biographical sketches are intended to provide certain kinds of information about individuals who appear in the three second session volumes of the correspondence series either as letter writers, recipients, or persons mentioned more than once in the text. (Those mentioned only once are identified in a footnote where they appear.) The information includes, when available: life dates; residence and occupation during the First Congress; prior significant political, military, economic, or social positions, including family ties to members of Congress and to each other; role in the first federal election; and any formal involvement with the First Congress, primarily as appointees or nominees to federal office, or petitioners. Information for the period after March 1791 is provided only if it directly relates to the First Congress or its members, such as the results of the second federal election. Military records include regimental assignments in the Continental Army as well as membership in the Society of the Cincinnati, in the belief that such affiliations may have contributed to mutual ties that affected correspondents' interactions with each other.

More extensive biographical data available in other volumes of the *DHFFC* is omitted and cross references are provided to those sources. Significant information deemed unreliable or inadequate subsequent to the publication of volume two of the *DHFFC* has been corrected here. Basic information drawn from the *Biographical Directory of the United States Congress*, the *Dictionary of American Biography*, the *Dictionary of National Biography*, or other standard encyclopedia sources is not cited. Lengthy sketches of all members of the First Congress can be found in *DHFFC* 14:487–932.

Most of the information made available here, drawn from sometimes very obscure sources, was brought to light through the notable efforts of Douglas E. Clanin, currently director of the Indiana Historical Society. Over the course of several years in the 1970s, Mr. Clanin exhaustively researched and compiled a biographical file for use in editing *The Documentary History of the First Federal Elections* and *The Documentary History of the Ratification of the Constitution*. These files have been very ably maintained and generously shared by the editors of the latter project. We heartily acknowledge the heavy debt owed to them and particularly to Mr. Clanin for his unique contribution to research.

ABEEL, JAMES (1733–1825), a native of Albany, was a New York City merchant by the outbreak of the Revolutionary War, during which he served as major in the state militia in 1776 and as deputy quartermaster general of the Continental Army, with the rank of lieutenant colonel, from 1777 until at least 1780. (*PNG* 2:314n)

ADAMS, ABIGAIL SMITH (1744–1818), of Braintree (now part of Quincy), Massachusetts, married John Adams in 1764. They took up residence at "Richmond Hill," in present-day Greenwich Village north of New York City, in the summer of 1789, residing there with their sons Charles and Thomas and Abigail's niece Louisa Smith (1773?–1857) during the first and second sessions of Congress. See also *DHFFC* 9:136n.

ADAMS, CHARLES (1770–1800), the second son of Abigail and John Adams, resided with his parents at "Richmond Hill" while studying law under John Laurance. See also *DHFFC* 17:1752. (*Adams* 3:54n, 234n, 4:191; *PAH* 5:363–64n)

ADAMS, JOHN (1735–1826), of Braintree (part of present-day Quincy), Massachusetts, was sworn in as Vice President of the United States on 21 April 1789. He championed and signed the Declaration of Independence while a member of Congress, 1774–77, and served in various diplomatic missions to France, The Netherlands, and Great Britain almost continuously thereafter until 1788. See also *DHFFC* 9:4n, 17:1752.

ADAMS, JOHN QUINCY (1767–1848), eldest son of John and Abigail Adams, practiced law in Boston after his admission to the bar in July 1790. See also *DHFFC* 17:1752–53.

ADAMS, SAMUEL (1722–1803), of Boston, an unsuccessful Antifederalist opponent of Fisher Ames in the first federal election, served as lieutenant governor of Massachusetts, 1789–93. See also *DHFFC* 17:1753. (*DHROC* 4:432)

ADAMS, THOMAS BOLYSTON (1772–1832), the youngest son of Abigail and John Adams, graduated from Harvard in 1790 and joined his parents at "Richmond Hill," outside New York City, during the second session. In late 1790 he followed them to Philadelphia where he began his legal studies.

ADGATE, MATTHEW (1737–1818), was a farmer and mill owner in Canaan, New York, where he became an early leader of the local revolutionary movement and later a legislator in the provincial congresses (1775–77) and state

Assembly (1780–85, 1788–89, and 1791). He voted against ratification of the Constitution as a delegate for Columbia County at the state convention, and ran unsuccessfully against Peter Silvester in the first federal election. (*DHFFE* 3:557)

ADLUM, JOHN (1759–1836), following a brief military career during the Revolutionary War, settled in Sunbury, Pennsylvania, in 1784 and met William Maclay, upon whose recommendation he served as a state surveyor (1787–90). Although an expert on the Six Nations, he failed to secure appointment as agent for Indian Affairs in the Northern Department in 1791. See also *DHFFC* 9:172n.

AERTSEN, GUILLIAM (1759–1806), a native of Philadelphia, served as a clerk in the treasury department's office of accounts from 1782 until his appointment as commissioner for settling accounts between South Carolina and the United States, 1784–89. (*PRM* 5:422n, 8:299n)

AITKEN, ROBERT (1734–1802), a native of Scotland, emigrated in 1771 to Philadelphia where he became a bookseller, stationer, and publisher of the *Pennsylvania Magazine, or American Monthly Museum* (1775–76). In 1782 he successfully sought Congress's official sanction for undertaking to print the first complete English Bible produced in America the year before. (*PGW* 5:495; *PBF* 21:517n)

ALBERTSON, ELIAS (b. 1763), of Pasquotank County, North Carolina, was appointed surveyor at Newbiggen Creek in 1790.

ALDEN, ROGER (1754–1836), served as chief clerk of the domestic division of the state department from 1789 until his resignation in July 1790. The Revolutionary War veteran and Society of the Cincinnati member studied law under William Samuel Johnson, whose daughter Gloriana Ann (1751–85) he married in 1783. In January 1790 Alden successfully petitioned Congress for expenses as keeper of the records of the Continental and Confederation Congresses. See also *DHFFC* 8:132–34, 9:264–65n, 17:1753.

ALLAIRE, PETER (1740–1820), was a New York City merchant secretly employed by the British Foreign Office, whose "Occurences" (reports) were enclosed in letters to Sir George Yonge. His role as secret agent was unknown even to the British foreign service in North America. See also *DHFFC* 17:1753–54.

ALLEN, JOHN (1763–1812), a native of Great Barrington, Massachusetts, studied law in Litchfield, Connecticut, where he practiced beginning in 1786.

ALLEN, JOSEPH (1749–1827), a Boston born 1774 graduate of Harvard and nephew of Samuel Adams, settled as a businessman in Worcester, Massachusetts, in 1776. In 1780 he participated in the Massachusetts State Constitutional Convention and was appointed Clerk of the Courts.

ALLEN, PAUL (ca. 1741–1800), was a sea captain in Providence, Rhode Island, which he represented in the state Assembly in 1778 and 1783–86. During the Revolutionary War his ships supplied military stores to the state. Despite the support of several prominent local figures, he failed in his bid for appointment as Providence's naval officer in 1790 and excise officer in 1791. (*PGW* 5:532n)

ALSOP, JOHN (1724–94), was a wealthy New York City merchant whose active participation in the revolutionary movement dated to the Stamp Act crisis of 1765. He was a member of the First and Second Continental Congress, but resigned from the latter in July 1776 out of opposition to Independence. Suspected of Loyalism, he retired to Middletown, Connecticut, for the remainder of the war but resumed his mercantile and philanthropic ventures in New York upon his return in 1784. A widower from 1772, Alsop had one child, Mary , who married Rufus King in March 1786. (John A. Stevens, Jr., ed., *Colonial Records of the New York Chamber of Commerce, 1768–1784* [New York, 1867], pp. 119–21)

AMBLER, JACQUELIN (1742–98), a merchant of Yorktown, Virginia, served on the Council of State, 1780–82, and as state treasurer thereafter until his death. (*PJM* 3:337n)

ANDERSON, JAMES (1739–1808), a Scottish lawyer, economist, scientist, and essayist, edited *The Bee*, a literary and scientific journal published in Edinburgh (1790–94).

ANDERSON, JOSEPH (1757–1837), served as federal judge for the Southern Territory, 1791–97. Although a native of Pennsylvania, he joined the Third New Jersey Regiment of the Continental Army at the outbreak of the Revolutionary War, rising from ensign to captain before transferring to the 1st Regiment in 1781. He retired as a brevet major at war's end, when he joined the Society of the Cincinnati. He remained in New Jersey to study law and was admitted to the Delaware bar in 1785. See also *DHFFC* 2:489, 7:578–79. (*PGW* 5:511n)

ANDREANI, COUNT PAOLO (1763–1823), of Milan, Italy, used his aristocratic family's connections to gain access to books forbidden by the Catholic Church and advance his scientific studies in the fields of mineralogy, geography, and meteorology. Having achieved some renown in 1784 for the first hot air balloon ascent to be performed outside France, he traveled extensively throughout Europe and the Mediterranean before touring North America from May 1790 to June 1792. (Cesare Marino and Karim M. Tiro, eds., *Along the Hudson and Mohawk: The 1790 Journey of Count Paolo Andreani* [Philadelphia, 2006])

ANDREWS, ELIZUR (1747–1829), of Southington, Connecticut, was a partner in a mercantile firm with Levi Hart.

ANDREWS, LORING (1769–1805), formerly co-editor of Boston's semiweekly *Herald of Freedom* (1788–89), published the *Western Star* at Stockbridge, Massachusetts, from 1 December 1789. (*Boston Printers*, p. 19)

ANDREWS, ROBERT (1744–1804), was, from 1779, professor of moral philosophy and mathematics at the College of William and Mary in Williamsburg, Virginia, representing that town in the state House of Delegates, 1790–99, and the surrounding James City County at the ratification convention in 1788, where he voted in favor of the Constitution. The Maryland native graduated from the College of Pennsylvania in 1766 and served as tutor to the children of John Page at "Rosewell," Virginia, until going to England in 1772 for ordination as an Anglican clergyman. Returning to Virginia, he served as chaplain of the state's 2nd Continental Regiment, 1776–79, before accepting his appointment at William and Mary. (*PJM* 3:312–13n; *DHROC* 8:516n)

ANDROSS (ANDROS), STEPHEN, served as selectman of Waldoboro, Maine, in 1780 and 1791.

ANSPACH, PETER, of New York City, served as attorney on behalf of Timothy Pickering when the former quartermaster general petitioned the First Congress for the settlement of his public accounts. Anspach had served as paymaster of the quartermaster's department from as early as 1778 until 1784. See also *DHFFC* 7:488.

ANTHONY, JOSEPH, SR. (1738–98), a native of Newport, Rhode Island, settled in Philadelphia in 1782 and became a merchant. His son, Joseph Jr. (1762–1814), married the daughter of United States Treasurer Michael Hillegas. (*PMHB* 53[1929]: 208–9)

APPLETON, NATHANIEL (1731–98), a Boston merchant, served as commissioner of loans for Massachusetts from 1775 until his death. See also *DHFFC* 2:500.

ARCHER, ABRAHAM, was appointed collector at York, Virginia, in 1789, having served as collector and naval officer there under the state, 1781–87. He became mayor in 1790. See also *DHFFC* 2:547.

ARMSTRONG, JOHN, JR. (1758–1843), defeated by William Maclay in the first federal election, settled in New York City upon his marriage to Alida Livingston (1761–1822), the younger sister of Chancellor Robert R. Livingston, in January 1789. See also *DHFFC* 9:180n.

ARNETT, SILAS W. (d. 1806), of New Bern, North Carolina, abandoned a career as a printer to take up the practice of law in about 1783. He voted in favor of the Constitution at the second ratifying convention in 1789. (*PGW* 5:357n)

ARNOLD, BENEDICT (1741–1801), was a Connecticut merchant and sea captain before joining the Continental Army in 1775, rising to the rank of major general and contributing significantly to the American success at Saratoga in 1777. After conspiring to surrender West Point to the British in 1780, the arch-traitor served as brigadier general in the British army until settling in England 1781, where he remained except for a period spent as a merchant in New Brunswick, Canada, 1785–91.

ARNOLD, PELEG (1752–1820), a lawyer of Smithfield, Rhode Island, served in the state House of Deputies, 1777–78 and 1782–83, in Congress, 1787–88, and in the state's upper chamber, or Council of Assistants, 1791–95. (*DHFFE* 4:431n)

ARNOLD, WELCOME (1745–98), was a wealthy merchant and distiller of Providence, Rhode Island, which he represented in the state House of Deputies almost continuously from 1778 until 1795, including five terms as speaker. An active Federalist, he voted to ratify the Constitution at the state convention in May 1790. See also *DHFFC* 17:1755.

ASHE, ELIZA MONTFORT (1762–ca. 1812), of Halifax County, North Carolina, married John Baptista Ashe in 1779 and resided with him in New York City during the First Congress.

ASHE, SAMUEL, JR. (1763–ca. 1831), of New Hanover County, North Carolina, was the younger brother of John Baptista Ashe. Joining the Continental Army at the earliest possible age, he rose from ensign of the 1st North Carolina Regiment in 1779 to lieutenant of the 3rd Regiment by war's end.

ATKINS, SARAH KENT (d. 1810), of Newburyport, Massachusetts, lived in poverty after the death of her husband Dudley Atkins in 1767. Among her six children were Mary Searle, Dudley Atkins Tyng, and her spinster daughter Rebecca (1767–1842), with whom she lived. (*JQA*, p. 35n)

ATLEE, ESTER SAYRE (1747–5 July 1790), of Lancaster, Pennsylvania, in 1763 married William Augustus Atlee (ca. 1735–1793), associate justice of the state supreme court from 1777 until his death. See also *DHFFC* 17:1755.

AUSTIN, BENJAMIN, JR. (1752–1820), was a Boston merchant and early activist in the revolutionary movement who became an Antifederalist publicist while serving in the state Senate in 1787–88 and 1789–97. (*DHROC* 4:433n)

AUSTIN, DAVID, JR. (1759–1831), was Presbyterian minister at Elizabeth, New Jersey, 1788–97. Brother-in-law to Roger Sherman's son John, the 1779 Yale graduate married Lydia Lathrop (d. 1818), daughter of Joshua Lathrop, in 1783. (*Yale Graduates* 4:91–97)

AUSTIN, DAVID, SR. (1732–1801), father-in-law of Roger Sherman's son John, was a merchant of New Haven, Connecticut, where he served as alderman in the 1780s. (*PGW* 3:264n; *Sherman's Connecticut*, p. 319)

AUSTIN, MOSES (1761–1821), a native of Connecticut, was a Philadelphia dry goods merchant by 1783. The next year he moved to Richmond and in 1789 he and his brother Stephen rented the Chiswell lead mines in southeastern Virginia, where he resided as its manager beginning in 1791. (*WMQ*, 2nd series, 2[1922]:199–200)

AUSTIN, STEPHEN (1747–1840), moved from Connecticut to Philadelphia before settling in Virginia, where he operated mines with his younger brother Moses by 1790. (*WMQ* 2nd series, 2[1922]:199–200)

AVERY, JAMES (1759–99), served as state naval officer and then excise officer at Machias, Maine.

AVERY, JOHN, JR. (1739–1806), a merchant and distiller of Boston, served as Massachusetts secretary of state, 1780–1806. See also *DHFFC* 17:1756.

BACON, JOHN (1738–1820), a native of Connecticut and 1765 graduate of the College of New Jersey (Princeton), was a Congregational minister at Boston's Old South Church from 1771 until his dismissal in 1775 for doctrinal differences. He settled as a farmer in Stockbridge, Massachusetts, which he represented in the state legislature intermittently over the next forty years. In 1787 Sedgwick succeeded him in the House and successfully challenged him in the widely publicized election for the town's delegate to the state ratification convention in 1788. Bacon succeeded Sedgwick in turn and served as state representative during the First Congress, and as county judge, 1789–1811. (*DHROC* 5:1034; *Princetonians, 1748–1768*, pp. 479–82)

BACON, WILLIAM (ca. 1740–1819), was a farmer of Sheffield, Massachusetts, which he represented in the state House of Representatives in 1777. (*Massachusetts Legislators*, p. 154)

BAGLEY, ABNER (1766–1851), was a weigher or gauger in Portland, Maine.

BAILEY, THEODORUS (1758–1828), opened a law practice in Poughkeepsie, New York, upon his admission to the bar in 1778. Although he held a commission in the state militia during the Revolutionary War, he had never held political office when he ran unsuccessfully as an Antifederalist against Egbert Benson in the first federal election. (*DHFFE* 3:557)

BAIRD, JOHN (ca. 1740–1800), represented Westmoreland County in the 1790–91 Pennsylvania House of Representatives after having served on the state's Supreme Executive Council and as an Antifederalist leader in the ratification convention. (*PMHB* 10:449–50; *DHROC* 2:241n, 639)

BAKER, JOHN, was appointed federal surveyor at Bennits Creek, Chowan County, North Carolina, in 1790. During the Revolutionary War he rose from lieutenant in the 7th North Carolina Regiment in 1776 to captain in 1778, when he accepted a colonel's commission in the state militia. He was a member of the state Assembly in 1787 and a delegate to the state's second ratification convention in 1789, where he voted in favor of the Constitution. See also *DHFFC* 2:526.

BALDWIN, DUDLEY (1753–94), older brother of Ruth and Abraham Baldwin, was a lawyer and farmer in Greenfield, Connecticut.

BALDWIN, ISAAC, JR. (1753–1830), represented Litchfield, Connecticut, in the state House of Representatives in 1783 and 1784.

BALDWIN, SIMEON (1761–1851), a lawyer of New Haven, Connecticut, married Roger Sherman's daughter Rebecca in 1787. See also *DHFFC* 17:1756.

BANGS, EDWARD (1756–1818), a Harvard graduate of 1777, studied law in Newburyport, Massachusetts, under Theophilus Parsons with his former classmate Rufus King and commenced the practice of law in Worcester in 1780. He served briefly as a soldier in 1775 and again in the forces raised by the state to suppress Shays' Rebellion in 1786–87. (D. Hamilton Hurd, ed., *History of Worcester County, Massachusetts* [2 vols., Philadelphia, 1889], 1:xxvi)

BARBÉ-MARBOIS, PIERRE FRANÇOIS, succeeded his older brother the marquis de Barbé-Marbois as French consul in Philadelphia in 1785 upon the latter's reassignment as intendant at St. Domingue (Haiti).

BARCLAY, THOMAS (1728–93), a Philadelphia merchant, performed diplomatic services for the United States between 1781 and 1787, some of which were the basis for his First Congress petition for compensation and the resulting unsuccessful Barclay Bill. The presence of his name on the Adamses' dinner list for 30 June indicates he was in New York City when the House began debating his petition on 1 July. See also *DHFFC* 8:119, 9:93n.

BARD, SAMUEL (1742–1821), professor of medicine at King's College (Columbia), commenced a medical practice in New York City with his father John (1716–99) in 1767. See also *DHFFC* 9:470n.

BARKER, JEREMIAH (1752–1835), a native of Cape Cod, served briefly on a privateer during the Revolutionary War before opening a medical practice in Gorham, Maine, in 1779. In 1790 he relocated his thriving practice to nearby Falmouth.

BARLOW, JOEL (1754–1812), European agent for the Scioto Land Company in 1788–92, was a close friend of Abraham Baldwin, whose sister Ruth he married in 1781. See also *DHFFC* 17:1757.

BARLOW, RUTH BALDWIN (1756–1818), of New Haven, Connecticut, was the younger sister of Abraham and Dudley Baldwin and wife of Joel Barlow. (*Yale Graduates* 4:4, 7)

BARNARD, JOSEPH (1748–1817), a native of Watertown, Massachusetts, was postmaster of Kennebunk and neighboring York, Maine, in 1789. (George Folsom, *History of Saco and Biddeford* [Saco, Me., 1830], p. 310)

BARNARD, THOMAS, was master of the packet that sailed between Boston and New York, the schooner *New York*, in 1790.

BARNEY, JOSHUA (1759–1818), a failed Baltimore merchant who had served as a Continental Navy captain, 1776–84, was appointed clerk of Maryland's federal courts in March 1790. See also *DHFFC* 7:458–60.

BARRELL, JOSEPH (1739–1804), brother of Nathaniel, Sr., and brother-in-law of John Langdon, was a prominent Federalist merchant and shipowner of Boston, involved in the Pacific northwest fur trade. See also *DHFFC* 17:1758.

BARRELL, NATHANIEL, SR. (1732–1831), brother of Joseph and brother-in-law of John Langdon, was an Antifederalist farmer of York, Maine. In 1758 he married Sally Sayward (d. 1805), only daughter of Jonathan Sayward; their daughter Olive married Samuel Emerson in 1791. See also *DHFFC* 17:1758–59.

BARRELL, NATHANIEL, JR. (d. 1792), nephew of John Langdon and Joseph Barrell, was a native of Portsmouth, New Hampshire, who had settled as a merchant in Martinique and Guadeloupe, West Indies, by 1790.

BARRELL, SARAH WEBB (1752–1832), sister of Samuel B. Webb, was the wife of Joseph Barrell (1739–1804) of Boston, a prominent Federalist merchant and brother-in-law of John Langdon. See also *DHFFC* 17:1758.

BARRETT, NATHANIEL (1743–93), a Boston merchant, was appointed consul to Rouen, France, in 1790. See also *DHFFC* 17:1759.

BARRY, JOHN (1745–1803), who emigrated from Ireland to Philadelphia about 1760, led an illustrious Continental Navy career before serving as a ship's captain in the China trade. An ardent Federalist with commercial ties to Robert Morris, he joined six other former navy and marine captains in an ultimately unsuccessful First Congress petition for compensation in 1790. See also *DHFFC* 7:438–39, 9:72n.

BARTLETT, BENJAMIN, of Suffolk, Virginia, served as a militia captain during the Revolutionary War.

BARTLETT, JOSIAH (1729–95), a physician of Kingston, New Hampshire, served as president (governor) of that state from 8 June 1790 to 1794. A longtime local, provincial, and state officeholder virtually from the time he moved to New Hampshire from his native Massachusetts in 1750, Bartlett went on to serve in Congress in 1775–76, when he signed the Declaration of Independence, and again in 1778 before accepting appointment as justice of the state superior court, 1782–90 (chief justice from 1788). He voted to ratify the Constitution at the state convention in 1788, but declined his election as a Senator later that year. (*PJB*, pp. xxxi–xxxvii; *DHFFE* 1:853)

BARTON, WILLIAM (1748–1831), a hatter by trade, represented Providence, Rhode Island, at the state ratification convention, where he voted in favor of the Constitution, and was subsequently appointed federal surveyor of that port in June 1790. See also *DHFFC* 17:1759.

BARTON, WILLIAM (1754–1817), a Philadelphia lawyer, unsuccessfully sought appointment as assistant secretary of the treasury and then as chief clerk of the State Department in 1790. See also *DHFFC* 17:1759.

BARTRAM, WILLIAM (1739–1823), was a prominent Quaker naturalist of Philadelphia, whose *Travels* (Philadelphia, 1791) related his botanical, zoological, and ethnological discoveries in the 1770s through the American southeast (present-day Carolinas, Georgia, Florida, and Alabama).

BASS, HENRY (1740–1813), was a merchant in his native Boston, where he was active in the revolutionary movement, most notably as a participant in the Boston Tea Party (1773). A brother-in-law of George Thatcher, he petitioned the First Congress unsuccessfully to reissue evidence of continental debt certificates accidentally lost. See also *DHFFC* 8:255.

BAUMAN, SEBASTIAN (d. 1803), a native of Germany, was a New York City grocer whose illustrious wartime career contributed to his appointment as the city's postmaster in late 1789. See also *DHFFC* 17:1759.

BAYARD, JOHN (1738–1807), a brother-in-law of William Paterson, abandoned his successful mercantile career in Philadelphia in 1788 and settled in New Brunswick, New Jersey, where he was serving as mayor in 1790. See also *DHFFC* 17:1759–60.

BAYLEY, JACOB (1728–1815), of Newbury, Vermont, was a local civic leader who served as a brigadier general in the New Hampshire militia and a

Continental deputy quartermaster general during the Revolutionary War. (*PGW: Revolution* 1:239n)

BAYLOR, JOHN (1752–1808), of New Market, Virginia, was executor for the estate of his brother George (1752–84), in which role he unsuccessfully petitioned the First Congress in 1790 for the settlement of his brother's wartime accounts. See also *DHFFC* 7:543.

BEAN, NATHANIEL (1750–1804), a native of Massachusetts, by 1775 settled in Warner, New Hampshire, where he became a farmer and mill owner. He served as town selectman, state representative (1782–83), and delegate to the state ratifying convention, where he voted in favor of the Constitution. (Walter Harriman, *History of Warner, New Hampshire* [Concord, N.H., 1879], pp. 235, 354)

BEATTY, READING (1757–1831), was a physician of Falsington, Bucks County, Pennsylvania, where he had settled in 1788 after a wartime career as a junior officer and army surgeon. The son of a colonial governor of New Jersey, through whom he was related to New York's Governor George Clinton, Beatty was also son-in-law to Henry Wynkoop by his marriage to Christina Wynkoop in 1786. See also *DHFFC* 17:1760.

BECKLEY, JOHN (1757–1807), was clerk of the House of Representatives from 1789 until his death, except between 1797 and 1801, when a Federalist majority kept him out of office. One of at least two sons and one daughter of John and Elizabeth Withers of England, he immigrated to Virginia about 1768 and embarked on a career clerking to various official bodies, as well as taking over the law practice of Edmund Randolph in 1779. Only one child was born by his marriage to Maria Prince (1772–1833) on 16 October 1790. See also *DHFFC* 9:11n.

BECKWITH, GEORGE (1753–1823), was a British army major entrusted with various intelligence missions to the United States on behalf of Great Britain between 1787 and 1792. In late 1781, while serving as General William von Knyphausen's aide-de-camp, he devised a plan to use a prisoner of war (a former clerk under Charles Thomson) to steal congressional papers. The plot failed when the would-be traitor informed on the British conspirators, who were either hanged or driven back to British occupied New York City. See also *DHFFC* 17:1761. (James Moody, *Lt. James Moody's Narrative of his Exertions and Sufferings* [London, 1783; reprint, New York, 1968], p. 43)

BEE, THOMAS (1740–1812), of Charleston, was appointed federal judge for the South Carolina district (1790–1812), following a long career in the colonial and state legislatures, Congress (1780–82), and as a delegate to the state ratifying convention, where he voted in favor of the Constitution. The Oxford educated lawyer and planter also served as lieutenant governor (1779–80) and as delegate to the state constitutional convention of 1790. See also *DHFFC* 2:542. (*PGW* 5:417n)

BELKNAP, JEREMY (1744–98), served as Congregational minister to Boston's Federal Street Church from 1787 until his death. The Harvard educated historian founded the Massachusetts Historical Society in 1791. See also *DHFFC* 17:1761.

BELL, WILLIAM (ca. 1739–1816), was a Philadelphia merchant, shareholder in the Bank of North America, and neighbor of Robert and Mary Morris. (*PRM* 7:325–26n)

BELLI, JOHN (d. 1809), established himself as a merchant in Alexandria, Virginia, upon his arrival from Italy in 1783. By 1786 he was settled in Danville, Kentucky, where he became a founding member of the Political Club with future Representative Brown, Harry Innes, Christopher Greenup, and Thomas Todd. (Nelson W. Evans, *History of Scioto County, Ohio* [Portsmouth, Ohio, 1903], pp. 652–56; *DHROC* 8:408–9n)

BELLOWS, BENJAMIN (1740–1802), a native of Worcester County, Massachusetts, settled in Walpole, New Hampshire, where he was town clerk, 1759–76. The longtime colonial and state legislator was also elected to Congress in 1781 but declined to attend. He served as a state militia general, 1781–92, and judge of the Cheshire County Court of Common Pleas, 1784–93. He voted to ratify the Constitution at the state convention and was a Presidential Elector in the first federal election. (*DHFFE* 1:854)

BENBURY, THOMAS, appointed federal collector at Edenton, North Carolina, in 1790, was a Federalist planter of Chowan County, which he represented as a colonial and state legislator, 1774–82. See also *DHFFC* 2:526.

BENEZET, DANIEL, SR. (1723–97), emigrated from his native London and became a merchant and local officeholder of Philadelphia. His older brother Anthony was a famous Quaker reformer who spoke against slavery. (*Drinker* 3:2115)

BENEZET, DANIEL, JR. (1760–98), a native of Philadelphia who served as a second lieutenant in the state militia during the last years of the Revolutionary War, owned mills in Gloucester County, New Jersey, where he settled by 1790. He was appointed federal collector at Great Egg Harbor in 1790. See also *DHFFC* 2:517. (*PGW* 5:361n)

BENNEHAM, RICHARD (1743–1825), was a merchant, planter, and tobacco industry pioneer of Orange County, North Carolina. (*Powell*)

BENSON, GEORGE (1752–1836), was the partner of Nicholas Brown in the Providence, Rhode Island, mercantile firm Brown and Benson. He served as deputy quartermaster general during the Revolutionary War. (*DHFFE* 4:438n)

BENSON, WILLIAM (d. 1802), a planter of Dobbs County, North Carolina, was appointed federal surveyor at Windsor in 1790. See also *DHFFC* 2:526.

BIDDLE, CHARLES (1745–1821), a Philadelphia merchant and sea captain, served Pennsylvania's Supreme Executive Council, first as a member, 1784–87 (the last two years as vice president or lieutenant governor of the state), and then as secretary until the new constitution of 1790 took effect. See also *DHFFC* 9:315.

BIDDLE, CLEMENT (1740–1814), was a Philadelphia merchant who served as federal marshal for Pennsylvania, 1789–93. See also *DHFFC* 2:533, 17:1762.

BINFORD, JOHN M. (1746–post 1807), represented Northampton County, North Carolina, in the state Senate between 1788 and 1808, when he moved to the Mississippi territory, in part of present-day Alabama.

BINGHAM, WILLIAM (1752–1804), was a wealthy Philadelphia banker and speculator in land and public securities who ran unsuccessfully for both Senator and Representative in the first federal election following two years in Congress, 1786–88. See also *DHFFC* 9:125n, 17:1762.

BIRD, HENRY M. (1755–1818), was principal partner in a London mercantile and banking firm heavily invested in South Carolina's war debt and rice trade. See also *DHFFC* 17:1762.

BISHOP, SAMUEL (1723–1803), was a longtime colonial and state legislator of New Haven, Connecticut, where he was appointed county court judge in 1789. (*Sherman's Connecticut*, pp. 46, 61, 83, 281n)

BISSETT, JOHN (ca. 1762–ca. 1810), born and educated in Scotland, was ordained an Episcopalian clergyman in Connecticut and assigned to the parish at Shrewsbury, Pennsylvania, in 1789, when he also served in the Church's General Convention at Philadelphia. After eight years ministering and teaching in New York City, he returned to Great Britain around 1800. (William B. Sprague, *Annals of the American Pulpit* [New York, 1861] 5:443n; William M. MacBean, *Biographical Register of Saint Andrew's Society* [New York, 1922] 1:295–96)

BIZE, HERCULES DANIEL (d. ca. 1800), a Swiss born British merchant and money lender, was Butler's most persistent creditor throughout the First Congress. (*Butler Letters*, pp. xxxvi–xxxvii, 19n)

BLACKBURN, THOMAS (1740–1807), of Prince William County, Virginia, was a former colonial legislator and an unsuccessful applicant for the office of federal collector at Dumfries. See also *DHFFC* 17:1763.

BLACKLEDGE, RICHARD, JR., was the son of the longtime business partner of Jacob Blount, and married Blount's daughter in 1786. He served as postmaster of Washington, North Carolina, in the 1780s, speculated in certificates, and served in the state legislature, 1791–95. See also *DHFFC* 7:63–64.

BLAIR, JOHN (1732–1800), of Williamsburg, Virginia, was a London trained lawyer and jurist who served as United States Supreme Court Justice, 1789–96. The signer of the Constitution voted for its ratification as a delegate for York County at the state convention. See also *DHFFC* 17:1763.

BLAND, MARTHA DANGERFIELD (d. 1804), married Theodorick Bland sometime between 1765 and 1771. During the First Congress she resided at "Cawsons," their plantation in Prince George County, Virginia.

BLEECKER, JOHN J. (1745–95), was a founding settler and farmer of Schaghticoke, New York. He served as a state militia captain during the Revolutionary War, and as an interpreter between the state and the Oneida Indians in the late 1780s. His late second wife was a distant relation of Philip Schuyler.

BLISS, MOSES (1735–1816), a lifelong resident of Springfield, Massachusetts, graduated from Yale in 1755 and was an ordained minister briefly before studying law under John Worthington (Fisher Ames's future father-in-law) and commencing practice in 1761. (*Yale Graduates* 2:365–66)

BLOUNT, JACOB (1760–1801), the younger brother of John Gray and William Blount, by whom he was schooled in the mercantile profession, was a merchant of Edenton, North Carolina. In 1789 he married Nancy, the only daughter of Josiah Collins of Edenton. (*Blount* 1:xxvii–xxviii)

BLOUNT, JOHN GRAY (1752–1833), brother of Jacob and William Blount, was a prominent merchant of Washington, Beaufort County, North Carolina, which he represented in the state House of Commons, 1782–89, and at both state ratification conventions, where he supported the Constitution. (*DHFFC* 4:353n)

BLOUNT, LEVI, a planter of Tyrrell County, North Carolina, was appointed surveyor at Plymouth in 1790. See also *DHFFC* 2:526.

BLOUNT, WILLIAM (1749–1800), was a planter, land speculator, and partner with his brothers Jacob and John Gray Blount in one of the largest mercantile operations in North Carolina before his appointment as both governor of the Southern Territory and superintendent of Indian Affairs for the Southern Department, 1790–96. Following service as paymaster of the 3rd Regiment of the North Carolina Line during the Revolutionary War, he sat in the state House of Commons for New Bern, 1780–81, and for Craven County, 1783–85 (speaker in 1784–85), in Congress, 1782–83 and 1786–87, and in the state Senate for Pitt County, 1788–89. He signed the Constitution as a member of the Federal Convention in 1787, and voted to ratify it at the second state convention in 1789. Benjamin Hawkins defeated him for Senator in the first federal election. See also *DHFFC* 2:526. (*DHFFE* 4:365–66)

BONDFIELD, JOHN, was a Canadian merchant in Bordeaux, France, where he served as Congress's commercial agent from 1787 until at least 1789. See also *DHFFC* 17:1764.

BOOTH, JAMES (1753–1828), a Federalist of New Castle, Delaware, served as secretary of state, 1778–90. (Emerson Wilson, *Forgotten Heroes of Delaware* [Cambridge, Mass., 1969], pp. 74–75)

BOUDINOT, ELISHA (1749–1819), a lawyer of Newark, New Jersey, was the younger brother of Elias Boudinot and Annis Boudinot Stockton. (*DHFFE* 3:36n)

BOUDINOT, HANNAH STOCKTON (1736–1808), of Elizabethtown, New Jersey, married Elias Boudinot in 1762. Her brother was Samuel W. Stockton, and her niece Julia Stockton married Benjamin Rush in 1776. See also *DHFFC* 14:683.

BOUNETHEAU, PETER (1742–98), of Charleston, South Carolina, served as clerk of the state Senate, 1778–80, and of the city council, ca. 1784–1798. (*South Carolina House* 1:160)

BOURDEAUX, DANIEL (ca. 1747–1815), a Charleston, South Carolina, merchant and land speculator, was a business partner with Butler in the 1770s. (*Butler Letters*, p. 19n)

BOURN, SILVANUS (ca. 1756–1817), a merchant of Barnstable, Massachusetts, served as consul to Hispaniola (Haiti), 1789–92. See also *DHFFC* 2:500–501, 8:710, 17:1764.

BOURNE, SHEARJASHUB (1746–1806), graduated from Harvard in 1764 and practiced law in Barnstable, Massachusettes, for several decades thereafter, except for a brief period during which he was engaged in mercantile pursuits in London, 1775–77. He represented Barnstable in the state House of Representatives, 1782–85 and 1788–90, and at the ratification convention, where he voted in favor of the Constitution. An ardent Federalist, he defeated George Partridge in the second federal election and served in the House, 1791–95. His wife was Hannah Doane, originally of Wellfleet, Massachusetts. Early in the second session, Bourne engaged Thatcher in a successful search for his runaway son-turned-seaman, John Doane Bourne (b. 1768). (*Harvard Graduates* 16:20–23)

BOWDOIN, JAMES (1726–1790), was a wealthy Boston merchant and Federalist governor of Massachusetts, 1785–87. See also *DHFFC* 17:1764.

BOWEN, JABEZ (1739–1815), a physician and jurist of Providence, Rhode Island, served as federal commissioner of loans for the state, 1790–1800. See also *DHFFC* 2:539, 17:1764–65.

BOWEN, OLIVER (ca. 1768–1804), son of Jabez Bowen, resided in Providence, Rhode Island, in 1790, when he unsuccessfully sought appointment as naval officer for that port.

BOWYER, HENRY (ca. 1760–1832), was clerk of Virginia's Botetourt County Court, 1788–1831. During the Revolutionary War he rose from second lieutenant in the 12th Virginia Regiment in 1777 to lieutenant of the 1st Continental Dragoons in 1781, serving until war's end. His wife, Agatha Madison, was the niece of both Patrick Henry and Bishop James Madison.

BOYD, JAMES (1732–98), was a Canadian refugee who settled in Boston in 1778 and subsequently lobbied to regain title to his holdings along the present-day Maine-New Brunswick border. See also *DHFFC* 17:1765. (*PGW* 4:329n)

BOYD, JOHN (ca. 1738–4 February 1790), a College of New Jersey (Princeton) graduate of 1757, commenced practice as a physician and druggist in Baltimore ten years later. He became an early activist in the local revolutionary movement. (*Princetonians, 1748–1768*, pp. 178–80)

BRACKETT, JOSHUA (1733–1802), a physician of Portsmouth, New Hampshire, served as judge of the state admiralty court, 1776–89. See also *DHFFC* 17:1765.

BRADFORD, RACHEL (1764–1805), of Philadelphia, was sister of William Bradford, Jr. and future wife (in 1799) of Elisha Boudinot. (George W. Corner, ed., *Autobiography of Benjamin Rush* [Princeton, N.J., 1948], p. 273n)

BRADFORD, WILLIAM (1729–1808), a physician and lawyer of Bristol, Rhode Island, served as deputy governor of that state, 1775–78. (*DHFFE* 4:422)

BRADFORD, WILLIAM, JR. (1755–95), of Philadelphia, served as attorney general of Pennsylvania from 1780 until his appointment to the state supreme court in August 1791. In October 1784 he married Elias Boudinot's only daughter, Susan Vergereau Boudinot (1764–1854). See also *DHFFC* 9:100n, 17:1765–66.

BRADLEY, ABRAHAM (ca. 1739–1817), of New Haven, Connecticut, was an early activist in that city's revolutionary movement and, with Roger Sherman, an influential member of its White Haven Congregational Church. He captained a state militia company during the Revolutionary War. (*Sherman's Connecticut*, p. 101n)

BRASHEAR, RICHARD, of Jefferson County in present-day Kentucky, served as a captain in George Rogers Clark's Illinois Company of Virginia militia, 1778–81. In 1787 he led an unsuccessful colony of American settlers to

Chickasaw Bluffs, present-day Vicksburg, Mississippi. (Lawrence Kinnaird, ed., "Spain in the Mississippi Valley, 1765–1794," *AHA* [1945] 3:236)

BREARLY, DAVID (1745–16 August 1790), a lawyer of Hunterdon County, New Jersey, served as federal district judge for New Jersey from September 1789 until his death, having previously served as the state's chief justice, 1779–89. See also *DHFFC* 17:1766.

BRECK, SAMUEL (1747–1809), represented Boston in the Massachusetts House of Representatives, 1784–91, after which he settled in Philadelphia. See also *DHFFC* 17:1766.

BRECKINRIDGE, ALEXANDER (d. 1801), brother of Robert Breckinridge, rose from first lieutenant of Nathaniel Gist's Additional Continental Regiment in 1777 to captain in 1779 before retiring at war's end. He settled near Louisville, Kentucky, which he represented at the statehood convention of 1787. (Washington and Lee University, *Historical Papers* 4[1893]:115)

BRECKINRIDGE, JAMES (1763–1833), a cousin of John Brown, was a surveyor and a lawyer who represented Botetourt County in the Virginia House of Delegates intermittently from 1789 to 1824. (*DHROC* 5:1090–91)

BRECKINRIDGE, ROBERT (1754–1833), originally of Virginia, settled near Louisville, Kentucky, in 1785 and served as a commissioner for veterans' land grants. He had served as a lieutenant in the 9th Regiment of the Virginia Line, 1777–78, and in the 4th Regiment thereafter until war's end. In 1788 he represented Jefferson County in the Virginia House of Delegates and at the ratifying convention, where he voted in favor of the Constitution. (*Kentucky in Retrospect*, p. 163)

BRÉHAN, MADAME, MARQUISE DE, left an unhappy marriage and, with her teenaged son, joined her brother Eléanor François Elie, comte de Moustier, during his tenure in New York City as French minister to the United States, 1788–89, to serve as the embassy's hostess while it occupied the Macomb Mansion on Broadway. A talented portraitist, who executed a miniature of Washington during a visit to Mount Vernon in November 1788, she was nevertheless perceived as haughty, depressed, and irritable. At the time Bréhan's "illicit" relationship with her brother was "universally known," according to James Madison, but her reputation had recovered by the time of the couple's return to France in 1790. (*PGW* 1:37–38n; *PJM* 11:383, 12:183, 186)

BRIESLER, JOHN, of Braintree (present-day Quincy), Massachusetts, and his wife Esther Field were devoted house servants of the Adams family in Europe and throughout the First Congress period. (*Adams* 3:156n)

BRIGGS, ISAAC (1763–1825), a surveyor, civil engineer, and promoter of steam navigation along the Savannah River, settled in Augusta, Georgia, after graduating from the University of Pennsylvania in 1782. He served as secretary of the state ratification convention and unsuccessfully challenged George Mathews for Representative in the first federal election. (*DHFFC* 2:481)

BRIGHT, FRANCIS (ca. 1746–ca. 1803), a captain in the Virginia state navy since 1776, undertook an active but unsuccessful campaign during the First Congress for appointment to command a federal revenue cutter. See also *DHFFC* 17:1767.

BRISBANE, WILLIAM (1759–1821), was a planter of St. John Parish, South Carolina.

BROMFIELD, HENRY (1751–1837), born to a Boston family of merchants, pursued his own mercantile interests there and in Amsterdam before relocating permanently to London in 1787. (*NEHGR* 26[1872]:38, 141)

BROOKS, ELEAZER (1727–1806), of Lincoln, Massachusetts, sat in the state House of Representatives (1774–78, 1780, and 1787–88), Senate (1780–87, 1788–91), and governor's Council (1791–99). He rose from captain to brigadier general in the state militia (1773–78), and voted to ratify the Constitution at the state convention in 1788 (*DHROC* 4:141n).

BROOM, JACOB (1752–1810), was a merchant, manufacturer, and postmaster, 1790–92, of Wilmington, Delaware. He served in the state House of Assembly, 1784–87 and 1788–89, and signed the Constitution in 1787. (*DHROC* 3:52n, 114)

BROOME, SAMUEL (1735–1810), was a New York City merchant who had resettled in New Haven, Connecticut by 1787, when he became involved in the minting of copper coins for Congress. (*LDC* 25:296)

BROUGH, ROBERT, was Virginia's port inspector for Hampton, 1788–89. See also *DHFFC* 17:1767.

BROWN, ANDREW (ca. 1744–1797), was printer of Philadelphia's *Federal Gazette* since its founding in 1788 as a pro-Constitution newspaper. See also *DHFFC* 17:1768.

BROWN, JAMES (1766–1835), a lawyer of Lexington, Kentucky, declined appointment as United States district attorney. He was the younger brother of Representative John Brown. See also *DHFFC* 2:494.

BROWN, JOHN (1736–1803), a merchant, slave trader, holder of securities, and wealthy businessman of Providence, Rhode Island, was a partner with his four brothers in the firm Nicholas Brown & Company, 1762–71. An early activist in the revolutionary movement, he sat in the state General Assembly throughout the war years and was elected to Congress, 1784 and 1785, but never attended; nevertheless in the latter year it elected him one of three commissioners to oversee the construction of a federal town on the Delaware River. In 1787 Brown partnered with John Francis (who married Brown's daughter Abigail the next year) to become the first Rhode Island merchants to engage in the China and East Indies trade.

BROWN, MOSES (1738–1836), of the prominent mercantile family of Providence, Rhode Island, which included his older brother John, became a strident abolitionist upon his conversion to Quakerism in 1774, helping to found the Providence Society for the Abolition of the Slave Trade in 1789. That same year he became partner in the state's first textile manufactory. Among the beneficiaries of his numerous philanthropic pursuits was the College of Rhode Island, later named for Brown's family. (*DHFFC* 4:405n; Charles Rappleye, *Sons of Providence: The Brown Brothers, the Slave Trade, and the American Revolution* [New York, 2006], pp. 253–54, 259–60)

BROWN, MOSES (1748–1820), a native of Newburyport, Massachusetts, settled as a merchant in Beverly in 1772, four years after his graduation from Harvard. During the Revolutionary War, he entered military service as captain of a local Minuteman company in 1775 and retired as captain in the 14th Continental Regiment in 1777. In 1789 he collaborated with his neighbor George Cabot in establishing Beverly's cotton manufactory. (*Harvard Graduates* 17:7–8)

BROWN, NICHOLAS (1729–91), the eldest of the surviving brothers of Providence, Rhode Island's foremost mercantile family, was a Federalist merchant and securities speculator. See also *DHFFC* 17:1768.

BROWN, SAMUEL (1769–1830), youngest brother of James and Representative John Brown, graduated from Dickinson College in 1789 and studied medicine in Staunton, Virginia, at the time of the First Congress. He went on to study at Edinburgh and established a medical practice in Bladensburg, Maryland, in the mid 1790s.

BRYAN, SAMUEL (1759–1821), a Philadelphia Antifederalist who authored the polemic Centinel essays, 1787–89, served as clerk of the state Assembly, 1784–85.

BUFORD, ABRAHAM (1749–1833) received his military training as an Indian fighter with the Virginia militia before the Revolutionary War. Commissioned major of the 14th Virginia Regiment in 1776, he transferred to the 5th Regiment and rose from lieutenant colonel to colonel in 1778, holding that rank in the 11th Regiment from 1778 to 1781, and in the 3rd Regiment thereafter until war's end. He settled on an extensive grant in Lincoln (part of present-day Mercer) County, Kentucky, where he became a member of Danville's Political Club, 1786–90, with future Representative John Brown, Harry Innes, and his father-in-law after 1788, Judge Samuel McDowell. (Thomas Speed, *The Political Club of Danville, Kentucky, 1786–1790* [Louisville, Ky., 1894], pp. 50–51)

BULL, JOHN (1740–1802), a Federalist planter of Prince William Parish, South Carolina, began his political career in a number of colonial offices before siding with the revolutionary movement and representing various parishes in the provincial and then state legislatures, 1775–80 and 1783–1800, serving simultaneously in Congress, 1784–87. He was defeated by Aedanus Burke in the first federal election. (*South Carolina Senate*, p. 190; *South Carolina House* 2:114–15; *DHFFE* 1:172)

BURBECK, HENRY (1754–1848), artillery captain in the federal army and posted in Georgia in 1790, rose from first lieutenant in Knox's Regiment of Continental Artillery in 1775 to captain in the 3rd Continental Artillery Regiment in 1777, to brevet major at war's end, when the Boston native enrolled as a member of the Society of the Cincinnati. See also *DHFFC* 2:501.

BURGES, BARTHOLOMEW (1740–1807), was an astronomer of Boston whose eclectic learning included East Indian affairs. His most famous works were *A Short Account of the Solar System* (Boston, 1789) and *A Series of Indostan Letters* (New York, 1790).

BURKE, EDMUND (1729–97), an Irish philosopher, political theorist, and member of Parliament, 1765–95, was a spokesman for liberal imperial policy in America and, after the Revolutionary War, in India.

BURR, JOSIAH (1753–95), was a merchant of New Haven, Connecticut. See also *DHFFC* 17:1769.

BURR, THEODOSIA PREVOST (d. 1794), married Aaron Burr in 1782. Their daughter Theodosia (1783–1812) was their only child to survive infancy. See also *DHFFC* 17:1769–70.

BURRAL, JONATHAN (1753–1834), of Connecticut, was appointed assistant postmaster general in 1789. See also *DHFFC* 17:1770.

BURRILL, JAMES, JR. (1772–1820), of Providence, Rhode Island, graduated from Brown in 1788 and studied law under Theodore Foster prior to being admitted to the bar in 1791.

BUTLER, EDWARD, son of Pierce Butler's oldest brother in Ireland, Sir Thomas Butler (1735–72), sold his army commission and settled in South Carolina in the late 1780s, when he began to involve his uncle in some financial embarrassment owing to unpaid debts. (*Butler*, pp. 49–50; *Butler Letters*, pp. 8–9n)

BUTLER, FRANCES, of Dublin, was the unmarried younger sister of Pierce Butler. Her brother's favorite, after whom he named his third daughter, she was his principal source of family news from Europe. (*Butler*, p. 499)

BUTLER, SENATOR PIERCE, family during the First Congress: Mary Middleton (m. 1771), who was the daughter of wealthy Charleston planter Thomas Middleton; their son Thomas; and four daughters: Sarah (1772?–1831), twins Anne Elizabeth or "Eliza" (1774–1854) and Frances (d. 1836), and Harriot Percy or "Henrietta" (1775?–1815). Sarah and Harriot seem to have lived with their parents during the second session; Anne and Frances, who had remained behind in South Carolina, moved to Philadelphia with their father after their mother's death in New York City on 13 November 1790. (*Butler*, pp. 484–87)

BUTLER, RICHARD (1743–91), a native of Ireland, represented Allegheny and Westmoreland counties in the 1790–91 session of the Pennsylvania state Senate. During the Revolutionary War he rose to the rank of brevet brigadier general in the Pennsylvania Line of the Continental Army and subsequently served as superintendent of Indian Affairs for the Northern Department, 1786–88. He returned to military duty as a major general of the federal army in 1791 and was killed in Arthur St. Clair's defeat by the Miami Indians in November. See also *DHFFC* 9:7n, 17:1770.

BUTLER, THOMAS (1778–1838), the only son of Pierce Butler to survive childhood, studied under Rev. Weeden Butler in England, 1784–95. See also *DHFFC* 17:1770–71.

BUTLER, WEEDEN (1742–1823), an Anglican minister of Margate, England, taught school for more than forty years in the Chelsea section of London, where the son of Pierce Butler (no relation) was enrolled as a student during the First Congress.

CABARRUS, STEPHEN (1754–1808), emigrated from France to North Carolina in 1776 and became a shipping merchant in Edenton, serving as Speaker of the state's House of Commons, 1789–93. His wife was Jeanne Henriette Damery Bodley. (*DHFFE* 4:355n)

CABELL, WILLIAM, SR. (1730–98), of "Union Hill," in present-day Amherst County, Virginia, was a surveyor, colonial militia officer, and longtime burgess, 1756–76, state senator, 1776–81, and member of the state House of Delegates from 1781 to 1783 and 1787 to 1788, when he voted against ratification of the Constitution in the state convention. In the first federal election he was an unsuccessful candidate for Presidential Elector. (*DHFFE* 2:410–11)

CABOT, FRANCIS (1757–1832), was a merchant of Salem, Massachusetts. See also *DHFFC* 17:1771.

CABOT, GEORGE (1752–1823), was a merchant of Beverly, Massachusetts, whose extensive business interests included banking and cotton manufacturing. On 22 June 1790 he was elected to succeed Tristram Dalton in the Second Federal Congress. See also *DHFFC* 17:1771.

CALDWELL, JOHN (1756–1838), of Hartford, Connecticut, was a banker, insurance officer, and prominent shipping merchant in the West Indies trade. He was a major in the state militia, 1788–92.

CALDWELL, JOHN (ca. 1757–1804), was a native of Virginia who settled in the area of Danville, Kentucky, in 1781 and represented Nelson County at the statehood conventions of 1787 and 1788.

CALDWELL, JOHN EDWARDS (1769–1819), was the orphaned son of Elias Boudinot's good friend, the Presbyterian minister of Elizabeth, New Jersey, Rev. James Caldwell. Boudinot made arrangements through the marquis de Lafayette for him to be educated in France, from which he returned to the United States in 1791. (George Adams Boyd, *Elias Boudinot: Patriot and Statesman* [New York, 1952], pp. 97, 145–46)

CALLENDER, THOMAS (d. 1828), was a merchant of Wilmington, North Carolina, where he was appointed federal surveyor in 1790. See also *DHFFC* 2:526–27.

CAMPBELL, ARTHUR (1743–1811), a land speculator and principal supporter of Kentucky statehood and the creation of the state of Franklin, represented Washington County in the Virginia House of Delegates, 1776–88. (*PJM* 4:126n)

CAMPBELL, DAVID (1750–1812), rose to major in the Virginia militia by 1778 and served briefly as clerk of the courts in Washington County, Virginia, before resettling to western North Carolina where he was elected chief judge of the state of Franklin. He represented Green County in the North Carolina House of Commons in 1787 and was appointed judge of the Southeast Territory, 1790–96. (*DHFFC* 2:548; *PGW* 5:423)

CAREY, MATHEW (1760–1839), was the Irish born printer and editor of the first successful American magazine, the *American Museum*, published monthly in Philadelphia, 1787–92. (Frank Luther Mott, *History of American Magazines, 1741–1850* [New York, 1930], p. 100)

CARMICHAEL, WILLIAM (ca. 1738–1795), was a lawyer of Queen Anne's County, Maryland, who gained diplomatic experience in Paris and Berlin before serving as chargé des affaires at Madrid, 1782–95. See also *DHFFC* 2:496.

CARNES, JOHN (1723–1802), was a merchant of Lynn, Massachusetts, which he represented in the state House of Representatives, 1785–93, and at the ratification convention, where he voted in favor of the Constitution. See *DHFFC* 17:1772.

CARR, THOMAS (1758–1820), was a surveyor and land speculator of Augusta, Georgia, where he settled after serving as a Virginia militia colonel, 1780–81. In 1789–90 he was director of the Tennessee Yazoo Company.

CARRINGTON, EDWARD (1749–1810), a lawyer of Powhatan County, Virginia, was federal marshal for the state, 1789–91, and supervisor of distilled spirits, 1791–94. See also *DHFFC* 17:1772.

CARROLL, DANIEL, of Duddington (1764–1849), the eldest son of Charles Carroll of Carrollton's first cousin, Charles Carroll of Duddington, was a large landowner in Prince George's County, Maryland, where his estate, "New Troy," was conveyed to the federal government in 1791 to become the site of the United States Capitol and surrounding neighborhood. (*CCP* 3:1523, 1526; Priscilla W. McNeil, "Rock Creek Hundred: Land Conveyed for the Federal City," *Washington History* vol. 3, 1[Spring/Summer 1991]:42–43)

CARTER, JOHN, SR. (1745–1814), of Providence, Rhode Island, was printer of the *Providence Gazette* from 1767 until his death.

CARTER, ROBERT, JR. (1728–1804), a planter of "Nomini Hall," in Westmoreland County, Virginia, served on the colony's Council of State from 1758 until the outbreak of the Revolutionary War when he retired from public life, except for an unsuccessful bid for a seat in the state ratification convention. His daughter Sarah Fairfax (b. 1773), courted by Richard Bland Lee in 1789, married Dr. Richard Chinn of Richmond in 1796. (*DH-ROC* 8:144n, 9:618n; Louis Morton, *Robert Carter of Nomini Hall* [Williamsburg, Va., 1941], pp. 220, 229)

CASS, JONATHAN (1752–1830), a blacksmith of Exeter, New Hampshire, was appointed a captain in the federal army in March 1791. See also *DHFFC* 17:1772.

CATON, MARY "POLLY" CARROLL (1770–1846), the eldest of Charles Carroll of Carrollton's three children to survive infancy, married Richard Caton of Baltimore in 1786.

CATON, RICHARD (1763–1845), a native of England, was a Baltimore merchant by 1785. The next year he married Mary "Polly" Carroll, elder daughter of Charles Carroll of Carrollton and in 1787 they settled on their estate "Castle Thunder," site of present day Catonsville, Maryland. In 1790 he became involved in cotton manufacturing.

CAZENOVE, THEOPHILE (1740–1811), was a leading Dutch broker who arrived in New York in March 1790 as a representative of Dutch firms Pieter Stadnitski & Son, Nicholas and Jacob Van Staphorst, and others interested in buying securities and other American investments. Boston merchant Thomas Russell introduced him to John Langdon during Cazenove's tour of New England in the autumn of 1790; Langdon may have been the unknown contact by whom Cazenove had access to secret Senate information in the winter of 1790–91. (*DGW* 6:49n; *PTJ* 18:235; Russell to Langdon, 27 September 1790, NhPoA)

CHADBOURN, BENJAMIN (1718–99), of Berwick, Maine, sat in the colonial legislature, 1756–71, the Massachusetts state Senate in 1780, and on the bench of the court of common pleas.

CHALONER, JOHN (1748–93), sometimes referred to as "Chalmer," was a prominent merchant of Philadelphia. See also *DHFFC* 17:1773.

CHAMPLIN, GEORGE (1738–1809), was a wealthy merchant of Newport, Rhode Island, which he represented in the state House of Deputies, 1784–92, and at the ratification convention, where he voted in favor of the Constitution. (*DHFFC* 4:422n)

CHAMPLIN, JABEZ (1728–1805), uncle of George Champlin, was a former high sheriff for Newport County, Rhode Island, who served with the state militia prior to his appointment as an assistant deputy quartermaster in the Continental Army. See also *DHFFC* 7:21–22.

CHANNING, WALTER (ca. 1758–1827), of Newport, Rhode Island, was the clerk of the county court. A younger brother of William Channing, he served as a lieutenant in the Rhode Island militia during the Revolutionary War.

CHANNING, WILLIAM (1751–93), a lawyer of Newport, Rhode Island, served as a federal district attorney, 1790–91, having served as state's attorney general, 1777–87 and again from 1791 until his death. The College of New Jersey (Princeton) graduate of 1769 was the brother of Walter, brother-in-law of Francis Dana, and son-in-law of William Ellery. See also *DHFFC* 2:539.

CHAPIN, ISRAEL, SR. (1757–1810), served as a militia brigadier general in his native Massachusetts during the Revolutionary War before settling on a farm in Canandaigua, New York, in 1789. (*PGW* 4:582n)

CHAPLIN, JOSEPH (1760–1812), of Washington, Massachusetts, was jailed for bankruptcy during the First Congress over failed speculation schemes with Ebenezer Kingsley, in which Theodore Sedgwick was involved as a surety. Kingsley was a relation through Chaplin's marriage to his cousin, Abigail Kingsley Messenger. (*DHSCUS* 6:176n)

CHAPMAN, HENRY, was a New York City merchant in 1789.

CHESTER, JOHN (1749–1809), was a farmer of Wethersfield, Connecticut, which he represented in the state House of Representatives, 1772–88, and at the ratification convention, where he voted in favor of the Constitution. After an unsuccessful bid for Representative in the first federal election, he served on the state Council of Assistants, 1788–92, and as federal supervisor of distilled spirits, 1791–1801. See also *DHFFC* 17:1774.

CHETWOOD, JOHN (1736–1807), a lawyer of Elizabeth, New Jersey, represented Essex County, New Jersey, at the ratification convention and in the state's upper house, or Legislative Council, in 1788. He served as associate justice of the state supreme court, 1789–97. (*DHFFC* 3:11n)

CHILD, FRANCIS (d. 1792) of Hillsboro, North Carolina, rose from first lieutenant of the 6th North Carolina Regiment in 1776 to captain in 1777, transferring to the 3rd Regiment in 1778 and retiring in 1781, when he became state comptroller for public accounts.

CHILDS, FRANCIS (1763–1830), established and published New York City's *Daily Advertiser*, 1785–96, simultaneously editing Philadelphia's *National Gazette*, 1791–93. See also *DHFFC* 17:1774.

CHIPMAN, NATHANIEL (1752–1843), of Rutland, was chief justice of Vermont's Supreme Court when he served on the New York-Vermont boundary commission in the summer of 1790. See also *DHFFC* 2:546.

CHOATE, STEPHEN (1727–1815), was a farmer and merchant of Ipswich, Massachusetts, which he represented in the state House, 1776–79, and Senate, 1780–83. (*Massachusetts Legislators*, p. 188)

CHURCH, EDWARD (1740–1816), younger brother of Benjamin Church, was a Boston merchant who by 1787 resettled in Georgia, where he engaged in the cotton trade. In 1790 he declined appointment as United States consul to Bilboa, Portugal. See also *DHFFC* 2:501, 17:1775.

CHURCH, JOHN B. (d. 1818), was a successful military contractor for the Continental Army during his sojourn in Philadelphia from his native England, to which he returned in 1783 and where he was elected a member of

Parliament in 1790. In 1777 he married Angelica Schuyler (b. 1756), eldest child of the future Senator, through whom he became Alexander Hamilton's brother-in-law in 1780. See also *DHFFC* 17:1775–76.

CHURCHMAN, JOHN (1753–1805), was a Quaker surveyor and cartographer from East Nottingham, Pennsylvania. See also *DHFFC* 8:8–9, 17:1776.

CLARK, ABRAHAM (1726–94), a lawyer of Rahway, New Jersey, was a long-time state legislator, member of Congress for nine years between 1776 and 1780, and unsuccessful candidate for Representative in the first federal election, who was appointed commissioner to settle New Jersey's accounts with the United States, 1789–90. See also *DHFFC* 17:1776.

CLARK, GEORGE ROGERS (1752–1818), of Louisville, Kentucky, was a Revolutionary War hero involved with the South Carolina Yazoo Company in an aborted plan to attack Spanish Louisiana in 1790–91. See also *DHFFC* 17:1776.

CLARKSON, MATTHEW (1733–1800), a native of New York City, became a Philadelphia merchant. He did not attend Congress when elected in 1785. In 1790 he was a member of the city council.

CLAY, JOSEPH, SR. (1741–1804), was a merchant and lawyer of Savannah, Georgia, which he represented in the state House of Assembly, 1782–83 and 1787–88. A native of England who settled in Georgia in 1760, his rapid rise owed much to his kinship with the powerful Habersham family, including his cousin and business partner Joseph Habersham. See also *DHFFC* 17:1777. (Frank Lambert, *James Habersham* [Athens, Ga., 2005], pp. 148–49)

CLAY, JOSEPH, JR. (1764–1811), only son of Joseph Clay, was born in Savannah, Georgia, where he returned to practice law after graduating first in his class from the College of New Jersey (Princeton) in 1784 and then studying with George Wythe at Williamsburg, Virginia. (*Princetonians, 1784–1790*, pp. 14–18)

CLAYPOOLE, DAVID, established Philadelphia's *Pennsylvania Packet* with John Dunlap in 1771.

CLINTON, CHARLES (1734–91), brother of George and James, was a physician of Little Britain, in present-day Orange County, New York. (*DHFFE* 3:212n)

CLINTON, DEWITT (1769–1828), son of James Clinton, graduated from Columbia College in 1786 and was admitted to the bar in 1788. He never actively practiced law, preferring to devote himself to the Antifederalist politics of his uncle, Governor George Clinton, to whom he became personal secretary in 1790.

CLINTON, GEORGE (1739–1812), of Ulster County, New York, was governor, 1777–95, and unsuccessful Antifederalist candidate for Vice President in the first federal election. See also *DHFFC* 9:136n, 17:1777.

CLINTON, JAMES (1733–1812), of present-day Orange County, New York, rose from colonel of the Third New York Regiment in 1775 and then of the Second New York Regiment in 1776, to brigadier-general later that year, winning notoriety for his campaign against the Iroquois in 1779 before retiring at war's end. Espousing the Antifederalist beliefs shared by his brother George and son DeWitt, he voted against the Constitution at the state ratification convention.

CLYMER, REPRESENTATIVE GEORGE, family during the First Congress: his wife, Elizabeth Meredith (m. 1765, d. 1815), of Philadelphia, sister of Samuel Meredith; and children Henry, Meredith (1771–94), Margaret (1772–99), Anne (d. 1810), and George, Jr. (1783–1848). (Jerry Grundfest, *George Clymer: Philadelphia Revolutionary* [New York, 1982], pp. 31–32n)

CLYMER, HENRY (1767–1830), eldest surviving son of George Clymer, graduated from the College of New Jersey (Princeton) in 1786 and became a Philadelphia lawyer who also managed the family's land investments. (Jerry Grundfest, *George Clymer: Philadelphia Revolutionary* [New York, 1982], p. 31n)

COATS, DAVID (1736–91), was a merchant and sea captain of Newburyport, Massachusetts. The longtime local and state officeholder also commanded some of the merchant marine involved in the unsuccessful Penobscot Expedition of 1779. (Marvin Sadik, *Christian Gullager: Portrait Painter to Federal America* [Washington, D.C., 1976], p. 50)

COBB, DAVID (1748–1830), a physician of Taunton, Massachusetts, served as judge of the Bristol County court of common pleas, 1784–96, speaker of the state House of Representatives, 1789–93, and an unsuccessful candidate for the seat won by George Leonard in the first federal election. See also *DHFFC* 17:1778.

COBB, MATHEW (1757–1824), like George Thatcher a native of Cape Cod, about 1780 settled in Biddeford, Maine, and became known as "King Cobb" for his fleet of merchant ships. ([Maine] *Portland Advertiser*, 27 March 1824)

COBHAM, THOMAS (d. post-1797), was a physician in North Carolina at the outbreak of the Revolutionary War, when his Loyalist sympathies led him to serve with the British Army in Charleston, South Carolina, and Florida. By 1786 he had resettled in London, where he worked at the Greenwich Hospital at the time of the First Congress.

COCHRAN, JOHN (1730–1807), commissioner of loans for New York, 1786–90, was a New York City physician who had served as surgeon general in the Continental Army, 1777–80, and director general of army hospitals thereafter until war's end, when he enrolled in the Society of the Cincinnati. In 1760 he married Philip Schuyler's sister Gertrude (1724–1813). (*DHFFC* 2:521–22)

CODMAN, JOHN (1755–1803), was a prominent Boston shipping merchant. (*DHSCUS* 2:329n)

CODMAN, RICHARD (1762–1806), a Harvard graduate of 1782, became a merchant based in France and a partner in his older brother John's Boston mercantile firm. (Cora Codman Wolcott, *Codmans of Charlestown and Boston* [Brookline, Mass., 1930], pp. 12, 15, 64)

COFFIN, ALEXANDER (1740–1839), originally of Nantucket, Massachusetts, was a sea captain and merchant in the East India trade who became one of the original proprietors of Hudson, New York, in 1783.

COFFIN, JOHN (1756–1838), was a large landowner of St. Johns, Nova Scotia (part of present-day New Brunswick), Canada. The Boston native became a Loyalist who commanded a cavalry unit in the southern theater for much of the Revolutionary War before retiring to Canada in 1783. His exploits won the respect of many in the Deep South, irrespective of ideology.

COGDELL, JOHN (1729–1807), was a merchant planter of Georgetown, South Carolina, where he was appointed collector in 1790. (*DHFFC* 2:542)

COLES, CATHERINE THOMPSON (1769–1848), daughter of wealthy New York City merchant James Thompson and sister of Elbridge Gerry's wife Ann, married Representative Isaac Coles on 2 January 1790.

COLLINS, JOHN (1717–95), a farmer of Newport, Rhode Island, served as governor, 1786–90, in which capacity he cast the deciding vote in the state Senate for calling a ratification convention in 1790. He sat in Congress, 1778–80 and 1782–83.

COLLINS, JOSIAH (1735-1819), was a native of England who settled in Edenton, North Carolina, in 1777, where he became a wealthy shipping merchant, planter, land speculator, and unsuccessful candidate for governor in 1788. In 1789 his only daughter Nancy married Jacob Blount, younger brother of John Gray and William Blount. (*Blount* 1:xxvii–xxviii, 177n)

COLLINS, STEPHEN (1733–94), was a Philadelphia Quaker merchant sympathetic to the revolutionary cause during the war. (*Drinker* 3:2129)

COMSTOCK, JOB (d. 1811), was a farmer of East Greenwich, Rhode Island, which he represented in the state House of Deputies, 1776–79, 1786–90. Collector of state revenues for Kent County, 1787–90, and state surveyor of the port of East Greenwich, 1789–90, he voted against the Constitution at the state ratification convention, ran unsuccessfully for Representative in the first federal election, and declined appointment as federal surveyor for the port in 1790. (*DHFFE* 4:448)

CONSTABLE, WILLIAM (1752–1803), a native of Dublin, Ireland, who became a prominent New York City merchant, a speculator in land and public securities, and a business associate of Robert Morris. In 1782 he married Ann White (1762–1826) of Philadelphia; their home at 39 Great Dock Street was Morris's residence. See also *DHFFC* 9:183n.

CONTEE, ALEXANDER (1752–1810), older brother of Benjamin Contee, was a merchant near East Nottingham, Pennsylvania, having headed a mercantile firm in London in the mid 1780s. (*PGW* 5:497n)

CONWAY, JOHN, a former sea captain of Perth Amboy and sheriff of Middlesex County, New Jersey, rose from captain in 1775 to lieutenant colonel of the First Regiment of the New Jersey Line in 1779 before retiring in 1781.

CONY, DANIEL (1752–1842), was a physician of Hallowell, Maine, which he represented in the Massachusetts House of Representatives from 1786 to 1789, when he was an unsuccessful candidate for Presidential Elector in the first federal election. He subsequently served in the state Senate, 1790–91. (*DHFFE* 1:745–46; *DHROC* 4:141n)

COOK, FRANCIS (ca. 1755–1832), was a merchant of Pownalborough, Maine, which he represented in the Massachusetts House of Representatives from 1787 until his appointment as collector at nearby Wiscasset in 1789, where he served until 1829. (*DHFFC* 2:502)

COOK, ORCHARD (1763–1819), a merchant of Newcastle, Maine, was a native of Salem, Massachusetts, who settled in Maine by 1786.

COOKE, SILAS, moved from Rhode Island to New Bern, North Carolina, in 1782 and became clerk of the Superior Court for the New Bern district.

COOMBS, WILLIAM (1736–1814), was a wealthy merchant of Newburyport, Massachusetts, where he had been a shipmaster and invested in privateers during the Revolutionary War. (Benjamin W. Labaree, *Patriots and Partisans* [Cambridge, Mass., 1962], pp. 209–10)

COPELAND, MOSES (ca. 1741–1817), a native of Massachusetts, settled in Warren, Maine, where he was postmaster during the First Congress.

CORBIN, FRANCIS (1759–1821), was a London trained lawyer of Middlesex County, Virginia, which he represented in the state House of Delegates, 1785–95, and at the ratification convention, where he voted in favor of the Constitution. (*DHROC* 8:525)

COTTRINGER, GARRETT (ca. 1759–1816), was a Philadelphia merchant and associate of Robert Morris. (Morris to Horatio Gates, 19 June 1787, Gates Papers, NHi)

COURTNEY, WILLIAM, represented Hillsborough in the North Carolina legislature, 1777–79 and 1781–90.

COX, JOHN (1731–93), was a prominent Philadelphia merchant and industrialist who retired to his estate, "Bloomsbury Farm," outside Trenton, New Jersey, shortly after the Revolutionary War. His daughter Catherine married Samuel W. Stockton, ca. 1783. See also *DHFFC* 17:1781.

COXE, TENCH (1755–1824), was a Philadelphia merchant, land speculator, economist, and Federalist essayist who became assistant secretary of the treasury on 10 May 1790. See also *DHFFC* 17:1781.

CRABTREE, ELEAZER, of Frenchman's Bay, Maine, served as a captain in the Massachusetts militia during the Revolutionary War. (*MSSR* 4:59)

CRAFTS, THOMAS, JR. (1740–99), was a Boston painter and "japaner," or furniture refinisher, who became one of the earliest activists in the revolutionary movement, and commanding colonel of Massachusetts's state artillery regiment. In 1763 he married Christopher Gore's sister Frances (1744–88).

CRAIGIE, ANDREW (1754–1819), brother-in-law of Bossenger Foster, Sr., was a Boston merchant deeply involved in public securities speculation. See also *DHFFC* 17:1781.

CRAIK, WILLIAM (1761–ca.1814), was a native of Port Tobacco, Maryland, where he practiced law before moving to Baltimore by 1793.

CRANCH, JOSEPH (d. 1815), was appointed armorer to the militia by the Massachusetts Provincial Congress in 1775, and was still working in the state's armory at Springfield, Massachusetts, at the time of the First Congress.

CRANCH, LUCY (1767–1846), of Braintree, Massachusetts, was the niece of John and Abigail Adams, and the daughter of Richard and Mary Smith Cranch.

CRANCH, MARY SMITH (1740–1811), elder sister of Abigail Adams, married John Adams's lifelong friend Richard Cranch (1726–1811) in 1762 and lived in Braintree (part of present-day Quincy), Massachusetts, during the First Congress. (*Adams* 1:122n)

CRÈVECOEUR, MICHEL-GUILLAUME ST. JOHN DE (1735–1813), was French consul in New York City from 1783 until his return to France in May 1790. See also *DHFFC* 17:1781–82.

CROCKER, JOSEPH (1749–97), was a Boston shopkeeper and merchant.

CROWNINSHIELD, GEORGE was a merchant and shipowner of Salem, Massachusetts. He was the father of George Crowninshield, Jr. (1766–1817).

CUMMING, JOHN NOBLE (1752–1821), a businessman of Newark, New Jersey, was appointed deputy federal marshal for that state in 1789. His sister Catherine (b. 1748) married Elias Boudinot's brother-in-law Philip Stockton (1746–92) in 1767. See also *DHFFC* 17:1782.

CURSON, RICHARD (ca. 1725–1805), was a Baltimore merchant and shipowner. See also *DHFFC* 17:1782–83.

CUSHING, HANNAH PHILLIPS (1754–1834), originally of Middletown, Connecticut, married William Cushing in 1774 and settled in Boston. (*DHSCUS* 1:27n)

CUSHING, WILLIAM (1732–1810), of Boston, was chief justice of the Massachusetts supreme judicial court from 1777 until his appointment to the United States Supreme Court in 1789, where he served until his death. In 1774 he married Hannah Phillips. See also *DHFFC* 17:1783.

CUSTIS, ELEANOR "NELLY" PARKE (1779–1852), and her brother George Washington "Washy" Parke Custis (1781–1857), youngest children of Martha Washington's deceased son and stepchildren of David Stuart, resided with the Washingtons throughout the First Congress. (*PGW* 1:4–5n)

CUTHBERT, ANTHONY (1751–1832), of Philadelphia, was captain in the city's artillery company in the last years of the Revolutionary War, after which he became a manufacturer of masts. (*PJM* 6:41n)

CUTLER, MANASSEH (1742–1823), was a Congregational minister as well as a practicing lawyer, physician, and amateur scientist of Ipswich, Massachusetts. In 1788–90 he lobbied Congress actively on behalf of Ohio River valley land companies in which he was co-investor. See also *DHFFC* 17:1783.

CUTTING, JOHN BROWN (ca. 1755–1831), served as an army apothecary during the Revolutionary War and in 1787–88 as secretary to John Adams while studying law in London, where he became an active lobbyist for American seamen's rights against impressment in 1790. See also *DHFFC* 17:1783.

CUYLER, JACOB (1742-1804), was a Federalist merchant of Albany, New York, who represented that town in the provincial and state legislatures, 1775–77, before serving as deputy commissary general of purchases for the Continental Army's Northern Department, 1778–82. After the war he was a business and political associate of Philip Schuyler and James Duane. (*PRM* 1:178n; Edward P. Alexander, *A Revolutionary Conservative: James Duane of New York* [New York, 1938], pp. 218, 232, 234)

DAKIN, THOMAS (ca. 1732–1802), was a blacksmith of Boston.

DALTON, RUTH HOOPER (1739–post-1817), of Newburyport, Massachusetts, married Tristram Dalton in 1758 and resided with him throughout the First Congress. Only three of their ten children survived infancy, of whom their daughter Ruth moved with them to Philadelphia for the third session. See also *DHFFC* 9:60n, 14:606–7.

DANA, FRANCIS (1743–1811), a Federalist lawyer of Boston who served as state legislator, member of Congress in 1777–78 and 1784, and diplomat, sat on the bench of the Massachusetts supreme judicial court, 1785–1806. See also *DHFFC* 17:1784.

DANA, SAMUEL WHITTLESEY (1760–1830), graduated from Yale in 1775, passed the bar in 1778, and commenced practice in Middletown, Connecticut, which he represented as a Federalist in the state House of Representatives, 1789–96. (*American Conservatism*, pp. 285–86)

DANE, NATHAN (1752–1835), was a lawyer of Beverly, Massachusetts, which he represented in the state House of Representatives, 1782–86, and Senate, 1790–91. He was the principal author of the Northwest Ordinance of 1787 while serving in Congress, 1785–88. See also *DHFFC* 17:1784.

DAVENPORT, FRANKLIN (1753–1832), named for his uncle Benjamin Franklin, was a Federalist lawyer of Woodbury, New Jersey, which he represented in the state General Assembly, 1786–89. During the Revolutionary War he was a major general in the state militia. (*DHFFE* 3:53n)

DAVES, JOHN (1748–1804), was a planter of New Bern, North Carolina, where he was appointed collector in 1790. A native of Virginia, he settled in North Carolina by the outbreak of the Revolutionary War, during which he rose from ensign in the 2nd North Carolina Regiment in 1776 to captain of the 3rd Regiment in 1781, retiring at war's end, when he enrolled in the Society of the Cincinnati. See also *DHFFC* 2:527.

DAVIE, WILLIAM R. (1756–1820), was a lawyer and planter of Halifax, North Carolina, which he represented in the state House of Commons almost continuously between 1784 and 1798. The Federalist veteran militia officer and member of the Federal Convention declined appointment as federal judge in 1790. See also *DHFFC* 17:1785.

DAVIES, WILLIAM (1749–1812), a veteran Continental Army officer of Mecklenburg County, Virginia, resided in New York City as commissioner for settling Virginia's accounts with the United States, 1789–90. See also *DHFFC* 17:1785.

DAVIS, DANIEL (1762–1835), moved to Maine in 1782, became a leader of the district's separatist movement, and represented Portland in the Massachusetts House of Representatives, 1789–91. See also *DHFFC* 17:1785–86.

DAVIS, JONATHAN (ca. 1728–1795), was a shipping merchant of Bath, Maine.

DAWES, THOMAS, JR. (1758–1825), was a Boston lawyer who ran unsuccessfully against Fisher Ames in both the first and second federal elections. The 1777 Harvard graduate sat in the Massachusetts House of Representatives, 1787–89, in the state convention, where he voted to ratify the Constitution, and on the bench of the Suffolk County probate court in 1790. See also *DHFFC* 17:1786.

DAWSON, JOHN (1762–1814), was a lawyer and planter of Spotsylvania County, Virginia, which he represented in the state House of Delegates, 1786–90, and at the ratification convention, where he voted against the Constitution. The 1782 Harvard graduate also attended Congress, 1788–89. (*DHROC* 8:17n, 355n)

DAWSON, PENELOPE JOHNSTON (1744—97), daughter of a colonial governor of North Carolina and first cousin of Samuel Johnston, was a wealthy widow of Edenton, North Carolina.

DAWSON, WILLIAM "BILLY" JOHNSTON (1765–96), the British educated son of Penelope Johnston Dawson of Edenton, North Carolina, served in the state House of Commons in 1791.

DAYTON, JONATHAN (1760–1824), was a lawyer of Elizabethtown, New Jersey, who served in the state Legislative Council in 1789 and the General Assembly in 1790. A 1776 College of New Jersey (Princeton) graduate, Continental Army veteran officer, and member of the Society of the Cincinnati, he served in Congress, 1787–88, and at the Federal Convention, where he signed the Constitution. Despite his defeat in a hotly contested first federal election for Representative, he was elected in the second federal election and served until 1799. See also *DHFFC* 18:1787.

DEANE, BARNABAS (1743–94), a merchant of Hartford, Connecticut, had been a business partner of his older brother, Silas.

DEANE, JAMES (1748–1823), a native of Connecticut, was sent as a missionary among the Iroquois before enrolling in Dartmouth's class of 1773.

During the Revolutionary War he served as an interpreter for the superintendent of Indian affairs of the Northern Department with the rank of major. In 1786 he settled permanently in present-day Westmoreland, New York, on land given him by the Oneida.

DEANE, SILAS (1737–89), a merchant and lawyer of Wethersfield, Connecticut, was an influential member of Congress, 1774–76, and was commissioned that body's first agent for conducting secret diplomatic and commercial negotiations with France, 1776–78. Robert Morris and Benjamin Franklin were among those who defended him against Congress's Adams-Lee faction intent on exposing profiteering and incompetence. He returned to Europe as a private citizen in 1780, became a bankrupt living in London, and died at sea en route back to the United States in September 1789.

DEARBORN, HENRY (1751–1929), federal marshal for Maine, 1789–93, was a physician of Pittston (present-day Gardiner), Maine, where he settled after long wartime service as an officer in Continental Army's New Hampshire Line. See also *DHFFC* 2:502, 17:1787.

DEAS, WILLIAM ALLEN (1764–post 1821), was a lawyer trained at London's Middle Temple who passed the bar in 1786 and settled in St. James Goose Creek Parish, South Carolina, which he represented in the state House of Representatives, 1790–92.

DELANY, SHARP (ca. 1739–1799), was an Irish immigrant who settled as an apothecary in Philadelphia before the Revolutionary War and served as federal collector there, 1789–99, having held that post under the state government since 1784. See also *DHFFC* 9:7n.

DEMING, JULIUS (1755–1838), was a merchant of Litchfield, Connecticut, which he represented in the state House, 1790–91. During the Revolutionary War he served as assistant commissary for the Eastern Department of the Continental Army.

DENNY, EBENEZER (1761–1822), of Carlisle, Pennsylvania, was commissioned a lieutenant in the federal army in 1787 and retained that rank in the establishment of 1789, serving as adjutant to Gen. Josiah Harmar at Fort Washington (Cincinnati), Ohio, 1790–91. During the Revolutionary War he rose from ensign in the 4th Regiment of the Pennsylvania Line in 1781 to lieutenant of the 3rd Regiment by war's end. See also *DHFFC* 2:533.

DENT, GEORGE (1756–1813), was a planter from Charles County, Maryland, which he represented in the state House of Delegates, 1782–90 (as speaker, 1788–90), and in the state Senate, 1791–92. From 1776 until 1779 he was an officer in the state militia. (*DHFFE* 2:236)

DERBY, ELIAS HASKET (1739–99), was a prominent merchant of Salem, Massachusetts. See also *DHFFC* 8:403–4.

DEROSSET, ARMAND JOHN (1767–1859), graduated from the College of Philadelphia (University of Pennsylvania) in 1790 and thereafter practiced medicine in Wilmington, North Carolina. (*Rush* 1:572n)

DEVENS, RICHARD (1721–1807), was a merchant of Charlestown, Massachusetts, who had served as a state legislator and commissary general of the militia during the Revolutionary War. See also *DHFFC* 17:1788.

DEXTER, AARON (1750–1839), was a Boston physician who graduated from Harvard in 1776 and became professor of chemistry there in 1783.

DEXTER, SAMUEL (1761–1816), a 1781 Harvard graduate and member of Boston's Wednesday Night Club, practiced law in Weston, Massachusetts, which he represented in the state House of Representatives in 1789. (*DHFFE* 1:641n)

DICKINSON, JOHN (1732–1808), one of the most influential essayists of the revolutionary and ratification movements, served as president (governor) of Delaware and then Pennsylvania in the 1780s, after serving both states as a congressman in the 1770s, during which time he was the principal author of the Articles of Confederation. The lawyer and planter from Kent County, Delaware, also represented that state at the Federal Convention, where he signed the Constitution. See also *DHFFC* 17:1788.

DOBBYN, HANNIBAL WILLIAM, arrived in New York City from Ireland in September 1789 to settle on the western frontier with some former tenants. In January 1790 he unsuccessfully petitioned Congress to purchase public lands. See also *DHFFC* 8:196–98.

DONALD, ALEXANDER (d. 1795), a Richmond tobacco merchant, came to Virginia shortly after the Revolutionary War as a partner in a Scottish mercantile firm. (*PJM* 12:48n; *John Marshall* 5:383n)

DORCHESTER, SIR GUY CARLETON, LORD (1724–1808), commander-in-chief of British forces in North America during the last year of the Revolutionary War, was governor general of Canada, 1775–78 and 1786–96. In the latter role he employed George Beckwith as the British foreign ministry's agent in New York City.

DOUGHTY, JOHN (ca. 1757–1826), of New Jersey, was a veteran officer commissioned as major in the federal army, 1789–91, in which role he was selected by Secretary of War Knox to conduct diplomatic negotiations with the Chickasaw and Choctaw nations in March 1790. See also *DHFFC* 2:518, 17:1789.

DOUW, VOLCKERT P. (1720–1801), of Greenbush, New York, was a lawyer and mayor of neighboring Albany, 1761–70, commissioner of Indian Affairs for the Northern Department from 1775 to 1784, and state Senator, 1786–93. (George Rogers Howell and Jonathan Tenney, *History of the County of Albany, New York, from 1609 to 1886* [New York, 1886], p. 661)

DRAYTON, STEPHEN (1736–1810), of Charleston, South Carolina, was a colonial legislator, an aide-de-camp to Nathanael Greene with the rank of major, 1777–78, and thereafter deputy quartermaster general for the Southern Department with the rank of colonel. (*PNG* 6:430n)

DROMGOOLE, ALEXANDER, a Virginia militia major during the Revolutionary War, became a trader with the Cherokee along the Tennessee and Little Tennessee rivers. He served as Virginia's emissary at the Cherokee nation's "capitol" of Chota (Echota), but Congress refused to appoint him superintendent of Indian affairs for the Southern Department in 1788. (*PJM* 10:273n; *LDC* 24:579n)

DROWNE, SOLOMON (1753–1834), a native of Providence, Rhode Island, graduated from the College of Rhode Island (Brown) in 1773 and served as surgeon's mate, then surgeon, in the state militia throughout the Revolutionary War. With a medical degree awarded by the College of Philadelphia (University of Pennsylvania) in 1781, he attended medical lectures throughout Europe from 1784 until 1788, when he returned to assist in the establishment of Marietta, Ohio. By 1790 he had resumed his medical practice in Providence. (*PMHB* 48[1924]:227–30)

DUANE, JAMES (1733–97), was a New York City lawyer who sat in Congress for part of every year between 1774 and 1783 and in the state Senate, 1782–85 and 1788–90, simultaneously serving as mayor, 1784–89, before being appointed federal judge for the New York district, 1789–94. See also *DHFFC* 17:1789–90.

DUER, WILLIAM (1747–99), a New York City merchant and speculator in public securities and land, and member of Congress, 1777–79, served as assistant secretary of the treasury from September 1789 until March 1790. His wife Catherine ("Lady Kitty") Alexander Duer (m. 1779) was related to the Livingstons, Schuylers, and Hamiltons. See also *DHFFC* 17:1790.

DUMAS, CHARLES GUILLAUME FRÉDÉRIC (1725–96), was a Swiss Frenchman residing at The Hague, where he served as Congress's agent and the unofficial chargé d'affaires to The Netherlands from 1775 until his death. (*PGW* 1:137n; *PRM* 5:532)

DUNLAP, JOHN (1747–1812), emigrated from Ireland to Philadelphia and, with David Claypoole, established there the *Pennsylvania Packet* in 1771. In 1791 he changed its name to *Dunlap's American Daily Advertiser.* An official printer to Congress during the late confederation and early federal Congresses, Dunlap also served on the Philadelphia common council, 1789–92. (*DHFFC* 8:603, 736, 14:xviii)

DUNN, SAMUEL (ca. 1724–1790), originally of Providence, Rhode Island, was a merchant and sea captain engaged in the West Indies trade. He died in Haiti. ([Providence, Rhode Island] *United States Chronicle*, 20 May 1790)

DWIGHT, HENRY WILLIAMS (1757–1804), of Stockbridge, Massachusetts, was the older brother of Pamela Sedgwick. A veteran of Col. John Fellows's Massachusetts Regiment of the Continental Army in 1775, he served as treasurer of Berkshire County from 1784 until his death.

DWIGHT, JOSIAH (1767–1820), younger brother of Thomas Dwight, graduated from Harvard in 1786 and became a merchant at Stockbridge, Massachusetts.

DWIGHT, THOMAS (1758–1819), a lawyer of Springfield, Massachusetts, and former state Representative, 1784–86, was a cousin of Theodore Sedgwick's wife Pamela. In April 1791 he married Hannah Worthington (1761–1833), an older sister of Fisher Ames's future wife, Frances. See also *DHFFC* 17:1791.

DWIGHT, TIMOTHY (1752–1817), was a 1769 graduate of Yale, where he remained as a tutor until joining the Continental Army's 1st Connecticut

Brigade as chaplain, 1777–78. He briefly represented his native Northampton in the Massachusetts House of Representatives, 1781–82, but his enduring fame rests on his membership in the "Connecticut Wits" (who included Joel Barlow and David Humphreys), and their literary contributions to the early American republic's "Rising Glory" movement. He held a Congregational church pulpit in Fairfield, Connecticut, from 1783 to 1795, when he succeeded Ezra Stiles as president of Yale. (*Yale Graduates* 3:321–33)

DYER, ELIPHALET (1721–1807), a lawyer of Windham, Connecticut, served on the state superior court, 1766–93, presiding as chief judge beginning in 1789. The 1740 Yale graduate and member of the Continental Congress, 1774–79 and 1782–83, put aside his Antifederalist views and voted in favor of the Constitution at the state convention. See also *DHFFC* 17:1791.

EARLE, WILLIAM (1727–1804), was a prominent merchant and shipowner of Providence, Rhode Island.

EASTON, JOHN (d. 1802), federal surveyor at Beaufort, North Carolina, from 1790 until his death, was a merchant of nearby New Bern, longtime county militia officer, 1781–89, and state legislator, 1778–87. See also *DHFFC* 2:527.

ECKLEY, JOSEPH (1750–1811), a native of London, immigrated to New Jersey in 1767, graduated from the College of New Jersey (Princeton) in 1772, and served as Congregational pastor of Boston's Old South Meetinghouse from 1779 until his death. He was also chaplain to the Massachusetts House of Representatives in 1783 and the state Senate in 1784. (*PJM* 1:67n, *Princetonians, 1769–1775*, pp. 206–9)

EDWARDS, JOHN (1755–1837), moved from Virginia to a farm in Fayette County, Kentucky, in 1780, which he represented in the Virginia House of Delegates, 1781–83, 1785, and 1786, and at several of the statehood conventions in the late 1780s.

EDWARDS, JONATHAN, JR. (1745–1801), son of the most famous colonial divine of the Great Awakening, was Congregational minister of New Haven, Connecticut's White Haven Church, 1768–95. He attended the College of New Jersey (Princeton), like his brothers Pierpont and Timothy, and graduated in 1765. (*Princetonians, 1748–1769*, pp. 492–96)

EDWARDS, PIERPONT (1750–1826), a 1768 graduate of the College of New Jersey (Princeton), was a Federalist lawyer in New Haven, Connecticut, which he represented in the state House of Representatives, 1787–89 (speaker in the last year), before his appointment as federal attorney for the state, 1789–1804. He declined his election to the Second Federal Congress. See also *DHFFC* 2:484, 17:1792.

EDWARDS, TIMOTHY (1738–1813), older brother of Jonathan, Jr., and Pierpont Edwards, was a shopkeeper, farmer, and land speculator of Stockbridge, Massachusetts. In addition to being a military supplier during the Revolutionary War, he served as a commissioner to the Iroquois, 1776–77. See also *DHFFC* 17:1792. (Barbara Graymont, *The Iroquois in the American Revolution* [Syracuse, N.Y., 1972], pp. 91, 149)

ELIOT, ANN TREADWELL (1766–1840), originally of Portsmouth, New Hampshire, was the wife of Rev. John Eliot of Boston.

ELIOT, JOHN (1754–1813), was Congregational pastor of Boston's New North Church from 1779 until his death. See also *DHFFC* 17:1792.

ELLERY, WILLIAM (1727–1820), was a lawyer and merchant of Newport, Rhode Island, where he served as federal collector from 1790 until his death, having resigned the post of continental loan officer he had held since 1786. See also *DHFFC* 17:1792–93.

ELLICE (ELLIS), ALEXANDER, was a partner with John Inglis in the London mercantile firm of Phyn, Ellice, and Inglis.

ELLICOTT, ANDREW (1754–1820), a surveyor from Ellicott City, Maryland, served as deputy to the geographer of the United States until the office expired in 1789. In February 1791 he was charged with surveying the boundaries of the new federal district. See also *DHFFC* 8:191–94, 9:35–36n, 17:1793.

ELLIOTT, BENJAMIN (1752–1835), was a merchant and large landowner of Huntingdon County, Pennsylvania. He represented Bedford County (of which Huntingdon then formed a part) in the state Assembly, 1776–77, and served as first sheriff when the new county was established in 1787. That same year he sat in the state convention where he voted in favor of the Constitution, for which he was pilloried in effigy in his home district. In December 1789 he took a seat on the state Supreme Executive Council. (*PHMB* 3[1879]:325–27; *DHROC* 2:718)

ELLIOTT, JOHN (1765–1824), originally of Killingworth, Connecticut, graduated from Yale in 1786 and was ordained pastor of the Congregational Church in Guilford, Connecticut, in November 1791.

ELLIOTT, ROBERT, was a partner with Elisha Otho "Elie" Williams as contractors for the federal army garrison at Fort Pitt (Pittsburgh), Pennsylvania.

ELLIS, JOSEPH (d. 1796), was a judge of Gloucester County, New Jersey, 1785–96, which he represented in the state General Assembly, 1778 and 1781–85, and on the Legislative Council, 1787–94. (*DHFFE* 3:29n)

ELLSWORTH, SENATOR OLIVER, family during the First Congress: his wife Abigail Wolcott (1756–1818), whom he married in 1772 and who was a first cousin of Connecticut's longtime Lieutenant Governor Oliver Wolcott, Sr.; and five children: Abigail, or "Nabby" (1774–1860); Oliver, or "Ollie" (1781–1805); Martin (1783–1857); Frances, or "Fanny" (1786–1868); and Delia (b. 23 July 1789–1840).

EMBREE, LAWRENCE (d. 1795), was a New York City merchant. (*Drinker* 3:2144)

EMERSON, SAMUEL (1764–1851), was a physician of Wells, Maine. In 1791 he married Olive Barrell, daughter of Nathaniel and Sally Sayward Barrell.

EMERY, SAMUEL (b. 1751), was a Boston merchant and 1774 Harvard graduate. See also *DHFFC* 17:1793.

EMLEN, SAMUEL, SR. (1730–99), was a Quaker merchant and antislavery activist of Philadelphia. He had two daughters and a son by his wife Sarah Mott (m. 1770). (*Drinker* 3:2144)

EPPES, FRANCIS (1747–1808), was a planter of Chesterfield County, Virginia. In ca. 1769 he married Elizabeth Wayles, younger half sister of Jefferson's wife Martha.

ERNEST, MATHEW (d. 1805), was a lieutenant in the United States Artillery Regiment posted at Fort Pitt (Pittsburgh), Pennsylvania, 1789–91. See also *DHFFC* 2:522.

EUSTIS, WILLIAM (1753–1825), a Harvard graduate of 1772, served as a regimental surgeon in the Continental Army, 1776–80, and army hospital surgeon thereafter until war's end, when he joined the Society of the Cincinnati. He represented Boston in the Massachusetts House of Representatives, 1788–94.

EVELEIGH, NICHOLAS (ca. 1748–1791), a merchant planter of Charleston, South Carolina, served as comptroller general of the United States treasury from 1789 until his death in April 1791. See also *DHFFC* 17:1793–94.

EVERETT, OLIVER (1752–1802), graduated from Harvard in 1779 and became pastor of Boston's New South Church, 1782–92. (*Massachusetts Bar* 2:485)

EVERTSON, NICHOLAS (ca. 1765–1807), a native New Yorker, graduated from Yale in 1787 and became an attorney in New York City. (*Yale Graduates* 4:543)

EWELL, MAXEY (ca. 1734–1800), of Charlottesville, Virginia, served as commissary to Gen. John Burgoyne's imprisoned "Convention Army" in Albemarle County in 1779–81.

EWING, JAMES (1744–1824), of Trenton, New Jersey, was appointed commissioner of loans for that state in 1790, having held the position under the Confederation, 1786–89. A veteran officer of the state militia, he served in the colonial and state legislature, 1774 and 1778. See also *DHFFC* 2:518.

FARLIE, JAMES (1757–1830), of Albany, was a clerk to the New York supreme court. (*DHSCUS* 1:650n)

FAW, ABRAHAM (1747–1828), was a merchant from Frederick County, Maryland, which he represented in the state House of Delegates, 1785–89, and at the state convention, where he voted to ratify the Constitution. He was an unsuccessful candidate for Representative in the first federal election. (*DHFFE* 2:237)

FAXON, JOHN (1763–1826), a native of Massachusetts, served as a musician and matross (artillery private) in the Continental Army and became a lawyer after his graduation from the College of Rhode Island (Brown) in 1787. (George L. Faxon, *History of the Faxon Family* [Springfield, Mass., 1880], pp. 126–27)

FENNER, ARTHUR (1745–1805), was a prosperous merchant of Providence, Rhode Island, whose only prior public office was as court clerk when he was elected as a compromise candidate for governor, serving from April 1790 until his death. His younger sister Lydia married Theodore Foster in 1771.

FENNO, JOHN (1751–98), a failed Boston merchant, moved to New York City in January 1789 to establish the *Gazette of the United States*. He married Mary Curtis (d. 1798) of Needham, Massachusetts, in 1777, with whom he had nine children. See also *DHFFC* 9:42n, 10:xxxiv–xxxviii, 17:1794.

FENWICK, JOSEPH (ca. 1765–1823), originally of St. Mary's County, Maryland, was a partner in a mercantile firm with George Mason's son John based in Bordeaux, France, when he was appointed United States consul there in June 1790. See also *DHFFC* 2:496, 17:1794–95.

FEW, CATHERINE NICHOLSON (1764–1854), daughter of the senior Continental Navy captain, "Commodore" James Nicholson of New York City, married William Few in June 1788, and resided with him in her parents' home at 91 Williams Street during the first two sessions of Congress. The first two of their three daughters were born during the First Congress: Frances (20 April 1789–1885) and Mary (1790–1873). Catherine's younger sister Frances married Joshua Seney on 1 May 1790. (Noble E. Cunningham, Jr., ed., "Diary of Frances Few, 1808–1809," *Journal of Southern History*, vol. 29, 3[Aug. 1963]:345n, 346n)

FINDLEY, WILLIAM (1741–1821), emigrated from Ireland to Cumberland County, Pennsylvania, in 1763, where he became a weaver, schoolteacher, lawyer, and militia officer. At war's end he settled in Westmoreland County, which he represented in the state Council of Censors, 1783–84; the General Assembly, 1784–88; the ratification convention where he voted against the Constitution; the Supreme Executive Council, 1789–90; the convention where he chaired the committee that drafted the new state constitution of 1790; and the state's first House of Representatives, 1790–91. An unsuccessful Antifederalist candidate for Representative in the first federal election, he subsequently won a seat in the second federal election and served until 1799. See also *DHFFC* 9:175n. (*DHROC* 2:728)

FINNIE, WILLIAM (1739–1804), of Norfolk, Virginia, was in New York in early 1789 and again in early 1790 unsuccessfully soliciting a government appointment and the settlement of his public accounts in the quartermaster department of Virginia, 1776–80. See also *DHFFC* 7:464–65, 17:1795.

FISHBOURN (FISHBOURNE), BENJAMIN (1759–8 November 1790), was rejected by the Senate as naval officer for Savannah, Georgia, in August 1789 after holding that position under the state since 1788. He served in the state House of Assembly, 1786–89, and as president of its Executive Council, 1788–89. See also *DHFFC* 2:491, 17:1795.

FISHER, JOSHUA (1748–1833), a cousin of Fisher Ames, graduated from Harvard in 1766 and, except for a brief career as a privateer during the Revolutionary War, enjoyed a flourishing medical practice in Beverly, Massachusetts, until he co-founded that town's cotton manufactory and became its superintendent in 1788. (*Harvard Graduates* 16:355–58)

FISHER, MIERS (1748–1819), a Philadelphia lawyer, city council member, and Quaker antislavery activist, played an important behind-the-scenes role in several legislative initiatives during the First Congress. See also *DHFFC* 17:1795.

FISK, JOHN (1744–97), was a merchant of Salem, Massachusetts, who served as a captain in the state navy during the Revolutionary War. (Robert McHenry, ed., *Webster's American Military Biographies* [New York, 1984], p. 124)

FITCH, ELIPHALET (b. ca. 1740), a distant relation of John Adams, whom he met in London in 1783, was a wealthy planter and receiver general for Great Britain in Kingston, Jamaica. (*PGW* 5:391n; *Adams*, 3:134)

FITCH, JOHN (1743–1798), of Bucks County, Pennsylvania, petitioned the First Congress four times regarding patent protection for various inventions utilizing steam for inland navigation. See also *DHFFC* 8:39–41.

FITZHUGH, WILLIAM "OF CHATHAM" (1741–1809), a planter of Stafford County, Virginia, served in the state House of Delegates, 1776–77, 1780–81, and 1787–88, and in the state Senate, 1781–85, in addition to attending Congress briefly in 1779. (*PJM* 1:297n)

FLINT, ROYAL (1754–97), was a New York City merchant, bookseller, and speculator in public securities and land. See also *DHFFC* 17:1796–97.

FOGG, JEREMIAH (1749–1808), interrupted legal studies to serve as an officer in the Revolutionary War, afterwards residing in Kensington, New Hampshire, which he represented as a Federalist at the state ratification convention. See also *DHFFC* 17:1797. (*Harvard Graduates* 17:21–24)

FOLGER, WILLIAM (d. 1815), a merchant originally from Nantucket, Massachusetts, was among the large colony that migrated from Cape Cod to Hudson, New York, in the 1780s. Through his wife he was a distant relation of Alexander Coffin.

FORREST, URIAH (1756–1805), a prominent merchant of Georgetown, Maryland (present-day D.C.), played an active role in negotiating the transfer of land titles from his fellow proprietors to form the core of Washington, D.C. The veteran officer of the Revolutionary War also served briefly in Congress in 1787. See also *DHFFC* 17:1797.

FOSDICK, NATHANIEL (1760–1819), a 1779 Harvard graduate, was a merchant and federal collector of Portland, Maine, 1789–1801, having held that position under the state since 1797. See also *DHFFC* 2:503. (*PGW* 2:329)

FOSTER, BOSSENGER, SR. (1743–1805), was a Boston merchant and speculator. In 1766 he married Andrew Craigie's sister Elizabeth, who died in 1778; the next year he married their sister Mary (d. 1805). (Frederick C. Pierce, *Foster Genealogy* [Chicago, 1899], pp. 936–37)

FOSTER, DWIGHT (1757–1823), younger brother of Theodore Foster, graduated from the College of Rhode Island (Brown) in 1774 and became a prosperous lawyer of Brookfield, Massachusetts, which he represented in the state House of Representatives, 1791–92. (*DHROC* 7:1529–30n; Frederick Clifton Pierce, *Foster Genealogy* [Chicago, 1899], p. 222)

FOSTER, LYDIA FENNER (1748–1801), of Providence, Rhode Island, sister of Governor Arthur Fenner, married Theodore Foster in 1771. Their surviving children at the time of the First Congress were Theodosia (b. 1772) and Theodore Dwight (b. 1780). (Rhode Island Historical Society *Collections*, 7[1885]:117)

FOX, EDWARD (1752–1822), was a native of Ireland who settled in Philadelphia by 1777 and studied law before serving as auditor general of Pennsylvania, 1778–83, commissioner for settling the accounts of the hospital department, 1782–86, and secretary to the board of treasury during the Revolutionary War. (*PRM* 4:253n; John H. Campbell, *History of the Friendly Sons of St. Patrick* [Philadelphia, 1892], p. 410)

FOX, JOHN (1749–95), was a merchant of Portland, Maine, where he served as selectman in 1786–89, as delegate to the convention where he voted to ratify the Constitution in 1788, and as state Representative in 1787–88 and 1790–92. (William Willis, *History of Portland, from 1632 to 1864* [Portland, Me., 1865], pp. 804–5; W. W. Clayton, *History of Cumberland County, Maine* [Philadelphia, 1880], pp. 167–68)

FRANCIS, JOHN (1763–96), son of Tench Francis and first cousin of Tench Coxe, moved from his native Philadelphia and became a partner in the Providence, Rhode Island, mercantile firm of Brown and Francis in 1786. In 1788 he married his partner John Brown's daughter Abigail (1766–1821). (*Rhode Island History* 6[1947]:101n; *PG*, 6 February 1788)

FRANCIS, TENCH (1730–1800), a Philadelphia merchant, acted as agent for the Penn family before the Revolutionary War, during which he served in the militia and loaned large sums of money for the cause. He was the first cashier of the Bank of North America, 1781–92. His sister Mary was the mother of Tench Coxe. (*Drinker* 3:2151)

FRANKLIN, BENJAMIN (1706–17 April 1790), the Boston born Philadelphia printer, writer, scientist, philanthropist, colonial legislator, postmaster general of British North America, 1753–74, colonial agent to Great Britain for Massachusetts, Georgia, New Jersey, and Pennsylvania, member of Congress, 1775–76, minister to France, 1776–85, and signer of both the Declaration of Independence and the Constitution, closed his lengthy public career as president (governor) of Pennsylvania, 1786–88. See also *DHFFC* 9:154–55, 17:1798.

FRANKLIN, WILLIAM TEMPLE (ca. 1760–1823), the illegitimate son of Benjamin Franklin's illegitimate son William Franklin, was born in Great Britain and educated there under the supervision of his grandfather, whose secretary he became while minister to France, 1776–85. Upon settling in New Jersey, he proved unsuccessful at both farming and procuring a diplomatic appointment, and returned to Great Britain shortly after his grandfather's death.

FRAZIER, NALBRO, a native Bostonian, was a partner in a Philadelphia mercantile firm with Tench Coxe from 1784 until it was dissolved in May 1790. See also *DHFFC* 17:1798–99.

FREDERICK II "THE GREAT" (1712–86), befriended and patronized many philosophes of the Enlightenment while acting as one of the great arbiters and military leaders in European politics during his reign as king of Prussia, 1740–86.

FREEMAN, CONSTANT, JR. (1757–1824), older brother of James and Ezekial Freeman, worked in his father Constant, Sr.'s mercantile firm, operating between Quebec and Boston, before the Revolutionary War. During the war he served in various Continental artillery units, rising from first lieutenant in 1776 to captain lieutenant in 1778 before retiring at war's end, when he joined the Society of the Cincinnati. In 1791 while serving as clerk in the war department, he declined appointment as captain of the additional federal regiment raised under the Military Establishment Act [HR-126A] (*PAH* 13:107). See also *DHFFC* 2:503.

FREEMAN, CONSTANT, SR., was a native of Cape Cod who became a merchant and sea captain trading between Massachusetts and Quebec. Although he supported the revolutionary cause, he resided in Quebec from 1776 to 1790, when he returned to Boston and became a distiller. He was the father of Ezekial, James, and Constant Freeman, Jr. (William Lee, "Record of the Services of Constant Freeman," *Magazine of American History with Notes and Queries* [New York, 1878], 2:349)

FREEMAN, EZEKIAL (b. 1762), son of Constant Freeman, Sr., and younger brother of James and Constant Freeman, Jr., was a native of Charlestown, Massachusetts, who clerked in the auditor's office during the First Congress.

FREEMAN, JAMES (1759–1835), son of Constant Freeman, Sr., and brother of Ezekial and Constant, Jr, graduated from Harvard in 1777 and was ordained minister of Boston's King's Chapel in 1787, where he oversaw its conversion from Anglicanism to the first Unitarian church in the United States. (Sydney E. Ahlstrom, *A Religious History of the American People* [New Haven, Conn., 1972], p. 388)

FRENCH, JAMES (d. post-1796), a deputy surveyor in Lincoln County, Kentucky, beginning in 1783, represented Madison County at the statehood convention of 1788. (*Sketches of Kentucky* 2:476, 516)

FRENEAU, PHILIP (1752–1832), became a close friend of James Madison while a student at the College of New Jersey (Princeton), class of 1771, after which he taught school, studied theology, and traveled the Caribbean briefly before enrolling in the New Jersey militia, 1778–80, and serving sporadically as a merchant sea captain and privateer. Throughout the 1770s he honed his skills as a poet to become a principal spokesman for an indigenous American literature, which was part of what he christened the "Rising Glory" movement. After assisting the publisher of Philadelphia's *Freeman's Journal*, 1781–82, he resumed a mercantile career but returned to publishing in 1790 with New York's *Daily Advertiser,* to which he contributed poems of social and political satire. Lured to Philadelphia by Jefferson's offer of a clerkship in the state department, Freneau simultaneously oversaw publication of the anti-administration *National Gazette,* 1791–93. (*Princetonians, 1769–1775,* pp. 149–56)

FREY, JOHN (1740–1833), a lawyer of Palatine, New York, was an early and active participant in the revolutionary movement as a local public officeholder and state militia officer, 1775–78. He represented Montgomery County at the state convention where he voted against the Constitution, and in the state Assembly during the First Congress. (Maryly B. Penrose, *Mohawk Valley in the Revolution* [Franklin Park, N.J., 1978], p. 253; *DHROC* 21:1477–79; *DHFFC* 3:510)

FROBISHER, WILLIAM, was a soap boiler in Boston in 1790.

FROTHINGHAM, JOHN (1750–1826), was a native of Massachusetts who graduated from Harvard in 1771, and in 1774 settled in Portland, Maine, where he taught school and studied law. Admitted to the bar in 1779, he was appointed state attorney for Cumberland County the next year as well as holding a variety of local public offices. (*Harvard Graduates* 17:520–21; William Willis, *History of the Law, Courts, and Lawyers of Maine* [Portland, Me., 1863], pp. 103–4)

GADSDEN, CHRISTOPHER (1723–1805), radical leader of the revolutionary movement in South Carolina, received his formal education in England and his mercantile training in Philadelphia before returning by 1746 to his native Charleston, where he became a merchant, planter, and colonial assemblyman, 1757–75. He attended the Stamp Act Congress in 1765 and Congress, 1774–76, simultaneously serving as colonel of the First South Carolina Regiment from 1775 until his promotion to brigadier general, 1776–77. While serving in the state House of Representatives in 1778, he helped to frame the state constitution under which he served as the first lieutenant governor until 1780. In that capacity he was taken prisoner at the surrender of Charleston in 1780, from which he never regained his health, continuing nevertheless to serve as state Representative until 1784. He voted for the Constitution at the state convention, was elected Presidential Elector in the first federal election, and attended the convention that drafted the state constitution of 1790. (*DHFFE* 1:220)

GALLATIN, ALBERT (1761–1849), emigrated from his native Geneva, Switzerland, in 1780 and resided briefly in Boston before settling permanently in Fayette County, Pennsylvania, in 1784. An Antifederalist spokesman during ratification, he served as delegate to the state constitutional convention of 1789–90, and as state Representative, 1790–91. See also *DHFFC* 9:380.

GAMBLE, ROBERT (1754–1810), was a merchant of Staunton, Virginia, before relocating to Richmond in 1790. During the Revolutionary War he rose from first lieutenant of the 12th Virginia Regiment in 1776 to captain of the 8th Regiment in 1778, serving until war's end, when he enrolled in the Society of the Cincinnati. (Alexander Brown, *The Campbells and their Kin* [Richmond, Va., 1939], pp. 278–79)

GANSEVOORT, LEONARD (1751–1810), was a lawyer and gentleman farmer of Albany, New York, which he represented in the provincial and state assemblies, 1775–79 and 1788, and in the state Senate, 1791–93. A political ally and confidant of Stephen van Rensselaer, he also served in Congress in 1788. (*DHFFC* 3:253)

GARDINER, JOHN (1737–93), represented Pownalboro, Maine, in the Massachusetts House of Representatives from 1789 until his death. The Glasgow trained lawyer had returned to his birthplace of Boston in 1783 after almost thirty years' residence in London, where he championed a number of liberal "Whig" causes, including as lawyer for the radical John Wilkes. (*Abigail Adams*, p. 38n)

GARDNER, WILLIAM (1751–1833), a merchant of Portsmouth, New Hampshire, served as state treasurer from 1789 until his appointment as federal commissioner of loans for the state, 1791–96. During the Revolutionary War he was a deputy clothier for the Continental Army as well as an officer in the state cavalry unit commanded by John Langdon, for whom Gardner served at the same time as private secretary. See also *DHFFC* 2:515. (*PJB*, p. 222n; Lawrence Shaw Mayo, *John Langdon of New Hampshire* [1937; reprint, Port Washington, N.Y., 1970], p. 143n)

GARDOQUI, DON DIEGO (JAMES) MARIA DE (1735–98), resided in New York City as Spain's *encargado de negocios*, or chief diplomatic representative to the United States, from 1785 until his return to Spain in October 1789. See also *DHFFC* 9:13n. (*PGW* 3:300)

GARNETT, MUSCOE (1736–1803), was a merchant planter of "Mount Pleasant," his estate near Loretto on the Rappahannock River below Fredericksburg, Virginia. (*PJM* 13:241)

GATES, HORATIO (1727–1806), a major general in the Continental Army, 1775–83, lived in semi-retirement on his plantation "Traveller's Rest" in Berkeley County, West Virginia, until he moved permanently to New York City in September 1790 and became an advocate for veterans' rights. See also *DHFFC* 17:1800.

GELSTON, DAVID (1744–1828), was an Antifederalist merchant from Suffolk County, Long Island, which he represented in the New York provincial and state assemblies, 1775–85 (speaker, 1784–85), and in the state Senate, 1791–94. In February 1789 he was one of the last delegates to present his credentials to the expiring Confederation Congress. (*DHFFE* 3:208n, 237n; *JCC* 34:605)

GEOGHEGAN, IGNATIUS (1743–97), a ship's surgeon for the South Carolina navy during the Revolutionary War, was Georgia's port health officer at Savannah from early 1789 throughout the First Congress. (*PTJ* 19:331–32)

GEORGE, DANIEL (ca. 1759–1804), was a schoolteacher, bookseller, and almanac publisher in Portland, Maine. See also *DHFFC* 17:1800.

GERRARD, CHARLES (ca. 1750–1797), managed John Gray Blount's store at Tarboro, North Carolina, before settling in Davidson County, Tennessee, which he represented at the state's 1789 ratification convention. During the Revolutionary War he served as first lieutenant in the 5th and 2nd North Carolina Regiments, 1777–81, before transferring to the 1st Regiment, where he served until war's end. (*Powell*)

GERRARD, JAMES (1749–1822), represented Bourbon County, Kentucky, in the Virginia Senate.

GERRY, ANN THOMPSON (1763–1849) daughter of New York City merchant James Thompson, married Elbridge Gerry on 12 January 1786 and resided with him at the seat of government during the first and second sessions. The first three of their nine children were alive during the First Congress: Catharine (1787–1850), Thomas (1788–1 November 1789), and Eleanor (b. July 1790). Gerry and Isaac Coles became brothers-in-law by the latter's marriage to Ann's sister Catherine on 2 January 1790. (George Athan Billias, *Elbridge Gerry: Founding Father and Republican Statesman* [New York, 1976], pp. 403–4)

GERRY, SAMUEL RUSSELL (1750–1807), younger brother of Elbridge Gerry, was appointed collector at his native Marblehead, Massachusetts, in 1790. See also *DHFFC* 2:504, 17:1800–1801. (*PGW* 6:124n)

GERRY, THOMAS, JR. (1735–ca. 26 April 1790), was a merchant of Marblehead, Massachusetts, as his younger brother Elbridge had been. He was often referred to as "Colonel" in family correspondence, for his rank of lieutenant colonel in the state militia. His death (dated approximately from an unlocated 26 April letter from Samuel to Elbridge Gerry, noting the event) followed spells of blindness beginning the year before. (George Athan Billias, *Elbridge Gerry: Founding Father and Republican Statesman* [New York, 1976], p. 129)

GIBBS, GEORGE (1735–1803), was a West Indian shipping merchant of Newport, Rhode Island, and brother-in-law of Walter Channing. (George Gibbs, *The Gibbs Family of Rhode Island*, [New York, 1933], pp. 11–18)

GIBBS, HENRY (1749–94), a Harvard graduate of 1766, was a merchant of Salem, Massachusetts, and a prominent Federalist. In 1781 he married Mercy Prescott (1755–1809), the younger sister of Roger Sherman's wife Rebecca. (*Harvard Graduates* 16:358; *DHROC* 4:174)

GILL, MOSES (1734–1800), a merchant of Princeton, Massachusetts, served on the governor's executive council, 1780–95, and as a presidential elector in the first federal election. (*DHFFE* 1:750)

GILLON, ALEXANDER (1741–94), emigrated from his native Holland and by 1766 had established a large mercantile business in Charleston, South Carolina. As commodore of the state navy, 1778–82, he was authorized to act as state purchasing agent in Europe. See also *DHFFC* 12:875n.

GILMAN, DANIEL (1770–1804), of Boston, Massachusetts, was the younger brother of John Taylor, Nathaniel, and Nicholas Gilman.

GILMAN, JOHN TAYLOR (1753–1828), eldest brother of Daniel, Nathaniel, and Nicholas Gilman, was a shipbuilder and merchant of Exeter, New Hampshire. A former member of Congress and state Representative, treasurer, and delegate to the state convention, where he voted to ratify the Constitution, he declined reappointment as commissioner for settling accounts between the federal government and the states when that board was reconstituted under the new Settlement of Accounts Act [HR-77] in 1790. See also *DHFFC* 2:515, 17:1801. (*PJB*, p. 181n)

GILMAN, NATHANIEL (1759–1847), of Exeter, New Hampshire, succeeded his father as continental loan officer for the state, 1783–89, but declined appointment as commissioner of loans in 1790. He was the brother of Daniel, John Taylor, and Nicholas Gilman. See also *DHFFC* 2:515, 17:1801–2. (*PJB*, p. 308n)

GILMER, GEORGE (1743–95), was a physician who resided at "Pen Park," his estate outside Charlottesville, Virginia. The University of Edinburgh graduate represented Albemarle County in the colony's last revolutionary convention of 1776 and in the state House of Delegates, 1778–80. (*DHROC* 8:258–59n)

GLASGOW, JAMES (d. 1820), was a land speculator and secretary of state for North Carolina, 1776–96. (*Blount* 3:101)

GLOVER, JOHN (1732–97), was a shipping merchant and fisherman of Marblehead, Massachusetts, who applied his civilian expertise to commanding "Glover's Regiment" of the Massachusetts Line (redesignated the 14th Continental Regiment) in 1775–76. Following his amphibious regiment's celebrated participation in the campaigns of 1776, he was promoted to brigadier general, 1777–82, and retired at war's end as a brevet major general.

GODDARD, MARY KATHERINE (1738–1816), a Baltimore drygoods and bookstore owner, was the sole proprietor and manager of the *Maryland Journal*, 1775–84, serving as the town's postmistress from 1775 until her dismissal in November 1789. See also *DHFFC* 8:231–32.

GOODHUE, FRANCES "FANNY" RITCHIE (1751–1801), originally of Philadelphia, married Benjamin Goodhue in 1775 and resided at their home in Salem, Massachusetts. By the time of the First Congress, she had given birth to the first seven of their eight children: Frances (b. 1778), Sarah (1780–96), Mary (b. 1781), Jonathan (b. 1783), Benjamin (1785–1814), Martha (b. 1787), and Stephen (27 August 1789–31 May 1790). (*DHFFC* 14:624; Jonathan E. Goodhue, *History and Genealogy of the Goodhue Family in England and America to the Year 1890* [Rochester, N.Y., 1891])

GOODHUE, STEPHEN (1739–1809), was a merchant of Salem, Massachusetts, who managed the business affairs of his older brother Benjamin during the First Congress. By his marriage in 1767 to Martha Prescott (b. 1744), he became the brother-in-law of both Roger Sherman and Henry Gibbs. See also *DHFFC* 17:1802.

GOODMAN, NOAH (1734–97), was an innkeeper in South Hadley, Massachusetts, which he represented as a Federalist at the state ratifying convention. During the Revolutionary War he rose to the rank of major in the state militia. (Sylvester Judd, *History of Hadley* [Springfield, Mass., 1905], p. 299)

GOODRICH, CHAUNCEY (1759–1815), a lawyer of Hartford, Connecticut, graduated from Yale in 1776 and taught there briefly before being admitted to the bar in 1781. He was brother-in-law to Oliver Wolcott, Jr. (*Yale Graduates* 2:139)

GOODWIN, SAMUEL (1716–1802), became a surveyor and agent for the Kennebec Company of land speculators and settled on their holdings in Pownalborough, Maine, in 1761.

GORDON, JAMES (1739–1810), emigrated from his native Ireland and by 1758 settled as a trader in Ballston Spa, Albany (part of present-day Saratoga) County, New York, which he represented in the state Assembly, 1777–80, 1786, and 1790. A lieutenant colonel in the county militia during the Revolutionary War, he succeeded Peter Silvester as a Federalist in the second federal election and served until 1795.

GORE, CHRISTOPHER (1758–1827), was a lawyer of Boston, which he represented in the Massachusetts House of Representatives from 1788 until he resigned his seat when it was deemed in conflict with his appointment as federal attorney for the state, 1789–96. See also *DHFFC* 2:504, 17:1803.

GORHAM, NATHANIEL (1738–96), a Federalist merchant and land speculator of Charlestown, Massachusetts, was a frequent state legislator, member of Congress, and member of the Federal Convention and state ratification convention before being appointed federal supervisor of distilled spirits for the state, 1791–96. See also *DHFFC* 2:504, 8:191–96, 17:1803.

GOUVERNEUR, ISAAC (1721–1807), uncle of Gouverneur Morris, was a successful New York City merchant.

GRAY, AMASA, a founding member of the Rhode Island Society of Mechanics and Manufacturers in 1789, represented Providence in the state House of Deputies, 1789–90.

GRAY, WILLIAM, JR. (1750–1825), a merchant of Salem, Massachusetts, represented that town at the state convention, where he voted to ratify the Constitution.

GRAYSON, WILLIAM SMALLWOOD (d. 1794), of Dumfries, Virginia, was the orphan son of Senator Grayson. He held a commission in the federal army for a few months before his death. (*PJM* 13:224n)

GREEN, ASHABEL (1762–1848), joined a state militia company in 1778 and served briefly as a sergeant before enrolling in the class of 1783 of the College of New Jersey (Princeton). In 1787, two years after his marriage to Elias Boudinot's niece Elizabeth Stockton (d. 1807), he commenced a popular and longtime pastorship at Philadelphia's Second Presbyterian Church.

GREEN, FREDERICK, published Annapolis's *Maryland Gazette* from 1772 to 1777 and, jointly with his brother Samuel (d. 1811), in 1779–1811.

GREEN, JOHN (b. 1736), was an Irish born Philadelphia sea captain who served as a captain in the Continental Navy. After the Revolutionary War he became a business associate of Robert Morris for whom he commanded the historic commercial voyage to China on the *Empress of China* in 1784–85. (*PRM* 3:217n, 8:862–65)

GREENE, CATHARINE "KITTY" LITTLEFIELD (1755–1814), widow of General Nathanael Greene, resided at their plantation "Mulberry Grove," outside Savannah, Georgia, except during the summer and part of the winter of 1789–90, when she stayed with the Knoxes in New York City while planning her successful petition to the First Congress for the settlement of her husband's public accounts. See also *DHFFC* 7:493–592, 17:1804.

GREENE, GRIFFIN (1749–1804), was involved in many business ventures with his first cousin, General Nathanael Greene, including as partner in the latter's iron forges, before serving briefly as his deputy quartermaster general. As a director of the Ohio Company, in 1788 he emigrated to Marietta, Ohio, where he became a local judge, and from which he founded the town of Belpre in 1790. (*PNG* 1:107n)

GREENLEAF, JAMES (1765–1843), a native of Boston, was a partner in the New York City mercantile firm of Greenleaf and Watson and served as the firm's agent as well as a government securities broker in Amsterdam, 1789–93. See also *DHFFC* 17:1804.

GREENUP, CHRISTOPHER (1750–1818), was a native of Virginia who settled in Danville, Kentucky, in 1783 and began to practice law. During the Revolutionary War he served as lieutenant in future Senator Grayson's Continental Regiment, 1777–78, subsequently commanding his own regiment of Virginia militia. Greenup was clerk of Virginia's district court of Kentucky, represented Fayette County in the state House of Delegates, 1785–86, and helped organize the Kentucky Manufacturing Society in 1789. He was also active in the statehood movement, one of the subjects frequently debated in Danville's Political Club, of which he was a founding member along with John Brown, Harry Innes, and Thomas Todd. (*DHROC* 8:408n, 434n)

GREGORY, ISAAC (1740–1800), a planter of Edenton, North Carolina, was appointed federal collector at Plankbridge (near present-day Elizabeth City) in 1790. See also *DHFFC* 2: 527–28.

GRENVILLE, WILLIAM WYNDHAM, LORD (1759–1834), Great Britain's secretary of state for the home department beginning in 1789, succeeded the Duke of Leeds as secretary of state for foreign affairs in 1791.

GRIFFIN, CYRUS (1748–1810), a London trained lawyer of Lancaster County, Virginia, served as United States district judge for that state from 1789 until his death. The former member of the state House of Delegates and of Congress (including as its president, 1787–88) was the younger brother of Samuel Griffin. See also *DHFFC* 2:549–50, 17:1804–5.

GRIMKÉ, JOHN FAUCHERAUD (1752–1819), a lawyer of Charleston, South Carolina, graduated from Cambridge in 1774 and studied at London's Middle Temple before returning to serve as an aide-de-camp in the Continental Army, 1777–78, and lieutenant colonel of the state artillery thereafter until 1780. While a state judge from 1783, he also sat in the state House of Representatives, 1784–89 (speaker, 1785–86), and at the ratifying convention where he voted in favor of the Constitution, under which he served as a Presidential Elector in the first federal election. (*DHFFE* 1:221)

GRISWOLD, MATTHEW (1714–99), was a Federalist lawyer and jurist of Lyme, Connecticut, which he represented in the colonial legislature from 1754 until 1769, serving simultaneously thereafter as deputy governor and chief judge of the superior court until his election as governor, 1784–86. After presiding over the ratifying convention where he voted in favor of the Constitution, he returned to the state House of Representatives, 1789–90. (*DHROC* 3:610)

GROVE, WILLIAM BARRY (1764–1818), was a lawyer of Fayetteville, North Carolina, which he represented in the state House of Commons (1786, 1788–89) and at both ratifying conventions, where he voted in favor of the Constitution. Running as a Federalist in the second federal election, he defeated Timothy Bloodworth and kept his seat until 1803.

HABERSHAM, JOSEPH (1751–1815), attended grammar school in Princeton, New Jersey, in the early 1760s and learned the mercantile trade in England before returning to his native Savannah, Georgia, in 1771, where he followed in the family line of successful merchant planters as a partner with his cousin Joseph Clay. He joined two brothers among the leadership of the revolutionary government, eventually serving in the 1st Regiment of the Georgia Line, where he rose from major to colonel between 1776 and his resignation in 1778. He declined a seat in Congress when elected in 1784, but did serve in the state House of Assembly in 1782, 1784–85, and 1787–90 (speaker in 1785 and 1790), in the ratifying convention, where he voted in favor of the Constitution, and as Savannah alderman, 1790–91. (*DHROC* 3:308–9; Frank Lambert, *James Habersham* [Athens, Ga., 2005], pp. 148–49)

HACKETT, JAMES (b. 1739), was a shipbuilder of Exeter, New Hampshire. During the war, he was employed by John Langdon to build the Continental Navy ships *Raleigh* and *America* in Portsmouth and in 1778 he served as lieutenant of the state militia's cavalry unit that Langdon raised and outfitted for the Rhode Island campaign. (*PJB*, p. 68n; Lawrence Shaw Mayo, *John Langdon of New Hampshire* [1937; reprint, Port Washington, N.Y., 1970], p. 173)

HALL, JOSIAS CARVIL (1746–1814), was a physician and planter of Baltimore County, Maryland, who became son-in-law to future Representative William Smith (Md.) by his marriage to Janet ("Jenny") Smith (1752–1812) sometime prior to 1775. See also *DHFFC* 17:1806.

HALL, LOTT (1757–1809), a native of Cape Cod, Massachusetts, followed in the steps of his childhood friend, George Thatcher, and studied law under Shearjashub Bourne. In 1782 he settled in Westminster, Vermont, which he represented in the state legislature. (Benjamin H. Hall, *The Halls of Eastern Vermont* [New York, 1858], pp. 658–66)

HALL, STEPHEN (1743–94), was a merchant and tanner of Portland, Maine. He married Mary Cotton Holt (1754–1808) in 1778. See also *DHFFC* 8:357–59, 17:1806.

HALL, WILLIAM (1759–18014), a captain in the South Carolina state navy during the Revolutionary War, was appointed commander of the federal revenue cutter for the state in October 1790. (*PGW* 6:101n)

HAMILTON, ALEXANDER (1757–1804), a New York City lawyer, served as secretary of the treasury, 1789–95. In state politics he was firmly allied to Philip Schuyler, whose daughter Elizabeth (1757–1854) he married in 1780. Four of their eight children were alive during the First Congress: Philip (1782–1801), Angelica (1784–1857), Alexander (1786–1875), and James Alexander (1788–1878). See also *DHFFC* 17:1807.

HAMILTON, JOHN (1764–1822), was a Scottish trained lawyer of Edenton, North Carolina, which he represented in the state House of Commons, 1789–93. He was a Federalist during the ratification of the Constitution. (*DHFFE* 4:355n)

HAMTRAMCK, JOHN F. (1756–1803), a native of Canada, served in the Continental Army as captain in the Fifth New York Regiment from 1776 until 1783 (when it was redesignated the 2nd Regiment). Rejoining the federal army with the same rank in 1785, he was commissioned major in 1789 and died in service with the rank of colonel. See also *DHFFC* 2:523.

HANCOCK, JOHN (1737–93), a wealthy Boston merchant, was an early leader of the revolutionary movement, member of Congress, 1775–78, and longtime governor, 1780–85 and 1787–93. Despite his Antifederalist leanings, he played a critical role in the state's ratification of the Constitution. See also *DHFFC* 17:1808.

HAND, EDWARD (1744–1802), was an Irish born physician and farmer of Lancaster County, Pennsylvania, who was nominated for Representative but won only as a Presidential Elector in the first federal election. See also *DHFFC* 17:1808.

HARDIN, JOHN (1753–92), a native of Virginia, served as a lieutenant in Pennsylvania's 2nd Continental Regiment from 1776 until his resignation in 1779. He settled in Nelson County, Kentucky, in 1786 and became lieutenant colonel of the militia, serving as second in command during Gen. Josiah Harmar's punitive expedition against the Native Americans of the Northwest Territory in late 1790.

HARDIN, JOSEPH (1734–1801), a native of Virginia, moved to Tryon County, North Carolina, which he represented in the provincial Congress,

1775–76, and in the state House of Commons, 1778–79. He served as a state militia major before settling on a farm near present-day Greeneville, Tennessee, which he also represented in the state House of Commons in 1782 and again in 1788. During the interlude, Hardin served as first Speaker of the House for the secessionist state of Franklin. (Clarence W. Griffin, *History of Old Tryon and Rutherford Counties, North Carolina* [Asheville, N.C., 1939], pp. 22–23)

HARDING, SETH (1734–1814), a native of Cape Cod, Massachusetts, moved to Norwich, Connecticut, in 1760 where he was a merchant and sea captain. He joined the state navy in 1776 and served as captain in the Continental Navy from 1778 until war's end, when he began an unsuccessful petition campaign to Congress for back pay and compensation. By 1786 he settled in New York City, where Roger Sherman and Benjamin Huntington were among the residents of the boardinghouse he ran at 59 Water Street during the first session. See also *DHFFC* 7:401, 447.

HARDY, JOSEPH (d. ca. 1815), a captain of marines from 1776 until 1781, served as chief clerk of the comptroller's office in the treasury department during the First Congress. In March 1790 he petitioned unsuccessfully with other former marine and naval officers for additional compensation for wartime services. See also *DHFFC* 7:439, 8:132, 17:1809.

HARMAR, JOSIAH (1753–1813), of Philadelphia, commanded the federal army on the northwest frontier as a lieutenant colonel, 1784–87, and as a brevet major general thereafter until March 1791. See also *DHFFC* 2:543, 9:342n, 17:1809.

HARRIS, RICHARD (1738–14 July 1790), a merchant of Marblehead, Massachusetts, and collector at that port under the state government from the mid 1780s, served as federal collector from 1789 until his death. See also *DHFFC* 2:504. (*PGW* 3:192)

HARRIS, ROBERT (1768–1851), of Harrisburg, Pennsylvania, was the younger half-brother of Mary Harris (1750–1809), whom William Maclay married in 1769. The local landowner and surveyor was in New York City for unspecified health reasons in February 1790. See also *DHFFC* 9:201n, 427.

HARRISON, BENJAMIN, SR. (1726–24 April 1791), of "Berkeley," was a planter who represented Charles County, Virginia, in the colonial and state legislature almost continuously from the 1750s until his death, except when he served in Congress, 1774–77, where he signed the Declaration of Independence, and as governor, 1781–84. An Antifederalist who voted against ratification of the Constitution, he ran unsuccessfully against Beverley Randolph for governor in December 1788. Anthony Singleton became his son-in-law in 1788. (*DHROC* 8:16n, 36n; *DHFFE* 2:361)

HARRISON, BENJAMIN, JR. (1755–99), eldest son of Benjamin Harrison (and older brother of future president William Henry Harrison), was a Richmond merchant who had been a deputy paymaster general for the Continental Army's Virginia Line and an agent for Superintendent of Finance Robert Morris, with whom he later partnered in a mercantile firm that included John Holker. Upon his father's death in 1791, Harrison settled on the family's James River estate "Berkeley" and became a planter. (*PRM* 8:563n; *PAH* 6:15n; Clifford Dowdey, *The Great Plantation: A Profile of Berkeley Hundred* [New York, 1957], p. 298)

HARRISON, GEORGE (1762–1845), a Philadelphia merchant, was a business associate of Robert Morris. (*PRM* 1:168n)

HARRISON, RICHARD HANSON (1750–1841), a native of Virginia, served as American agent in Spain, 1784–89. He returned briefly to the United States before returning to serve as consul at Cadiz, 1789–91. See also *DHFFC* 2:550.

HART, JONATHAN (1748–4 November 1791), served as a captain in the federal army from 1783 until his death during Arthur St. Clair's expedition against the Indians of the Northwest Territory. During the Revolutionary War he rose from ensign in the 22nd Continental Regiment in 1776 to captain in the 1st Connecticut Regiment in 1781 before retiring as major in 1783. See also *DHFFC* 2:484.

HART, THOMAS (1730–1808), was a native of Virginia who settled in North Carolina in 1755 and became a planter and major land speculator in Kentucky lands. After serving as state legislator and militia colonel early in the Revolutionary War, he migrated to Hagerstown, Maryland, where he established himself as a merchant and manufacturer. An unsuccessful petition to Congress in June 1790 sought compensation for supplies furnished to the Southern Army in 1780. During the First Congress he apparently had business interests in Kentucky, where he settled permanently in 1794. See also *DHFFC* 7:51.

HARTLEY, CATHERINE HOLTZINGER, of York, Pennsylvania, married future Representative Thomas Hartley ca. 1770.

HARVIE, JOHN (1742–1807), was a merchant and landowner in Richmond, Virginia, where he was mayor, 1785–86. Prior to settling there in 1780, he had a prominent law practice and several estates in Albemarle County, Virginia, which he represented in the state House of Delegates in 1777, and for which he served as colonel of the county militia, 1776–81. He attended Congress, 1777–78, served as state register for the land office, 1780–91, and voted as a Presidential Elector in the first federal election. (*DHFFE* 2:414)

HARWOOD, THOMAS (1743–1804), a merchant of Annapolis, Maryland, and longtime treasurer for the state's Western Shore, was appointed commissioner of loans for Maryland in 1790, having held that post under the Confederation government since 1777. (*PGW* 4:455–56n)

HASKELL, ELNATHAN (1755–1825), rose from sergeant to brigadier major in various regiments of the Massachusetts Line from 1775 until war's end, when he was retained in Henry Jackson's Continental Regiment until 1784. A founding member of the state Society of the Cincinnati, he settled in South Carolina in 1789 and became an agent for buyers and sellers of government securities. (Bradford A. Whittemore, *Memorials of the Massachusetts Society of the Cincinnati* [Boston, 1964], pp. 239–40)

HAWKINS, JOHN (d. 1805), rose from ensign to captain in the 3rd Regiment of the Virginia Line in 1776–77 before his capture at Charleston, South Carolina, in 1780. Paroled, he resigned because of poor health and settled in Fayette County, Kentucky, which he represented in the Virginia House of Delegates in 1789. (F. L. Brackett, *The Lodge of Washington* [Alexandria, Va., 1899], p. 106; *Register of the Virginia General Assembly, 1776–1918*, p. 385)

HAY, JOHN (ca. 1757–1809), a lawyer of Fayetteville, North Carolina, emigrated from his native Ireland and settled in North Carolina in 1779. Admitted to the state bar in 1783, he represented Cumberland County in the state House of Commons, 1786–87 and 1790, and at the second ratification convention, where he voted in favor of the Constitution. (*DHFFE* 4:320n; *PGW* 5:185n)

HAYS, ROBERT (1758–1819), was one of the principal landowners of Davidson County, in present-day Tennessee, which he represented in the North Carolina House of Commons in 1787. (*PGW* 5:477n)

HAYWOOD, JOHN (1755–1827) of Edgecombe County, North Carolina, was state treasurer from 1788 to 1827.

HAZARD, EBENEZER (1745–1817), a historian and documentary editor of New York City, served as United States postmaster general from 1782 until September 1789. Langdon resided with Hazard, his wife Abigail Arthur (m. 1783), and their three children during the second session of the First Congress. See also *DHFFC* 9:184–85n.

HAZARD, JONATHAN (ca. 1728–1812), of Kingston, Rhode Island, was a member of Congress in 1788 and a longtime state representative who led the fight against ratification at the state convention in 1790 and lost the first federal election for Senator. See also *DHFFC* 17:1811. (*DHFFE* 4:448)

HEDGE, TEMPERANCE. See Lee, Temperance Hedge.

HEATH, WILLIAM (1737–1814), was a farmer of Roxbury, Massachusetts, which he represented in the colonial legislature and Provincial Congresses, 1770–75. From militia general, he was commissioned brigadier general of the Continental Army, 1775–83, and became an ardent supporter of war veterans' benefits. He represented Suffolk County in the state Senate, 1784–85 and 1791–93. Although he voted to ratify the Constitution at the state convention, he was credited with authoring Antifederalist tracts during the first federal election, where he came in seventh (in a field of fifteen) for the Suffolk District seat in Congress won by Fisher Ames. (*DHROC* 4:67n; *DHFFE* 1:455n, 609; *DHFFC* 7:177)

HENRY, PATRICK (1736–99), a lawyer of Prince Edward and Henry counties, Virginia, and Antifederalist leader in the state, served as a Presidential Elector in the first federal election. See also *DHFFC* 9:114–15n, 17:1812.

HENSHAW, SAMUEL (1744–1809), was a lawyer of Northampton, Massachusetts, which he represented in the state House, 1788–91. The 1773 Harvard graduate was a Presidential Elector and campaign manager for Theodore Sedgwick in the first federal election. (*DHFFE* 1:751–52)

HERON, WILLIAM (1742–1819), a native of Ireland, was a schoolteacher and surveyor of Redding Ridge, Fairfield County, Connecticut, which he represented in the state House, 1778–82 and 1784–96. Secret dealings he conducted with the British during the Revolutionary War led some historians until recently to portray him as a double agent. (*PGW* 6:127–28)

HETFIELD, MARY ("Polly"), of Elizabeth, New Jersey, was the daughter of Abner Hetfield and Boudinot's younger sister Mary (1742–1801).

HIGGINSON, STEPHEN (1743–1828), a wealthy Federalist Boston merchant, made a fortune as a privateer during the Revolutionary War and served in the Massachusetts House of Representatives, 1781–82, and in Congress, 1783. See also *DHFFC* 17:1813. (*DHROC* 7:1770)

HILL, HENRY (1732–98), was a Philadelphia wine merchant who received his mercantile training in Scotland and the Madeira Islands before returning to his native city in 1763, where he became director of the Bank of North America, 1781–92. As an Anticonstitutionalist member of the state Assembly, 1780–84, and Supreme Executive Council, 1785–88, he was a political ally of Robert Morris and George Clymer; he became Clymer's brother-in-law when he married Anne Meredith in 1773. (*PRM* 2:361n; *Drinker* 3:2162)

HILL, JEREMIAH (1747–1820), was a merchant of Biddeford, Maine, which he served as town clerk, 1780–88, state representative, 1787–88, and federal collector, 1789–1809. In 1772 he married Mary Emery (1752–1837), also of Biddeford. See also *DHFFC* 2:505, 17:1813–14.

HILL, WILLIAM HENRY (1767–1809), a lawyer and planter of Wilmington, North Carolina, served as federal district attorney, 1790–94. See also *DHFFC* 2:528.

HILLEGAS, MICHAEL (1729–1804), a former Philadelphia sugar refiner and iron manufacturer, served as treasurer of the United States from 1775 to 1789. See also *DHFFC* 9:266n.

HILLER, JOSEPH (1748–1814), was a jeweler of Salem, Massachusetts, where he served as collector, 1789–1802, having held that post under the state government since 1784. See also *DHFFC* 2:505.

HINCKLEY, SAMUEL (1757–1840), a lawyer of Northampton, Massachusetts, graduated from Yale College in 1781 and studied law under Caleb Strong, whose youngest sister he married in 1786. Hinckley served as register of probate, 1786–1815. (*Yale Graduates* 4:188)

HINKLING, THOMAS (1745–1834), a Boston native, became a merchant at St. Michaels, the Azores.

HITCHCOCK, ENOS (1744–1803), was a Congregational minister in Providence, Rhode Island. In May 1790 he petitioned Congress for copyright protection. See also *DHFFC* 8:32.

HITE, CATHERINE (1766–1849), was the youngest daughter of John Hite (d. 1777) of Winchester, Virginia.

HITE, GEORGE (1761–1816), of Berkeley County, West Virginia, was the grandnephew of Madison's aunt Frances Madison Beale. Their distant cousin Isaac Hite married Madison's sister, Nelly Conway Madison, in 1783.

HOBART, SAMUEL (1734–98), was a West Indies merchant of Portsmouth, New Hampshire. From 1776 until at least 1778 he operated a gunpowder mill in nearby Exeter, which he represented in the state House of Representatives until he was expelled in 1779 under suspicion of communicating with the British. (*PJB*, pp. 115n, 273n)

HOBBY, JOHN (ca. 1720–1802), was a shopkeeper in Portland, Maine.

HODGDON, ALEXANDER (1741–97), of Boston, was Massachusetts state treasurer, 1787–92. (Oliver Roberts, *History of the Military Company of . . . Massachusetts, 1637–1888* [2 vols., Boston, 1897], 1:207)

HODGDON, SAMUEL (1745?–1824), a Philadelphia merchant and business partner of Timothy Pickering at the time of the First Congress, served as quartermaster of the federal army, 1791–92. See also *DHFFC* 17:1814.

HODGE, ABRAHAM (1755–1805), a native of New York City, settled in North Carolina where he published the Federalist *State Gazette* at New Bern, 1785–88, and at Edenton thereafter until 1793. (*American Conservatism*, p. 388; Clarence S. Brigham, *History and Bibliography of American Newspapers* [2 vols., Worcester, Mass., 1947], 2:1431)

HODGE, MICHAEL (1743–1816), a merchant of Newburyport, Massachusetts, was an insurance officer, 1787–92, town clerk, 1780–90, and port surveyor, 1789–92, having held that post under the state government throughout the Revolutionary War and intermittently during the Confederation. See also *DHFFC* 2:505. (*PGW* 3:148–49)

HOLDEN, THOMAS (1741–1823), of Warwick, Rhode Island, served in the state House of Deputies, 1776, 1778–81, and 1786, and upper chamber or Council of Assistants, 1790–92. He was a brigadier general in the Kent

County militia in the 1780s and major general in the state militia during the First Congress. Although he was elected to Congress in 1788 and 1789, he never attended. (*DHFFE* 4:431n)

HOLKER, JOHN (1745–1822), was born in England and raised as the son of a cotton manufacturer in France. He first visited the United States in 1777 as an "observer" for the French government, returning the next year as consul of France at Philadelphia and purchasing agent for the French navy. In 1782 he became France's consul general for New York, New Jersey, Pennsylvania, and Delaware. Both as purchasing agent and as a speculator in currency and commodities for his own profit, he was a close business associate of Robert Morris, with whom he and Benjamin Harrison, Jr., partnered in Richmond, Virginia, in 1783. (*PJM* 5:95; *PRM* 8:563n)

HOLLINGSWORTH, HENRY (1737–1803), older brother of Levi Hollingsworth, was a merchant, mill owner, and arms manufacturer of Elkton, Maryland. He sat in the state convention, where he voted to ratify the Constitution, and in the House of Delegates from 1789 to 1794. (*PGW* 5:485n; *DHFFE* 122n)

HOLLINGSWORTH, LEVI (1739–1824), a Philadelphia merchant and manufacturer, enjoyed lucrative government contracts during the last years of the Revolutionary War, awarded by his close friend and business associate, Superintendent of Finance Robert Morris. He was the younger brother of Henry Hollingsworth. See also *DHFFC* 17:1815.

HOLLIS, THOMAS BRAND (ca. 1719–1804), was a wealthy British radical, philanthropist, and supporter of the United States who became the friend and frequent host of the Adamses at his home in London. (*Adams* 3:188)

HOLMES, ABIEL (1763–1837), a native of Connecticut, graduated from Yale in 1783 and served as a Congregational minister at Midway, Georgia, 1785–91. On 29 August 1790 he married Polly Stiles, the daughter of Yale's President Ezra Stiles.

HOLMES, ABRAHAM (1754–1839), of Rochester, Massachusetts, was a Shays sympathizer who went on to serve in the state House of Representatives, 1787–91, and at the ratifying convention, where he voted against the Constitution. (*DHROC* 4:171n)

HOLTEN, SAMUEL (1738–1816), was a former physician of Danvers, Massachusetts, who served in Congress, 1778–80, 1783–85, and 1787. He ran unsuccessfully as an Antifederalist for both Representative and Senator in the first federal election, after which he served in the state Senate, 1789–90, and Executive Council, 1789–92. See also *DHFFC* 17:1815.

HOOKER, JOHN (1760–1829), was a prominent lawyer and judge in Springfield, Massachusetts. He married Pamela Sedgwick's first cousin Sarah Dwight (1764–1842) in February 1791. See also *DHFFC* 17:1815.

HOOKER, NOADIAH (ca. 1737–1823), of Farmington, Connecticut, which he frequently represented in the state House of Deputies throughout the 1780s, served as captain in the Second Regiment of the Connecticut Line in 1775 before transferring to the state militia later that year and rising to the rank of colonel.

HOOMES, JOHN (d. 1805), was a planter and stagecoach line owner of Bowling Green, Virginia, which he served as postmaster, 1790–96, and member of the state House of Delegates, 1791–95. See also *DHFFC* 17:1815.

HOOPER, DANIEL (1720–1802), was a merchant of Biddeford, Maine, where he served as postmaster, 1789–98. (George Folsom, *History of Saco and Biddeford* [Saco, Me., 1830], p. 310)

HOOPER, GEORGE (1744–1821), a native of Boston and younger brother of William Hooper, a signer of the Declaration of Independence, became a prominent merchant of Wilmington, North Carolina until allegations of Loyalism led him to settle in South Carolina in the latter part of the Revolutionary War. He returned to Wilmington by May 1790, when he signed a merchants' petition to the First Congress. His wife was the daughter of Archibald Maclaine. (*Powell*; *DHFFC* 8:399)

HOOPS, ROBERT (ca. 1750–ca. 1800), was a millowner and military contractor of Belvidere, New Jersey. The longtime county judge, 1779–94, member of the state's Legislative Council, 1784–85 and 1789–90, and delegate to the state ratification convention, was an unsuccessful candidate for Representative in the first federal election. (*DHFFE* 3:184)

HOPKINS, JOHN, JR. (ca. 1757–1827), a merchant of Richmond, was appointed commissioner of loans for Virginia in 1789, having served as the state continental loan officer since 1780. See also *DHFFC* 2:550. (*PRM* 1:202n)

HOPKINS, SAMUEL (1721–1803), was minister to a sect of Independent Calvinists in Newport, Rhode Island.

HOPKINS, THEODORE, originally of Hartford, Connecticut, was a London merchant.

HOPKINS, THOMAS (ca. 1740–1809), was a merchant of Portland, Maine.

HOPKINSON, FRANCIS (1737–9 May 1791), a Federalist lawyer and jurist of Philadelphia, most noted as a propagandist and Signer of the Declaration of Independence during the Revolutionary War, served as federal district judge for Pennsylvania from 1789 until his death. See also *DHFFC* 2:534, 9:100n, 17:1816.

HORRY, HARRIOT PINCKNEY (1748–1830), was the widow of South Carolina militia Colonel Daniel Horry (d. 1785) and maintained their large rice plantation "Hampton" on the Santee River, south of Georgetown, South Carolina. (*DGW* 6:126)

HOUSER, GEORGE, represented Stokes County in the North Carolina House of Commons in 1790. (*Steele* 1:62n)

HOUSTOUN, JOHN (1744–96), of "White Bluff," outside Savannah, Georgia, was a lawyer and planter who served as a member of the Provincial Congress and the Continental Congress in 1775, the state Executive Council in 1777, governor in 1778 and 1784–85, chief justice in 1786, and mayor of Savannah, 1789–90.

HOWARD, JOHN EAGER (1752–1842), of "Belvedere," Baltimore County, Maryland, followed an illustrious wartime military career by serving as a member of Congress in 1788, governor, 1788–91, and state Senator thereafter until 1796. See also *DHFFC* 2:157n, 17:1816.

HOWELL, ABNER (1744–97), a native of New Jersey, served as a captain in the Pennsylvania militia before settling in Mason (part of present-day Bracken) County, Kentucky.

HOWELL, DAVID (1747–1824), a lawyer of Providence, Rhode Island, served as state attorney general, 1789–90. See also *DHFFC* 17:1816.

HOWELL, JOSEPH, JR. (1750–98), of Pennsylvania, served as commissioner of army accounts, 1788–92, after five years as deputy commissioner. See also *DHFFC* 9:265n.

HOWLAND, BENJAMIN (1755–1821), was a farmer of Tiverton, Rhode Island.

HUBBARD, DUDLEY (1763–1816), began the practice of law in Berwick, Maine, in 1789, three years after graduating from Harvard. (*Maine Bar*, pp. 144–45)

HUBBARD, NEHEMIAH (d. 1837), was a merchant of Middletown, Connecticut, who had served as a deputy quartermaster general in the Continental Army, 1778–83.

HUBBARD, NICHOLAS, was a native of Great Britain who settled in Amsterdam and, with the Van Staphorsts and Willinks, represented the United States' banking interests in The Netherlands.

HULL, AGRIPPA (1759–1838), was a free Black who lived in Stockbridge, Massachusetts, from 1765 until his death. In 1777 he enlisted in the Continental Army and acted as a manservant to Gen. John Paterson and Gen. Tadeusz Kosciuszko before his discharge at war's end, after which he was employed as a domestic servant to the Sedgwicks.

HULL, WILLIAM (1753–1825), a lawyer of Newton, Massachusetts, was a Yale graduate of 1772 who trained for the ministry before turning to law, which he studied under Tapping Reeve until joining the Continental Army as captain in the 7th Connecticut Regiment in 1775, redesignated the 19th Continental Regiment in 1776. Transferring to the 8th Regiment of the Massachusetts Line in 1777, he rose to lieutenant colonel in the 3rd Regiment by 1783, and was retained in the federal army until 1784, when he commenced his legal practice. (*Yale Graduates* 3:444–48)

HUME, DAVID (1711–76), was a Scottish philosopher and historian and a principal figure of the Scottish Enlightenment centered in Edinburgh.

HUMPHREYS, DAVID (1752–1818), was a native of Connecticut who graduated from Yale in 1771 and became a principal author of the "Rising Glory" movement in American literature. A presidential aide and member of Washington's official family, he was selected for a number of diplomatic missions to Native Americans and various European Courts. See also *DHFFC* 2:485, 8:45n, 17:1817.

HUNEWELL (HUNNEWELL), RICHARD (1758–1823), was a merchant of Penobscot, Maine, who served as first sheriff of Hancock County, 1790–98. During the Revolutionary War he rose to the rank of lieutenant in the state militia. (*Maine Historical Magazine* 8[1893]:239)

HUNTER, HENRY (1751–1837), who served as a private in the Revolutionary War, was appointed surveyor at Skewarkey, present-day Williamston, North Carolina, in 1790.

HUNTER, JOHN (d. 1802), was a farmer in Laurens County, South Carolina, which he represented in the state House, 1785–92.

HUNTINGTON, BENJAMIN, family during the First Congress: wife Anne (b. 1740, m. 1765), of Norwich, Connecticut, who died on 6 October 1790, after suffering from an undisclosed illness through much of the first and second sessions; and the five of their eight children known to have been alive at the time of the First Congress: Henry (1766–1846), a Norwich lawyer and 1783 graduate of Dartmouth; Gurdon (1768–1840); George (1770–1842); Nancy (1775–1842); and Benjamin (1777–1850). See also *DHFFC* 14:503. (*The Huntington Family in America* [Hartford, Conn., 1915], pp. 150, 897–99, 903)

HUNTINGTON, EBENEZER (1754–1834), of Norwich, Connecticut, was a Federalist merchant, banker, speculator in land and public securities. During the Revolutionary War he rose from lieutenant to major in the 2nd Regiment of the Connecticut Line, 1775–76, to lieutenant colonel in Webb's Continental Regiment, the 3rd and 1st Connecticut Regiments, and Swift's Connecticut Battalion, 1776–83. (*Yale Graduates* 3:565–67; *American Conservatism*, pp. 289–90)

HUNTINGTON, JEDEDIAH (1743–1818), was a Federalist merchant of Norwich, Connecticut, who relocated to New London as its federal collector from 1789 until his death. The Harvard graduate of 1763 married future Representative Jonathan Trumbull's sister Faith (d. 1775) in 1766. An early activist in the revolutionary movement, he was commissioned colonel of the 8th Regiment of the Connecticut Line in 1775, of the 17th Continental Regiment in 1776, and of the 1st Connecticut Regiment in 1777. Promoted to brigadier general later that year, he served until war's end, when he retired as brevet major general and helped to organize and head the Society of the

Cincinnati. He represented Norwich in the state House of Deputies in 1786 and at the ratifying convention where he voted in favor of the Constitution, served as New London County sheriff, 1788–1789, and held the post of state treasurer briefly before accepting his federal appointment. See also *DHFFC* 2:485. (*Harvard Graduates* 15:408–18)

HUNTINGTON, SAMUEL (1731–96), a lawyer of Norwich, Connecticut, and the first cousin of Benjamin Huntington, served as governor from 1786 until his death. He was also a longtime state superior court judge and member of Congress in 1776, 1778–81, and 1783, who voted to ratify the Constitution at the state convention. See also *DHFFC* 17:1818.

HURD, JOHN (1727–1809), a Harvard graduate of 1747, served as secretary to New Hampshire's last colonial governor before moving to the New Hampshire frontier to speculate in lands. After retiring as militia colonel, he settled in Boston in 1779 and became a merchant, insurance broker, and investor in the Ohio Company. (*Harvard Graduates* 12:164–71)

HURT, JOHN (1752–1824), was appointed a chaplain in the federal army in March 1791, having served in that capacity with the 6th Regiment of the Virginia Line from 1776 until the war's end in 1783, when he enrolled in the Society of the Cincinnati. See also *DHFFC* 2:550.

HUTCHINSON, JAMES (1752–93), a former Continental Army surgeon, was a Philadelphia physician and medical professor. See also *DHFFC* 17:1818.

HUTSON, RICHARD (1748–95) was elected, with Mathews and John Rutledge, to the South Carolina Court of Chancery in 1784 and served until he resigned in 1794 under threat of impeachment. The 1765 graduate of the College of New Jersey (Princeton) took up the practice of law in Charleston, which he represented in the state's House of Representatives (1776–79, 1781–82, 1785, and 1788). He also served as a member of the state's legislative council (1780–82), lieutenant governor (1782–83), member of Congress (1778–79) where he signed the Articles of Confederation, and at the state convention where he voted to ratify the Constitution. (*Princetonians, 1748–1768*, pp. 499–502)

HYDE, CALEB (1739–1820), of Lenox, Massachusetts, was brigadier general of the state militia after the Revolutionary War, where he rose from captain in 1775, to major in 1776, to lieutenant colonel in 1778, before retiring in 1781, the same year that he became sheriff of Berkshire County. He was also a major investor in the Phelps-Gorham Genessee Tract. (*DHROC* 5:644n; *MSSR* 8:595–96)

HYNES, ANDREW, settled in Nelson County (in present-day Elizabethtown), Kentucky, in 1780, which he represented in the Kentucky statehood convention of 1785. (*Sketches of Kentucky* 1:354, 2:307, 371)

IMLAY, WILLIAM (1742–1807), was a Hartford merchant who served as commissioner of loans for Connecticut almost continuously from 1780 until his death. See also *DHFFC* 17:1819.

IMLAY, WILLIAM EUGENE (1755–1803), a merchant and physician of Upper Freehold, New Jersey, graduated from the College of New Jersey (Princeton) in 1773 and served as a captain in the state militia and the 3rd Regiment of the New Jersey Line between 1775 and the end of the war. About 1780 he became active as a lay minister in the Universalism movement, participating with John Murray and Benjamin Rush in the general convention in Philadelphia in May–June 1790. (*Princetonians, 1769–1775*, pp. 297–99)

INGLIS, JOHN, the son of a prominent Scottish born Philadelphia merchant, settled in London as a partner with Alexander Ellice in the mercantile firm of Phyn, Ellice, and Inglis.

INNES, HARRY (1752–1816), a lawyer from Danville, Kentucky, and an active member of the town's Political Club during ratification, served as federal district court judge from 1789 until his death. He married Elizabeth Calloway (1757–91) in 1775. See also *DHFFC* 17:1819.

INNES, JAMES (1754–98), attorney general of Virginia, 1786–96, was a lawyer of Williamsburg, which he represented in the state House of Delegates in the 1780s and at the ratifying convention where he supported the Constitution, unlike his older brother Harry. See also *DHFFC* 17:1819.

IREDELL, HANNAH (1747–1826), sister of Samuel Johnston, married James Iredell of Edenton, North Carolina, in 1773. By the time of the First Congress, they had two surviving children: Annie (1785–1816) and James (1788–1853).

IREDELL, JAMES (1751–99), an emigrant from England who married Samuel Johnston's sister Hannah in 1773, was a lawyer of Edenton, North Carolina, who served as associate justice of the United States Supreme Court from 1790 until his death. See also *DHFFC* 17:1819.

IRVINE, WILLIAM (1741–1804), was a physician of Carlisle, Pennsylvania, who served as a commissioner for settling the accounts between the United States and the individual states, 1788–93. The former Continental Army brigadier general, with extensive service on Pennsylvania's western frontier, sat in Congress, 1787–88, but lost bids as an Antifederalist candidate for both Senator and Representative in the first federal election. See also *DHFFC* 17:1820.

IRVINE, WILLIAM (1750–1820), was a native of Virginia who settled in Madison County, Kentucky, in 1778, and became the first clerk of the county court and a delegate to the statehood conventions of 1787–88.

IZARD, HENRY (1771–1826), third child and eldest son of Ralph Izard, graduated from Columbia College in May 1789 but remained with his parents during the First Congress, serving as a witnessing signatory to the Treaty of New York.

JACKSON, JONATHAN (1743–1810), a merchant of Newburyport, Massachusetts, was federal marshal for the state, 1789–91, and federal inspector of revenue for the northern district, 1791–96. See also *DHFFC* 17:1820.

JACKSON, WILLIAM (1759–1828), a Philadelphia lawyer and secretary to the Federal Convention, served as a presidential aide from September 1789 until 1791. See also *DHFFC* 17:1820.

JARDINE, ALEXANDER (d. 1799), of London, was a social reformer who served as British consul at Galicia in 1791.

JARVIS, CHARLES (1748–1807), was a prominent physician of Boston, which he represented in the Massachusetts House of Representatives, 1787–97. See also *DHFFC* 17:1821.

JARVIS, LEONARD, JR. (1742–1813), Massachusetts's comptroller general during the First Congress, served as a deputy Continental prize agent during the Revolutionary War and state Representative for Boston in 1782 and 1787. In March 1791 he was appointed federal revenue inspector for Boston and southern Massachusetts. See also *DHFFC* 17:1821. (*LDC* 6:492n; *PGW* 7:568)

JASPER, SAMUEL (d. 1801), a merchant of Edenton, North Carolina, was appointed surveyor at Currituck Inlet in 1790. See also *DHFFC* 2:528.

JAY, JOHN (1745–1829), a New York City lawyer, was secretary for foreign affairs, 1784–89, before his appointment as chief justice of the United States Supreme Court, 1789–95, serving simultaneously as interim secretary of state until March 1790. See also *DHFFC* 17:1821.

JAY, SARAH (1756–1802), daughter of New Jersey's longtime governor, William Livingston, married John Jay in 1774.

JEFFERSON, THOMAS (1743–1826), a lawyer and planter of Albemarle County, Virginia, assumed the duties of secretary of state on 21 March 1790 and served until 1793. See also *DHFFC* 17:1821–22.

JEFFRIES, JOHN (1745–1819), graduated from Harvard in 1763 and studied in London before returning to establish a medical practice in his native Boston in 1770. Although a friend of most of the city's revolutionary leaders, he accompanied the British in the evacuation of Boston and served as a military surgeon in Nova Scotia, 1776–79. After a brief tour of duty during the southern campaigns of 1780, he established a highly lucrative private practice in London, where he also became a celebrated aerialist, co-manning the first balloon flight across the English Channel in 1785. He was family physician to the Adamses during their sojourn in England beginning in 1786, and indeed never severed his ties to Boston's political elite, who welcomed him back for what was intended to be a short visit in November 1789 but turned into a lifelong stay that included a visit to New York City from 24 July until mid-August 1790. (*Harvard Graduates* 15:419–27)

JENIFER, DANIEL OF ST. THOMAS (1723–16 November 1790), was a merchant planter of Annapolis and Charles County, Maryland, who enjoyed an uninterrupted career as a colonial judge and legislator over the two decades preceding the Revolutionary War. The "Major" (a title acquired by 1765) then served in the state Senate, 1776–81, simultaneously serving in Congress, 1779–81, and attended the Federal Convention where he signed the Constitution.

JENKINS, MARSHALL, was a merchant who left his native Martha's Vineyard, Massachusetts, and became one of the original proprietors of Hudson, New York, in 1783.

JOHNSON, ANNE BEACH (1729–96), of Stafford, Connecticut, married William Samuel Johnson in 1749. Three of their seven children were still alive during the First Congress: Charity (1751–1810), Samuel William, and

Robert Charles. A fourth, Elizabeth Verplank (b. 1763) died on 26 February 1789. Another daughter, Gloriana Ann (b. 1757), married Roger Alden in 1783 but died in 1785.

JOHNSON, CHARLES (d. 1802), was a planter of Chowan County, North Carolina, which he represented in the state Senate, 1780–81, 1783, and 1788–93, in the state's House of Commons in 1782, and at both state conventions, where he voted in favor of ratifying the Constitution. He was elected to Congress in 1781, 1784, and 1785, but never attended. (*DHFFE* 4:324n; *LDC* 26:xxxi)

JOHNSON, JOSHUA (1742–1802), a Maryland born merchant and younger brother of Thomas Johnson, served as United States consul in London, 1790–97. See also *DHFFC* 2:497, 17:1822.

JOHNSON, ROBERT CHARLES (1766–1806), son of William Samuel Johnson, graduated from Yale in 1783 and, like his older brother, Samuel William, practiced law in Stratford, Connecticut. He was an active Federalist. (*Yale Graduates* 4:285–87)

JOHNSON, SAMUEL WILLIAM (1761–1846), elder son of William Samuel Johnson, graduated from Yale in 1779 and practiced law in Stratford, Connecticut, which he represented in the state House of Representatives, 1790–97. (*Yale Graduates* 4:118)

JOHNSON, THOMAS (1732–1819), a planter and lawyer of Frederick County, Maryland, declined appointment as a federal district judge in 1789, serving instead as chief judge of the state's general court from 1790 until his appointment to the United States Supreme Court in August 1791, where he sat until his resignation in 1793. See also *DHFFC* 17:1823.

JOHNSTON, FRANCES CATHCART (1752–1801), married Samuel Johnston in 1770 and resided at their plantation, "Hayes," in Chowan County at the time of the First Congress. Five of their nine children survived infancy: Samuel (b. 1770), Penelope (1771–1820), James Cathcart (1782–1865), Frances (1785–1837), and Helen (1787–1842).

JOHNSTON, JOHN (1735–1791), brother of Samuel Johnston, was a planter from Bertie County, North Carolina. A militia captain, 1779–81, he also served periodically in the state legislature. (*Iredell* 1:137n)

JOHNSTON, ZACHARIAH (1742–1800), was a planter of Augusta County, Virginia, which he represented in the state House of Delegates, 1778–92. See also *DHFFC* 17:1823.

JONES, ALLEN (1739–98) of Halifax County, North Carolina, served as speaker of the state Senate in 1778, delegate to Congress, 1779–80, and member of the Council of State in 1782. (*Powell*)

JONES, EDWARD (1762–1841), emigrated from Ireland and in 1786 settled in Wilmington, North Carolina, where he was admitted to the bar in 1788. He served in the state House of Commons from that year until his appointment as state solicitor general in 1791. (*PGW* 5:478n)

JONES, JOHN (1729–91), was a Quaker physician of Philadelphia, where he was an attending physician at the Pennsylvania Hospital and the first vice president of the city's College of Physicians. The native New Yorker took his medical degree from Rheims, France, in 1751 and taught surgery at King's College (Columbia) before moving to Philadelphia in 1780. (*Drinker* 3:2173)

JONES, JOHN COFFIN (ca. 1750–1829), a Harvard graduate of 1768, became a wealthy merchant and banker of Boston, which he represented in the Massachusetts House of Representatives, 1786–88, and 1790–94. Although he declined his appointment to the Annapolis Convention in 1786, he played an active role in the state convention, where he voted to ratify the Constitution. (*DHROC* 6:1221)

JONES, JOSEPH (1727–1805), uncle of James Monroe, was a London trained lawyer of Fredericksburg, Virginia. He served frequently in the state House of Delegates and Congress before serving on the state Executive Council from 1785 until 1789, when he took a seat on the state's general court, remaining until his death. See also *DHFFC* 17:1824. (*DHFFE* 2:261n)

JONES, ROBERT STRETTEL (1745–92), was a merchant of Brunswick, New Jersey, which he represented in the state General Assembly, 1787–89, and in the town's common council, 1788–90. From 1771 to 1779 he was secretary of the American Philosophical Society. (*DHFFE* 3:59n)

JONES, TIMOTHY (1737–1800), was a merchant militia captain of New Haven, Connecticut, which he represented in the state House in the 1786 session. Although a member of Yale's class of 1757, he was visiting Boston during commencement and received the actual degree from Harvard. (*Harvard Graduates* 14:182)

JONES, WALTER (1745–1815), was a planter and physician of Northumberland County, Virginia, which he represented in the state Senate, 1785–97, and at the ratifying convention, where he voted in favor of the Constitution. See also *DHFFC* 17:1824.

JORDAN, JEREMIAH (ca. 1733–1806), a planter of St. Mary's County, Maryland, was appointed port surveyor at Lewellensburg, Maryland, in 1789. See also *DHFFC* 2:498, 17:1824.

JORDAN, MELITIAH (1753–1818), a lumberer and merchant of Trenton, Maine, was collector at Frenchman's Bay from 1789 until his death. See also *DHFFC* 2:507.

JORDAN, TRISTRAM (1731–1821), was a prominent merchant of Biddeford, Maine, where he was a longtime selectman and justice of the peace. He served as a state militia colonel during the Revolutionary War and represented York County in the Massachusetts Senate, 1787–88.

JUDD, WILLIAM (1743–1804), a Yale graduate of 1763, became a lawyer of Farmington, Connecticut, which he represented in the state House of Representatives, 1786–94, and at the ratifying convention, where he voted in favor of the Constitution. See also *DHFFC* 17:1824.

KALTESSEN (KALTEIZEN), MICHAEL (1729–1807), emigrated from the German state of Wurttenburg and by 1755 settled in Charleston, South Carolina, where he became a lumber merchant. He served in the Provincial Congress, 1775–76, the state House of Representatives for St. Philip and St. Michael Parish, 1776–78 and 1783–90, and the state convention where he voted to ratify the Constitution. (*South Carolina House* 3:390–91)

KAMMERER, HENRY (HEINRICH) (d. 1798), was a Philadelphia stationer who supplied paper to the Senate during the First Congress. In 1789 he was president of the city's German Society, succeeding Peter Muhlenberg and being succeeded by Frederick A. Muhlenberg.

KEAIS, NATHAN (1740–95), was a merchant of Washington, North Carolina, where he served as collector, 1790–96. He sat in the state House of Commons in 1777 and at the first ratifying convention in 1788, where he supported the Constitution. See also *DHFFC* 2:528.

KEAN, JOHN (1756–95), a merchant of Charleston, South Carolina, was a member of Congress, 1785–87, and in August 1789 was appointed to replace Abraham Baldwin as one of three commissioners for settling accounts between the United States and the individual states. See also *DHFFC* 13:1522n.

KEARNY, SUSANNA (d. 1799), daughter of Rev. Ravaud Kearny of Perth Amboy, New Jersey, married John Richardson Bayard Rodgers on 5 July 1790, after a courtship in which William Paterson frequently acted as go-between. (*Princetonians, 1769–1775*, p. 520)

KENNEDY, SAMUEL, JR. (ca. 1744–1803), was a physician of Basking Ridge, New Jersey. (*Princetonians, 1748–1768*, pp. 100–101)

KILHAM, DANIEL (1753–1841), graduated from Harvard in 1777 and abandoned the practice of medicine in Salem, Massachusetts, to become an apothecary in nearby Newburyport, which he represented in the state House, 1787–88. He lost reelection bids in 1788 and 1789 on account of his fervent antifederalism. (*DHROC* 4:141n; *JQA* 32n, 105–6n)

KILLEN, WILLIAM (1722–1803), of Kent County, Delaware, was chief justice of the state Supreme Court, 1777–93. (*DHFFE* 2:79n)

KING, CYRUS (1772–1817), originally of Scarsborough, Maine, lived with his older half-brother and guardian Rufus King while attending Columbia College beginning in the summer of 1790, having previously attended Phillips Academy in Andover, Massachusetts.

KING, ELIZABETH "BETSY" (1770–1817), of Scarborough, Maine, was the younger half-sister of Rufus King. She married Dr. Benjamin Jones Porter on 16 November 1791. (*Maine Historical and Genealogical Recorder* 1[1889]:8)

KING, GEORGE (1754–1831), was a merchant of Sharon, Connecticut.

KING, MARY ALSOP (1770–94), the only child of a wealthy New York City merchant, married Rufus King in 1786 and together they lived with her widowed father at 38 Smith Street. Their children during the First Congress were John Alsop (1788–1867), Charles (16 March 1789–1867), and Caroline (1790–93). A fourth child, James Gore King, was born on 8 May 1791 (d. 1853).

KINGSLEY, EBENEZER, (1758–92), was a merchant and land speculator of Becket, Massachusetts. His family's prominence in local church and civil affairs did not prevent the scandal that followed his bankruptcy in 1790 over failed securities speculation schemes with Joseph Chaplin, a relation by marriage. (Esther T. Moulthrop, ed., *Bicentennial History of Becket, Berkshire County, Massachusetts* [Pittsfield, Mass., 1965], pp. 32–34, 52–53, 64; *DHSCUS* 6:176–77, 182n)

KINSEY, JAMES (ca. 1731–1803), a Quaker lawyer of Burlington, New Jersey, was appointed chief justice of the state Supreme Court in 1789. See also *DHFFC* 17:1826.

KIRBY, EPHRAIM (1757–1804) was a lawyer of Litchfield, Connecticut, who published the first volume of his *Reports of Cases Adjudged in the Superior Court . . . of Connecticut* in 1789. (*DHSCUS* 1:658n)

KIRKLAND, SAMUEL (1741–1808), a native of Norwich, Connecticut, graduated from the College of New Jersey (Princeton) in 1765 and was ordained a Congregational minister the next year. Throughout the First Congress period he lived in the area of Utica, New York, as a missionary to the Oneida Indians. He is credited with having preserved favorable relations between the United States and the Oneida during the Revolutionary War, despite their Iroquois brethren's hostility. He also served as brigade chaplain in General John Sullivan's 1779 campaign. (*Princetonians, 1748–1768*, pp. 502–7; *PAH* 26:511n)

KNOX, HENRY (1750–1806), formerly a Boston bookseller who rose to major general during the Revolutionary War, served as secretary of war, 1785–94. See also *DHFFC* 2:507, 9:52n, 17:1826.

KNOX, HUGH (d. 1817), a merchant of Edenton, North Carolina, was appointed surveyor at Nixonton in 1790. (*Pasquotank County Records: Estates Records, 1757–1866*, Nc-Ar)

KNOX, LUCY FLUCKER (1757–1824), who married Henry Knox in 1774, became a principal hostess of the Republican Court at the seat of government.

KNOX, WILLIAM (1756–95), formerly a Boston merchant, was employed under his older brother Henry as a clerk in the War Department before his appointment as United States consul to Dublin, 1790–92. See also *DHFFC* 2:507.

KUNZE, JOHN CHRISTOPHER (1744–1807), a New York City Lutheran minister from 1774, in 1771 married Margaretha Henrietta "Peggy" Muhlenberg (1751–1831), sister of the two Representatives, who resided in the Kunze household during the first two sessions. William Maclay joined them during the second session. See also *DHFFC* 9:178n.

LACAZE, JAMES, was the French born Philadelphia agent for a Spanish mercantile firm that traded in military stores in the last years of the Revolutionary War. He returned to Europe following the firm's bankruptcy in 1786. (*PRM* 3:94–95n, 4:498)

LAFAYETTE, MARIE-JOSEPH, MARQUIS DE (1757–1834), was a wealthy French nobleman who became the highest ranking foreign volunteer in the Continental Army, serving as major general, 1777–82. At the outbreak of the French Revolution he headed the moderate party of liberals and in 1790 served as vice president of the National Assembly and commander of the Paris National Guard.

LA FOREST, RENÉ-CHARLES-MATHURIN, COMTE DE (1756–1846), served as French vice consul at Savannah, Georgia, and Charleston, South Carolina, before assuming the duties of acting consul general at New York City, 1785–91, and as full consul general thereafter, until his recall in 1793.

LALUZERNE, ANNE-CÉSAR, CHEVALIER DE (1741–91), served as French minister plenipotentiary to the United States from 1779 until his appointment as minister to Great Britain, 1784–91.

LAMB, JOHN (1735–1800), was a New York City merchant and leader of the revolutionary movement who served as collector at that port, 1789–97, having held the post under the state government since 1784. He opposed ratification of the Constitution and coordinated interstate Antifederal efforts. See also *DHFFC* 2:524. (*DHFFE* 3:216)

LAMOTTE, ——, a native merchant of Le Havre, France, was appointed United States vice consul at that port in 1790.

LAMOTTE, JAMES, was a British merchant who remained in Charleston, South Carolina, after the British evacuated in 1782. (George C. Rogers, Jr.,

Evolution of a Federalist: William Loughton Smith of Charleston [Columbia, S.C., 1962], pp. 100, 109)

LANGDON, ELIZABETH SHERBURNE (ca. 1760–1813), sister of Samuel Sherburne, married John Langdon in 1777 and resided thereafter in Portsmouth, New Hampshire. She and their only child, Elizabeth (b. 1777), joined Langdon at the seat of government for most of the first and third sessions. See also *DHFFC* 14:650.

LANGDON, HENRY SHERBURNE (1766–1857), of Portsmouth, New Hampshire, graduated from Yale in 1785 and was admitted to the bar in 1792. Son of Woodbury and nephew of John Langdon, he married the sister of William Eustis in 1792. (*Yale Graduates* 4:422–23)

LANGDON, SAMUEL (1723–97), was Congregational minister at Hampton Falls, New Hampshire, from 1781 until his death. A native of Boston who graduated from Harvard in 1740, he served as minister at Portsmouth, 1747–74, before accepting an appointment as wartime president of his alma mater, 1774–80. His leadership proved essential at the state convention for ratifying the Constitution in 1788. (*Harvard Graduates* 10:508–28)

LANGDON, WOODBURY (1739–1805), older brother of John Langdon and, like him, a merchant of Portsmouth, New Hampshire, accepted appointment as commissioner for settling accounts between the United States and the individual states in 1790, upon resigning from the state superior court following his impeachment for neglect of duty. See also *DHFFC* 2:516, 17:1828.

LANGHAM, ELIAS (1759–1830), served as state commissary for military stores at Point of Fork (present day Columbia), Virginia. See also *DHFFC* 17:1828.

LANSDOWNE, MARQUIS OF. See Shelburne, William Petty, earl of.

LATHROP, JOSHUA (1723–1807), graduated from Yale in 1743 and became a wealthy pharmacist and physician of Norwich, Connecticut. (*Yale Graduates* 1:741–42)

LATIMER, GEORGE (1750–1825), was a Philadelphia merchant active in Pennsylvania's Republican, or Anti-constitutionalist, circles who voted to ratify the Constitution at the state convention. (*DHROC* 2:590; *Rush* 2:833n)

LATIMER, HENRY (1752–1819), was a physician of Newport, Delaware. After graduating from the College of Philadelphia (University of Pennsylvania) in 1773 and pursuing advanced medical studies at Edinburgh, he served as a Continental Army hospital surgeon, 1777–83. He was a member of the state House of Assembly, 1787–88, and was elected its Speaker in 1790 despite his failed candidacy for Presidential Elector in the first federal election. (*PGW* 6:158n; *DHFFE* 2:83n)

LAURANCE, ELIZABETH, daughter of New York City merchant Alexander McDougall, married John Laurance in 1772. She died after a lingering illness on 16 August 1790.

LAWRENCE, NATHANIEL (1761–97), was a native of Long Island who attended the College of New Jersey (Princeton) from 1776 until joining the Second Regiment of the Continental Army's North Carolina Line as a second lieutenant in 1778. He retired as a captain at war's end and took his degree from Princeton before studying law under Egbert Benson. Admitted to the New York bar in 1786, he was practicing law in New York City by 1789, although he represented Queens County, Long Island, at the state convention in 1788, when he voted to ratify the Constitution despite his antifederalism, and also in the state Assembly, 1791–92. (*Princetonians, 1776–1783*, pp. 425–29)

LAWSON, ALEXANDER (d. 1798), graduated from the College of Philadelphia (University of Pennsylvania) in 1759 and pursued legal training at London's Inns of Court before returning to his native Baltimore to become county clerk and town commissioner. Although he was relieved of these public trusts because of his Loyalism during the Revolution, he continued to reside in Baltimore. (*Inns of Court*)

LEA, THOMAS (d. 1793), was a Philadelphia merchant and a founding member of the Hibernian Society there in 1790.

LEAR, TOBIAS (1762–1816), a native of Portsmouth, New Hampshire, graduated from Harvard in 1783 and, upon Benjamin Lincoln's recommendation, was hired by George Washington in 1786 as his private secretary and tutor to his adopted grandchildren at Mount Vernon. He remained part of the President's "official family" throughout the First Congress. See also *DHFFC* 17:1829. (*DGW* 4:337; Stephen Decatur, Jr., *Private Affairs of George Washington* [Boston, 1933], p. vi)

LEE, ARTHUR (1740–92), younger brother of Richard Henry Lee and second cousin of Richard Bland Lee, whom he failed to unseat in the second federal election, was a planter of Prince William County, Virginia. A congressman from 1782 to 1784 and member of the board of treasury, 1785–89, Arthur Lee was an inveterate foe of Robert Morris and became an Antifederal essayist. See also *DHFFC* 9:178n, 17:1829.

LEE, CHARLES (1758–1815), was a lawyer of Alexandria, Virginia, where he served as federal collector, 1789–93, having served there as state naval officer since 1779. The College of New Jersey (Princeton) graduate of 1775 was a brother of Richard Bland and Henry Lee, and son-in-law to their second cousin Richard Henry Lee by his marriage to Anne "Nancy" Lee (1770–1804) in February 1789. Another brother, Edward Jennings Lee (1772–1843), would marry another daughter of R. H. Lee, Sarah Caldwell "Sally" (1775–1837). See also *DHFFC* 2:551, 17:1830.

LEE, HENRY "LIGHT-HORSE HARRY" (1756–1818), older brother of Richard Bland and Charles Lee, was a land speculator and planter of "Stratford Hall," in Westmoreland County, Virginia, of which he became proprietor upon his marriage to his cousin, Richard Henry Lee's niece Matilda Lee (1764–16 August 1790) in 1782. The College of New Jersey (Princeton) graduate of 1773 enjoyed a celebrated career in the Continental Army, 1777–82, before serving in Congress, 1786–88, and becoming a Federalist leader at the state convention, where he voted to ratify the Constitution. See also *DHFFC* 17:1830.

LEE, HENRY (1758–1854), was a farmer and surveyor of Bourbon County, Kentucky, which he represented at the statehood convention of 1787, in the Virginia House of Delegates in 1788, and at the state ratifying convention that same year, when he voted against the Constitution. (Hugh Blair Grigsby, *History of the Virginia Federal Convention of 1788* [Richmond, Va., 1890–91] 2:368; *Register of the Virginia General Assembly, 1776–1918*, p. 397)

LEE, JOHN (1751–1812), older brother of Silas Lee and a merchant of Penobscot, Maine, was collector of that port, 1789–1801, having served as naval officer there under the state government. See also *DHFFC* 2:507.

LEE, LUDWELL (1760–1836), second son of Richard Henry Lee, was an attorney and planter of "Shutter's Hill," Alexandria, Virginia. He was an aide-de-camp to General Lafayette briefly in 1781, attended the College of William and Mary, and studied law under George Wythe. (*PRM* 6:507n)

LEE, SILAS (1760–1814), was the brother of John Lee and a lawyer of Wiscasset, Maine. After graduating from Harvard in 1784 he studied law under George Thatcher and became his nephew by marriage, as well as his professional and political protégé. (*American Conservatism*, p. 261)

LEE, TEMPERANCE HEDGE "TEMPY" (d. 1845), daughter of John Hedge and Thatcher's oldest sister Temperance, married Silas Lee in early 1790. See also *DHFFC* 17:1811.

LEE, THEODORICK (1766–1849), a planter of Loudoun County, Virginia, and brother of Charles, Henry, and Richard Bland Lee, helped oversee the latter's estate during the First Congress.

LEE, THOMAS (1758–1805), the eldest son of Richard Henry Lee, was a lawyer in Dumfries, Virginia. He married George Washington's niece and Corbin Washington's sister, Mildred, in 1788. (*PGW* 3:247n)

LEE, THOMAS LUDWELL, JR. (d. 1807), a planter of "Berry Hill," Stafford County, Virginia, was the son of Richard Henry Lee's oldest brother and first cousin of Thomas Lee Shippen.

LEE, WILLIAM (1739–95), younger brother of Richard Henry and Arthur Lee, was a merchant planter of "Green Spring," near Williamsburg, Virginia. He was serving as Congress's commercial agent in Nantes when commissioned to represent the United States at Berlin and Vienna in 1778. Never recognized by those courts, his commission was revoked in 1779 and he spent the remainder of the war in Brussels.

LEEDS, FRANCIS OSBORNE, FIFTH DUKE OF (1751–99), also the marquis of Carmarthen until 1790, was Great Britain's secretary of state for foreign affairs under William Pitt the Younger from 1783 until his resignation in April 1791.

LEFFINGWELL, CHRISTOPHER (1734–1810), was a merchant and manufacturer of Norwich, Connecticut, where he was appointed naval officer under the state government in 1784. During the Revolutionary War he served as a state militia colonel. (*PGW* 3:209–10n)

LEMONT, JOHN (d. 1837), of Kennebec, Maine, rose from lieutenant to captain in the Massachusetts militia, 1775–76, before transferring to captain in the 14th Regiment of the state's Continental Line, 1777–78. (*MSSR* 9:674)

LETOMBE, PHILIPPE-ANDRÉ-JOSEPH DE (1738–1833), was appointed French consul for New Hampshire, Massachusetts, Rhode Island, and Connecticut in 1779 (although he was not formally recognized by Congress until 1781), and served continuously, except for a one year leave in 1785–86, until his recall to France in 1793.

LEVY, MOSES (1757–1826), graduated from the College of Philadelphia (University of Pennsylvania) in 1772 and became a prominent Philadelphia lawyer. (*University of Pennsylvania Alumni Book*)

LEWIS, GEORGE (d. ca. 1803), immigrated from Virginia to Mason County, Kentucky, in 1780, settling near Maysville in 1789. (William P. Drake, et al., *Kentucky in Retrospect* [Frankfort, Ky., 1942], p. 168)

LEWIS, HOWELL (b. 1759), of Goochland County, Virginia, received a captain's commission in the United States Army in 1792, resigning in 1797. (*PJM* 13:235n)

LEWIS, THOMAS (1749–1809), a native of Fairfax County, Virginia, settled in Fayette County, Kentucky, after the Revolutionary War, where he rose from second lieutenant in the 15th Virginia Regiment in 1776 to first lieutenant in 1777 before retiring in 1781. (*Kentucky in Retrospect*, p. 169)

LEWIS, WILLIAM (1751–1819), a Quaker lawyer of Philadelphia and a prominent abolitionist, served as United States attorney for Pennsylvania from 1789 until his appointment as federal judge for the eastern district of the state in 1791. See also *DHFFC* 2:535, 9:78n. (*DHROC* 2:729)

L'HOMMEDIEU, EZRA (1734–1811), a lawyer of Southold, Long Island, New York, was at the midpoint of a long state legislative career when he lost his bid for Representative (against his brother-in-law William Floyd), and then for Senator, in the first federal election. The Yale graduate of 1754 also served in Congress, 1777–83 and 1788. See also *DHFFC* 17:1832.

LIBBEY, JEREMIAH (1748–1824), was postmaster of Portsmouth, New Hampshire.

LINCOLN, BENJAMIN (1733–1810), a farmer of Hingham, Massachusetts, with a distinguished wartime military career, served as collector for Boston and Charlestown, 1789–1809. He was also given the additional duties of superintendent of lighthouses in Massachusetts on 10 March 1790. See also *DHFFC* 2:507–8, 9:129n, 17:1832.

LINCOLN, LEVI (1749–1820), a native of Hingham, Massachusetts, and distant relation of Benjamin Lincoln, graduated from Harvard in 1772 and three years later commenced a successful legal practice in Worcester, where he also became a major promoter of scientific agriculture. With Caleb Strong, he successfully argued the case of Quok Walker that in 1783 ruled slavery unconstitutional in Massachusetts. That same year he was elected to Congress but declined to serve. (*Harvard Graduates* 18:121–28)

LINCOLN, MARY OTIS (1764–1807), of Boston, the daughter of James Otis, Jr., and the niece of Samuel Allyne Otis, Joseph Otis, and Mercy Otis Warren, married Benjamin Lincoln, Jr. (1756–88) in 1785. He was the eldest of Benjamin and Ruth Lincoln's seven children to survive infancy, graduated from Harvard in 1777, and practiced law before his untimely death. (David B. Mattern, *Benjamin Lincoln and the American Revolution* [Columbia, S.C., 1995], pp. 35, 179; Thomas Bouvé, et al., *History of the Town of Hingham, Massachusetts* [Hingham, Mass., 1893], pp. 10, 277)

LINDSAY, WILLIAM (1743–97), a merchant of Norfolk, Virginia, served as collector of that port and adjoining Portstmouth, 1789–97, having held the post of state naval officer for that district upon his predecessor Josiah Parker's election to the First Congress. See also *DHFFC* 2:551, 17:1832.

LINN, WILLIAM (1752–1808), minister of New York City's largest congregation, the Collegiate Reformed Presbyterian Dutch Church, 1786–1805, served as chaplain of the House of Representatives from 1 May 1789 until Congress removed to Philadelphia. In 1774 he married Rebecca Blair, daughter of the former vice president of his alma mater, the College of New Jersey (Princeton). See also *DHFFC* 9:53n.

LITHGOW, WILLIAM, JR. (1750–96), a lawyer of Hallowell and Georgetown (present-day Bath), Maine, served as United States attorney for the Maine district, 1789–94. See also *DHFFC* 2:508, 17:1833.

LITTLE, JOSIAH (ca. 1747–1830), of Newbury, Massachusetts, had business interests in shipping and real estate. (George T. Little, *The Descendants of George Little* [Auburn, Me., 1882], pp. 109–10)

LITTLEFIELD, WILLIAM (1753–1822), of Block Island, Rhode Island, was the brother of Catharine "Kitty" Greene. During the Revolutionary War he rose from ensign of the 12th Continental Regiment in 1776, to captain of the 2nd Rhode Island Regiment in 1777. He served as aide-de-camp to his brother-in-law General Nathanael Greene by 1779 before retiring the next year and returning to Block Island, which he represented in the state House of Deputies, 1785 and 1792. (*PGW* 4:74n; *PNG* 4:331)

LIVINGSTON, HENRY BROCKHOLST (1757–1823), son of New Jersey Governor William Livingston, was a land speculator and prominent lawyer in his native New York City. The College of New Jersey (Princeton) graduate of 1774 rose to the rank of lieutenant colonel and aide-de-camp to Gen. Philip Schuyler before accepting a furlough in 1779 to serve as private secretary to his brother-in-law John Jay during the latter's diplomatic mission to Spain. He formally retired from the official families of both men in 1782, and by the end of the First Congress had become a political enemy of each. He passed the bar in 1783 and was elected to a single term in the state Assembly, 1788–89. (*Princetonians, 1769–1775*, pp. 397–407)

LIVINGSTON, JOHN (1750–1822), a member of one of New York's preeminent political dynasties, was a major landowner and speculator of Columbia County, New York, which he represented in the state Assembly, 1787–88 and 1789–90. He was brother-in-law of James Duane, brother of Walter Livingston, and cousin of Robert R. Livingston, who headed the rival Livingstons "of Clermont."

LIVINGSTON, JOHN HENRY (1746–1825), second cousin of Chancellor Robert R. Livingston, was minister of New York City's Dutch Reformed Church. (*PGW* 4:434)

LIVINGSTON, PHILIP PETER (1740–1810), was a land and securities speculator, banker, and manufacturer of Greenburgh, New York. After graduating from the College of New Jersey (Princeton) in 1758 he trained in the law at London's Inns of Court where he established contacts that provided him with a number of administrative posts in colonial New York and British West Florida before and during the Revolution. He returned to New York after the war, represented Westchester County at the state convention where he voted to ratify the Constitution, and served in the state Senate in 1789–93. (*Princetonians, 1748–1768*, pp. 232–35)

LIVINGSTON, ROBERT, JR. (1708–28 November 1790), was the third lord of "Livingston Manor," a large patrimonial estate comprising parts of present day Dutchess and Columbia counties, New York. In state and national politics he was a Federalist.

LIVINGSTON, ROBERT R. (1746–1813), chancellor of New York State, 1777–1801. See also *DHFFC* 17:1834.

LIVINGSTON, WALTER (1740–97), principal heir of New York's "Livingston Manor," served on the board of treasury from 1785 to 1789. By his marriage to Philip Schuyler's daughter Cornelia, he was the brother-in-law of Alexander Hamilton, John B. Church, and James Duane. See also *DHFFC* 17:1834.

LIVINGSTON, WILLIAM (1723–25 July 1790), of Elizabethtown, New Jersey, was governor of that state from 1776 until his death. His daughter Sarah married John Jay in 1774. See also *DHFFC* 9:70–71n.

LLOYD, EDWARD, IV (1744–96), was a planter of Talbot County, Maryland, and patriarch of Maryland's wealthiest family before the Revolution. After serving in the colonial and provincial legislatures, he sat in the state Executive Council, 1777–79, and Senate, 1780–88 and 1791–96. He also attended Congress, 1783–84. (*CCP* 1:371n)

LLOYD, THOMAS (1756–1827), was a British born reporter and stenographer from Philadelphia who published the *Congressional Register* in the first and second sessions of the First Congress. See also *DHFFC* 10:xxix–xxxiii, 12:xix–xxi.

LOCKE, JOHN (1632–1704) was a British philosopher who developed his social contract theory of revolution in *Two Treatises of Government* (1689), which summarized the gains of the Glorious Revolution of 1688–89 and profoundly influenced the American revolutionary movement.

LOGAN, BENJAMIN (1743–1802), was a Virginia native who migrated to Kentucky at the outbreak of the Revolutionary War and rose to brigadier general in the state militia by war's end. He represented Lincoln County in the state House of Delegates in 1781–82 and 1785–87, and at the statehood conventions of 1785, 1787, and 1788. (*DHROC* 8:434n; Thomas Marshall Green, *Historic Families of Kentucky* [Cincinnati, Ohio, 1889], pp. 120–41)

LOGAN, GEORGE (1753–1821), a Quaker physician and gentleman farmer of Germantown, Pennsylvania, represented Philadelphia County in the state Assembly, 1785–89. He supported the Constitution during ratification but soon thereafter left the Federalist party. See also *DHFFC* 9:209n. (*DHROC* 2:729)

LOMAX, THOMAS (1746–1811) was a prominent planter of "Port Tobago," Caroline County, Virginia. (*PGW* 5:463)

LOMBAERT, HERMAN JOSEPH (ca. 1756–1793), a Philadelphia merchant, was the son-in-law of Henry Wynkoop. See also *DHFFC* 9:32n.

LORD, LYNDE (ca. 1733–1801), was sheriff of Litchfield, Connecticut. (Dwight Kilbourne, *Bench and Bar of Litchfield County, Connecticut, 1709–1909* [Litchfield, Conn., 1909], p. 263)

LORING, EUNICE (b. 1767), and her cousin Sarah (d. September 1790), operated a boardinghouse for congressmen in New York City. Sarah was previously known to some of the Massachusetts delegation as the proprietor of Boston's Golden Ball Tavern. See also *DHFFC* 17:1835.

LOTHROP, ELISHA (1745–23 September 1790), a native of Norwich, Connecticut, was a merchant in Demerara (present-day Georgetown), Guyana. His second wife, Lydia Huntington Fitch (1735–1810), was a distant relative of Benjamin Huntington.

LOUDON, SAMUEL (1727–1813), of New York City, published the *New York Packet*, 1776–92, in partnership with his son John from 1785 until the latter's death in late 1789. See also *DHFFC* 8:737.

LOVELL, JAMES (1737–1814), of Boston, served as the federal naval officer for that city and nearby Charlestown, Massachusetts, 1789–1814, having held the post of state's revenue collector at Boston from 1788. See also *DHFFC* 2:508, 17:1835–36.

LOW, NICHOLAS (1739–1826), was a land speculator, merchant, and banker of New York City, which he represented in the state Assembly, 1788–89, and at the state convention where he voted to ratify the Constitution. (*DHFFE* 3:322n)

LOWELL, JOHN (1743–1802), a lawyer of Boston, served as United States judge for the Massachusetts district, 1789–1801. See *DHFFC* 2:508, 17:1836.

LOWTHER, MARGARET (ca. 1759–post 1824), daughter of New York City merchant William Lowther, married John Page on 27 March 1790 and returned with him to Virginia at the end of the second session of the First Congress. The first of their eight children was born at Page's plantation "Rosewell" in February 1791. See also *DHFFC* 14:922–23.

LOWTHER, WILLIAM (d. 1794), a native of Great Britain, settled as a merchant sea captain in New York City in 1771 for reasons of health, after a fifteen year residence in Edenton, North Carolina, and remained in New York throughout the British occupation. His Loyalist sympathies temporarily exiled him to Canada in 1783, but he returned and divided his time thereafter between New York and Edenton, where he died. By his wife, Barbara Gregory (d. 1794), he had a son and two daughters, one of whom, Margaret, married John Page. (William M. MacBean, *Biographical Register of Saint Andrew's Society* [New York, 1922] 1:142; [Edenton] *State Gazette of North Carolina*, 26 Sept. 1794)

LUX, GEORGE, JR. (1753–97), was a merchant and planter of "Chatsworth," his family's estate outside Baltimore. His wife, Catherine Biddle Lux, died 9 February 1790. See also *DHFFC* 17:1836.

LYDE, NATHANIEL BYFIELD (b. 1735), was a Boston sea captain after the Revolutionary War. He married Hannah, younger sister of Bossenger Foster, Sr., in 1777. (*Harvard Graduates* 7:206–14)

LYMAN, DANIEL (1756–1830), was a lawyer and manufacturer of Newport, Rhode Island, where he was appointed federal surveyor of the port, 1790–1802. He served briefly in the Massachusetts militia after graduating from Yale in 1776, but spent the duration of the war as aide-de-camp to General William Heath, 1777–83, retiring as brevet major and a member of the Society of the Cincinnati. See also *DHFFC* 2:540.

LYMAN, SAMUEL (1749–1802), a native of Connecticut, graduated from Yale in 1770 and abandoned divinity studies to take up law. He opened a legal practice in Hartford but in 1784 resettled in Springfield, Massachusetts, which he represented in the state House, 1786–88, and Senate, 1790–93. He was an unsuccessful candidate for Presidential Elector and for Representative in the first and second federal elections. Senator Strong was his first cousin. (*Yale Graduates* 3:388; *DHFFE* 1:532, 754)

LYMAN, WILLIAM (1755–1811), a Yale graduate of 1776, became a merchant of Northampton, Massachusetts, which he represented in the state House, 1787–88, and Senate, 1789–90. (*DHROC* 4:114n)

LYNCH, DOMINICK (1754–1825), was an Irish immigrant who settled in New York City in 1785 and became a wealthy partner in a mercantile firm with Diego de Gardoqui, Spain's consul general by 1788. On behalf of the Catholic laity, he joined Thomas Fitzsimons and the two Carroll cousins, Daniel and Charles of Carrollton, in signing, and probably presenting, the Church's (undated) complimentary address to George Washington on 15 March 1790. (*PGW* 1:47, 5:300)

McCall, Heath (d. 1792), was a lawyer of Charleston, South Carolina, who attended London's Inns of Court early during the Revolutionary War. (*Inns of Court*)

McConnell, Matthew (ca. 1743–1816), was a Philadelphia merchant and stockbroker of Philadelphia. His *Essay on the Domestic Debts*, previously dated 1787, may have been printed in early 1790. See also *DHFFC* 9:336n.

McCormick, Daniel, was a New York City merchant, alderman, and director of the Bank of New York.

McCullough, John (d. 1799), a master carpenter of Swansborough, North Carolina, was appointed federal surveyor there, 1790–95, having been its collector of customs under the state government from 1788. See also *DHFFC* 2:529.

McDowell, Joseph (1758–99), represented Burke County in North Carolina's House of Commons, 1780–89, Senate, 1790–94, and at both state ratification conventions, where he opposed the Constitution. He declined nomination as Senator in the first federal election and may have been the McDowell who received votes for the House seat won by John Steele. He was admitted to the bar in 1791. (*DHFFE* 4:368)

McDowell, Samuel, Sr. (1735–1817), represented Augusta County, Virginia, in the colonial and state legislature, 1772–78, Rockbridge County in 1778, and sat on the state Council of State in 1781 while serving as a colonel of the state militia. Appointed judge of Virginia's district court for Kentucky in 1783, he migrated to Danville and became a founding member of that town's Political Club with John Brown, Harry Innes, Christopher Greenup, and Thomas Todd. McDowell also presided over all the statehood conventions between 1784 and 1790. (Thomas Marshall Green, *Historic Families of Kentucky* [Cincinnati, Ohio, 1889], pp. 31–39; *DHROC* 8:408)

McDowell, Samuel, Jr. (1764–1834), was appointed United States marshal for the Kentucky district in 1789. See *DHFFC* 2:494.

McGillivray, Alexander (1759–93), "Great Beloved Man" of the Creek Indians, served as their principal commercial agent and trade negotiator with Spain and the United States by the late 1780s. From his plantation in

Little Tallassee (near present-day Montgomery, Alabama), he led a Creek delegation to New York City to sign the federal government's first treaty with a foreign power in August 1790.

MCKEAN, THOMAS (1734–1817), of Philadelphia, served as chief justice of Pennsylvania, 1777–99. See also *DHFFC* 9:79n, 17:1838.

MCKENZIE, WILLIAM, a planter of Martin County, North Carolina, married Senator Johnston's sister-in-law, Margaret "Peggy" Cathcart, in 1781. (*Iredell* 1:103n)

MCKINLY, JOHN (1721–96), an Irish born physician of Wilmington, Delaware, served as first president (governor) of the state in 1777. See also *DHFFC* 17:1838.

MCKNIGHT, CHARLES, JR. (1750–1791), a New York City physician, graduated from the College of New Jersey (Princeton) in 1771 and held high medical posts in the Continental Army, 1778–82. See also *DHFFC* 9:202–3n, 17:1838.

MACLAINE, ARCHIBALD (d. 1791), was a lawyer of Wilmington, North Carolina, which he represented in the provincial congresses, intermittently in the state House and Senate, 1777–87, and at the first state convention where he supported the Constitution. (*DHFFE* 4:320n)

MACLAINE, BARBARA LOWTHER (b. 1767), of New York City, was the younger sister of Margaret Lowther Page. She married British Army Lieut. Archibald Maclaine in 1784, but was left a widow after only a few months when he was killed in a brawl while en route to England to contest his court martial for insubordination and dismissal from active duty in Quebec. ([Inverness, Scotland] *Celtic Magazine* 13[1888]:442)

MACLAY, JOHN HARRIS (b. 1770), the oldest of William Maclay's eight children to survive infancy, managed the family farm at Sunbury, Pennsylvania. See also *DHFFC* 9:343n.

MACLAY, SAMUEL (1741–1811), younger brother and confidant of William Maclay, was a large landowner of Northumberland County, Pennsylvania, which he represented in the state Assembly, 1787–91. In 1773 he married the daughter of Maclay's friend, William Plunket. (*DHFFC* 9:213)

McLean, Archibald (d. 1798), originally from Scotland, was a book dealer and Federalist printer who published the *New-York Daily Gazette* during the First Congress. He had previously published the city's *Independent Journal*, the first newspaper to carry the *Federalist* essays. See also *DHFFC* 9:196n.

McLellan, Joseph (1732–1820), was a merchant and sea captain of Portland, Maine. Before the Revolution he was involved mostly in the West Indian trade, but in the 1790s his shipping firm expanded into one of the largest in the district. See also *DHFFC* 17:1838.

McNairy, John (1762–1837), served as judge of the Southeast Territory, 1790–96, having served as judge of the superior court of Davidson County, Tennessee, since 1787. The Pennsylvania native was admitted to the bar in 1784. (*PGW* 5:478n)

McPherson, John (1756–1806), represented Prince William Parish, South Carolina, in the state's House, 1781–84 and 1786–92, and at its ratification convention, where he voted in favor of the Constitution. He was commissioned a brigadier general in the state militia in 1790. (*South Carolina Senate*, p. 271)

McQueen, John (1757–1807), was a planter and land speculator of Georgia. He became Don Juan McQueen when he fled to Spanish Florida in 1791 to avoid debts that had been guaranteed by his friend, Pierce Butler. (*Butler*, p. 536)

McToksin, Jehoiakim, was a member of the Stockbridge, or Moheconnuck, Indian Nation in Stockbridge, Massachusetts. During the Revolutionary War he served as a scout in General John Sullivan's campaign against the Iroquois, compensation for which he successfully petitioned the First Congress in February 1790. See also *DHFFC* 7:6–7.

Madison, Ambrose (1755–93), a planter of Orange County, Virginia, was a younger brother of James Madison. Like his father and brother, he speculated in Kentucky lands. (*DHROC* 9:604; *PJM* 15:363, 378)

Madison, James, Sr. (1723–1809), also known as "the Colonel," was father of the Representative. "Montpelier," his plantation in Orange County, Virginia, was the lifelong home of the younger Madison, who inherited it upon his father's death.

MANDRILLON, JOSEPH (1743–94), was a French banker based in Amsterdam, who had traveled in America before the Revolution and published frequently on American affairs. (*PGW* 1:68n)

MANIGAULT, GABRIEL (1758–1809), was a prominent planter and securities speculator of St. James Goose Creek Parish, South Carolina, which he represented in the state House, 1785–93, and at the state convention, where he voted to ratify the Constitution. He became the son-in-law of Ralph Izard and the brother-in-law of William Smith (S.C.) by his marriage to Margaret Izard in 1785. (*South Carolina House* 3:470–73)

MANIGAULT, JOSEPH (1763–1843), younger brother of Gabriel Manigault, entered London's Middle Temple in 1781 and became a lawyer and planter of Charleston, South Carolina. (*DGW* 6:126n; *Inns of Court*)

MANLEY, JOHN (ca. 1734–1793), a Boston sea captain, had served in the British Navy before joining the Continental Navy, where he commanded the *Hancock* in 1777 and *The Hague* in 1782–83. (*PGW: Revolution* 2:295–96n; John F. Millar, *American Ships of the Colonial and Revolutionary Periods* [New York, 1978], pp. 104, 152)

MANNING, JAMES (1738–91), was a native of New Jersey who in 1764 settled in Providence, Rhode Island, where he became a Baptist minister and first president of the College of Rhode Island (Brown). See also *DHFFC* 8:389–91, 17:1839–40.

MANSFIELD, ISAAC (1750–1826), a native of Marblehead, Massachusetts, and 1767 graduate of Harvard, served as a Congregational pastor in Exeter, New Hampshire, from 1776 until he was released for doctrinal reasons in 1787. He was still residing there as a schoolteacher when he petitioned the First Congress in December 1790 for a settlement of his accounts as a Continental Army chaplain in 1775–76. See also *DHFFC* 7:577. (*Harvard Graduates* 16:499–502)

MAPPA, ADAM GERARD (1754–1828), was a type foundry maker whose revolutionary activities forced him to flee his native Holland and settle in New York City in December 1789, where he resumed the manufacture of type. (*PGW* 4:197)

MARCHANT, HENRY (1741–96), was a lawyer of Newport, Rhode Island, who served as federal district judge for that state, 1790–96. He also represented the town at the state convention where he voted to ratify the Constitution. See also *DHFFC* 2:540, 8:389–90, 17:1840.

MARSHALL, JOHN (1755–1835), was a leading lawyer in Richmond, Virginia, which he represented in the state House of Delegates, 1787–88 and 1789–91, and at the state convention, where he voted to ratify the Constitution. See also *DHFFC* 2:551–52, 17:1840.

MARSHALL, WILLIAM (1735–1809), was a native of Virginia whose conversion experience in 1768 led him to become a Baptist evangelist. In ca. 1780 he settled in Lincoln County, Kentucky.

MARTIN, ALEXANDER (1740–1807), a native of New Jersey, graduated from the College of New Jersey (Princeton) in 1756 and settled as a merchant in Salisbury, North Carolina, by 1764. Within the next decade he moved to Guilford County, which he represented in the colonial House of Commons, 1773–74, the provincial congress in 1775–76, and intermittently in the state Senate, 1778–82, 1785, and 1787–88. During the Revolutionary War he rose from lieutenant colonel of the 2nd Regiment of the North Carolina Line in 1775 to commanding colonel in 1776, resigning the next year. He was governor in 1782–85 and again in 1789–92. Although he declined to serve in Congress when elected in 1786, he did serve in the Federal Convention the next year, and was the only Signer who was later defeated for a seat at a state ratification convention. By 1790 he had transferred his official residence to his plantation "Danbury" in Rockingham County. (*DHFFE* 4:336n; *Princetonians, 1748–1768*, pp. 157–60; Charles D. Rodenbough, *Governor Alexander Martin* [Jefferson, N.C., 2004], pp. 126, 142)

MARTIN, JOSEPH (1740–1808), the Confederation Congress's sole agent to the Cherokee and Chickasaw nations in the late 1780s, returned to his native Virginia in 1789 and served in the state legislature, 1791–99. See also *DHFFC* 17:1840–41.

MASON, GEORGE (1725–92), an early leader of the revolutionary movement and then the antifederalist movement in Virginia, was a planter of "Gunston Hall" in Fairfax County, Virginia, which he represented in the state House of Delegates, 1776–81 and 1787–88. See also *DHFFC* 17:1841.

MASON, JOHN (1766–1849), seventh child of George Mason, became a partner of Joseph Fenwick in a mercantile firm based on Bordeaux, France, in 1788. He returned in 1791 and settled in Georgetown, Maryland (present-day D.C.). (*PGW: Retirement* 2:2n)

MASON, JONATHAN, SR. (1725–98), was a prosperous Boston merchant who had been active in the Revolutionary movement as a town selectman and Son of Liberty. In 1786 he became a director of the Massachusetts Bank.

MASSEY, LEE (1732–1814), a planter of "Bradley," Fairfax County, Virginia, and confidant of his neighbor, George Mason, gave up a legal practice to be ordained in the Anglican Church in 1766 and serve as rector of the county's Truro Parish from 1767 to 1777. (*DGW* 2:235–36; *PGM* 1:lxxviii)

MATHEWS (MATTHEWS), JOHN (1744–1802), was a London trained lawyer and jurist of Charleston, South Carolina, which he represented in the colonial legislature, provincial congresses, and state House of Representatives, 1776–80 and 1784 (as speaker, 1777–78). In addition to captaining a county militia company during the Revolutionary War, he served as delegate to Congress, 1778–81, and governor, 1782–83, prior to his appointment to the state's court of chancery in 1784.

MATHEWS, THOMAS (1742–1812), was a merchant and planter of Norfolk, Virginia, which he represented in the state House of Delegates, 1781–82 and 1784–93 (as speaker, 1788–93). Although he voted to ratify the Constitution at the state convention, he lost to his recently converted fellow Federalist Josiah Parker in the first federal election. See also *DHFFC* 17:1841–42.

MAURY, FONTAINE (1761–1824), of Fredericksburg, Virginia, was a merchant whose store often served as a post office. (*PGW* 1:244n)

MAURY, JAMES (1746–1840), was a former merchant of Fredericksburg, Virginia, who became a tobacco importer at Liverpool, England, by 1788 and served as United States consul there, 1789–1830. (*DHFFE* 2:406n)

MAXWELL, CORNELIUS (1755–1809), appointed messenger for the Senate in April 1789, was a native of Scotland who immigrated to New York in time to serve as a sergeant in the 3rd Regiment of the state's Continental Line during the Revolutionary War. See also *DHFFC* 8:523.

MAY, JOHN (b. 1744), was a major land speculator, developer, and surveyor of Jefferson County, Kentucky, which he represented in the Virginia House of Delegates in 1782. Founder and namesake of Maysville, Kentucky, in 1787, he was killed by Shawnee at the mouth of the Scioto River on 20 March 1790. (Benjamin H. Coke, *John May, Jr., of Virginia* [Baltimore, 1975], pp. 243–50)

MAYBERRY, RICHARD, of Windham, Maine, served as captain in the 11th Massachusetts Regiment from 1776 to 1778, when he transferred to the state militia. (*MSSR* 10:386)

MAYO, EBENEZER (b. 1764), a merchant of Portland, Maine, served as Massachusetts' excise collector for Cumberland County in 1790.

MAZZEI, PHILIP (1730–1816), was an Italian physician and merchant who immigrated to Virginia in 1773 at the head of a colony of Italian planters and became Thomas Jefferson's friend and neighbor. He acted as the state's agent and military arms procurer in Italy, 1779–83, and except for a brief return visit in 1785 remained in Europe as a promoter of the United States and republican ideas. During the First Congress he resided in Paris as a representative of the Polish government.

MEAD, DAVID (1752–1816), a native of New York, moved to Pennsylvania by 1769 and became an innkeeper and distiller in Sunbury. He moved to Cussewago (present-day Meadville), Pennsylvania, in 1788. (Robert Ilisevich, *David Mead: Pennsylvania's Last Frontiersman* [Meadville, Penn., 1988])

MEADE, GEORGE (1741–1808), a Philadelphia merchant and banker, served on the city council, 1789–91. He was a close business associate of Robert Morris and Thomas Fitzsimons, and married the latter's sister Catherine in 1761. See also *DHFFC* 17:1842.

MEALS, JOHN, served as Georgia's state treasurer until his death in December 1791. (*DHFFC* 5:526n)

MELCHER, ISAAC (1749–90), a native of Pennsylvania and barrackmaster of the Continental Army, 1779–80, became a gentleman farmer and land speculator in New York and Ohio. See also *DHFFC* 17:1842.

MENTGES, FRANCIS (d. 1805), immigrated from his native France to Philadelphia by the outbreak of the Revolutionary War, during which he served in the 11th, 7th, and 5th Regiments of the Pennsylvania Line, rising from first lieutenant to lieutenant colonel, 1776–83, and serving as inspector of the southern army in the last years of the war, after which he enrolled in the Society of the Cincinnati. As inspector general of the state militia, he formed part of the delegation that escorted George Washington into Philadelphia for the Federal Convention. He was appointed inspector of federal troops under the Military Establishment Act in 1790, and in the same year he petitioned Congress unsuccessfully for compensation for military service. See also *DHFFC* 7:246–49.

MERCER, ARCHIBALD (1747–1814), was a Federalist businessman of Millstone, New Jersey, where he owned several large flour mills. During the Revolutionary War he invested in privateers outfitted in New Hampshire, among which John and Woodbury Langdon were co-owners.

MERCER, JAMES (1736–93), of Fredericksburg, Virginia, had represented Hampshire County in the colonial legislature before serving on the bench of the state General Court, 1779–89, and Court of Appeals thereafter until his death. (*PJM* 1:164n)

MEREDITH, SAMUEL (1741–1817), a Philadelphia merchant, was appointed port surveyor in August 1789 but accepted the more lucrative appointment as United States treasurer the next month and served until 1801. His brothers-in-law in the First Congress included Lambert Cadwalader, Philemon Dickinson, and George Clymer, who also became a close business associate. His children during the First Congress, by his marriage to Margaret "Peggy" Cadwalader (b. 1748) in 1772, were Martha, Elizabeth or "Betsey" (ca. 1775–1826), Anne (b. ca. 1776), Margaret (1781–1824), and Maria (1783–1854). The Merediths' estate, "Green Hill," then on the outskirts of Philadelphia, was located at present-day 17th and Girard streets. See also *DHFFC* 17:1843.

MERRILL, HEZEKIAH (1750–1801), was a merchant of Hartford who served as receiver of Continental taxes for Connecticut, 1782–88. (*PRM* 5:132n)

MEYER, JOHN, originally of Philadelphia, served as one of two principal clerks in the treasury department. In August 1790 he applied unsuccessfully to succeed John Pintard as "clerk for foreign languages" in the state department. It has been suggested that Hamilton urged his subordinate's transfer in order to plant a spy in his rival's department. (*PTJ* 17:351–53n)

MIFFLIN, THOMAS (1744–1800), a retired merchant of Philadelphia, served as president of Pennsylvania, 1788–90, and as governor, 1790–99. The Continental Army major general attended Congress, 1774–75, 1783–84 (as its president), and the Federal Convention, where he signed the Constitution. In 1767 he married Sarah Morris (d. 1790). See also *DHFFC* 9:79n, 17:1843.

MIFFLIN, WARNER (1745–98), a Quaker planter of Camden, Delaware, was an active abolitionist and lobbyist during the Confederation and First Congress. He married Ann Emlen (d. 1815) in 1788. See also *DHFFC* 8:317–19. (*Drinker* 3:2184)

MILES, SAMUEL (1739–1805), was a member of the Pennsylvania Supreme Executive Council, 1788–90, and mayor of Philadelphia from April 1790 to April 1791. See also *DHFFC* 9:217n.

MILLER, ASHER (1753–1821), was a lawyer of Middletown, Connecticut, where he served as federal surveyor, 1789–90. The Yale graduate of 1778 had previously been state Representative, 1785 and 1788–93, state attorney, 1785–94, and delegate to the state convention, where he voted to ratify the Constitution. See also *DHFFC* 2:486.

MILLER, GEORGE, was the Charleston based British consul for North Carolina, South Carolina, and Georgia from 1787.

MILLER, JOHN (d. 1808), a captain in the Virginia militia in 1779, represented Madison County, Kentucky, at the statehood convention of 1787 and in the Virginia House of Delegates, 1789–90. (*Sketches of Kentucky* 1:354, 365, 366)

MILLER, PHINEAS (1764–1803), a Connecticut born graduate of Yale in 1785, was employed by Catharine Greene as a tutor for her children and co-manager of her Georgia plantations. See also *DHFFC* 17:1844.

MILLIGAN, JACOB, served as a privateer and junior officer in the South Carolina state navy during the Revolutionary War and subsequently became harbor master of Charleston. (*PGW* 4:250)

MINOT, GEORGE R. (1758–1802), a Boston lawyer and historian, was clerk of the Massachusetts House of Representatives, 1782–91. The 1778 Harvard graduate was admitted to the bar in 1781, having studied in the offices of William Tudor where he formed a lifelong friendship with fellow law student Fisher Ames. See also *DHFFC* 17:1844.

MINOT, JONAS CLARK (1735–1813), older brother of George R., was inspector of customs for the Boston district, 1789–1802. See also *DHFFC* 17:1844.

MIRÓ, ESTEBAN (1744–95), became governor of Spanish Louisiana in 1785, with the rank of brigadier general after 1789.

MITCHELL, GEORGE R. (d. 1799), was a planter of Sussex County, Delaware, which he represented in the state's House of Assembly, 1784–88. He served as speaker of the Legislative Council, 1788–92, and a Presidential Elector in 1789. (*DHFFE* 2:97)

MITCHELL, JOHN HINKLEY (1741–1816), was a West Indies merchant who settled in Philadelphia by 1769. He held various state militia posts, 1776–80, despite poor relations with the state government, after which he relocated to Charleston, South Carolina, where he was a merchant planter and became a city warden by 1787. See also *DHFFC* 8:504–9. (*PGW* 2:347–48n)

MITCHELL, JUSTUS (1754–1806), graduated from Yale in 1776 and served as a Congregational minister in New Canaan, Connecticut, from 1783 until his death. In 1779 he married Martha, the daughter of Roger Sherman's younger brother Josiah. (*Yale Graduates* 3:622–24)

MITCHELL, STEPHEN MIX (1743–1835), a lawyer of Wethersfield, Connecticut, was a member of the state Council of Assistants, 1784–93, and a judge of the Hartford County court, 1789–95. Despite long service in the state House, in Congress, and at the state convention, where he voted to ratify the Constitution, he failed in his bid for Representative in the first federal election. See also *DHFFC* 17:1845.

MONROE, JAMES, family during the First Congress: wife Elizabeth Kortright (1768–1830) of New York, whom he married in 1786, and their daughter Eliza Kortright Monroe (b. 1787).

MONTESQUIEU, CHARLES LOUIS, BARON DE (1689–1755), was a French jurist, political philosopher, and author of the vastly influential *Spirit of the Laws* (1748).

MONTGOMERIE, THOMAS (1754–1818), was a merchant of Dumfries, Virginia. (*PGW* 1:63n)

MONTGOMERY, JOHN (1722–1808), immigrated from his native Ireland to Carlisle, Pennsylvania, about 1740 and became a merchant, representing Cumberland County in the state House, 1790–91. See also *DHFFC* 9:327–28n.

MONTMORIN DE SAINT-HEREUR, ARMAND-MARC, COMTE DE (1745–92), was France's foreign minister, 1787–91.

MOORE, ALFRED (1755–1810), a lawyer and planter of Brunswick County, North Carolina, served as state attorney general, 1782–91. During the Revolutionary War he was a captain in the 1st Regiment of the state's line, 1775–77. (*DHSCUS* 1:137–39)

MOORE, BENJAMIN (1748–1816), graduated from King's College (Columbia) in 1768, was ordained an Anglican minister in 1774, and served as assistant minister at New York City's Trinity Church, 1784–1800. (*New York*, pp. 140–41)

MOORE, STEPHEN (1734–99), a native of New York City, was a Canadian merchant who resettled in Caswell (now Person) County, North Carolina, at the outbreak of the Revolutionary War, during which he rose to the rank of lieutenant colonel in the state militia. After the war he resumed his mercantile activities near Hillsboro, North Carolina. His petition to the First Congress in May 1790, seeking compensation for wartime damages to land he owned along the Hudson in New York State, resulted in the federal government's purchase of West Point. See also *DHFFC* 7:110–13.

MORGAN, DANIEL (1736–1802), a hero of the Revolutionary War battles of Saratoga and Cowpens, captained one of the first non-New England units to join what became the Continental Army in 1775 and rose to colonel of the 11th Regiment of the Virginia Line, 1776–79. After a brief retirement, he rejoined the army as a brigadier general, 1780–83, returning at war's end to his farm "Soldier's Rest" outside Winchester, Virginia.

MORGAN, GEORGE (1743–1810), a merchant, land speculator, and farmer of "Prospect," near Princeton, New Jersey, launched a settlement of American colonists at New Madrid in Spanish Louisiana (in present-day Missouri) in 1788–89. In the 1760s he was a partner in a mercantile firm active in the Illinois country. See also *DHFFC* 17:1846.

MORRIS, GOUVERNEUR (1752–1816), was a New York City lawyer who played a major role at the Federal Convention before serving as George Washington's unofficial representative to the British government in London beginning in January 1790. His five square mile estate "Morrisania" (in present-day south Bronx) served as an occasional retreat for Robert Morris during the First Congress. See also *DHFFC* 2:116, 451–67, 9:390, 17:1846.

MORRIS, LEWIS III (1726–98), was the third and last lord of the manorial estate "Morrisania," in present-day south Bronx, from 1762 until he sold it to his younger half-brother Gouverneur in 1787, four years after Congress declined to accept it as the federal seat of government. The Yale graduate of 1746 attended the colonial and provincial legislatures before taking a seat in Congress, 1775–77, where he signed the Declaration of Independence. He was a brigadier general of the Westchester County militia throughout the war, while also serving intermittently in the state Senate, 1777–90. At the state convention of 1788 he voted to ratify the Constitution.

MORRIS, LEWIS IV, JR. (1752–1824), son of Lewis III, nephew of Gouverneur Morris, and brother-in-law of Daniel Huger, married into South Carolina's planter aristocracy in 1783 and settled in Charleston upon retiring as a brevet lieutenant colonel in the Continental Army. The 1774 graduate of the College of New Jersey (Princeton) and member of the Society of the Cincinnati voted to ratify the Constitution at the state convention in 1788 and went on to serve in the state House of Representatives, 1789–94. See also *DHFFC* 17:1846.

MORRIS, LEWIS R. (1760–1825), was a local and state officeholder, businessman, and landowner of Springfield, Vermont, where he settled by 1785. Birth into the influential New York dynasty of Morrises (which included his uncle Gouverneur) probably aided his appointment as undersecretary of domestic affairs in Robert R. Livingston's department of foreign affairs, 1781–83. He was Windsor County court clerk, 1789–96, and clerk of Vermont's House of Representatives, 1790–91, before his appointment as federal marshal for Vermont, 1791–1801. His marriage in 1786 to Mary, sister of Timothy Dwight, ended in divorce shortly thereafter. See also *DHFFC* 2:547. (George Dangerfield, *Chancellor Robert R. Livingston* [New York, 1960], p. 145)

MORRIS, MARY WHITE (1749–1827), of Philadelphia, married Robert Morris in 1769. During the First Congress, their family consisted of: Robert, Jr. (1769–ca. 1804); Esther ("Hetty"); Thomas (1771–1849), who frequently stayed with his father while Congress sat in New York; William White (1772–98); Charles (b. 1777); Maria (1779–1852); and Henry (1784–1842). See also *DHFFC* 9:60n, 17:1846–47.

MORRIS, ROBERT (ca. 1745–1815), was a lawyer born in New Brunswick, New Jersey, who served as federal district court judge for the state from 1789 until his death. The son of one of the colony's supreme court justices, he became in turn chief justice of the state Supreme Court, 1777–79. (*DHFFE* 3:53n)

MORRIS, STAATS (1765–1827), was the son of Lewis Morris III of "Morrisania" (in present-day south Bronx), New York, and nephew of Gouverneur Morris. His travels through Europe in the 1780s coincided with those of his friend Thomas Lee Shippen.

MORRISON, ISAAC, represented Nelson County, Kentucky, at the statehood convention of 1788 and in the Virginia House of Delegates in 1790. (*Sketches of Kentucky* 1:354, 366)

MORSE, JEDIDIAH (1761–1826), was a Congregational minister of Charlestown, Massachusetts, who graduated from Yale in 1783. In May 1789 he married the niece of his fellow historian, Ebenezer Hazard. See also *DHFFC* 8:30. (*DHFFC* 17:1847)

MORTIMER, CHARLES, was a physician of Fredericksburg, Virginia, who attended George Washington's mother during her terminal illness in August 1789. He was mayor intermittently throughout the 1780s. (*PGW* 5:540n)

MORTON, SARAH WENTWORTH (1759–1846), of Boston, in 1781 married Perez Morton (1751–1837), state attorney for Suffolk County, Massachusetts. (*PGW* 4:450; Howard Haycroft and Stanley Kunitz, *American Authors, 1600–1900* [New York, 1938], pp. 545–46)

MOTLEY, JOHN, was master of the brig *Betsey*, a packet boat that sailed between New York and Charleston, South Carolina.

MOTT, JAMES (1739–1823), a farmer of Middletown, New Jersey, served as state treasurer, 1783–99. In addition to captaining a militia company during the Revolutionary War, he sat in the state General Assembly, 1776–79.

MOULTRIE, ALEXANDER (ca. 1750–1807), studied at London's Inns of Court before returning to his native Charleston, South Carolina, by 1772, when he was admitted to the bar. He served in the city militia from 1774 until at least 1782, when he was promoted to colonel. State representative from 1776 to 1786, he simultaneously served as state attorney general from 1776 until 1792, when he was impeached for embezzlement. He was one of four initial investors in the South Carolina Company's scheme for settling Georgia's Yazoo lands in 1789–90. (*Inns of Court*)

MOULTRIE, WILLIAM (1730–1805), was a planter of St. John's Berkeley, South Carolina, who served as state Senator in 1791, having held the offices of Representative, lieutenant governor, and then governor, 1783–87. The Revolutionary War hero also voted for the Constitution at the state convention in 1788. See also *DHFFC* 17:1848.

MOYLAND, STEPHEN (1737–1811), immigrated from his native Ireland in 1768 and settled in Philadelphia, where he became an owner of merchant vessels. During the Revolutionary War he served briefly as aide-de-camp to George Washington and quartermaster general before being commissioned colonel of the 3rd Regiment of Continental Dragoons in 1777, where he served until his retirement as brevet brigadier general at war's end. See also *DHFFC* 9:263n.

MURFREE, HARDY (1752–1809), was a planter of Murfreesboro, North Carolina, where he was appointed federal surveyor in 1790. During the Revolutionary War he rose from captain in the 2nd Regiment of the North Carolina Line in 1775, to lieutenant colonel of the 1st Regiment in 1778, retiring in 1782 and subsequently joining the Society of the Cincinnati. He voted in favor of the Constitution at the second ratification convention in 1789. See also *DHFFC* 2:529.

MURRAY, ALEXANDER (1755–1821), of Philadelphia, was a lieutenant in the Continental Navy from 1781. His wife was Mary ("Polly").

MURRAY, JOHN (1741–1815), a native of England, was a preacher in Gloucester, Massachusetts, where he co-founded Universalism. In 1788 he married the widow Judith Sargent Stevens, who accompanied him to the Convention of Societies of Universal Baptists that he helped organize for seventeen delegates from four states, held in Philadelphia between 25 May and 8 June 1790.

MURRAY, JOHN JR. (1758–1819), a Quaker distiller of New York City, married Catherine Bowne (ca. 1763–1834) in 1784. (*Drinker* 3:2190)

MURRAY, JUDITH SARGENT (1751–1820), sister of Winthrop and cousin of Epes Sargent, married the prominent theologian and preacher John Murray of Gloucester, Massachusetts, in 1788. Many of this poet, playwright, and novelist's letters that discuss the First Congress describe events she witnessed during her journey to and from the Universalist Convention organized by her husband and held in Philadelphia in the summer of 1790.

Murray, William Vans (1760–1803), was enrolled in London's Middle Temple in 1784 and returned in 1787 to practice law in his native Dorchester County, Maryland, which he represented in the state House of Delegates, 1788–90. Unsuccessful in his bid for the seat won by George Gale in the first federal election, Murray defeated him in the second election and served until 1797. (*DHFFE* 2:239–40)

Myers, Moses (ca. 1752–1835), was a prominent merchant of Norfolk, Virginia. (*PRM* 6:215n)

Nasson, Samuel (1745–1800), was a farmer and miller of Sanford, Maine, which he served as selectman, 1786–90, member of the Massachusetts House of Representatives, 1787–89, and delegate to the state convention, where he voted against ratification of the Constitution. See also *DHFFC* 17:1849.

Necker, Jacques (1732–1804), a Geneva born banker, served as France's minister of finance from 1776 until his dismissal in 1781. He returned to office from 1788 to 1790.

Neilson (Nelson), John (1745–1833), left the College of Philadelphia (University of Pennsylvania) before graduating with the class of 1761 and became a shipping merchant in New Brunswick, New Jersey. During the Revolutionary War he rose to the rank of brigadier general of the state militia, serving also as state Representative in 1779 and state deputy quartermaster general, 1780–83. He declined to serve in either Congress or the Federal Convention when elected, in 1778 and 1787 respectively, but he did attend the state convention where he voted to ratify the Constitution, and was named a Presidential Elector although he lost a bid for Representative in the first federal election. (*DHFFE* 3:186)

Nelson, Thomas (b. 1764), son of Virginia's Governor Thomas Nelson, Jr. (d. January 1789), served as George Washington's aide and personal secretary from October 1789 until November 1790. See also *DHFFC* 9:240n.

Nelson, William, Jr. (1754–1813), a lawyer of Richmond, served as federal attorney for Virginia from 1789 until 1791, when he became judge of the state General Court. See also *DHFFC* 2:552. (*PJM* 6:500n)

Neufville, John (1727–1804), a Charleston merchant, served as federal commissioner of loans for South Carolina, 1790–93. See also *DHFFC* 2:544.

NICHOLAS, GEORGE (ca. 1749–1799), brother-in-law of Attorney General Edmund Randolph, was a lawyer of Danville, Kentucky, where he settled in early 1789 and became a leader of the statehood movement. He previously resided in Albemarle County, Virginia, which he represented in the state House of Delegates, 1786–87, and at the state convention, where he voted to ratify the Constitution. See also *DHFFC* 17:1850.

NICHOLS (NICHOLLS), WILLIAM (1754–1804), a Philadelphia lawyer, served as a municipal court clerk in 1790. During the Revolutionary War he rose from ensign to second lieutenant and quartermaster of the 7th Pennsylvania Regiment in 1776, before transferring to Thomas Hartley's Regiment as a captain, 1777–78. (*PGW* 6:132n)

NICHOLSON, JAMES (1737–1804), of New York City, was the retired "commodore" or senior captain of the Continental Navy and a municipal officeholder, 1788–89. By his marriage to Frances Witter (1744–1832) in 1763, he had four daughters, of whom Catherine and Frances married William Few and Joshua Seney, respectively. See also *DHFFC* 7:438, 17:1851.

NICHOLSON, JOHN (1757–1800), immigrated from Wales to Pennsylvania, where he became state comptroller general, 1782–94, and an Antifederalist leader. His politics and extensive land speculations made him a controversial figure whom William Maclay nevertheless employed as a conduit for his own anonymous newspaper pieces, and as a source for information during the debate over Alexander Hamilton's funding plan. See also *DHFFC* 9:194n.

NICKOLLS (NICHOLS), JAMES B., brother-in-law of John Swanwick, apprenticed under Thomas Fitzsimons at Philadelphia prior to settling as a merchant in Portsmouth, Virginia, in 1785. (*PGW* 2:143–44n)

NIVISON, JOHN (1760–1820), a former student at the College of William and Mary, was a prominent lawyer and landowner of Norfolk, Virginia.

NIXON, JOHN (1733–1808), a Philadelphia merchant and financier, signed the two petitions from that city's public creditors to Congress, in August 1789 and December 1790. He was a director of the Bank of Pennsylvania when it was founded in 1780. See *DHFFC* 17:1851.

NORTH, WILLIAM (1755–1836), son-in-law of New York City Mayor James Duane, was a merchant of Duanesburg, New York. His military career during the Revolutionary War was distinguished by his close friendship with Baron von Steuben, whom he served as aide-de-camp, 1779–83. See also *DHFFC* 17:1851–52.

NORTON, ELIZABETH (1763–1811), of Weymouth, Massachusetts, was the daughter of Mary and Richard Cranch and the niece of John and Abigail Adams. She married Rev. Jacob Norton in 1789. (*Adams* 3:231n)

O'BRYEN, RICHARD (1758–1824), of Maine, was master of the *Dauphin* at the time of the ship's capture by Algerine "pirates" in 1785. From Algiers he corresponded with the United States government as spokesman for himself and his fellow captive Americans, including by a petition presented to the House in May 1790. See also *DHFFC* 2:425–49, 9:366n, 8:2–4.

O'FALLON, JAMES (1749–ca. 1794), was a native of Ireland who trained for medicine in Edinburgh before immigrating to North Carolina in 1774. After serving as an army surgeon during the Revolutionary War, he settled in South Carolina with Pierce Butler's encouragement and in 1789 became general agent for the South Carolina Yazoo Company. In 1790 he was in Kentucky, home of his brother-in-law George R. Clark, fomenting a separatist movement for colonizing territory claimed by both Spain and the United States in present-day Mississippi. See also *DHFFC* 9:368n. (*McGillivray*, p. 269n)

OGDEN, ABRAHAM (1743–98), federal attorney for New Jersey, 1791–98, was a land speculator and lawyer of Newark, New Jersey, which he represented in the state General Assembly in 1790. He married Sarah F. Ludlow in 1767. See also *DHFFC* 2:520.

OGDEN, SAMUEL (1746–1810), owned and operated ironworks in Morris County, New Jersey. In 1775 he married Euphemia Morris, sister of Gouverneur and Lewis Morris III. See also *DHFFC* 17:1852.

OLIVER, ROBERT (1738–1810), a native of Massachusetts, served in the Revolutionary War as a captain in Ephraim Doolittle's Massachusetts Regiment in 1775, transferred to the 2nd Continental Regiment in 1776, to the 3rd Regiment of the Massachusetts Line in 1777 where he was promoted to major, and to the 3rd Regiment of the state line in 1783, retiring at war's end as a brevet lieutenant colonel. Investing in the Ohio Company, he built mills in Waterford, Ohio, in 1789 before resettling in Marietta as a director of the company in 1791. (S. P. Hildreth, *Memoirs of the Pioneer Settlers of Ohio* [Cincinnati, Ohio, 1858], pp. 391–95)

OLNEY, JEREMIAH (1749–1812), of Smithfield, Rhode Island, served as federal collector at neighboring Providence, 1790–1809. During the Revolutionary War he rose from captain of the 2nd Regiment of the Rhode Island Line in 1775 and of the 11th Continental Regiment in 1776, to lieutenant colonel of the 2nd Rhode Island Regiment from 1777 until 1781 when he transferred to the 1st Regiment, resigning as colonel of the Rhode Island Battalion at war's end, when he joined the Society of the Cincinnati. See also *DHFFC* 2:540–41.

OLYPHANT, DAVID (1720–1805), was a Scottish born physician who had a distinguished military and political career in South Carolina before retiring to Newport, Rhode Island, in 1785. In March 1790 he unsuccessfully petitioned Congress for compensation for his service as director general of army hospitals in South Carolina, 1776–81. In 1786 he married Nancy Vernon, niece of William Vernon. See also *DHFFC* 7:302–7.

ORNE, AZOR (1731–96), was a merchant of Marblehead, Massachusetts, which he served as selectman, 1787–89, state Representative in 1787 and 1789, and delegate to the state convention, where he voted to ratify the Constitution. See also *DHFFC* 17:1852.

ORR, ALEXANDER (1761–1835), was a farmer of Mason County, Kentucky, which he represented in Virginia's House of Delegates in 1790.

ORTON, JAMES (1765–ca. 1840), graduated from Dartmouth College in 1787 and studied law prior to becoming a tavern keeper in Stockbridge, Massachusetts, in 1790. He purchased the tavern from his mother, Anna Bingham, in order to protect it from confiscation in the Kingsley-Chapin bankruptcy case that enmeshed Sedgwick in financial troubles that year. (Lion G. Miles, "Anna Bingham: From the Red Lion Inn to the Supreme Court," *New England Quarterly*, vol. 69, 2[June 1996]:287–99; George T. Chapman, *Sketches of Alumni of Dartmouth College* [Cambridge, Mass., 1867], p. 46)

OSBORNE, GEORGE JERRY, JR. (1761–1800), was editor of Portsmouth's *New-Hampshire Spy* from 1786–92. (Clarence S. Brigham, *History and Bibliography of American Newspapers* (2 vols., Worcester, Mass, 1947), 2:1462; [Portsmouth] *New-Hampshire Gazette*, 10 June 1800)

OSBORNE, HENRY (1751–1800), immigrated from his native Ireland to Pennsylvania before settling in Camden County, Georgia, where he practiced law and filled several public offices, including: state revenue collector,

1785–91; chief justice, 1787–89; Presidential Elector in 1789; treaty commissioner to the southern Indians later that same year; and state Senator, 1789–90. See also *DHFFC* 17:1853.

OSBORNE, JOHN C. (1766–1819), was a native of Connecticut who practiced medicine in Newbern, North Carolina, from 1787 to 1807.

OSGOOD, JOSHUA BAILEY (1753–91), a 1772 Harvard graduate, was a merchant and large landowner of Fryeburg, Maine, which he represented in the Massachusetts House of Representatives in 1790. (*Harvard Graduates* 18:138–40)

OSGOOD, SAMUEL (1748–1813), a former member of the board of treasury, 1785–89, settled permanently in New York City in 1786, became an active Antifederalist and served as postmaster general, 1789–90. See also *DHFFC* 2:509, 9:167n, 17:1853.

OSWALD, ELEAZER (1755–95), was the Antifederalist editor of Philadelphia's *Independent Gazetteer* from 1782 until his death. See also *DHFFC* 9:210n.

OTIS, HARRISON GRAY (1765–1848), eldest child of Samuel Allyne Otis, graduated from Harvard in 1783, studied law under John Lowell, and commenced practice in his native Boston in 1786. He married Sally Foster on 31 May 1790.

OTIS, JOSEPH (1726–1809), was a merchant of Barnstable, Massachusetts, where he served as collector, 1789–92, having held the post under the state government since 1776. He was the brother of Samuel Allyne Otis and Mercy Otis Warren. See also *DHFFC* 2:509. (*PGW* 5:225n)

OTIS, SAMUEL ALLYNE (1740–1814), served as secretary of the Senate from 1789 until his death. He was father to Harrison Gray Otis, and brother to Joseph Otis and Mercy Otis Warren. His daughter Abigail (b. 1774) died in Boston in March 1790. See also *DHFFC* 9:5n, 17:1854.

OTTO, LOUIS GUILLAUME (1754–1817), a native of the German state of Baden, first came to America as secretary to La Luzerne, 1779–84, and returned as France's chargé d'affaires in Philadelphia in 1785. He moved to New York City to become acting minister upon the comte de Moustier's return to France in October 1789, serving until his own departure in late 1792. Long a favorite in the Republican Court of the Confederation period, Otto married America Frances ("Fanny"), daughter of St. Jean de Crèvecoeur, in April 1790. See also *DHFFC* 9:198n. (*PGW* 4:185n; *PTJ* 16:356; Arthur Lee to Anne Hume Shippen Livingston, 12 February 1784, Shippen Family Papers, DLC)

OVERTON, JOHN (1766–1833), originally of Virginia, settled in Mercer County, Kentucky, in 1787, where he began the study of law and became active in Danville's Political Club with Brown, Innes, and other prominent Federalists. In 1789 he moved to Nashville, Tennessee, where he practiced law and would become a confidante of another frontier lawyer, Andrew Jackson. (*DHROC* 8:415)

OWEN, DANIEL (1731–1812), owner of a forge and iron mill in Glocester, Rhode Island, served as a colonial assemblyman, 1775–76, on the Council of Assistants, 1781–82, as deputy governor, 1786–90, and justice of the state supreme court, 1790–95. In 1790 he attended the ratification convention but did not vote in his capacity as its presiding officer. (*DHFFE* 4:399n)

OWEN, JOHN (d. 1815), was a merchant and attorney of Charleston, South Carolina. In 1782 he represented St. Philip's and St. Michael's Parish in the state House of Representatives. (*PRM* 1:366n; *South Carolina House*)

PAGE, MANN, JR. (ca. 1749–1803), younger brother of John Page, was a lawyer and planter of "Mannsfield" in Spotsylvania County, Virginia, which he alternated representing along with Gloucester County in the state House of Delegates between 1776 and 1790. He also attended Congress in 1777. (*DHROC* 8:195n)

PAGE, WILLIAM (1749–1810), a physician of Charlestown, New Hampshire, served in the state House of Repreesentatives, 1788–92. In June 1790 he sat on the committee that drew up articles of impeachment against John Langdon's brother, Superior Court Justice Woodbury Langdon. (*PJB*, p. 331n)

PAINE, THOMAS (1737–1809), became the most notable propagandist of America's revolutionary movement following his immigration to Philadelphia from his native England with Benjamin Franklin's encouragement in 1774 and the publication, with Benjamin Rush's encouragement, of *Common Sense* and the first installment of *The Crisis* essays in 1776. He served as a volunteer aide to General Nathanael Greene before his appointment as secretary to Congress's committee on foreign affairs, 1777–79, to the Pennsylvania Assembly as clerk in 1779, and to a subordinate role in a diplomatic mission to Europe in 1781. He resided in Bordentown, New Jersey, after the war until returning to Europe to promote his invention of an iron bridge. Exiled from England for more propagandistic writings in support of the French Revolution in 1792, he settled in France thereafter, until his return and retirement to New York in 1802.

PARISH, JOHN (1734–1807), of Philadelphia, was a traveling Quaker minister who joined the antislavery petition delegation to the second session of the First Congress. He married his second wife, Abigail Halloway Bissell, in 1773. (*Drinker* 3:2193)

PARISH, JOHN (1742–1829), a native of Scotland, moved to Hamburg where he became a partner in his father's mercantile firm in 1760. He served as United States vice consul there, 1790–93, and consul, 1793–96.

PARISH, ROBERT (1727–1815), of Philadelphia, was a Quaker carpenter and shopkeeper. (*Drinker*, 3:2194)

PARKER, DANIEL (1754–1829), a native of Massachusetts, was a major subcontractor and military supplier to the French and Continental armies during the Revolutionary War, in association with Jeremiah Wadsworth, William Duer, and others. Despite some share in the lucrative China trade launched by the successful voyage of the *Empress of China*, which he co-owned with Robert Morris, the threat of bankruptcy induced him to settle in Europe in 1784. (*PRM* 4:497–98n)

PARKER, JOHN, SR. (1735–1802), a planter of Berkeley County, South Carolina, who lost much of his wealth during the Revolutionary War, represented neighboring St. James Goose Creek Parish in the state Senate, 1776–80 and 1789–90. Despite his reduced circumstances, his family was closely connected with the state's elite: his son John, Jr. (1759–1832), a former member of Congress and state representative, was a school friend of William Smith (S.C.), and became brother-in-law to Charles Cotesworth Pinckney and Edward Rutledge. (*South Carolina Senate*; George C. Rogers, Jr., *Evolution of a Federalist: William Loughton Smith of Charleston* [Columbia, S.C., 1962], pp. 28, 126)

PARKER, MARY PIERCE BRIDGES, was a widow when she married Josiah Parker in 1773. She and their only child, Ann Pierce Parker (ca. 1780–1849), resided on their plantation, "Macclesfield," in Isle of Wight County, Virginia. Her brother, Thomas Pierce, was a Federalist elected to represent the county at the ratification convention, but he never attended. (*DVB* 3:495–97; *DHROC* 10:1670n)

PARKINSON, GEORGE, emigrated from England to Philadelphia with a weaver's training and industrial secrets. On 11 January 1790 he signed a partnership agreement with Tench Coxe to reconstruct Sir Richard Arkwright's water frame mill in exchange for shared profits from its use, guarantee of a patent, and the expense of bringing Parkinson's family from England. He was subsequently an employee of the Society for Establishing Useful Manufactures, founded by Alexander Hamilton. (*Coxe*, pp. 189–90)

PARSONS, SAMUEL HOLDEN (1737–November 1789), a director of the Ohio Company beginning in 1787, was appointed judge of the Northwest Territory that same year and retained the post until his death, apparently by drowning. The Harvard graduate of 1756, Continental Army general, and Indian treaty commissioner had practiced law in Middletown, Connecticut. See also *DHFFC* 17:1856.

PARSONS, WILLIAM WALTER (1762–1801), of Middletown, Connecticut, served as high sheriff of Middlesex County in 1789. He was the eldest son of Samuel Holden Parsons. (*PGW* 6:215n)

PARTRIDGE, OLIVER (ca. 1751–1837), began his medical practice in 1771 in Stockbridge, Massachusetts, where he was the lifelong friend, housemate, and frequent partner in practice of his brother-in-law, Dr. Erastus Sergeant. (*Harvard Graduates* 17:89)

PATERSON, EUPHEMIA WHITE (1746–1832), of New Brunswick, New Jersey, became the second wife of William Paterson in 1785. His letters during the First Congress frequently addressed her as "Affy." Their family at the time of the First Congress included two surviving children from his previous marriage in 1779 to Cornelia Bell (d. 1783): Cornelia (b. 1780) and William (b. 1783). (*DHSCUS* 1:86–87n; John E. O'Connor, *William Paterson, Lawyer and Statesman* [New Brunswick, N.J., 1979], pp. 116, 117)

PATTERSON, ROBERT (1743–1824), a native of Ireland, immigrated to Pennsylvania in 1768 and became a teacher, specializing in navigation; Andrew Ellicott was among his pupils. During the Revolutionary War he served briefly as a military instructor in the Delaware militia. Following the reorganization of the College of Philadelphia into the University of Pennsylvania, he was appointed professor of mathematics, 1782–1813.

PATTERSON, ROBERT (1753–1827), a native of Pennsylvania, migrated to Kentucky in 1775, from where he participated in George Rogers Clark's successful campaign in the Illinois Country in 1778. The next year he helped found Lexington, Kentucky, where he resided until 1804. He served as sheriff of surrounding Fayette County, which he represented in the Virginia House of Delegates in 1790. (John S. Williams, ed., *The American Pioneer* [Cincinnati, Ohio, 1843] 2:343–47; *Register of the Virginia General Assembly, 1776–1918*, p. 415)

PATTON, ROBERT, was a Scottish immigrant and merchant of Fredericksburg, Virginia. (*DHROC* 10:1584)

PAYNE, EDWARD (ca. 1726–1806), represented Fayette County at the Kentucky statehood convention of 1795. (*Sketches of Kentucky* 1:354)

PAYNE, MICHAEL, a merchant of Chowan County, North Carolina, served in the state House of Commons, 1781–83 and 1784–85, and at the state's first ratification convention in 1788, where he supported the Constitution. During the Revolutionary War he served as captain in the 2nd Regiment of the North Carolina Line. (*North Carolina Historical Review* 27[1950]:130; John L. Cheney, Jr. *North Carolina Government, 1585–1974* [Raleigh, N.C., 1975], pp. 208–9, 213–15, 766; Louise I. Trenholme, *Ratification of the Constitution in North Carolina* [New York, 1932], p. 163n)

PEABODY, OLIVER (1752–1831), an attorney of Exeter, New Hampshire, served as judge of probate for Rockingham County, 1790–93. The 1773 Harvard graduate studied law under Nathaniel Peaslee Sargeant with fellow students Rufus King and Christopher Gore. (*Harvard Graduates* 18:275–83)

PEARSON, SAMUEL, was a merchant of Portland, Maine, where he operated a ropewalk by 1800.

PECK, WILLIAM (1755–1832), of Providence, was appointed federal marshal for the Rhode Island district in 1790, a position he held for almost two decades. The former Continental Army officer was also a member of the Society of the Cincinnati. See also *DHFFC* 2:541. (*DHFFE* 4:407n)

PECKHAM, GEORGE HAZARD (1739–99), of South Livingston, Rhode Island, served as clerk of the Court of Common Pleas of Washington County, 1782–86 and 1788–90 . (*PGW* 6:149n)

PEERY, WILLIAM (1732–1800), a prominent lawyer and frequent state assemblyman from Lewes, Delaware, served as a treaty commissioner to the Southern Indians in 1785, for which he sought compensation in an unsuccessful petition to the First Congress in June 1790. He had declined appointment as federal judge for the Southern Territory the year before. See also *DHFFC* 2:490, 8:102.

PEIRCE, EBENEZER (1745–1802), represented Partridgefield (present-day Peru), Massachusetts, in the state House, 1782–86, 1788, and 1789, and at the state convention, where he voted against the Constitution. (*DHROC* 6:1212n)

PEMBERTON, JAMES (1723–1809), brother of John, was a Philadelphia merchant prince and leader of that city's large and influential Quaker community. He coordinated the antislavery petitions to Congress during the second session as vice president of the Pennsylvania Abolition Society and chairman of its committee of correspondence. See also *DHFFC* 8:220, 315–17.

PEMBERTON, JOHN (1727-1795), of Philadelphia, was a traveling Quaker minister and a leading member of the antislavery petitions delegation to the second session of the First Congress, who regularly reported its progress in letters to his brother James. He married Hannah Zane (1734–1811), in 1766. (*Drinker* 3:2196)

PENDLETON, EDMUND (1721–1803), a lawyer of Caroline County, Virginia, former member of congress, 1774–75, and supporter of the Constitution at the state convention, was serving on the bench of the state supreme court of appeals, 1779–1803, when he declined appointment as federal district judge. See also *DHFFC* 2:553, 17:1857–58.

PENDLETON, NATHANIEL, JR. (1756–1821), a native of Virginia like his uncle Edmund Pendleton, was elected chief justice of Georgia shortly before his appointment as federal judge for the Georgia district, 1789–96. See also *DHFFC* 2:493, 17:1858.

PENHALLOW, SAMUEL (1757–1805), of Portsmouth, New Hampshire, was the son of John Penhallow (1723–1809), a privateer during the Revolutionary War and one of the city's most prominent revolutionaries.

PEPOON, SILAS (1754–1817), was a storekeeper in Stockbridge, Massachusetts. A native of Connecticut, he settled in Stockbridge in 1776, served as captain of the town militia during Shays' Rebellion, and became one of Theodore Sedgwick's political lieutenants in Berkshire County. (Richard E. Welch, Jr., *Theodore Sedgwick, Federalist* [Middletown, Conn., 1965], p. 114; *DHSCUS* 6:182)

PERKINS, THOMAS H. (1764–1854), amassed a fortune as a Boston merchant in partnership with his brother James beginning in 1786.

PETERS, RICHARD (1744–1828), a wealthy lawyer and gentleman farmer of "Belmont," his estate outside Philadelphia, was speaker of Pennsylvania's last General Assembly, 1789–90, and a member of its Senate, 1790–91. See also *DHFFC* 9:61n, 17:1858–59.

PETERSON, EDWARD, was a sea captain who resided in Newport, Rhode Island, in 1790.

PETIT, CHARLES (1736–1806), was a Philadelphia merchant, financier, and one of the largest public securities holders in the country. See also *DHFFC* 8:258, 264, 290, 9:137n, 17:1859.

PHELPS, OLIVER (1749–1809), was a merchant and land speculator of Granville, Massachusetts. He held elective state office almost continuously between 1778 and 1788, when he joined Nathaniel Gorham as a principal investor in the six million acre Genessee Purchase in New York, where he frequently resided during the First Congress. See also *DHFFC* 8:191–200, 9:20n, 17:1859.

PHILLIPS, GEORGE (1750–1802), was a merchant of Middletown, Connecticut, which he represented in the state General Assembly in 1787. A Yale graduate of 1769, he married the sister of William Wetmore the following year, and rose from ensign to colonel in the state militia during the Revolutionary War. (*Yale Graduates* 3:354)

PHILLIPS, NATHANIEL (1756–1832), of Warren, Rhode Island, was appointed federal surveyor for that port and Barrington in 1790. See also *DHFFC* 2:541.

PHILLIPS, SAMUEL, SR. (1715–21 August 1790), a 1734 Harvard graduate and the father of Samuel Phillips, Jr., was a retired merchant of Andover, Massachusetts, which he represented in the colonial and state House of Representatives, 1759–78. (*Harvard Graduates* 9:431–36)

PHILLIPS, SAMUEL, JR. (1752–1808), the only surviving child of Samuel Phillips, Sr., was a gunpowder and paper manufacturer of Andover, Massachusetts, who represented Essex County in the state Senate, 1780–1801 (as its president, 1788–1801). See also *DHFFC* 17:1860.

PICKERING, JOHN (1737–1805), a lawyer of Portsmouth, New Hampshire, served as state president (governor), 1789–90, and chief justice of the state supreme court thereafter until 1795. See also *DHFFC* 17:1860.

PICKERING, JOHN (1740–1811), of Salem, Massachusetts, graduated from Harvard in 1759 and abandoned school teaching for farming until chronic ill health forced his retirement from all but public duties in 1783. He was a longtime member of the colonial and state House of Representatives, serving until 1780 (as speaker in 1778). In 1776 he began a thirty-year long tenure as register of deeds for Essex County. He was the older brother of Timothy Pickering and Paine Wingate's wife, Eunice. (*Harvard Graduates* 14:481–85)

PICKERING, TIMOTHY (1745–1829), formerly a lawyer of Salem, Massachusetts, settled in Luzerne County, Pennsylvania, after a distinguished career in the Continental Army and held various local and state offices, including a seat at the state convention, where he voted to ratify the Constitution. He successfully petitioned the First Congress in July 1790 for the settlement of his wartime accounts. In 1765 his older sister Eunice married Paine Wingate, a distant cousin through Pickering's mother. In 1776 he himself married Rebecca White (1754–1828), with whom he had seven children by the time of the First Congress: John (b. 1777), Timothy (b. 1779), Henry (b. 1781), Charles (b. 1784), William (b. 1786), Edward (b. 1787), and Octavius (b. ca. 1790). See also *DHFFC* 7:486–93, 17:1860–61.

PICKETT, MARTIN (1740–1804), was a planter and merchant of Fauquier County, Virginia, which he served as member of the state House of Delegates, 1776–81, Federalist delegate to the state ratification convention in 1788, and county sheriff, 1789–90. (*VMHB* 23[1915]:437–38; *DHROC* 9:588n)

PIERCE, JOHN (1750–98), joined fellow Bostonian Henry Knox's Continental Army artillery regiment in 1776 and rose from second lieutenant to captain-lieutenant by 1778 before retiring at war's end. In 1786 he was commissioned lieutenant in the artillery battalion under the Confederation and retained that post under the federal establishment from 1789 until his promotion to captain in 1791. In 1790 his unit was transferred from West Point to a garrison on St. Marys River, Georgia. See also *DHFFC* 2:510.

PIERCE, JOSEPH (1745–1828), older brother of John Pierce and brother-in-law of Thomas Dawes, Jr., was a Boston merchant and shopkeeper in 1790. See also *DHFFC* 17:1861.

PIERSON, SAMUEL (1759–1852), was a Revolutionary War veteran of New Gloucester, Maine.

PIKE, NICHOLAS (1743–1819), was a teacher of Newburyport, Massachusetts, when he petitioned Congress in June 1789 for copyright protection. See also *DHFFC* 8:30–31, 36–37.

PIKE, WILLIAM (1748–1804), of Newburyport, Massachusetts, began his military career as a private in the 2nd Continental Light Dragoons Regiment in 1777, shortly before seeing action at Saratoga. He rose to cornet by 1781 and served until the war's end.

PINCKNEY, CHARLES (1757–1824), a lawyer and planter of Charleston, South Carolina, served several terms in Congress and the state House of Representatives before declining nomination for Senator in the first federal election and serving instead as governor, 1789–92. Charles Cotesworth and Thomas Pinckney were his second cousins. See also *DHFFC* 17:1862. (*DHFFE* 1:217–18)

PINCKNEY, CHARLES COTESWORTH (1746–1825), a lawyer and planter of Charleston, South Carolina, like his second cousin Charles and brother Thomas Pinckney, enjoyed a distinguished wartime military career while simultaneously holding office as state Representative in 1778 and 1782, and state Senator in 1779. A strong Federalist at both the Federal Convention and state convention, he went on to serve as Presidential Elector in the first federal election but declined to succeed his brother-in-law John Rutledge, Sr., as justice on the United States Supreme Court in May 1791. See also *DHFFC* 17:1862.

PINCKNEY, THOMAS (1750–1828), a Charleston, South Carolina, lawyer and planter, declined appointment as federal district judge in 1789. Trained in London, like his brother Charles Cotesworth, he preceded his second cousin Charles Pinckney as governor, 1787–89, presided over the state convention where he voted to ratify the Constitution, and sat in the state House of Representatives in 1791. See also *DHFFC* 2:544, 17:1862.

PINKNEY, WILLIAM (1764–1822), a native of Annapolis, was admitted to the Maryland bar in 1786 after studying under Samuel Chase and practiced in Harford County. An Antifederalist at the state ratification convention, he went on to serve in the state House of Delegates, 1788–92. His election as Representative to the Second Federal Congress was contested on grounds of residency eligibility and he resigned his seat in November 1791.

PINTARD, JOHN (1759–1844), a New York City merchant like his cousin John Marsden Pintard, graduated from the College of New Jersey (Princeton) in 1776 and served as deputy commissary of prisoners at New York during the Revolutionary War. The State Department employed him as clerk for foreign languages until the government moved to Philadelphia in 1790, the same year he was elected to the New York State Assembly. (*PTJ* 17:352–53n)

PINTARD, JOHN MARSDEN (d. 1811), a New York City wine merchant like his father Lewis Pintard and cousin John Pintard, was appointed United States consul at Madeira, 1789–99, and returned there in mid 1790. Elias Boudinot, who married the older sister of Pintard's mother Susannah Stockton (b. 1742), resided at his nephew's home at 12 Wall Street for much of the first two sessions of the First Congress. See also *DHFFC* 2:524, 14:686, 17:1862–63.

PINTARD, SAMUEL (1742–1805), uncle of John and John Marsden Pintard, was an invalided British army captain who retired to Hempstead, Long Island, New York. At the outbreak of the Revolutionary War he declined a commission in both the British and Continental armies. In 1770 he married Hannah Stockton Boudinot's younger sister Abigail (b. 1738), while his older brother Lewis married her younger sister Susannah. (Thomas C. Stockton, *The Stockton Family* [Washington, D.C., 1911], pp. 24, 48; *Princetonians, 1791–1794*, pp. 208–9)

PITT, WILLIAM, THE YOUNGER (1759–1806), a member of the British House of Commons from 1781, became Chancellor of the Exchequer the next year and simultaneously held the office of Prime Minister, 1783–1801, and again from 1804 until his death.

PLATT, RICHARD (1755–1830), a New York City businessman and one of the largest public securities holders in the United States, was involved with William Duer and Alexander Hamilton in many financial and political ventures. He married Sarah Aspinwall on 5 September 1790. See also *DHFFC* 17:1863.

PLEASANTS, THOMAS, JR. (ca. 1737–1804), a planter and merchant of Goochland County, Virginia, served as commercial agent for that state in the last years of the Revolutionary War. (*PJM* 3:87n; *PRM* 2:214n)

PLUMER, WILLIAM (1759–1850), a native of Massachusetts, moved in 1768 to Epping, New Hampshire, where he opened a legal practice upon being admitted to the bar in 1787, and which he represented in the state House, 1785–86, 1788, and 1790–91 (as speaker in 1791).

POLLOCK, OLIVER (ca. 1737–1823), was an Irish merchant who settled in Philadelphia around 1760 and in New Orleans by 1768. He was appointed the United States agent there in 1778 and in Havana in 1783. Imprisoned for debt, he was released in 1785, returned to Philadelphia where he successfully pressed claims against Congress, and returned to New Orleans in 1790. (*PRM* 2:226n)

POMEROY, RALPH (1737–1819), a lawyer and businessman of Hartford, Connecticut, succeeded Oliver Wolcott, Jr., as state comptroller in 1789. The College of New Jersey (Princeton) graduate of 1758 gave up teaching to study law, passing the bar in 1768. During the Revolutionary War, he served in the 3rd Regiment of the Connecticut Line from 1777 until retiring as first lieutenant in 1781, and thereafter served as deputy quartermaster general of the state until war's end. It was in the latter role that he worked closely with Jeremiah Wadsworth, in whose cotton manufactory he later invested. (*Princetonians, 1748–1768*, pp. 240–43; *PRM* 3:300n)

POOLE, ABIJAH (d. 1820), of Portland, Maine, served as ensign in the Massachusetts militia in 1776 before transferring to lieutenant in the 13th Regiment of the state's Continental Line, 1777–79. (*MSSR* 12:540)

PORTER, BENJAMIN JONES (1763–1847), was a physician of Falmouth, Maine. In 1790 he was involved in the lumbering business with William King, Rufus King's half-brother. He married their sister Elizabeth ("Betsy") on 16 November 1791. See also *DHFFC* 17:1864.

POSEY, THOMAS (1750–1818) of Fredericksburg, Virginia, rose from captain in the 7th Virginia Regiment in 1776 to major in the 2nd and 7th regiments in 1778 to lieutenant colonel in the 7th Regiment in 1782, retiring from the 1st Regiment with that rank at war's end.

POTTER, SAMUEL (ca. 1750–1804), a lawyer of South Kingston, Rhode Island, served as deputy governor, 1790–99. (*DHFFE* 4:406n)

POWELL, LEVEN (1737–1810), was a merchant, miller, and farmer of Loudoun County, Virginia, which he represented in the state House of Delegates, 1779, 1787–88, 1791–92, and at the convention where he voted to ratify the Constitution. In addition to investing heavily in western lands, he became a charter trustee of Henry Lee's and James Madison's speculative venture at Great Falls, Virginia, in 1790. See also *DHFFC* 17:1864. (Robert A. Rutland, ed., *The Papers of George Mason, 1725–1792* [3 vols., Chapel Hill, N.C., 1970], 1:lxxxviii)

PRICE, RICHARD (1723–91), was a British moral philosopher and nonconformist minister who became a major champion of the American Revolution.

PRIESTLEY, JOSEPH (1733–1804), a teacher, philosopher, and scientist of Birmingham, England, was best known to America's revolutionary generation, whose efforts he supported, as a religious reformer of the nonconformist tradition, like his friend Richard Price.

PRIOR, EDMUND (1755–1841), a prominent New York City merchant, was clerk of the New York Yearly Meeting of Friends (Quakers), 1784–86. In February and March 1790 he hosted and assisted the delegation of Philadelphia Quakers in lobbying for the antislavery petitions to the First Congress. (Zephaniah W. Pease, ed., *Diary of Samuel Rodman* [New Bedford, Mass., n.d.], p. 226; [Philadelphia] *Friend* 15[20 Nov. 1841]:64; John Cox, Jr., *Quakerism in the City of New York, 1657–1930* [New York, 1930], p. 139)

PROVOOST, SAMUEL (1742–1815), named Episcopalian bishop of New York in 1786, was elected by the Senate as one of Congress's two chaplains at the opening of the first session and served until Congress moved to Philadelphia. See also *DHFFC* 2:215, 8:781, 9:7n.

PUTNAM, BARTHOLOMEW (1738–1824), was a mariner and shipowner of Salem, Massachusetts, where he was federal surveyor for the port, 1789–1809. See also *DHFFC* 2:511.

PUTNAM, RUFUS (1738–1824), of Rutland, Massachusetts, was appointed judge of the Northwest Territory, 1790–96, having served as superintendent of the Ohio Company based in Marietta, Ohio, which he helped found in 1788. See also *DHFFC* 2:511, 17:1865–66.

RAMSAY, DAVID (1749–1815), was a historian and physician of Charleston, South Carolina, where he settled at the outbreak of the Revolutionary War, after graduating from the College of New Jersey (Princeton) in 1765 and studying medicine under Benjamin Rush. He served in Congress from 1782 to 1783 and again from 1785 to 1786, the next year marrying Martha, daughter of the former president of Congress, Henry Laurens. He became a strong Federalist and voted for the Constitution at the state convention in 1788, but lost election as a Representative to William Smith in the first federal election. His *History of the American Revolution* (1789–90) followed an earlier two volume *History of the Revolution in South Carolina* (Trenton, N.J., 1785), which James Jackson is known to have read sometime in 1790. See also *DHFFC* 8:27–29, 17:1866.

RANDALL, THOMAS (1723–97), an Irish born sea captain, became a leader of the revolutionary movement in New York City and held a number of municipal offices during the 1780s. In April 1789 he served as coxswain of the ceremonial barge that brought Washington from New Jersey to New York City for his inauguration. (*PGW* 2:196n; John Stevens, Jr., *Colonial Records of the New York Chamber of Commerce, 1768–84* [New York, 1867], pp. 157–58)

RANDOLPH, BEVERLEY (1754–97), a planter of Cumberland County, Virginia, served as governor, 1788–91. Previously he was a member of the state House of Delegates, 1777–78, 1779–81, and of the Executive Council, 1781–88, over which he presided as lieutenant governor, 1783–88. (*DHROC* 8:11–12n)

RANDOLPH, DAVID MEADE (1760–1830), a planter of Chesterfield County, Virginia, succeeded Edward Carrington as federal marshal for the Virginia district in October 1791. In 1777 he captained a state militia company of dragoons. (*PGW* 3:104n)

RANDOLPH, EDMUND (1753–1813), was a lawyer of Williamsburg, Virginia, which he represented in the state House of Delegates from November 1788 until his appointment as United States attorney general, 1789–94. In 1776 he married Elizabeth Carter Nicholas (d. 1810). See also *DHFFC* 2:553. (*PJM* 4:147–48n)

RANDOLPH, JOHN, "OF ROANOKE" (1773–1833), left the College of New Jersey (Princeton), where he had enrolled in the class of 1791, and attended Columbia College from 1788 until the summer of 1790. His stepfather and legal guardian was St. George Tucker, brother of Thomas Tudor Tucker and brother-in-law of Theodorick Bland; Attorney General Edmund Randolph was his uncle. (*Princetonians, 1791–1794*, pp. 90–92)

RANDOLPH, THOMAS MANN, JR. (1772–1836), a planter of "Varina," in Henrico County, Virginia, was the son of a childhood friend of Thomas Jefferson, whose elder daughter Martha, also known as "Patsy" (1772–1836), married the younger Randolph on 23 February 1790. The marriage settlement brought the couple the additional estate of "Poplar Forest" in Bedford County. (Dumas Malone, *Jefferson and the Rights of Man* [Boston, 1951], p. 252)

RAWLE, WILLIAM (1759–1836), was a Loyalist who studied law in British occupied New York City and in London during the Revolutionary War. He returned to his native Philadelphia where he passed the bar in 1783 and served in the Assembly, 1789–90.

RAYNAL, GUILLAUME-THOMAS-FRANÇOIS (1713–96), of France, was a defrocked priest and radical philosopher and revolutionary whose *Philosophical and Political History of the Settlements and Trade of the Europeans in the East and West Indies* (6 vols., 1770) went through thirty editions by 1789.

REA (REESE), JAMES, moved from Mecklenberg County, North Carolina, to the Holston settlements (in present-day east Tennessee) in 1784. A lawyer, he served in the general assembly of the short lived "state" of Franklin. (S. C. Williams, *History of the Lost State of Franklin* [Johnson City, Tenn., 1924], p. 318)

READ, GEORGE, family during the First Congress: his wife Gertrude Ross Till (ca. 1730–1802), married in 1763 and residing in New Castle, Delaware; and their children George, Jr. (1765–1836), a lawyer of New Castle, Delaware; William (1767–1846); John (1769–1854), a College of New Jersey (Princeton) graduate of 1787 who studied law under his father before commencing practice in New Castle in 1791; and Mary or "Maria" (1770–1816).

READ, JAMES (d. 1803), was a planter of Wilmington, North Carolina, where he was appointed collector in 1790. See also *DHFFC* 2:529–30.

READ, NATHAN (1759–1849), was a Harvard graduate of 1781 who operated an apothecary shop in Salem, Massachusetts. He started experimenting with steam powered inland navigation in 1787 and tried capitalizing on his innovations by petitioning and lobbying the First Congress in person during the second session. See also *DHFFC* 8:43–44.

READ, THOMAS (1738–1817), of Ingleside, Virginia, served as Charlotte County clerk from 1770 until his death. He studied at the College of William and Mary and worked as a surveyor before becoming active in the revolutionary movement as delegate to the Virginia Conventions, 1774–76, and lieutenant in the county militia. Although described by some contemporaries as a Federalist, he voted against ratification at the state convention. (*DHROC* 9:630n, 762n; James Grant Wilson and John Fiske, *Appleton's Cyclopedia of American Biography* [New York, 1880] 5:200)

REEVE, TAPPING (1744–1823), a native of Long Island, graduated from the College of New Jersey (Princeton) in 1763 and taught school before turning to the study of law in Hartford in 1770. He passed the Connecticut bar in 1772, the same year he married the sister of his former pupil, Aaron Burr, and settled permanently in Litchfield, Connecticut, where he established his famous law school in 1784. An ardent Federalist, he was nominated for Representative in the second federal election. (*Princetonians, 1748–1766*, pp. 440–44)

REID, GEORGE (d. 1799), originally of North Carolina, served as assistant commissioner of army accounts and deputy paymaster general during the later Confederation period. By 1788 he was settled in Greene County, Georgia.

REMSEN, HENRY, JR. (1762–1843), the son of a New York City dry goods merchant, served as undersecretary in the department of foreign affairs from 1784 until he succeeded Roger Alden as chief clerk in the domestic branch of the department of state, 1790–92. (*Emerging Nation* 3:136n)

REYNOLDS, JAMES (b. 1759), assisted his father, a deputy commissary of purchases under Jeremiah Wadsworth, during the Revolutionary War, while also engaged in mercantile activities along the Hudson River. He failed to secure a revenue appointment in 1789 and turned to speculating in veterans' war claims. In 1783 he married Maria Lewis (b. 1768), whose adulterous relations with Alexander Hamilton, beginning probably in July 1791, led to Reynolds's successful blackmailing of the secretary of the treasury until December 1792, when Hamilton himself acknowledged the arrangement rather than risk being implicated in Reynolds's other illicit activities. (*PAH* 21:121–27; *PTJ* 18:626–30)

RHODES, ZACHARIAH (b. 1755), of Cranston, Rhode Island, was appointed surveyor at Patuxet in 1790. See also *DHFFC* 2:541.

RICE, THOMAS (1734–1812), was a physician of Pownalborough (present-day Wiscasset), Maine. Against the instructions of that town, he voted in favor of the Constitution at the state convention. See also *DHFFC* 17:1868.

RIDDICK, WILLIS (1757–1800), represented Nansemond County in the Virginia House of Delegates from 1784 until his death. (*PGW* 1:177n)

RITTENHOUSE, DAVID (1732–96), was an internationally known scientist and inventor and a prominent Philadelphia Antifederalist who ran unsuccessfully for the state ratification convention and for Presidential Elector. See also *DHFFC* 17:1869. (*DHFFE* 1:425–26)

RIVINGTON, JAMES (1724–1802), was a New York City bookseller and stationer. He remained in the city throughout the British occupation, when he published the first American daily newspaper. See also *DHFFC* 17:1869.

ROBINSON, WILLIAM, JR., was a Philadelphia lawyer who sat in the Pennsylvania Assembly, 1785–89. In 1791 he was appointed a judge of the Court of Common Pleas. (*DHROC* 2:95n)

ROBISON, THOMAS (1747–1806), was a prosperous merchant of Portland, Maine, where he immigrated from Scotland before the Revolutionary War. He returned to Great Britain as a Loyalist, but resettled in Portland in 1783.

RODGERS, JOHN RICHARDSON BAYARD (1757–1833), was a College of New Jersey (Princeton) graduate of 1775 who studied medicine in Philadelphia and Edinburgh before opening a practice in his native New York City in early 1789. On 5 July 1790 he married Susan Kearny (d. 1799). See also *DHFFC* 9:147n.

RODNEY, THOMAS (1744–1811), was a planter and jurist of Kent County, Delaware, who had opposed ratification on the grounds that the Constitution left too much power to the states. He served in Congress, 1781–82 and 1786, and in the state House of Assembly, 1787–88. See also *DHFFC* 17:1870.

ROGERS, DANIEL DENISON (1751–1825), was a Boston merchant. His wife is variously listed as Abigail or Elizabeth Bromfield.

ROGERS, HEZEKIAH (1753–1811), was appointed federal surveyor at New Haven, Connecticut, in 1789. He represented Norwalk in the state House, 1786–88, and at the state convention, where he voted to ratify the Constitution. See also *DHFFC* 2:487, 17:1870.

ROGERS, NATHANIEL (1745–1829), of Newmarket, New Hampshire, succeeded John Parker as federal marshal for the state in 1791, at which time he was serving as a member of the state Executive Council. See also *DHFFC* 17:1870.

ROGERS, SAMUEL (ca. 1747–1804), a Boston merchant before the Revolutionary War, resettled in London as a merchant, banker, and agent for other Loyalists. His banking business failed in 1791. (*Harvard Graduates* 16:211–12)

ROMAINE (ROMAYNE), NICHOLAS (1756–1817), began the study of medicine at King's College (Columbia) in 1774 and took his degree at Edinburgh in 1780. In 1783 he resettled in his native New York City, where he practiced medicine and in 1781 opened a private medical school. (Brian Stookey, "Nicholas Romayne," *Bulletin of the New York Academy of Medicine*, vol. 43, 7[July 1967]:576–97)

ROSS, GEORGE, JR. (1752–1832), was a lawyer of Lancaster, Pennsylvania, which he represented in the state Assembly, 1786–87. He sat on the state Supreme Executive Council, 1787–90, as vice president (lieutenant governor) from November 1788 to October 1790.

ROUSSEAU, JEAN JACQUES (1712–78), was one of the most renowned French philosophes of the Enlightenment, most noted for his writings on political theory and education.

ROWLAND, ZACHARIAH (1745–1802), a merchant of Richmond, Virginia, was appointed surveyor of that port in 1790.

RUSH, BENJAMIN (1745–1813), was a prominent Philadelphia physician, social reformer, and political activist who maintained an extensive correspondence with the Pennsylvania congressional delegation during the first and second sessions of the First Congress. In January 1776 he married Julia Stockton (1759–1848), the niece of Elias and Hannah Boudinot. See also *DHFFC* 8:312, 9:85n, 17:1871.

RUSSELL, BENJAMIN (1761–1845), edited Boston's *Massachusetts Centinel*, a Federalist newspaper, from 1784 to 1790, when he changed its name to the *Columbian Centinel* (16 June 1790–1820). See also *DHFFC* 17:1871–72.

RUSSELL, ELEAZER (ca. 1720–1798), served as federal naval officer at Portsmouth, New Hampshire, 1789–98, after filling that office continuously under the colonial and state governments from the late 1760s. See also *DHFFC* 2:516. (*PGW* 3:225)

RUSTON, THOMAS (ca. 1740–1804), a former physician, was a prominent Philadelphia manufacturer, financier, and speculator. See also *DHFFC* 8:365, 371–73, 9:91n, 17:1872.

RUTHERFURD, JOHN (1760–1840), the son of Walter Rutherfurd, had formerly been a New York City lawyer who studied under William Paterson. He was a merchant and landowner of Sussex (part of present-day Warren) County, New Jersey, which he represented in the state General Assembly, 1789–90. Although unsuccessful as a candidate for Representative in the first federal election, he served as Presidential Elector in 1789 and succeeded Jonathan Elmer as Senator in 1791. (*DHFFE* 3:187)

RUTHERFURD, WALTER (1723–1804), of Paterson, Bergen County, New Jersey, was the father of John Rutherfurd. See also *DHFFC* 17:1872.

RUTLEDGE, EDWARD (1749–1800), younger brother of John Rutledge, Sr., and a signer of the Declaration of Independence, was a London trained lawyer of Charleston, South Carolina, which he represented at the state convention, where he voted to ratify the Constitution. In 1774 he married Henrietta Middleton (d. 1792), whose sister Sarah married Charles Cotesworth Pinckney in 1773, and first cousin Mary married Pierce Butler in 1771. See also *DHFFC* 17:1872–73.

RUTLEDGE, HENRY MIDDLETON (1775–1844), was the eldest son of Edward and Henrietta Middleton Rutledge.

RUTLEDGE, JOHN, SR. (1739–1800), a London trained lawyer of Charleston, South Carolina, like his younger brother Edward, served as associate justice of the United States Supreme Court from 1789 until his resignation in March 1791 to serve as chief justice of the state Supreme Court. His children, by his marriage to Elizabeth Grimké in 1763, included Martha (1764–1816), John, Jr., and Eliza (1776–1842). See also *DHFFC* 2:545, 17:1873.

RUTLEDGE, JOHN, JR. (1766–1819), like his father John and uncle Edward Rutledge, was a lawyer in Charleston, South Carolina. He traveled through Europe between 1787 and mid 1790, when he was in New York City and acted as a witnessing signatory to the Treaty of New York. (*DHSCUS* 1:859n, *PGW: Confederation* 5:220–21n)

RYERSON, THOMAS (1753–1835), a native of New Jersey, rose from ensign to second lieutenant in the 2nd Continental Regiment, 1775–76, and after the war settled in Washington County, Pennsylvania, which he represented in the state Assembly, 1789–90, and House, 1790–91.

St. Clair, Arthur (1734–1818), governor of the Northwest Territory, 1787–1802, was appointed major general of the federal army on the last day of the First Congress. See also *DHFFC* 2:536, 9:6–7n, 17:1873.

Sargeant, Nathaniel Peaslee (1731–91), a Harvard graduate of 1751, was associate justice of the Massachusetts supreme judicial court, 1776–90, and chief justice thereafter until his death. In 1776 he married his second wife, Mary Leavitt (d. 1805), the older sister of Eunice Wingate and Timothy Pickering. (*Harvard Graduates* 12:574–80; *Adams* 1:321–22n)

Sargent, Epes (1748–1822), was a merchant of Gloucester, Massachusetts, where he served as collector, 1789–95. See also *DHFFC* 2:511.

Sargent, Mary Turner (1743–1818), a native of Salem, Massachusetts, married Daniel Sargent, brother of Epes Sargent, in 1763 and settled in Boston in 1778. (Barbara N. Parker and Anne B. Wheeler, *John Singleton Copley: American Portraits* [Boston, 1938], pp. 170–71)

Sarly, Jacob, was a merchant sea captain and partner in the New York City firm of Sarly and Barnewell, engaged in the East Indies trade. He captained the *America*, whose return from Canton in 1790 helped launch the China trade. (*PAH* 10:389n)

Sarmento, Francisco, was a Spanish merchant who settled on Teneriffe in the Canary Islands. His nomination as the United States vice consul there was rejected by the Senate in August 1790.

Saunders, Roger Parker (d. 1795), a planter of Charleston, South Carolina, who, like Pierce Butler, owned large holdings in Georgia, worked with Alexander Gillon in resolving Butler's indebtedness problems in 1790. During the Revolutionary War he served as captain in the first South Carolina Regiment. (*Butler*, p. 543)

Savage, George (d. 1824), was appointed collector at Cherry Stone, Northampton County, Virginia, 1789–90, having served as the state's naval officer and commissioner of wrecks since 1782. See also *DHFFC* 2:554.

Savage, Joseph (1756–1814), son of Samuel Phillips Savage, brother of Samuel Savage, and brother-in-law of George Thatcher, was commissioned a captain in the federal army in September 1789, having held that position under the Confederation's military establishment since 1786. In March 1790 he was sent with his unit from West Point to the garrison at Beard's Bluff on Georgia's Altamaha River, as a precaution against the renewal of hostilities with the Creeks, and served until his resignation in October 1791. See also *DHFFC* 2:512, 17:1874.

SAVAGE, SAMUEL (1748–1831), was a physician of Barnstable, Massachusetts, where he settled in 1773. He was the son of Samuel Phillips Savage and brother-in-law of George Thatcher. See also *DHFFC* 17:1875.

SAVAGE, SAMUEL PHILLIPS (1718–97), a farmer of Weston, Massachusetts, was a retired Boston merchant who served as a Middlesex County judge from 1776 until his death. His children by his first marriage, to Sarah Tyler (1718–64) in 1742, included Joseph, Samuel, and Sarah, who married George Thatcher in 1784. At the time of the First Congress, Savage was married to Bathsheba Johnston (1725–92). See also *DHFFC* 17:1875.

SAWYER, EDMUND, a merchant of Camden County, North Carolina, was appointed surveyor at Pasquotank in 1790. See also *DHFFC* 2:530.

SAYRE, STEPHEN (1736–1818), a native of Long Island, New York, immigrated to London, where he became a merchant and banker and a supporter of his native countrymen's revolutionary cause. He was the lord mayor of London, 1773–74. (*LDC* 3:238n, 13:352n)

SAYWARD, JONATHAN (1713–97), a wealthy merchant of York, Maine, served as a colonial legislator and probate court judge before the outbreak of the Revolutionary War. Although branded a Loyalist, he remained in York and enjoyed close ties with the political and social elite until his death. (*DHROC* 4:335n)

SCHOONMAKER, CORNELIUS (1745–96), was a farmer and surveyor of Ulster County, New York, which he represented in the state Assembly, 1777–81 and 1782–90, and at the state convention, where he voted against the Constitution. In the second federal election he won the seat held by John Hathorn and served until 1793. (*DHFFE* 3:561)

SCHUYLER, CATHERINE VAN RENSSELAER (1734–1803), of Albany and Saratoga, New York, married Philip Schuyler in 1755. Eight of their eleven children survived to the time of the First Congress: Angelica, wife of John B.

Church; Elizabeth, wife of Alexander Hamilton; Margarita, wife of Stephen Van Rensselaer; John Bradstreet; Philip Jeremiah (1768–1835), who married Sarah Rutsen in 1788 and had a son, Philip (b. 5 April 1789–1822); Rensselaer (1773–1847); Cornelia (1776–1808); and Catherine (1781–1857).

SCHUYLER, JOHN BRADSTREET (1765–95), the eldest surviving son of Philip Schuyler, managed his father's estate at Saratoga, New York. By his marriage in 1787 to Stephen Van Rensselaer's sister Elizabeth, he had two children: Philip (1788–1865) and Stephen Van Rensselaer, who was born on 4 May 1790 and died later that month.

SCOTT, CHARLES (ca. 1739–1813), a native of Virginia and veteran of the French and Indian War under George Washington's command, rose from lieutenant colonel of the 2nd Regiment of the Virginia Line, to commanding colonel of the 5th Regiment in 1776, to brigadier general the next year, to brevet major general at war's end, when he became a charter member of the Society of the Cincinnati. In 1785 he settled in Fayette County (part of present-day Woodford County), Kentucky, which he represented in Virginia's House of Delegates in 1789 and 1790. In 1791 he participated in Gen. Josiah Harmar's unsuccessful campaign against the Indians of the Northwest Territory. In 1762 he married Frances Sweeney (d. 1804).

SCRIBA, GEORGE LUDWIG CHRISTIAN (1753–1836), was a New York City merchant and land speculator. With William Constable as a silent partner, he petitioned Congress in March 1790 to purchase up to four million acres of western lands. See also *DHFFC* 8:198–99, 17:1875–76.

SEABURY, SAMUEL (1729–96), a native of Connecticut, graduated from Yale in 1748 and studied medicine in Edinburgh while awaiting his final ordination in the Anglican Church in 1753. Because of his Loyalism, he was driven from his pulpit in Westchester, New York, and spent the Revolutionary War as a refugee in British occupied New York City. In 1784 he was consecrated the first American bishop in the Episcopalian Church, and served as minister in New London, Connecticut, from 1785 until his death. (*Yale Graduates* 2:179–88)

SEAGROVE, JAMES (ca. 1747–1812), was an Irish born merchant in New York City before relocating in 1786 to Georgia, where he became collector at St. Marys, 1789–91. The former army supplier had close business ties to William Constable. See also *DHFFC* 2:493–94, 17:1876.

SEARLE, GEORGE (ca. 1751–1796), was a merchant of Newburyport, Massachusetts. In 1779 he married Mary (1753–1836), daughter of Sarah Kent Atkins and older sister of Dudley Atkins Tyng. (*JQA*, p. 134n)

SEBASTIAN, BENJAMIN (1745–1834), a clergyman and lawyer of Kentucky, was offered trading privileges by Governor Miró in exchange for promoting the settlement of Spanish Louisiana. See also *DHFFC* 17:1876.

SEDAM, CORNELIUS (1759–1823), served as an ensign in the 1st New Jersey Regiment, 1782–83, and held the same rank in the federal army from 1786 until his promotion to lieutenant on 4 March 1791. See also *DHFFC* 2:520.

SEDGWICK, ANN THOMPSON (1719–93), of Cornwall, Connecticut, was the mother of Theodore Sedgwick and the widow of Deacon Benjamin Sedgwick (ca. 1716–57). Theodore Sedgwick's older brother John (ca. 1741–1820) had the care of their mother; her other children were Sarah (ca. 1739–1766), Benjamin (ca. 1743–1778), Mary Ann (1749–1826) and Lorraine (1755–1823).

SEDGWICK, PAMELA DWIGHT (ca. 1753–1807), of Stockbridge, Massachusetts, became the second wife of Theodore Sedgwick in 1774. At the time of the First Congress they had six children: Eliza Mason (1775–1827); Frances Pamela (1778–1842); Theodore, Jr. (1780–1839); Henry Dwight (1785–1831); Robert (1787–1841); and Catharine Maria (28 December 1789–1868). See also *DHFFC* 17:1876.

SEDGWICK, THEODORE, III (1768–1843), son of Theodore Sedgwick's brother Benjamin and Mary Tuttle of Litchfield County, Connecticut, was appointed ensign in the federal army in 1791. See also *DHFFC* 2:512.

SENEY, FRANCES NICHOLSON (1771–1854), daughter of "Commodore" James Nicholson of New York City, married Joshua Seney in New York City on 1 May 1790. Her older sister Catherine had married William Few in June 1788.

SERGEANT, ERASTUS (1742–1814), opened a medical practice in his native Stockbridge, Massachusetts, in 1768, frequently consulting with his lifelong friend, brother-in-law, partner in practice, and housemate, Dr. Oliver Partridge. During the Revolutionary War he rose from captain to major in the state militia, 1776–77. Yale bestowed an honorary degree in 1784, and

Harvard made him an honorary member of the class of 1768. John Sergeant, Jr., was his brother and Pamela Sedgwick was their younger half-sister. (*Harvard Graduates* 17:89–90)

SERGEANT, JOHN, JR. (1747–1824), following his father's career, served as Congregational missionary to the Housatonic (Mohegan) Indians in his native Stockbridge, Massachusetts, from 1775 until the tribe relocated to New Stockbridge (present-day Stockbridge), New York, in 1786. Thereafter he divided his time between the two towns. In 1752 his widowed mother married Joseph Dwight, through whom Sergeant became half-brother to their daughter, Pamela Sedgwick.

SETON, ANNA MARIA (b. 1772), daughter of New York City merchant William Seton, married John Vining in New York City on 24 November 1790. She died of an overdose of medicine sometime before Vining's death in 1802.

SETON, WILLIAM (1746–98), a native of Scotland, immigrated to New York City where he was established as a merchant by 1768, and where he remained throughout the British occupation during the Revolutionary War. He became cashier of the Bank of New York in 1784 and director two years later. Anna Maria Seton, who married John Vining on 24 November 1790, was Seton's daughter by his first marriage in 1767 to Rebecca, daughter of business associate Richard Curson of Baltimore. After Rebecca's death, Seton married her sister Anna Maria in 1776.

SEWALL, DANIEL (1755–1842), was a longtime clerk of the York County, Maine, courts and published an almanac in Portsmouth, New Hampshire.

SEWALL, DAVID (1735–1825), a lawyer and jurist of York, Maine, served as a justice of the Massachusetts supreme judicial court from 1781 until his appointment as federal judge for the Maine district, 1789–1819. See also *DHFFC* 2:512, 17:1877.

SEWALL, DUMMER (1737–1832), a farmer and miller of Bath, Maine, was a state Senator, 1788–89, 1790–91, and postmaster, 1791–1806. See also *DHFFC* 17:1877.

SEWALL, HENRY (1752–1845), a merchant of Hallowell, Maine, served as clerk of the United States district court for Maine, 1789–1818. See also *DHFFC* 17:1877.

SEXTON, DAVID (1744–1800), of Deerfield, Massachusetts, was a state senator for Hampshire County in 1790.

SEYMOUR, THOMAS (1735–1829), first mayor of Hartford, Connecticut, 1784–1812, served in the colonial and state House of Representatives, 1774–93 (as speaker, 1790–92). The Yale graduate of 1755 also served as a lieutenant colonel in the colonial and state militia. (*Yale Graduates* 2:378–79)

SHANNON, WILLIAM (1752–94), was a native of Pennsylvania who settled in Jefferson County (part of present-day Shelby County), Kentucky, after the Revolutionary War, in which he served as commissary and quartermaster in the Western Department under George Rogers Clark, 1778–83.

SHAW, ELIZABETH SMITH (1750–1815), youngest sister of Abigail Adams, married Reverend John Shaw of Haverhill, Massachusetts, in 1777.

SHAW, SAMUEL (1754–94), a merchant of his native Boston, served as United States consul at Canton, China, 1786–94. He first traveled to China as supercargo on Robert Morris's *Empress of China*, which opened the China trade to United States shipping in 1784. Shaw was back in the United States from July 1789 until his third voyage to Canton in March 1790. During the Revolutionary War he rose from second lieutenant in Henry Knox's Regiment of Continental Artillery in 1775 to first lieutenant of the 3rd Continental Artillery Regiment in 1777, to captain in 1780, retiring in 1783 as Knox's aide-de-camp with the rank of major. See also *DHFFC* 2:512. (Josiah Quincy, ed., *Journals of Major Samuel Shaw* [Boston, 1847])

SHEAFE, JAMES (1755–1829), was a merchant of Portsmouth, New Hampshire, which he served as state Representative, 1788–90, town selectman, 1789–92, and state Senator in 1791. See also *DHFFC* 17:1878.

SHELBURNE, WILLIAM PETTY, EARL OF (1737–1805), served as Great Britain's secretary of state for the southern department, 1766–68, in which office he advocated a conciliatory policy towards the American colonies. He returned to the ministry in 1782 with a commitment to recognize the independence of the United States, and was created marquis of Lansdowne upon successfully negotiating the Treaty of Paris in 1783, after which he ceased to play an active role in politics.

SHELBY, ISAAC (1750–1826), was a native of Maryland who in 1773 migrated to Bristol, then considered far southwestern Virginia, in present-day east Tennessee. He served as both a commissary and officer in the Virginia militia, 1776–81, frequently sharing command with John Sevier. After the boundary between Virginia and North Carolina was drawn, Shelby's holdings fell in Sullivan County, North Carolina, which he represented in the state House of Commons in 1782. The next year he settled permanently in Lincoln County, Kentucky, which he represented in several of the statehood conventions of the 1780s.

SHELDON, JAMES (1726–1818), represented Richmond, Rhode Island, in the state House of Deputies, 1785–91, and at the state convention, where he voted against ratification of the Constitution. The unsuccessful candidate for Representative in the first federal election was a member of the Providence (Rhode Island) Abolition Society. (*DHFFE* 4:449)

SHEPARD, LEVI (1744–1805), was the most successful merchant in Northampton, Massachusetts, in the late 1780s, having started his career as a druggist (hence his title "Doctor"). In November 1787 he served on the six-man committee that drafted the instructions for his wife's second cousin, Caleb Strong, at the state ratifying convention. (*DHROC* 5:996)

SHEPARD, WILLIAM, was a wealthy planter of New Bern, North Carolina. (*Powell* 5:329)

SHERBURNE, HENRY (1747–1824), a Federalist of Newport, Rhode Island, served during the Revolutionary War as major of the 3rd Rhode Island Regiment in 1775, of the 15th Continental Regiment in 1776, and of the 1st Rhode Island Regiment briefly in 1777 before being commissioned colonel of one of the Sixteen Additional Continental Regiments, 1777–81. In 1783 Congress appointed him a commissioner for settling accounts between New York and the United States. (*DHFFE* 4:417n)

SHERBURNE, JOHN SAMUEL (formerly Samuel) (1757–1830), brother-in-law of John Langdon, was a Portsmouth lawyer who served as federal attorney for the New Hampshire district, 1789–93, while also serving in the state legislature, 1790–93. See also *DHFFC* 2:516–17, 17:1878.

SHERIDAN, RICHARD BRINSLEY (1751–1816), was an Irish born playwright and prominent Whig member of Parliament, 1788–1812.

SHERMAN, ISAAC (1753–1819), the third son of Roger Sherman, had been appointed by Congress as a surveyor in the Northwest Territory in 1785, but accompanied his brother John to Georgia in 1789 to seek greater economic opportunities. See also *DHFFC* 8:93–96, 17:1878.

SHERMAN, JOHN (1750–1802), brother of Isaac, was Roger Sherman's eldest child by his first marriage. During the Revolutionary War he served as paymaster of the 6th Connecticut Regiment, 1777–81, and of the 4th Regiment thereafter until war's end, carrying the rank of first lieutenant from 1780. Unsuccessful in a retail business, he embezzled his regiment's final settlement certificates and, bailed out by his father, sought a second and equally unsuccessful start as a businessman in Georgia in 1789. His first wife Rebecca, whom he divorced in 1792, was the daughter of Roger Sherman's good friend, David Austin. (*Sherman's Connecticut*, pp. 173–74, 317–19, 329)

SHERMAN, REBECCA PRESCOTT (ca. 1743–1793), of New Haven, Connecticut, became Roger Sherman's second wife in 1763. She added seven children to the four from Sherman's first marriage in 1749 to Elizabeth Hartwell (1735–60). Sherman's eleven children alive during the First Congress were: John; William (1751–89); Isaac; Chloe (1758–1840); Rebecca (1764–95), who married Simeon Baldwin in 1787; Elizabeth (1765–1850); Roger, Jr. (1768–1856), who graduated from Yale in 1787; Mehetabel (1774–1851); Oliver (1770–1820); Martha (1779–1806); and Sarah (1783–1866). Her sister Martha married Benjamin Goodhue's brother Stephen in 1767, and her sister Mercy married Henry Gibbs in 1781.

SHIPPEN, THOMAS LEE (1765–98), the son of William Shippen, Jr., and nephew of Richard H. Lee, spent several months in New York City in the winter and spring of 1790, en route home to his native Philadelphia after a long European sojourn that included studying law at London's Inner Temple. He visited New York City again in July and August 1790, when he was a witnessing signatory to the Treaty of New York. Later that year he began courting Elizabeth Farley Banister of Virginia, whom he married on 10 March 1791 at her family's plantation, "Nesting," in Charles City County, Virginia. (*PGW* 2:35n; Charles Royster, *The Fabulous History of the Dismal Swamp Company* [New York, 1999], pp. 315, 339)

SHIPPEN, WILLIAM, JR. (1736–1808), a prominent Philadelphia physician, married Richard H. Lee's sister Alice (1736–1817) in 1762; Thomas Lee Shippen was their son. See also *DHFFC* 17:1879.

SHORT, PEYTON (1761–1815), younger brother of William Short, declined appointment as collector at Louisville, Kentucky, in 1789. Two years earlier he married Maria (b. 1762), daughter of the federal judge for the Northwest Territory, John Cleves Symmes. See also *DHFFC* 2:554.

SHORT, WILLIAM (1759–1849), brother of Peyton, served as secretary of the American legation in Paris under Thomas Jefferson, upon whose return to the United States he became chargé des affaires, 1789–92. See also *DHFFC* 2:1880, 17:1880.

SHOTWELL, WILLIAM (1762–1840), was a Quaker ironmonger of New York City who hosted Warner Mifflin during the antislavery petition campaign in the spring of 1790. (*Drinker* 3:2212)

SHUTE, WILLIAM (1750–1841), kept a store in Elizabeth, New Jersey, where he served as postmaster, 1789–93. During the Revolutionary War he rose from captain in the 2nd New Jersey Regiment to colonel in the 2nd New Jersey Battalion.

SIBLEY, JOHN (1757–1837), opened a medical practice in Fayetteville, North Carolina, after serving as a surgeon's mate in the militia of his native Massachusetts in 1776.

SINGLETON, ANTHONY (d. 1795), was Virginia's agent for its sinking fund, established in 1787. During the Revolutionary War, he served as captain in the 1st Continental Artillery Regiment, 1777–83, and in 1788 he married Lucy Randolph (1760–1809), the widowed daughter of Benjamin Harrison, Sr. (*PJM* 13:64n)

SITGREAVES, JOHN (1757–1802), a lawyer of New Bern, North Carolina, served as federal district attorney from June 1790 until his appointment as federal judge for the North Carolina district, December 1790–1802. A native of England, he served as lieutenant in the state militia, 1776–80, a member of Congress in 1785, and a state Representative, 1784, 1786–89. See also *DHFFC* 2:530.

SIZER, WILLIAM (b. 1746), a native of Connecticut, served in Jeduthan Baldwin's Continental Regiment of Artillery Artificers (engineers) as lieutenant in 1777 and as captain, 1778–82. In 1786 he resettled in West Springfield, Massachusetts, where he was elected town treasurer in 1790.

SKERRETT, CLEMENT, a tavern keeper in Baltimore County, had served as a lieutenant in the Continental Artillery Regiment, 1778–83.

SKINNER, JOHN (1760–1819), a nephew of William Skinner and, like him, a planter of Edenton, North Carolina, served as a federal marshal, 1790–94. The former state Representative and Senator supported the Constitution at the first ratification convention in 1788. See also *DHFFC* 2:530–31. (*PGW* 5:269n)

SKINNER, JOSHUA (d. 1798), a planter of Edenton, North Carolina, was appointed federal surveyor at Hartford in 1790, while serving as state Senator, 1790–94. See also *DHFFC* 2:531.

SKINNER, THOMPSON (1752–1809), a carpenter and contractor of Williamstown, Massachusetts, served in the state House of Representatives, 1781–85, Senate, 1785–87, on the Berkshire County court of common pleas, 1788–1807, and at the state convention, where he voted to ratify the Constitution. In the first federal election, the veteran militia captain was an unsuccessful candidate for the seat won by Theodore Sedgwick. (*DHFFE* 1:758; *DHROC* 5:1070)

SKINNER, WILLIAM (1728–98), a planter of Edenton, North Carolina, was appointed federal commissioner of loans for the state, 1790–98. He rose to the rank of brigadier general in the state militia during the Revolutionary War, held a number of colonial and state offices, and supported the Constitution at the state's first ratification convention in 1788. John Skinner was his nephew. See also *DHFFC* 2:531.

SKIPWITH, FULWAR (1765–1839), had conducted business in London and Paris for his father, a Richmond tobacco merchant, before settling as a merchant himself in Martinique, where he served as United States consul, 1790–99. (*PJM* 9:29n)

SLOUGH, MATHIAS (ca. 1733–1812), a merchant and tavern keeper of Lancaster, Pennsylvania, served in the colonial and state Assembly, 1774–75, 1777, and 1780–83. A supply agent for Pennsylvania troops as early as 1776, he was also commanding colonel of the Pennsylvania Battalion of the Continental Army's Flying Camp that same year. (*PRM* 1:262–63n; Alexander Harris, *Biographical History of Lancaster County* [Baltimore, 1974], pp. 539–40)

SMEAD, DAVID (1732–1806), was a deacon and selectman of Greenfield, Massachusetts, which he represented in the state House, 1780–93. In 1786 he had been an active supporter of the Shaysites. (*Political Parties*, p. 417)

SMITH, ABIGAIL "NABBY" ADAMS (1765–1813), the only daughter of John and Abigail Adams to survive infancy, married William Stephens Smith in 1786 while living with her parents in London. The Smiths resided at the

Adamses' "Richmond Hill" estate with their two infant sons during most of the first and second sessions of the First Congress, before relocating to their own quarters in New York City.

SMITH, ADAM (1723–90), was a Scottish political economist whose *Inquiry into the Nature and Causes of the Wealth of Nations* (2 vols., London, 1776), presented a detailed critique of the British political and economic system in the eighteenth century.

SMITH, CHARLOTTE IZARD (1770–92), daughter of Ralph Izard and sister-in-law of Gabriel Manigault, married William Smith (S.C.) in 1786. She resided with him throughout the First Congress, during which their son Thomas Loughton (February 1790–1817) was born. See also *DHFFC* 14:847.

SMITH, DANIEL (1748–1818), a surveyor and planter of Sumner County, North Carolina (which then included all of present-day north central Tennessee), was appointed secretary of the Southern Territory, 1790–96. The Virginia native was a veteran officer of the state militia before moving to Tennessee, which he represented in the North Carolina Senate in 1789 and at the state's second convention that same year, where he voted to ratify the Constitution. See also *DHFFC* 2:555)

SMITH, EBENEZER (1734–1807), the largest landowner of Meredith, New Hampshire, held many local and state offices, including state Senator, 1784–85 and 1787–91 (as presiding officer, 1790), and member of the Governor's Council, 1788–89. The state militia colonel and county court judge was an unsuccessful candidate for Presidential Elector in the first federal election. (*DHFFE* 1:858)

SMITH, ISRAEL (1759–1810), represented Vermont in the boundary commission with New York state in the summer of 1790. Like his fellow commissioner Nathaniel Chipman, he was born in Connecticut, graduated from Yale (1781), and commenced the practice of law in Rutland. He served in the Vermont legislature in 1785 and 1788–91, prior to his election to Congress in the second federal election.

SMITH, JEREMIAH (1759–1842), was a lawyer of Peterborough, New Hampshire, which he represented in the state House, 1788–91, before unseating Abiel Foster in the second federal election. He attended Harvard briefly in 1777, participated with the state militia in the Saratoga campaign, graduated from Queen's College (Rutgers) in 1780, and passed the bar in 1786.

SMITH, JOHN "of Mastic" (1752–1816), was a farmer at Brookhaven, Long Island, New York, who represented Suffolk County in the state Assembly, 1784–85 and 1787–94. He overcame his Antifederalist leanings to vote in favor of the Constitution at the state convention. (*DHFFE* 3:204)

SMITH, JOHN COTTON (1765–1845), a Yale graduate of 1783, practiced law in Sharon, Connecticut.

SMITH, JONATHAN (ca. 1740–1802), a farmer and state militia colonel of Lanesborough, Massachusetts, served in the provincial and state House of Representatives, 1775–83 and 1787–88, the state Senate, 1783–84, and the state convention, where he voted to ratify the Constitution. (*DHROC* 6:1233n)

SMITH, JOSEPH ALLEN (1769–1828), younger half-brother of William Smith (S.C.), was present in New York City in the summer of 1790, when he was a witnessing signatory to the Treaty of New York.

SMITH, MELANCTON (1744–98), was active in the revolutionary movement in Poughkeepsie before expanding his successful mercantile business to New York City about 1785, when he began two years of service in Congress. He retained his upstate political connections with Gov. George Clinton, but was a sufficiently moderate Antifederalist to help broker many of the successful compromises of the ratification convention, where he voted for the Constitution as a delegate for Dutchess County. During the first federal election he was an unsuccessful candidate for the Senate. (*DHROC* 19:499; *DHFFE* 3:212, 259)

SMITH, REUBEN (1737–1804), graduated from Yale in 1757 and about 1759 commenced practice as a druggist and physician in Litchfield, Connecticut, where he resided the rest of his life. He held several local elective and judicial posts, including county treasurer, 1779–1801. (*Yale Graduates* 2:498)

SMITH, ROBERT (1732–1801), was an Anglican minister who settled in Charleston in 1757, and was elevated to Episcopalian bishop for South Carolina in 1795. His daughter Sarah married John Rutledge, Jr., in 1791. (George C. Rogers, Jr., *Evolution of a Federalist: William Loughton Smith of Charleston* [Columbia, S.C., 1962], pp. 388, 405; Albert S. Thomas, "Robert Smith: First Bishop of South Carolina," *Historical Magazine of the Protestant Episcopalian Church* 15[March 1946]:15–29)

SMITH, SAMUEL (1752–1839), moved with his family in 1757 from his native Pennsylvania to Baltimore, where he became a wealthy shipping merchant. During the Revolutionary War he rose from captain in the 4th Regiment of the Maryland Line, to lieutenant colonel by the time of his resignation in 1779, ending the war as a full colonel in the state militia.

SMITH, THOMAS (d. 1793), of Philadelphia, served as a commissioner for the Continental loan office for Pennsylvania from 1776 until his death.

SMITH, WILLIAM (1727–1803) was an Episcopalian minister of Philadelphia who served as rector of the College of Philadelphia (University of Pennsylvania), 1755–79 and 1789–91. See also *DHFFC* 9:177n, 17:1882.

SMITH, WILLIAM, of Boston, graduated from Harvard in 1775, became a merchant, and served as town treasurer during the First Congress. See also *DHFFC* 8:272, 302, 17:1882.

SMITH, WILLIAM STEPHENS (1755–1816), was federal marshal for the New York district from 1789 until Washington appointed him supervisor of excises for the New York district on 4 March 1791. The 1774 College of New Jersey (Princeton) graduate abandoned legal studies at the start of the Revolutionary War and embarked on a military career that culminated in serving as Washington's aide-de-camp, 1781–83. While secretary to the United States legation in London in 1786, he married the Adamses' daughter, Abigail. Although he played a gentleman farmer on his estate in Jamaica, Long Island, Smith and his family resided at the Adamses' "Richmond Hill" for much of the first and second sessions of the First Congress, before moving into New York City. See also *DHFFC* 2:130, 525, 17:1882.

SNELL, THOMAS, was master of the sloop *Catharine*, the packet boat between Charleston, South Carolina, and New York, during the second session of the First Congress.

SNOW, SAMUEL (1758–1838), served as a captain in the Rhode Island militia until 1780 and settled in Providence as a merchant.

SODERSTROM, RICHARD (d. 1815), served as Swedish consul for the northern states beginning in 1784, while engaging in the shipping trade there and in New York City. See also *DHFFC* 17:1882–83.

SOHIER, MARTIN BRIMMER (d. 1792), of Boston, was appointed ensign in the federal army in 1791. See also *DHFFC* 2:513.

SOUTHGATE, ROBERT (1741–1833), was a physician and farmer of Scarborough, Maine. In 1773 he married Rufus King's younger sister Mary (1756–1824), and became executor of their father's estate. (Leonard B. Chapman, *Monograph of the Southgate Family* [Portland, Me., 1907], pp. 8–10; Robert Ernst, *Rufus King: American Federalist* [Chapel Hill, N.C., 1968], p. 16)

SPENCE, KEITH (d. 1809), was a Scottish born merchant of Portsmouth, New Hampshire, and business partner with John Langdon's brother-in-law Henry Sherburne. When revelations of his bankruptcy surfaced in late 1790, he was no longer considered for appointment as commissioner of loans for New Hampshire. (*PGW* 6:585–86n)

SPENCE, PETER, was a physician who settled in Kensington, London, after the Revolutionary War, when he was banished from his native Charleston, South Carolina, and much of his property confiscated because of his Loyalism. He spent the war as a surgeon to the British army. (*Butler*, p. 546)

SPENCER, SAMUEL (1734–93), was a lawyer of Anson County, North Carolina. The 1759 College of New Jersey (Princeton) graduate was appointed to the state superior court in 1777 and became an Antifederalist leader during the ratification period. (*Princetonians, 1748–1768*, pp. 289–92)

STACEY, GEORGE (d. 1808), graduated from Harvard in 1784 and became a lawyer in Newburyport, Massachusetts. (*JQA*, p. 37n)

STANWOOD, WILLIAM (1752–1829), was a shipbuilder of Brunswick, Maine. During the Revolutionary War he served as lieutenant in the 11th Regiment of the Massachusetts Line, 1776–78.

STARKE, BURWELL, son of the colonial vice admiralty judge in Virginia, studied at the College of William and Mary with the class of 1773 and was admitted to the bar in London in 1783. By 1790 he had returned to Dinwiddie County, Virginia, where he practiced law. (*John Marshall* 1:236n; *Inns of Court*)

STELLE, BENJAMIN (1746–1819), a native of New Jersey, graduated from the College of New Jersey (Princeton) in 1766 and moved to Providence, Rhode Island, where he established a Latin school with the support of James Manning, a friend of his family and president of the College of Rhode Island (Brown). During the Revolutionary War, Stelle served as adjutant of two Rhode Island militia regiments, 1775–77, and as deputy paymaster, 1779–81. (*PGW* 5:195n)

STEPHENS, ISAAC, was master of the *Maria* out of Boston when it was captured by Algerine pirates in 1785. He remained a captive in Algiers until his release in 1796. He was one of the signatories of the 1788 petition that may have been submitted to the First Congress in May 1790. See also *DHFFC* 2:426, 435, 444, 448, 8:2–4. (*Emerging Nation* 3:59n)

STERRET, SAMUEL (1756–1833), was a merchant of Baltimore, which he represented in the Maryland House of Delegates in 1789. In the first federal election he lost to William Smith (Md.), but was elected to the Second Congress when Smith retired. See also *DHFFC* 9:206n, 17:1884.

STEUBEN, FREDERICK WILLIAM, BARON VON (1730–94), was a Prussian military officer who settled in New York City after a distinguished military career as volunteer Inspector General of the Continental Army, 1778–84, for which service he petitioned for and received compensation under the Steuben Act of 1790. See also *DHFFC* 7:201–6, 9:260–61n.

STEVENS, DANIEL (1746–1835), a Charleston, South Carolina, merchant and planter, served as federal supervisor of excise from 4 March 1791 until 1801. See also *DHFFC* 2:545, 17:1884.

STEWART, CHARLES (1729–1800), immigrated from Ireland and settled as a farmer in Hunterdon County, New Jersey, in 1755. He served in Congress in 1784–85. See also *DHFFC* 9:173n, 17:1885. (Oscar Jewel Harvey, *A History of Wilkes-Barre, Luzerne County, Pennsylvania* [6 vols., Wilkes-Barre, Penn., 1909], 1:459)

STEWART, WALTER (1756–96), a native of Ireland, settled in Philadelphia before the outbreak of the Revolutionary War, during which he rose from captain to major of the 3rd Pennsylvania Battalion, 1776–77, to colonel of the 13th Regiment of the Pennsylvania Line from 1777 to 1778, when he transferred to the 2nd Pennsylvania Regiment, retiring at war's end as brevet brigadier general. He had commercial dealings with Robert Morris while inspector of the Northern Department of the Continental Army, 1782–83, and as a fellow merchant after the war. In the first federal election he was an unsuccessful Antifederalist candidate for Presidential Elector. (*DHFFE* 1:427; *PRM* 5:12n)

STILLMAN, GEORGE, of Westerly, Rhode Island, voted to ratify the Constitution at the state convention and was subsequently appointed federal surveyor at Pawcatuck River in 1790. See also *DHFFC* 2:541.

STOCKTON, ANNIS BOUDINOT (1736–1801), older sister of Elias Boudinot, married Richard Stockton, Sr., of "Morven," in Princeton, New Jersey, in 1757. Stockton (1730–81), a Signer of the Declaration of Independence, was also older brother to Elias Boudinot's wife, Hannah. Among their six children were Richard, Jr., and Julia (1759–1848), who married Benjamin Rush in 1776.

STOCKTON, RICHARD, JR. (1764–1828) of "Morven," in Princeton, New Jersey, graduated from the College of New Jersey (Princeton) in 1779 and studied law under his maternal uncle, Elias Boudinot. He married Mary Field in 1788.

STOCKTON, SAMUEL W. (1751–95), younger brother of Hannah Stockton Boudinot, was a land speculator and lawyer of Trenton, New Jersey. After graduating from the College of New Jersey (Princeton) in 1767 and passing the bar in 1772, he embarked on some unknown business ventures in England before serving as secretary to William Lee's unsuccessful diplomatic mission to Germany and Austria, 1777–79. He married Catherine Cox (d. 1823) ca. 1783. See also *DHFFC* 17:1885.

STOCKTON, SUSAN (1761–1821), of Princeton, New Jersey, was the daughter of Boudinot's sister Annis and Richard Stockton, Sr. Richard, Jr. and Benjamin Rush's wife Julia were her siblings.

STODDERT, BENJAMIN (1751–1813), was a merchant of Georgetown, Maryland (in present-day D.C.). See also *DHFFC* 17:1885–86.

STOKES, JOHN (1756–12 October 1790), was a veteran officer of the Virginia Line of the Continental Army, who settled in Montgomery County, North Carolina, and practiced law. He served in the state Senate, 1786–87, and in 1789 represented Salisbury in both the state House of Commons and second ratification convention, where he voted for the Constitution. An unsuccessful candidate for Senator in the first federal election, he served only a few months of his appointment as federal district judge before his death. See also *DHFFC* 2:531. (*DHFFE* 4:371)

STONE, FREDERICK (ca. 1769–1793), orphaned son of Michael Jenifer Stone's older brother Thomas (1743–87), was his uncle's ward during the First Congress. Although he suffered from an unknown illness at the time, he entered the College of New Jersey (Princeton) in July 1789 and graduated in August 1791, presumably residing with his uncle during his frequent absences from school. (*Princetonians, 1791–1794*, pp. 112–13)

STONE, JOHN HOSKINS (1750–1804), younger brother of Michael Jenifer Stone, was a merchant of Annapolis, Maryland, which he represented in the state House of Delegates, 1785–87 and 1790. See also *DHFFC* 17:1886.

STONE, WALTER (d. 1791), brother of Michael Jenifer Stone, was a merchant of Port Tobacco, Maryland, where he raised the two orphaned daughters of his deceased brother Thomas: Margaret "Peggy" (1771–1809) and Mildred "Milly" (1771–1836).

STORER, CHARLES (1761–1829), was a Boston native who served as John Adams's private secretary in Europe after graduating from Harvard in 1779. See also *DHFFC* 8:709–10n.

STORER, HANNAH QUINCY (1736–1826), whom John Adams had courted before marrying her distant cousin Abigail, married Ebenezer Storer, Jr., sometime before 1790. (*Adams* 1:71n)

STORER, SAMUEL, was a merchant of Portsmouth, New Hampshire, and a brother-in-law of Tobias Lear. (*DGW* 5:491n)

STORY, DANIEL (1756–1804), a native of Boston, was sent by the Ohio Company to Marietta, Ohio, in 1790 to serve as the first licensed preacher in the Northwest Territory. (Martin R. Andrews, ed., *History of Marietta and Washington County, Ohio* [Chicago, Ill., 1902], pp. 884–85)

STREET, JOHN (d. 1807) was appointed the United States vice consul to Fayal, in the Azores, in 1790.

STREET, SAMUEL (1753–1813), a native of Connecticut, became an Indian trader in central New York State. During the Revolutionary War he supplied British forces from Fort Niagara (in present-day Ontario, Canada), where he remained as a storekeeper after the war and also engaged in land speculation.

STRONG, NATHAN (b. 1748), was a Congregational clergyman of Hartford, Connecticut, who by 1790 was engaged in mercantile pursuits and distilleries. After graduating from Yale in 1769 he abandoned law studies and became licensed to preach, serving as parson of Hartford's First Church in 1774 and chaplain of the 22nd Continental Regiment in 1776. (*Yale Graduates* 3:357–63)

STRONG, SIMEON (1736–1805), was a prominent lawyer of Amherst, Massachusetts, which he had represented in the colonial House of Representatives, 1767 and 1769. The Yale graduate of 1756 was forced for health reasons to leave the ministry and took up the law, passing the bar in 1762. (*Yale Graduates* 1:437–39)

STROTHER, FRENCH (1733–1800), was a planter of Culpeper County, Virginia, which he represented in the state House of Delegates, 1776–91, Senate, 1791–1800, and the state convention, where he voted against ratification of the Constitution. (*DHROC* 9:578n)

STUART, DAVID (1753–ca. 1814), was a physician and planter of "Abingdon," Fairfax County (part of present-day Arlington County), Virginia, which he represented in the state House of Delegates, 1785–88, and at the state convention, where he voted to ratify the Constitution. He became a neighbor and confidant to the Washingtons after his marriage in 1783 to Eleanor Calvert Custis (1754–1811), the widow of Martha's son, and served as a Presidential Elector in 1789. See also *DHFFC* 17:1887.

SULLIVAN, JAMES (1744–1808), younger brother of New Hampshire's President (governor) John Sullivan and husband of John Langdon's sister Martha, was a lawyer who moved from Maine to Boston in 1782 and followed a long career as state legislator and supreme court justice by serving as Massachusetts's attorney general, 1790–1807. See also *DHFFC* 17:1887.

SULLIVAN, JOHN (1740–95), served as federal judge for the New Hampshire district from 1789 until his death. The older brother of James Sullivan studied law under Samuel Livermore and practiced in Durham, New Hampshire, before serving as president (governor), 1786–88, and again as interim governor after John Langdon's resignation in 1789. See also *DHFFC* 17:1887–88.

SUMNER, DAVIS (1761–1826), a native of Milton, Massachusetts, fought in the Rhode Island militia during the Revolutionary War and settled in Bath, Maine, where he married Dummer Sewall's daughter Lydia in 1785.

SWAINE, JOHN (ca. 1762–1794), co-published Francis Childs's [New York] *Daily Advertiser* from July 1789 until his death. See also *DHFFC* 10:xxxix.

SWAN, CALEB (d. 1809), a native of Maine, served as a noncommissioned officer in the 9th and 8th Massachusetts Regiments from 1777 until retiring from Henry Jackson's Continental Regiment in 1784. He seems to have served as a clerk in the Confederation's war department, and was retained during the First Congress until journeying to Georgia as deputy Indian agent to the Creeks from October 1790 to January 1791.

SWAN, JOHN (1750–1824), a Baltimore financier and businessman, emigrated from his native Scotland in 1766. He served throughout the Revolutionary War as captain of Continental dragoons, 1777–78, and as major thereafter until war's end, when he joined the Society of the Cincinnati and became a state militia general. (Richard H. Spencer, ed., *Geneological and Memorial Encyclopedia of Maryland* [New York, 1919], pp. 629–30)

SWANWICK, JOHN (1740–98), a Philadelphia merchant, clerked under Superintendent of Finance Robert Morris, who appointed him receiver of continental taxes in Pennsylvania in 1782 and accepted him into the partnership of Willing and Morris in 1783. (*PRM* 1:8n)

SYMMES, JOHN CLEVES (1742–1814), a native of New Jersey, resided at North Bend (in present-day Ohio) as judge of the Northwest Territory, 1789–1803, having held that position under the Confederation since 1788. Peyton Short became his son-in-law in 1787. See also *DHFFC* 2:521.

TALBOT, SILAS (1751–1813), a native of Massachusetts, settled in Providence, Rhode Island in 1772 and served as captain in the 2nd Rhode Island Regiment in 1775, the 11th Continental Regiment in 1776, and the 1st Rhode Island in 1777, before being promoted to major that year, and lieutenant colonel in 1778. In 1779 he exchanged his uniform for that of a Continental Navy captain, in which he served until war's end, after which he settled in Johnstown, New York. (*PGW* 5:75n)

TALLMADGE, BENJAMIN (1754–1835), a merchant of Litchfield, Connecticut, employed his familiarity with his native Long Island to serve as Washington's head "spy master" operating in the crucial theater of Long Island Sound. His formal military commissions included captain and then major of the 2nd Continental Dragoons between 1776 and 1783, when he was breveted a lieutenant colonel. In 1784 he married future Representative William Floyd's daughter Mary (1763–1805).

TATUM, HOWELL (1753–1822), was a native of North Carolina who migrated to western North Carolina (present-day Tennessee) by 1787 and commenced practicing law in Nashville in 1789. During the Revolutionary War he rose to the rank of captain in the 1st Regiment of the North Carolina Line, 1775–83. (*PGW* 5:423–24)

TAYLOR, FRANCIS (1747–99), James Madison's second cousin, was a planter of Orange County, Virginia, with large land holdings in Kentucky and the Northwest Territory. Commissioned a captain of the 2nd Virginia Regiment in 1776, he rose to major of the 15th Regiment in 1778, retiring later that year but returning to duty as colonel of the state troops guarding Gen. John Burgoyne's Convention Army imprisoned in Virginia, 1779–81. (*PJM* 1:125n)

TAYLOR, JOHN (ca. 1734–94), was a physician who unsuccessfully led the Antifederalist forces at Massachusetts's ratification convention as a delegate from Douglas, before moving across the state line to Smithfield, Rhode Island. See also *DHFFC* 17:1889.

TAYLOR, JOHN, of Albany, New York, was a land speculator who contracted to sell nine hundred acres in the Mohawk Valley to James Madison and James Monroe in 1786. Madison made the final payment in late 1790. Taylor served in the state Assembly, 1777–81 and 1786–87. (*PJM* 12:297n)

TAYLOR, JOHN "OF CAROLINE" (1753–1824), was a lawyer and planter of Caroline County, Virginia, which he represented in the state House of Delegates, 1779–85. Last enrolled in the College of William and Mary in 1771, he then studied law, was admitted to the bar in 1774, and employed his expertise as judge advocate of the Continental troops in Virginia, with the rank of major, 1776–79. Thought to have opposed the Constitution during ratification, he was one of the unsuccessful challengers of John Page during the second federal election, but filled the Senate seat left vacant when Richard H. Lee resigned in 1792 and went on to become a principal theoretician and apologist for states' rights.

TAYLOR, RICHARD (1744–1826), a planter of Jefferson County, Kentucky, was appointed collector at Louisville in 1790. During the Revolutionary War, the native of Orange County, Virginia, rose from first lieutenant of the 1st Virginia Regiment in 1775, to captain in 1776, to major of the 13th then the 9th regiments in 1778, to lieutenant colonel of the 2nd Regiment from 1779 until his retirement in 1781. He settled in Kentucky in 1785, and attended statehood conventions in that year and in 1788. See also *DHFFC* 2:495. (*Kentucky in Retrospect*, pp. 173, 175)

TELFAIR, EDWARD (ca. 1735–1794), a native of Scotland who became a merchant of Richmond and Burke counties, Georgia, served as governor in 1786 and 1789–93. Previously he had served in Congress, the state Assembly, and the state convention that voted unanimously to ratify the Constitution. He married Sally Gibbons in 1774. See also *DHFFC* 17:1889.

TELLES, JOHN, a native of Portugal, became a prominent Philadelphia merchant in the 1780s, associated with Robert Morris, among others, in the Portuguese flour trade. (*PTJ* 19:308–12)

TEMPLE, SIR JOHN (1732–98), Boston born but raised in Great Britain, held political appointments in colonial New England, including as lieutenant governor of New Hampshire and surveyor general of customs for Northern America, 1761–74. He returned to England where he filled a high customs post before being dismissed again, presumably because of his pro-American sympathies, although upon his return to Massachusetts in 1778 he was denied state citizenship on grounds of his Loyalism. He returned to America in 1781–82, during part of which he was involved in secret diplomatic negotiations for Great Britain, and returned again as Great Britain's first consul general at New York, 1785–98; for the first six of those years he was that country's highest diplomatic posting in its former colonies. Sir John (created a baronet in 1786) was very popular in New York City social circles, despite his near deafness. In 1767 he married James Bowdoin's only daughter, Elizabeth (1750–1809). (*MHSC* 9[1897]:xiii–xvii; *PJM* 5:3–4; *New York*, p. 87)

TEN BROECK, ABRAHAM (1734–1810), served an apprenticeship in the New York City mercantile firm of his brother-in-law, Philip Livingston, before establishing himself as a merchant in his native Albany. A former colonial legislator, he represented the western district in the state Senate, 1779–83, during much of which time he also served as a colonel and then brigadier general in the state militia. In the first federal election he ran unsuccessfully as a Federalist against Jeremiah Van Rensselaer, the near-kinsman of his father-in-law, Stephen Van Rensselaer. (*DHFFE* 3:563)

TENNEY, SAMUEL (1748–1816), was a physician of Exeter, New Hampshire. (*PJB*, p. 363n)

THACHER, JOSIAH (1733–99), a native of Connecticut, settled in Gorham, Maine, in 1767, serving as its Congregational minister until 1781, when he resigned and began a public service career that included state Representative, 1783–85, Senator, 1786–91, and judge of the Cumberland County court of common pleas, 1784–99. See also *DHFFC* 17:1889–90.

THATCHER, MARY (ca. 1741–1817), of Boston, was the wife of Elisha Thatcher, originally of Barnstable, Massachusetts, who operated a boardinghouse in Boston at the time of his death sometime before 1817.

THATCHER, SARAH SAVAGE (1760–1843), sister of Joseph and Samuel, and daughter of Samuel Phillips Savage, married George Thatcher in 1784. During his absence at the Confederation and First Federal Congresses, she raised the first three of their ten children at their home in Biddeford, Maine: Samuel Phillips Savage (1785–1842), Sarah (1787–1827), and George (7 September 1790–1857).

THATCHER, THOMAS (1757–1806), younger brother of George Thatcher, was a schoolteacher of Barnstable, Massachusetts.

THAYER, SIMEON (1737–1800), a native of Massachusetts, was trained as a wigmaker but established himself as a tradesman and then innkeeper in Providence, Rhode Island. With military experience gained during the French and Indian War, he was commissioned captain lieutenant of the 2nd Rhode Island Regiment in 1775 and was promoted to major in 1777 before retiring in 1781. (*PGW* 5:529n)

THEOBALD, PHILIP (1750–1808), a native of Hesse-Cassel, Germany, who graduated from the University of Gottingen in 1774, practiced medicine in Pownalborough (part of present-day Dresden), Maine, following his release on parole as a chaplain and surgeon for Hessians captured at Saratoga in 1777. (*Collections and Proceedings of the Maine Historical Society*, series 2, 1[1890]:317–18).

THOMAS, ABISHAI C., left Georgia as a young man and settled in Washington, North Carolina, where he worked for John Gray Blount. He was a deputy quartermaster general of the Continental Army, sat in the state House of Commons in 1787, and served with Hugh Williamson as North Carolina's agents for settling the state's accounts with the United States, beginning in 1788. Through the first two sessions of the First Congress he simultaneously served as Blount's business agent at the seat of government, despite an acknowledged problem with gambling. (*Blount* 1:391n, 501–2)

THOMAS, ISAIAH (1749–1831), was editor and printer of the [Worcester] *Massachusetts Spy*, 1775–76 and 1778–1801, an influential organ of revolutionary sentiments during the 1770s and of Federalist sentiments during the ratification debates. (*DHROC* 4:lv–lvi)

THOMAS, PHILIP (1747–1815), was a physician of Frederick, Maryland. See also *DHFFC* 17:1890.

THOMAS, SAMUEL, of Maine, served as an ensign in Col. Edmund Phiney's Regiment of Massachusetts Continental Line in 1775.

THOMPSON, CATHERINE (1768–1848), daughter of New York City merchant James Thompson, became the second wife of widower Isaac Coles on 2 January 1790; they had one child, Walter (8 December 1790–1857). Gerry had married Catherine's older sister Anne in 1786.

THOMPSON, EBENEZER (1733–1805), was appointed federal naval officer for Providence, Rhode Island, in 1790. The veteran militia officer and state legislator was also a member of the town council, 1783–92. See also *DHFFC* 2:541. (*DHFFE* 4:404n)

THOMPSON, GEORGE (ca. 1751–1834), represented Fluvanna County in Virginia's House of Delegates, 1779–80, 1782, 1785–87, and 1790–91. See also *DHFFC* 17:1890.

THOMPSON, THOMAS (1739–1809), a native of England, became a sea captain, ship builder, and merchant after settling in Portsmouth, New Hampshire, about 1767. See also *DHFFC* 17:1891.

THOMSON (THOMPSON), THOMAS, was an Irish merchant who settled in Virginia in 1783 after spending seventeen years in the Madeira Islands. He was named United States consul for the Canary Islands in 1790 but declined the appointment. See also *DHFFC* 17:1891.

THORNTON, WILLIAM (1759–1828), heir to sugar plantations in his native West Indies, trained in medicine in Edinburgh, took his degree in 1784, and two years later settled in Philadelphia where he practiced medicine and became a steamboat promoter, abolitionist, and architect. Shortly after his marriage there to Anna Maria Brodeau, daughter of Ann Brodeau (d. 1836), on 13 October 1790, he returned to Tortola, West Indies, until 1792.

THORPE, JOHN (1726–92), a native of Maryland, entered the Catholic Church's Society of Jesus (Jesuits) in 1747 and in 1760 became an agent for the English Jesuits in Rome, where he undoubtedly remained after the Society was suppressed in the 1770s. (*CCP* 1:49n)

TICHENOR (TICKNOR), ISAAC (1754–1838), was a lawyer of Bennington, Vermont, where he settled in 1777 and which he represented in the state legislature, 1781–85 and 1787–92. During the First Congress, he served as one of the state's commissioners to Congress for facilitating its admission into the Union. See also *DHFFC* 16:1114–15n.

TILGHMAN, PEREGRINE (1741–1807), of the plantation "Hope," in Talbot County, Maryland, represented the Eastern Shore in the state Senate, 1787–88. During the Revolutionary War he served as colonel of the county militia.

TODD, LEVI (1756–1807), moved with his older brother Robert from Pennsylvania to Kentucky in 1776 and fought in the Virginia militia under George Rogers Clark and Benjamin Logan before becoming a founding settler of Lexington. He served in the statehood conventions of 1785 and 1787, and as Fayette County clerk at the time of the First Congress. (Thomas Marshall Green, *Historic Families of Kentucky* [Cincinnati, Ohio, 1889], p. 212)

TODD, ROBERT (1754–1814), a native of Pennsylvania, settled permanently with his brother Levi in Kentucky in 1776. He captained a Virginia militia company during George Rogers Clark's campaigns in the Old Northwest, 1778–82.

TODD, THOMAS (1765–1826), migrated from Virginia to Danville, Kentucky, in 1784, where he studied law under his cousin Harry Innes. Clerk of every statehood convention of the 1780s and a founding member of Danville's Political Club (1786–90) with future Representative John Brown, Innes, and Christopher Greenup, Todd later clerked under Innes in the federal district court for the Kentucky district of Virginia (1790–92). He was no relation of the Todd brothers, Levi and Robert. (Thomas Marshall Green, *Historic Families of Kentucky* [Cincinnati, Ohio, 1889], pp. 190–91)

TOWNSEND, SAMUEL (1717–24 November 1790), a wealthy Quaker merchant of Oyster Bay, Long Island, represented the Southern District in the New York Senate from 1784 and was Floyd's successor as Representative-elect at the time of his death.

TRACY, JOHN (1753–1815), like his older brother Nathaniel, was a once wealthy merchant of Newburyport, Massachusetts, who was thrown into bankruptcy in the mid 1780s. After graduating from Harvard in 1771 he joined his brother and Jonathan Jackson in a short lived mercantile partnership, 1774–75, but privateering restored his fortunes during the Revolutionary War and enabled him to operate as sole partner of Tracy and Tracy, 1780–85. See also *DHFFC* 17:1892.

TRACY, NATHANIEL (1751–96), was a bankrupt merchant of Newburyport, Massachusetts, who proved unsuccessful in persuading the First Congress to create a national bankruptcy law. The 1769 Harvard graduate made a fortune with his brother John as co-owner of a fleet of privateers during the Revolutionary War, but declared bankruptcy in 1786. Between 1779 and 1784 he served first in the state House of Representatives and then in the Senate. See also *DHFFC* 8:86–89.

TRACY, URIAH (1755–1807), graduated from Yale in 1778, was admitted to the bar in 1781, and became a lawyer in Litchfield, Connecticut, which he represented in the state House of Representatives, 1788–93. (*Yale Graduates* 4:63–66)

TREDWELL, THOMAS (1743–1831), graduated from the College of New Jersey (Princeton) in 1764, studied law, and established a practice in his native Suffolk County, Long Island, to which his activism in the revolutionary movement forced him to flee during the British occupation, 1776–83. He served in the New York Assembly, 1777–83, and resettled in New York City briefly before returning to Suffolk County, which he represented in the state Senate, 1786–89. A prominent partisan of Gov. George Clinton, he became a leading Antifederalist at the state convention, where he voted against ratification. He was considered for United States Senator in the first federal election and was unsuccessful in winning William Floyd's House seat in the second federal election, but was ultimately elected to replace fellow Antifederalist William Townsend, who died before he could assume his seat in the Second Congress. In 1765 Tredwell married Ann Hazard, first cousin of Ebenezer Hazard. (*DHFFE* 3:212n; *Princetonians, 1748–1768*, pp. 468–72)

TRESCOTT, EDWARD (d. 1818), of the parish of St. Philip's and St. Michael's outside Charleston, South Carolina, had been revenue collector for the state before 1789.

TREVETT, RICHARD (d. 1793), a former ship captain of York, Maine, served as collector at that port from 1791 until his death. See also *DHFFC* 2:513.

TRIST, ELIZA HOUSE, was the mistress of a boardinghouse at Fifth and Market streets in Philadelphia, where James Madison and other members of

Congress, principally from New York and Virginia, regularly resided while in that city. (*PJM* 2:92n)

TROTTER, JAMES (1753–1827), of Fayette County, Kentucky, was a commander of the Kentucky militia deployed in Gen. Josiah Harmar's expedition in late 1790.

TROWBRIDGE, ISAAC (1758–1822), a native of Oxford, Connecticut, and a veteran of the 1st Regiment of the Massachusetts Line, 1777–83, contracted to carry the mail between Hartford and New York City beginning in 1788, from which contract he asked to be relieved in an unsuccessful petition submitted to Congress in February 1790. See also *DHFFC* 8:230–31.

TRUMBULL, DAVID (1751–1822), brother of the painter John and Representative Jonathan Trumbull, was a farmer as well as merchant in his prominent family's firm based in Lebanon, Connecticut. See also DHFFC 17:1893.

TRUMBULL, JOHN (1750–1831), was a lawyer of Hartford, Connecticut, where he served as state's attorney, 1789–95. The Yale graduate of 1767 passed the bar in 1773 but continued his studies under John Adams in Boston before returning to New Haven to open his own law practice in 1774. He became an influential essayist on behalf of the revolutionary movement, and, upon resettling in Hartford in 1781, he joined David Humphreys and Joel Barlow in forming the nationalist literary circle known as the "Connecticut Wits." (*Yale Graduates* 3:251–57)

TRUMBULL, JOHN (1756–1843), younger brother of David and Representative Jonathan Trumbull, was already a prominent London trained portrait painter upon his arrival in New York City in December 1789, where he boarded with his brother and Jeremiah Wadsworth throughout the second session while executing portraits of the leading figures of the "Republican Court." The Harvard graduate of 1773 gave the first known evidence of his future craft by supplying drawings of British fortifications while serving in the 1st Connecticut Regiment, 1775–77. (*Harvard Graduates* 18:331–48)

TRUXTON, THOMAS (1755–1822), was a native of Long Island, New York, who led a successful career as a privateer during the Revolutionary War before turning to merchant shipping, most prominently in Philadelphia's China trade. See also *DHFFC* 9:72n.

TUCKER, JOHN, SR. (1719–92), father of United States Supreme Court clerk John Tucker, Jr., graduated with Harvard's class of 1741 and in 1745 settled permanently in Newbury, Massachusetts, where, despite some sharp doctrinal disputes, he served as minister of the First Congregational Church for the remainder of his life. (*JQA*, p. 49n; *DHSCUS* 1:704n)

TUCKER, JOHN, JR. (1753–1825), a Boston lawyer, was the first clerk of the United States Supreme Court from 1790 until his resignation in August 1791. He simultaneously served as clerk to the Massachusetts supreme judicial court, having held that post since 1783. See also *DHFFC* 17:1893.

TUCKER, JOSEPH (1754–1804), was a merchant from York, Maine, who served as paymaster of the 7th Massachusetts Regiment, 1778–83, and thereafter as agent for the state's troops stationed at West Point. He served in the Massachusetts House of Representatives, 1791–93. See also *DHFFC* 8:99.

TUCKER, ST. GEORGE (1752–1827), younger brother of Thomas Tudor Tucker, husband of Theodorick Bland's sister Frances (d. 1788), and confidant of John Page throughout the First Congress, was a lawyer of Williamsburg, Virginia, where he also served as professor of law at the College of William and Mary beginning in 1790. See also *DHFFC* 17:1893.

TUCKER, SAMUEL (1747–1833), was a sea captain from Marblehead, Massachusetts, with business ties to Benjamin and Stephen Goodhue. See also *DHFFC* 17:1894.

TUCKER, SARAH HENSHAW (d. 1822), of Boston, married John Tucker, Jr., in 1785.

TUDOR, WILLIAM (1750–1819), was a Boston lawyer who had studied law under John Adams and in turn trained Fisher Ames. See also *DHFFC* 17:1894.

TUFTS, COTTON (1732–1815), a physician of Weymouth, Massachusetts, represented Suffolk County in the state Senate, 1781–82 and 1783–92. Abigail Adams's uncle by marriage, he undertook to administer some of the Adamses' business interests during the First Congress. (*DHROC* 4:174n)

TURBERVILLE, GEORGE LEE (1760–98), was a planter of Richmond County, Virginia, which he represented in the state House of Delegates, 1785–90. See also *DHFFC* 17:1894.

TURNER, GEORGE (ca. 1750–1843), of Philadelphia was appointed judge of the Northwest Territory in 1789. See also *DHFFC* 17:1894–95.

Tyler, William (1751–1826), was surveyor of the port of Providence, Rhode Island, under the state government, 1789–90. (*DHFFE* 4:437n)

Tyng, Dudley Atkins (1760–1829), was a lawyer of Newburyport, Massachusetts. He graduated from Harvard in 1781 and tutored briefly in Virginia, where he began to study law, before returning to Massachusetts in 1784. The son of the widow Sarah Kent Atkins, he adopted the last name "Tyng" in 1790 in order to inherit an estate from a rich relation. (*Massachusetts Bar* 1:137; *JQA*, pp. 34–35n)

Updike, John (1729–1804), brother-in-law of the newspaper publisher John Carter, Sr., merchant and ship owner of Providence, Rhode Island.

Van Berckel, Franco Petrus (b. 1760), succeeded his father as minister plenipotentiary to the United States from The Netherlands between 10 May 1789 and 1795. (*New York*, p. 86)

Van Berckel, Pieter Johan (1725–1800), served as minister plenipotentiary to the United States from The Netherlands from 1783 until his son replaced him in 1789. See also *DHFFC* 17:1895.

Vanderbilt, John (1739–96), a merchant of Kings County, New York, served in the state Assembly (1784–86) and the state Senate (1786–90).

Van Der Kemp, Francis Adrian (1752–1829), was a Mennonite clergyman and author in Kingston, New York, whose political activities had forced him into exile from his native Netherlands in 1788. He met John Adams while the latter was minister at The Hague in 1781. (*Adams* 2:456n)

Van Rensselaer, Stephen (1764–1839), became the eighth patroon of the vast Rensselaerswyck estate in Albany and Rensselaer counties, New York, in 1769. The Harvard graduate of 1782 married Philip Schuyler's daughter Margarita (1758–1801) in 1783 and was closely allied politically to his father-in-law while serving in the state Assembly, 1789–90, and Senate, 1791–95. (*LDC* 25:42n; *DHFFE* 3:253n)

Van Schaack, Cornelius (1734–97), brother of Jane Silvester and Henry and Peter Van Schaack, was a merchant of Kinderhook, New York, with large land holdings in Stockbridge, Massachusetts.

Van Schaack, David (b. 1736), was a wealthy fur trader of Kinderhook, New York, with large land holdings in Stockbridge, Massachusetts. Jane

Silvester and Cornelius, Henry, and Peter Van Schaack were his siblings. During the Revolutionary War he was proscribed as a Loyalist by the New York legislature, which did not restore his citizenship until 1786. (*DHROC* 4:185n)

VAN SCHAACK, HENRY (1733–1823), a former fur merchant of northern New York, was banished for his Loyalism during the Revolutionary War and settled in Pittsfield, Massachusetts. In 1760 he married Jane Holland (d. ca. 1815). His younger brother was Peter Van Schaack, and Peter Silvester became their brother-in-law by his marriage to their sister Jane (b. 1739) in 1764. See also *DHFFC* 17:1895.

VAN SCHAACK, PETER (1747–1832), practiced law in Kinderhook, New York, having studied under his brother-in-law, Peter Silvester. Proscribed as a Loyalist during the Revolutionary War, he resided in England from 1778 to 1785, and his citizenship was restored the next year. (*DHFFE* 3:502n)

VAN STAPHORST, NICHOLAS AND JACOB, were brothers and partners in one of Amsterdam's most important banking firms. They belonged to the syndicate of bankers that negotiated loans with John Adams for the Confederation Congress. Nicholas Hubbard joined the partnership in 1789. (*Adams* 2:445n; *PTJ* 13:185–86)

VANS, WILLIAM (ca. 1730–1820), was a merchant and state legislator of Salem, Massachusetts, who was appointed state excise collector in March 1790. (*PGW* 5:317n)

VAUGHAN, SAMUEL, JR. (1762–1802), was the son of a wealthy Jamaican plantation owner who brought his entire family to Philadelphia in 1783. Samuel, Jr., traveled frequently between there and New York in 1789–90. (*PJM* 12:85n)

VAUGHN, WILLIAM, was a merchant of Portland, Maine.

VERNON, WILLIAM (1719–1806), was a merchant of Newport, Rhode Island. He served as president of the naval board of the Eastern Department from 1777 until its dissolution in 1782. (*NEHGR* 33[1879]:317; *PRM* 1:190n)

VERPLANCK, GULIAN (1751–99), a Dutch trained New York City merchant, served as speaker of the state assembly, 1789–90. The King's College (Columbia) graduate of 1768 was the uncle of William Samuel Johnson's son-in-law, Daniel C. Verplanck. (William E. Ver Planck, *The History of Abraham Isaacs Ver Planck* [Fishkill Landing, N.Y., 1892], pp. 104, 162–68)

VIAR, JOSÉ IGNACIO, served on the staff of the Spanish legation to the United States until the departure of Don Diego de Gardoqui in October 1789, when he became acting *encargado*, or chargé des affaires, until 1794. (*PGW* 3:300n)

VILLEMANZY, JACQUES-PIERRE ORILLARD, COMTE DE (1751–1830), was commissary to the French army in the United States commanded by the viscount de Rochambeau in the latter years of the Revolutionary War.

VOIGT (VOIGHT), HENRY (1738–1814), trained as a watchmaker in his native Germany, immigrated to Pennsylvania about 1760 and established himself in that trade in Philadelphia in 1780. In the late 1780s he became an active collaborator and promoter of John Fitch's steam engine. (Silvio Bedini, "History Corner: Henry Voigt," *Professional Surveyor* vol. 17, 1[October 1997])

VOLTAIRE, the pen name of François-Marie Arouet (1694–1778), was a French essayist and the foremost proponent of the liberal philosophy of the European Enlightenment.

VREDENBURGH, WILLIAM J. (1760–1813), a native of New York City, was a ship chandler before 1788, when he became a merchant engaged in the coasting trade. He served as a private in the 1st Canadian Regiment of the Continental Army. By 1790 he was a broker and speculating heavily in government securities and land warrants. (*PTJ* 18:618–19n)

WADSWORTH, ASAHEL (ca. 1743–1817), was an innkeeper of Farmington, Connecticut.

WADSWORTH, DECIUS (1768–1821), a native of Farmington, Connecticut, graduated from Yale in 1785 and studied law with John Trumbull in Hartford. (*Yale Graduates* 4:443–44)

WADSWORTH, HARRIET (1769?–1793), was the eldest of the three children who were born to Jeremiah Wadsworth and Mehitable Russell (1734–1817) following their marriage in 1767, and who lived with their mother in Hartford, Connecticut, during the First Congress. The other two children were Daniel (1771–1848) and Catherine (1774–1841).

WADSWORTH, PELEG (1748–1829), was a large landowner and merchant of Portland, Maine. The Harvard graduate of 1769 taught school and kept a store before joining the Continental Army, where he served as a captain with Theophilus Cotton's Regiment in 1775 and with the 23rd Continental Regiment in 1776. In 1777 he returned to his native Duxbury, Massachusetts, which he represented in the state House that year. After residing briefly in Boston in 1778, he accepted a commission as brigadier general in the state militia, 1779–81, serving mostly in Maine, where he settled in 1784. See also *DHFFC* 17:1897. (*Harvard Graduates* 17:291–303)

WAIT, THOMAS B. (1762–1830), was publisher of Portland, Maine's *Cumberland Gazette*, 1785–91. See also *DHFFC* 17:1897–98.

WAITE, STEPHEN (1759–post 1834), was a native of Portland, Maine, where he served as federal weigher and gauger.

WALDO, SAMUEL (d. 1798), brother-in-law of William Wetmore, was a merchant of Portland, Maine.

WALKER, BENJAMIN (1753–1818), a British born merchant and securities broker of New York City, served as federal naval officer for that port, 1789–97, except for a leave of absence in the winter of 1790–91, when he was in Europe as an agent for the Scioto Land Company. The veteran Continental Army officer and close associate of baron von Steuben and Alexander Hamilton was a commissioner for settling various departments' accounts during the Confederation period, including Robert Morris's finance office accounts. See also *DHFFC* 2:525, 17:1898.

WALKER, JOHN (1755–1841), was appointed federal naval officer in Wilmington, North Carolina in 1790. See also *DHFFC* 2:531.

WALLACE, GUSTAVUS BROWN (1751–1802), of Stafford County, Virginia, was a member of the state House of Delegates, 1786–87. See also *DHFFC* 17:1898.

WALLIS, SAMUEL (1736–98), was a Philadelphia merchant and land speculator with a home and extensive land holdings near Muncy, Pennsylvania, about twenty-five miles north of Sunbury on the West Branch of the Susquehanna River. His contemporaries were unaware that he spied for the British during the Revolutionary War. (John Bakeless, *Turncoats, Traitors, and Heroes* [Philadelphia, 1959], pp. 294–302; *Northumberland County Historical Society Proceedings* 4:48–59)

WALN, RICHARD (c. 1737–1809), was a Quaker merchant of Philadelphia, with an estate, "Walnford," near Crosswicks, New Jersey. (*Drinker* 3:2225)

WALTON, GEORGE (ca. 1741–1804), a Virginia born lawyer of Burke County, Georgia, served as governor, 1779–80 and again from January to November 1789, when he became justice of the state superior court, western circuit, until 1792. See also *DHFFC* 17:1899.

WALTON, MATTHEW (d. 1819), emigrated from his native Virginia, like his cousin George Walton, and settled on extensive holdings in Nelson County, Kentucky, which he represented in the statehood conventions of 1785 and 1787, at the Virginia convention, where he voted against the Constitution, and in the Virginia House of Delegates in 1789 and 1790. (*Kentucky in Retrospect*, p. 175; *DHROC* 10:1541)

WANTON, GIDEON, the namesake son of a colonial governor of Rhode Island, was a Newport merchant who served in the House of Deputies in 1776 and as the state's naval officer of that port, 1788–90. (*PGW* 5:447n)

WARD, JOSEPH (1737–1812), was a Boston real estate developer and investor in government securities. The former schoolteacher and veteran Continental Army officer was a Federalist like his protégé and pupil, the editor John Fenno. See also *DHFFC* 8:272, 17:1899.

WARD, SAMUEL (1756–1832), moved from his native Rhode Island to New York City in 1787 and became a merchant active in opening up the China trade. The son of a colonial governor who was a leader of the revolutionary movement, he rose from captain to lieutenant colonel in the 1st Rhode Island Regiment, 1775–81, and was elected to the Annapolis Convention, although it adjourned before his arrival. (*PAH* 22:235–36n)

WARREN, JAMES (1726–1808), a merchant and gentleman farmer of Plymouth, Massachusetts, served as speaker of the state House of Representatives, 1787–99. In 1754 he married Mercy Otis, who became, like him, a prominent Antifederalist. See also *DHFFC* 7:1–4, 17:1900.

WARREN, MERCY OTIS (1728–1814), of Plymouth, Massachusetts, was a poet, playwright, historian, and prominent Antifederalist essayist. She was the sister of Samuel A., James, Jr., and Joseph Otis, and, after 1754, the wife of James Warren. (*DHROC* 4:438)

WARREN (WARING), THOMAS (1752–1818), a native of Virginia, settled in Maysville, Kentucky, in 1785, where he served as Mason County justice in 1789 and sheriff in 1790. (*Kentucky in Retrospect*, p. 168)

WARVILLE, JACQUES-PIERRE BRISSOT DE (1754–93), was a French journalist and social reformer who had been touring the United States since July 1788 in preparation for writing a history. He succeeded in writing one of the most famous travelogues of America before Tocqueville. See also *DHFFC* 17:1900.

WASHINGTON, CORBIN (1765–99), a planter of "Prospect Hill," in Berkeley County, West Virginia, was the youngest son of George Washington's deceased brother, John Augustine, and Hannah Bushrod. At the time of the First Congress, he was married to Hannah Lee (1765–1801), daughter of Richard Henry Lee. Corbin's sister Mildred had married another of R. H. Lee's children, Thomas Lee (1758–1804) in 1788.

WASHINGTON, GEORGE (1732–99), of Mount Vernon, in Fairfax County, Virginia, President of the United States, 1789–97, was a planter, colonial legislator, land speculator, advocate of Potomac River navigation, and former commander-in-chief of the Continental Army. See also *DHFFC* 9:4n, 17:1900–1901.

WASHINGTON, HANNAH BUSHROD (1731–1801), of "Bushfield," in Westmoreland County, Virginia, was the widowed wife of George Washington's younger brother John Augustine (d. 1787), and mother of Corbin Washington.

WASHINGTON, LUND (1737–96), managed Mount Vernon, the estate of his distant cousin George Washington, from 1765 until taking up residence on the neighboring plantation of "Hayfield" in 1784. (*PGW* 1:4n)

WASHINGTON, MARTHA DANDRIDGE CUSTIS (1731–1802), a wealthy widow when she married George Washington in 1759, helped to establish the "Republican Court" shortly after her arrival at New York City on 27 May 1789. Her two youngest grandchildren, Eleanor Parke "Nelly" (1779–1852) and George Washington Parke "Washie" Custis (1781–1857), lived with the Washingtons throughout the First Congress.

WATERS, PHILEMON (1734–96), was a native Virginian who fought under Washington's command during the French and Indian War. Shortly after he settled as a planter in Newberry County, South Carolina, which he represented in the state House in 1779–80, 1782, and 1786–88, the Senate in 1783–84, and at the ratification convention, where he voted in favor of the Constitution. He served as a captain in the state militia during the Revolutionary War and as colonel in 1783–94. (*South Carolina House* 3:752–53)

WATSON, MARSTON (1756–1800), was a shipowner of Marblehead, Massachusetts. See also *DHFFC* 17:1901.

WATSON, THOMAS, was master of the *New York*, the packet ship that sailed between New York and London in 1790.

WATTS, JOHN, JR. (1749–1836), graduated from King's College (Columbia) in 1766 and until the Revolutionary War held a government office under the Crown in his native New York City, which he then represented in the state Assembly, 1788–93 (as speaker, 1791–93). (*New York Genealogical and Biographical Record* 25[1894]:180–81; William M. MacBean, *Biographical Register of the Saint Andrew's Society of New York* [New York, 1922], 1:252–53)

WAYNE, ANTHONY (1745–96), originally of Pennsylvania, moved in early 1788 to the rice plantation, "Richmond," outside Savannah, which had been presented to him by the state of Georgia in recognition of his celebrated Revolutionary War record. He defeated James Jackson in the second federal election, but the seat was declared vacant when questions arose about voting fraud and his legal residence. See also *DHFFC* 9:245n, 17:1901–2.

WEBB, SAMUEL BLACHLEY (1753–1807), a native of Connecticut, was living in New York City by 1789 as an agent for the Boston merchant, Joseph Barrell. The distinguished Continental Army veteran and prominent Federalist married Catherine Hogeboom on 3 September 1790 and retired to a farm in Claverack, New York. See also *DHFFC* 17:1902.

WEBB, WILLIAM (ca. 1764–1822), served as collector at Bath, Maine, 1789–1804, having held that office under the state government since 1779. (Patrick M. Reed, *History of Bath and Environs* [Portland, Me., 1894], p. 183)

WEBB, WILLIAM CRITTENDEN (1732–1815), served as overseer of roads and deputy sheriff of Orange County, Virginia. (*PJM* 13:306)

WEBSTER, NATHANIEL (1749–1830), a Harvard graduate of 1769, was minister of the Second Congregational Church of Biddeford, Maine, 1779–1828. (*Harvard Graduates* 17:303–5)

WEBSTER, NOAH (1758–1843), a Yale graduate of 1778, was a lexicographer, educational reformer, and political essayist of Hartford, Connecticut, where he practiced law, 1789–93. (*Yale Graduates* 4:66–79)

WEBSTER, PELATIAH (1726–95), a graduated from Yale in 1746 and became a Philadelphia merchant, political economist, and essayist. See also *DHFFC* 17:1902. (*DHROC* 13:294n; *Yale Graduates* 2:97–102)

WEED, JACOB (d. 24 March 1791), was a Sea Island cotton planter of Camden County, Georgia, where he settled by 1787 and helped found the city of St. Marys. The state militia colonel served in the state ratification convention in 1787, the state Assembly, 1787 and 1789–90, and in the executive council in 1789. (*DHROC* 3:274n)

WELLS, NATHANIEL (1740–1816), a 1760 Harvard graduate and former schoolteacher of Wells, Maine, served in the Massachusetts Senate, 1782–97, and in the state convention, where he voted to ratify the Constitution. See also *DHFFC* 17:1903.

WELLS, RICHARD, a merchant of Burlington, New Jersey, was one of the twelve original managers of the United Company of Philadelphia for Promoting American Manufactures, founded in 1775. Knowing the advantages of imitating British inventions, in March 1790 he petitioned the Senate against the broad incorporation of patent protection. See also *DHFFC* 8:42–43.

WELSH, THOMAS (1752–1831), a Boston physician, graduated from Harvard in 1772 and served as a Massachusetts militia surgeon when war broke out three years later. In 1777 he married Abigail Adams's first cousin Abigail Kent and was a close friend of the Adamses thereafter. (*JQA*, p. 2n; *Adams* 3:234n)

WENDELL, JOHN (1731–1808), a 1750 Harvard graduate, was a land speculator and lawyer of Portsmouth, New Hampshire. (*PRM* 1:179n; *Harvard Graduates* 12:592–97)

WETMORE, WILLIAM (1749–1830), graduated from Harvard in 1770 and was a leading lawyer in Essex County, Massachusetts, until 1788 when he settled in Boston and became a speculator in land and government securities. See also *DHFFC* 17:1904.

WEYMAN, EDWARD (ca. 1730–1793), served as federal port surveyor at Charleston, South Carolina, 1789–93. See also *DHFFC* 2:545.

WHIPPLE, JOSEPH (1738–1816), was a merchant of Portsmouth, New Hampshire, where he served as collector, 1789–98, having held that post under the state government since 1786. He was brother-in-law to Joshua Brackett. See also *DHFFC* 2:517.

WHIPPLE, OLIVER (1734–1813), graduated from Harvard in 1766 and served as a customs officer for the Crown in Georgia briefly before returning to his native Rhode Island to open a law practice in 1771. The next year he moved to Portsmouth, New Hampshire, where his law practice was temporarily suspended while he was imprisoned for suspected Loyalism, 1776–77. In 1774 he married Abigail, the sister of Massachusetts's gadfly legislator during the First Congress, John Gardiner. (*Harvard Graduates* 16:430–34)

WHITE, ANTHONY WALTON (1750–1803), younger brother of Paterson's wife Euphemia, escaped poor business investments in his native New Brunswick, New Jersey, and settled in New York City, 1788–93, where he had many close ties to the Federalist leadership not only through family but also his own distinguished service in the Continental Army. See also *DHFFC* 7:543–44.

WHITE, PHILLIPS (1729–1811), a native of Haverhill, Massachusetts, served in the French and Indian War before settling permanently as a merchant and farmer in South Hampton, New Hampshire, which he represented in the colonial and state House, 1775–82 (speaker in the first and last of those years). The Rockingham County probate judge, 1776–90, also served as a member of Congress, 1782–83.

WHITE, WILLIAM (1748–1836), Episcopal bishop of his native Philadelphia since 1787 and chaplain to Congress, 1790–1800, became Robert Morris's brother-in-law by the latter's marriage to Mary White in 1762. See also *DHFFC* 9:343n.

WHITNEY, ABEL (1756–1807), was a merchant of Westfield, Massachusetts. The Harvard graduate of 1773 also served as aide-de-camp to the county militia general, 1787–93. (*Harvard Graduates* 18:349–50)

WHITTEMORE, SAMUEL (1733–1806), was a schoolmaster of his native Gloucester, Massachusetts, where he served as federal surveyor of the port, 1789–92. The Harvard graduate of 1751 served in the state House of Representatives in 1776 and 1783–84. See also *DHFFC* 2:514.

WICKHAM, JOHN (1763–1839), was admitted to the bar in 1786 after studying at the College of William and Mary and commenced to practice law in Williamsburg, Virginia. (*John Marshall* 2:36n)

WIDGERY, WILLIAM (ca. 1753–1822), a native of England, was a lawyer in New Gloucester, Maine, which he represented in the Massachusetts House, 1787–94, and in the state convention, where he voted against ratification of the Constitution. He was also town selectman, 1789–90. (*DHROC* 4:439n)

WIGGIN, MARY WINGATE (1766–1840), daughter of Paine Wingate, married Andrew Wiggin of Stratham, New Hampshire, in 1788. Their family at the time of the First Congress consisted of daughters Harriet (1788–1836) and Caroline (1790–1817). (*Wingate*, pp. 153–57)

WILBERFORCE, WILLIAM (1759–1833), was a British philanthropist who became leader of the campaign against the slave trade as a member of Parliament, 1780–1824.

WILCOCKS, ALEXANDER (1741–1801), a Philadelphia lawyer, was city recorder in 1791. (*DHSCUS* 1:185n)

WILDER, ABEL (1741–92), was a native of Leominster, Massachusetts, but by 1762 settled in nearby Winchendon, which he served as town clerk, state Representative, 1779–85, and state Senator, 1786–92. (Ezra Hyde, *History of the Town of Winchendon* [Worcester, Mass., 1849], pp. 33, 48, 51)

WILKINS, NATHANIEL, of Gloucester County, Virginia, was appointed federal collector at Cherry Stone in 1790. During the Revolutionary War he rose from second lieutenant of the 9th Virginia Regiment in 1776 to first lieutenant in 1777, before resigning in 1778 after the loss of a hand. (*PGW* 5:420–21n)

WILKINSON, JAMES (1757–1825), originally of Maryland, practiced medicine briefly before embarking on a busy wartime career as aide-de-camp to Nathanael Greene, Benedict Arnold, and Horatio Gates, 1776–77, lieutenant colonel of Thomas Hartley's Additional Continental Regiment in 1777, brevet brigadier general, 1777–78, secretary to the board of war in 1778, and clothier general of the army, 1779-81. He represented Bucks County in the Pennsylvania General Assembly, 1781–83, before settling permanently near Lexington, Kentucky, in 1784. In 1787 he conspired with Louisiana's

Governor Miró to establish an independent republic of Kentucky allied to Spain. The plan, abandoned by late 1789, may have involved Representative John Brown, Harry Innes, Benjamin Sebastian, and others. There is evidence that Wilkinson was, throughout the episode, a double agent, working simultaneously for the United States. See also *DHFFC* 9:245–46n. (*DHROC* 8:291n; *Westward Expansion*, pp. 232–33)

WILLARD, JOSEPH (1738–1804), a noted scientist and astronomer, graduated from Harvard in 1765 and served as a Congregational minister in Beverly, Massachusetts, from 1773 until his appointment as president of his alma mater in 1781. (*Harvard Graduates* 16:253–65)

WILLIAMS, BENJAMIN (1757–1814), was a farmer of Johnston and Craven counties, North Carolina, representing the latter at the first state convention (1788) where he voted against ratifying the Constitution, and the former in the state's House of Commons in 1789. During the Revolutionary War he rose from first lieutenant in the 2nd North Carolina Regiment in 1775 to captain in 1776, before retiring at war's end. (*DHFFE* 4:355n)

WILLIAMS, EPHRAIM (1760–1835), of Stockbridge, Massachusetts, was admitted to the bar in 1787, having studied under Theodore Sedgwick, and subsequently became his law partner and political protégé. Pamela Sedgwick was a first cousin. (*Massachusetts Bar* 2:449; Richard E. Welch, Jr., *Theodore Sedgwick, Federalist: A Political Portrait* [Middletown, Conn., 1965], p. 160)

WILLIAMS, GEORGE (1731–97), was a sea captain and merchant of Salem, Massachusetts, which he represented in the state House, 1776–79, 1783, and 1785. (*Massachusetts Legislators*, p. 383)

WILLIAMS, JOHN FOSTER (ca. 1744–1814), of Boston, served as commander of the federal revenue cutter for Massachusetts from 1790 until his death. During the Revolutionary War he commanded various vessels of the state navy. (*PGW* 6:520n)

WILLIAMS, OTHO HOLLAND (1749–94), was a distinguished Continental Army veteran appointed as collector of Baltimore, 1789–94. He became the son-in-law of William Smith (Md.) by his marriage in 1785 to Mary "Polly" Smith (ca. 1764–1795). At the time of the First Congress, their children were Robert (1786–93), William Elie (1787–1833), and Edward Greene (23 March 1789–1829). See also *DHFFC* 2:499, 9:47n, 17:1908.

WILLIAMS, THOMAS, was appointed federal surveyor at Indiantown, North Carolina, in 1790. The former state Representative, 1788–89, supported the Constitution at the first ratification convention in 1788. See also *DHFFC* 2:531.

WILLIAMS, WILLIAM (1731–1811), a merchant of Lebanon, Connecticut, attended Congress in 1775–76, where he signed the Declaration of Independence; the state House of Representatives in 1780–84; the state convention, where he voted to ratify the Constitution; and the state Council of Assistants, 1784–1803. See also *DHFFC* 17:1909.

WILLIAMSON, MARIA APTHORPE (ca. 1766–14 October 1790), daughter of the wealthy merchant Charles W. Apthorpe of New York City, married Hugh Williamson there on 3 January 1789. Their son Charles was born on 18 October of that year and she died a year later, after the birth of their second child.

WILLINK, WILHELM, the Younger (1750–1841), was an Amsterdam merchant who served as one of the Dutch bankers to the United States government.

WILSON, JAMES (1742–98), was a Philadelphia lawyer and land speculator who served as an associate justice of the United States Supreme Court, 1789–98. The native of Scotland became, like his law teacher John Dickinson, a pamphleteer for the revolutionary movement, a frequent member of Congress, and an active member of the Federal Convention. He was also a leader of the state's Republicans or Anti-Constitutionalists, responsible for the Pennsylvania constitution of 1790. See also *DHFFC* 17: 1909–10.

WILSON, JOSEPH (d. 1809), was a Philadelphia merchant in the 1780s before returning to his native Ireland, where he served as United States consul at Dublin, 1794–1809. (*PRM* 6:159n)

WILSON, STEPHEN (d. 1794), was a Baltimore merchant.

WINDER, WILLIAM (d. 1808), was originally a merchant of Somerset County, Maryland, which he represented in the state House of Delegates before his appointment to the naval board of the middle department, 1778–80. Named commissioner for settling accounts between Delaware and the United States in 1783, he was reassigned as commissioner of accounts for Virginia and North Carolina in 1787. (*PRM* 7:54n)

WINGATE, EUNICE (1742–1843), sister of Timothy Pickering, married Paine Wingate in 1765 and resided at their home in Stratham, New Hampshire, during the First Congress. Their children were: Mary Wiggin; Sarah, or "Sally" (1769–1808), who married Josiah Bartlett's son, Josiah, in 1792; George (1778–1852); John (1781–1831); and Elizabeth (1783–1829). (C. E. L. Wingate, *History of the Wingate Family in England and America* [Exeter, N.H., 1886], pp. 153–57; *PJB*, p. 382n)

WINGATE, HANNAH VEAZIE, of Stratham, New Hampshire, was the wife of Paine Wingate's cousin Joshua. (*Wingate*, p. 213)

WINSTON, JOSEPH (1756–1815), was a native Virginian who settled in Surry (part of present-day Stokes) County, North Carolina, by 1770. A major in the state militia, 1775–81, he also served in both the state House of Commons, 1777, 1779, and 1782–83, and Senate, 1787–89, and in both state ratifying conventions, where he supported the Constitution.

WOLCOTT, FREDERICK (1767–1837), of Litchfield, Connecticut, was the youngest brother of Oliver Wolcott, Jr. After graduating from Yale in 1786 he studied law but never practiced owing to ill health. (*Yale Graduates* 4:519–20)

WOLCOTT, OLIVER, SR. (1726–97), lieutenant governor of Connecticut, 1786–96, was a physician of Litchfield, Connecticut, with lengthy experience in both the colonial and state legislatures, and the pre-federal Congresses. See also *DHFFC* 17:1910.

WOLCOTT, OLIVER, JR. (1760–1833), was a Hartford lawyer appointed auditor of the United States treasury, 1789–91. The son of Connecticut's lieutenant governor, brother of Frederick Wolcott, and brother-in-law of Chauncey Goodrich, he married in 1785 Elizabeth Stoughton (1766–1805), originally of Windsor, Connecticut, who resided with him in New York City after November 1789. See also *DHFFC* 17:1911. (*DGW* 5:505n)

WOOD, JAMES, JR. (1741–1813), of Frederick County, Virginia, was the brother-in-law of Alexander White. During the Revolutionary War he served as colonel of the 12th Virginia Regiment (1776–78) and of the 8th Regiment thereafter until war's end. He married Jean Moncure (1753–1835) about 1775.

WOOD, LEIGHTON (1740–1805), of Hanover County, Virginia, served as state commissioner to investigate accounts of public trade, 1777–78, and state auditor of public accounts in 1780 before accepting appointment as state solicitor general later that year. (*PJM* 2:79n)

WOOD, MARY RUTHERFORD (1718–98), was the wife of James Wood, Sr. (ca. 1707–1759), founder of Winchester, Virginia. Their eldest daughter Elizabeth (1739–pre 1784) was Alexander White's first wife. (K. G. Greene, *Winchester, Virginia, and Its Beginnings* [Strasburg, Va., 1926], p. 352)

WOOD, WILLIAM (1748–1810), served in the militia of his native Virginia during the Revolutionary War before co-founding the town of Washington (part of present-day Maysville), Kentucky, where he became a Baptist minister in 1785.

WOODBRIDGE, DUDLEY, SR. (1705–90), was a physician of Stonington, Connecticut.

WOODBRIDGE, DUDLEY, JR. (1747–1823), was a lawyer of Marietta, Ohio, where he moved from Norwich, Connecticut.

WOODBRIDGE, THEODORE (d. 1811), of Glastonbury, Connecticut, was a Continental Army veteran who had served as first lieutenant in the 4th Connecticut Regiment in 1775, captain in David Wooster's Continental Regiment, 1775–76, and major of the 7th Connecticut Regiment, 1778–81, and 2nd Connecticut Regiment thereafter until the war's end.

WOODWARD, JOSEPH (ca. 1758–1838), resided in Boston, Massachusetts, in 1790.

WOODWORTH, JOHN (1768–1858), originally of Albany, New York, graduated from Yale in 1788 and commenced the practice of law in Troy, New York, in 1791.

WORMELEY, RALPH, JR. (1744–1806), was a planter of "Rosegill," in Middlesex County, Virginia, which he represented in the state House of Delegates, 1788–90, and at the state convention, where he voted to ratify the Constitution. (*DHROC* 9:787–88n)

WORTHINGTON, FRANCES (1764–1837), daughter of John Worthington, the noted Loyalist lawyer of Springfield, Massachusetts, was courted throughout the First Congress by Fisher Ames, whom she married on 15 July 1792. Her older sister Mary married Jonathan Bliss in July 1790, and another older sister Hannah married Thomas Dwight in April 1791.

WRAY, GEORGE, JR. (d. 1810), was appointed federal collector at Hampton, Virginia, in 1790. See also *DHFFC* 2:555.

WYNKOOP, ANNE (1765–1815), was Henry Wynkoop's second oldest daughter. On 17 August 1790 she married James Raguet (b. 1756) of Newtown, Pennsylvania, a French Huguenot who immigrated to America in 1783. Their first child, Susannah (d. 1793), was born on 22 July 1791.

WYNKOOP, PETER (1755–1835), originally of Kingston, New York, moved to New York City in 1785 and became a baker and tobacco merchant.

WYNKOOP, SARAH NEWKIRK (d. 1813), became Henry Wynkoop's third wife in 1782 and resided at their estate "Vredens Berg," near Newtown in Bucks County, Pennsylvania. In addition to their daughter Susannah (1784–1849), their family during the First Congress consisted of seven children by Wynkoop's first marriage in 1761 to Susanna Wanshaer (d. 1776): Christina (1763–1841), who married Reading Beatty in 1786; Anne; Margaretta (b. 1768), who married Philadelphia merchant Herman J. Lombaert in November 1789; Nicholas (1770–1815); Mary Helen, or "Maria" (1772–1809); John W. (1774–93); and Jonathan (1776–1842). (*Collection of Papers Read before the Bucks County Historical Society* 3[1909]:212–15)

WYNNS, WILLIAM, was a planter of Hertford County, North Carolina, which he served as sheriff, 1790–94, and which he had represented in the state House of Commons, 1779–80 and 1782. He was appointed surveyor at Winton, North Carolina, in 1790. See also *DHFFC* 2:531.

YATES, ROBERT (1738–1801), of Albany, New York, served as associate justice of the state supreme court, 1777–90, and chief justice, 1790–98. He was an outspoken critic of the Constitution at both the Federal Convention, which he left early in protest, and at the state ratification convention. See also *DHFFC* 17:1913.

YEATES, JASPER (1745–1817), was a lawyer of Lancaster, Pennsylvania, which he represented at the state convention, where he voted to ratify the Constitution. His wife was Sarah Burd Yeates (1749–1829). See also *DHFFC* 17:1913.

YEATON, HOPLEY (ca. 1739–1812), a sea captain of Portsmouth, Massachusetts, served during the Revolutionary War as a privateer as well as an officer on the Continental Navy's frigate *Raleigh*, constructed under John Langdon's supervision in 1776. (*PJB*, p. 103n; Lawrence Shaw Mayo, *John*

Langdon of New Hampshire [1937; reprint, Port Washington, N.Y., 1970], p. 136)

YONGE, SIR GEORGE (1731–1812), was a member of Parliament, 1754–61 and 1763–96, while serving as Great Britain's secretary at war, 1782–94.

YOUNG, NOTLEY (1738–1802), was a planter of "Non Such," in Prince George's County, Maryland (part of present-day D.C.). His second wife, whom he married in 1782, was Mary Carroll, younger sister of Representative Daniel Carroll.

YOUNG, THOMAS (1731–77), was a New York City physician who moved to Boston in the 1760s and became active in the revolutionary movement as one of the founders of the "Sons of Liberty." After moving to Philadelphia in 1775, he helped to draft the state's first constitution of 1776; he died the next year of camp fever while serving as a senior Continental Army surgeon. (Merrill Jensen, *The Founding of a Nation: A History of the American Revolution, 1763–1776* [New York, 1968], p. 412)

SECOND SESSION HOUSE BILLS

No.	*Short Title*	*Long Title*	*Date Introduced*	*Date Signed by President*
		SECOND SESSION: JANUARY 4, 1790–AUGUST 12, 1790		
34	ENUMERATION	An Act providing for the actual enumeration of the inhabitants of the United States	Jan. 18	Mar. 1 46053
35	FOREIGN INTERCOURSE	A Bill providing the means of intercourse between the United States and foreign nations	Jan. 21	Recommitted See [HR–52]
36	NORTH-CAROLINA	An Act for giving effect to the several acts therein mentioned, in respect to the State of North Carolina, and other purposes	Jan. 25	Feb. 8 22956 46035
37	NATURALIZATION	A Bill establishing an uniform rule of naturalization	Jan. 25	Recommitted See [HR–40]
38	MITIGATION OF FINES	A Bill to provide for the remission or mitigation of fines, forfeitures, and penalties in certain cases	Jan. 26	Recommitted See [HR–45]
39	COPYRIGHT	A Bill for securing the copyright of books to authors and proprietors	Jan. 28	Recommitted See [HR–43]
40	NATURALIZATION	A Bill to establish an uniform rule of naturalization, and to enable aliens to hold lands under certain restrictions	Feb. 16	Mar. 26
		An Act to establish an uniform rule of naturalization		MWA
41	PATENTS	An Act to promote the progress of useful arts	Feb. 16	Apr. 10 DLC (Mss. Div.)
42	POST OFFICE	A Bill for regulating the post-office of the United States	Feb. 23	Recommitted See [HR–74]
43	COPYRIGHT	A Bill for the encouragement of learning, by securing the copies of maps, charts, books, and	Feb. 25	May 31

No.	Short Title	Long Title	Date Introduced	Date Signed by President
		other writings, to the authors and proprietors of such copies, during the times therein mentioned		
		An Act for the encouragement of learning, by securing the copies of maps, charts, books, to the authors and proprietors of such copies, during the times therein mentioned		46038
44	BAILEY	An Act to vest in Francis Bailey, the exclusive privilege of making, using, and vending to others, punches for stamping the matrices of types, and impressing marks on plates, or any other substance, to prevent counterfeits, upon a principle by him invented, for a term of years	Feb. 26	Not passed—S See [HR–41]
45	MITIGATION OF FINES	An Act to provide for the remission or mitigaiton of fines, forfeitures, and penalties, in certain cases	Mar. 3	Not passed See [HR–57]
46	SALARIES OF CLERKS	An act for encreasing the salaries of clerks in the office of the Commissioners for settling accounts, between the United States and individual states	Mar. 8	Not passed—S
47	APPROPRIATIONS	An Act making appropriations for the support of government for the year one thousand seven hundred and ninety	Mar. 8	Mar. 26 46044
48	INSPECTION	An act to prevent the exportation of goods not duly inspected according to the laws of the several States	Mar. 8	Apr. 2 Sc-Ar

No.	Short Title	Long Title	Date Introduced	Date Signed by President
49	Ely	A Bill to allow compensation to John Ely, for his services and expences as a regimental surgeon in the late army of the United States	Mar. 11	Not passed—HR See [HR–56]
50	Collection	An Act further to suspend part of an Act, entitled, "An Act to regulate the collection of the duties imposed by law on the tonnage of ships or vessels, and on goods, wares, and merchandizes, imported into the United States"	Mar. 26	Apr. 15
		An Act, further to suspend part of an Act, entitled, "An Act to regulate the collection of the duties imposed by law on the tonnage of ships or vessels, and on goods, wares, and merchandizes, imported into the United States;" and to amend the said Act		22962
[50a]	Military Establishment	An Act for regulating the military establishment of the United States	Mar. 25, passed by House	Apr. 30 22958
[50b]	Indian Treaty	An Act providing for holding a treaty or treaties, to establish peace with certain Indian tribes	Mar. 29, received by Senate	July 22 22966 46051
51	Indian Trade	A Bill to regulate trade and intercourse with the Indian Tribes	Mar. 30	Recommitted See [HR–65]
52	Foreign Intercourse	An Act providing the means of intercourse between the United States and foreign nations	Mar. 31	July 1 46055
53	Officers	An Act for the relief of a certain description of officers therein mentioned	Apr. 5	Not passed See [HR-59]

No.	Short Title	Long Title	Date Introduced	Date Signed by President
54	SALARIES-EXECUTIVE	An Act supplemental to the Act for establishing the salaries of the executive officers of government, with their assistants and clerks	Apr. 13	June 4 46056
55	See [HR-50a]			
56	ELY	An Act to allow compensation to John Ely, for his attendance as a physician and surgeon on the prisoners of the United States	Apr. 22	Not passed—S
57	MITIGATION OF FORFEITURES	An Act to provide for mitigating or remitting the forfeitures and penalties accruing under the revenue laws, in certain cases therein mentioned	Apr. 27	May 26 Sc-Ar
58	AUTHENTICATION	An Act to prescribe the mode in which the public acts, records, and judicial proceedings in each state shall be authenticated, so as to take effect in every other State	Apr. 28	May 26 22968
59	INVALID OFFICERS	An Act to authorize the issuing of certificates to a certain description of invalid officers	Apr. 30	Not passed—S
60	STEUBEN	An Act for finally adjusting and satisfying the claims of Frederick William Steuben	Apr. 30	June 4 46033
61	MERCHANT SEAMEN	An Act for the government and regulation of seamen in the merchants service	May 3	July 20 22959
62	DUTIES ON DISTILLED SPIRITS	A Bill for repealing, after the last day of —— next, the duties heretofore laid upon distilled spirits imported from abroad, and laying others in their stead, and also upon spirits distilled within the United States, as well to discourage the excessive	May 5	Not passed See [HR–83]

No.	Short Title	Long Title	Date Introduced	Date Signed by President
		use of those spirits, and promote agriculture, as to provide for the support of the public credit, and for the common defence and general welfare		
63	FUNDING	An Act making provision for the debt of the United States	May 6	Aug. 4 46048
64	DUTIES ON WINES	A Bill repealing, after the last day of —— next, the duties heretofore laid upon wines imported from foreign ports or places, and laying others in their stead	May 11	Not passed See {HR–83}
65	INDIAN TRADE	An Act to regulate trade and intercourse with the Indian tribes	May 14	July 22 22972
66	TRADE AND NAVIGATION	A Bill concerning the navigation and trade of the United States	May 17	Not passed—HR
67	JENKINS	An Act for the relief of Thomas Jenkins and company	May 20	June 14 Sc-Ar
68	NORTH CAROLINA JUDICIARY	An Act for giving effect to an Act, entitled, "An Act to establish the Judicial Courts of the United States," within the State of North-Carolina	May 21	June 4 Ct
69	SETTLEMENT OF ACCOUNTS	A Bill to provide for the settlement of the accounts between the United States and the individual States	May 27	Recommitted—HR
70	MCCORD	An Act to satisfy the claims of John McCord, against the United States	June 2	July 1
71	RHODE ISLAND	An Act for giving effect to the several Acts therein mentioned, in respect to the State of Rhode-Island and Providence Plantations	June 2	June 14 22957

No.	Short Title	Long Title	Date Introduced	Date Signed by President
72	TWINING	An Act for the relief of Nathaniel Twining	June 3	July 1
73	RHODE ISLAND JUDICIARY	An Act for giving effect to an Act, entitled, "An Act to establish the Judicial Courts of the United States" within the State of Rhode-Island and Providence Plantations	June 4	June 23 Sc-Ar
74	POST OFFICE	An Act to establish the Post-Office and Post-Roads within the United States	June 7	Not passed
75	RHODE ISLAND ENUMERATION	An Act for giving effect to an Act, entitled, "An Act, providing for the enumeration of the inhabitants of the United States," in respect to the State of Rhode-Island and Providence Plantations	June 7	July 5 46034
76	WEST POINT	An Act to authorize the purchase of a tract of land [at West Point] for the use of the United States	June 15	July 5 46062
77	SETTLEMENT OF ACCOUNTS	An Act to provide more effectually for the settlement of the accounts between the United States and individual States	June 17	Aug. 5 22969
78	TONNAGE	An Act imposing duties on the tonnage of ships or vessels	June 22	July 20 22963
79	GOULD	An Act to satisfy the claim of the representatives of David Gould, deceased, against the United States	June 23	Not passed—S
80	INVALID PENSIONERS	An Act further to provide for the payment of the invalid pensioners of the United States	June 29	July 16 46043
81	MILITIA	A Bill more effectually to provide for the national defence, by establishing a uniform militia throughout the United States	July 1	Not passed—HR

No.	*Short Title*	*Long Title*	*Date Introduced*	*Date Signed by President*
82	COLLECTION	An Act to provide more effectually for the collection of the duties imposed by law on goods, wares, and merchandize, imported into the United States, and on the tonnage of ships or vessels	July 8	Aug. 4 22970
83	WAYS AND MEANS	An Act making further provision for the payment of the debts of the United States	July 13	Aug. 10 22965 46046
84	LIGHTHOUSES	An Act to amend the Act for the establishment and support of light-houses, beacons, buoys and public piers	July 14	July 22 22967
85	VIRGINIA CESSION	An Act to enable the officers and soldiers of the Virginia line, on the continental establishment, to obtain titles to certain lands lying north-west of the river Ohio, between the Little Miami and Sciota	July 15	Aug. 10 46065
86	CONSULS AND VICE CONSULS	A Bill for establishing the fees and perquisites to be received by Consuls and Vice-Consuls of the United States in foreign parts, and for other purposes An Act concerning consuls and vice consuls of the United States, in foreign parts	July 15	Postponed—S
87	See [HR-50b]			
88	DISABLED SOLDIERS AND SEAMEN	An Act for the relief of disabled soldiers and seamen lately in the service of the United States, and of certain other persons	July 16	Aug. 11 46042

No.	Short Title	Long Title	Date Introduced	Date Signed by President
89	COASTING	A Bill for registering ships or vessels, for regulating those employed in the coasting trade and fisheries, and for other purposes	July 22	Postponed—HR
90	STEWART AND DAVIDSON	An Act for the relief of John Stewart and John Davidson	July 27	Aug. 4 22961
91	BARCLAY	An Act to compensate Thomas Barclay for various public services	July 28	Not passed
92	POST OFFICE	An Act to continue in force for a limited time, an Act, entitled, "An Act for the temporary establishment of the post-office"	July 28	Aug. 4 46063
93	NAVIGATION	An Act declaring the assent of Congress to certain Acts of the States of Maryland, Georgia, and Rhode-Island	Aug. 3	Aug. 11 Sc-Ar
94	GEORGIA	A Bill making further provision for the debt of the United States, so far as respects the assumption of the debt of the State of Georgia	Aug. 3	Not passed—HR
95	SETTLING ACCOUNTS	An Act for adding two Commissioners to the board established for settling the accounts between the United States and the individual States	Aug. 4	Not passed—S
96	STIRLING	An Act making an appropriation for discharging the claim of Sarah Alexander, the widow of the late Major General Lord Stirling, who died in the services of the United States	Aug. 4	Aug. 11
		An Act for the relief of the persons therein mentioned or described		CtY (Franklin)

No.	*Short Title*	*Long Title*	*Date Introduced*	*Date Signed by President*
97	PORTLAND HEAD LIGHTHOUSE	An Act authorizing the Secretary of the Treasury to finish the lighthouse on Portland Head in the district of Maine	Aug. 5	Aug. 10 22955
98	SURVEYOR GENERAL	A Bill providing for the appointment of a surveyor-general for the United States	Aug. 6	Not passed—HR
99	CALDWELL	An Act for the relief of Adam Caldwell	Aug. 6	Postponed—S
100	SPECIAL APPROPRIATIONS	An Act making certain appropriations therein mentioned	Aug. 9	Aug. 12 46045
101	SINKING FUND	An Act making provision for the reduction of the public debt	Aug. 9	Aug. 12 46050

SECOND SESSION SENATE BILLS

No.	*Short Title*	*Long Title*	*Date Introduced*	*Date Signed by President*
		SECOND SESSION: JANUARY 4, 1790–AUGUST 12, 1790		
6	PUNISHMENT OF CRIMES	A Bill defining the crimes and offences that shall be cognizable under the authority of the United States, and their punishment	Jan. 26	Apr. 30
		An Act for the punishment of certain crimes against the United States		46041
7	NORTH CAROLINA CESSION	An Act to accept a cession of the claims of the State of North-Carolina, to a certain district of western territory	Mar. 3	Apr. 2 Sc-Ar
8	SOUTHERN TERRITORY	An Act for the government of the territory of the United States south of the River Ohio	Apr. 9	May 26 22960 46039
9	COURTS	An Act to continue in force an Act passed at the last session of Congress, entitled, "An Act to regulate processes in the courts of the United States"	Apr. 23	May 26 Sc-Ar
10	NORTH CAROLINA JUDICIARY	An Act for giving effect to the Acts therein mentioned, in respect to the State of North-Carolina, and to amend the said Act	Apr. 29	Not passed See [HR–68]
11	RHODE ISLAND TRADE	An Act to prevent bringing goods, wares, and merchandizes from the State of Rhode-Island and Providence Plantations, into the United States, and to authorize a demand of money from the said State	May 13	Not passed—HR

No.	*Short Title*	*Long Title*	*Date Introduced*	*Date Signed by President*
12	RESIDENCE	A Bill to determine the permanent seat of Congress, and the government of the United States	May 31	July 16
		An Act for establishing the temporary and permanent seat of the Government of the United States		46032
13	CIRCUIT COURTS	A Bill for altering the time of holding the courts in South Carolina and Georgia	Aug. 7	Aug. 11
		An Act to alter the times for holding the Circuit Courts of the United States in the districts of South-Carolina and Georgia, and providing that the District Court of Pennsylvania shall in future be held in the city of Philadelphia only		46061

INDEX

The contents of volumes 18–20 make up part of the single richest documentary archive on the history of the post–Federal Convention founding period, an archive gathered over the last half of the twentieth century for the documentary histories of the Ratification of the Constitution and of the First Federal Congress (FFC). The index that follows has been compiled with the aim of providing access to the wide variety of information to be found there. For example, the editors have indexed as broadly as possible all references to newspaper articles and their distribution in order to trace the manner and paths by which information was reported throughout the United States in 1790. Similarly, this index reveals much about how correspondence was transmitted in the eighteenth century.

The correspondence of members of the FFC transcends regional or even national significance and offers perspectives on the social, economic, cultural, and intellectual, no less than the political and constitutional, history of the period. The complexity necessarily involved in such an undertaking has been reduced by certain space- and time-saving arrangements that bear pointing out.

- Constituent relations—embracing in a most direct way citizens' expectations of their government—constitute an especially large and challenging theme for indexing. Though most federal offices had been filled by the beginning of the Second Session, office seeking is still the most common category of members' constituent relations. In most cases all actions by members relating to office seekers have been grouped under "constituent relations: and office seeking."
- Entries under First Federal Congress, House of Representatives, and Senate relate to general and organizational references to those bodies, while most references relating to their deliberations and actions on a particular topic will be found under the name of the subject.
- In recognition of the nuances of eighteenth-century language and the evolution of constitutional terms, index entries employ original wording as nearly as possible (e.g., Union, as distinct from United States).
- Because of his unique constitutional standing in the Senate, John Adams is treated as a member of Congress in all cases except constituent relations.
- "Constituent" is understood to include "correspondent," even when the correspondent in question is not a constituent per se.
- The subentry "opinion on" is provided only for members. The subentries "debate" and "role" override "opinion" under a member's name

when they cover the same pages. The subentry "role" refers only to activities actually performed (e.g., political negotiations and committee service). All of these subentries are used only for FFC-related issues.

• Writers and recipients are specified by name under "letters to" and "letters from" only in the case of members, high level government officials (e.g., John Jay), and other non-members with copious correspondence (e.g., Tench Coxe).

• The subentry "relations with" is interpreted broadly to include friendly ties, conversations, etc. Names are specified only when the relations are between members or members and high level government officials (e.g., Thomas Jefferson).

• The entry "[*a state or section*] delegation" is used to indicate an unspecified number, or all, of a state's or section's Representatives or Senators in the FFC. There is an implied cross reference from every individual member to his respective state's delegation.

• The subentry "correspondence" under an individual's name indicates letters that are mentioned, as opposed to printed, excerpted, or calendared.

• Places take their present state name (e.g., Maine).

• Printed works (books, plays, and pamphlets) are indexed under their author, when known.

• Daily weather index entries do not include the accounts that are printed in the heading of most days' printed correspondence.

• FFC and NYC are used as abbreviations, when possible, for the First Federal Congress and New York City.

• New York City and Philadelphia institutions, neighborhoods, and other sites are indexed under New York City and Philadelphia.

In addition to those interns and volunteers acknowledged in the introduction, the following George Washington University undergraduates assisted with the preparation of this index: Annie Dobberteen, Carly Gibbs, Conor MacCaffrey, Heather Naviasky, Megan Vijiarungam, and Daniel Waters. George Mason University graduate student Amanda Roberts also contributed to this effort. We are much indebted to them for their diligent work on the tedious necessities of index entry and checking.